# Final Report of the Thirty-fourth Antarctic Treaty Consultative Meeting

ANTARCTIC TREATY
CONSULTATIVE MEETING

# Final Report
# of the Thirty-fourth
# Antarctic Treaty
# Consultative Meeting

Buenos Aires,
20 June – 1 July 2011

---

Secretariat of the Antarctic Treaty
Buenos Aires
2011

Antarctic Treaty Consultative Meeting (34th : 2011 : Buenos Aires)
   Final Report of the Thirty-fourth Antarctic Treaty Consultative Meeting.
   Buenos Aires, Argentina, 20 June–1 July 2011.
   Buenos Aires : Secretariat of the Antarctic Treaty, 2011.
   348 p.

ISBN 978-987-1515-26-4

1. International law – Environmental issues. 2. Antarctic Treaty system.
3. Environmental law – Antarctica. 4. Environmental protection – Antarctica.

DDC 341.762 5

ISBN 978-987-1515-26-4

# Contents

## VOLUME 1 (in hard copy and CD)

# VOLUME 2 (in CD and online-purchased copies)

## PART II. MEASURES, DECISIONS AND RESOLUTIONS (Cont.)

### 4. Management Plans

## PART III. OPENING AND CLOSING ADDRESSES AND REPORTS

### 1. Statements at the Session on Commemoration of the 50th Anniversary of the entry into force of the Antarctic Treaty

# PART IV. ADDITIONAL DOCUMENTS FROM ATCM XXXIV

# Acronyms and Abbreviations

| | |
|---|---|
| ACAP | Agreement on the Conservation of Albatrosses and Petrels |
| ASOC | Antarctic and Southern Ocean Coalition |
| ASMA | Antarctic Specially Managed Area |
| ASPA | Antarctic Specially Protected Area |
| ATS | Antarctic Treaty System or Antarctic Treaty Secretariat |
| ATCM | Antarctic Treaty Consultative Meeting |
| ATCP | Antarctic Treaty Consultative Party |
| CAML | Census of Antarctic Marine Life |
| CCAMLR | Convention on the Conservation of Antarctic Marine Living Resources and/or Commission for the Conservation of Antarctic Marine Living Resourcess |
| CCAS | Convention for the Conservation of Antarctic Seals |
| CEE | Comprehensive Environmental Evaluation |
| CEP | Committee for Environmental Protection |
| COMNAP | Council of Managers of National Antarctic Programs |
| EIA | Environmental Impact Assessment |
| HCA | Hydrographic Committee on Antarctica |
| HSM | Historic Site and Monument |
| IAATO | International Association of Antarctica Tour Operators |
| ICG | Intersessional Contact Group |
| ICSU | International Council for Science |
| IEE | Initial Environmental Evaluation |
| IHO | International Hydrographic Organization |
| IMO | International Maritime Organization |
| IOC | Intergovernmental Oceanographic Commission |
| IP | Information Paper |
| IPCC | Intergovernmental Panel on Climate Change |
| IPY | International Polar Year |
| IPY-IPO | IPY Programme Office |
| IUCN | International Union for Conservation of Nature and Natural Resources |
| RFMO | Regional Fishery Management Organisation |
| SATCM | Special Antarctic Treaty Consultative Meeting |
| SCAR | Scientific Committee on Antarctic Research |

| | |
|---|---|
| SCALOP | Standing Committee for Antarctic Logistics and Operations |
| SC-CAMLR | Scientific Committee of CCAMLR |
| SP | Secretariat Paper |
| SPA | Specially Protected Area |
| UNEP | United Nations Environment Programme |
| UNFCCC | United Nations Framework Convention on Climate Change |
| WG | Working Group |
| WMO | World Meteorological Organization |
| WP | Working Paper |
| WTO | World Tourism Organization |

# PART I
# Final Report

# 1. Final Report

# Final Report of the Thirty-fourth Antarctic Treaty Consultative Meeting

**Buenos Aires, June 20th – July 1st, 2011**

(1)     Pursuant to Article IX of the Antarctic Treaty, Representatives of the Consultative Parties (Argentina, Australia, Belgium, Brazil, Bulgaria, Chile, China, Ecuador, Finland, France, Germany, India, Italy, Japan, the Republic of Korea, the Netherlands, New Zealand, Norway, Peru, Poland, the Russian Federation, South Africa, Spain, Sweden, Ukraine, the United Kingdom of Great Britain and Northern Ireland, the United States of America, and Uruguay) met in Buenos Aires from 20 June to 1 July 2011, for the purpose of exchanging information, holding consultations and considering and recommending to their Governments measures in furtherance of the principles and objectives of the Treaty.

(2)     The Meeting was also attended by delegations from the following Contracting Parties to the Antarctic Treaty which are not Consultative Parties: Colombia, Cuba, Czech Republic, Greece, Monaco, Romania, Switzerland and Venezuela. A delegation from Malaysia was present by invitation of ATCM XXXIII to observe the Meeting.

(3)     In accordance with Rules 2 and 31 of the Rules of Procedure, Observers from the Commission for the Conservation of Antarctic Marine Living Resources (CCAMLR), the Scientific Committee on Antarctic Research (SCAR) and the Council of Managers of National Antarctic Programs (COMNAP) attended the Meeting.

(4)     In accordance with Rule 39 of the Rules of Procedure, Experts from the following international organisations and non-governmental organizations attended the Meeting: the Antarctic and Southern Ocean Coalition (ASOC), the International Association of Antarctica Tour Operators (IAATO), the International Hydrographic Organization (IHO) and the United Nations Environment Programme (UNEP).

(5) The Host Country Argentina fulfilled its information requirements towards the Contracting Parties, Observers and Experts through the Secretariat Circulars, letters and a website with public and members only sections.

## Item 1: Opening of the Meeting

(6) The Meeting was officially opened on 20 June 2011. On behalf of the Host Government, in accordance with Rules 5 and 6 of the Rules of Procedure, the Executive Secretary of the Host Government Secretariat Mr Jorge Roballo called the meeting to order and proposed the candidacy of the distinguished jurist and Ambassador Ariel Mansi as Chair of ATCM XXXIV. The proposal was accepted.

(7) The Chair warmly welcomed all Parties, Observers and Experts to Buenos Aires. He reminded delegates that 2011 was the 50th anniversary of the entry into force of the Antarctic Treaty, the 20th anniversary of the signing of the Protocol on Environmental Protection and on a longer time scale, the centenary of the year in which the Norwegian expedition lead by Roald Amundsen was the first to reach the South Pole. These anniversaries constituted a milestone upon which the Antarctic community could reflect about the future.

(8) Dr Lino Barañao, the Minister of Science, Technology and Productive Innovation of Argentina, officially welcomed delegates to the Meeting on the 50th anniversary of the entry into force of the Antarctic Treaty. He recalled the continued scientific challenges provided by the Antarctic and how the principle of consensus at the Treaty meetings had engendered a spirit of cooperation between those working in the region. Since its establishment of the first permanent Antarctic scientific station – Orcadas – in 1904, Argentina had maintained its interest in scientific investigations in Antarctica, and just 60 years ago had established the Instituto Antártico Argentino, recently recognised by the Ministry of Science, Technology and Productive Innovation as one of the most important science and technology organizations in the country.

(9) The Chair thanked the Minister for his recognition of the scientific importance of Antarctica. He noted that the agenda of this meeting covered a wide range of subjects including governance of the Antarctic, management of its environment, science and the implications of climate change, as well as operational matters and bioprospecting.

(10) Argentina noted that the recent deaths of Ambassador Jorge Berguño of Chile and Dr Teodor Negoita of Romania had deprived the Antarctic community of their considerable talents and experience. Recalling that Ambassador Berguño had attended 19 Consultative Meetings and had represented Chile at many other international meetings, Argentina paid tribute to his many important contributions to the development of the Antarctic Treaty over several decades. His extensive knowledge and wisdom in Antarctic law and governance will be sorely missed by his many colleagues and friends from around the world. Chile thanked Argentina for its fine words and commented that his legal excellence and personal experience could not be replaced. Romania spoke about how Dr Negoita had contributed to Antarctic science. The Meeting stood in silence to commemorate their contributions.

## Item 2: Election of Officers and Creation of Working Groups

(11) Mr Richard Rowe, Representative of Australia (Host Country of ATCM XXXV) was elected Vice-chair. In accordance with Rule 7 of the Rules of Procedure, Dr Manfred Reinke, Executive Secretary of the Antarctic Treaty Secretariat, acted as Secretary to the Meeting. Mr Jorge Roballo, head of the Host Country Secretariat, acted as Deputy Secretary. Dr Yves Frenot of France had been elected as Chair of the Committee for Environmental Protection at CEP XIII.

(12) Three Working Groups were established:

- Working Group on Legal and Institutional Affairs;
- Working Group on Tourism and Non-governmental Activities;
- Working Group on Operational Matters.

(13) The following Chairs of the Working Groups were elected:

- Legal and Institutional Affairs: Mr Richard Rowe of Australia;
- Tourism and Non-governmental Activities: Ambassador Donald Mackay of New Zealand;
- Operational Matters: Dr José Retamales of Chile.

## Item 3: Adoption of the Agenda and Allocation of Items

(14) The following Agenda was proposed:

1. Opening of the Meeting
2. Election of Officers and Creation of Working Groups
3. Adoption of the Agenda and Allocation of Items
4. Operation of the Antarctic Treaty System: Reports by Parties, Observers and Experts
5. Operation of the Antarctic Treaty System: General Matters
6. Operation of the Antarctic Treaty System: Review of the Secretariat's Situation
7. Report of the Committee for Environmental Protection
8. Liability: Implementation of Decision 1 (2005)
9. Safety and Operations in Antarctica
10. Tourism and Non-Governmental Activities in the Antarctic Treaty Area
11. Inspections under the Antarctic Treaty and the Environment Protocol
12. Science Issues, Science Cooperation and Facilitation, including the Legacy of the International Polar Year 2007-2008
13. Implications of Climate Change for the Management of the Antarctic Treaty Area
14. Operational Issues
15. Education Issues
16. Exchange of Information
17. Biological Prospecting in Antarctica
18. Development of a Multi-year Strategic Work Plan
19. Commemoration of the 50th Anniversary of the entry into force of the Antarctic Treaty
20. Preparation of the 35th Meeting
21. Any Other Business
22. Adoption of the Final Report

(15) Deputy Secretary Mr Jorge Roballo described the activities involved in agenda item 19, which included a visit to the historic corvette *Uruguay*, a meeting session attended by several high representatives and a celebratory reception organised by the Argentine Foreign Ministry. Given the limited time available it was clear from the comments of several Parties that careful planning would be needed to allow for all those who wished to make statements.

(16)  The Meeting adopted the following allocation of agenda items:
- Plenary: Items 1, 2, 3, 4, 7, 18, 19, 20, 21, 22
- Legal and Institutional Working Group: Items 5, 6, 8, 17, 18 and review of draft measures of CEP report, Item 7
- Tourism Working Group: Items 9, 10
- Operational Matters Working Group: Items 9, 11, 12, 13, 14, 15, 16

Some documents submitted under Items 9 and 10 would be discussed in a joint meeting of the Tourism Working Group and the Operational Matters Working Group.

(17)  The Meeting decided to allocate draft instruments arising out of the work of the Committee for Environmental Protection and the Working Groups on Operational Matters and Tourism to the Legal and Institutional Working Group for consideration of their legal and institutional aspects.

## Item 4: Operation of the Antarctic Treaty System: Reports by Parties, Observers and Experts

(18)  Mr Michel Rocard (former Prime Minister of France), together with Mr Robert Hawke (former Prime Minister of Australia) and Mr Felipe González, (former President of the Government of Spain) were closely involved in the rejection of the ratification of the Convention for the Regulation of Antarctic Mineral Resources Activities (CRAMRA) and the initiation and development of the Protocol on Environmental Protection to the Antarctic Treaty (Protocol). This year marked the 20th anniversary of the adoption of the Protocol on Environmental Protection to the Antarctic Treaty. Recalling the history of the negotiation of the Protocol after the failure to ratify CRAMRA, Mr Rocard highlighted the need to extend the protection of the Antarctic environment by increasing the number of parties to the Protocol. Knowing that 14 of the Non-Consultative Parties had not yet acceded to the Protocol France, together with Australia and Spain, had decided that it would be important to persuade as many of them as possible to embrace the Protocol, and proposed that the Meeting should adopt a Resolution urging these States to accede to the Protocol. Both Italy and Chile strongly supported this initiative to increase the effectiveness of the regime.

(19)  Australia thanked Mr Rocard, reflecting on the instrumental role that Mr Rocard, Mr Hawke and Mr González had played in the development of

the Protocol. Australia expressed its regret that Mr Hawke was unable to attend the ATCM due to illness. Australia conveyed a personal message from Mr Hawke which highlighted the significance of the Protocol, which places environmental protection at the front of our attention. Mr Hawke noted the progress made over the past 20 years on protecting and managing Antarctica's remarkable natural values, and that it is imperative for those Non-Consultative Parties who have not acceded to the Protocol to do so. Australia confirmed that it remained strongly committed to the Protocol noting that it was co-sponsoring, together with France and Spain, a Resolution to appeal to Non-Consultative Parties who have not yet acceded to the Protocol to do so. Australia commended the Resolution to the Meeting.

(20) Pursuant to Recommendation XIII-2, the Meeting received reports from: The United States in its capacity as Depositary of the Antarctic Treaty and the Protocol; the United Kingdom in its capacity as Depositary of the Convention for the Conservation of Antarctic Seals (CCAS); Australia in its capacity as Depositary of the Convention on the Conservation of Antarctic Marine Living Resources (CCAMLR) and Depositary of the Agreement on the Conservation of Albatrosses and Petrels (ACAP); the Commission for the Conservation of Antarctic Marine Living Resources (CCAMLR); the Scientific Committee on Antarctic Research (SCAR), and the Council of Managers of National Antarctic Programs (COMNAP).

(21) The United States, in its capacity as Depositary Government, reported on the status of the Antarctic Treaty and the Protocol on Environmental Protection to the Antarctic Treaty (IP 22).

(22) No new States had acceded during the year and there were now 48 Parties to the Antarctic Treaty and 34 Parties to the Protocol (see Vol. 2).

(23) The United Kingdom, as Depositary for the Convention on the Conservation of Antarctic Seals, reported that there had been no accessions to the Convention since ATCM XXXIII. No seals were killed during the period between March 2009 and February 2010 (IP 3). The United Kingdom expressed its appreciation to Parties to the Convention for meeting the 30 June yearly deadline for reporting the information referenced in paragraph 6 of the Annex to the Convention to SCAR and the Contracting Parties (see Vol. 2, Part III, section 3).

(24) Australia, in its capacity as Depositary for the Convention for the Conservation of Antarctic Marine Living Resources, reported that there had been no new accessions to the Convention since ATCM XXXIII and that there were currently 34 Parties to the Convention (IP 67).

(25)  Australia, in its capacity as Depositary for the Agreement on the Conservation of Albatrosses and Petrels, reported that there had been no new accessions to the Agreement since ATCM XXXIII and that there were currently 13 Parties to the Agreement (IP 66).

(26)  The CCAMLR observer introduced IP 80 *Report by the CCAMLR Observer to the Thirty-Fourth Antarctic Treaty Consultative Meeting*, a report on the outcomes of CCAMLR XXIX which was held in Hobart, Australia in October-November 2010. He reported that six CCAMLR Members harvested 211,974 tonnes of krill in 2009/2010, noting that Subarea 48.1 was closed when the catch reached 99% of the trigger level for the subarea. Catches of toothfish in 2009/2010 were 14,518 tonnes and the reported catch of icefish was 363 tonnes. He summarised the CCAMLR Scientific Committee's priorities over the next two to three years, which included feedback management for the krill fishery, assessment of toothfish fisheries, MPAs and climate change. He reported on plans for CCAMLR's MPA Workshop to be held in Brest, France in August 2011, and informed the Meeting that the Commission was working to establish a CCAMLR Scientific Scholarship. Finally, he advised that Norway had been selected as the current Chair of the Commission and highlighted that 7 April 2012 would mark the 30th anniversary of the entry into force of the Convention for the Conservation of Antarctic Marine Living Resources.

(27)  The President of the Scientific Committee on Antarctic Research introduced the SCAR Report (IP 81), which included the main activities of SCAR from 2010, many covered in more detail in other agenda items. Highlighting some key items, he mentioned that in 2009 SCAR underwent an external review, had recently published a new six year strategic plan, and is in the process of renewing its major science program. The next Antarctic Earth Sciences symposium will be held in Edinburgh in 2011. The last SCAR Open Science Conference was held in Buenos Aires in 2010, whilst the next one will be held in 2012 in Portland, Oregon, U.S. SCAR was pleased to announce the second recipient of the Martha Muse Prize for Science and Policy, Professor Helen Fricker of the United States of America. Monaco had become the latest member of SCAR, bringing the total membership to 36 countries. With various partners, SCAR had developed the Southern Ocean Observing System plan, whilst a new science plan had been recently jointly published with IASC on ice sheet mass balance for both poles. SCAR had recently held an initial workshop to develop a new initiative on Antarctic conservation for the 21st century.

(28) The Executive Secretary of the Council of Managers of National Antarctic Programs introduced the COMNAP Report (IP 10). She highlighted several features including the new COMNAP Research Fellowship, a very successful symposium titled "Responding to change – new approaches" and good practice workshops on energy management and on the implications of dealing with the results from the IPY project on aliens in Antarctica.

(29) In relation to Article III-2 of the Antarctic Treaty, the Meeting received reports from the International Hydrographic Organization (IHO), the Antarctic and Southern Ocean Coalition (ASOC), the International Association of Antarctica Tour Operators (IAATO) and the United Nations Environment Programme (UNEP). These reports can be found in Vol. 2.

(30) The International Hydrographic Organization introduced IP 114 *Report by the International Hydrographic Organization (IHO) on "Cooperation in Hydrographic Surveying and Charting of Antarctic Waters."* It highlighted the continued use of seminars given to a wide variety of audiences to draw attention to the way in which others could contribute to the work. Whilst IHO was concerned with the slow rate of data gathering it appreciated that survey work in Antarctica was very expensive. It paid tribute to the support from IAATO ships and said that more data collection by ships of opportunity would be welcomed. Progress with Electronic Navigation Charts for the Southern Ocean continues.

(31) The representative of the Antarctic and Southern Ocean Coalition introduced the ASOC report (IP 129). ASOC noted that it had submitted a range of papers on key topics this year including papers on ocean acidification, climate change, a review of the first twenty years of the Environment Protocol, Marine Protected Areas and the Ross Sea, as well as developments in tourism.

(32) The International Association of Antarctica Tour Operators introduced its annual report, IP 108. IAATO expressed that it appreciates engaging with Treaty Parties in developing tourism management policies that are pragmatic and justifiable as it addresses important safety and environmental concerns. For the 2010-11 season, overall tourist activities from IAATO member operators continued to decline due to the worldwide economic downturn. IAATO remains committed to a policy of transparency and openness regarding its activities to ensure effective management and, where incidents are concerned, noted that lessons can be learned. It also noted its members' logistical support to the scientific community, and monetary support to Antarctic conservation organizations. It invited ATCM attendees to the next IAATO Annual Meeting in Providence, Rhode Island, U.S., 1-4 May 2012.

(33)   The representative of UNEP drew attention to the joint paper with ASOC (IP 113) reviewing the effectiveness of annual reporting by Parties on steps taken to implement the Protocol.

## Item 5: Operation of the Antarctic Treaty System: General Matters

(34)   Argentina introduced WP 24 *Progress Report of the Intersessional Contact Group on Review of ATCM Recommendations*. The ICG was established by ATCM XXXIII to examine and review the status of ATCM recommendations on protected areas and monuments; operational matters; and environmental issues other than area protection and management. WP 24 is an initial report listing those recommendations which could be designated as no longer current. The results of the review are summarised in WP 24 Appendix 1: List of recommendations proposed to be considered as no longer current; and WP 24 Appendix 2: List of recommendations that require further advice.

(35)   It was noted that the CEP was also considering WP 24. It was agreed to refer Appendix 2 to the CEP and SCAR for their review and advice.

(36)   Following discussion on how to deal with recommendations determined to be no longer current, the Meeting agreed that they should be archived for reference by the Secretariat and clearly identified as no longer current.

(37)   There was some discussion on how to address certain Recommendations related to Antarctic seals adopted prior to the Convention on the Conservation of Antarctic Seals (CCAS), particularly for those States that were not party to CCAS. Argentina, following consultation with other delegations, suggested that in order to avoid confusion, the four recommendations in Item 3 of Appendix 2 should appear as current.

(38)   Sweden sought clarification regarding Appendix 1, point 8, in relation to measures that preceded the Protocol on Environmental Protection to the Antarctic Treaty (Protocol). Argentina noted that this point was not addressed by the ICG and suggested that further consideration may be required. The United Kingdom clarified that all Consultative Parties were members of the Protocol and in light of Article 22 of the Protocol, this would remain the case.

(39)   Consequently, and after checking that there were no Non-Consultative Parties that had approved these four recommendations of Appendix 1.8, the Meeting noted that these recommendations could be declared as no longer current.

(40)  Argentina reported on the informal consultations considering the proposals of the Intersessional Contact Group on the Review of the ATCM Recommendations and noted that the CEP, after discussion of the recommendations, had advised that Recommendations III-8, III-10, IV-22, X-4, X-7, XII-3, and XIII-4 should be considered no longer current.

(41)  Sweden recalled the discussion by the Meeting of the status of Recommendation IV-22 on sealing which predated the adoption of the Convention on the Conservation of Antarctic Seals. The Meeting was of the view that Recommendation IV-22 should remain current to avoid confusion about the obligations of the Consultative Parties with respect to sealing in the Antarctic.

(42)  The Meeting agreed to adopt Decision 1 (2011), indicating clearly which measures were no longer current.

(43)  Argentina noted that the Intersessional Contact Group (ICG) on the Review of the ATCM Recommendations still had work outstanding in consideration of the papers referred to in SP 6 (2010), specifically in relation to recommendations on operational issues. The Meeting thanked Argentina for the work it had undertaken as convenor. Viewing the completion of this work as important and following further discussion, the Meeting welcomed the offer by the Executive Secretary for the Secretariat to undertake this intersessional work in relation to recommendations on operational issues. The Secretariat would convene an ICG to carry out this review and would report to ATCM XXXV.

(44)  The Netherlands and Germany introduced WP 22 *An Additional Procedure for Intersessional Consultations among ATCPs*. They drew attention to requests by outside bodies, specifically mentioning requests from certain UN Secretariat Divisions regarding the provision of relevant information from the Antarctic Treaty Secretariat, pointing out that the Secretariat had neither a mandate to respond, nor any intersessional mechanism to organise a consultation procedure. The Netherlands highlighted the relevance of the Antarctic Treaty to international actors, and the need to provide the international community with timely and up to date substantive responses. The Netherlands considered that Rule 46 was insufficient for this purpose and was seldom used. It suggested that the point of contact for the future Host Country might be best placed to provide a substantive response following consultation with Treaty Parties.

(45) While endorsing the general aim of WP 22 to improve efficiency in the intersessional work of the ATCM, several Parties drew attention to the need to respect the principle of the consensus decision-making process, and to take into consideration the need for Parties to have adequate time to consider and draft responses. Norway noted the lack of clarity regarding the relationship between the UN and ATCM in the request from the UN referred to in WP 22 and that this could raise questions relating to Article IV of the Treaty. China emphasised the need to ensure that a Party had seen the information and proposed that the Secretariat be required to keep a copy of the receipt of a given draft response from that Party.

(46) Following further discussion, the Netherlands noted there were four main points of concern: the importance of upholding the principle of consensus; the need to allow adequate time for delegations to consider draft responses; clarity regarding the nature and relevance of information requests from appropriate international organisations; and the role of the host State *vis-a-vis* the role of the Executive Secretary. Following informal consultations conducted by Germany and the Netherlands, the Meeting agreed to amend the Rules of Procedure.

(47) The Meeting agreed to consider two WPs together, WP 25 *The Timely Submission of Papers in Advance of ATCMs*, and WP 36 *A Proposed New Approach to the handling of Information Papers*, and to keep in mind the interest of the Committee on Environmental Protection in the two papers.

(48) Introducing WP 25 *The Timely Submission of Papers in Advance of ATCMs*, Germany and the United States noted the need to establish incentives for the timely submission of papers by a fixed deadline. They proposed a three step approach: amendment of the ATCM Rules of Procedure; amendment of the CEP Rules of Procedure; and the replacement of the existing guidelines for submission of documents with a new set of procedures, including new mechanisms.

(49) France introduced WP 36 *A Proposed New Approach to the handling of Information Papers* on behalf of Australia and New Zealand, and commented that by combining the ideas in the two papers, the efficiency of preparation of documents would be enhanced. The steady increase in the number of Information Papers was creating difficulties and expense. Categorising IPs into three types – Information Papers, Expert Papers and Background Papers – would make it easier for Working Groups to decide how to use them. Australia drew attention to the urgent need to streamline the handling

of Information Papers to improve the efficiency of meetings, and noted there would be no change to Working Papers or Secretariat Papers.

(50) Several Parties agreed on the need to restrict the number of Information Papers presented, and emphasised a need to focus on establishing firm submission deadlines. Norway and Japan both expressed concern regarding the joint consideration of these papers as they believed they were trying to achieve different objectives. They highlighted the need to focus on achieving simplification. China noted the need to establish a clear definition of an Information Paper. Sweden supported the intent of the respective papers, while registering its concern about WP 25, paragraph 2, regarding the translation of late papers.

(51) Germany urged discussion of whether a Meeting or a Meeting Chairman should be involved in deciding if a document was late, stating that exceptions allowing for late submissions would have to be carefully drafted. Following open-ended contact group discussions, Germany reported that while preliminary agreement among participants had been established for change as indicated in WP 25, consensus had not yet been reached regarding the precise wording.

(52) Following a contact group meeting involving both the ATCM and the CEP, New Zealand noted how the draft proposal regarding WP 36 on the designation and handling of papers prepared for the ATCM differed from the current approach. In addition to the current designation of Secretariat Papers, Working Papers and Information Papers, the contact group supported the use of Background Papers (BG). BGs would be intended to provide a formal route for information to other Meeting participants. BGs would, however, be included on the list of ATCM meeting documents listed in the Final Report and archived on the Secretariat website. New Zealand advised that the contact group had consulted the CEP on where BGs were expected to be most useful.

(53) During further discussion, the Meeting agreed with the proposed approach in a revised version of WP 36, and that WP 25 should be merged with it as appropriate. The proponents of the two papers agreed to work on the production of a single draft Decision, revising the ATCM and CEP Rules of Procedure as well as the Guidelines for the Submission, Translation and Distribution of Documents for the ATCM and the CEP. The Netherlands noted that such a revision should also incorporate the amendments required as a result of the Meeting's endorsement of WP 22. The Meeting adopted Decision 2 (2011) containing "Revised ATCM Rules of Procedure (2011)" and "Revised CEP Rules of Procedure (2011)".

(54) Introducing WP 40 *Strengthening Support for the Madrid Protocol*, France noted the importance of paying tribute to the twentieth anniversary of the adoption of the Protocol. France noted the personal nature of Mr Rocard's speech. France emphasised that the intention of the proposal provided in WP 40 was to inform the Meeting of the desire of France, Australia and Spain to establish coordinated diplomatic action that would encourage the fourteen Non-Consultative Parties that were not yet Party to the Protocol, to become so. As co-sponsors of this proposal, Australia and Spain noted the importance of commemorating and reinforcing the fundamental principles of the Protocol, and emphasised the importance they attached to appealing to all Non-Consultative Parties to become Party to the Protocol, as was proposed in the draft resolution presented in WP 40.

(55) The United States drew attention to the major contributions made by many Consultative Parties to the development of the Protocol and indicated that it supported launching an effort by Consultative Parties to convince remaining Non-Consultative Parties to become Party to the Protocol. It noted that the message to these Non-Consultative Parties needs to be from and acceptable to all Consultative Parties.

(56) Norway thanked the proponents of WP 40, and echoed the concerns of the United States regarding the consistency of the message. It suggested that one way forward might be for the Chairman of the Meeting to write to those Parties that have not already acceded to the Protocol.

(57) As there was strong support for the objective of WP 40, and given the variety of possible mechanisms for promoting accession to the Protocol (including contact by individual Treaty Parties, a letter from the Chairman of the ATCM, a letter from the Executive Secretary on behalf of the Treaty Parties, changes to the text of the draft resolution presented in WP 40, and the suggested addition of a paragraph to the Declaration on Antarctic Cooperation on the Occasion of the 50th Anniversary of the Entry into Force of the Antarctic Treaty agreed at this ATCM, referring also to the 20th anniversary of the Madrid Protocol and urging additional accessions to the Protocol), an open-ended contact group was set up to consider the best way forward.

(58) France, Australia and Spain offered to take the lead in organising the representations on behalf of the Consultative Parties that would be made to the 14 Non-Consultative Parties not Party to the Protocol. They indicated that they planned to organise demarches in Non-Consultative Party capitals, to which all Consultative Parties would be invited to participate. At each demarche, the representatives of the participating Consultative Parties would

provide a copy of the Resolution concerning this initiative, the Declaration adopted at this ATCM and an aide-memoire providing reasons for acceding to the Protocol. The three countries indicated that they would draft an aide-memoire and coordinate its content with the Consultative Parties in advance of the demarches. The *aide-memoire* would be available sufficiently in advance of the demarches so that embassies of participating Consultative Parties would have adequate time for preparation. Norway proposed that the contents of the aide-memoire be equal to that of the Resolution.

(59) The Meeting welcomed the offer by France, Australia and Spain and agreed that the procedures proposed by the three Parties would be followed. The Meeting then adopted Resolution 1 (2011).

(60) On adoption of this Resolution, the United Kingdom highlighted that the procedure adopted in relation to this initiative, namely, the practice of naming Consultative Parties in the operative paragraphs of a Resolution, should not be regarded as a precedent.

(61) The Russian Federation introduced WP 55 *On a strategy for the development of the Russian Federation activities in the Antarctic for the period until 2020 and longer-term perspective.* The Russian Federation noted that its activities are designed, among other objectives, to strengthen the economic capacity of the Russian Federation by enhanced use of the marine biological resources of the Southern Ocean and complex investigations of Antarctic mineral, hydrocarbon and other natural resources. It clarified that these investigations would be purely scientific and consistent with the statement it made at ATCM XXV (Warsaw) on exploratory research, and would not contravene Article 7 of the Environment Protocol.

(62) The Russian Federation noted that its activities would also include research related to assessing the role and place of the Antarctic in global climate change; activities related to the GLONASS navigational satellite system; construction and modernisation of Russia's Antarctic stations; the construction of two large-tonnage ice-class research vessels to conduct integrated fishing and oceanographic research; and a new vessel for geological-geophysical studies of the Southern Ocean.

(63) The Meeting took note of the Russian Federation's proposal. The United Kingdom thanked the Russian Federation for its clarification that the references in WP 55 relating to minerals and hydrocarbons were consistent with ATCM XXV - IP 14 (Russian Federation) and with paragraph 125 of the Final Report of ATCM XXV.

(64)   ASOC presented IP 89 rev. 1 *The Antarctic Environmental Protocol, 1991-2011*, noting the accomplishments of the Parties since the entry into force of the Protocol. These included the scope and depth of compliance with the Protocol by some Parties; the development of the CEP as a robust body; the approval of a reviewed Annex II; and the agreement of a Liability Annex.

(65)   ASOC also identified several concerns, including the need to identify and protect the wilderness values of the Antarctic; the proliferation of national stations; uneven implementation of Environmental Impact Assessments; inconsistent use of the electronic information exchange system; the cumulative impact of human activities in the Antarctic; and the need to develop an effective matrix of protected areas. It noted the need to enhance synergies between the ATCM-CEP and CCAMLR to establish appropriate MPAs and ASPAs in the Southern Ocean. ASOC suggested that IP 89 rev.1 might be used as the basis for a review of the implementation of the Protocol for the 25$^{th}$ anniversary of its signature in five years (2016).

(66)   The Netherlands introduced IP 95 *Paying for Ecosystem Services (PES) of Antarctica?*, noting that ecosystem services could be viewed as the dividend society receives from natural capital. While there were limited human activities in Antarctica, the Netherlands saw it as an ecosystem with great potential for future use. To investigate the options for implementation of a PES scheme in Antarctica it was relevant to ask: Who would be the sellers of Antarctic ecosystem services? What was a well-defined service? Who would be the eligible buyers? What are the transaction costs of the implementation of payment schemes?

(67)   The Netherlands indicated its hope that this paper, the first ever on this subject in the ATCM, would give rise to a debate and an exchange of views that could mature over the following years. The Meeting noted the usefulness of the paper for future consideration of this subject area.

## Item 6: Operation of the Antarctic Treaty System: Review of the Secretariat's Situation

(68)   The Chairman introduced agenda item 6 by referring the Working Group to SP 2 rev. 2 *Secretariat Report 2010/11*; SP 3 *Secretariat Programme 2011/12*; and SP 4 *Contributions Received by the Antarctic Treaty Secretariat 2008-2012*.

(69)   The Executive Secretary thanked Parties for their support and expressed appreciation to the Government of Argentina for its excellent and continuing

efforts in preparing for ATCM XXXIV and in supporting the activities of the Secretariat.

(70) The Executive Secretary noted improvements to the ATS website including the addition of all measures and procedures adopted at ATCM XXXIII and CEP XIII, a clearer view of the site on its home page with easier access to other sections of the site from the home page; and a re-organisation enabling users to download all meeting documents in one step.

(71) The Executive Secretary reported that the Secretariat had realised a number of significant cost savings associated with editing, printing and distribution. The Final Report of the ATCM had been distributed through the Parties' representatives in Buenos Aires. Additional print-ready copies are available through Amazon (*http://www.amazon.com*). The CEP Handbook had been updated and a *Compilation of Key Documents of the Antarctic Treaty System*, in two volumes, had been produced. The Executive Secretary noted that because of the number of pages required to include the Antarctic Treaty, Environment Protocol, CCAMLR, CCAS and Secretariat-related documents in a single volume, it had not proved possible to produce a pocket-sized version. The Rules of Procedure and Administrative Regulations had been printed in a slimmer volume, Volume 2, which would allow the Secretariat to revise the smaller volume, to take account of changes and revisions without reissuing Volume 1. Additional copies of both volumes are available through Amazon.

(72) The Executive Secretary reported that the Secretariat had entered into a two-year contract with the company ONCALL Conference Interpreters and Translators for interpretation and translation at ATCM XXXIV and XXXV, with cost savings of approximately US$168,000 – US$303,000 compared to the costs of the previous firm which provided the services at ACTM XXXII and XXXIII. ONCALL had organised the language services for CCAMLR in Hobart since 2002 and is certified under ISO quality management standards.

(73) The Executive Secretary informed the Meeting of the relocation of the Secretariat to its new premises provided by Argentina located at Maipú 757, in Buenos Aires. He underscored that the new premises were more spacious and a considerable improvement to the Secretariat's working conditions. He also pointed out that Argentina had provided strong support to the Secretariat towards securing the new space and commended the Host Country's close cooperation with the Secretariat and timely intervention on this matter. Argentina advised the Meeting that it had finalised arrangements to cover all expenses associated with the relocation of the Secretariat. The Meeting expressed appreciation to Argentina for its support and generosity.

(74) The Executive Secretary reported on several personnel matters including an upgrade in the position of the Finance Officer to a G-2 rank, as agreed by ACTM XXXIII; the extension of the contract of the Assistant Executive Secretary to 2014; and the injury of a staff member while at work. In the latter case, he advised that the Staff Regulations of the Secretariat did not address accidents in the workplace. The Secretariat had received advice from its legal advisors and was in consultation with the Argentine authorities on the matter.

(75) The Executive Secretary noted that the Auditor's report of the period up to 31 March 2010 indicated, in customary language, that the Secretariat's financial statements were presented fairly in all respects.

(76) The Executive Secretary reported that the former Executive Secretary, Mr Jan Huber, in a letter dated 25 January 2011, clarified that since he would receive pension benefits from the Netherlands Foreign Service there was no need for him to request termination and pension benefits from the Secretariat as per regulation 10.4 of the Staff Regulations.

(77) In presenting SP 3 *Secretariat Programme 2011/12*, the Executive Secretary noted a requirement for travel to attend meetings of COMNAP and CCAMLR, plans to publish the decisions and Report of ACTM XXXIV and support intersessional contact groups organised by the ATCM and CEP, as well as the anticipated continued use and expansion of modern means of communication. The Secretariat requested Parties to provide past Reports and other documents for the ATCM archives, particularly in languages other than English.

(78) The Executive Secretary emphasised that it was his goal to have absolute zero real growth in the budget for 2012/13. He indicated that the budget should remain stable through 2013-2015, from which time he predicted a rise of approximately 2%.

(79) Japan requested clarification of how the figure shown as Working Capital Fund in Appendix 1 of SP 3 had been calculated. The Executive Secretary replied that the Working Capital Fund represented one sixth of the contributions of the Parties, in accordance with the Financial Regulations.

(80) Japan also welcomed the forecast budget for 2012/13 as it showed zero nominal growth and noted that the forecast budgets after 2013 as indicated in SP 3 did not mean any commitment by the Parties.

(81) Germany thanked the Secretariat for its activities in general and for the budget draft for the coming year, noting that any increase in salaries would use the same methodology that had been applied in the previous two years.

(82)  The Meeting commended the Executive Secretary on his excellent work in many aspects, including the budget, and particularly for achieving a decrease in interpretation and translation costs, and expressed its wishes for zero nominal growth in the budget to be maintained.

(83)  The Executive Secretary introduced SP 4 *Contributions received by the Antarctic Treaty Secretariat 2008-2012,* noting that the Secretariat was in receipt of most of the contributions for 2010 and 2011, and confirming that there were no outstanding contributions due from previous years. He urged Parties with outstanding payments for this year to provide their contributions as soon as possible.

(84)  Peru advised the Meeting that governmental approval had recently been given for payment of its contribution, which would be made within weeks.

(85)  The Meeting thanked the Executive Secretary for his comprehensive and clear presentation of SP 2 rev. 2, SP 3 and SP 4, and for his continued efforts and innovative ideas for keeping costs down. The Meeting approved the Audited Financial Report 2009/10 (presented in SP 2 rev. 2). It agreed to take note of the five year forward budget profile for 2011 to 2016 and to approve all other components of the Secretariat Programme (SP 3) including the budget for 2011/12 and the Forecast Budget for 2012/13. The Meeting adopted Decision 3 (2011).

(86)  Noting that the Electronic Information Exchange System (EIES) was useful in the context of search and rescue operations in Antarctica, the Executive Secretary recommended that Parties make greater use of the EIES. He indicated that only 17 Parties had added information to it during the past year. He also noted that the CEP had some concerns about the ease of use of the system. Improvements to the system may be needed as well as further encouragement to Parties to add to the information contained in the system.

(87)  In a response to a request from the United Kingdom, the Secretariat circulated a list of which Parties had been using the EIES over the past three years, in order to facilitate discussions about the issues which were preventing its wider use. Several Parties noted that in its current form the system was already relatively easy to use and proposed an increase in real time use of this system by all Parties.

(88)  New Zealand noted that if the Norwegian vessel *Berserk* had obtained a permit and this information had been available through the EIES, then this might have assisted search and rescue efforts. New Zealand encouraged all Parties to post the information that was available to them.

(89) France drew attention to WP 11 *Follow-up to the unauthorised presence of French yachts within the Treaty area and damage caused to the hut known as Wordie House - Observations on the consequences of the affair*, noting that only a few Parties used the EIES.

(90) The United States commended use of the EIES for all Parties that had expedition or tourist-related activity to report; however, the United States also shared the concerns raised in the CEP on the ease of use of the system, especially for Parties with numerous expeditions involving many landings. Sweden suggested that those Parties not engaged in non-Governmental or tourist Antarctic activity in a given year make a nil return in EIES.

## Item 7: Report of the Committee for Environmental Protection

(91) Dr Yves Frenot, Chair of the Committee for Environmental Protection, introduced the report of CEP XIV. The CEP considered 46 Working Papers, 68 Information Papers and 4 Secretariat Papers (the full list of papers is provided as an Annex to the Report of CEP XIV).

### *Strategic Discussions on the Future of the CEP (CEP Agenda Item 3)*

(92) The Committee revised and updated its Five-year Work Plan. It discussed in detail the issue of wastes and clean-up of sites of past activities and decided to give higher priority to such issues in the future. Additionally, in order to answer to the ATCM request contained in Decision 4 (2010), it added to its work plan a special task on repair or remediation of environmental damage with the highest priority.

### *Operation of the CEP (CEP Agenda Item 4)*

(93) The Committee noted that the level of compliance in the submission of annual reports on the implementation of the Protocol remained low, even twelve years after ratification. In order to increase this level of compliance, some Members pointed out that the Electronic Information Exchange System (EIES) could be more user-friendly.

(94) The Secretariat agreed to convene an informal contact group on the CEP Discussion Forum to coordinate technical proposals from Members on this matter.

## Climate Change Impact for the Environment (CEP Agenda Item 5)

(95)  The Committee considered a proposal by the United Kingdom and Norway to track actions to address the recommendations arising from the 2010 Antarctic Treaty Meeting of Experts on Climate Change (ATME Climate Change). It endorsed the proposal that the Secretariat continue to record the actions related to each of the 30 ATME recommendations, by both the CEP and the ATCM.

(96)  The Committee considered a methodology proposed by the United Kingdom and Norway to assess possible impacts of climate change on ASPAs. It noted the wide interest of such an approach and encouraged interested Members to contribute to work to further develop and define such methodology.

## Environmental Impact Assessment (CEP Agenda Item 6)

### Draft Comprehensive Environmental Evaluations

(97)  Two draft Comprehensive Environmental Evaluations (CEEs) were circulated in advance of CEP XIV and examined by the Committee:

*1. Draft Comprehensive Environmental Evaluation for the Proposed Exploration of Subglacial Lake Ellsworth, Antarctica (United Kingdom)*

(98)  The Committee discussed in detail this draft CEE prepared by the United Kingdom as well as the report by Norway of the intersessional contact group (ICG) established to consider the draft CEE in accordance with the *Procedures for intersessional CEP consideration of draft CEEs,* and additional information provided by the United Kingdom in response to issues raised in the ICG. The Committee advised the Meeting that:

(99)  The draft CEE and the process followed by the United Kingdom generally conform to the requirements of Article 3 of Annex I to the Protocol on Environmental Protection to the Antarctic Treaty.

(100) The information contained in the draft CEE supports its conclusions that the proposed activity will have no more than a minor or transitory impact on the Antarctic environment, taking into account the rigorous preventative and mitigation measures prepared and adopted by the proponent. Furthermore, the proposed activity is justified on the basis of the global scientific importance and value to be gained by the exploration of Lake Ellsworth.

(101) When preparing the required final CEE, the proponent should consider, and address as appropriate, all comments raised by Members. In particular, the

ATCM's attention is drawn to the suggestions that the final CEE should provide further detail regarding: assessment of the activities of the support contractor, further documentation/consideration as to the issue of potential mixing at break-through; further discussion as to how to minimise the disturbance of the water column as a result of the presence of the scientific equipment; assessment of risk of equipment loss in the lake; consideration of the size of the on-ice team in light of project safety; and considerations relating to international collaboration.

(102) The draft CEE is clear and well-structured, well written and with high quality graphs and figures.

(103) The CEP recommended that the ATCM endorse these views and the Meeting accepted the CEP's advice.

*2. Draft Comprehensive Environmental Evaluation for the construction and operation of the Jang Bogo Antarctic Research Station, Terra Nova Bay, Antarctica (Republic of Korea)*

(104) The Committee discussed in detail this draft CEE and also discussed the report by Australia of the ICG established to consider the draft CEE in accordance with the *Procedures for intersessional CEP consideration of Draft CEEs*, and additional information provided by the Republic of Korea in response to issues raised in the ICG. The Committee advised the meeting that:

(105) The draft CEE generally conforms to the requirements of Article 3 of Annex I to the Protocol on Environmental Protection to the Antarctic Treaty.

(106) The information contained in the draft CEE supports the proponent's conclusion that the construction and operation of Jang Bogo station is likely to have more than a minor or transitory impact on the environment. The information provided also supports the proponent's conclusion that these impacts will be outweighed by the knowledge and information to be gained through the research activities that will be supported by the station.

(107) When preparing the required final CEE, the proponent should consider, and address as appropriate, the comments raised by Members. In particular, the ATCM's attention is drawn to the suggestions that the final CEE should provide further detail regarding: the possible cumulative impacts of activities by multiple operators in the Terra Nova Bay region; the ancillary station infrastructure; the wastewater treatment system; the management of sewage and food wastes; oil spill prevention; measures to prevent impacts on the

skua colony; measures to prevent the introduction of non-native species; and plans for decommissioning the station.

(108) The draft CEE is clear, well structured, and well presented.

(109) The CEP recommended that the ATCM endorse this view and the Meeting accepted the CEP's advice.

## Other EIA Matters

(110) The Committee was informed on the progress of the CEP Tourism Study conducted by New Zealand, recalling the ATCM's interest in the CEP's proposal to examine the environmental aspects and impacts of tourism and non-governmental activities in Antarctica. The work which has been identified as a priority by the CEP will be completed in the coming year and a report will be presented at CEP XV.

(111) In addition, the Committee was informed on the circulation of two final CEEs:

- *Final Comprehensive Environmental Evaluation (CEE) of New Indian Research Station at Larsemann Hills* (India)
- *Final Comprehensive Environmental Evaluation of the "Water Sampling of the Subglacial Lake Vostok"* (Russian Federation)

(112) The Russian Federation also provided information on the technology for investigating water of the subglacial Lake Vostok.

## Area Protection and Management (CEP Agenda Item 7)

*Management Plans for Protected and Managed Areas*

(113) The Committee had before it 12 revised management plans for 11 ASPAs and one ASMA. One of these had been subject to review by the Subsidiary Group on Management Plans (SGMP) and 11 revised management plans had been submitted directly to CEP XIV.

(114) Accepting the CEP's advice, the Meeting adopted the following Measures on Protected and Managed Areas:

- Measure 1 (2011): Antarctic Specially Protected Area No 116 (New College Valley, Caughley Beach, Cape Bird, Ross Island): Revised Management Plan
- Measure 2 (2011): Antarctic Specially Protected Area No 120 (Pointe-Géologie Archipelago, Terre Adélie): Revised Management Plan

- Measure 3 (2011): Antarctic Specially Protected Area No 122 (Arrival Heights, Hut Point Peninsula, Ross Island): Revised Management Plan
- Measure 4 (2011): Antarctic Specially Protected Area No 126 (Byers Peninsula, Livingston Island, South Shetland Islands): Revised Management Plan
- Measure 5 (2011): Antarctic Specially Protected Area No 127 (Haswell Island): Revised Management Plan
- Measure 6 (2011): Antarctic Specially Protected Area No 131 (Canada Glacier, Lake Fryxell, Taylor Valley, Victoria Land): Revised Management Plan
- Measure 7 (2011): Antarctic Specially Protected Area No 149 (Cape Shirreff and San Telmo Island, Livingston Island, South Shetland Islands): Revised Management Plan
- Measure 8 (2011): Antarctic Specially Protected Area No 165 (Edmonson Point, Wood Bay, Ross Sea): Revised Management Plan
- Measure 9 (2011): Antarctic Specially Protected Area No 167: (Hawker Island, Vestfold Hills, Ingrid Christensen Coast, Princess Elizabeth Land, East Antarctica): Revised Management Plan
- Measure 10 (2011): Antarctic Specially Managed Area No 2: (McMurdo Dry Valleys, Southern Victoria Land): Revised Management Plan

(115) Noting that substantial changes were proposed to the management plan for ASPA 140, Parts of Deception Island, South Shetland Islands, the Committee decided to refer the management plan to the SGMP for intersessional review.

## CEP Subsidiary Group on Management Plans

(116) The Committee reviewed the report from its Subsidiary Group on Management Plans (SGMP) convened by Australia. During the intersessional period, the SGMP had reviewed and revised the *Guide to the Preparation of Management Plans for Antarctic Specially Protected Areas* (adopted under Resolution 2 (1988)), including to incorporate standard wording and a template for ASPA management plans.

(117) The Committee agreed to:

- endorse the revised *Guide to the Preparation of Management Plans for Antarctic Specially Protected Areas* and incorporated template and standard wording for ASPA management plans, and

- encourage proponent Parties of management plans that have not yet provided information on the status of ASPA management plans overdue for review to provide such information.

(118) The Committee also adopted a work plan for the SGMP's activities during the 2011/12 intersessional period.

(119) The Meeting adopted Resolution 2 (2011): Revised Guide to the Preparation of Management Plans for Antarctic Specially Protected Areas.

(120) Several other issues were discussed under this item, including proposed monitoring activities within ASPA No 107 (Emperor Island, Dion Islands, Marguerite Bay, Antarctic Peninsula). The Secretariat agreed to issue a reminder to Parties responsible for an ASPA/ASMA management plan that is due for a review during the next year.

## Historic Sites and Monuments

(121) The Committee was informed of the outputs of the informal intersessional discussions convened by Argentina on Historic Sites and Monuments (HSMs). The discussion focussed on: a) the different ways in which Parties define and apply the concept of "historic heritage" and the existing agreed definitions in the Antarctic context, and b) the adequacy of the existing mechanisms available in the Antarctic Treaty System for the protection of historic sites. Given the broad variety of concepts and views on these issues, the Committee agreed that the informal discussions on Historic Sites and Monuments had been useful and should continue.

(122) The Committee had before it one proposal for a new HSM and a proposal to revise the description of HSM 82. Accepting the CEP's advice, the Meeting adopted the following Measures on Historic Sites and Monuments:

- Measure 11 (2011): Antarctic Historic Sites and Monuments: Monument to the Antarctic Treaty and Plaque
- Measure 12 (2011): Antarctic Historic Sites and Monuments: No 1 Building at Great Wall Station

(123) Whilst accepting Measure 11 (2011), the UK reiterated its concern, expressed previously, about the use of double designations in listing historic sites.

(124) The Committee noted that the latest list of HSMs was very outdated and suggested that the ATCM task the Secretariat with updating the list annually.

(125) The Meeting considered the request from the CEP and agreed to task the Secretariat with maintaining an up to date list of Historic Sites and Monuments on the Secretariat's website.

## Site Guidelines

(126) The Committee discussed the report of the open-ended Intersessional Contact Group on the revision of environmental elements of Recommendation XVIII-1 convened by Australia. The ICG had developed updated guidelines for visitors based on Recommendation XVIII-1 (1994), but in a format suitable for use as a generic cover to accompany site specific guidelines.

(127) The Meeting considered and approved the General Guidelines for Visitors to the Antarctic with the adoption of Resolution 3 (2011).

(128) The Committee discussed proposals for two revised site guidelines and proposals for three new site guidelines. The Committee endorsed the revised versions of the site guidelines for Whalers Bay and Hannah Point and the new site guidelines for Taylor Valley, Ardley Peninsula and Mawson's Hut.

(129) The Meeting considered and approved two revised Site Guidelines and three new Site Guidelines by means of Resolution 4 (2011).

## Human footprint and wilderness values

(130) The Committee discussed the concepts of footprint and wilderness related to protection of the Antarctic environment and recognised the interest in the development of terminology. It also supported the concept of inviolate areas which could serve as reference sites.

## Marine spatial protection and management

(131) The Committee congratulated the Secretariat for the production of its excellent summary of the work of the CEP on Marine Protected Areas. It agreed to request that the Secretariat provide regular updates of the report online at the ATS website.

(132) The Committee was informed about the CCAMLR MPA Workshop which will be held in Brest, France from 29 August to 2 September 2011. The Committee recalled its previous agreement to engage constructively with CCAMLR on these matters and noted that it looks forward to a report on the upcoming CCAMLR MPA Workshop in Brest. The Committee thanked

CCAMLR for its invitation to attend the Workshop. Polly Penhale from the United States will be the CEP Representative.

*Other Annex V Matters*

(133) The Committee considered the proposal from Australia for enhancing the Antarctic Protected Areas Database. It agreed:

- that the Antarctic Protected Areas Database should be expanded to include fields representing: (1) primary reason for designation; and (2) main Environmental Domain represented;
- to encourage proponents to make ASPA and ASMA boundaries available in a digital format suitable for use in a GIS where possible, and to provide this information to the Secretariat for central management and access via the Antarctic Protected Areas Database;
- to request the Secretariat to modify the Antarctic Protected Areas Database as necessary to accommodate these changes; and
- to recommend that the ATCM modify the coversheet for Working Papers presenting ASPAs and ASMAs appended to Resolution 1 (2008) to allow the Secretariat to capture the relevant information for inclusion in the database.

(134) The Meeting adopted Resolution 5 (2011): Revised Guide to the Presentation of Working Papers Containing Proposals for Antarctic Specially Protected Areas, Antarctic Specially Managed Areas or Historic Sites and Monuments.

(135) The CEP also discussed the report of the CEP Workshop on Marine and Terrestrial Antarctic Specially Managed Areas held in Montevideo, Uruguay, on 16-17 June 2011. The Committee congratulated the workshop co-conveners from Australia and Uruguay, and thanked Uruguay for hosting the workshop.

(136) The Committee supported the four recommendations arising from the workshop, and agreed to:

1. Request the Secretariat to establish links from the ATS website to ASMA websites, where available.

2. Promote further exchange of information on good practice in ASMA management. In particular, ASMA Management Groups could be encouraged

to share information regarding initiatives that may be of broader interest for application in other ASMAs.

3. Seek to identify opportunities to draw on COMNAP's broader experience and responsibilities to help facilitate cooperation and coordination in the development, implementation and management of ASMAs. In addition, the CEP seeks to draw on SCAR with respect to scientific activities, IAATO with respect to tourism activities, and SC-CAMLR with respect to good practice in the identification, management and monitoring of marine areas.

4. Encourage interested Members to review the provisions of existing ASMA management plans, with a view to preparing a suggested work plan and supporting materials to aid efforts by the SGMP to develop guidance for establishing ASMAs and for preparing and reviewing ASMA management plans.

## Conservation of Antarctic Fauna and Flora (CEP Agenda Item 8)

### Quarantine and non-native species

(137) The issue of non-native species in Antarctica remains a priority 1 issue on the CEP's five-year work plan. The Committee reviewed the work of an ICG established at CEP XII and convened by New Zealand. The major outcomes of the ICG's second year of work included the completion of the overall objective and key guiding principles for Parties' actions to address risks posed by non-native species and the completion of the Non-Native Species Manual.

(138) The Committee supported the ICG's recommendations to:

1. Endorse the overall objective and key guiding principles for Parties' actions to address risks posed by non-native species;

2. Encourage the dissemination and use of the Manual;

3. Continue to develop the Non-Native Species Manual with the input of SCAR and COMNAP on scientific and practical matters, respectively; and

4. Task the Secretariat with posting the Manual in all four Treaty languages on the ATS website.

(139) The Meeting adopted Resolution 6 (2011): Non-Native Species.

(140) The Committee discussed the checklists prepared by COMNAP and SCAR for supply chain managers to reduce the risk of introduction of non-native species. The CEP approved the recommendations including addition of the checklists into the "Non-Native Species Manual".

(141) The Committee also discussed measures to reduce the risk of non-native species introductions to the Antarctic Region associated with fresh foods, proposed by SCAR. The Committee accepted an offer from SCAR to moderate an informal discussion on this issue during the intersessional period with the intention of submitting a revised paper to CEP XV.

## Other Annex II matters

(142) The Committee was informed of the wish of Germany to host a 2nd Workshop of the "Discussion Forum of Competent Authorities" on the impacts of anthropogenic underwater sound on the Antarctic environment. The Committee indicated an interest in developing its understanding of this topic, and welcomed offers from SCAR and ASOC to submit a summary of new information on this topic to the CEP XV in order to facilitate further discussion.

(143) The Committee noted the production of two new Codes of Conducts by SCAR:

- SCAR's Code of Conduct for the exploration and Research of Subglacial Aquatic Environments
- SCAR's Code of Conduct for the Use of Animals for Scientific Purposes in Antarctica

## Environmental Monitoring and Reporting (CEP Agenda Item 9)

(144) The Committee discussed the potential use of remote sensing techniques for improved monitoring of environment and climate change in Antarctica. The discussion was based on WP 15 rev. 1 produced by the United Kingdom and which recommended that the CEP:

1. notes and endorses the potential for remote sensing to contribute significantly to future environmental monitoring programmes, including in the context of protected area management and monitoring the impacts of climate change;

2. considers how else the utilisation of remote sensing data can support the CEP's work and that of the ATCM; and

3. continues to explore opportunities to use and investigate new monitoring applications.

(145) The Committee agreed to support these recommendations and encouraged information exchange to benefit all Parties that work in the Antarctic region, and to avoid duplication of efforts.

## *Inspection Reports (Agenda Item 10)*

(146) The Committee considered the Inspection Report from Japan (WP 1 and IP 4). Japan emphasised the results on waste management and disposal, treatment of sewage and domestic liquid wastes in several stations, and made recommendations including improvements of waste water treatment and oil tank facilities at some stations.

(147) The Committee also considered the Inspection Report from Australia (WP 51 and IP 39, IP 40). Australia noted that its inspections had raised some areas of environmental concern, and referred the meeting to its recommendations that Parties should:

- endeavour to manage currently operating facilities in compliance with the Protocol;
- maintain and regularly assess temporarily unoccupied facilities to ensure that environmental harm is not occurring;
- give due consideration to the removal of facilities and equipment no longer in use and the removal of accumulated waste materials;
- make efforts to share with the operating Party information on unoccupied facilities; and
- share knowledge and experience about addressing the challenges of dealing with the legacies of past activities.

(148) With respect to observations made on the need for stronger waste water management measures, particularly at inland stations, the Committee called on COMNAP to submit information on best practices on waste water management to CEP XV. The Committee also welcomed the information provided by the Russian Federation in response to the observations made by Australia's inspection team in 2010, and its intention to report at a future meeting on additional action taken in relation to issues identified.

## Cooperation with Other Organisations (CEP Agenda Item 11)

(149) The Committee received the annual reports from COMNAP, SCAR, CCAMLR and the report from the CEP Observer to SC-CAMLR's Working Group on Ecosystem Monitoring and Management.

## General Matters (CEP Agenda Item 12)

### Practicality of repair and remediation of environmental damage

(150) The Committee considered the request from ATCM XXXIII for advice on environmental issues related to the practicality of repair and remediation of environmental damage. Australia produced a Working Paper (WP 28) to stimulate discussion and assist the CEP to provide a timely and helpful response to Decision 4 (2010), and identified eight points that Australia considered the CEP should build on in preparing such a response.

(151) The Committee encouraged Members to submit papers and proposals on this issue to CEP XV with a view to establishing an ICG on repair or remediation of environmental damage at that meeting.

### Review of ATCM Recommendations

(152) The CEP noted that the ATCM had considered WP 24 *Progress Report on the Intersessional Contact Group on Review of ATCM Recommendations* (Argentina), and had requested advice on outstanding components of several Recommendations that address environmental matters other than area protection and management.

(153) The Committee advised the Meeting that the following Recommendations referred by the ATCM for its consideration could be considered no longer current:

- Recommendation III-8
- Recommendation III-10
- Recommendation IV-22
- Recommendation X-7
- Recommendation XII-3
- Recommendation XIII-4

(154) The Committee further advised the Meeting that elements of the Guidelines for Scientific Drilling in the Antarctic Treaty Area presented in Recommendation

XIV-3 have not been replaced or superseded, and that there could be some benefit in retaining such guidelines.

(155) The Meeting accepted the advice of the Committee.

### Election of Officers (CEP Agenda Item 13)

(156) The Committee re-elected Verónica Vallejos from Chile as Vice-chair for a second two-year term.

### Preparation for CEP XV (CEP Agenda Item 14)

(157) The Committee adopted the provisional agenda for CEP XV contained in Appendix to the CEP's report. It also supported the proposal, as outlined in WP 8 by Australia, to hold CEP XV in 2011 over a period of five days.

(158) A new agenda item has been added to reflect the necessity for the Committee to answer to the ATCM request on the practicality of repair and remediation of environmental damage - Decision 4 (2010).

(159) The Meeting thanked Dr Frenot for his excellent chairmanship and congratulated the Committee for presenting a high quality report.

(160) With regards to the EIES, Several Parties acknowledged that the current system could be more user-friendly, and welcomed the Secretariat's efforts to make technical improvements. However, these Parties reminded the Meeting that the exchange of information was nevertheless a requirement under the Protocol.

(161) Several Parties reiterated their support for the CEP's advice to endorse the draft CEEs presented by the United Kingdom and the Republic of Korea, and remarked that they looked forward to receiving the finalised CEEs.

(162) New Zealand drew attention to the importance of the CEP continuing to take a strategic approach to its work and suggested this could be a reference point for the ATCM in its consideration of a multi-year strategic work plan. New Zealand welcomed the CEP's finalization of generic environmental advice to visitors and the development of the Non-native Species Manual. New Zealand reinforced the importance of a continued interaction between the CEP and ATCM.

(163) In endorsing the CEP report, the UK highlighted a number of points including that information exchange is a formal requirement under the Protocol and that such information collected under the EIES contributes significantly

to the work of other parts of the ATCM including the Tourism Working Group. The UK also noted that the revised advice for visitors based on Recommendation XVIII-1 was intended to enhance and supplement and not replace it. The Meeting encouraged the one remaining Party to implement Recommendation XVIII-1 as soon as possible so that it would enter into force.

(164) The US noted the pro-active approach of the Secretariat in its willingness to lead an informal discussion group to address technical issues related to the Electronic information Exchange system. These efforts should facilitate improved use of the EIES. With regard to the CEEs presented by the UK and the Republic of Korea, the US commented on the high quality of the EIA process employed by both Parties and commended their responsiveness to questions and recommendations presented by the CEP. The Guidelines for Visitors to the Antarctic was viewed as an important contribution to the reduction of environmental impact. In addition, this work by the CEP was recognised furthering the work of the Tourism Working Group. The US looks forward to continued collaboration between the CEP and SC-CCAMLR in the area of marine spatial management and awaits with interest the outcome of the CCAMLR MPA workshop.

## Item 8: Liability: Implementation of Decision 1 (2005)

(165) The Meeting noted that five Parties (Finland, Peru, Poland, Spain, Sweden) had already approved Measure 1 (2005). In accordance with Decision 4 (2010) (which replaced Decision 1 (2005)) other Parties provided an update of their progress since ATCM XXXIII in approving Annex VI to the Protocol on Environmental Protection relating to Liability arising from Environmental Emergencies.

(166) The majority of Parties, while noting the importance of ratifying Annex VI, reported that their respective Governments were still in various stages of preparing the implementation measures necessary for approval.

(167) Australia, the Netherlands, the United Kingdom and New Zealand informed the Working Group that they were well advanced towards the ratification of Annex VI. The United Kingdom and New Zealand noted that their draft legislation was available on the internet. The United States informed the meeting that the President had submitted Annex VI to the U.S. Senate for

advice and consent to ratification and was nearing completion of related legislation to be presented to Congress.

(168) In thanking Parties for their updates and the progress made so far, ASOC suggested that the domestic legislative packages developed by those Parties most advanced in the processes of ratification of Annex VI could provide advice and assistance to other Parties in order to facilitate their progress. The Netherlands, expressing concern at the lack of progress in relation to Annex VI, supported this proposal by ASOC.

(169) The Meeting discussed the appropriateness of placing Parties' legislation or draft legislation onto a discussion forum as a way to advance discussions on this matter. The Secretariat agreed to facilitate this.

(170) Finland introduced IP 34 *Implementation of Annex II and VI of the Protocol on Environmental Protection to Antarctic Treaty and Measure 4 (2004)*. The Meeting thanked Finland for its update.

## Item 9: Safety and Operations in Antarctica

(171) Argentina introduced WP 2 rev. 1 *Early Warning System for Antarctica of the arrival of waves generated by earthquakes*, noting that recent large-magnitude seismic events including earthquakes in Chile and Japan generated tsunamis which crossed the oceans for thousands of kilometres, reaching the coasts of distant continents. Although Antarctica is not considered a highly seismic continent, high-magnitude earthquakes have been recorded with their hypocentres below the seabed in the Antarctic region (in the South Orkney Islands in 2007) or close to it (in the South Sandwich Islands in 2011), with the potential to generate tsunamis.

(172) Given that the majority of stations in Antarctica are coastal and that a significant number of scientific, logistical and tourism activities are carried out in coastal areas, Argentina noted the critical importance of making information available on the arrival time of tsunamis along the Antarctic coast.

(173) Argentina noted that there is a system of buoys serving as a tsunami early warning system (EWS). Scientific institutions, such as the United States' National Oceanic and Atmospheric Administration (NOAA) produce and publish numerical models for calculating the estimated height and arrival time of tsunami waves. However, these models do not usually include the Antarctic coasts.

(174) Therefore, Argentina proposed that the Antarctic Treaty Secretariat contact the institutions which produce numerical models for the arrival times and wave heights of tsunamis to request that they extend their outputs to include the coast of Antarctica. It also proposed that requests be made of SCAR to report on the risks associated with earthquakes and tsunamis along the coasts of Antarctica and to COMNAP to analyse the risks to Antarctic stations and operations and consider the establishment of an EWS for the arrival of tsunamis along the coasts of Antarctica.

(175) The Meeting expressed its thanks and strong support to Argentina for its paper and proposals. Several Parties and organizations noted a willingness to contribute to improving EWS to extend their application to Antarctica. The Meeting noted the considerable importance of improved bathymetric charting in order to provide data for use by EWS models in accurately estimating the arrival times and wave heights of tsunamis reaching the coasts of Antarctica.

(176) The United States welcomed the paper and indicated its willingness to provide tsunami warnings, noting that time may be required to initiate this process. It urged other countries to join the PTWS (Pacific Tsunami Warning System) and CARIBE-EWS (Intergovernmental Coordinating Group for the Tsunami and Other Coastal Hazards Warning System for the Caribbean and Adjacent Regions).

(177) Germany noted that following the tsunami event in Indonesia, it developed an EWS for the region. India added that it too has established a tsunami warning system for Indian Ocean rim countries and that the system is working well. India is also contributing seismic and GPS data through its observatories to WMO. The Russian Federation added that it has considered installing its own EWS system in the Russian Far East.

(178) Germany stressed the importance of improved bathymetric charting, especially for "white spots" on the charts, in calculating wave height. It endorsed the importance of SCAR and COMNAP work on EWS and indicated its willingness to join in that work.

(179) New Zealand reported that it had maintained tide gauges in the Ross Sea over a long period at Cape Roberts and has a great deal of data available on wave heights. The gauges, for example, registered wave details of the April earthquake in Japan within 24 hours.

(180) COMNAP noted that it had already begun work on a project regarding risk to coastal Antarctic infrastructure and personnel from tsunamis, and will

present a project report to the August COMNAP Annual General Meeting. If the Meeting finds it useful, COMNAP will be in a position to present the report as a working paper at ATCM XXXV. The Meeting agreed that the report would be useful and requested that COMNAP, with assistance from SCAR, would provide it to ATCM XXXV to assist with further discussion of this topic.

(181) The United Kingdom suggested that it would be useful if the United States were to include a representative from NOAA on its delegation to ATCM XXXV to present information on its global tsunami EWS. The UK observed that the system has proven extremely useful to the British Antarctic Survey and does provide some predictions for Antarctica. The UK used predictions from the system in evacuating personnel from Rothera Station during the Chilean earthquake.

(182) The UK noted that both SCAR and COMNAP have scientific and operations information that could prove useful and stressed the importance of approaching the Hydrographic Commission for Antarctica (part of the International Hydrographic Organisation) on the need for improved bathymetric charting. The Chairman agreed to write to the IHO telling them about the issue, and inviting them to contribute information on bathymetric charting for tsunami prediction at ATCM XXXV.

(183) SCAR also supported the need for improved bathymetry, noting it has an Action Group on the "International Bathymetric Chart of the Southern Ocean".

(184) Chile was keen to support this initiative and share its considerable experience with others, and also with working groups that might work on these issues, indicating that the highest importance should be given to these matters.

(185) Ecuador noted that it is installing a tsunami warning centre in the Galapagos that can provide data upon request. In addition, Ecuador felt that it was important to generate a global communication system for tsunami warning in Antarctica.

(186) France noted the effects in reproductive failures and impacts on breeding behaviour in penguin colonies on its sub-antarctic islands following the 2004 tsunami in Sumatra. France is prepared to integrate data from its observatories in the Indian Ocean into a larger EWS.

(187) Argentina thanked the Meeting for its support and mentioned that the record of the five stations belonging to the Argentine-Italian Antarctic

Seismic Network (ASAIN) is online for use. It also noted that the Argentine Hydrographic Service is engaged in bathymetric charting using the *Puerto Deseado* research vessel. It further suggested that the inclusion of links to all the alert system web pages would be valuable.

(188) The Russian Federation introduced WP 56 *Ensuring* safety *of shipping in Antarctic waters adopted in the Russian Federation*, citing growing concern in the international Antarctic community with the increased frequency of accidents by marine vessels in the Southern Ocean, occasionally resulting in environmental emergencies.

(189) The Russian Federation has been actively present in the Southern Ocean since its 1946-47 summer season whaling cruise. Since then Russian vessels have operated in large numbers in Antarctic waters and have extensive experience of Antarctic conditions.

(190) Russian vessels are frequently chartered and Russian masters and crew are used by other countries to support their national research programs. Russian vessels and Russian experience in ice navigation have been used to support Chinese and Korean vessels operating in the Antarctic. The Republic of Korea acknowledged this support and noted its appreciation. Argentina remarked on the professionalism of the crew on the Russian vessels it had chartered.

(191) The Russian Federation, as a country which regularly navigates in these waters, is willing to share its experience and advice on safe shipping. Russia has adopted a system of training providing a large number of highly qualified polar masters, ship officer and ice pilots. The details of its training and certification are described in WP 56.

(192) The Russian Federation called the attention of the Meeting to a little known, but very useful, publication of the World Meteorological Organization (WMO) on ice shipping – WMO Report 35 in Marine Meteorology and Related Oceanographic Activities series (WMO/TD no 783, 1996).

(193) The Meeting expressed its appreciation to the Russian Federation for its paper and for highlighting the importance of training specific to the conditions which vessels, masters and crew face in Antarctica. Germany suggested that as far as possible national programs should use crews experienced in operating in Antarctic conditions. Argentina noted the importance of training the crews of all vessels, especially those small non-IAATO members, and reported on the Course of Navigation in Antarctic Waters, which it holds annually.

(194) New Zealand commented on the considerable value of the COMNAP ship reporting system to ensuring the safety of vessels supporting national programs.

(195) Chile informed the Meeting that the Captains of Chilean vessels that operate in the Antarctic area, according to national maritime laws, were required to complete the course "Navigation and Operations in Antarctic Waters", developed at the Maritime Training and Instruction Center, CIMAR. Anyone interested in obtaining more information on this course can find it in *www.cimar.cl*.

(196) Chile introduced IP 134 *Situación SAR en los últimos 5 años en el área de la Antártida de responsabilidad de Chile.* The statistics in the paper, although possibly incomplete, identify the number of vessels docking at important ports and stations designated to collect vessel information. The report also includes medical evacuations from tourist vessels. Chile has made efforts to ensure the presence as necessary of the Chile and Argentina Combined Antarctic Naval Patrol with its naval vessels in areas in the Antarctic where Chile has SAR responsibilities. Chile noted that often there is not enough information on the position of vessels in the area to come to their aid. Exact information is necessary to ensure salvage, rescue and environmental protection. Resolution 6 (2010) directs Party vessels to report their position and movements. Chile has been providing this information and urges other Parties to contribute to this effort.

(197) China, in commenting on its IP6 *Report on the Evacuation of an Altitude Sickness – Suffered Expeditioner at the Kunlun Station in Dome A,* thanked colleagues for their assistance in effecting the evacuation and spoke in memory of William Colston.

(198) Norway reported on a successful evacuation on June 22 from Troll Station using a Gulfstream G 550 (without refuelling on the Antarctic legs), a small aircraft which flew from Cape Town to the station and returned to Cape Town within 12 hours.

(199) Norway introduced IP 59 *The grounding of the Polar Star*, and reported that the grounding (by striking a rock) was a minor incident sustained without damage to passengers or the environment. Though minor, Norway stressed the importance of reporting all incidents in order to have complete data for use in developing future risk assessments and considering possible regulations.

(200) Norway introduced IP 60 *Working Group on the development of a mandatory code for ship operating in polar waters, IMO.* The task is the work of the IMO

51

Subcommittee on Design and Equipment. Taking into account the urgent need for mandatory requirements, the Polar Code would initially apply to SOLAS passenger and cargo ships. The report of its March 2011 meeting, annexed to IP 60, contained information on the status of current discussions in IMO and background for discussion on possible future guidelines for fishing vessels and yachts.

(201) ASOC thanked Chile for IP 134 and Norway for IP 59, and urged all Antarctic Treaty Parties who flag, permit or licence vessels which have had similar incidents to report on these to the ATCM.

(202) ASOC presented IP 85 *Developing a Mandatory Polar Code – Progress and Gaps*. ASOC called on the ATCM to adopt a Resolution on collaborative action to ensure that the Mandatory Polar Code provides appropriate safety and environmental protection standards for vessel operations in Antarctic waters.

(203) ASOC presented IP 91 *Vessel Protection and Routing – Options Available to Reduce Risk and Provide Enhanced Environmental Protection*. ASOC recommends that the ATCM adopt a Resolution on the need for a review of measures to address collisions, groundings and protection of vulnerable areas.

(204) Many Parties congratulated Norway on its work in chairing the IMO Working Group developing the Mandatory Polar Code.

(205) The Meeting supported New Zealand's call for Parties to actively participate and follow the work programme of the IMO's Mandatory Polar Code, as the development of the mandatory code was at the request of the ATCM, it must ensure the Antarctic perspective is properly represented. It noted that such action would be consistent with Resolution 5 (2010) on coordination among Antarctic Treaty Parties on Antarctic proposals under consideration in the IMO.

(206) The United Kingdom stressed the importance of Parties sending delegates to the IMO Working Group to ensure they are properly briefed on ship operations in Antarctica. The United Kingdom informed the ATCM that it has taken its own IMO delegate to the Antarctic on HMS Scott, to offer a first-hand experience of the unique ice conditions of the region.

(207) Argentina encouraged Parties to work closely with COMNAP on issues of navigation, search and rescue with respect to the development of the Mandatory Polar Code.

(208) COMNAP informed the ATCM that it is paying careful attention to the development of the Code, and invites National Antarctic Programmes (NAPs) to participate in its Shipping Expert Group.

(209) Norway was grateful for the support shown on the work for the Mandatory Polar Code, while underlining that the IMO is the place for decision making on Antarctic shipping requirements.

(210) Chile presented IP 135 *Patrulla de rescate terrestre Argentina-Chilena PARACACH (Bases Antárticas "Esperanza" y "O'Higgins").*

(211) Another paper submitted under this agenda item was:

- IP 44 *Exploration, Search and Rescue Training Activities in Support of the Scientific, Technical and Logistical Operational Tasks* (Uruguay)

## Item 10: Tourism and Non-Governmental Activities

### *Overview of Antarctic Tourism in the 2010/11 season*

(212) IAATO introduced IP 106 rev. 1 *Overview of Antarctic Tourism*, noting that the overall number of tourists carried by IAATO operators during the 2010-11 season was 33,824, an eight percent decrease from 2009-2010. For the 2011-12 season, IAATO forecasts a further decrease of 25% to 25,319 visitors, due primarily to withdrawal from the market of several IAATO members that are affected by new IMO fuel regulations. Despite the decrease, IAATO noted trends increasing in several smaller segments: air-cruise, land programs and yacht expeditions. It expressed concern about activities of some non-IAATO yachts, pointing to the great value of the competent authority process and action against those who do not comply with Treaty Party requirements.

(213) Argentina introduced IP 20 *Report on Antarctic tourist flows and cruise ships operating in Ushuaia during the 2010/2011 austral summer season*, reporting that a total of 33,656 visitors went to Antarctica through Ushuaia. Argentina noted the importance of this paper as a source of information originating outside the industry sector.

(214) The Meeting thanked Argentina and IAATO for presenting their papers, noting that the effective management of tourism activities required the availability of comprehensive data on these activities.

## Tourism rules and regulations

(215) The United States introduced WP 26 *ATCM Review of Tourism Rules and Regulations,* jointly submitted with France, Germany, the Netherlands and New Zealand. These Parties believed that the ATCM should conduct a review of the adequacy of current international rules related to tourism in Antarctica with the objective of identifying gaps in regulation, noting that previous ATCMs had acknowledged the need to address this issue. The United States emphasised that this effort would assist the Meeting in determining which tourism issues are of greatest priority and thus which issues should be focussed on in coming years.

(216) The Meeting thanked the U.S. and co-sponsors for this paper and stated that, in principle, they supported the development of a strategic approach to the management of tourism activities in Antarctica.

(217) India, supported by several other Parties, suggested that it was important for the ATCM to focus not only on the adequacy of current measures, but also on the adequacy of their implementation by national authorities.

(218) Norway highlighted the point made in WP 26, that some of the topics of relevance to this discussion could be referred to other international bodies such as IMO and IHO. Norway also emphasised the importance of considering the implications for tourism activities of the mandatory Polar Code for shipping, when it is approved by the IMO.

(219) ASOC thanked the United States of America and the other contributors to WP 26. It noted that the tourism issue required strategic perspectives, which meant anticipating developments. Current tourism, although involving fewer tourists than the recent peak, had changed in recent years, for instance in terms of the activities that take place in the interior of Antarctica and the number of semi-permanent tourism camps. ASOC endorsed the content of WP 26, particularly the reference to the need to use a precautionary approach.

(220) The Netherlands introduced WP 21 *Antarctic Tourism: Towards a strategic and pro-active approach via an inventory of outstanding questions,* submitted jointly with the United Kingdom. The Netherlands' proposed approach was to identify the most important questions requiring attention by the ATCM, to consider the most appropriate forms of action in response to these questions, and to identify which of these questions were priorities for discussion at the next ATCM.

(221) As the paper's co-author, the United Kingdom reminded the Meeting that in 2008 it had tabled a proposal at ATCM XXXI to consider a strategic vision for the development of Antarctic tourism over the next decade. The United Kingdom noted that despite the actions arising from this earlier paper there were still some questions that needed to be addressed by the ATCM. The sixteen questions highlighted in WP 21 represented a tool for focussing discussion and should facilitate the setting of priorities.

(222) Many Parties agreed that WP 21 and WP 26 would benefit from joint consideration.

(223) Argentina and Sweden, while expressing support for WP 21, suggested that the paper would benefit from some clarification on its intended outcomes. Sweden suggested that a survey or inventory on the implementation of existing tourism regulations by national authorities might be a useful outcome.

(224) France, noting that WP 21 raised a number of important questions, highlighted the need for the WG to adopt a long term perspective in relation to the regulation of tourism activities. France noted that safety was a particular concern.

(225) Belgium highlighted the equal importance of implementing measures already adopted at previous Meetings as well as continuing to develop regulation. Several Parties sought clarification that the list of questions is an agenda for future discussion on the subject, and added the value of considering Antarctic tourism regulation in wider international fora. Some Parties also highlighted the importance of considering the effects of climate change in relation to tourism regulation mechanisms in the future.

(226) China expressed its support for a discussion in the next ATCM and for identifying priority issues regarding tourism, taking into account questions listed in WP 21 and other issues that may be presented by Consultative Parties.

(227) Brazil advised that it had recently approved national legislation on the regulation of tourist activities in Antarctica.

(228) The United States noted the importance of considering issues related to maritime safety in addition to matters addressed in Resolution 7 (2009).

(229) Australia noted that the CEP tourism study is likely to come to fruition next year, and that this will facilitate informed discussions on the topic in the future.

(230) IAATO welcomed the discussions raised in WPs 21 and 26, suggesting that future discussion on the adequacy of current tourism management measures should take into account that, while tourism numbers had decreased over the past few years, the nature of tourism activities was currently evolving.

(231) ASOC thanked the authors of WP 21 for providing a practical way forward by producing a pertinent list of questions that would contribute to clarifying the issue of tourism. In particular, ASOC endorsed questions addressing Principle II of Resolution 7 (2009) stating that tourism should not be allowed to contribute to the long term degradation of the Antarctic environment and other values of Antarctica.

(232) The Meeting agreed that it was highly desirable to take a more strategic approach to the ATCM's review of tourism policies, identify gaps, and set priorities for future discussion, taking into account existing regulatory instruments and guidelines and implementation thereof. It agreed that ATCM XXXV would discuss further work related to tourism with the aim of agreeing to key priorities, including by considering:

- The report of the Intersessional Contact Group referred to in paragraph 261;
- Issues for which it may be appropriate to develop new international regulatory instruments or guidelines, such as Measures or Resolutions;
- The outcomes of the study by the Committee on Environmental Protection on the environmental impact of tourism in the Antarctic Treaty area, if available, and its implications for further work on tourism policy.

(233) The Meeting requested the Secretariat to remind Consultative Parties of this agreement three months prior to ATCM XXXV via circular.

(234) The Meeting agreed to convene an open-ended Intersessional Contact Group (ICG) working until ATCM XXXV to prepare for the ATCM's review of tourism policies with the following terms of reference. The ICG will identify:

- policy questions relating to the management and regulation of tourism, including those identified in ATCM XXXIV-WP 21;
- issues for which it may be appropriate to develop new regulatory instruments or guidelines, such as Measures or Resolutions; and
- a list of priority issues that may be considered at the ATCM, including but not limited to safety and environmental protection.

(235) It was further agreed that:

- Observers and Experts participating in ATCM XXXIV would be invited to participate in the ICG;
- The Secretariat would develop an interactive electronic discussion forum and provide assistance to the ICG; and
- The Netherlands would act as convener, and would report to ATCM XXXV on the progress made in the ICG.

(236) France introduced WP 46 *Limitation of tourism and non-governmental activities to sites under Guidelines for Site Visits only,* with the objective of encouraging Tour Operators to limit their visitations only to sites with agreed Guidelines. The proposed resolution sought to improve the analysis of landing impacts, to ensure better the safety of tourists and to limit risks and accidents.

(237) Some Parties expressed their support for the sentiment of France's proposal, although they suggested that the wording be amended. France later clarified that there had been a problem of translation to English, and that the draft resolution was not intended to be mandatory. France suggested that the word "invites" was more reflective of the spirit of the proposal than "urges".

(238) While thanking France for submitting the paper and emphasising the need to continue developing Site Guidelines, some Parties expressed a series of concerns.

(239) Argentina noted that limiting visits only to sites with Guidelines could increase the pressure on those sites and ultimately prove counterproductive, especially taking into account that sites with existing Guidelines are usually the most vulnerable, or the sites that already receive most visitors. Argentina also urged Parties to prepare more such site guidelines in the future.

(240) Following Argentina's intervention, several Parties expressed concerns regarding the potential negative environmental impacts of limiting tourism activities to specific sites.

(241) Uruguay suggested that the CEP should urge members to develop Site Guidelines for those sites that do not have them and thus make them available for tour operators.

(242) With respect to WP 46, Ukraine reminded Parties about previous recommendations (ATCM XXXIII Final Report, paragraphs 242-248) encouraging Parties to prepare clearly stated policies related to visitors to their research stations. In connection to this, the policy regarding visits

by tourists to Vernadsky Station, prepared by Ukraine in the format of the Visitor Site Guidelines for the management of tourists, might be considered a contribution germane to this discussion.

(243) The Netherlands pointed out that because of climate change there are now more places becoming available for visitation and that if guidelines were to become stricter tour operators might be encouraged to land on sites without guidelines.

(244) Several Parties drew attention to the Madrid Protocol and other Measures and Resolutions on tourism in place to manage tourism activities, highlighting that when visitors land at sites without guidelines, they do not arrive in a place exempt from overall regulation. The United Kingdom also noted that these site guidelines applied to all visitors.

(245) In this respect, IAATO suggested that there are some advantages in considering Antarctica area management in the context of all human activities as a whole, instead of just restricting visits to sites with guidelines.

(246) Australia noted that the suite of sites with guidelines had not been selected as the only places where tourism should occur, so the notion of concentrating all tourist activities at those sites may be problematic.

(247) The United States shared the environmental protection sentiments behind WP 46 and the concerns expressed over the potential unintended consequences of concentrating tourism at locations with site guidelines. Furthermore, the proposal appeared not to take into account that there are no site guidelines for land-based tourism.

(248) Attention was drawn to papers IP 30 *Areas of tourist interest in the Antártica Peninsula (Antarctic Peninsula) and Orcadas del Sur Islands (South Orkney Islands) region. 2010/2011 austral summer season*, submitted by Argentina, and IP 105 *Report on IAATO Operator use of Antarctic Peninsula Landing Sites and ATCM Visitor Guidelines 2009-2010 and 2010-11 seasons*, submitted by IAATO, which were considered relevant in light of the issues being discussed.

(249) ASOC thanked France for WP 46 and highlighted several useful concepts in this document that are important for tourism management. It noted that the idea of encouraging visitation at some sites and not in others is something already applied in some management plans, for instance at the Deception Island ASMA and at the Dry Valleys ASMA. It also noted that questions of dispersing or concentrating tourism needed to be looked at from a holistic

perspective including groups of sites where landings take place, perhaps across Antarctic regions, rather than at sites isolated from each other.

(250) Most Parties agreed that the proposal submitted by France raised some important questions that needed to be further discussed in the future.

(251) Norway introduced IP 75 *The legal aspects of the Berserk Expedition* and stated that, whilst the expedition in question lacked the necessary approval from Norwegian authorities, it was nevertheless a concern of the Norwegian government in so far as it involved a Norwegian registered sailboat and four Norwegian nationals.

(252) Members acknowledged Norway's thorough and transparent handling of the matter, and New Zealand's prompt search and rescue response to the incident.

(253) Many Parties highlighted the need for appropriate and timely exchange of information.

(254) On this note, and as one of the crew of the *Berserk* was of joint British nationality, the United Kingdom recalled Resolution 3 (2004), that recommends to those Parties that become aware of expeditions involving vessels or nationals of another Treaty Party that they promptly consult those relevant Parties.

(255) New Zealand suggested that a review of port state controls might also be worth exploring in this context.

(256) IAATO noted the usefulness of the communication between Norway and other parties, including IAATO, which took place prior to the commencement of the *Berserk* expedition, and acknowledged Norway's efforts to pursue a prosecution in response to the *Berserk* incident, noting that a successful prosecution might prove an effective deterrent to future incidents.

(257) ASOC introduced IP 84 *Antarctic Tourism – What Next? Key Issues to Address with Binding Rules*, noting that in its view current trends suggest that without regulatory constraints tourism will continue to expand and diversify, adopting new modalities and penetrating further into the Antarctic mainland and along its coasts. This may have consequences, *inter alia*, on the environment, the conduct of science, the safety of tourists, and other values of the Antarctic region recognised by the Antarctic Treaty and its Protocol. It is therefore important that Antarctic Treaty states take proactive steps to constrain tourism developments within ecologically sustainable limits

appropriate for the Antarctic. For this, making use of existing mechanisms would be a good first step.

(258) ASOC referred to its paper IP 87 *Land-Based Tourism in Antarctica*, which examined the interface between commercial land-based tourism and the use of national programme infrastructure, as well as recent developments in land-based tourism. Those operations rely directly or indirectly on some form of state support, including permits, use of runways, and use of facilities and terrain adjacent to research stations. The broad array of land activities now available to tourists shows that land-based tourism is growing. ASOC believes that if no actions are taken soon, land-based tourism may well become consolidated as a major activity.

(259) The United States indicated that it disagreed with ASOC's conclusion that the operation of Antarctic Logistics and Expeditions Union Glacier Camp had more than a minor or transitory impact. It also noted that the activity is similar in size and operation to other summer camps operated by the United States Antarctic Program that also have no more than a minor or transitory impact. It advised that IEEs of US non-governmental operators were available from the US Environmental Protection Agency.

(260) Responding to comments by the US, ASOC noted that the EIA for the UNION Glacier Camp was not available at the Secretariat website at the time of writing IP 87, and that its comments about the impact of this facility were based on the large area of operations of the activities conducted from the Camp extending to the Ellsworth Mountains, Patriot Hills, and the South Pole, and its assumption that an activity operating for more than two decades was bound to have more than a transitory impact.

## Supervision and Management of Tourism

(261) Argentina introduced WP 48 *Report of the Intersessional Contact Group on Supervision of Antarctic Tourism*, summarising the main points discussed in the ICG, and highlighting that the views of all participant Parties were reflected in this paper. Argentina noted that 6 Parties, IAATO and ASOC have actively participated in these debates, which focussed on the variety of mechanisms currently available within the Antarctic Treaty system, and their implementation by Parties, for ensuring more appropriate supervision of tourism on board cruise ships, small vessels and yachts in Antarctica.

(262) The Meeting thanked Argentina for convening the ICG, acknowledging the value of the work that had been carried out by this ICG.

(263) While many Parties commented that they found the use of existing inspection checklists very useful, some Parties noted that the scope of these checklists could still be broadened, for example, to apply to the types of tourist activities that are not currently covered by the existing inspection checklists.

(264) Many Parties highlighted the importance of inspections for regulating activities in Antarctica. Brazil suggested that tourism operators could contribute to the funding of such inspections. Uruguay and Ecuador noted that scientific stations located in proximity to sites visited by tourists also played an important role in the inspection of tourism activities.

(265) The Netherlands, noting the need for more inspections of tourism activities, encouraged Parties to include inspections of tourist activities as part of their national inspections.

(266) In response to this comment, Germany stated that, while National Antarctic Programs could help with inspection procedures, it was the competent authorities responsible for issuing permits that should ultimately be responsible for leading inspections.

(267) ASOC thanked Argentina for WP 48 and stated that inspections are a useful mechanism to verify what occurs on the ground, but that in the case of tourism, this mechanism is in its view somewhat under-applied and under-developed. All activities should be inspected and their impact assessed as appropriate, but a focus on tourism was in ASOC's view appropriate. ASOC stressed the importance of identifying the precise footprint of commercial tourism and that inspections were one of the means of doing this.

(268) The Meeting agreed on the importance of inspections and observer programmes and the need to continue improving inspection mechanisms. Argentina agreed to continue to convene the Intersessional Contact Group on the Supervision of Antarctic Tourism for the following intersessional period.

(269) The Terms of Reference for an ICG were agreed as follows:

- To further elaborate a checklist covering visitors' activities at landing sites, taking as a model the draft checklist produced by the ICG during the intersessional period 2010-11, to support inspections under Article VII of the Antarctic Treaty and Article 14 of the Madrid Protocol.
- To consider the development of further checklists to cover other types of visitors' activities in Antarctica.
- To submit a report to ATCM XXXV (Hobart, 2012).

(270) It was further agreed that:

- Observers and Experts participating in ATCM XXXIV will be invited to participate in the ICG;
- The Secretariat would develop an interactive electronic discussion forum and provide assistance to the ICG; and
- Argentina would act as convener, and would report to ATCM XXXV on the progress made in the ICG.

(271) IAATO brought the meeting's attention to their work to enhance their organisations observer scheme outlined in IP 107 *Towards an IAATO Enhanced Observer Scheme*, noting that the initiative is one of a suite of efforts which aim to ensure that the organisation can have confidence in its systems. The enhanced scheme involves a three part process involving two desktop exercises (an internal and external review) and field observations. The scheme is going through a pilot phase this coming season. IAATO submitted the checklists associated with these various processes to the ATCM for their information and as a contribution to the discussion.

(272) In introducing IP 105 *Report on IAATO operator use of Antarctic Peninsula Landing Sites and ATCM Visitor Site Guidelines, 2009-2010 and 2010-11 Seasons* IAATO noted that they intended to continue to provide this information on their members' activities each season. The paper suggests that two additional sites be considered for the development of site guidelines and noted that each season IAATO member operators encounter visits at these sites from non-IAATO visitors.

(273) Parties thanked IAATO for the work done on IP 107, and Australia and Argentina highlighted the robust approaches and mechanisms taken by IAATO for assessing its members' activities.

(274) Ecuador introduced IP 126 *Manejo turístico para la isla Barrientos* and acknowledged IAATO's support of their work to monitor tourist activities in the Barrientos Islands.

(275) Argentina and Uruguay expressed their support for Ecuador's efforts.

(276) Other papers submitted under this agenda item were:

- IP 9 *Antarctic Site Inventory: 1994-2011* (United States)
- IP 23 *Antarctic Peninsula Compendium, 3rd Edition* (United States and United Kingdom)

(277) New Zealand and IAATO thanked the US and UK for their information papers, noting the importance of research and monitoring for informing the ATCM's work.

## Yacht Activities in the Antarctic

(278) The Chairman noted that WP 37 *Yacht guidelines to complement safety standards of ship traffic around Antarctica* and WP 20 *Data Collection and Reporting on Yachting Activity in Antarctica in 2010/11* are to some extent complementary, and proposed their joint consideration.

(279) China suggested that a first step was to regulate the activities of yacht activities in the Antarctic waters within the competence of the ATCM, and then the related regulations can be suggested to the IMO for its consideration in the development of the Polar Code.

(280) Introducing WP 37, Germany noted that yachts are not included in the negotiations for the first tranche of the IMO Polar Code, which, when concluded, will relate to some sea-based activities in the Treaty Area. WP 37 proposes a checklist for those intending to conduct yachting activities in Antarctica.

(281) The United Kingdom introduced WP 20 *Data Collection and Reporting on Yachting Activity in Antarctica in 2010/11,* intending to provide information to Parties regarding the number of yachts around the Antarctic Peninsula in the 2010/11 season. IAATO noted that their members were pleased to contribute to this list regarding sightings of non-IAATO member yachts, many of which appeared to be unauthorised. The importance of on-going information sharing in this regard was highlighted.

(282) Many Parties thanked the authors of both WPs for their information and acknowledged that both the checklist provided in WP 37 and the data reported in WP 20 were useful, and provided a good basis for further discussions on the subject. Parties noted, however, that the checklist is not exhaustive, and that some refinement to the text will be necessary.

(283) Several Parties also suggested that the ATCM should advise the IMO that it would like to see yachting activities considered in the second stage of the mandatory Polar Code for shipping under discussion in the IMO.

(284) IAATO noted that IAATO yacht operators were in the minority of the yachts reported in the area, and drew attention to the importance of experience and training, given the challenges of the Antarctic environment, in order to minimise risks.

(285) Australia endorsed the proposals set out in both WPs, and noted in relation to WP 20 that one yacht listed as a non-IAATO member was Australian, and had been duly authorised by Australia.

(286) France added, in relation to WP 37, the need for a refined clarity of terms. In relation to WP 20, it was noted that the table only provided the names of the vessels, with no indication of where the vessels were registered.

(287) In response to France's query, the United Kingdom noted that WP 20 did not include specific flag State information owing to the fact that it was difficult to be 100% certain on such registration. Similarly WP 20 did not indicate whether the vessels had been authorised as each country has its own domestic legislation and standards of authorisation. In this regard, the UK highlighted the need for enhanced levels of co-ordination between Parties.

(288) In relation to WP 37, Chile noted that each country has its own legal system that requires vessels to comply with safety regulations, and emphasised the importance of information exchange between Parties in this regard.

(289) In relation to WP 37, Argentina expressed its support for intersessional initiatives aimed at discussing guidelines for yachts. It also noted that the wording of this proposed checklist included the use of verbs that suggested different degrees of compliance, some of which would not be appropriate for a checklist.

(290) It was agreed to establish an Intersessional Contact Group for the preparation of yacht guidelines and data sharing with the Terms of Reference listed below.

(291) In order to promote good practice, protect the environment and help improve safety standards of yachts visiting Antarctica, pending introduction of appropriate measures taken by the IMO, the following issues should be discussed during the intersessional period:

- Assess existing ATCM, relevant national and international regulations to define the need of improvements for safe yacht expeditions in Antarctica;
- Further develop the proposed yacht checklist presented in WP 37 and discuss options for its wider use;
- Develop yacht-specific guidelines on the basis of the above mentioned checklist and existing guidelines and consider how best to disseminate and consult among the yachting community;
- Propose a mechanism to share data on vessel yacht sightings; and
- Report to ATCM XXXV on the outcome of the ICG.

(292) It was further agreed that:

- Observers and Experts participating in ATCM XXXIV will be invited to participate in the ICG;
- The Secretariat would develop an interactive electronic discussion forum and provide assistance to the ICG; and
- Germany would act as convener, and would report to ATCM XXXV on the progress made in the ICG.

(293) Argentina introduced IP 21 rev. 1 *Non-commercial pleasure and/or sport vessels which travelled to Antarctica through Ushuaia during the 2010/2011 season.*

(294) The United Kingdom took IP 15 *Training Course for Yachts intending to visit Antarctica* as read by Parties, but highlighted that the training courses implemented in the UK proved very successful, and the UK would be happy to engage with any other Party wishing to conduct such courses.

(295) IAATO introduced IP 14 *IAATO Yacht Outreach Campaign.* Commenting on IP 15, IAATO confirmed they had taken part in the training courses, and that this has been effective in relation to increasing awareness across the yachting community. In relation to IP 14, IAATO drew attention to the outreach campaign that was intended to raise awareness amongst non-IAATO operators.

(296) Parties' attention was drawn to IP 28 *Technical safety standards and international law affecting yachts with destination Antarctica* submitted by Germany, in relation to its relevance to the work being done by the ICG on yacht guidelines.

(297) Norway introduced IP 94 *Use of dogs in the context of a commemorative centennial expedition*, and Argentina introduced IP 122 *Perceptions of Antarctica from the modern travellers' perspective.*

### *Other Matters*

(298) Argentina made the following statement: "With regard to incorrect references to the territorial status of the Malvinas Islands, South Georgias and South Sandwich Islands made in documents available and presentations made at this Antarctic Treaty Consultative Meeting, Argentina rejects any reference to these islands as being a separate entity from its national territory, thus giving them an international status that they do not have. Furthermore, it rejects the shipping register operated by the alleged British authorities thereof and any other unilateral act undertaken by such colonial authorities, which are not recognised by Argentina. The Malvinas, South Georgias and South

Sandwich Islands and the corresponding maritime areas are an integral part of the Argentine national territory, are under illegal British occupation and are the subject of a sovereignty dispute between the Argentine Republic and the United Kingdom of Great Britain and Northern Ireland."

(299) In response, the United Kingdom stated that it had no doubt about its sovereignty over the Falkland Islands, South Georgia and the South Sandwich Islands and their surrounding maritime areas, as is well known to all delegates. In that regard, the United Kingdom has no doubt about the right of the government of the Falkland Islands to operate a shipping register for UK & Falkland flagged vessels.

(300) Argentina rejected the statement by the United Kingdom and reaffirmed its legal position.

(301) Following the conclusion of all agenda items, the Chairman invited Parties to make general comments on issues that have come before the Meeting.

(302) Opening the discussion, France expressed deep concern that at present the Meeting was not engaging in substantive debate on major key issues related to tourism development, and noted the importance of new types of Antarctic tourism, particularly adventure tourism. Attention was also drawn to questions on environmental protection, security and safety. Addressing medium and long term issues should not rule out taking action in the short term.

(303) Several Parties concurred with the major points raised by France, highlighting the need to reassess issue priorities, increase the number of Working Papers on substantive issues, and suggested that WP 21 and WP 26 could provide much of the basis for discussions at the next ATCM. Parties noted the considerable benefits of working jointly with both the Operations and Legal Working Groups on these issues.

(304) Parties emphasised that increased cooperation between Consultative Parties should provide the basis for moving forward on these issues, recognising the importance of both information exchange and continuing and developing dialogue. Fundamental to progress would be Working Papers with enhanced factual and contextual content and an improved analysis of topical issues. Parties needed to come to the ATCM well prepared to work on substantive issues related to tourism, and to focus less on process.

(305) Australia noted that as host of ATCM XXXV it was looking forward to focussed discussion on tourism issues in Hobart at the next meeting, and that it was supportive of proposals for a strategic approach to questions of

tourism management, and the work planned for the intersessional period. Australia associated itself with the remarks of other Parties relating to the need for papers to make a clear argument identifying a problem or proposal, based on available facts.

(306) The United States emphasised that it was necessary to improve the ATCM's approach to working on tourism issues and that the key is greater involvement and participation, both at Meetings and intersessionally. It added that it was essential to establish priorities in the future.

(307) Several Parties noted the value of ICGs as fora for discussion, which contribute to reaching more robust results before ATCMs, and encouraged improved participation among Parties. Several Parties also emphasised the pre-eminent importance of the Tourism Working Group Meeting as the primary platform for discussion.

(308) India, supported by several Parties, referred to the importance of considering Antarctic issues within a wider global context, and highlighted the value of developing linkages with other relevant international instruments and organisations. Brazil suggested that this approach could be developed through a workshop to develop a strategic framework on broader general tourism matters before the next ATCM.

(309) Belgium suggested that the ATCM's work on tourism should evolve similarly to the CEP, with a rolling work program for example, and should have a strategic discussion at the beginning of its consideration of tourism at its meetings.

(310) IAATO noted the challenge posed by inconsistent application of the Protocol and the method of dealing with unauthorised activities, a theme taken up by Germany which suggested that regulations contained in the Protocol make it difficult to forbid some activities.

(311) The Netherlands felt that the development of certain forms of extreme tourist activities in Antarctica should be discouraged. It feared that the ATCM, by not developing tourism policies fast enough to keep up with developments in the industry, would face shifting baselines for decision making. It felt that the Parties have the right to withhold permits for activities they deem incompatible with the intrinsic or wilderness values of Antarctica, even if such activities do not cause direct environmental harm, and that the ATCPs should, in the Netherlands' view, jointly or individually, prevent that Antarctica become a playground for extreme activities that Parties would prohibit in their own national natural reserves.

(312) New Zealand noted that its approach on tourism and non-governmental activities was partly informed by its large SAR area. There had been loss of life from a yachting expedition and a fishing vessel in the recent season. New Zealand encouraged Treaty Parties to actively advocate for Antarctic specific considerations in the IMO's Mandatory Polar Code for Shipping.

(313) ASOC noted a lack of information on land-based tourism as the consequence of an apparent lack of focus on substantive issues in the tourism debate, and drew attention to upholding policy decisions consistent with Resolution 7 (2009). ASOC suggested that both WP 21 and WP 26 provided a good framework for a strategic discussion of tourism.

## *Joint Tourism – Operations Working Group*

(314) France introduced WP 11, *Follow-up to the unauthorised presence of French yachts within the Treaty area and damage caused to the hut known as Wordie House - Observations on the consequences of the affair*, about the actions taken by France in relation to this incident, and to facilitate wider discussion among Parties on the subject.

(315) France informed the Meeting that as neither yacht involved in the incident had received authorisation from France, under French law it was possible for French authorities to take action against the two Captains involved. France confirmed that legal action had been undertaken by the Prefect to activate the Paris Court for judgement on this issue.

(316) In light of the incident, France emphasised the importance of improving clarity with respect to the provision of safety documentation requested from yachts by port authorities of Parties. It also indicated that this documentation does not constitute an authorisation to undertake activities in Antarctic waters.

(317) France enquired about the possibility of searching the EIES by vessel name, and asked the Secretariat to obtain the necessary information.

(318) France raised questions about the capacity of national laws to deal with future potential incidents of a similar nature. Further work on that issue could be necessary in line with the possibilities given to Parties by Art. 9 of the Antarctic Treaty. France offered to produce a WP on this topic at the next ATCM.

(319) France encouraged collaboration amongst Parties and with the Secretariat in dealing with these issues, and urged Parties to use the ATS website to good effect.

(320) The Secretariat Information and Technology expert confirmed that the filter "by vessel name" can be included in the EIES, but noted that it is up to the Parties to decide on the appropriateness or otherwise of the provision of information in relation to the rejection of applications for authorisation. He welcomed suggestions from Parties on how the summarised reports section of the EIES could be further developed to provide other facilities that would be useful to them.

(321) Chile noted that documentation issued by its relevant maritime authority related to crew and vessel safety for search and rescue purposes, and did not constitute authorisation to enter Antarctic waters. Chile added that in order to deny a vessel from departing, a court order or document from a competent authority must be provided.

(322) The United Kingdom supported France's call to search the EIES by vessel. It also noted that following similar experiences with unauthorised yachts, a list of all British yachts authorised to enter Antarctic waters is now provided to Chile. In the UK's view this incident highlighted the importance of further dialogue between competent authorities to study existing authorisations and infringements. The UK thanked France for its extensive efforts to investigate this incident and to pursue action against those involved.

(323) The Russian Federation noted that only a few Parties issue authorisations to enter Antarctica, and that, in most cases, authorisation procedures did not exist. Russia highlighted the need for national procedures of the Consultative Parties to be applied in accordance with Art. 1 of Annex 1, and noted the difficulty of applying Annex VI.

(324) The Russian Federation suggested raising the liability of the port State last visited by yachts journeying to Antarctica, and suggested enhanced co-ordination and information sharing between competent national authorities charged with issuing authorisations, the Secretariat, and the port State of last call.

(325) The Republic of Korea expressed privacy concerns in relation to Recommendation 2 on refusals of authorisations relating to its legal ability to release such information.

(326) In relation to the refusal of authorisation, Norway noted that if a vessel was not listed as authorised Parties should understand that it was unauthorised. Norway added that it is the responsibility of flag States to ensure that vessels flying their flags are acting in accordance with international law, and that it is up to the flag States to take necessary action. Norway noted the collective challenge posed by testimonies, and that this needs to be considered in a wider perspective.

(327) Japan expressed concern regarding the inclusion of the refusals of authorisation into the EIES, noting that it was cautious about adding new items to the EIES which were not explicitly required of Parties.

(328) The United States offered to share information regarding its experience of dealing with infractions, and confirmed the existence of US legislation to deal with these issues.

(329) IAATO noted it used the EIES as a first port of call for information on authorisations and it was problematic when this information was incomplete. IAATO noted the value of prosecution in these kind of incidents, so as not to undermine environmental and safety efforts made by authorised groups.

(330) Chile and Argentina summarised the procedures that they have in place for issuing permits and authorisations for private or national activities.

(331) The Chair highlighted that all Parties need to contribute information to the EIES in accordance with previous Decisions of the ATCM. France indicated that it would submit a more detailed proposal in terms of jurisdiction and evidential issues, and the problems associated with potential prosecution procedures.

(332) Chile referred to the current categories of the EIES of "pre-season information" and "post-season reports" and suggested the development of the EIES into a system designed to incorporate real-time updates of information.

(333) Norway commented that Resolution 3, 2004 has not been fully implemented, and that under Recommendation 1, all Parties needed to nominate a single contact point for information on tourism. The Meeting highlighted the benefits of nominating contact points on tourism issues.

(334) Several Parties advocated caution in respect of making any substantial changes to the current EIES, and noted the issue should be further discussed in the future.

(335) The Secretariat confirmed that the issue of refusals can be managed in parallel to the EIES.

(336) The United Kingdom introduced WP 19 *Assessment of Land-Based Activities in Antarctica,* which proposed a checklist to assist with the assessment of these activities against the provisions of the Protocol and other relevant Treaty instruments. This had been developed in line with the UK's specific procedures to deal with authorisations for land-based activities. The UK invited other Parties to collaborate in enhancing and adapting the checklist.

(337) Many Parties thanked the United Kingdom for introducing WP 19 and expressed their support for the checklist.

(338) In response to a query from China, the United Kingdom replied that the checklist referred specifically to non-governmental activities and not to national scientific activities.

(339) Germany informed the Meeting that it had developed a questionnaire for authorising land-based activities which was very similar to the proposed checklist and encouraged the UK to consult it. Germany raised several issues relevant to developing the UK checklist, including methods of access to inland areas and exit from them, visits to ASMA and ASPA sites, introduction of materials and the need to define the term 'vehicle'.

(340) Japan noted that the paper used two similar expressions to identify the activities in question, and suggested that only "non-governmental land-based activities" be used.

(341) France and Argentina suggested that the issue of non-native species could be added to the checklist.

(342) Argentina pointed out that there were other issues that needed to be included on the checklist and that further discussions about this topic were necessary.

(343) The Russian Federation noted it had also experienced some difficulties when issuing authorizations for land-based activities and echoed Germany's concerns about the access points to land-based activities. Russia also raised the point that if such activities are conducted in the areas where national Antarctic Programmes facilities are located it should be previously agreed with the national Antarctic Programmes concerned.

(344) The United States reported that it had experience in this matter and that the proposed checklist was broadly consistent with its own practice. It stated that would be happy to work with the UK intersessionally to provide additional input.

(345) The Netherlands expressed concern with formalising these guidelines because they included references to the usage of vehicles and tractors and suggested caution in this matter. The Netherlands is concerned that including such references in the guidelines could implicitly authorise and encourage such activities, reducing the national capability to control them.

(346) Many Parties expressed support for the checklist while suggesting that several improvements could be made. Several Parties and IAATO offered to work with the United Kingdom intersessionally with this work, and that the ATS forum would be utilised.

(347) The Netherlands, while acknowledging that a checklist could be useful, believed that strategic discussions were required in order to determine what kinds of tourist activities were acceptable to the ATCM.

(348) ASOC thanked the UK for the proposed checklist and noted that to a degree lack of clarity about land-based tourism is a result of insufficient exchange of information and discussion. For instance, there had been no ATCM or CEP discussion of environmental impact assessments for the establishment of land-based tourism facilities, whereas the establishment of new research stations had been discussed.

(349) New Zealand introduced IP 18 *The Berserk Incident, Ross Sea, February 2011,* submitted jointly with Norway and United States, about the Search and Rescue operation and the contribution EIA authorisation processes can make to not only environmental protection, but also safety at sea and search and rescue efficiency. New Zealand expressed concern that the *Berserk* expedition organiser could make a further unauthorised expedition to the Antarctic Treaty area, and noted the inherent difficulties in preventing such unauthorised expeditions.

(350) The co-authors expressed their gratitude to New Zealand for presenting this paper, highlighting the importance of sharing this kind of information with a view to learning lessons and improving policy.

(351) Chile considered that it would be more efficient in future meetings to have an annotated agenda, structured under specific items, prepared in advance for both Tourism and the joint meeting between Tourism and Operations WG. It recommends that the Secretariat consider this in planning the next meeting.

(352) Another paper submitted under this agenda item was:

- IP 28 *Technical safety standards and international law affecting yachts with destination Antarctica* (Germany)

## Item 11: Inspections under the Antarctic Treaty and the Environment Protocol

(353) Japan introduced WP 1 *Inspection Undertaken by Japan in Accordance with Article VII of the Antarctic Treaty and Article XIV of the Protocol on Environmental Protection* and made recommendations on: i) addressing NGO activities, ii) DROMLAN logistics, iii) waste management and disposal, iv) treatment of sewage and domestic liquid wastes, v) renewable

energy, vi) cooperation on effective use of facilities and equipment, and vii) scientific international cooperation.

(354) The ATCM thanked Japan for the detailed and professional manner of its station inspections, and for its valuable contribution to the inspection mechanism of the Antarctic Treaty.

(355) The Russian Federation noted it will present a report to the next ATCM on the comments it received from the inspection of its stations by Japan and Australia. It will also present a report on the DROMLAN network to the COMNAP meeting in Sweden in August 2011.

(356) New Zealand commended Japan for the inspection of non-native species, which reflects the priorities of the CEP. New Zealand added that the idea of inspections could be extended to the potential impacts on the marine zone.

(357) The United Kingdom congratulated Japan on their Antarctic Treaty inspection, which was the first one they had undertaken in Antarctica. The United Kingdom supported the recommendations in the inspection report.

(358) The Republic of Korea supported the recommendations by Japan for waste management and the sourcing of alternative energy.

(359) South Africa thanked Japan for the detailed and positive report from the inspection of SANAE IV station.

(360) India, while thanking Japan for its detailed inspection of Maitri Station, pointed out that it is using a biodegradation plant to treat waste water before it is discharged.

(361) Belgium thanked Japan for the inspection of its station, and the resulting recommendations. Belgium also expressed its willingness to share their experience and information regarding renewable energy alternatives with interested Parties.

(362) Several Parties noted that, given the state of current technology, it is impossible for stations to run solely on renewable energy during winter. They reported that this type of energy can be used as a supplement for other existing types. Some Parties indicated experiencing technical problems with wind turbines due to extreme meteorological conditions.

(363) Germany pointed out that, notwithstanding the need for alternative energy, the main concern must be the safety of the station and its population. Germany remained convinced that it was not at present safe to rely entirely on renewable energy. Information about the failure of sustainable energy

systems should be included in reports to allow others to assess reliability before installation.

(364) Ecuador confirmed that renewable energy will be a priority for its station, and noted that, in its view, the use of renewable energy should be a priority for all countries.

(365) Norway commented that renewable energy has not been implemented as widely as it could be but it has finalised a project described in IP 74 *Assessment of Wind Energy Potential at the Norwegian Research Station Troll* (agenda item 13) that will assess the potential for this.

(366) Norway noted that the activities regarding satellite data downloaded at Troll are to the benefit of society, in particular in relation to weather forecasting, pollution and climate change research. Several Parties expressed their encouragement of the exchange of information and collaboration on removal of waste or remains of old stations.

(367) Japan noted that the first inspection was quite a valuable experience and expressed its intention to continue to contribute to the ATCM.

(368) Australia presented WP 51 *Australian Antarctic Treaty and Environmental Protocol Inspections: January 2010 and January 2011*. For each on-ground inspection of an occupied station, the inspection team had included a person who was fluent in the language used at the station. Australia noted that the main observations and recommendations were related to environmental matters. These matters had been considered in detail by the Committee for Environmental Protection. The inspectors had been impressed by the commitment to scientific activity at the facilities inspected, and had assessed that the drilling project at Lake Vostok appeared to be proceeding in accordance with the final CEE circulated by the Russian Federation. The inspectors had not observed any instances of non-conformance with the provisions of the Antarctic Treaty.

(369) The United Kingdom thanked Australia for their two Antarctic Treaty inspection reports. The United Kingdom noted that the inspection team had visited very remote locations in East Antarctica which are difficult to reach. The United Kingdom noted that the inspection team had visited Vostok Station (Russian Federation) and had observed that the drilling project to enter subglacial Lake Vostok was proceeding in large part in accordance with the final CEE. The United Kingdom supported the recommendations in the inspection reports.

(370) Germany expressed regret for the unavailability of its station (Gondwana) for interior inspections due to unforeseen circumstances and highlighted that collaboration in clean-up of old stations could be a valuable cost saver.

(371) Japan welcomed the inspection report on Syowa Station. It provided Japan with a different image of their station from the viewpoint of different Parties and will contribute to its station management.

## Item 12: Science Issues, Scientific Cooperation and Facilitation, Including the Legacy of the International Polar Year 2007-2008

(372) Argentina presented IP 5 *60ᵗʰ Anniversary of the Argentine Antarctic Institute* and IP 17 *Bioremediation of Antarctic Soils Contaminated with Hydrocarbons. Rational Design of Bioremediation Strategies.* Regarding IP 17, it was mentioned that different bioremediation strategies were studied in order to reduce hydrocarbon levels in Antarctic soils. Biostimulation strategies proved to be efficient in improving the breakdown of these compounds of environmental concern.

(373) Japan presented IP 41 *Japan's Antarctic Research Highlights in 2010-2011 Including Those Related to Climate Change.* The major topic was the installation and the first observation of a large atmospheric radar system (PANSY).

(374) SCAR presented IP 51 *The Southern Ocean Observing System (SOOS): An Update* as well as IP 55 *Summary Report on IPY 2007-2008 by the ICSU-WMO Joint Committee.*

(375) Norway and the Russian Federation commented on IPY legacy issues in IP 58 *IPY Legacy Workshop,* and IP 101 rev. 1, *Russian Proposals for an International Polar Decade.*

(376) Norway reported on the Legacy Workshop held in conjunction with the IPY Science Conference in Norway in June 2010. The holding of such a workshop was discussed and supported at ATCM XXXII. The Workshop was attended by 60 representatives from a large number of countries and organisations. The report is appended to IP 58. The recommendations of the workshop relating to the International Polar Decade (IPD) had more recently been moved forward through a joint WMO-Roshydromet workshop on the IPD initiative held in St. Petersburg in April 2011 and also at the WMO Congress in May 2011.

(377) The Russian Federation noted that the St. Petersburg workshop was an informal scientific exchange. However, resolutions adopted in May 2011 at

the Sixteenth Hydrological Congress and at the Seventh Ministerial Meeting of the Arctic Council have both supported the concept of an IPD. SCAR and COMNAP will be asked to consider support for an IPD to begin in 2014.

(378) The Republic of Korea introduced IP 77 *Scientific and Science-related Collaborations with Other Parties during 2010-11.* These collaborations included a Korean Polar Research Institute (KOPRI) joint research expedition with the United States using the ice-breaking research vessel *Araon* in the Amundsen Sea. The joint expedition to search for Antarctic meteorites between KOPRI and Italy's PNRA recovered 113 meteorites and will be extended. KOPRI and the United States collaborated on a marine and quaternary geosciences project on abrupt environmental change in the Larsen Ice Shelf system. KOPRI conducted a short survey of the Antarctic Ridge in early 2011 in cooperation with participating US scientists. Korea supported the international collaborative study by Japan on magnetism in the King George Island. Finally, KOPRI and Italy conducted a collaborative initial study on Antarctic gas hydrates. Korea hopes to widen collaboration to include other Parties in the future.

(379) New Zealand acknowledged the work by the Republic of Korea and in particular the exciting work on gas hydrates. It also congratulated Korea on its new ice-breaker enabled work.

(380) Russian Federation reported on the work described in IP 97 *Current status of the Russian drilling project at Vostok station.* Although the Russian Federation had planned to penetrate the ice through to Lake Vostok, due to technical problems with the drill bit and the presence of ice crystals at the bottom of the bore, drilling was discontinued at 3720 metres. The further drilling of the remaining 20-30 metres of ice will resume in December 2011, when it will be able to ascertain the actual thickness of the glacier above the lake.

(381) The Russian Federation stressed that its drilling was conducted pursuant to a permit issued by the Government of Russia and was conducted in full compliance with a final environmental impact assessment (EIA) which had been provided to the CEP. The EIA requires that all necessary measures are taken to control penetration into the lake and drilling will automatically stop when the lake is reached. Any liquid in the bore hole will be extracted. Russia will present documents describing its work once drilling is complete.

(382) Germany thanked the Russian Federation for its open discussion and presentation and expressed the hope that the project would in future be seen by everyone as an example of how to inform the community on project progress, including all of its difficulties. It noted that the work was conducted

under very difficult conditions, and also noted that the monocrystals recovered may be helpful in better understanding ice on earth.

(383) Chile noted that its scientific activities conducted in 2010/11 are presented in IP 118 *Contribuciones chilenas al conocimiento científico de la Antártica: Expedición 2010/11.*

(384) Ecuador presented IP 125 *Cooperación en investigación científica entre Ecuador y Venezuela.* Ecuador noted three bi-national projects conducted with Venezuela in 2011. These included an updating of nautical charts in the South Shetland Islands which will be continued by hydrographers during stage 2 in 2012. The second and third projects were a study of palaeontology on Dee Island and a study of bioprospecting of Antarctic organisms. Ecuador thanked Brazil, Argentina and Chile for logistical and other support to the projects.

(385) In commenting on its IP 119 *Programa Chileno de ciencia Antartica PROCIEN: Un Programa Abierto al Mundo,* Chile noted the importance of opening Antarctic science to the world and the improvement of science when submitted to international review and scrutiny. Chile urged increased scientific collaboration as a means to involve other scientist and reduce costs.

(386) The following papers were also submitted to this session:

- IP 7 *Brief Introduction of the Fourth Chinese National Arctic Expedition* (China)
- IP 36 *ERICON AB Icebreaker FP7 Project. A New Era in Polar Research* (Romania)
- IP 37 *Law-Racovita Base. An Example of Co-operation in Antarctica.*(Romania)
- IP 42 *Legacy of IPY 2007-2008 for Japan* (Japan)
- IP 61 *The SCAR Antarctic Climate Evolution (ACE) Programme* (SCAR)
- IP 70 *The Dutch Science Facility at the UK's Rothera Research Station* (Netherlands & UK)
- IP 96 *Scientific Workshop on Antarctic Krill in the Netherlands* (Netherlands)
- IP 100 *Preliminary Results of the Russian Scientific Studies in the Antarctic in 2010* (Russian Federation)
- IP 112 *Ukrainian Research in Antarctica 2002-2012* (Ukraine)

- IP 132 *Report on the Research Activities: Czech Research Station J.G.Mendel, James Ross Island and the Antarctic Peninsula, Season 2010/11* (Czech Republic)
- IP 133 *Report on All-Terrain Vehicles Impact on Deglaciated Area of James Ross Island, Antarctica* (Czech Republic)

## Item 13: Implications of Climate Change for Management of the Antarctic Treaty Area

(387) The United Kingdom introduced WP 44, *Progress Report on the ATME on Climate Change*. The UK noted that Norway and the UK developed WP 44 to facilitate the ATCM's on-going consideration of the conclusions and recommendations arising from the 2010 Climate Change Antarctic Treaty Meeting of Experts (ATME). The summary table at Annex A recorded the actions taken to date by the CEP and ATCM against each of the thirty recommendations of the ATME.

(388) The UK and Norway proposed that the ATCM task the Secretariat with maintaining and updating the table to inform future discussions on the ATME recommendations until they have all been closed. The Meeting agreed that the Secretariat would maintain the table and provide regular updates to future CEP meetings and ATCMs.

(389) New Zealand and Australia praised the work of the ATME and supported its recommendations. New Zealand acknowledged the substantive work of SCAR. Australia commented that discussions and agreements at this ATCM and CEP may need to be reflected in the progress report.

(390) Argentina noted it had no objection with respect to the proposal of WP 44, though also noted that such a proposal does not imply the adoption, by the ATCM, of the recommendations listed in WP 44.

(391) Norway noted that some ATME recommendations relate to SCAR's work on climate change, particularly the Antarctic Climate Change and the Environment (ACCE) publication. Norway drew the Meeting's attention to IP 83, ASOC's Antarctic climate change communication plan, which is directed to address climate change ATME Recommendation 2 (2010). Norway announced that the UK, Norway and ASOC will be providing financial support to facilitate communication of future updates and publications related to the ACCE Report. Norway noted that such future updates would

include topics such as "Southern Ocean Change", "Antarctica 2100", "Ice Sheets and Sea Level Rise" and "Recovery of the Ozone Hole".

(392) SCAR thanked the UK, Norway and ASOC for their assistance and later introduced IP 52 *Antarctic Climate Change and the Environment – 2011 Update,* the second update since the ACCE was completed. SCAR's group promoting the ACCE now includes the Russian Federation and China; it hopes to add other members from other countries in the future.

(393) The United Kingdom thanked SCAR for the update on the Antarctic Climate Change and Environment (ACCE). The United Kingdom noted the importance of issuing regular updates as science is rapidly developing. For example, United States and British researchers had just published research in *Nature* that the Pine Island Glacier in West Antarctica was now melting 50% faster than 15 years ago. The United Kingdom reiterated the importance of getting the ACCE report to decision makers and the public and was pleased to be able to provide financial support to SCAR, along with Norway and ASOC, to help communicate climate change in Antarctica.

(394) Bulgaria introduced IP 11 *Permafrost and Climate Change in the Maritime Antarctic: 5 Years of Permafrost Research at the St Kliment Ohridksi Station in Livingston Island,* commenting on its joint work and monitoring with Spain and Portugal.

(395) COMNAP introduced IP 8 *COMNAP Energy Management Workshop*. The workshop was one example of COMNAP's efforts to share experience of energy efficiency and alternative energy practices. This work, along with other work of COMNAP, including, for example, the 2010 Symposium, also addresses the ATME Recommendation 4, bullet point 2.

(396) Norway introduced IP 74 *Assessment of Wind Energy Potential at the Norwegian Research Station Troll.* In consultation with two private firms, Norway has collected data from 2008, 2009 and 2010 on the operation of the wind energy complex. Winds at Troll alternate between short periods of very strong winds and longer periods of very low winds. Wind generation may have the potential to meet 10-15% of Norway's energy needs at Troll but, while promising, it has its limitations. Phase 2 of Norway's consideration of alternative energy will explore the use of other sources, including solar power.

(397) Australia welcomed Norway's paper, which contributed directly to Recommendation 6 from the 2010 Climate ATME. It also recalled ATCM XXX - IP 48, which reported on Australia's experience with operating a wind farm at Mawson station. Of particular relevance to Recommendation

6, that paper provided details about engineering and design aspects of the wind farm, as well as information about important considerations for the application of wind energy to remote locations such as Antarctic stations.

(398) The Russian Federation introduced IP 98 *New Approach to Study of Climate Change based on Global Albedo Monitoring.* It indicated that global albedo monitoring adds an important parameter to atmospheric monitoring and noted its use by the NOAA in the United States. The Russian Federation urged its use in Antarctica as a very useful supplement to existing methods.

(399) SCAR commented that the method used to measure global albedo in the Russian paper was an interesting technique that warranted further investigation.

(400) ASOC thanked COMNAP for IP 8 and Norway for IP 74 and for the proactive efforts to move forward recommendations from the ATME on climate change. ASOC also introduced IP 92 *The Ross Sea: A Valuable Reference Area to Assess the Effects of Climate Change*, which explains how IPCC predictions indicate that the Ross Sea will be the last portion of the Southern Ocean with sea ice year-round. Protection of the Ross Sea will therefore provide a reference area for scientists to assess the magnitude of the changes occurring elsewhere in the Southern Ocean.

(401) Additional papers submitted to this session were:

- IP 88 *Ocean Acidification and the Southern Ocean* (ASOC)
- IP 103 *IAATO Climate Change Working Group: Report of Progress* (IAATO)
- IP 111 *Installation of new meteorological equipment at Vernadsky Station* (Ukraine)

## Item 14: Operational Issues

(402) The Republic of Korea presented IP 19 *The Draft Comprehensive Environmental Evaluation for the Construction and Operation of the Jang Bogo Antarctic Research Station, Terra Nova Bay, Antarctica* which had been discussed at the CEP.

(403) Several Parties congratulated the Republic of Korea on its contribution to scientific research in West Antarctica, reiterating comments made at the CEP. France requested that information be shared on waste water management and the water recycling system as it could be valuable for other Antarctic stations. Korea indicated it would be happy to do so.

(404) Australia presented IP 49 *Renewable Energy and Energy Efficiency Initiatives at Australia's Antarctic Stations.* The paper responded to Recommendation 4 from the 2010 Climate ATME by providing an overview of selected examples of Australia's Antarctic energy management practices. Australia indicated that it would be pleased to provide further information to interested parties.

(405) The Republic of Korea presented IP 78 *The First Antarctic Expedition of Araon (2010/2011).*

(406) India enquired what maximum ice thickness the ship had experienced and was designed to break. The Republic of Korea replied that *Araon* was designed to break a thickness of 1.5m of sea ice at a speed of 3 knots. It has been tested at 1.5m, but it is believed it could break more than that thickness at a slower speed.

(407) ASOC presented IP 82 *An Antarctic Vessel Traffic Monitoring and Information System.* ASOC called on the ATCM to adopt a Resolution or Decision on the development of an Antarctic Vessel Traffic Monitoring and Information System (VTMIS).

(408) IAATO noted that all its members operating SOLAS passenger vessels must participate in IAATO vessel monitoring system.

(409) The United States noted that the development of any mandatory vessel traffic system/reporting system would be under the jurisdiction of the International Maritime Organisation (IMO) as the appropriate international body, not the ATCM. However, the ATCM or a Contracting Government could refer a proposal to the IMO. The United States reaffirmed its support of maximum participation in the voluntary systems already operated by COMNAP and IAATO.

(410) Argentina presented IP 121 *Medical Evacuation Reported by the Combined Antarctic Naval Patrol.* Sweden thanked Chile and Argentina for having assisted Swedish nationals in distress in a timely fashion.

(411) Brazil offered thanks for the support provided by the Chilean ship *Lautaro* in December 2010, for the transport of equipment and researchers from the Chilean station President Frei to the Brazilian station Comandante Ferraz.

(412) Bulgaria thanked Brazil for their support and use of their ship for the opening of the Bulgarian St. Kliment Ohridski station.

(413) Another paper submitted to this session was:

- IP 63 *Renovación del Parque de Tanques de combustible de la Base Científica Antártica Artigas* (Uruguay)

## Item 15: Education Issues

(414) Ecuador presented IP 124 *I Concurso Intercolegial sobre Temas Antárticos (CITA, 2010)*, noting that this exercise was an important tool for getting young people interested in Antarctica. Ecuador thanked the Chilean Antarctic Institute for its collaboration.

(415) Bulgaria introduced IP 128 *The Excitement "Antarctic" Distance In Itself Invisible* and presented video material related to its exhibition.

(416) Papers submitted under this agenda item included:

- IP 45 *Publication of the book "The Elephant Island. The Adventure of the Uruguayan Pioneers in Antarctica"* (Uruguay)
- IP 46 *Publication of the book "Antarctic Verses" in occasion of the 25ᵗʰ anniversary of* "Uruguay Consultative Member of the Antarctic Treaty" (Uruguay)
- IP 47 *Commemorative postage stamp issue: "25ᵗʰ anniversary of Uruguay consultative member of the Antarctic Treaty"* (Uruguay)

## Item 16: Exchange of Information

(417) ASOC presented IP 113 *Review of the implementation of the Madrid Protocol: Annual Report by Parties (Article 17)* (already presented in CEP).

## Item 17: Biological Prospecting

(418) Argentina and the Netherlands introduced papers related to bioprospecting in the Antarctic: respectively IP 16 *Report on the recent bioprospecting activities carried out by Argentina during the period 2010-2011* and IP 62 *A case of Biological Prospecting*. Both papers were noted by the Working Group.

(419) The Netherlands reported verbally on international developments on bioprospecting since ATCM XXXIII. The first development was the conclusion on 30 October 2010 of the Nagoya Protocol to the Convention on Biological Diversity (CBD).

(420) Broad support was expressed by the Meeting for the view that the Nagoya Protocol did not apply to bioprospecting in Antarctica. Several other Parties

agreed on the need to ensure that there was no ambiguity on the issue and noted that the Antarctic Treaty system was the appropriate forum for dealing with Antarctic bioprospecting.

(421) The second development was the outcome of a United Nations General Assembly (UNGA) Ad Hoc Informal Working Group meeting on the conservation and sustainable use of marine biological diversity in areas beyond national jurisdiction. The Ad Hoc Working Group made recommendations to the UNGA for addressing this issue in that forum, including questions with respect to marine genetic resources.

(422) The Netherlands urged the Meeting to begin to address the legal and policy implications of the Nagoya Protocol and the UN process.

(423) Japan stated that the forthcoming intergovernmental negotiations on the Nagoya Protocol, in which the issue of the need for and modalities of a global multilateral benefit-sharing mechanism would be discussed, should also be taken into consideration.

(424) Several Parties noted the proposals at ATCM XXXIII, including by the Netherlands and Chile, to focus attention on bioprospecting in Antarctica and that, given developments by the CBD and the UNGA, there was now a sense of urgency on this issue. Sweden proposed the establishment of an intersessional contact group.

(425) The Netherlands was requested to consult informally on the development of terms of reference of a possible intersessional contact group. While several Parties were supportive of this approach, it appeared during these consultations that, in the absence of a Working Paper on the issue, there should be a more specific understanding of the approach and process by which the Meeting would progress the issue. Following consultations, the Netherlands reported that it had not been possible to agree to the formation of an intersessional contact group on bioprospecting. Several Parties urged that informal contacts between various interested Parties should continue.

(426) The Russian Federation introduced IP 99 *Microbiological monitoring of coastal Antarctic stations and bases as a factor of study of anthropogenic impact on the Antarctic environment and the human organism*. The Russian Federation noted that it had identified pathogenic fungi in snow, ice, air, open and enclosed spaces, and soil. These fungi are potentially dangerous to humans and were collected in areas not visited by humans for a number of years. The Russian Federation invited cooperation on its work and noted the potential for its findings to assist in battling the spread of diseases.

## Item 18: Development of a Multi-year Strategic Work Plan

(427) New Zealand opened the discussion, noting that a multi-year work plan had served the CEP well. Although it would be a difficult challenge, New Zealand saw merit in developing a multi-year strategic work plan for the ATCM. Such a work plan would provide an opportunity each year to pause and consider our collective vision for Antarctica, while helping guide our work from year to year. Such a plan should be flexible enough to incorporate emerging issues as well as issues currently on the ATCM's agenda. Discussions on developing a multi-year strategic work plan should be part of ongoing discussions about how the Meeting structures its work.

(428) Australia saw great value in work to agree on the most important issues warranting the collective attention of the Parties, and to develop a structured approach to addressing those issues. It emphasised that further discussions on the development of a multi-year strategic work plan should be informed and supported by clear and considered proposals. Australia noted that a key benefit of a strategic work plan would be to forecast dedicated consideration of issues, allowing Parties to thoroughly prepare for a substantive and constructive debate. It further noted that it would be useful to identify principles or criteria to guide Parties' collective consideration of and agreement on priorities. It would also be important for a strategic work plan to have flexibility and be dynamic to accommodate emerging issues.

(429) Belgium considered that a current weakness, one that could be addressed by the strategic plan, was the lack of institutional memory and continuity of discussions, and also agreed that when developing the strategic work plan clarity of purpose was essential. In its view climate change, renewable energy, bio-prospecting and marine protected areas were priorities. Belgium suggested that the Meeting could work more closely with other organizations and with national governments, and that the CEP was a good example to follow when building up a strategy, which needed to be both flexible and succinct.

(430) While supporting the idea of developing a strategic work plan, the United Kingdom said that it was important to remember the aims of the Antarctic Treaty, under Article IX. The United Kingdom suggested bringing in experts to deal with particular issues and emphasised that policy development should be based on data and science, for example, by drawing on the advice of the CEP under each relevant agenda item, rather than just taking the whole CEP report in one session.

(431) Argentina noted that such a plan would be useful because it could enable the ATCM to establish a clear direction, defining priorities and making the meetings more efficient. Argentina also highlighted the importance of ICGs and encouraged more Parties to participate in them.

(432) For Germany Article IX of the Treaty provided an appropriate basis from which to develop the plan, and it saw the development of a collective vision amongst Parties as being an important goal. Germany noted the importance of frequent re-evaluation of the ATCM agenda in order to be able to respond to new and emerging issues. It suggested that the Host Party could propose one or two priority issues for detailed consideration among Parties, experts and observers at each Meeting, from which an agreed document containing outcomes could be developed both for action by the ATCM and for providing better links to the wider international community. Germany raised the questions of how to translate the main results of ongoing scientific research into action, and how to communicate these results and ATCM outcomes to the public.

(433) The Netherlands agreed with the idea of a strategic vision and with the concept of dedicating a Meeting day to the consideration of a specific issue. It affirmed the continuing importance of the Protocol, and drew attention to human impact issues including possible future human settlement on the continent and the likelihood of more stations being established, suggesting that Ny Alesund could provide a valuable model for mitigating future impacts and enhancing science cooperation in Antarctica. The Netherlands noted that the Wordie House incident highlighted the need for the development of a joint monitoring and compliance mechanism.

(434) Japan highlighted the need to enhance the efficiency of Meetings, noting that Working Papers should frame and stimulate debate among Parties, rather than be informative. It made a concrete proposal that Working Papers should include proposals of decisions or resolutions, except for urgent cases.

(435) Ecuador felt that intersessional work should be strengthened, that better use should be made of EIES, and that the participation of professionals from different disciplines could enhance Meeting discussions.

(436) The United States noted the importance of both prioritising topics, as well as identifying specific issues for consideration within these topics. It supported the idea of devoting part of an ATCM to a specific theme but noted the importance of maintaining consensus on the selection of issues for discussion.

(437) Sweden suggested that emerging issues needed to be considered in the strategic plan, in addition to present issues. It agreed with other Parties on the usefulness of intersessional work, with the help of the electronic tools at our disposal on the Secretariat website, and noted the need for discussing the interface between the ATCM and CCAMLR regarding MPAs. Sweden added that the ATCM would benefit from greater use of the competencies of SCAR and COMNAP, and their participation in collective work and in outreach would be very useful.

(438) Brazil supported the points already made, especially the suggestions made by the Netherlands and the priority points presented by Belgium. It highlighted the importance of avoiding duplication of work in the ATCM which was undertaken in other fora. Brazil supported the idea of having an agreed theme for the ATCMs, agreed with shortening the meeting, and stressed the importance of Parties preparing their papers in a timely fashion.

(439) Uruguay noted that the development of a multi-year strategic work plan needed a clear baseline, and stated that the reduction to eight working days should not be matched by an increase in the number of delegates, or more Working Groups and/or costs. As final points it suggested that intersessional and expert meetings take place electronically, and that the key theme for each meeting be determined by consensus.

(440) India believed that a multi-year strategic plan will give ATCM a clear direction whilst also identifying priority issues. At also emphasised the need for tabling a Working Paper on this issue in the next ATCM.

(441) China proposed that the plan must have a vision defined by the principles of the Antarctic Treaty which should highlight the role of scientific research. It identified the challenge produced by the increase of human activities in the Antarctic as a key area of concern. China noted that scientific research was of primary importance and should be more extensively discussed in order to ensure that policies and action were based on good evidence.

(442) ASOC considered that the objective and environmental principles of the Protocol provided a vision for the future. ASOC expressed concern about emerging pressures at all levels that threaten the natural reserve status of Antarctica. Supporting suggestions that advanced planning for ATCMs would help ensure that discussions produce clear outcomes, it also encouraged Parties to provide tangible evidence that the natural condition of Antarctica is protected, the pressures on the environment minimised and managed, and that action is based on scientific evidence and/or the precautionary approach.

## Item 19: Commemoration of the 50ᵗʰ Anniversary of the entry into force of the Antarctic Treaty

(443) The Chairman reported that the text of the Declaration on Antarctic Cooperation on the Occasion of the 50ᵗʰ Anniversary of the Entry into Force of the Antarctic Treaty had been examined and discussed at length among the Parties. All contributions to the text made by the Parties had been incorporated and a consensus reached on the text in English. Text in the other official languages will reflect the consensus wording. The Declaration is annexed as Appendix 1.

(444) The Chairman submitted the Declaration for adoption, noted the consensus of the Meeting and reported the Declaration adopted.

(445) The Chairman noted with pleasure the attendance of Minister Hector Timerman, Minister for Foreign Relations, International Trade and Worship of Argentina, Minister Alfredo Moreno Charme, Minister for Foreign Relations for Chile and Minister Luis Almagro Lemes, Minister for Foreign Relations for Uruguay, as well as Ambassador Luiz Alberto Figueiredo Machado, Under Secretary of Environment, Energy, Science and Technology, Ministry of Foreign Relations, as the Special Representative from Brazil, and Mr Michel Rocard as the Special Representative for France to present statements on behalf of their governments on this anniversary milestone of the Antarctic Treaty. The statements of these senior representatives are annexed in full at Vol. 2, Part III, section 1 together with the statements from the Consultative Parties.

## Item 20: Preparation of the 35ᵗʰ Meeting

### a. Date and place

(446) The Meeting welcomed the kind invitation of the Government of Australia to host ATCM XXXV in Hobart from June 4-13, 2012.

(447) For future planning, the Meeting took note that the following likely timetable of upcoming ATCMs:

- 2013 Belgium
- 2014 Brazil

(448) The Meeting welcomed the intention of the Government of the Kingdom of Belgium to host the ATCM XXXVI in Brussels.

(449) Australia presented WP 8 *Proposed schedule for the 35th Antarctic Treaty Consultative Meeting, Hobart, 2012,* noting the importance of ensuring that the reduction in length of the Meeting from ten to eight days would allow adequate time for the CEP, the ATCM and the established Working Groups to undertake necessary work. Australia noted the proposal included the possibility of establishing new Working Groups, and emphasised the importance of retaining a focus on environmental protection. The Committee for Environmental Protection also considered the proposed schedule for the Hobart meeting in this regard.

(450) Norway introduced WP 60 *Proposal for shortening the Antarctic Treaty Consultative Meetings.* Norway noted that its proposal to reduce the length of the Meeting to six and a half working days sought to improve the efficiency and working methods of Meetings through a variety of methods – the merging of agenda items, increased use of expert meetings intersessionally, shorter meetings, and a reconsideration of the structure of working groups. Norway noted that the ATCM may decide to pursue its proposal further following the 2012 Meeting in Hobart.

(451) The Meeting welcomed the proposed schedule in WP 8 for ATCM XXXV.

(452) The Meeting noted that there were common points of interest in both papers. Several Parties drew attention to the need to re-prioritise the work agenda in light of the reduced meeting time frame planned for ATCM XXXV, and to consider the restructuring of Working Groups. The United Kingdom noted the importance of delegations having the capacity to field experts for all areas in order to avoid making decisions in isolation. It suggested the establishment of a broader Human Impact Working Group. The Meeting considered it needed to retain Working Groups in their current form for the next meeting.

(453) Several Parties expressed concern that six and a half days may be too short, adding that a further reduction in Meeting days may inhibit efficiency, and suggested there be a re-examination of the length of the meeting following ATCM XXXV. It was also noted that the savings that could accrue through reducing the length of the meetings to less than eight days might be lost through the need for additional intersessional expert meetings. Some Parties considered it worth exploring the concept of meetings of experts in conjunction with ATCMs in order to avoid additional time and travel

costs, and to enable all Parties to participate in such meetings. Chile and Germany both noted the potential benefits of including "Arctic and Antarctic Developments" as a separate agenda item. However, Japan questioned the inclusion of this item. The United States noted that the need for meetings of experts is independent of the length of ATCMs.

(454) While supporting the proposed schedule for ATCM XXXV, Argentina noted that shorter ATCMs should not lead to additional expert meetings due to budget and travel limitations, as well as reduced participation and lack of translation / interpretation at these meetings.

(455) Some Parties raised the question of whether the CEP needed to meet for the full five days of the Meeting, while some others emphasised the importance of the CEP having adequate time to consider the important issues it deals with. Others suggested the possibility of conducting informal contact group meetings on the Saturday of the middle weekend. Several Parties noted the importance of ensuring that evenings and weekends remained free from work commitments to allow adequate rest periods for all those participating in the Meeting.

(456) Other suggestions included the possibility of ATCM Meetings taking place biannually, as had been the case in earlier years. Other Parties noted their continued preference for an annual Meeting. It was also suggested that the first Heads of Delegation meeting take place on the Monday in advance of the first Plenary.

(457) The Meeting noted it would be useful to assess the efficacy of an eight day meeting following the conclusion of ATCM XXXV. Australia, as ATCM XXXV host, indicated it would provide for this. Belgium noted that, in preparation for ATCM XXXVI which it would host in 2013, it would analyse the proposals outlined in both Working Papers.

## b. Invitation of International and Non-Governmental Organisations

(458) In accordance with established practice, the Meeting agreed that the following organisations having scientific or technical interest in Antarctica should be invited to send experts to attend ATCM XXXV: the ACAP Secretariat, ASOC, IAATO, IHO, IMO, IOC, the Intergovernmental Panel on Climate Change (IPCC), IUCN, UNEP, WMO and WTO.

### c. Invitation to Malaysia

(459) The Chair reported on informal contact with the Delegation of Malaysia. Recalling that Malaysia had been invited to observe the ATCM on several occasions, if Malaysia has not acceded by the time of ATCM XXXV the Host Country of the ATCM will follow the procedure of previous years regarding participation, if Malaysia so requests.

### d. Preparation of the Agenda for ATCM XXXV

(460) The Meeting approved the Preliminary Agenda for ATCM XXXV.

### e. Organisation of ATCM XXXV

(461) Pursuant to Rule 11, the Meeting decided as a preliminary matter to propose the same Working Groups at ATCM XXXV as at this Meeting.

### f. The SCAR Lecture

(462) Taking into account the valuable series of lectures given by SCAR at a number of ATCMs, the Meeting decided to invite SCAR to give another lecture on scientific issues relevant to ATCM XXXV.

## Item 21: Any Other Business

(463) There was no other business.

## Item 22: Adoption of the Final Report

(464) The Meeting adopted the Final Report of the 34th Antarctic Treaty Consultative Meeting.

(465) The Chair of the Meeting Ambassador Ariel Mansi made closing remarks.

(466) The Meeting was closed on Friday, 1 July at 13:40.

# 2. CEP XIV Report

# Report of the Committee
# for Environmental Protection (CEP XIV)

Buenos Aires, June 20-24, 2011

## Item 1: Opening of the Meeting

(1) The CEP Chair, Dr Yves Frenot, opened the meeting on Monday 20 June 2011 and thanked Argentina for arranging and hosting the meeting in Buenos Aires.

(2) The Chair recalled the various significant anniversaries being celebrated at the ATCM XXXIV, including the 20th anniversary of the opening for signature of the Madrid Protocol in 1991. He also offered his condolences for the loss of Ambassador Jorge Berguño (Chile) and Dr Teodor Negoiţă (Romania), both valued members of the Antarctic community.

(3) The Chair summarised the work undertaken during the intersessional period. This included four intersessional contact groups (among them two for the evaluation of draft CEEs circulated during the period), one workshop and other studies contributing to the papers before CEP XIV. Most of the planned work decided at the end of CEP XIII was achieved.

## Item 2: Adoption of the Agenda

(4) The Committee adopted the following agenda and confirmed the allocation of 46 Working Papers, 68 Information Papers and 4 Secretariat Papers to Agenda Items:

1. Opening of the Meeting
2. Adoption of the Agenda
3. Strategic Discussions on the Future Work of the CEP
4. Operation of the CEP
5. Climate Change Implications for the Environment: Strategic Approach

6. Environmental Impact Assessment (EIA)

   a. Draft Comprehensive Environmental Evaluations

   b. Other EIA Matters

7. Area Protection and Management Plans

   a. Management Plans

   b. Historic Sites and Monuments

   c. Site Guidelines

   d. Human Footprint and Wilderness Values

   e. Marine Spatial Protection and Management

   f. Other Annex V Matters

8. Conservation of Antarctic Flora and Fauna

   a. Quarantine and Non-Native Species

   b. Specially Protected Species

   c. Other Annex II Matters

9. Environmental Monitoring and Reporting

10. Inspection Reports

11. Cooperation with Other Organisations

12. General Matters

13. Election of Officers

14. Preparation for Next Meeting

15. Adoption of the Report

16. Closing of the Meeting

(5) The Chair drew attention to the continuous increase in the extent and volume of the CEP Final Reports with each meeting. He proposed to reduce the size of this report by focussing on the key issues discussed, the decisions taken, and the Committee's advice to the ATCM, as well as future work targets.

## Item 3: Strategic Discussions on the Future Work of the CEP

(6) ASOC introduced IP 89 rev. 1 *The Antarctic Environmental Protocol, 1991-2011.* While noting the Protocol's many achievements, ASOC raised concerns that the Protocol is not consistently applied by all Parties and that some of its more innovative and progressive aspects of environmental management, such as international collaboration, EIA for all activities, and dependent and associated ecosystems, are much less adequately realised than might be expected. ASOC recommended that a better and more consistent implementation of the Protocol's letter and intent is required, including greater transparency in national implementation, and a greater commitment to international management of the Antarctic region.

(7) The Committee noted the value of independent reviews and thanked ASOC for its paper, which was a useful reference for new reflections on the continued work of the CEP, including through its five-year work plan. Some Members noted that IP 89 rev. 1 could form the basis for a possible review of the implementation of the Protocol in 2016 at the 25th anniversary of the Protocol. It was also suggested that it would be a useful document for assisting Parties in assessing internally how well they were performing with respect to the Protocol objectives.

(8) During this discussion, the Russian Federation reminded the Committee of the importance of the consistent application of EIAs, and offered to work with interested Parties.

(9) The Committee revised and updated the Five-Year Work Plan (Appendix 3).

## Item 4: Operation of the CEP

(10) The Chair noted that the two Working Papers to be presented under this Agenda Item were also submitted for discussion by the Legal and Institutional Working Group.

(11) The United States introduced WP 25, jointly elaborated with Germany, entitled *Timely Submission of Papers in Advance of ATCMs,* which aimed to improve the efficiency and effectiveness of ATCM and CEP work, by including in the Rules of Procedure clear rules related to submission of papers in advance of ATCMs.

(12)  Australia presented WP 36, co-authored with France and New Zealand, entitled *A proposed new approach to the handling of Information Papers*. This paper was intended to improve the efficiency of meetings by modifying the procedures for the handling of Information Papers, including the provision that papers not material to discussions under the ATCM / CEP agenda be made available only via the ATS website and not be circulated or introduced during the meeting.

(13)  These documents were not discussed in detail by the Committee and were addressed by the Legal and Institutional Working Group.

(14)  The United Nations Environment Program (UNEP) introduced IP 113 *Review of the Implementation of the Madrid Protocol: Annual Report by Parties (Article 17)*, jointly submitted with ASOC. UNEP emphasised that the level of compliance in the production of annual reports on the implementation of the Protocol remained low even twelve years after ratification.

(15)  Many Members agreed that the level of compliance required considerable improvement and reiterated that all Parties should submit their annual reports. Some Members pointed out that the platform to do so, the Electronic Information Exchange System (EIES), could be more user-friendly.

(16)  The Secretariat agreed to convene an informal contact group on the CEP Discussion Forum to coordinate technical proposals from Members on this matter.

(17)  Other papers submitted under this agenda item were:

- IP 71 *Annual Report pursuant to Article 17 of the Protocol on Environmental Protection to the Antarctic Treaty. 2009-2010* (Italy)

- IP 93 *Annual Report Pursuant to Article 17 of the Protocol on Environmental Protection to the Antarctic Treaty* (Ukraine)

## Item 5: Climate Change Implications for the Environment: Strategic Approach

(18)  The United Kingdom introduced a joint paper with Norway, WP 44 *Progress Report on ATME on Climate Change,* which tracked actions on the conclusions and recommendations arising from the *2010 Antarctic Treaty Meeting of Experts on Climate Change (ATME Climate Change).*

(19) SCAR informed the Committee that it had already incorporated Recommendation 17 on the identification of key regions, habitats and species at greatest risk from climate change effects of the ATME into its research programmes.

(20) South Africa noted that the impact of climate change on biodiversity is one of its key current Antarctic research challenges.

(21) Australia noted that the ATME recommendations may be best managed by incorporating them into relevant aspects of the Committee's business, including the five-year work plan. It noted that combining or grouping the recommendations by subject matter (e.g. non-native species, area protection) could assist with such an approach.

(22) Several Members considered that such a framework like the one proposed in WP 44 would be a useful tool to inform the management activities of the CEP through its five-year work plan.

(23) IAATO referred to IP 103 *IAATO's Climate Change Working Group: Report on Progress* and stated that it would continue to provide information to the CEP on this work and raise awareness of climate change in the Antarctic to other interested Members, noting the successful collaboration with SCAR earlier this year.

(24) CCAMLR added that its Scientific Committee had considered ATME Recommendations 19, 26, 28 and 1, 2, 4, 5, 6, and agreed that future Working Groups should continue to focus on ecosystem management. CCAMLR also noted its continued participation in the Committee with the submission of IP 31 *Report by the SC-CAMLR Observer to the Fourteenth Meeting of the Committee for Environmental Protection.*

(25) COMNAP remarked that ATME Recommendations 4 and 5, which refer directly to COMNAP, had been addressed in IP 8 *COMNAP Energy Management Workshop*, to be discussed under ATCM Item 13. COMNAP is able to provide updates to ATME Recommendations 4 and 5 to include in this progress report.

(26) The Committee agreed to task the Secretariat to update on a regular basis the summary table at Annex A of WP 44, recording the actions *vis à vis* each of the 30 ATME recommendations, by both the CEP and the ATCM.

(27) The United Kingdom introduced first steps towards developing a simple and rapid assessment of vulnerability of 12 ASPAs to climate change (WP 43 *Developing a Single Methodology for Classifying Antarctic Specially Protected Areas According to their Vulnerability to Climate Change jointly submitted by the United Kingdom and Norway)*. The United Kingdom explained that this paper assessed possible impacts in terms of two components: vulnerability of their key values and regional exposure to climate change. The United Kingdom drew attention to two of the most vulnerable of these 12 ASPAs to emerge from the analysis, namely ASPA 107 Dion Islands and ASPA 151 Lions Rump.

(28) India congratulated the United Kingdom for this excellent paper but raised concerns that there was a bias towards only assessing the impacts on the biology and vegetation of the ASPAs rather than a more general biodiversity approach. It suggested that the assessment lacked information on mineral species and glacial retreat and how such threats in these cases might be identified.

(29) The USA noted that the methodology had promise, but would benefit from implementing the ecosystem approach, rather than the simpler approach of focussing on a single species or a single ASPA characteristic in placing the ASPA in the matrix. This could be included in the Five-Year Work Plan for the CEP.

(30) Argentina agreed with the views of the USA, and suggested that the preliminary variables proposed by WP 43 were too different in terms of spatial scale (regional vs. ASPA area) and weight. Therefore, in Argentina's opinion, this matrix needs more refinement.

(31) Australia noted that the methodology proposed by the United Kingdom and Norway could be combined with an understanding of the impacts of local activities to better understand the risks to protected areas and the values they are designated to protect. It further noted that such a methodology could assist with identifying and protecting areas that are of scientific value as climate change reference sites or sites to observe and track climate change.

(32) Argentina, Chile, Germany, South Africa, France and ASOC all supported further work to develop the range and comparability of variables in such a project.

(33) New Zealand, thanking the United Kingdom and Norway for these very helpful papers, noted the important role that protected areas will play in building resilience to climate change. It also noted that the risk-based

approach was very helpful, and a range of parameters (variables) can be used to more fully assess vulnerability and risk.

(34) The Chair noted the wide interest in this approach and suggested that, whilst it could already be seen as a useful tool for the management plans of the protected areas, with an increase in the number of parameters it would be even more useful. The Chair encouraged the United Kingdom, Norway and interested Members to continue the work.

(35) SCAR briefly introduced IP 52 *Antarctic Climate Change and the Environment – 2011 Update*. SCAR pointed out that membership of the new SCAR ACCE Expert Group has been expanded to include a wider range of expertise and to include experts from the Russian Federation, China and other countries. It is SCAR's intention to continue to attract new members to ensure as broad a representation as possible. Over the short to medium term SCAR is also planning to put together a series of targeted publications building on the ACCE Report.

(36) ASOC presented IP 83 *An Antarctic Climate Change Communication Plan* and IP 88 *Ocean Acidification and the Southern Ocean*.

(37) The United Kingdom thanked ASOC for both Information Papers, and noted that regardless of whether this information was disseminated by the CEP or ATCM as a whole, or by individual Parties, it was important to raise awareness of the issues. The Committee agreed to encourage Parties to develop research in this field.

(38) SCAR informed the Committee that an Action Group on Ocean Acidification would produce a comprehensive report in two years, focussing on both ecosystem and species responses to ocean acidification.

(39) Other papers presented under this agenda item were:

- IP 8 *COMNAP Energy Management Workshop* (COMNAP)

- IP 56 *Marine Spatial Protection and Management under the Antarctic Treaty System: New Opportunities for Implementation and Coordination* (IUCN)

- IP 65 *Frontiers in understanding Climate Change and Polar Ecosystems Workshop Report* (United States)

## Item 6: Environmental Impact Assessment (EIA)

### *6a) Draft Comprehensive Environmental Evaluation*

(40)  The United Kingdom presented WP 16 *Draft Comprehensive Environmental Evaluation (CEE) for the Proposed Exploration of Subglacial Lake Ellsworth, Antarctica* on behalf of the Lake Ellsworth Consortium. The United Kingdom expressed its gratitude to Norway for convening the ICG, and to all ICG participants for their constructive comments on the draft CEE, noting that a preliminary response to their comments is set out in IP 13 *The Draft Comprehensive Environmental Evaluation (CEE) for the Proposed Exploration of Subglacial Lake Ellsworth, Antarctica.*

(41)  Norway presented WP 14 *Report of the Intersessional Open-ended Contact Group to Consider the Draft CEE for the "Proposed Exploration of Subglacial Lake Ellsworth, Antarctica".*

(42)  Norway remarked that, having reviewed the United Kindom's draft CEE for the "Proposed Exploration of Subglacial Lake Ellsworth, Antarctica" in accordance with the *Procedures for intersessional CEP consideration of draft CEEs*, the ICG advised the CEP that:

1) The draft CEE and the process followed by the United Kingdom generally conformed to the requirements of Article 3 of Annex I to the Protocol on Environmental Protection to the Antarctic Treaty.

2) There was general agreement with the proponent's conclusion that it will entail less than minor or transitory impact taking into account the rigorous preventative and mitigation measures proposed and adopted by the proponent. These have substantially mitigated the risks which justified preparing the CEE. There was, furthermore, general agreement that the proposed activity is justified on the basis of its global scientific importance and value to be gained by the exploration of Lake Ellsworth.

3) The draft CEE is clear and well-structured.

4) When preparing the required final CEE, the proponent should closely consider and address, as appropriate, the comments raised by participants in Appendix A of WP 14.

5) The final CEE could furthermore be improved by taking into consideration participants' editorial suggestions (identified in Appendix B of WP14).

(43) Several Members underscored the importance of the CEE, and thanked Norway for leading the ICG. France noted that during this intersessional work, a number of participants had commented that the CEE lacked details on logistics aspects of the proposal.

(44) Germany thanked the United Kingdom for IP 13. Germany wanted to highlight the purpose of utilising low impact drilling techniques that limit environmental impacts, and looks forward to the final CEE.

(45) The Netherlands raised a point of clarification with respect to the next step after consultation on the draft CEE. The Netherlands asked whether the United Kingdom was required to take into consideration the issues raised by the ICG and the Committee, before presenting the final CEE to the ATCM for approval.

(46) The Chair clarified that Annex I to the Protocol requires the proponent to address comments on a draft CEE received from other Parties. Accordingly, the CEP will offer technical advice to the ATCM on the adequacy of this CEE, as per the requirements under the Environment Protocol.

(47) The Russian Federation agreed with the Chair's comments, and suggested that the United Kingdom should take on board the advice of the CEP on the draft CEE in accordance with established national procedures. Russia asserted that the United Kingdom needs to mitigate all potential problems, and provide explanations for why it has chosen the methodology it will employ.

(48) ASOC mentioned reference to its comments during the ICG on this draft CEE, and added that the impact to the environment and adequate compliance with the Environment Protocol might be better addressed if the United Kingdom was to consider conducting an independent audit project of the drilling project such as that which New Zealand undertook for the ANDrill CEE. It suggested that after entry a pristine subglacial lake could be considered to have been permanently altered and was no longer pristine.

(49) The United Kingdom expressed gratitude for the comments from many Members, and indicated that it would make every effort to respond to these comments when preparing the final CEE next year. The United Kingdom also thanked Norway as chair of the ICG.

## CEP advice to the ATCM

(50) The Committee discussed in detail the draft Comprehensive Environmental Evaluation (CEE) prepared by the United Kingdom for the "Proposed Exploration of Subglacial Lake Ellsworth, Antarctica" (WP 16 and IP 13). It also discussed the report by Norway of the ICG established to consider the draft CEE in accordance with the Procedures for intersessional CEP consideration of Draft CEEs (WP 14), and additional information provided by the United Kingdom in response to issues raised in the ICG (IP 13). Those discussions are summarised in paragraphs 40-50 above.

(51) Having fully considered the draft CEE, the Committee advised ATCM XXXIV that:

- The draft CEE and the process followed by United Kingdom generally conform to the requirements of Article 3 of Annex I to the Protocol on Environmental Protection to the Antarctic Treaty.

- The information contained in the draft CEE supports its conclusions that the proposed activity will have no more than a minor or transitory impact on the Antarctic environment, taking into account the rigorous preventative and mitigation measures prepared and adopted by the proponent. Furthermore, the proposed activity is justified on the basis of the global scientific importance and value to be gained by the exploration of Lake Ellsworth.

  When preparing the required final CEE, the proponent should consider, and address as appropriate, all comments raised by Members. In particular, the ATCM's attention is drawn to the suggestions that the final CEE should provide further detail regarding: assessment of the activities of the support contractor, further documentation/consideration as to the issue of potential mixing at break-through, further discussion as to how to minimise the disturbance of the water column as a result of the presence of the scientific equipment, assessment of risk of equipment loss in the lake, consideration of the size of the on-ice team in light of project safety and considerations relating to international collaboration.

- The draft CEE is clear and well-structured, well written and with high quality graphs and figures.

(52)   The CEP recommended that the ATCM endorse these views.

(53)   The Republic of Korea introduced WP 42 *The Draft Comprehensive Environmental Evaluation for the construction and operation of the Jang Bogo Antarctic Research Station, Terra Nova Bay, Antarctica* and IP 19 containing the full draft CEE. Highlighting the main scientific objectives of the project, which include the study of climate change issues and long term studies of the ocean and different ecosystems, Korea noted that the draft CEE was intended to show clearly how the impact on the Antarctic environment would be minimised, and to share the benefits of construction and research with the wider international community, by promoting international global scientific cooperation.

(54)   The Republic of Korea was grateful for the valuable work of the ICG in reviewing the draft CEE. The Republic of Korea thanked Norway for its suggestion to source an alternative solution to waste incineration, which will save a projected 50 tons of fuel annually.

(55)   Australia introduced WP 7 *Report of the intersessional open-ended contact group to consider the draft CEE for the "Construction and Operation of the Jang Bogo Station, Terra Nova Bay, Antarctica"*. It noted that the ICG had expressed strong support for the proponent's plans to minimise and mitigate the environmental impacts of the project, and had recognised that environmental considerations had clearly been a key consideration in the project planning. Australia briefly introduced the outcomes of the ICG, highlighting the opportunities that participants had identified to enhance the final CEE, in keeping with the objectives of the CEE process established under Annex I of the Protocol.

(56)   Many Members supported the Republic of Korea's plans, highlighting the importance of future international collaborations that this project will bring for research in East Antarctica. Some Members also noted with approval the use of alternative energy sources in the operation of the station.

(57)   China supported and congratulated the Republic of Korea's plan of constructing a new research station in Antarctica and believed it would serve the purpose of the Antarctic Treaty. China agreed with the ICG's conclusion regarding the draft CEE for Jang Bogo station and expected the final CEE would have good considerations of the comments from other Parties.

(58)   The proposed station will lie only 10km from the Italian Mario Zucchelli Station and will be close to the German Gondwana Station. France and

Germany reported that Republic of Korea had visited their Antarctic research centres after completing the draft CEE to discuss many of the technical comments. Italy had proposed potential collaboration with Korea for the establishment of a marine protected area in Terra Nova Bay. The United States commended Korea for addressing questions and concerns raised in WP 7, through the timely submission of IP 76 and through additional information contained in its presentation to the CEP. The US offered to share pier building experiences at McMurdo Station with Korea.

(59) Belgium pointed to the necessary collaboration between the new Korean station and the existing stations in the surrounding areas so as to reduce the cumulative impact on the environment. It showed interest in collaborating with the Republic of Korea on undertaking long-term monitoring of the terrestrial and marine ecosystems in the region, including in the Amundsen Sea where few studies have yet been conducted; it indicated that the fact that the station will be constructed on the border of the Ross Sea will put Korea under a special responsibility should the Ross Sea or part of it receive a protection status.

(60) ASOC noted that since the station will operate year-round, its environmental impacts will be substantive. However, ASOC expressed appreciation for the decisions taken by the Republic of Korea to minimise environmental impacts since the first draft was circulated, such as by eliminating incineration and by using precast concrete foundations. ASOC expressed hopes that now that Korea will be active in that part of Antarctica it will collaborate with Italy on the establishment of marine protection in the Ross Sea.

(61) The Republic of Korea expressed its appreciation for the Committee's support of its draft CEE.

## CEP advice to the ATCM

(62) The Committee discussed in detail the draft Comprehensive Environmental Evaluation (CEE) prepared by the Republic of Korea for "Construction and Operation of the Jang Bogo Station, Terra Nova Bay, Antarctica" (WP 42 and IP 19). It also discussed the report by Australia of the ICG established to consider the draft CEE in accordance with the *Procedures for intersessional CEP consideration of Draft CEEs* (WP 7), and additional information provided by the Republic of Korea in response to issues raised in the ICG (IP 76). Those discussions are summarised in paragraphs 56 and 57 above.

(63)   Having fully considered the draft CEE, the Committee advised ATCM XXXIV that:

- The draft CEE generally conforms to the requirements of Article 3 of Annex I to the Protocol on Environmental Protection to the Antarctic Treaty.

- The information contained in the draft CEE supports the proponent's conclusion that the construction and operation of Jang Bogo station is likely to have more than a minor or transitory impact on the environment. The information provided also supports the proponent's conclusion that these impacts will be outweighed by knowledge and information to be gained through the research activities that will be supported by the station.

- When preparing the required final CEE, the proponent should consider, and address as appropriate, the comments raised by Members. In particular, the ATCM's attention is drawn to the suggestions that the final CEE should provide further detail regarding: the possible cumulative impacts of activities by multiple operators in the Terra Nova Bay region; the ancillary station infrastructure; the wastewater treatment system; the management of sewage and food wastes; oil spill prevention; measures to prevent impacts on the skua colony; measures to prevent the introduction of non-native species; and plans for decommissioning the station.

- The draft CEE is clear, well structured, and well presented.

(64)   The CEP recommended that the ATCM endorses this view.

### 6b) Other EIA matters

(65)   The Russian Federation introduced WP 54 *Technology for Investigating Water Strata of Subglacial Lake Vostok.*

(66)   China thanked the Russian Federation and encouraged the continued exchange of information on the use of technology in Antarctica. The United States thanked Russia for keeping the CEP updated on the progress and changes to the project.

(67)   Belgium asked about the precautionary measures in place if there is some technological failure, for example if the drill unit becomes stuck or the lake

is contaminated. The Russian Federation responded that all questions on risks will be considered in the environmental impact assessment for the study.

(68)   New Zealand updated the Committee on the progress with the CEP Tourism Study, recalling the ATCM's interest in the CEP's proposal to examine the environmental aspects and impacts of tourism and non-governmental activities in Antarctica. Good progress has been made on the study, but it was not able to be completed in time for the meeting. New Zealand informed the Committee that the draft report had been uploaded to the CEP forum, and that it intended to complete the work in the coming year, with the support of the Management Group.

(69)   The Committee thanked New Zealand for the update and encouraged New Zealand to continue to pursue this work which has been identified as a priority by the CEP, and encouraged Members to participate in the Management Group.

(70)   ASOC presented IP 84 *Antarctic Tourism – What Next? Key Issues to Address with Binding Rules;* and IP 87 *Land-Based Tourism in Antarctica.*

(71)   Chile noted a correction to IP 87, informing the Committee that Chile did not promote commercial tourism in the Antarctic Peninsula, nor operate a hotel facility in the region. Chile does however offer refuge for people from other national programmes who are in transit to other areas of the Antarctic Peninsula. Chile added it would be keen to respond to ASOC's questionnaire if asked, to provide information on its land-based infrastructure in Antarctica.

(72)   With reference to the ALE Camp at Union Glacier, the United States objected to ASOC's assumption that the field camp would have more than a minor or transitory impact on the surrounding environment. The United States suggested that ASOC should not draw such generalised conclusions, as understanding the full extent of the impact would require a review of the environmental impact assessment that includes the details regarding the proposed activity as well as mitigation measures that will be implemented.

(73)   Uruguay informed the Committee that it has not participated in any land-based tourism activities since 2008, and would also like to fill out the ASOC questionnaire.

(74)   The United Kingdom informed the Committee that the two UK-based companies mentioned in the paper undergo a very stringent permit process to make sure they fully comply with the Environment Protocol.

(75)   ASOC responded to Chile by noting that the reference to Chile's alleged support of commercial tourism in IP 87 was from information supplied by another Party when responding to the ASOC questionnaire, and not ASOC's own assessment.

(76)   ASOC responded to the US that conclusions in the report have been based on as much accurate information as possible, but added that the content of IEE itself is not available on the ATS EIA database.

(77)   India introduced IP 64 *Final Comprehensive Environmental Evaluation (CEE) of New Indian Research Station at Larsemann Hills, Antarctica and Update on Construction Activity.*

(78)   The Russian Federation expressed support for this project.

(79)   Belgium offered to collaborate on the efforts to evaluate the impact of the station on the area lakes, as it had been studying the biodiversity of those lakes near to the new station.

(80)   Other papers submitted under this agenda item were:

- SP 5 rev. 1 *Annual list of Initial Environmental Evaluations (IEE) and Comprehensive Environmental Evaluations (CEE) prepared between April 1ˢᵗ 2010 and March 31ˢᵗ 2011*

- IP 72 *Methodology for Clean Access to the Subglacial Environment Associated with the Whillans Ice* (United States)

- IP 123 *Estudio de impacto ambiental ex-post de la estación científica ecuatoriana "Pedro Vicente Maldonado". Isla Greenwich-Shetland del Sur-Antártida, 2010-2011* (Ecuador)

## Item 7: Area Protection and Management Plans

### *7a) Management Plans*

*i) Draft Management Plans which have been reviewed by the Subsidiary Group on Management Plans*

(81)   In its capacity as convenor of the Subsidiary Group on Management Plans (SGMP), Australia introduced WP 47 *Subsidiary Group on Management Plans – Report on Terms of Reference #1 to #3: Review of Draft Management Plans.*

The SGMP had reviewed the plan for ASPA 126 and recommended that the proponents make some structural amendments to the management plan and improvements to the maps, and had sought clarification on a number of other matters. The SGMP considered that the revised plan adequately addressed these comments, and it recommended that the CEP approve the revised management plan prepared by the United Kingdom, Chile and Spain for ASPA 126.

(82) The Committee endorsed the SGMP's recommendation and agreed to forward the revised management plan for ASPA 126 to the ATCM for adoption.

ii) *Draft revised Management Plans which had not been reviewed by the Subsidiary Group on Management Plans*

(83) The Committee considered revised management plans for ten Antarctic Specially Protected Areas (ASPAs) and one Antarctic Specially Managed Area (ASMA) under this category:

- WP 3 *Review of the management plan for ASPA No 120, Pointe-Géologie Archipelago, Terre Adélie* (France)

- WP 4 *Management Plan for ASPA No 166, Port-Martin, Terre Adélie. Proposal to extend the existing Management Plan* (France)

- WP 6 *Revised Management Plan for Antarctic Specially Protected Area No 149 Cape Shirreff and San Telmo Island, Livingston Island, South Shetland Islands* (USA & Chile)

- WP 9 *Revised Management Plan for Antarctic Specially Protected Area No 122 Arrival Heights, Hut Point Peninsula, Ross Island* (USA)

- WP 23 *Revision of the Management Plan for Antarctic Specially Protected Area (ASPA) No 140 Parts of Deception Island, South Shetland Islands* (UK)

- WP 29 *Revised management plan for Antarctic Specially Protected Area No 167, Hawker Island, Princess Elizabeth Land* (Australia)

- WP 31 *Revision of Management Plan for Antarctic Specially Protected Area No 116: New College Valley, Caughley Beach, Cape Bird, Ross Island* (NZ)

- WP 33 *Revision of Management Plan for Antarctic Specially Protected Area No 131: Canada Glacier, Lake Fryxell, Taylor Valley, Victoria Land* (NZ)

- WP 39 *Revised Management Plan for Antarctic Specially Managed Area No 2 McMurdo Dry Valleys, Southern Victoria Land* (USA & NZ)

- WP 50 *Revised Management Plan for Antarctic Specially Protected Area (ASPA) No 165 Edmonson Point, Ross Sea* (Italy)

- WP 58 *Revised Management Plan for Antarctic Specially Protected Area No 127 "HASWELL ISLAND" (Haswell Island and Adjacent Emperor Penguin Rookery on Fast Ice) Revised Management Plan* (Russian Federation)

(84) With respect to WP 3 and WP 4, France informed the Committee that it had conducted a five-yearly review of the management plans for ASPA 120 and ASPA 166. In light of these reviews, France proposed that the revised management plan for ASPA 120 be approved with only minor changes and that the management plan for ASPA 166 be approved without modification for a period of five years. The Committee noted France's advice that the management plan for ASPA 166 had been reviewed and did not require revision.

(85) With respect to WP 6, the USA informed the Committee that only minor changes had been made to the management plan for ASPA 149.

(86) In response to an enquiry from ASOC, the USA and Chile provided further details on the educational and historical values of ASPA 149 including archaeological artefacts present within the Area.

(87) With respect to WP 9, the USA explained that some major changes had been made to the management plan for ASPA 122 including several revisions of the boundaries, new values, amendments to some maps and access to the area. The USA remarked that, while changes to the text of the management plan were major, changes to the values being protected and implementation were only minor.

(88) With respect to WP 23, the United Kingdom proposed major changes to the management plan for ASPA 140 and asked the Committee to send this management plan for intersessional review by the SGMP. The Committee supported this proposal and agreed to refer the draft revised management plan to the SGMP for intersessional review.

(89)   With respect to WP 29, Australia informed the Committee that only minor amendments to the management plan for ASPA 167 were required. It had modified the provisions for access to the Area to provide the opportunity for more frequent censuses of the southern giant petrel colony, conducted in an appropriate manner such as through the use of automated digital cameras. This would improve the chances of developing a more detailed understanding of population status and trends, consistent with Resolution 5 (2009).

(90)   With respect to WP 31 and WP 33, New Zealand informed the Committee that the revised management plans for ASPA 116 and ASPA 131 included only minor updates and editorial changes and more detailed biodiversity information.

(91)   With respect to WP 39, the USA informed the Committee of several important modifications in the revised management plan for ASMA 2 following a review process over three years. Changes were made to the boundaries of the Area, new values to be protected were identified, updated maps and photographs were produced, and the appendices were reorganised and updated. In addition, Scientific Zones and Restricted Zones had also been introduced to replace the former category of 'Special Features' and the former category of 'Tourist Zone' had been reclassified as Visitor Zone, the latter being considered more inclusive.

(92)   IAATO welcomed the intention of the proponents to consider additional visitor zones. Without undermining the importance of the area for scientific research, IAATO considers the current zoning to be overly restrictive given that the ASMA area amounts to 17500 km$^2$ and that the visitor zone is limited to an area of only 0.1 km$^2$, and noted the value to Antarctic science and the conservation of safe and environmentally responsible, high quality visitor experiences.

(93)   Italy introduced WP 50, *Revised Management Plan for Antarctic Specially Protected Area (ASPA) No 165 Edmonson Point, Ross Sea*. No substantial changes had been made to the existing management plan.

(94)   The Russian Federation introduced WP 58 *Revised Management Plan for Antarctic Specially Protected Area No 127 "Haswell Island" (Haswell Island and Adjacent Emperor Penguin Rookery on Fast Ice)*. Minor changes had been made to the existing plan, including new information from research conducted in the last five years on subsection 6(i), and an update of the bibliography in section 8.

(95) The Committee approved all the revised Management Plans other than ASPA 140, which it forwarded to the SGMP for intersessional review.

**Advice to the ATCM**

(96) In reviewing the advice of the SGMP and following the Committee's assessment the Committee agreed to forward the following management plans to the ATCM for adoption:

| # | Name |
|---|------|
| ASMA 2 | Antarctic Specially Managed Area No 2 McMurdo Dry Valleys, Southern Victoria Land |
| ASPA 116 | New College Valley, Caughley Beach, Cape Bird, Ross Island |
| ASPA 120 | Pointe-Géologie Archipelago, Terre Adélie |
| ASPA 126 | Byers Peninsula, Livingstone Island, South Shetland Islands |
| ASPA 122 | Arrival Heights, Hut Point Peninsula, Ross Island |
| ASPA 127 | "HASWELL ISLAND" (Haswell Island and Adjacent Emperor Penguin Rookery on Fast Ice) Revised Management Plan |
| ASPA 131 | Canada Glacier, Lake Fryxell, Taylor Valley, Victoria Land |
| ASPA 149 | Cape Shirreff and San Telmo Island, Livingston Island, South Shetland Islands |
| ASPA 165 | Edmonson Point, Ross Sea |
| ASPA 167 | Hawker Island, Princess Elizabeth Land |

(97) The United States introduced WP 10 *Developing a plan for Special protection at Taylor Glacier and Blood Falls, Taylor Valley, McMurdo Dry Valleys, Victoria Land.* The USA proposed the establishment of an informal International Working Group to discuss area protection at Taylor Glacier and Blood Falls and to develop a draft ASPA Management Plan to be submitted to the CEP in 2012. The United States offered to coordinate this group and Norway and SCAR noted their interest in contributing to the discussions. Norway also noted the usefulness of having such an open process in developing new ASPAs.

(98)  Australia introduced WP 13 *Subsidiary Group on Management Plans – Report on Terms of Reference #4 and #5: Improving Management Plans and the Process for their Intersessional Review* on behalf of the SGMP. The SGMP invited the CEP to consider the outcomes of its intersessional work, which had been conducted in accordance with the work plan adopted by CEP XIII.

(99)  During the intersessional period, the SGMP had reviewed and revised the *Guide to the Preparation of Management Plans for Antarctic Specially Protected Areas* (adopted under Resolution 2 (1988)), including to incorporate standard wording and a template for ASPA management plans. The modifications introduced had, among other things, addressed a range of matters referred to the SGMP by CEP XIII for consideration. The SGMP had also consulted with relevant Members to review the status of management plans that were overdue for five-yearly review.

(100) The United States stressed that the SGMP should be seen as an important resource for those Members needing help in writing or reviewing management plans. Australia urged other Members to participate in SGMP to enhance its expertise and value.

(101) Argentina and Chile noted that this management plan template should not be prescriptive, and should allow Members to be innovative when preparing management plans for ASPAs.

(102) Australia reiterated that the suggested standard wording and template for ASPA management plans, and the revised Guide, prepared by the SGMP were intended as tools to assist consistency between management plans. They were not intended to be prescriptive or to discourage proponents from developing and implementing site-specific or creative and innovative approaches to area protection and management.

(103) The Committee thanked the SGMP for its work and agreed to:

- endorse the revised *Guide to the Preparation of Management Plans for Antarctic Specially Protected Areas* and incorporated template and standard wording for ASPA management plans presented at Attachment A to WP 13; and

- encourage proponent Parties of management plans that have not yet provided information on the status of ASPA management plans overdue for review to provide such information.

(104) The Meeting also adopted a work plan for the SGMP's activities during the 2011/12 intersessional period as identified in Attachment C of WP 13 (see Appendix 1).

## CEP Advice to the ATCM

(105) The Committee recommends that the ATCM adopt a Resolution approving the new *Guide to the Preparation of Management Plans for Antarctic Specially Protected Areas.*

(106) The United Kingdom presented WP 18 *Proposed Monitoring Activities Within Antarctic Specially Protected Area (ASPA) No 107 Emperor Island, Dion Islands, Marguerite Bay, Antarctic Peninsula.* The United Kingdom noted that the continued existence of the emperor penguin colony within this ASPA is in doubt, and that further research is necessary to access its status. The occurrence of this colony represents the sole value worthy of protection within this ASPA and led to its designation.

(107) The United States and Australia commented that further monitoring of the Dion Islands ASPA seems a sensible way to move forward. Australia noted that, as a general rule, well documented areas such as ASPAs which are highly vulnerable to climate change may be of value to science for observing and tracking the impacts of climate change, and the possible existence of such new or emerging values should be closely considered when determining the benefits of continued designation of an Area.

(108) The Committee supported the approach planned by the United Kingdom and looked forward to receiving further information on the status of the values at ASPA 107.

(109) The Secretariat presented SP 7 *Status of Antarctic Specially Protected Area and Antarctic Specially Managed Area Management Plans.* The CEP was asked if this register was still required, since this information is now available from the online ASPA/ASMA Database on the Secretariat website.

(110) Chile and Germany moved for keeping and improving this register. Germany inquired what happens when the review date has been passed without any review of the management plans.

(111) The Chair thanked Germany and noted that this point was brought up by the ICG. The Chair emphasised the necessity of the Secretariat reminding Members of the status of the ASPA/ASMA management plans and their responsibilities for initiating subsequent reviews.

(112) Norway noted that the review process does not necessarily need to result in the tabling of a revision of the ASPA/ASMA management plans. Germany asked if the "next revision" column could be used more proactively.

(113) Australia suggested that the Secretariat could send a reminder to those Parties responsible for an ASPA/ASMA management plan that is due for a review during the next year, and in doing so could draw attention to the revised *Guide to the Preparation of Management Plans for Antarctic Specially Protected Areas* (WP 13) to help facilitate the review.

(114) The United Kingdom commented that it has initiated or completed field work for the review process of six ASPAs, which will put the United Kingdom in a good position to be fully up to date with the upcoming review process of the corresponding management plans.

(115) Chile noted that its reviews of three outstanding ASPA management plans would be ready for presentation next year.

(116) IP 79 (Australia, China, India, Romania, Russian Federation): *Report of the Larsemann Hills Antarctic Specially Managed Area (ASMA) Management Group* was also presented under this Agenda item.

(117) The United States presented IP 73 *Amundsen-Scott South Pole Station, South Pole Antarctica Specially Managed Area (ASMA No 5) 2011 Management Report*, and noted that more visitors each year present a challenge for combining tourist activities with research activities. IP 73 was not presented as a Working Paper because the USA needed to determine if the changes made so far would work (for example the moving of the tourist camping site away from the main research station). The United States mentioned that it has an excellent collaboration with IAATO.

(118) The United Kingdom suggested that the process of developing the ASMA guidelines could have started earlier and that the lack of a formal process or changes to the management plan could create problems in advising visitors of the new rules or guidelines. The USA noted that it expected to revise the

guidelines in the coming year, and would appreciate assistance from any interested Members. It intended to present a more formal set of guidelines next year.

(119) India introduced IP 79 *Report of the Larsemann Hills Antarctic Specially Managed Area (ASMA) Management Group* on behalf of ASMA 6 Management Group (Australia, China, India, Romania, Russian Federation) highlighting the need for the establishment of an ASPA on this region. Belgium and Romania supported the proposal and offered collaboration.

(120) Regarding IP 131 *Deception Island Specially Managed Area (ASMA) Management Group Report* (Argentina, Chile, Norway, Spain, United Kingdom, United States), Spain informed the Meeting that it will present a new management plan revision next year for ASMA No 4.

(121) The Republic of Korea introduced IP 115 *Survey of the ASPA 171 Narębski Point, ASPA 150 Ardley Island and ASPA 132 Potter Peninsula in 2010-11* and also introduced IP 109 *Cooperation Management Activities at ASPAs in King George Island (Isla 25 de Mayo), South Shetland Islands*, submitted jointly with Argentina. Both are related to Korean efforts to improve the environmental management plan for ASPA 171.

### 7b) Historic Sites and Monuments

(122) Argentina noted that during the 13ᵗʰ CEP meeting Argentina offered to coordinate an informal debate during the intersessional period on Historical Sites and Monuments. Argentina thanked several Members for their significant contributions during the debate, the results of which are summarised in WP 27 *Report of the Informal Discussions on Historic Sites and Monuments*.

(123) During these debates, work focussed on two main lines: a) the different ways Parties define and apply the concept of "historic heritage" and on the existing agreed definitions on the Antarctic context, and b) the adequacy of the existing mechanisms available in the Antarctic Treaty system for the protection of historic sites. Concerning the former, the informal discussion group had concluded that a wide range of definitions existed on what can be considered a HSM, while in reference to the latter, some participants considered that the existing criteria are broad enough to accommodate

different views on heritage, while others saw this flexibility as a limitation to define the historic character of a site.

(124) Given the broad variety of concepts and views on these issues, the group concluded that it would be beneficial to continue discussing these matters on the CEP forum.

(125) While thanking Argentina for its work, China noted that caution was necessary as in the diversity of cultures that exist in the Antarctic community any rigid definition might not prove helpful. China announced that it would like to participate in further discussions.

(126) Several Members expressed their appreciation for Argentina's work and encouraged further debates on this issue. Norway noted that there are a number of relevant issues to discuss further to achieve a common understanding of how to classify historical sites and monuments. The United States expressed the need to make listings more transparent and accessible to a wider audience. The United Kingdom pointed out that a rigid definition of 'historical monuments' was unlikely to be possible and probably not necessary given the diversity of the Antarctic community.

(127) The Committee agreed that the informal discussions on Historic Sites and Monuments had been useful and should continue.

(128) Argentina concluded that the main objective of these debates was not to reach agreement on specific definitions, but to exchange different points of view on an issue that is complex, especially because it deals with social sciences where cultural differences may lead to diverse interpretations on historic heritage. Argentina expressed its gratitude for the Committee's confidence in the work of this group.

(129) China presented WP 5 *Proposed addition of No 1 Building Commemorating China's Antarctic Expedition at Great Wall Station to the List of Historic Sites and Monument,* highlighting the value of Building No 1 and suggesting that its inclusion on the list would be a positive enhancement.

(130) Japan drew attention to the size of Building No 1 and expressed concerns over its potential impact on the surrounding environment, but wished to support the designation of this important building.

(131) The United Kingdom drew attention to comments in its 2005 Inspection Report which highlighted the need for repair work to prevent further deterioration and asked if this had been carried out. Several Members, while showing their support for the proposal, requested more information on the maintenance and conservation of the building.

(132) China thanked the Members for their support and assured the Committee that the maintenance and conservation plan was in progress, and that further details of this would be provided in the future.

(133) The Committee approved the proposals presented in WP 5 and passed them to be considered by the ATCM.

(134) Chile presented WP 59 *Proposal of Modification for the Historic Monument No 82 Installation of Commemorative Plaques at the Monument to the Antarctic Treaty.* Chile informed the Committee that, in accordance with Measure 3 (2007), four plaques in commemoration of the International Polar Year had been installed in each of the official languages of the Antarctic Treaty System at the "Monument to the Antarctic Treaty" near Frei, Bellingshausen and Escudero stations at King George Island. The proposed modification relates to a minor change in wording of the HSM 82.

(135) The Committee approved Chile's request and its submission to the ATCM.

---

**Advice to the ATCM**

(136) The Committee recommends that the ATCM approve the addition of the following new site to the list of Historic Sites and Monuments in Measure 3 (2003):

- No 1 Building Commemorating China's Antarctic Expedition at Great Wall Station

(137) The Committee also recommends that the ATCM approve the proposed modification of the HSM 82 Monument to the Antarctic Treaty.

---

(138) The Secretariat noted that the latest list of Historic Sites and Monuments was very outdated and suggested that the ATCM task the Secretariat with updating the list annually. The United Kingdom and France expressed their support for the Secretariat's proposal and the Committee agreed to ask the

ATCM to decide whether the Secretariat should be tasked with updating the Historic Sites and Monuments list.

**Advice to the ATCM**

(139) The Committee recommends that the ATCM ask the Secretariat to keep the official lists of ASPAs, ASMAs and HSMs updated according to Measures taken at the ATCM.

(140) Argentina referred to IP 130 *Update on enhancement activities for HSM 38 "Snow Hill"*, noting that this paper provides continuity to the series of papers presented by Argentina to the CEP over years on the management and conservation activities at HSM 38.

(141) Also submitted under this agenda items was:

- IP 117 *Inauguración de la instalación de Placas Conmemorativas en el Monumento al Tratado Antártico* (Chile)

*7c) Site Guidelines*

(142) In its capacity as convener, Australia presented WP 45 *Report of the open-ended intersessional contact group on revision of environmental elements of Recommendation XVIII-1*. Australia informed the Committee that the ICG had developed updated guidelines for visitors based on Recommendation XVIII-1 (1994), but in a format suitable for use as a generic cover to accompany site specific guidelines.

(143) Australia reported that several issues were left unresolved in the ICG's discussions, such as the inclusion of specific minimum distances for approaches to wildlife.

(144) The ICG recommended that the CEP:

1. endorse the attached guidelines, and forward them to the ATCM for adoption by means of a Resolution;

2. agree that an ICG be convened to consider new site guidelines requiring detailed discussion;

3. decide that, in general, site guidelines should be periodically reviewed at least every five years;

4. request the Secretariat to develop a review schedule for site guidelines based on a five-yearly review period, for consideration by CEP XV; and

5. encourage Members bringing forward new site guidelines to give consideration to the generic guidelines, and to focus on matters specific to the circumstances of each site.

(145) New Zealand and Chile expressed their support for the guidelines and the ICG's recommendations. Ecuador expressed an interest in participating in future work of the ICG given its experience of managing visitors to the Galapagos Islands.

(146) Several Members showed in-principle support for the ICG's recommendations while raising some specific concerns. The USA was uncertain about the relationship between the updated guidelines and Recommendation XVIII-1 (1994) and believed that further discussion on this topic should be referred to the Legal and Institutional Working Group. Germany expressed a view that the guidelines should identify specific minimum approach distances from wildlife, hence advocating a precautionary approach.

(147) In response to Germany, the Chair noted the advice from SCAR, presented in 2008 at ATCM XXXI in WP 12 *Human disturbance to wildlife in the broader Antarctic region: a review of findings*. Given the range of variables likely to have an influence on susceptibility to disturbance, SCAR had reported that it was difficult to identify specific wildlife approach distances.

(148) The United Kingdom indicated its overall support for work to update the generic site guidelines while expressing concerns that the site guidelines, as drafted, were not ready for consideration by the ATCM. The United Kingdom emphasised that the provisions of Recommendation XVIII-1 (1994), which had not yet entered into force, would be mandatory while the guidelines developed by the ICG would remain voluntary. The United Kingdom strongly encouraged ratification of Recommendation XVIII-1 (1994) by all Parties so that it would come into force. The United Kingdom did not agree with the proposal for a formal mandatory and automatic review of specific site guidelines by the original proponents. Instead, site guidelines should be reviewed and revised as and when necessary and by any Party.

(149) Having reminded the Committee that Recommendation XVIII-1 (1994) was divided into two parts, IAATO suggested that the guidelines developed by the ICG could be used to replace the second part of Recommendation

XVIII-1 (1994). IAATO also encouraged the outstanding ratification to Recommendation XVIII-1 (1994) to be made as soon as possible.

(150) The CEP considered WP 45 and agreed that the provision of general environmental advice to visitors, based on the current understanding of the CEP, would complement the site specific guidelines. The CEP again noted the desirability of Recommendation XVIII-1 (1994) entering into force.

(151) After comments raised by some members, Australia convened work in a contact group, and the CEP subsequently finalised *Guidelines for Visitors to the Antarctic.*

(152) In considering the other recommendations of the ICG, the CEP decided that its present practice of considering new guidelines, and reviewing existing guidelines as they are brought forward would suffice.

## CEP advice to the ATCM

(153) The CEP finalised environmental advice to visitors in the form of Guidelines for visitors to the Antarctic, suitable for use as a cover sheet to accompany site specific guidelines. The CEP recommended that the ATCM adopt them by means of a Resolution, and that the Secretariat make them available alongside the site specific guidelines.

(154) The CEP also encouraged Members, in bringing forward new site guidelines to give consideration to the generic guidelines, and focus on matters specific to the circumstances of each site.

(155) United Kingdom introduced WP 17 *Revision of Site Guidelines for Whalers Bay, Deception Island, South Shetland Islands* on behalf of the ASMA Management Group for Deception Island. The paper proposed minor changes to the existing site guidelines including the correction of minor typographical errors, clarification of landing site location and revision of maps.

(156) New Zealand introduced WP 30 *Site Guidelines for the Taylor Valley Visitor Zone, Southern Victoria Land,* jointly prepared with the USA.

(157) As part of the review of the McMurdo Dry Valleys ASMA, the Management Group agreed to re-format the existing tourism provisions in that Plan into site guidelines format. The guidelines reflect the existing management

provisions. New Zealand noted that there had been a minor change to a boundary of the zone following concerns raised by scientists about the sensitivity of the site.

(158) The United Kingdom thanked New Zealand and the United States for their work and asked about monitoring at the site and about the size of the area relative to the visitation rate.

(159) New Zealand noted that the site was the subject of long term monitoring of visitor impacts through its VISTA monitoring programme as well as other scientific research in the area, and that the site was only accessible by helicopter, limiting the number of visitors at the site at any one time.

(160) IAATO expressed concern over the revision of the boundary, and welcomed the opportunity to discuss other possible visitor zones in the Dry Valleys ASMA in the future.

(161) ASOC noted the need for environmental impact assessment for the establishment of any proposed new visitor zones.

(162) Chile presented WP 49 *Guidelines for the north-east beach of the Ardley Peninsula (Ardley Island), King George Island (Isla 25 de Mayo), South Shetland Islands*, jointly elaborated with Argentina.

(163) Several Members expressed their support for the proposal while some Members sought further clarification on the guidelines. China suggested that the guidelines include a precise definition of the term "Visitor". In response to China's enquiry, Chile clarified that "Visitor" is understood as any person who lands on the beach and is not required to conduct any scientific work there.

(164) Australia introduced WP 52 rev. 1 *Visitor site guide for Mawson's Huts and Cape Denison, East Antarctica*. Australia noted that Cape Denison is one of six sites remaining from the 'heroic era' of Antarctic exploration, and is designated as Historic Site and Monument No 77, and ASMA 3. Within the ASMA, the four timber huts of the Australasian Antarctic Expedition and immediate surrounds are designated as ASPA 162. The values of the site are significant, and the site is sensitive to the potential impacts associated with visits. Australia therefore regards a visitor site guide as a useful adjunct to the existing management arrangements. The proposed visitor site guide does not replace or extend the provisions of the ASPA and ASMA management plans.

(165) IAATO welcomed the proposed new site guidelines.

(166) IAATO presented IP 104 *Proposed Amendment to Antarctic Treaty Site Guidelines for Hannah Point* informing the Meeting that, following an incident in which an elephant seal, possibly disturbed by visitors, went over a cliff, IAATO had internally adopted a precautionary extension to closed Area B in the Site Guidelines for Hannah Point, should elephant seals be hauled out in the area at the time of a visit. IAATO informed that immediately following the incident, it circulated a message to all IAATO vessels still operating in the area to alert them to the incident and ask them to keep away from the cliff edge area if elephant seals were present. The incident was discussed at the IAATO Meeting in 2011, where the members agreed to an additional precautionary measure to the application of the site guidelines for Hannah Point. IAATO suggested the Committee consider and adopt this amendment. After a broad discussion the Committee agreed to amend the site guidelines for Hannah Point in line with IAATO's suggestion.

(167) The Committee approved the revised versions of the site guidelines for Whalers Bay and Hannah Point and the new site guidelines for Taylor Valley, Ardley Peninsula and Mawson's Hut.

**Advice to the ATCM**

(168) The Committee approved the revised guidelines for Whalers Bay and Hannah Point, and the new site guidelines for Taylor Valley, Ardley Peninsula, and Mawson's Hut, and agreed to forward them to the ATCM for adoption by means of a Resolution.

(169) Ukraine briefly introduced IP 110 *Ukraine policy regarding visits by tourists to Vernadsky Station* and invited interested Members to submit comments in the course of the work.

(170) The USA introduced IP 23 *Antarctic Peninsula Compendium, 3ʳᵈ Edition* (USA & UK) and announced the availability of the third edition of the Antarctic Peninsula Compendium, which compiles data and site descriptive information from the 142 locations the Antarctic Site Inventory has visited and censused in 17 field seasons from November 1994-February 2011. The Compendium is available on disc and at the Oceanites website *(http://www.oceanites.org)*.

(171) Bulgaria briefly introduced IP 12 *Guidelines of environmental behavior of the expedition participants and visitors to the Bulgarian Base in Antarctica* and hoped that these guidelines would prove useful for other stations in Antarctica.

(172) Other papers submitted under this agenda item included:

- IP 9 *Antarctic Site Inventory: 1994-2011* (USA)

- IP 105 *Report on IAATO Operator use of Antarctic Peninsula Landing Sites and ATCM Visitor Site Guidelines, 2009-10 & 2010-11 Seasons* (IAATO)

- IP 126 *Manejo turístico para la isla Barrientos* (Ecuador)

## 7d) Human footprint and wilderness values

(173) New Zealand introduced WP 35 *Understanding concepts of Footprint and Wilderness related to protection of the Antarctic environment.* New Zealand recommended that CEP XIV aim for agreement among the Members on practical definitions of footprint and wilderness in the Antarctic context. It suggested that the CEP should consider medium term goals for improving planning and environmental impact assessment to minimise footprint and give greater protection to inviolate areas and wilderness values through Annex V measures.

(174) Australia highlighted that any definitions of footprint and wilderness should be able to be practically applied. For example, it recalled that most references to footprint in past CEP discussions had referred to the spatial extent of physical disturbance, which would be beneficial in environmental terms, including to prioritise action to minimise impacts on rare and environmentally sensitive ice-free areas. Australia expressed its willingness to continue informal discussions with New Zealand during the intersessional period.

(175) The United Kingdom agreed in principle with the definition suggested, but noted wilderness did not automatically exclude science. It noted that the concept of planning for areas never visited as inviolate reference and wilderness areas has been called for for over 40 years and should be advanced.

(176) The USA and Belgium also supported the work, agreeing that setting aside inviolate reference areas could be valuable.

(177) Argentina mentioned that it would prefer a general approach rather than a specific definition of footprint and wilderness, as it is often used on a case by case basis. Argentina also noted that international cooperation encouraged the retention of wilderness values in Antarctica, by avoiding the duplication of efforts, leading to a more reduced footprint from such activities.

(178) The Chair noted the interest of the Committee in the development of terminology and the support for the concept of inviolate areas.

(179) ASOC introduced IP 86 *Evolution of Footprint: Spatial and Temporal Dimensions of Human Activities.* ASOC encouraged the CEP to seek consensus on the definitions for footprint and wilderness, and approve these definitions.

(180) Other papers submitted under this Agenda item were:

- IP 1 *Temporal and spatial patterns of anthropogenic disturbance at McMurdo Station, Antarctica* (United States)

- IP 2 *The Historical Development of McMurdo Station, Antarctica, An Environment Perspective* (United States)

- IP 43 *Discovery of human activity remains, pre-1958 in the north coast of the King George Island (Isla 25 de Mayo)* (Uruguay)

- IP 133 *Report on all-terrain vehicles impact on deglaciated area of James Ross Island, Antarctica* (Czech Republic)

### 7e) Marine spatial protection and management

(181) The Secretariat introduced SP 6 *Summary of the Work of the CEP on Marine Protected Areas.*

(182) Several Members commended the excellent report, and noted that it would have been very useful had it been available at the time of the joint CEP/CCAMLR Workshop in 2009.

(183) A number of Members referenced a CEP decision at the 2009 Baltimore ATCM/CEP Meeting, which committed the CEP to promote a harmonised approach for the protection of the Antarctic marine environment through the establishment of MPAs within, but not exclusively limited to, 11 priority areas by 2012.

(184) The Committee requested the Secretariat to provide regular updates of the report on the ATS website, so Parties can be kept up to date with this issue.

(185) The Secretariat confirmed that the request could be fulfilled.

(186) The Committee noted that a number of scientists from Members will participate in the CCAMLR MPA Workshop to be held in Brest, France from August 29th to September 2nd 2011.

(187) Belgium fully supported the creation of a representative network of MPAs. Belgium noted that it hosts and coordinates the SCAR-MARBIN database used by the Antarctic community.

(188) The Committee recalled its previous agreement to engage constructively with CCAMLR on these matters and noted that it looks forward to a report on the upcoming CCAMLR MPA Workshop in Brest, France. The Committee thanked CCAMLR for its invitations to attend the Workshop. Polly Penhale from the United States will be the CEP Representative.

(189) ASOC (on behalf of IUCN) introduced the IP 56 *Marine Spatial Protection and Management under the Antarctic Treaty System: New Opportunities for Implementation and Coordination.*

(190) ASOC presented IP 90 *The Southern Ocean MPA Agenda – Matching Words and Spirit with Action*; and IP 92 *The Ross Sea: A Valuable Reference Area to Assess the Effects of Climate Change.*

(191) Thanking the Secretariat for the MPA paper, ASOC noted that at the 2009 joint CEP / SC-CAMLR workshop, both bodies agreed to cooperate in establishing a representative network of MPAs in the Southern Ocean. CCAMLR agreed on a work plan towards the creation of the MPA network by the 2012 target date. This timetable is reflected in the CEP five-year work plan. The first milestone of the proposed work plan is for Members to collate relevant data for the 11 priority areas and others as appropriate and characterise each region in terms of biodiversity patterns and ecosystem processes, physical environmental features. However, there appears to have been little progress so far on this milestone. The second milestone is the special MPA workshop this coming August in Brest, France. ASOC urged ATCPs and CCAMLR Members to make effective use of this opportunity to address milestone one and present robust MPA proposals.

(192) Turning to IP 92 ASOC noted that it had put forward a number of papers making the 'science case' for supporting full protection of the Ross Sea slope and shelf in the context of establishing an important component of a representative network of MPAs in the Southern Ocean. This particular paper focuses on the climate reference zone potential of the Ross Sea. Since models used by the International Panel on Climate Change predict that the Ross Sea will be the last portion of the Southern Ocean with sea ice year round, the Ross Sea will be a 'refugium' for the study of normal ice processes and associated biota, and can serve as an important reference area to help understand the magnitude and the ecological and economic significance of changes elsewhere in the Southern Ocean.

### 7f) Other Annex V matters

(193) Australia introduced WP 32 *Enhancing the Antarctic Protected Areas Database to help assess and further develop the protected areas system.* Australia proposed that the CEP agree that the Antarctic Protected Areas Database should be expanded to include further relevant information (to be provided by proponents when submitting management plans), encourage proponents to make Area boundaries available in a digital format suitable for use in a geographic information system (GIS) where possible, and request the Secretariat to take the steps necessary to accommodate these changes.

(194) The Committee supported the recommendations presented in WP 32 and agreed:

- that the Antarctic Protected Areas Database should be expanded to include fields representing: (1) primary reason for designation; and (2) main Environmental Domain represented;

- to recommend that the ATCM modify the coversheet for Working Papers presenting ASPAs and ASMAs appended to Resolution 1 (2008) to allow the Secretariat to capture the relevant information for inclusion in the database;

- to encourage proponents to make ASPA and ASMA boundaries available in a digital format suitable for use in a GIS where possible, and to provide this information to the Secretariat for central management and access via the Antarctic Protected Areas Database; and

- to request the Secretariat to modify the Antarctic Protected Areas Database as necessary to accommodate these changes.

(195) Several Members noted that, due to technical and resource constraints, not all Members were in a position to implement all of these recommendations at this time.

(196) In response to these concerns, Australia emphasised the voluntary nature of this aspect of the proposal. It encouraged those Members with the capacity to implement all recommendations to do so while offering assistance and support to those Members who lacked this capacity. Australia also reassured the Committee that issues of data compatibility and exchange could be addressed and that it would consult with the Secretariat to find practical solutions to these challenges.

(197) Norway also noted that there may be issues relating to exchange format standards, etc, that need to be discussed further in the future.

(198) Australia announced that it was in consultation with a private company that had prepared a comprehensive dataset of spatial information representing the boundaries of all existing ASPAs and ASMAs. Australia planned to purchase this dataset and convey it to the Secretariat with a view to making the data widely available. Australia will work with the Secretariat during the intersessional period to that end.

(199) In order to allow the Secretariat to capture the relevant information for inclusion in the database, the Committee drafted modifications to the coversheet for Working Papers presenting ASPAs and ASMAs appended to Resolution 1 (2008) in the form of a Resolution.

**CEP Advice for the ATCM**

(200) The Committee recommends that the ATCM adopt the Revised Guide to the Presentation of Working Papers containing proposals for ASPA/ASMA/HSM by means of a Resolution.

(201) Germany introduced WP 41 *Fourth Progress Report on the Discussion of the International Working Group about Possibilities for Environmental Management of Fildes Peninsula and Ardley Island.*

(202) The co-authors proposed a meeting of the IWG during the CEP XIV Buenos Aires for further discussion, and encouraged interested Members to continue to work and revise the document, and contribute information and feedback to the continued work of the IWG.

(203) Uruguay encouraged the Parties who are active in the Fildes Peninsula to participate in the discussion with respect to the IWG to continue the protection of this region.

(204) China agreed to continue participation, and informed the committee that it had sent its comments to the IWG. China agreed to the present version of Annex 3 to WP 41.

(205) The Chair noted that the CEP would continue to discuss the work of the IWG at the next CEP meeting in Hobart.

(206) The Russian Federation introduced WP 57 *On the Need of Constant Monitoring of the Values of Antarctic Specially Protected Areas and Antarctic Specially Managed Areas.*

(207) A number of Members supported this Working Paper, but several noted caution was required when asserting the monitoring should be made mandatory, as visiting a site for monitoring purposes might cause further harm to the values the ASPA/ASMA is trying to protect.

(208) The Russian Federation responded that monitoring was intended to be mandatory, but would not necessarily require a site visit, as even remote monitoring is very important for reviewing management plans of ASPAs/ASMAs

(209) France noted that in most management plans submitted this year the values for each site had been revised.

(210) The Committee agreed to return to discussion of this topic at the next CEP meeting.

(211) Australia presented WP 61 rev. 1 *Report of the CEP Workshop on Marine and Terrestrial Antarctic Specially Managed Areas. Montevideo, Uruguay, 16-17 June 2011.*

Australia noted that CEP XIII had endorsed a proposal by the SGMP to convene an ASMA workshop to exchange good practice and work towards producing guidelines for preparing management plans for ASMAs.

(212) The workshop co-conveners, Juan Abdala (Uruguay) and Ewan McIvor (Australia) thanked all participants for their involvement and expressed regret that several other colleagues had been unable to attend due to flight cancellations. WP 61 rev. 1 and IP 136 presented the recommendations arising and key points raised under the four terms of reference for the workshop, which were:

1. Share good practice by examining common issues arising and lessons learnt from different approaches to site management in Antarctica, and drawing upon relevant approaches to the management of multiple use areas elsewhere.

2. Develop guidelines for the preparation of ASMA management plans.

3. Identify the characteristics of potential new ASMAs.

4. Prepare a report for CEP XIV.

(213) The Committee congratulated the organisers of the Workshop and Uruguay for hosting the Workshop, and strongly emphasised the importance of continuing this work.

(214) Uruguay informed the Committee that the most important aim of this workshop was to consolidate a system for creating management plans for marine and terrestrial ASMAs. Uruguay cautioned that facilitation of information exchange between operators and bureaucrats needed to be practical; otherwise, there would be a risk of unrealistic expectations in the application of the protection measures required of the region.

(215) The Committee supported the four recommendations arising from the workshop, and agreed to:

1. Request the Secretariat to establish links from the ATS website to ASMA websites, where available.

2. Promote further exchange of information on good practice in ASMA management. In particular, ASMA Management Groups could be encouraged to share information regarding initiatives that may be of broader interest for application in other ASMAs.

3. Seek to identify opportunities to draw on COMNAP's broader experience and responsibilities to help facilitate cooperation and coordination in the development, implementation and management of ASMAs. In addition, the CEP agreed to seek to draw on SCAR with respect to scientific activities, IAATO with respect to tourism activities, and SC-CAMLR with respect to good practice in the identification, management and monitoring of marine areas.

4. Encourage interested Members to review the provisions of existing ASMA management plans, with a view to preparing a suggested work plan and supporting materials to support work by the SGMP to develop guidance for establishing ASMAs and for preparing and reviewing ASMA management plans.

(216) COMNAP also congratulated the organisers and was pleased to have participated in the Workshop. It also noted it was pleased to see inclusion of Recommendation 3 of WP 61.

(217) ASOC thanked Australia and Uruguay for organising and coordinating the ASMA workshop. ASOC noted that in its view the diversity of current ASMAs highlights the flexibility of the ASMA as an instrument for area protection, as well as the potential to expand its use beyond current applications in the establishment of new marine and terrestrial ASMAs.

(218) The following IPs were also submitted under this agenda item:

- IP 24 *Progress Report on the Research Project "Current Environmental Situation and Management Proposals for the Fildes Region (Antarctic)"* (Germany)

- IP 69 *Summary of Key Features of Antarctic Specially Managed Areas* (Australia)

- IP 102 *Present Zoological Study at Mirny Station Area at ASPA No 127 "Haswell Island"* (Russian Federation)

(219) The Chair noted that IP 109 *Cooperation Management Activities at ASPAs in King George Island (Isla 25 de Mayo), South Shetland Islands* (Republic of Korea and Argentina) had already been introduced earlier in the week under Agenda Item 7(a).

## Item 8: Conservation of Antarctic Flora and Fauna

### 8a) Quarantine and Non-native Species

(220) In its capacity as convenor, New Zealand introduced WP 34 *Report of the Intersessional Contact Group on Non-Native Species 2010-2011*. New Zealand summarised the major outcomes of the ICG's second year of work, including completion of the overall objective and key guiding principles for Parties' actions to address risks posed by non-native species and of the Non-Native Species Manual.

(221) The Committee congratulated New Zealand and ICG participants for their work, noting the complexity of discussing issues related to non-native species. Many Members thanked the ICG for producing such comprehensive and practical outcomes.

(222) Several Members agreed that the Manual should be posted on the ATS website and remain a living document to be updated from time to time as required.

(223) Chile and Uruguay emphasised the need to have the Manual and related documents available in all four Treaty languages, to facilitate the use of the Manual.

(224) In light of discussions on WP 34, Germany drew the Committee's attention to IP 26 *Progress Report on the Research Project "The role of human activities in the introduction of non-native species into Antarctica and in the distribution of organisms within the Antarctic"*. Germany informed the Committee that it would bring the results of this research project to the attention of the next CEP.

(225) In response to a suggestion from India, COMNAP agreed to facilitate the dissemination of the Manual to managers of National Antarctic Programmes.

(226) IAATO informed the Committee that it would include a link to the Manual in the IAATO Field Operations Manual.

(227) Netherlands encouraged examples and case studies to be included on the ATS website alongside the Manual.

(228) Following discussion of WP 34, the Committee agreed to support the ICG's recommendations to:

1. Endorse the overall objective and key guiding principles for Parties' actions to address risks posed by non-native species;

2. Encourage the dissemination and use of the Manual;

3. Continue to develop the Non-Native Species Manual with the input of SCAR and COMNAP on scientific and practical matters, respectively; and

4. Task the Secretariat with posting the Manual in all four Treaty languages on the ATS website.

(229) The Committee considered and endorsed a Resolution prepared by ICG participants which encourages the use and further development of the Manual.

---

**CEP Advice to the ATCM**

(230) The Committee recommends the ATCM to adopt the Manual on Non-native Species in Antarctica by means of a resolution.

---

(231) COMNAP introduced WP 12 *Raising awareness of non-native species introductions: Workshop results and checklists for supply chain managers*, submitted in conjunction with SCAR. The Working Paper made two recommendations to the CEP, including that the CEP consider the inclusion of the checklist to reduce the risk of introduction of non-native species into the proposed "Non-Native Species Manual".

(232) Most Members highlighted the practicality of the ranking of actions and the style of the checklist.

(233) China expressed its concerns about the applicability of some of the points proposed in the checklist. In particular, China noted that some aspects of the checklist are too strict to be implemented, and they might benefit from review to be more practical.

(234) COMNAP thanked China, and noted that, even though some of the standards proposed in the checklist would be difficult to achieve, the adoption of these standards would be voluntary.

(235) Argentina noted that these checklists had been developed after extensive consultations amongst COMNAP members.

(236) IAATO and some members of COMNAP intend to use the checklists next summer season.

(237) The Meeting extended its congratulations to COMNAP and SCAR for the development of this comprehensive work in WP 12. The Chair reminded the Meeting that the list is intended to advise and facilitate the work of operators, but it is not mandatory to adopt it.

(238) The CEP approved the recommendations including addition of the checklists into the "Non-Native Species Manual", and recommended the addition of the comments made by China.

(239) SCAR introduced WP 53 *Measures to Reduce the Risk of Non-Native Species Introductions to the Antarctic Region Associated with Fresh Foods*. SCAR recommended the CEP discuss the adoption of these measures.

(240) China expressed concern with Section 3b) which recommended fresh food in transit to the Antarctic by boat or air should be accompanied with insecticide spray to eradicate insects. China noted that insecticides are banned substances on aircraft due to their flammable nature, and therefore the recommendation could compromise onboard safety. Chile noted that there may be an alternative to flammable aerosol insecticides which would minimise the concern with onboard safety.

(241) The United Kingdom supported the adoption of the three main recommendations and Annex A of the report, while noting that the measures are not proposed to become mandatory.

(242) Argentina was concerned with the report's use of the words 'banning' and 'prohibiting' of the transport of fresh fruit or food in the Antarctic region. Argentina noted clarification was needed in reference to section 2c) as 'seasonal produce' was a confusing term given that Parties receive food from both hemispheres. Argentina also noted that irradiation of food by UV light would shorten its durability, and it strongly opposes gamma irradiation of produce. It suggested that the SCAR/COMNAP medical group could be consulted on this issue.

(243) The United States suggested the adoption of these measures would require too much discussion and clarification during this meeting for all Members to express concerns. The United States noted that the intersessional review of these measures would be a good task to ensure the continued work of

the Non-Native Species ICG, and suggested the inclusion of COMNAP to explore practical issues, such as food safety, transport safety and nutrition of people.

(244) South Africa highlighted its concern with biosecurity matters, reflecting that practical and cost-saving measures would have the most chance of success.

(245) New Zealand thanked SCAR for its work and noted that the guidelines could be included in the annex to the Manual as a resource which could be applied as appropriate to assist Parties in meeting their requirements under Annex II.

(246) COMNAP accepted the invitation to participate in the discussions and asked for more time to consider the practical consequences of such measures.

(247) SCAR thanked all Members for their comments, and added several points of clarification. These measures were at the draft stage, and will require consultation on content and development of wording before formal adoption. The banning of fresh produce is not intended to be part of this approach, as these guidelines are designed only to mitigate the introduction of non-native species.

(248) The Committee accepted an offer from SCAR to moderate an informal discussion on WP 53 during the intersessional period with the intention of submitting a revised paper to CEP XV.

(249) Australia introduced IP 68 *Alien Species Database*, jointly submitted with SCAR, recalling the Committee's earlier agreement to encourage use of the Alien Species database maintained by the Australian Antarctic Data Centre (AADC) as the central repository of Antarctic alien species records, and reporting on work by the AADC to enhance the database to provide a standard online form for entering records and to allow images to be uploaded. Australia noted that the Non-Native Species Manual reiterated the Committee's earlier agreements, and encouraged Members to submit information on non-native species to the database.

(250) In response to an enquiry from Chile, Australia assured the Committee that the database could be modified to accommodate a continuous record for all non-native species events.

(251) The United Kingdom suggested that the information contained in IP 50 *Colonisation status of known non-native species in the Antarctic terrestrial environment (updated 2011)* could be added to the database.

(252) Other papers submitted under this item included:

- IP 32 *Report on IPY Oslo Science Conference Session on Non-Native Species* (France)

- IP 26 *Progress Report on the Research Project "The role of human activities in the introduction of non-native species into Antarctica and in the distribution of organisms within the Antarctic* (Germany)

### *8b) Specially Protected Species*

(253) No papers were submitted under this item.

### *8c) Other Annex II Matters*

(254) Germany introduced WP 38 *Antarctic Discussion Forum of Competent Authorities (DFCA) – Impacts of underwater sound to Antarctic waters.* Germany offered to host a 2nd workshop of the DFCA in the autumn of 2011 on the impacts of anthropogenic underwater sound on the Antarctic environment. This would follow on from the 1st workshop held in 2006 and reported in XXIX ATCM IP 43.

(255) The Committee thanked Germany for its paper and indicated an interest in continuing to develop its understanding of this topic.

(256) Some Members expressed an interest in attending the proposed workshop. Other Members stated that, based on the highly technical nature of underwater acoustics, the DCFA was not the most appropriate forum through which the CEP should be exploring this issue at this point in time.

(257) The United Kingdom drew a clear distinction between scientific evidence, which was the basis for this Committee's work, and the activities of Competent Authorities which were not necessarily relevant. However, the United Kingdom noted the value of holding such a workshop to cover a range of topics, including some topics to be discussed by other working groups.

The Russian Federation noted that this topic had been fully explored at previous meetings. The USA noted that Competent Authorities are not under the jurisdiction of the CEP and therefore the CEP should not consider this question. Instead, the United States proposed that advice should be sought from SCAR and noted the importance of understanding the underwater noise profile which would benefit from monitoring. ASOC reminded the Committee that it had provided four IPs on this subject to earlier meetings and would be happy to provide an update for the Committee.

(258) The Committee welcomed offers from SCAR and ASOC to submit a summary of new information on this topic to the CEP XV in order to facilitate further discussion.

(259) SCAR introduced IP 33 *SCAR's code of conduct for the exploration and research of subglacial aquatic environments* and IP 53 *SCAR's Code of Conduct for the Use of Animals for Scientific Purposes in Antarctica.*

(260) The United Kingdom noted that IP 33 had been useful in the drafting of its CEE on the exploration of Subglacial Lake Ellsworth.

(261) In reference to IP 53, the United Kingdom expressed the view that researchers should not wait until the end of an experiment to painlessly kill animals used for scientific purposes that would otherwise suffer permanent pain, distress, discomfort, or disablement that could not be relieved.

(262) Other papers submitted under this item:

- IP 27 *Progress Report on the Research Project 'Whale Monitoring Antarctica'* (Germany)

- IP 29 *Potential of Technical Measures to Reduce the Acoustical Effects of Airguns* (Germany)

- IP 94 *Use of dogs in the context of commemorative centennial expedition* (Norway)

## Item 9: Environmental Reporting

(263) The United Kingdom introduced WP 15 rev. 1 *Remote Sensing Techniques for Improved Monitoring of Environment and Climate Change in Antarctica.*

(264) The United Kingdom recommended that the CEP:

1. note and endorse the potential for remote sensing to contribute significantly to future environmental monitoring programmes, including in the context of protected area management and monitoring the impacts of climate change;

2. consider how else the utilisation of remote sensing data can support the CEP's work and that of the ATCM; and

3. continue to explore opportunities to use and investigate new monitoring applications.

(265) Many Members expressed their acknowledgement to the United Kingdom for the preparation of WP 15 rev. 1 and showed support for the recommendations listed.

(266) Some of these Members also highlighted that WP 15 does not cover several alternative examples of remote sensing, or other techniques that could be used for remote collection of data or monitoring aside from satellite derived data. Norway suggested that work should be done to examine the data sets and monitoring themes in ongoing international remote sensing initiatives, and bring this information back to the CEP for reference. Norway would be happy to work with other Members in this regard.

(267) Some Members also made comments on the difficulties of using remote sensing for monitoring. The Russian Federation announced that it had submitted IP 98 (ATCM agenda item 13) on the use of different techniques for monitoring, which compares the advantages and limitations of several different techniques.

(268) Germany pointed out how useful satellite monitoring could be in determining trends in climate change.

(269) Australia recommended information exchange of the current and planned remote sensing activities of all Members in the Antarctic region, to share experience, data and results and avoid any duplication between the studies being undertaken. Chile and Ecuador expressed their agreement with this recommendation. Ecuador mentioned that it would appreciate any collaboration in database sharing, especially on long time series data that are not currently available for all Members.

(270) Several Members informed the Committee of their use of remote sensing techniques each season for environmental monitoring purposes, some which are not always satellite based due to the high expense. Argentina informed the Committee of the recent launch of a new satellite which will allow for more effective monitoring of the Antarctic and sub-Antarctic regions. India also informed the Committee about its launch of polar satellites.

(271) The Committee agreed to support the recommendations of WP 15 rev. 1, with the addition of another recommendation suggested by Australia on encouraging information exchange to benefit all Parties that work in the Antarctic region, and avoid duplication of efforts. The Chair highlighted that other techniques of remote collection of data or monitoring, other than satellite remote sensing, are also important and should be taken into account when planning for monitoring.

(272) Romania introduced IP 35 *Environmental Monitoring and Ecological Activities in Antarctica, 2010-2012.*

(273) SCAR introduced IP 51 *The Southern Ocean Observing System (SOOS): An Update*, submitted in conjunction with Australia. Australia noted that despite the importance of the Southern Ocean, it was one of the least studied marine areas in the world. Recognising that several Parties are already closely engaged in this programme, Australia encouraged all Parties to support and contribute to the SOOS programme. Australia announced that it was hosting the secretariat for this programme. The United States mentioned its support for the SOOS programme, and stated that it will collaborate on this effort.

## Item 10: Inspection Reports

(274) Japan introduced WP 1 *Inspection undertaken by Japan in accordance with Article VII of the Antarctic Treaty and Article XIV of the Protocol on Environmental Protection* and IP 4 containing the full inspection report. During its inspection in January and February 2010, Japan visited six stations: Maitri Station (India), Princess Elisabeth Station (Belgium), Neumayer Station III (Germany), SANAE IV Base (South Africa), Troll Station (Norway) and Novolazarevskaya Station (Russian Federation).

(275) Japan introduced the results of the inspection including waste management and disposal, treatment of sewage and domestic liquid wastes. Following

the introduction of the results, Japan recommended that at some stations, waste water treatment and oil tank facilities etc. should be improved.

(276) Australia introduced WP 51 *Australian Antarctic Treaty and Environmental Protocol inspections: January 2010 and January 2011* and IP 39 and IP 40 containing the full inspections reports. In January 2010, Australian observers conducted inspections of Syowa Station (Japan), Druzhnaya IV and Soyuz Stations (Russian Federation) and Mount Harding Antarctic Specially Protected Area (ASPA) 168, as well as an aerial observation of Molodezhnaya Station (Russian Federation). In January 2011, Australian observers conducted on-ground inspections of Gondwana Station (Germany) and Vostok Station (Russian Federation), and an aerial observation of Leningradskaya Station (Russian Federation).

(277) Australia noted that the inspection teams were impressed by the evident commitment to science, as well as activities to remove accumulated wastes at a number of stations inspected. Australia noted that its inspections had raised some areas of environmental concern, and referred the Meeting to its recommendations that Parties should: ensure current facilities operate in compliance with the Protocol; maintain and regularly assess temporarily unoccupied facilities to ensure that environmental harm is not occurring; give due consideration to the removal of facilities and equipment no longer in use and the removal of accumulated waste materials; make efforts to share with the operating Party information on unoccupied facilities; and share knowledge and experience about addressing the challenges of dealing with the legacies of past activities.

(278) Those Parties whose stations were inspected thanked Japan and Australia for their visits and for providing them with constructive feedback.

(279) The Russian Federation welcomed the outcomes of the reports as useful and constructive, and noted that the outcomes would assist Russia in taking specific actions. Russia informed the Meeting that in response to the observations made by Australia's inspection team in 2010, it had sent a team to Soyuz Station to conduct repairs in the 2010/11 season. Russia offered to report at a future meeting on additional action taken in relation to issues identified. The Russian Federation referred to WP 55 *On strategy for the development of the Russian Federation activities in the Antarctic for the period until 2020 and longer-term perspective* which provided further

details of its plans for addressing some issues identified at the stations that had been inspected.

(280) The Committee agreed that inspections are highly valuable, noting that they facilitated the effective implementation of the Protocol.

(281) ASOC thanked Australia and Japan for their inspections. As noted in ATCM XXVI - IP 118 rev. 1 produced by ASOC and UNEP, some sites and facilities have not received inspection, and the inspections conducted by Japan and Australia help to fill that gap. According to ASOC, the inspections reports further confirm some of the conclusions of ASOC's ATCM XXXIV - IP 89 rev.1 that there are poor implementation standards of the Protocol. ASOC recommended that the findings of these inspections be considered by the Parties that had been inspected and also in the future work of the CEP.

(282) The Russian Federation welcomed the outcomes of the reports and suggested that future inspections should take into account national and cultural aspects, highlighting that email exchanges in preparation for Australia's inspection of Vostok station had coincided with the Orthodox Christmas.

(283) With respect to observations made on the need for stronger waste water management measures, particularly at inland stations, the Committee called on COMNAP to submit information on best practices on waste water management to CEPXV. It was also noted that the Committee had previously acknowledged the practical challenges in meeting the requirements of the Protocol in this regard.

(284) As a response to Japan's observation with regards to use of alternative energy at stations, Norway drew the Committee's attention to IP 74 *Assessment of wind energy potential at the Norwegian research station Troll,* noting the potential for harnessing wind and solar energy in Antarctic stations.

(285) Given that the Committee had made no specific policies on the use of hydroponics at Antarctic stations, Argentina proposed that the CEP initiate some informal discussions on this matter.

(286) Some Members remarked that, while they endeavored to fulfill their Protocol obligations, it was difficult and expensive to fully maintain and regularly assess temporarily unoccupied facilities, as well as to manage waste and deteriorating structures.

(287) In this regard, the United States noted that it has had some successful experience in removing material from sites of past activities and announced that it would present an information paper on this to CEP XV.

(288) The Committee supported Australia's recommendation on how Parties might deal with the legacies of past activities, and the maintenance of long-established facilities. It also agreed to incorporate this into the five-year work plan.

(289) Japan expressed its hope to all the Parties inspected that the report be fully utilised to improve their facilities in Antarctic stations for environmental protection to implement the Environment Protocol in the near future.

## Item 11: Cooperation with other Organisations

(290) Papers submitted under this agenda item were:

- IP 10 *The Annual Report for 2010 of the Council of Managers of National Antarctic Programs* (COMNAP)

- IP 31 *Report by the SC-CAMLR Observer to the Fourteenth Meeting of the Committee for Environmental Protection* (CCAMLR)

- IP 54 *Summary of SCAR's Strategic Plan 2011-2016* (SCAR)

- IP 57 *Report of the CEP Observer to SC-CAMLR's Working Group on Ecosystem Monitoring and Management (WG-EMM)* (CCAMLR)

## Item 12: General Matters

(291) In response to a request from ATCM XXXIII for advice on environmental issues related to the practicality of repair and remediation of environmental damage, Australia introduced WP 28 *Environmental issues related to the practicality of repair or remediation of environmental damage.* The paper was intended to stimulate discussion and assist the CEP to provide a timely and helpful response to Decision 4 (2010), and identified eight points that Australia considered the CEP should build on in preparing such a response.

(292) The Committee thanked Australia for initiating work on a challenging and important issue and expressed an interest that this issue be discussed by the CEP.

(293) The Netherlands suggested that the topic on repair or remediation of environmental damage be integrated into the CEP's Five-Year Work Plan. The Netherlands and ASOC also raised concerns that some approaches could allow considerable delay in reacting to a problem.

(294) ASOC further noted poor practices with regards to abandoned facilities and waste management reported at this ATCM in WP 1, WP 51 and IP 24.

(295) Argentina expressed their support to all points presented in WP 28 and referred to IP 17 presented to ATCM XXXIV where studies describing the development of a process for bioremediation of hydrocarbon contaminated soils, which exhibited positive results, were briefly described. Argentina also mentioned that bioremediation processes have been included in the action plan against oil spills for Jubany station.

(296) In response to a request from the Committee, SCAR agreed to provide advice to the CEP on technical matters relating to repair and remediation of environmental damage.

(297) The Committee encouraged Members to submit papers and proposals on this issue to CEP XV with a view to establishing an ICG on repair or remediation of environmental damage at that meeting.

(298) Other papers submitted under this agenda item were:

- IP 48 *Thala Valley Waste Removal* (Australia)
- IP 49 *Renewable Energy and Energy Efficiency Initiatives at Australia's Antarctic Stations* (Australia)
- IP 61 *The SCAR Antarctic Climate Evolution (ACE) Programme* (SCAR)
- IP 95 *Paying for Ecosystem Services of Antarctica?* (Netherlands)
- IP 127 *The Construction of an Orthodox Chapel at Vernadsky Station* (Ukraine)

(299) The CEP noted that the ATCM had considered WP 24 *Progress Report on the Intersessional Contact Group on Review of ATCM Recommendations* (Argentina), and had requested advice on outstanding components of the following Recommendations that address environmental matters other than area protection and management:

- Recommendation III-8

- Recommendation III-10

- Recommendation IV-22

- Recommendation X-7

- Recommendation XII-3

- Recommendation XIII-4

- Recommendation XIV-3

(300) An open-ended contact group was convened by Australia to consider whether, in the Committee's view, these Recommendations could be considered no longer current.

(301) The Committee supported the advice of the contact group. It noted that the outstanding components of Recommendations III-10, IV-22, X-7, XII-3, XIII-4 related to encouraging SCAR to provide advice to inform the Parties' deliberations on: conservation of Antarctic fauna and flora; matters relating to Antarctic pelagic sealing; monitoring of hydrocarbons in the marine environment; environmental impacts of scientific and logistic activities; and waste management.

(302) The Committee agreed that these Recommendations were out of date and could be considered no longer current, but noted SCAR's ongoing and valuable role in providing scientific advice to the ATCM and CEP, as embodied in Articles 10.2 and 12 of the Environment Protocol.

(303) With respect to Recommendation XIII-4, the Committee noted that COMNAP would be best placed to provide advice regarding procedures for waste management.

(304) The Committee noted that the guidelines for scientific drilling presented in Recommendation XIV-3 had not been replaced or superseded. It agreed that,

in accordance with Article 8 and Annex I of the Protocol, such activities would be subject to prior environmental impact assessment, but that there could be some benefit in retaining information to guide the planning, conduct and environmental assessment of drilling activities. The Committee agreed to give further attention to this matter, with due consideration to the experiences arising from several existing and planned drilling activities.

(305) The Committee noted that, in practical terms, the provisions of the Environment Protocol and its Annexes had superseded the provisions of the Agreed Measures for the Conservation of Antarctic Fauna and Flora appended to Recommendation III-8.

---

**CEP advice to the ATCM:**

(306) The Committee advises that the following Recommendations referred by the ATCM for its consideration could be considered no longer current:

- Recommendation III-8

- Recommendation III-10

- Recommendation IV-22

- Recommendation X-7

- Recommendation XII-3

- Recommendation XIII-4

(307) The Committee further advises that elements of the Guidelines for Scientific Drilling in the Antarctic Treaty Area presented in Recommendation XIV-3 have not been replaced or superseded, and that there could be some benefit in retaining such guidelines. The Committee will give further attention to this matter, with due consideration to the experiences arising from several existing and planned drilling activities.

---

## Item 13: Election of Officers

(308) The Committee congratulated Verónica Vallejos from Chile on her re-election as Vice-chair for a new two-year term.

## Item 14: Preparation for the Next Meeting

(309) Australia introduced WP 8 *Proposed schedule for the 35th Antarctic Treaty Consultative Meeting, Hobart, 2012.*

(310) While ATCM XXXV would be held over an eight-day period, Australia noted that the duration of the CEP meeting had not been reduced.

(311) The Committee adopted the provisional agenda for CEP XV (Appendix 2).

## Item 15: Adoption of the Report

(312) The Committee adopted its Report.

## Item 16: Closing of the Meeting

(313) The Chair closed the Meeting on Friday 24th June 2011.

**Annex 1**

# CEP XIV Agenda and Summary of Documents

| 1. OPENING OF THE MEETING | |
|---|---|
| | |

| 2. ADOPTION OF THE AGENDA | |
|---|---|
| SP 1 | ATCM XXXIV AND CEP XIV AGENDA AND SCHEDULE. |

| 3. STRATEGIC DISCUSSION ON THE FUTURE WORK OF THE CEP | |
|---|---|
| IP 89<br>ASOC | THE ANTARCTIC ENVIRONMENTAL PROTOCOL, 1991-2011. This paper reflects on Antarctic environmental protection since the signature of the Protocol on Environmental Protection, noting significant accomplishments, issues, events, and challenges. |

| 4. OPERATION OF THE CEP | |
|---|---|
| WP 25<br>Germany<br>and USA | TIMELY SUBMISSION OF PAPERS IN ADVANCE OF ATCMs. This paper considers that the ATCM and CEP can improve the efficiency and effectiveness of their work by including in their Rules of Procedure clear provisions related to the submission of papers prior to ATCMs. It proposes to provide firm deadlines for the submission of WPs and incentives for meeting those deadlines, and to replace the current guidelines contained in Decision 3 (2009) with the adoption of a new set of procedures. |
| WP 36<br>Australia,<br>France and<br>New Zealand | A PROPOSED NEW APPROACH TO THE HANDLING OF INFORMATION PAPERS. This paper proposes modifications to the categories of official document for the ATCM and CEP, with the objective of ensuring a focus on Working Papers raising substantive matter for discussion and/or decision, while retaining a formal means for sharing valuable information between Parties and other meeting participants. A draft Decision and suggested revision to the Guidelines for the Submission, Translation and Distribution of Documents for the ATCM and the CEP are presented. |
| IP 71<br>Italy | ANNUAL REPORT PURSUANT TO ARTICLE 17 OF THE PROTOCOL ON ENVIRONMENTAL PROTECTION TO THE ANTARCTIC TREATY. 2009-2010. |
| IP 93<br>Ukraine | ANNUAL REPORT PURSUANT TO ARTICLE 17 OF THE PROTOCOL ON ENVIRONMENTAL PROTECTION TO THE ANTARCTIC TREATY |
| IP 113<br>UNEP &<br>ASOC | REVIEW OF THE IMPLEMENTATION OF THE MADRID PROTOCOL: ANNUAL REPORT BY PARTIES (ARTICLE 17). This paper addresses the annual reporting duty set out in Article 17 of the Madrid Protocol, analysing the level of compliance by Parties with their annual reporting duty since the entry into force of the Madrid Protocol. |

| 5. CLIMATE CHANGE IMPLICATIONS FOR THE ENVIRONMENT: STRATEGIC APPROACH | |
|---|---|
| WP 43<br>UK and<br>Norway | DEVELOPING A SIMPLE METHODOLOGY FOR CLASSIFYING ANTARCTIC SPECIALLY PROTECTED AREAS ACCORDING TO THEIR VULNERABILITY TO CLIMATE CHANGE. Considering that the protected areas system is an important tool for managing the implications of climate change, the UK and Norway propose a first attempt to develop a methodology to classify existing protected areas according to their vulnerability and risk to climate change. |
| WP 44<br>UK and<br>Norway | PROGRESS REPORT ON ATME ON CLIMATE CHANGE. The UK and Norway have developed this paper to facilitate the ATCM's ongoing consideration of the conclusions and recommendations arising from the 2010 Climate Change ATME. The summary table at Annex A records the actions taken to date by the CEP and the ATCM against each of the 30 ATME recommendations. The UK and Norway propose that the ATCM task the Secretariat to maintain and update this table to inform future discussions on the ATME recommendations, until they have all been closed. |
| IP 52<br>SCAR | ANTARCTIC CLIMATE CHANGE AND THE ENVIRONMENT – 2011 UPDATE. This paper is the second update to the ATCM since the publication of the SCAR Antarctic Climate Change and the Environment report, and highlights some recent advances in Antarctic climate science and associated impacts on the environment. |
| IP 56<br>IUCN | MARINE SPATIAL PROTECTION AND MANAGEMENT UNDER THE ANTARCTIC TREATY SYSTEM: NEW OPPORTUNITIES FOR IMPLEMENTATION AND COORDINATION. IUCN requires that Parties work closely with CCAMLR to identify relevant, broad-scale areas which are of interest to both bodies. |
| IP 65<br>United States | FRONTIERS IN UNDERSTANDING CLIMATE CHANGE AND POLAR ECOSYSTEMS WORKSHOP REPORT. This paper informs on a Workshop attended by polar and non-polar scientists to explore whether there are new capabilities available to study ecosystems in different ways that might shed light on questions related to species movement, changes in seasonality, feedbacks and how changes in these patterns might be related to climate change. |
| IP 83<br>ASOC | AN ANTARCTIC CLIMATE CHANGE COMMUNICATION PLAN. In this paper, ASOC provides a draft communication plan to help implement Recommendation 2 from the ATME on Climate Change. |
| IP 88<br>ASOC | OCEAN ACIDIFICATION AND THE SOUTHERN OCEAN. ASOC informs on the impact of acidification on the Southern Ocean's chemistry and organisms. It recommends increased research on the uptake and distribution of $CO_2$ in the Southern Ocean, as well as the establishment of a network of MPAs and marine reserves as a tool for eliminating other stressors in order to help build ecosystem resilience. |

| IP 103 IAATO | IAATO's CLIMATE CHANGE WORKING GROUP: REPORT OF PROGRESS. This paper reports on the objectives and activities of the IAATO's Climate Change WG, matters discussed in the last IAATO General Meeting, and initiatives for the future. |
|---|---|

## 6. ENVIRONMENTAL IMPACT ASSESSMENT
### 6a) Draft Comprehensive Environmental Evaluations

| WP 7 Australia | REPORT OF THE INTERSESSIONAL OPEN-ENDED CONTACT GROUP TO CONSIDER THE DRAFT CEE FOR THE "CONSTRUCTION AND OPERATION OF THE JANG BOGO STATION, TERRA NOVA BAY, ANTARCTICA". This paper informs on the result of the intersessional review by an ICG coordinated by Australia, according to the CEP Procedures, of the draft CEE prepared for the new Korean station. |
|---|---|
| WP 14 Norway | REPORT OF THE INTERSESSIONAL OPEN-ENDED CONTACT GROUP TO CONSIDER THE DRAFT CEE FOR THE "PROPOSED EXPLORATION OF SUBGLACIAL LAKE ELLSWORTH, ANTARCTICA". This paper reports the results of the intersessional review by an ICG coordinated by Norway, according to the CEP procedures, of the draft CEE prepared for the proposed exploration of Subglacial Lake Ellsworth. |
| WP 16 United Kingdom | DRAFT COMPREHENSIVE ENVIRONMENTAL EVALUATION (CEE) FOR THE PROPOSED EXPLORATION OF SUBGLACIAL LAKE ELLSWORTH, ANTARCTICA. This paper describes the antecedents and objectives of the exploration of Subglacial Lake Ellsworth and the process of the preparation, circulation, and conclusions of the draft CEE. |
| WP 42 Republic of Korea | THE DRAFT COMPREHENSIVE ENVIRONMENTAL EVALUATION FOR THE CONSTRUCTION AND OPERATION OF THE JANG BOGO ANTARCTIC RESEARCH STATION, TERRA NOVA BAY, ANTARCTIC. This paper informs on the preparation and circulation process of the Draft CEE, as well as its contents, and includes the non-technical summary as an attachment. |
| IP 13 United Kingdom | THE DRAFT COMPREHENSIVE ENVIRONMENTAL EVALUATION (CEE) FOR THE PROPOSED EXPLORATION OF SUBGLACIAL LAKE ELLSWORTH, ANTARCTICA. This paper presents the complete version of the Draft CEE. |
| IP 19 Rep. of Korea | THE DRAFT COMPREHENSIVE ENVIRONMENTAL EVALUATION FOR THE CONSTRUCTION AND OPERATION OF THE JANG BOGO ANTARCTIC RESEARCH STATION, TERRA NOVA BAY, ANTARCTICA. This paper presents the complete version of the Draft CEE. |
| IP 76 Rep. of Korea | THE INITIAL RESPONSES TO THE COMMENTS ON THE DRAFT COMPREHENSIVE ENVIRONMENTAL EVALUATION FOR CONSTRUCTION AND OPERATION OF THE JANG BOGO ANTARCTIC RESEARCH STATION, TERRA NOVA BAY, ANTARCTICA. This paper provides preliminary responses to several comments raised by Parties on the Draft CEE. |

| 6b) Other EIA Matters | |
|---|---|
| WP 54<br>Russian<br>Federation | TECHNOLOGY FOR INVESTIGATING WATER STRATA OF SUBGLACIAL LAKE VOSTOK. This paper informs that during February 2011 the ice borehole at Vostok station closely approached the ice/water interface, and that the opening to lake water will more likely occur in the summer season of 2011-12 using the technology designed by the Russian Federation in 2001, and in compliance with the Final CEE approved in 2010. |
| SP 5 rev 1<br>Secretariat | ANNUAL LIST OF INITIAL ENVIRONMENTAL EVALUATIONS (IEE) AND COMPREHENSIVE ENVIRONMENTAL EVALUATIONS (CEE) PREPARED BETWEEN APRIL 1ST 2010 AND MARCH 31ST 2011. The Secretariat will report on the list of IEEs and CEEs for the most recent reporting period. |
| IP 64<br>India | FINAL COMPREHENSIVE ENVIRONMENTAL EVALUATION (CEE) OF NEW INDIAN RESEARCH STATION AT LARSEMANN HILLS, ANTARCTICA AND UPDATE ON CONSTRUCTION ACTIVITY. India informs on the incorporation of suggestions received regarding the Final version of the CEE and its circulation to Parties, and on the Station construction process. |
| IP 72<br>USA | METHODOLOGY FOR CLEAN ACCESS TO THE SUBGLACIAL ENVIRONMENT ASSOCIATED WITH THE WHILLANS ICE STREAM. This paper informs on a project focussed on addressing the potential for the West Antarctic Ice Sheet to make a large contribution to near-future global sea level rise, and the presence of microorganisms and microbial habitats in dark and cold subglacial aquatic environments. |
| IP 84<br>ASOC | ANTARCTIC TOURISM – WHAT NEXT? KEY ISSUES TO ADDRESS WITH BINDING RULES. This paper addresses three issues ASOC has identified as requiring particular attention from regulatory entities: Antarctic tourism as a multi-scalar, dynamic issue; environmental pressures from tourism; and the application of existing instruments. |
| IP 87<br>ASOC | LAND-BASED TOURISM IN ANTARCTICA. This paper examines the interface between commercial land-based tourism and the use of national programme infrastructure, as well as recent developments in land-based tourism. |
| IP 123<br>Ecuador | ESTUDIO DE IMPACTO AMBIENTAL EX-POST DE LA ESTACIÓN CIENTÍFICA ECUATORIANA "PEDRO VICENTE MALDONADO". ISLA GREENWICH-SHETLAND DEL SUR-ANTÁRTIDA, 2010-2011. This paper informs on the environmental impact assessment associated with the XIV and XV Ecuadorian Antarctic expeditions, and presents an Environmental Management Plan to conduct Ecuadorian activities in Antarctica. |

| 7. AREA PROTECTION AND MANAGEMENT | |
|---|---|
| 7a) Management Plans | |
| i. | Draft management plans which had been reviewed by the Subsidiary Group on Management Plans |
| WP 47 Australia | SUBSIDIARY GROUP ON MANAGEMENT PLANS – REPORT ON TERMS OF REFERENCE #1 TO #3: REVIEW OF DRAFT MANAGEMENT PLANS. The SGMP reviewed one draft ASPA management plan referred by the CEP for intersessional review. The SGMP recommends that the CEP approve the revised management plan prepared by the United Kingdom, Chile and Spain for ASPA 126 Byers Peninsula. |
| ii. | Draft revised management plans which had not been reviewed by the Subsidiary Group on Management Plans |
| WP 3 France | REVIEW OF THE MANAGEMENT PLAN FOR THE ANTARCTIC SPECIALLY PROTECTED AREA NO. 120, POINTE-GÉOLOGIE ARCHIPELAGO, TERRE ADÉLIE. France informs on the five-yearly review of the management plan for ASPA 120, noting that only minor changes have been made in order to clarify the text and to remove some of the ambiguities present in the previous version. It is recommended that the CEP approve the attached revised Management Plan for this Area. |
| WP 4 France | MANAGEMENT PLAN FOR ANTARCTIC SPECIALLY PROTECTED AREA NO. 166, PORT-MARTIN, TERRE ADÉLIE. PROPOSAL TO EXTEND THE EXISTING MANAGEMENT PLAN. France has conducted the five-yearly review of the management plan for ASPA 166 and, in light of this review, it suggests to renew the management plan without any modification for a period of five years. |
| WP 6 USA and Chile | REVISED MANAGEMENT PLAN FOR ANTARCTIC SPECIALLY PROTECTED AREA NO. 149 CAPE SHIRREFF AND SAN TELMO ISLAND, LIVINGSTON ISLAND, SOUTH SHETLAND ISLANDS. This paper informs that only minor changes were made on the revised Management Plan, including a brief introduction, updates to the agreed provisions under CCAMLR, a requirement for National programmes operating in the Area, and editorial corrections. |
| WP 9 United States | REVISED MANAGEMENT PLAN FOR ANTARCTIC SPECIALLY PROTECTED AREA NO. 122 ARRIVAL HEIGHTS, HUT POINT PENINSULA, ROSS ISLAND. Some major changes were introduced in this Management Plan, including several revisions of the boundaries, a brief introduction, new values, amendments to some maps, descriptions of the Area and access to the Area, and editorial changes. |

| | |
|---|---|
| WP 23<br>United Kingdom | REVISION OF THE MANAGEMENT PLAN FOR ANTARCTIC SPECIALLY PROTECTED AREA (ASPA) NO. 140 PARTS OF DECEPTION ISLAND, SOUTH SHETLAND ISLANDS. The proposed changes to the revised Management Plan include an introduction, revision of boundaries, access to the area, maps, and the inclusion of photographs. Given the substantial changes introduced in the revised version, the UK asks the Committee to send this MP for intersessional review for the SGMP. |
| WP 29<br>Australia | REVISED MANAGEMENT PLAN FOR ANTARCTIC SPECIALLY PROTECTED AREA NO. 167, HAWKER ISLAND, PRINCESS ELIZABETH LAND. Australia informs that it has determined that only minor amendments to the Management Plan are required, including an introduction, some additional requirements for visitors, improved maps, reference to the EDA, and updates to the bibliography. Australia recommends that the CEP approve the revised Management Plan. |
| WP 31<br>New Zealand | REVISION OF MANAGEMENT PLAN FOR ANTARCTIC SPECIALLY PROTECTED AREA NO. 116: NEW COLLEGE VALLEY, CAUGHLEY BEACH, CAPE BIRD, ROSS ISLAND. New Zealand informs that the revised version of the Management Plan includes updated information on vegetation cover, invertebrates, and glacier boundaries, and proposes that the CEP approve the revised Management Plan. |
| WP 33<br>New Zealand | REVISION OF MANAGEMENT PLAN FOR ANTARCTIC SPECIALLY PROTECTED AREA (ASPA) NO. 131: CANADA GLACIER, LAKE FRYXELL, TAYLOR VALLEY, VICTORIA LAND. New Zealand informs that for the revised Management Plan it assessed the glacier boundary location, lake edge, and meltwater streams in relation to potential changes due to climate change, and conducted a vegetation survey to ensure that the algal biodiversity of the Area is well characterised. New Zealand proposes that the CEP approve the revised Management Plan. |
| WP 39<br>UK and NZ | REVISED MANAGEMENT PLAN FOR ANTARCTIC SPECIALLY MANAGED AREA NO. 2 MCMURDO DRY VALLEYS, SOUTHERN VICTORIA LAND. This paper informs on several important modifications introduced in the ASMA 2 Management Plan during the review process. Changes were made in the boundaries of the Area, the description of values to be protected, restrictions to activities within the Area, maps and photographs. |
| WP 50<br>Italy | REVISED MANAGEMENT PLAN FOR ANTARCTIC SPECIALLY PROTECTED AREA (ASPA) N° 165 EDMONSON POINT, ROSS SEA. Italy informs that boundaries, maps and descriptions of the Area remain without changes and that only minor changes were made in the revised Management Plan, mainly related to a review of activities conducted in the Area, an update to the population numbers of breeding birds and permit conditions, and an introduction of key management issues related to the protection of potentially sensitive features of the site. |

| | |
|---|---|
| WP 58<br>Russian<br>Federation | REVISED MANAGEMENT PLAN FOR ANTARCTIC SPECIALLY PROTECTED AREA NO. 127 "HASWELL ISLAND" (HASWELL ISLAND AND ADJACENT EMPEROR PENGUIN ROOKERY ON FAST ICE) REVISED MANAGEMENT PLAN. The Russian Federation informs that only minor changes were introduced in the revised Version of the Management Plan for ASPA 127. |

| | |
|---|---|
| iii. | New draft management plans for protected/managed areas |

| | |
|---|---|
| iv. | Other matters relating to management plans for protected/managed areas |
| WP 10<br>United States | DEVELOPING A PLAN FOR SPECIAL PROTECTION AT TAYLOR GLACIER AND BLOOD FALLS, TAYLOR VALLEY, MCMURDO DRY VALLEYS. The United States proposes the establishment of an International Working Group to discuss area protection at Taylor Glacier and Blood Falls and to develop a draft ASPA Management Plan to be submitted to the CEP XV in 2012. |
| WP 13<br>Australia | SUBSIDIARY GROUP ON MANAGEMENT PLANS – REPORT ON TERMS OF REFERENCE #4 AND #5: IMPROVING MANAGEMENT PLANS AND THE PROCESS FOR THEIR INTERSESSIONAL REVIEW. This paper reports on tasks undertaken by the SGMP during the intersessional period. In particular, it reports the revision of the Guide to the Preparation of Management Plans for Antarctic Specially Protected Areas, the finalisation of a template suggesting standard wording for ASPA Management Plans, and the development of an outline for the CEP Workshop on Marine and Terrestrial ASMAs. |
| WP 18<br>United<br>Kingdom | PROPOSED MONITORING ACTIVITIES WITHIN ANTARCTIC SPECIALLY PROTECTED AREA (ASPA) NO. 107 EMPEROR ISLAND, DION ISLANDS, MARGUERITE BAY, ANTARCTIC PENINSULA. Noting that the continued existence of the emperor penguin colony within the ASPA is now in doubt, the UK proposes delaying the revision of the current ASPA Management Plan for 5 years to enable the status of the colony to be confirmed, after which appropriate management action will be considered. |
| SP 7<br>Secretariat | STATUS OF ANTARCTIC SPECIALLY PROTECTED AREA AND ANTARCTIC SPECIALLY MANAGED AREA MANAGEMENT PLANS. Information on the status of ASPA and ASMA management plans according to the review requirements of Annex V to the Protocol. |
| IP 73<br>USA | AMUNDSEN-SCOTT SOUTH POLE STATION, SOUTH POLE ANTARCTICA SPECIALLY MANAGED AREA (ASMA NO. 5) 2011 MANAGEMENT REPORT. This paper summarises the continuing challenges in managing diverse activities in the ASMA, particularly in relation to the expected increase in non-governmental activities associated with celebrations of the Centenary of Amundsen and Scott reaching the South Pole. |

| | |
|---|---|
| IP 79<br>Australia,<br>China, India,<br>Romania,<br>Russian<br>Federation | REPORT OF THE LARSEMANN HILLS ANTARCTIC SPECIALLY MANAGED AREA (ASMA) MANAGEMENT GROUP. Parties active in the Larsemann Hills established a Management Group to oversee the implementation of the ASMA Management Plan. This paper gives a brief report on the Management Group's activities during 2010-11. |
| IP 109<br>Rep. of<br>Korea &<br>Argentina | COOPERATION MANAGEMENT ACTIVITIES AT ASPAS IN 25 DE MAYO (KING GEORGE) ISLAND, SOUTH SHETLAND ISLANDS. This paper informs on activities between the Republic of Korea and Argentina to initiate a review of the environmental management in two ASPAs on King George Island, South Shetland Islands: ASPA 132 and ASPA 171. |
| IP 115<br>Rep. of<br>Korea | FAUNA SURVEY OF THE ASPA 171 NARĘBSKI POINT, ASPA 150 ARDLEY ISLAND AND ASPA 132 POTTER PENINSULA IN 2010-11. This paper informs on a survey aimed to formulate a comprehensive management plan for the ASPA 171. |
| IP 131<br>Argentina,<br>Chile,<br>Norway,<br>Spain,<br>UK, USA | DECEPTION ISLAND SPECIALLY MANAGED AREA (ASMA) MANAGEMENT GROUP REPORT |

| 7b) Historic Sites and Monuments | |
|---|---|
| WP 5<br>China | PROPOSED ADDITION OF No.1 BUILDING COMMEMORATING CHINA'S ANTARCTIC EXPEDITION AT GREAT WALL STATION TO THE LIST OF HISTORIC SITES AND MONUMENT. This paper proposes the addition of the first permanent building constructed by China in Antarctica as a new HSM. |
| WP 27<br>Argentina | REPORT OF THE INFORMAL DISCUSSIONS ON HISTORIC SITES AND MONUMENTS. This paper informs on the results of the informal discussions on Historic Sites and Monuments, which focussed on both the evaluation of what is considered to be "historic" and the inclusion of the more holistic concept of "enhancement" for dealing with HSMs in Antarctica. |
| WP 59<br>Chile | PROPOSAL OF MODIFICATION FOR THE HISTORIC MONUMENT No. 82. INSTALLATION OF COMMEMORATIVE PLAQUES AT THE MONUMENT TO THE ANTARCTIC TREATY. Chile informs on the installation of a commemorative plaque for the International Polar Years at the "Monument to the Antarctic Treaty" that had been erected near the Frei, Bellingshausen & Escudero bases, King George Island, according to what was set forth through Measure 3 (2007). |

| | |
|---|---|
| IP 117<br>Chile | INAUGURACIÓN DE LA INSTALACIÓN DE PLACAS CONMEMORATIVAS EN EL MONUMENTO AL TRATADO ANTÁRTICO. This paper provides the speech by Ambassador Fernando Schmidt, Deputy Foreign Minister of Chile, at the unveiling of the plaques commemorating the International Polar year. The plaques were installed on 1 February 2011 at the Monument to the Antarctic Treaty located on King George Island. |
| IP 130<br>Argentina | UPDATE ON ENHANCEMENT ACTIVITIES FOR HSM 38 "SNOW HILL" |

### 7c) Site Guidelines

| | |
|---|---|
| WP 17<br>UK,<br>Argentina,<br>Chile,<br>Norway,<br>Spain and<br>USA | REVISION OF SITE GUIDELINES FOR WHALERS BAY, DECEPTION ISLAND, SOUTH SHETLAND ISLANDS. This paper informs on the changes proposed in the revised guidelines related to a better identification of the landing area, revisions in maps and in the Cautionary Notes, and the correction of minor typographical errors. |
| WP 30<br>NZ and USA | SITE GUIDELINES FOR THE TAYLOR VALLEY VISITOR ZONE, SOUTHERN VICTORIA LAND. This paper proposes the adoption of site guidelines for this area in the McMurdo Dry Valleys which aim to minimise the risk of visitor related pressures at this site of outstanding natural and scenic value, and are to be used in conjunction with the ASMA 2 Management Plan. |
| WP 45<br>Australia | REPORT OF THE OPEN-ENDED INTERSESSIONAL CONTACT GROUP ON REVISION OF ENVIRONMENTAL ELEMENTS OF RECOMMENDATION XVIII-1. This paper informs on the conclusions of the ICG convened by Australia to: review existing environmental advice to visitors; develop revised and updated guidance; and consider how the CEP might best assess new site guidelines and periodically review existing guidelines. The ICG developed updated guidelines for visitors based on Rec. XVIII-1, which are presented for consideration by the CEP, together with a draft Resolution for adoption by the ATCM. The paper also provides recommendations on how the CEP might effectively and efficiently consider new guidelines and review existing guidelines. |
| WP 49<br>Chile and<br>Argentina | SITE GUIDELINES FOR THE NORTHEAST BEACH OF ARDLEY PENINSULA (ARDLEY ISLAND), KING GEORGE ISLAND (25 DE MAYO ISLAND), SOUTH SHETLAND ISLANDS. Having received and considered the comments received by Parties during the intersessional period, Chile and Argentina propose these revised guidelines aimed to optimise management of the increasing number of visitors in the area. |

| | |
|---|---|
| WP 52 Australia | VISITOR SITE GUIDE FOR MAWSON'S HUTS AND CAPE DENISON, EAST ANTARCTICA. This paper proposes to adopt the site guidelines, which are aimed to assist in managing visits to this place of outstanding historical, archaeological, technical, social and aesthetic value. |
| IP 9 United States | ANTARCTIC SITE INVENTORY: 1994-2011. This paper provides updated information on the Antarctic Site Inventory, which has collected biological data and site-descriptive information in the Antarctic Peninsula since 1994. |
| IP 12 Bulgaria | GUIDELINES OF ENVIRONMENTAL BEHAVIOR OF THE EXPEDITION PARTICIPANTS AND VISITORS TO THE BULGARIAN BASE IN ANTARCTICA. This paper informs on a comprehensive set of guidelines for staff and visitors to St. Kliment Ohridski Base. |
| IP 23 USA & UK | THE ANTARCTIC PENINSULA COMPENDIUM 3RD EDITION. This compendium includes information on 142 sites that are regularly visited by tourists or other visitors, sites with historic census data, national research stations, sites within ASMAs, and a few ASPAs. |
| IP 104 IAATO | PROPOSED AMENDMENT TO ANTARCTIC TREATY SITE GUIDELINES FOR HANNAH POINT. This paper proposes an amendment to the Site Guidelines as a result of an incident in which an elephant seal, possibly disturbed by visitors, went over a cliff. |
| IP 105 IAATO | REPORT ON IAATO OPERATOR USE OF ANTARCTIC PENINSULA LANDING SITES AND ATCM VISITOR SITE GUIDELINES, 2009-10 & 2010-11 SEASON. IAATO reports that most of the landings were covered by Site Guidelines or under National Program management through their proximity to stations. IAATO suggests that two sites should adopt site guidelines for visitors in the near future. |
| IP 110 Ukraine | UKRAINE POLICY REGARDING VISITS BY TOURISTS TO VERNADSKY STATION. This paper informs on policies oriented to visitors to the station, prepared in a format of Visitor Site Guidelines, facilitating tourist vessel expedition crew comprehension and use. |
| IP 126 Ecuador | MANEJO TURÍSTICO PARA LA ISLA BARRIENTOS. This paper informs on observations of tourist activities in the vicinity of Pedro Vicente Maldonado station and a monitoring programme aimed to improve guidelines for tourists in the area. |

### 7d) Human footprint and wilderness values

| | |
|---|---|
| WP 35 New Zealand | UNDERSTANDING CONCEPTS OF FOOTPRINT AND WILDERNESS RELATED TO PROTECTION OF THE ANTARCTIC ENVIRONMENT. This paper defines the terms "Footprint" and "Wilderness in the Antarctic" and proposes the possibility of outlining ways in which the CEP might consider more active management of wilderness according to the Environmental Principles set out in Article 3 of the Protocol. |

| IP 1<br>United States | TEMPORAL AND SPATIAL PATTERNS OF ANTHROPOGENIC DISTURBANCE AT McMURDO STATION, ANTARCTICA. This paper informs that the National Science Foundation has funded a long-term monitoring programme that examines the impacts of science and logistics at McMurdo Station, Antarctica's largest scientific base. |
|---|---|
| IP 2<br>United States | THE HISTORICAL DEVELOPMENT OF McMURDO STATION, ANTARCTICA, AN ENVIRONMENTAL PERSPECTIVE. Report based on a scientific publication on a long-term monitoring programme that examines the impacts of science and logistics at McMurdo Station. |
| IP 43<br>Uruguay | DISCOVERY OF HUMAN ACTIVITY REMAINS, PRE-1958 IN THE NORTH COAST OF THE KING GEORGE ISLAND / 25 DE MAYO. In a beach in the north coast of King George, there were found remains of human activity pre-1958, and these are being studied in order to start a multi-task research line, including the archaeology, anthropology, history and environmental protection areas. |
| IP 86<br>ASOC | EVOLUTION OF FOOTPRINT: SPATIAL AND TEMPORAL DIMENSIONS OF HUMAN ACTIVITIES. By providing several examples of cases of the study of human footprint in Antarctica, ASOC considers that human activities have not only a spatial dimension but also a temporal dimension and that, together, both dimensions define the evolution of footprint through time, which can expand or contract, and be more or less lasting depending on the case. |

### 7e) Marine Spatial Protection and Management

| SP 6<br>Secretariat | SUMMARY OF THE WORK OF THE CEP ON MARINE PROTECTED AREAS. This paper summarises discussions at the CEP on Marine Protected Areas, and analyses the cooperation between the CEP and CCAMLR through a review of CEP and Workshop reports and documents submitted to those meetings. |
|---|---|
| IP 56<br>IUCN | MARINE SPATIAL PROTECTION AND MANAGEMENT UNDER THE ANTARCTIC TREATY SYSTEM: NEW OPPORTUNITIES FOR IMPLEMENTATION AND COORDINATION. IUCN requires that Parties work closely with CCAMLR to identify relevant, broad-scale areas which are of interest to both bodies. |
| IP 90<br>ASOC | THE SOUTHERN OCEAN MPA AGENDA – MATCHING WORDS AND SPIRIT WITH ACTION. ASOC asks ATCPs and CCAMLR Members to make effective use of the upcoming CCAMLR Marine Protected Areas workshop to be held in August 2011 in Brest, France, to make progress on the work that is necessary to ensure that a representative system of MPAs can be designated by 2012. |

| | |
|---|---|
| IP 92<br>ASOC | THE ROSS SEA: A VALUABLE REFERENCE AREA TO ASSESS THE EFFECTS OF CLIMATE CHANGE. This paper proposes that the Ross Sea shelf and slope be included in the network of marine protected areas now being instituted in the Southern Ocean, and that Ross Sea foodweb and ecosystem processes should be protected from extractive activities that will compromise its value as a reference area. |

**7f) Other Annex V Matters**

| | |
|---|---|
| WP 32<br>Australia | ENHANCING THE ANTARCTIC PROTECTED AREAS DATABASE TO HELP ASSESS AND FURTHER DEVELOP THE PROTECTED AREAS SYSTEM. Following its proposal at CEP XIII and after intersessional consultation, Australia proposes that the CEP: agree that the APA Database be expanded to include further relevant information to be provided by proponents when submitting management plans; encourage proponents to make Area boundaries available in a digital format suitable for use in GIS where possible; and request the Secretariat to take the steps necessary to accommodate these changes. |
| WP 41<br>Chile and<br>Germany | FOURTH PROGRESS REPORT ON THE DISCUSSION OF THE INTERNATIONAL WORKING GROUP ABOUT POSSIBILITIES FOR ENVIRONMENTAL MANAGEMENT OF FILDES PENINSULA AND ARDLEY ISLAND. This paper informs on the progress made by the IWG on the management in Fildes peninsula and the pending tasks to finalise it. The Convenors propose to hold an IWG Meeting during CEP XIV in Buenos Aires in order to continue the discussion of all aspects related to the nature, scope and characteristics of a management scheme for the region. |
| WP 57<br>Russian<br>Federation | ON THE NEED OF CONSTANT MONITORING OF THE VALUES OF ANTARCTIC SPECIALLY PROTECTED AREAS AND ANTARCTIC SPECIALLY MANAGED AREAS. This paper suggests that, in order to know whether the measures taken are sufficient to preserve the living nature values protected in ASPAs or ASMAs, management decisions to be considered during the review of the management plans should be based on the data on the state of living nature values as a result of proper monitoring programmes. |
| IP 24<br>Germany | PROGRESS REPORT ON THE RESEARCH PROJECT "CURRENT ENVIRONMENTAL SITUATION AND MANAGEMENT PROPOSALS FOR THE FILDES REGION (ANTARCTIC)". This paper describes the antecedents of this research project and informs on the future steps. |
| IP 69<br>Australia | SUMMARY OF KEY FEATURES OF ANTARCTIC SPECIALLY MANAGED AREAS. This paper presents a summary of the key features of the seven existing Antarctic Specially Managed Areas, using information drawn from management plans. |

| IP 102 Russian Federation | PRESENT ZOOLOGICAL STUDY AT MIRNY STATION AREA AND AT ASPA No 127 "HASWELL ISLAND". This paper reports on zoological studies and monitoring programmes in the area since 1955, noting that sea mammals and birds prove to be sensitive indicators of environmental changes and primarily changes in the ocean ecosystem. |
|---|---|
| IP 109 Rep. of Korea | COOPERATION MANAGEMENT ACTIVITIES AT ASPAs IN 25 DE MAYO (KING GEORGE) ISLAND, SOUTH SHETLAND ISLANDS. This paper informs on joint activities between the Republic of Korea and Argentina to initiate a review of the environmental management in two ASPAs King George Island, South Shetland Islands: ASPA 132 and ASPA 171. |

## 8. CONSERVATION OF ANTARCTIC FLORA AND FAUNA

### 8a) Quarantine and Non-native Species

| WP 12 COMNAP and SCAR | RAISING AWARENESS OF NON-NATIVE SPECIES INTRODUCTIONS: WORKSHOP RESULTS AND CHECKLISTS FOR SUPPLY CHAIN MANAGERS. This paper informs on the results of a workshop held in 2010 which discussed the preliminary results of the IPY project "Aliens in Antarctica". COMNAP and SCAR encourage the CEP to consider the inclusion of the COMNAP/SCAR checklists into the proposed "Non-Native Species Manual" which is currently under discussion. |
|---|---|
| WP 34 New Zealand | REPORT OF THE INTERSESSIONAL CONTACT GROUP ON NON-NATIVE SPECIES 2010-2011. New Zealand reports on the second year of work of the ICG. The paper reports on the conclusion of the group of the overall objective and key guiding principles for Parties' actions to address risks posed by NNS. A NNS Manual is presented, containing generally applicable guidelines and resources to support the prevention and monitoring of and response to NNS introductions. |
| WP 53 SCAR | MEASURES TO REDUCE THE RISK OF NON-NATIVE SPECIES INTRODUCTIONS TO THE ANTARCTIC REGION ASSOCIATED WITH FRESH FOODS. SCAR informs on the development of simple practical measures to reduce the risk of introductions of non-native species into the Antarctic Treaty area via fresh foods, and requires comments on these guidelines as the basis for the development and eventual adoption of formal CEP guidelines via the Non-native Species Intersessional Contact Group. |
| IP 26 Germany | PROGRESS REPORT ON THE RESEARCH PROJECT "CURRENT ENVIRONMENTAL SITUATION AND MANAGEMENT PROPOSALS FOR THE FILDES REGION (ANTARCTIC)". This paper describes the preliminary results of the research project. |
| IP 32 France | REPORT ON IPY OSLO SCIENCE CONFERENCE SESSION ON NON-NATIVE SPECIES. The scientific outputs of the IPY Oslo Science Conference related to Non-Native Species in the Polar Regions are compiled in this Information Paper for contribution to the discussion of the Committee on this issue. |

| IP 50 UK & Uruguay | COLONISATION STATUS OF KNOWN NON-NATIVE SPECIES IN THE ANTARCTIC TERRESTRIAL ENVIRONMENT (UPDATED 2011). This paper reports on the developments of knowledge of terrestrial NNS and provides data on new locations reported and efforts necessary to eradicate those species. |
|---|---|
| IP 68 Australia & SCAR | ALIEN SPECIES DATABASE. Australia informs that the Antarctic Data Centre has added to the database an online record entry form and a facility to upload images of observations / collections. |

## 8b) Specially Protected Species

## 8c) Other Annex II Matters

| WP 38 Germany | ANTARCTIC DISCUSSION FORUM OF COMPETENT AUTHORITIES (DFCA) – IMPACTS OF UNDERWATER SOUND TO ANTARCTIC WATERS. Based on the importance of the threat of anthropogenic underwater sound for the marine ecosystem, Germany proposes to give fresh impetus to the DFCA by organising a Workshop to discuss the evaluation by Competent Authorities of this particular matter and report back to the CEP XV. |
|---|---|
| IP 27 Germany | PROGRESS REPORT ON THE RESEARCH PROJECT 'WHALE MONITORING ANTARCTICA'. This project is aimed to enhance the understanding of the distribution and abundance of Antarctic whales, and to provide reliable data to assess the impact of sound on these whales. |
| IP 29 Germany | POTENTIAL OF TECHNICAL MEASURES TO REDUCE THE ACOUSTICAL EFFECTS OF AIRGUNS. This paper reports on recent information on noise reduction for airgun based systems as well as possible alternative acoustic methods and equipment. |
| IP 33 SCAR | SCAR'S CODE OF CONDUCT FOR THE EXPLORATION AND RESEARCH OF SUBGLACIAL AQUATIC ENVIRONMENTS. SCAR provides guidance to the scientific community with interests in exploring and conducting research on and in Antarctic subglacial aquatic environments. |
| IP 53 SCAR | SCAR'S CODE OF CONDUCT FOR THE USE OF ANIMALS FOR SCIENTIFIC PURPOSES IN ANTARCTICA. SCAR's proposed code of conduct provides guiding principles to the scientific community for research involving animals. |
| IP 94 Norway | USE OF DOGS IN THE CONTEXT OF A COMMEMORATIVE CENTENNIAL EXPEDITION. This paper informs that the Norwegian authorities received and considered a notification for an expedition in Antarctica involving the use of dogs. This action is banned through Annex II and Norwegian legislation, and an exemption from the ban was not granted. |

| 9. Environmental Monitoring and Reporting | |
|---|---|
| WP 15 rev. 1 United Kingdom | Remote Sensing Techniques for Improved Monitoring of Environment and Climate Change in Antarctica. The United Kingdom informs on the advantages of remote sensing compared with other techniques for monitoring the Antarctic environment and studying the effects of regional climate change. It recommends the CEP to endorse the potential of this tool and to continue to explore further applications. |
| IP 8 COMNAP | COMNAP Energy Management Workshop. This document summarises the outcomes of the Workshop held in Buenos Aires in 2010 during the COMNAP Annual Meeting. |
| IP 35 Romania | Environmental Monitoring and Ecological Activities in Antarctica, 2010-2012. This paper reports on research that will focus on climate change consequences in both polar area bio/ecosystems. |
| IP 51 SCAR & Australia | The Southern Ocean Observing System (SOOS): An update. This paper presents an update to an IP presented last year, and summarises progress with the design and implementation of a Southern Ocean Observing System (SOOS) over the last year. |

| 10. Inspection reports. Progress to the International Polar Year | |
|---|---|
| WP 1 Japan | Inspection undertaken by Japan in accordance with Article VII of the Antarctic Treaty and Article XIV of the Protocol on Environmental Protection. This paper informs on the results of the inspections conducted by Japan of six Antarctic stations between January 29th and February 10th 2010. |
| WP 51 Australia | Australian Antarctic Treaty and Environmental Protocol inspections: January 2010 and January 2011. This paper reports on the results of the inspections conducted by Australia of three Antarctic stations and one Protected Area, and one aerial observation in 2010; and the inspections of three Antarctic stations in 2011. |
| IP 4 Japan | Japanese Inspection Report 2010. Full report of the inspection conducted by Japan in 2010. (see also WP 1) |
| IP 39 Australia | Australian Antarctic Treaty and Environmental Protocol inspections January 2010. Full report of the inspection. (see also WP 51) |
| IP 40 Australia | Australian Antarctic Treaty and Environmental Protocol inspections January 2011. Full report of the inspection. (see also WP 51) |

| 11. Cooperation with Other Organizations ||
|---|---|
| IP 10 COMNAP | Council of Managers of National Antarctic Programs (COMNAP) Report to ATCM XXXIII |
| IP 31 CCAMLR | Report by the SC-CAMLR Observer to the Fourteenth Meeting of the Committee for Environmental Protection. This paper reports on matters of common interest between the SC-CAMLR and the CEP, discussed at the last SC-CAMLR Meeting. |
| IP 54 SCAR | Summary of SCAR's Strategic Plan 2011-2016. SCAR describes its mission to be the leading non-governmental, international facilitator and advocate of research in and from the Antarctic region, to provide objective and authoritative scientific advice to the Antarctic Treaty and others, and to bring emerging issues to the attention of policy makers. |
| IP 57 CCAMLR | Report of the CEP Observer to SC-CAMLR's Working Group on Ecosystem Monitoring and Management (WG-EMM). This paper reports on matters of common interest between the SC-CAMLR WG-EMM and the CEP, discussed at the last Meeting. |

| 12. General Matters ||
|---|---|
| WP 28 Australia | Environmental issues related to the practicality of repair or remediation of environmental damage. In Decision 4 (2010) the ATCM requested the CEP to consider environmental issues related to the practicality of reparation or remediation of environmental damage in the circumstances of Antarctica. This paper briefly reviews relevant past discussions and identifies several suggested points for inclusion in the Committee's response to that Decision. |
| IP 48 Australia | Thala Valley Waste Removal. This paper provides a progress report on the removal of waste from the old Thala Valley waste disposal site near Casey station. |
| IP 49 Australia | Renewable Energy and Energy Efficiency Initiatives at Australia's Antarctic Stations. In response to Recommendation 4 of the 2010 ATME on Climate Change, this paper provides an overview of selected examples of Australia's energy management experience to date. |
| IP 61 SCAR | The SCAR Antarctic Climate Evolution (ACE) Programme. The SCAR ACE Programme represents the interests of a large land and marine geoscience research community focussing in deciphering the record of the onset and the response of the Antarctic ice sheets to past climate changes across a range of timescales. ACE coordinates the integration between geophysical and geological records of past ice sheet behavior and coupled climate, ocean, and ice sheet models. |

| IP 95<br>Netherlands | PAYING FOR ECOSYSTEM SERVICES OF ANTARCTICA? This paper describes the options for introducing payment for ecosystem schemes in Antarctica against the background of the concept of ecosystem services and the concept of Payment for Ecosystem Services (PES) with some general examples. |
|---|---|
| IP 127<br>Ukraine | THE CONSTRUCTION OF AN ORTHODOX CHAPEL AT VERNADSKY STATION. Ukraine informs on the construction process of the chapel and the environmental procedures followed in advance. |

### 13. ELECTION OF OFFICERS

### 14. PREPARATION FOR NEXT MEETING

| WP 8<br>Australia | PROPOSED SCHEDULE FOR THE 35TH ANTARCTIC TREATY CONSULTATIVE MEETING, HOBART, 2012. This paper requests the consideration of the Committee on a proposed schedule for the CEP XV. |
|---|---|

### 15. ADOPTION OF THE REPORT

### 16. CLOSING OF THE MEETING

**Appendix 1**

# Draft SGMP work plan for 2011/12

| Terms of Reference | Suggested tasks |
|---|---|
| ToR 1 to 3 | Review draft management plans referred by CEP for intersessional review and provide advice to proponents |
| ToR 4 and 5* | Work with relevant Parties to ensure progress on review of management plans overdue for five-yearly review* |
| | As appropriate, consider actions arising from ASMA workshop* |
| | Review and update SGMP work plan |
| Working Papers | Prepare report for CEP XV against SGMP ToR 1 to 3 |
| | Prepare report for CEP XV against SGMP ToR 4 and 5 |

**Appendix 2**

# Provisional Agenda for CEP XV

1. Opening of the Meeting
2. Adoption of the Agenda
3. Strategic Discussions on the Future Work of the CEP
4. Operation of the CEP
5. Climate Change Implications for the Environment: Strategic approach
6. Environmental Impact Assessment (EIA)
    a. Draft Comprehensive Environmental Evaluations
    b. Other EIA Matters
7. Area Protection and Management Plans
    a. Management Plans
    b. Historic Sites and Monuments
    c. Site Guidelines
    d. Human footprint and wilderness values
    e. Marine Spatial Protection and Management
    f. Other Annex V Matters
8. Conservation of Antarctic Flora and Fauna
    a. Quarantine and Non-native Species
    b. Specially Protected Species
    c. Other Annex II Matters
9. Environmental Monitoring and Reporting
10. Inspection Reports
11. Cooperation with Other Organisations
12. Repair and Remediation of Environment Damage
13. General Matters
14. Election of Officers
15. Preparation for Next Meeting
16. Adoption of the Report
17. Closing of the Meeting

**Appendix 3**

# CEP Five Year Work Plan

| Issue / Environmental Pressure Actions | CEP Priority | *Intersessional Period* | CEP XV 2012 | *Intersessional Period* | CEP XVI 2013 | *Intersessional Period* | CEP XVII 2014 | *Intersessional Period* | CEP XVIII 2015 | *Intersessional Period* | CEP XIX 2016 |
|---|---|---|---|---|---|---|---|---|---|---|---|
| **Introduction of non-native species** | 1 | NNS manual uploaded onto websites. SCAR lead informal group on draft guidelines for fresh food. COMNAP to provide advice | Discuss further preventive measures for inclusion in NNS manual including revised SCAR guidelines | Interested Members, experts, NAPs work on monitoring measures | Discuss further monitoring measures for inclusion in NNS manual | Interested members, experts, NAPs work on response measures | Discuss further response measures for inclusion in NNS manual | Prepare for review of manual--consider informal discussion group | Review non-native species manual | | |
| **Actions:** 1. Continue developing practical guidelines & resources for all Antarctic operators. 2. Continue advancing recommendations from climate change ATME. | | | | | | | | | | | |
| **Tourism and NGO activities** | 1 | NZ pursue feedback and prepare final draft of Report | Consideration of CEP report and other ATME outcomes | | | | | | | | |
| **Actions:** 1. Provide advice to ATCM as requested. 2. Advance recommendations from ship-borne tourism ATME. | | | | | | | | | | | |
| **Global Pressure: Climate Change** | 1 | UK and Norway lead development of methodology to classify ASPA vulnerability and risk. SCAR to participate | 1) Discuss the results of intersessional work on methodology with a view to presenting draft classification of (ASPAs, 2) progress on ATME recommendations | | Standing agenda item. SCAR provides yearly update | | Standing agenda item. SCAR provides yearly update | | Standing agenda item. SCAR provides update | | Standing agenda item. SCAR provides update |
| **Actions:** 1. Consider implications of climate change for management of Antarctic environment. 2. Advance recommendations from climate change ATME. | | | | | | | | | | | |

169

| Issue / Environmental Pressure Actions | CEP Priority | Intersessional Period | CEP XV 2012 | Intersessional Period | CEP XVI 2013 | Intersessional Period | CEP XVII 2014 | Intersessional Period | CEP XVIII 2015 | Intersessional Period | CEP XIX 2016 |
|---|---|---|---|---|---|---|---|---|---|---|---|
| **Processing new and revised protected / managed area management plans** | 1 | SGMP / conducts work as per agreed work plan. Members review & Experts advise on provisions and practices of ASMA Management Plans. Secretariat establish website links | Develop guidance for establishing ASMAs. Consideration of SGMP / report | SGMP / conducts work as per agreed work plan | Consideration of SGMP / report | SGMP / conducts work as per agreed work plan | Consideration of SGMP / report | SGMP / conducts work as per agreed work plan | Consideration of SGMP / report | SGMP / conducts work as per agreed work plan | Consideration of SGMP / report |
| **Actions:** 1. Refine the process for reviewing new and revised management plans. 2. Update existing guidelines. 3. Advance recommendations from climate change ATME. | | | | | | | | | | | |
| **Marine spatial protection and management** | 1 | 1. Send relevant papers to SC-CAMLR MPA workshop (Aug 2011). 2. CEP Observer to attend MPA Workshop and WG-EMM | Review CEP Observer reports to WG-EMM, MPA workshop and provide advice to SC-CAMLR | | Review outcome of CCAMLR MPA decisions and review SC-CAMLR Plan of Work for further coordination | | | | | | |
| **Actions:** 1. Cooperate with CCAMLR on Southern Ocean bioregionalisation and other common interests and agreed principles. 2. Identify and apply processes for spatial marine protection. 3. Advance recommendations from climate change ATME. | | | | | | | | | | | |
| **Operation of the CEP and Strategic Planning** | 1 | | Standing item Review and revise work plan as appropriate | | Standing item Review and revise work plan as appropriate | | Standing item Review and revise work plan as appropriate | | Standing item Review and revise work plan as appropriate | | 25th anniversary of Protocol. Review and revise work plan as appropriate |
| **Actions:** 1. Keep the 5 year plan up to date based on changing circumstances and ATCM requirements. 2. Identify opportunities for improving the effectiveness of the CEP. 3. Consider long-term objectives for Antarctica (50-100 years time). | | | | | | | | | | | |

| Issue / Environmental Pressure Actions | CEP Priority | Intersessional Period | CEP XV 2012 | Intersessional Period | CEP XVI 2013 | Intersessional Period | CEP XVII 2014 | Intersessional Period | CEP XVIII 2015 | Intersessional Period | CEP XIX 2016 |
|---|---|---|---|---|---|---|---|---|---|---|---|
| **Repair or Remediation of Environmental Damage** | 1 | Members prepare papers on dealing with legacy of past activities. SCAR, develop advice; COMNAP report on its experience. | Discuss content of advice to ATCM on environmental risk, repair and remediation | Possible ICG to develop advice. Members prepare further papers | Review year 1 work of possible ICG. | Possible ICG to develop advice | Provide advice to ATCM | | Secretariat requested to develop and maintain an inventory | | |
| **Actions:** 1. Develop advice in response to request from ATCM Decision 4 (2010). 2. Establish Antarctic-wide inventory of sites of past activity. 3. Consider guidelines for repair and remediation. | | | | | | | | | | | |
| **Human footprint / wilderness management** | 2 | Consideration by interested Parties | Discuss future actions based on papers including Annex 1 and Annex 5 measures | Secretariat summary report of information exchanged on inventory of past activities, with input from COMNAP? | Continue discussion of concepts and terms 'footprint' and 'wilderness' | | | | | | |
| **Actions:** 1. Develop an agreed understanding of the terms "footprint" and "wilderness". 2. Develop methods for improved protection of wilderness under Annexes I and V. | | | | | | | | | | | |
| **Maintain the list of Historic Sites and Monuments** | 2 | Secretariat update list of HSMs | Standing item. Progress on informal discussions on HSM | Secretariat update list of HSMs | Standing item | Secretariat update list of HSMs | Standing item | Secretariat update list of HSMs | Standing item | | |
| **Actions:** 1. Maintain the list and consider new proposals as they arise. 2. Consider strategic issues as necessary. | | | | | | | | | | | |
| **Monitoring and state of the environment reporting** | 2 | SCAR review | Report from SCAR regarding SC-ADM support for CEP work | | | | | | | | |
| **Actions:** 1. Identify key environmental indicators and tools. 2. Establish a process for reporting to the ATCM. 3. Advance recommendations from climate change ATME. | | | | | | | | | | | |

| Issue / Environmental Pressure Actions | CEP Priority | Intersessional Period | CEP XV 2012 | Intersessional Period | CEP XVI 2013 | Intersessional Period | CEP XVII 2014 | Intersessional Period | CEP XVIII 2015 | Intersessional Period | CEP XIX 2016 |
|---|---|---|---|---|---|---|---|---|---|---|---|
| **Exchange of Information** | 2 | Informal discussion lead by the Secretariat | Secretariat Report | | Secretariat Report | | Secretariat Report | | Secretariat Report | | Secretariat Report |
| **Actions:**<br>1. Assign to the Secretariat.<br>2. Monitor and facilitate easy use of the EIES. | | | | | | | | | | | |
| **Biodiversity knowledge** | 2 | SCAR prepare review of science since 2004 of biotic effects of underwater acoustic noise | Discussion of SCAR update on underwater noise | | | | | | | | |
| **Actions:**<br>1. Maintain awareness of threats to existing biodiversity.<br>2. Advance recommendations from climate change ATME | | | | | | | | | | | |
| **Site specific guidelines for tourist-visited sites** | 3 | | Standing agenda item; Parties to report on their reviews of site guidelines | | Standing agenda item; Parties to report on their reviews of site guidelines | | Standing agenda item; Parties to report on their reviews of site guidelines | | Standing agenda item; Parties to report on their reviews of site guidelines | | Standing agenda item; Parties to report on their reviews of site guidelines |
| **Actions:**<br>1. Review site specific guidelines as required.<br>2. Provide advice to ATCM as required. | | | | | | | | | | | |
| **Implementing and Improving the EIA provisions of Annex I** | 3 | Establish ICG to review draft CEEs as required | Consideration of ICG reports on draft CEE, as required | Establish ICG to review draft CEEs as required | Consideration of ICG reports on draft CEE, as required | Establish ICG to review draft CEEs as required | Consideration of ICG reports on draft CEE, as required | Establish ICG to review draft CEEs as required | Consideration of ICG reports on draft CEE, as required | Establish ICG to review draft CEEs as required | Consideration of ICG reports on draft CEE, as required |
| **Actions:**<br>1. Refine the process for considering CEEs and advising the ATCM accordingly.<br>2. Develop guidelines for assessing cumulative impacts.<br>3. Keep the EIA Guidelines under review.<br>4. Consider application of strategic environmental assessment in Antarctica.<br>5. Advance recommendations from climate change ATME | | | | | | | | | | | |

| Issue / Environmental Pressure Actions | CEP Priority | Intersessional Period | CEP XV 2012 | Intersessional Period | CEP XVI 2013 | Intersessional Period | CEP XVII 2014 | Intersessional Period | CEP XVIII 2015 | Intersessional Period | CEP XIX 2016 |
|---|---|---|---|---|---|---|---|---|---|---|---|
| **Specially protected species** | 3 | | | | | | | | | | |
| **Actions:** 1. Consider listing / de-listing proposals as required. | | | | | | | | | | | |
| **Overview of the protected areas system / EDA** | 3 | Secretariat modify database as in Resolution XXV WP32. Members begin working towards expansion of database for spatial data, Secretariat to maintain PA Database. | | | | | Discuss possible implications of an updated gap analysis based on EDA | | | | |
| **Actions:** 1. Apply the Environmental Domains Analysis (EDA) to enhance the protected areas system. 2. Advance recommendations from climate change ATME. 3. Maintain and develop Protected Area database. | | | | | | | | | | | |
| **Emergency response action and contingency planning** | 3 | Members consider experience and possible papers to progress advice to ATCM | Discuss work and relevance to Repair and Remediation issue in relation also to request from ATCM | Discuss Work | ICG | Discussion | ICG | Discussion | ICG | Final Recs to the ATCM | |
| **Actions:** 1. Advance recommendations from ship-borne tourism ATME. 2. Develop advice in response to request from ATCM Decision 4 (2010). | | | | | | | | | | | |
| **Updating the Protocol and reviewing Annexes** | 3 | | | | Requires CEP discussion on the need and aims for reviewing Protocol annexes | | | | | | |
| **Actions:** 1. Prepare a prioritised timetable for the review of the remaining annexes. | | | | | | | | | | | |
| **Inspections (Article 14 of the Protocol)** | 3 | | Standing item | | Standing item | | Standing item | | Standing item | | |

173

| Issue / Environmental Pressure Actions | CEP Priority | Intersessional Period | CEP XV 2012 | Intersessional Period | CEP XVI 2013 | Intersessional Period | CEP XVII 2014 | Intersessional Period | CEP XVIII 2015 | Intersessional Period | CEP XIX 2016 |
|---|---|---|---|---|---|---|---|---|---|---|---|
| **Actions:** 1. Review inspection reports as required. | | | | | | | | | | | |
| **Waste** | 3 | | COMNAP provides information for improved waste management | | | | COMNAP reviews information from 2006 waste management workshop | | | | |
| **Actions:** 1. Develop guidelines for best practice disposal of waste including human waste. | | | | | | | | | | | |
| **Energy management** | 4 | | | | | | | | | | |
| **Actions:** 1. Develop best-practice guidelines for energy management at stations and bases. | | | | | | | | | | | |
| **Outreach and education** | 4 | | [Pending ATCM 34 discussion] | | | | Dedicated time for discussion | | | | |
| **Actions:** 1. Review current examples and identify opportunities for greater education and outreach. | | | | | | | | | | | |

174

# 3. Appendices

# Declaration on Antarctic Cooperation on the Occasion of the 50th Anniversary of the Entry into Force of the Antarctic Treaty

On the occasion of the 50th Anniversary of the entry into force of the Antarctic Treaty on June 23, 1961, the Consultative Parties to the Antarctic Treaty,

**Noting** that 2011 is also the year of the 50th Anniversary of the first Antarctic Treaty Consultative Meeting and the 20th Anniversary of the opening for signature of the Protocol on Environmental Protection to the Antarctic Treaty,

**Reaffirming** the Washington Ministerial Declaration of 6 April 2009 on the 50th Anniversary of the signing of the Antarctic Treaty (ATCM XXXII),

**Highlighting** that the Consultative and Non-Consultative Parties have been consistently applying the provisions of the Antarctic Treaty, including Article IV, both individually and collectively, thus consolidating the culture of Antarctic international cooperation in peace and harmony enshrined in the Treaty,

**Affirming** that the Protocol on Environmental Protection to the Antarctic Treaty and its Annexes are playing a significant role in protecting the Antarctic environment and its dependent and associated ecosystems,

**Appreciating** the dynamic and pragmatic evolution of the Antarctic Treaty system that is focused on achieving concrete results, especially in the fields of scientific research and environmental protection,

**Noting** that the abovementioned international cooperation has contributed to furthering the principles and purposes of the Charter of the United Nations,

**Acknowledging** that this cooperation has contributed to the preservation of peace and the prevention of conflicts in the region,

**Recognising** that over the past 50 years the Antarctic Treaty has successfully met its objective that Antarctica "be used exclusively for peaceful purposes and not become the scene or object of international discord",

Hereby:

**Reaffirm** their continued commitment to upholding the Antarctic Treaty and all the other elements of the Antarctic Treaty system that have evolved since the Treaty's entry into force,

**Reaffirm also** their intention to continue their strong and effective cooperation under the Antarctic Treaty and all the other elements of the Antarctic Treaty system by:

- Continuously enhancing scientific research and exchanging and making freely available scientific observations and data from Antarctica as provided for in Article III of the Antarctic Treaty;

- Enhancing logistical and scientific cooperation among national Antarctic programmes while minimising environmental impact;

- Approving, in a timely manner, all Measures adopted by the Antarctic Treaty Consultative Meeting in accordance with the Antarctic Treaty;

- Proactively addressing future environmental, scientific, management and operational challenges including, where necessary, by further enhancing the Treaty system's regulatory framework;

- Pursuing a coherent approach within the Antarctic Treaty system;

- Continuing to identify and address emerging environmental challenges and strengthening the protection of the Antarctic environment and its dependent and associated ecosystems, particularly in relation to global climate change and human activities in the region, including tourism;

- Further refining and enhancing the exchange of information between Parties;

- Interacting with international governmental and non-governmental organisations that have an interest in the Antarctic Treaty area;

- Enhancing understanding in the wider community - including academia, decision makers and the general public - of the significance of international cooperation under the Antarctic Treaty system, its operation and the global importance of scientific research in Antarctica; and

- Appeal to States that are Antarctic Treaty Parties but not yet Party to the Protocol on Environmental Protection to the Antarctic Treaty, to become Party to the Protocol.

Buenos Aires, June 23rd 2011

# Preliminary Agenda for ATCM XXXV

1. Opening of the Meeting

2. Election of Officers and Creation of Working Groups

3. Adoption of the Agenda and Allocation of Items

4. Operational of the Antarctic Treaty System: Reports by Parties, Observers and Experts

5. Operation of the Antarctic Treaty System: General Matters

6. Operation of the Antarctic Treaty System: Review of the Secretariat's Situation

7. Development of a Multi-Year Strategic Work Plan

8. Report of the Committee for Environmental Protection

9. Liability: Implementation of Decision 4 (2010)

10. Safety and Operations in Antarctica

11. Tourism and Non-Governmental Activities in the Antarctic Treaty Area

12. Inspections under the Antarctic Treaty and the Environment Protocol

13. Science Issues, Scientific Cooperation and Facilitation, including the Legacy of the International Polar Year 2007-2008

14. Implications of Climate Change for Management of the Antarctic Treaty Area

15. Operational Issues

16. Education Issues

17. Exchange of Information

18. Biological Prospecting in Antarctica

19. Preparation of the 36th Meeting

20. Any Other Business

21. Adoption of the Final Report

# PART II

# Measures, Decisions and Resolutions

# 1. Measures

# Antarctic Specially Protected Area No 116
## (New College Valley, Caughley Beach, Cape Bird, Ross Island): Revised Management Plan

**The Representatives,**

*Recalling* Articles 3, 5 and 6 of Annex V to the Protocol on Environmental Protection to the Antarctic Treaty providing for the designation of Antarctic Specially Protected Areas ("ASPA") and approval of Management Plans for those Areas;

*Recalling*

- Recommendation XIII-8 (1985), which designated Caughley Beach as Site of Special Scientific Interest ("SSSI") No 10 and annexed a Management Plan for the site;

- Recommendation XIII-12 (1985), which designated New College Valley as Specially Protected Area ("SPA") No 20;

- Recommendation XVI-7 (1991), which extended the expiry date of SSSI 10 to 31 December 2001;

- Recommendation XVII-2 (1992), which annexed a Management Plan for SPA 20;

- Measure 1 (2000), which expanded SPA 20 to incorporate Caughley Beach, annexed a revised Management Plan for the Area, and provided that thereupon SSSI 10 shall cease to exist;

- Decision 1 (2002), which renamed and renumbered SPA 20 as ASPA 116;

- Measure 1 (2006), which adopted a revised Management Plan for ASPA 116;

*Recalling* that Recommendation XVI-7 (1991) and Measure 1 (2000) have not become effective, and that Recommendation XVII-2 (1992) was withdrawn by Measure 1 (2010);

*Recalling* that Recommendation XIII-12 (1985) and Recommendation XVI-7 (1991) are designated as no longer current by Decision 1 (2011);

*Noting* that the Committee for Environmental Protection has endorsed a revised Management Plan for ASPA 116;

*Desiring* to replace the existing Management Plan for ASPA 116 with the revised Management Plan;

**Recommend** to their Governments the following Measure for approval in accordance with paragraph 1 of Article 6 of Annex V to the Protocol on Environmental Protection to the Antarctic Treaty:

That:

1.  the revised Management Plan for Antarctic Specially Protected Area No 116 (New College Valley, Caughley Beach, Cape Bird, Ross Island), which is annexed to this Measure, be approved; and

2.  the prior Management Plans for ASPA 116, namely those annexed to Recommendation XIII-8 (1985), Measure 1 (2000) and Measure 1 (2006), shall cease to be effective.

# Antarctic Specially Protected Area No 120
## (Pointe-Géologie Archipelago, Terre Adélie):
## Revised Management Plan

**The Representatives,**

*Recalling* Articles 3, 5 and 6 of Annex V to the Protocol on Environmental Protection to the Antarctic Treaty providing for the designation of Antarctic Specially Protected Areas ("ASPA") and approval of Management Plans for those Areas;

*Recalling*

- Measure 3 (1995), which designated Pointe-Géologie Archipelago as Specially Protected Area ("SPA") No 24 and annexed a Management Plan for the Area;

- Decision 1 (2002), which renamed and renumbered SPA 24 as ASPA 120;

- Measure 2 (2005), which adopted a revised Management Plan for ASPA 120;

*Recalling* that Measure 3 (1995) has not become effective;

*Noting* that the Committee for Environmental Protection has endorsed a revised Management Plan for ASPA 120;

*Desiring* to replace the existing Management Plan for ASPA 120 with the revised Management Plan;

**Recommend** to their Governments the following Measure for approval in accordance with paragraph 1 of Article 6 of Annex V to the Protocol on Environmental Protection to the Antarctic Treaty:

That:

1.  the revised Management Plan for Antarctic Specially Protected Area No 120 (Pointe-Géologie Archipelago, Terre Adélie), which is annexed to this Measure, be approved;

2.  the Management Plan for ASPA 120 annexed to Measure 2 (2005) shall cease to be effective; and

3.  Measure 3 (1995), which has not become effective, be withdrawn.

# Antarctic Specially Protected Area No 122
## (Arrival Heights, Hut Point Peninsula, Ross Island): Revised Management Plan

**The Representatives,**

*Recalling* Articles 3, 5 and 6 of Annex V to the Protocol on Environmental Protection to the Antarctic Treaty providing for the designation of Antarctic Specially Protected Areas ("ASPA") and approval of Management Plans for those Areas;

*Recalling*

- Recommendation VIII-4 (1975), which designated Arrival Heights, Hut Point Peninsula, Ross Island as Site of Special Scientific Interest ("SSSI") No 2 and annexed a Management Plan for the site;

- Recommendation X-6 (1979), which extended the expiry date of SSSI 2 from 30 June 1981 to 30 June 1985;

- Recommendation XII-5 (1983), which extended the expiry date of SSSI 2 from 30 June 1985 to 31 December 1985;

- Recommendation XIII-7 (1985), which extended the expiry date of SSSI 2 from 31 December 1985 to 31 December 1987;

- Recommendation XIV-4 (1987), which extended the expiry date of SSSI 2 from 31 December 1987 to 31 December 1997;

- Resolution 3 (1996), which extended the expiry date of SSSI 2 from 31 December 1997 to 31 December 2000;

- Measure 2 (2000), which extended the expiry date of SSSI 2 from 31 December 2000 to 31 December 2005;

- Decision 1 (2002), which renamed and renumbered SSSI 2 as ASPA 122;

- Measure 2 (2004), which adopted a revised Management Plan for ASPA 122;

*Recalling* that Measure 2 (2000) was withdrawn by Measure 5 (2009);

*Recalling* that Recommendation VIII-4 (1975), Recommendation X-6 (1979), Recommendation XII-5 (1983), Recommendation XIII-7 (1985), Recommendation XIV-4 (1987), and Resolution 3 (1996) are designated as no longer current by Decision 1 (2011);

*Noting* that the Committee for Environmental Protection has endorsed a revised Management Plan for ASPA 122;

*Desiring* to replace the existing Management Plan for ASPA 122 with the revised Management Plan;

**Recommend** to their Governments the following Measure for approval in accordance with paragraph 1 of Article 6 of Annex V to the Protocol on Environmental Protection to the Antarctic Treaty:

That:

1. the revised Management Plan for Antarctic Specially Protected Area No 122 (Arrival Heights, Hut Point Peninsula, Ross Island), which is annexed to this Measure, be approved; and

2. the Management Plan for ASPA 122 annexed to Measure 2 (2004) shall cease to be effective.

# Antarctic Specially Protected Area No 126
## (Byers Peninsula, Livingston Island, South Shetland Islands): Revised Management Plan

**The Representatives,**

*Recalling* Articles 3, 5 and 6 of Annex V to the Protocol on Environmental Protection to the Antarctic Treaty providing for the designation of Antarctic Specially Protected Areas ("ASPA") and approval of Management Plans for those Areas;

*Recalling*

- Recommendation IV-10 (1966), which designated Byers Peninsula, Livingston Island, South Shetland Islands as Specially Protected Area ("SPA") No 10;

- Recommendation VIII-2 (1975), which terminated SPA 10, and Recommendation VIII-4 (1975), which redesignated the area as Site of Special Scientific Interest ("SSSI") No 6 and annexed the first Management Plan for the site;

- Recommendation X-6 (1979), which extended the expiry date of SSSI 6 from 30 June 1981 to 30 June 1985;

- Recommendation XII-5 (1983), which extended the expiry date of SSSI 6 from 30 June 1985 to 31 December 1985;

- Recommendation XIII-7 (1985), which extended the expiry date of SSSI 6 from 31 December 1985 to 31 December 1995;

- Recommendation XVI-5 (1991), which adopted a revised Management Plan for SSSI 6;

- Measure 3 (2001), which extended the expiry date of SSSI 6 from 31 December 1995 to 31 December 2005;

- Decision 1 (2002) which renamed and renumbered SSSI 6 as ASPA 126;

191

- Measure 1 (2002), which adopted a revised Management Plan for SSSI 6;

*Recalling* that Recommendation XVI-5 (1991) and Measure 3 (2001) have not become effective;

*Recalling* that Recommendation VIII-2 (1975), Recommendation X-6 (1979), Recommendation XII-5 (1983), Recommendation XIII-7 (1985) and Recommendation XVI-5 (1991) are designated as no longer current by Decision 1 (2011);

*Noting* that the Committee for Environmental Protection has endorsed a revised Management Plan for ASPA 122;

*Desiring* to replace the existing Management Plan for ASPA 126 with the revised Management Plan;

**Recommend** to their Governments the following Measure for approval in accordance with paragraph 1 of Article 6 of Annex V to the Protocol on Environmental Protection to the Antarctic Treaty:

That:

1. the revised Management Plan for Antarctic Specially Protected Area No 126 (Byers Peninsula, Livingston Island, South Shetland Islands), which is annexed to this Measure, be approved;

2. the prior Management Plans for ASPA 126, including the one annexed to Measure 1 (2002), shall cease to be effective; and

3. Recommendation XVI-5 (1991) and Measure 3 (2001), which have not become effective, be withdrawn.

# Antarctic Specially Protected Area No 127
## (Haswell Island): Revised Management Plan

**The Representatives,**

*Recalling* Articles 3, 5 and 6 of Annex V to the Protocol on Environmental Protection to the Antarctic Treaty providing for the designation of Antarctic Specially Protected Areas ("ASPA") and approval of Management Plans for those Areas;

*Recalling*

- Recommendation VIII-4 (1975), which designated Haswell Island as Site of Special Scientific Interest ("SSSI") No 7 and annexed a Management Plan for the site;

- Recommendation X-6 (1979), which extended the expiry date of SSSI 7 from 30 June 1981 to 30 June 1983;

- Recommendation XII-5 (1983), which extended the expiry date of SSSI 7 from 30 June 1983 to 31 December 1985;

- Recommendation XIII-7 (1985), which extended the expiry date of SSSI 7 from 31 December 1985 to 31 December 1991;

- Recommendation XVI-7 (1987), which extended the expiry date of SSSI 7 from 31 December 1991 to 31 December 2001;

- Measure 3 (2001), which extended the expiry date of SSSI 7 from 31 December 2001 to 31 December 2005;

- Decision 1 (2002), which renamed and renumbered SSSI 7 as ASPA 127;

- Measure 4 (2005), which extended the expiry date of the Management Plan of ASPA 127 from 31 December 2005 to 31 December 2010;

- Measure 1 (2006), which adopted a revised Management Plan for ASPA 127;

*Recalling* that Recommendation VIII-4 (1975), Recommendation X-6 (1979), Recommendation XII-5 (1983), Recommendation XIII-7 (1985) and Recommendation XVI-7 (1987) are designated as no longer current by Decision 1 (2011);

*Noting* that the Committee for Environmental Protection has endorsed a revised Management Plan for ASPA 127;

*Desiring* to replace the existing Management Plan for ASPA 127 with the revised Management Plan;

**Recommend** to their Governments the following Measure for approval in accordance with paragraph 1 of Article 6 of Annex V to the Protocol on Environmental Protection to the Antarctic Treaty:

That:

1. the revised Management Plan for Antarctic Specially Protected Area No 127 (Haswell Island), which is annexed to this Measure, be approved; and

2. the prior Management Plans for ASPA 127, namely those annexed to Recommendation VIII-4 (1975) and Measure 1 (2006), shall cease to be effective.

# Antarctic Specially Protected Area No 131
## (Canada Glacier, Lake Fryxell, Taylor Valley, Victoria Land): Revised Management Plan

**The Representatives,**

*Recalling* Articles 3, 5 and 6 of Annex V to the Protocol on Environmental Protection to the Antarctic Treaty providing for the designation of Antarctic Specially Protected Areas ("ASPA") and approval of Management Plans for those Areas;

*Recalling*

- Recommendation XIII-8 (1985), which designated Canada Glacier, Lake Fryxell, Taylor Valley, Victoria Land as Site of Special Scientific Interest ("SSSI") No 12 and annexed a Management Plan for the site;

- Recommendation XVI-7 (1987), which extended the expiry date of SSSI 12 to 31 December 2001;

- Measure 3 (1997), which adopted a revised Management Plan for SSSI 12;

- Decision 1 (2002), which renamed and renumbered SSSI 12 as ASPA 131;

- Measure 1 (2006), which adopted a revised Management Plan for ASPA 131;

*Recalling* that Measure 3 (1997) has not become effective;

*Recalling* that Recommendation XVI-7 (1987) has not become effective and that it is designated as no longer current by Decision 1 (2011);

*Noting* that the Committee for Environmental Protection has endorsed a revised Management Plan for ASPA 131;

*Desiring* to replace the existing Management Plan for ASPA 131 with the revised Management Plan;

**Recommend** to their Governments the following Measure for approval in accordance with paragraph 1 of Article 6 of Annex V to the Protocol on Environmental Protection to the Antarctic Treaty:

That:

1.  the revised Management Plan for Antarctic Specially Protected Area No 131 (Canada Glacier, Lake Fryxell, Taylor Valley, Victoria Land), which is annexed to this Measure, be approved;

2.  the prior Management Plans for ASPA 131, including the one annexed to Measure 1 (2006), shall cease to be effective; and

3.  Measure 3 (1997), which has not become effective, be withdrawn.

# Antarctic Specially Protected Area No 149
## (Cape Shirreff and San Telmo Island, Livingston Island, South Shetland Islands): Revised Management Plan

**The Representatives,**

*Recalling* Articles 3, 5 and 6 of Annex V to the Protocol on Environmental Protection to the Antarctic Treaty providing for the designation of Antarctic Specially Protected Areas ("ASPA") and approval of Management Plans for those Areas;

*Recalling*

- Recommendation IV-11 (1966), which designated Cape Sherriff and San Telmo Island, Livingston Island, South Shetland Islands as Specially Protected Area ("SPA") No 11;

- Recommendation XV-7 (1989), which terminated SPA 11 and redesignated the area as Site of Special Scientific Interest ("SSSI") No 32 and annexed a Management Plan for the site;

- Resolution 3 (1996), which extended the expiry date of SSSI 32 from 31 December 1999 to 31 December 2000;

- Measure 2 (2000), which extended the expiry date of SSSI 32 from 31 December 2000 to 31 December 2005;

- Decision 1 (2002), which renamed and renumbered SPA 11 as ASPA 149;

- Measure 2 (2005), which adopted a revised Management Plan for ASPA 149;

*Recalling* that Recommendation XV-7 (1989) and Measure 2 (2000) have not become effective, and that Measure 2 (2000) was withdrawn by Measure 5 (2009);

*Recalling* that Recommendation XV-7 (1989) and Resolution 3 (1996) are designated as no longer current by Decision 1 (2011);

197

*Noting* that the Committee for Environmental Protection has endorsed a revised Management Plan for ASPA 149;

*Desiring* to replace the existing Management Plan for ASPA 149 with the revised Management Plan;

**Recommend** to their Governments the following Measure for approval in accordance with paragraph 1 of Article 6 of Annex V to the Protocol on Environmental Protection to the Antarctic Treaty:

That:

1. the revised Management Plan for Antarctic Specially Protected Area No 149 (Cape Sheriff and San Telmo Island, Livingston Island, South Shetland Islands), which is annexed to this Measure, be approved; and

2. the Management Plan for ASPA 149 annexed to Measure 2 (2005) shall cease to be effective.

# Antarctic Specially Protected Area No 165
## (Edmonson Point, Wood Bay, Ross Sea):
## Revised Management Plan

**The Representatives,**

*Recalling* Articles 3, 5 and 6 of Annex V to the Protocol on Environmental Protection to the Antarctic Treaty providing for the designation of Antarctic Specially Protected Areas ("ASPA") and approval of Management Plans for those Areas;

*Recalling* Measure 1 (2006), which designated Edmonson Point, Wood Bay, Ross Sea as ASPA 165 and annexed a Management Plan for the Area;

*Noting* that the Committee for Environmental Protection has endorsed a revised Management Plan for ASPA 165;

*Desiring* to replace the existing Management Plan for ASPA 165 with the revised Management Plan;

**Recommend** to their Governments the following Measure for approval in accordance with paragraph 1 of Article 6 of Annex V to the Protocol on Environmental Protection to the Antarctic Treaty:

That:

1. the revised Management Plan for Antarctic Specially Protected Area No 165 (Edmonson Point, Wood Bay, Ross Sea), which is annexed to this Measure, be approved; and

2. the Management Plan for ASPA 165 annexed to Measure 1 (2006) shall cease to be effective.

# Antarctic Specially Protected Area No 167
## (Hawker Island, Vestfold Hills, Ingrid Christensen Coast, Princess Elizabeth Land, East Antarctica): Revised Management Plan

**The Representatives,**

*Recalling* Articles 3, 5 and 6 of Annex V to the Protocol on Environmental Protection to the Antarctic Treaty providing for the designation of Antarctic Specially Protected Areas ("ASPA") and approval of Management Plans for those Areas;

*Recalling* Measure 1 (2006), which designated Hawker Island, Vestfold Hills, Ingrid Christensen Coast, Princess Elizabeth Land, East Antarctica as ASPA 167 and annexed a Management Plan for the Area;

*Noting* that the Committee for Environmental Protection has endorsed a revised Management Plan for ASPA 167;

*Desiring* to replace the existing Management Plan for ASPA 167 with the revised Management Plan;

**Recommend** to their Governments the following Measure for approval in accordance with paragraph 1 of Article 6 of Annex V to the Protocol on Environmental Protection to the Antarctic Treaty:

That:

1.  the revised Management Plan for Antarctic Specially Protected Area No 167 (Hawker Island, Vestfold Hills, Ingrid Christensen Coast, Princess Elizabeth Land, East Antarctica), which is annexed to this Measure, be approved; and

2.  the Management Plan for ASPA 167 annexed to Measure 1 (2006) shall cease to be effective.

# Antarctic Specially Managed Area No 2
## (McMurdo Dry Valleys, Southern Victoria Land): Revised Management Plan

**The Representatives,**

*Recalling* Articles 4, 5 and 6 of Annex V to the Protocol on Environmental Protection to the Antarctic Treaty, providing for the designation of Antarctic Specially Managed Areas ("ASMA") and the approval of Management Plans for those Areas;

*Recalling* Measure 1 (2004), which designated McMurdo Dry Valleys, Southern Victoria Land as ASMA 2 and annexed a Management Plan for the Area;

*Noting* that the Committee for Environmental Protection has endorsed a revised Management Plan for ASMA 2;

*Desiring* to replace the existing Management Plan for ASMA 2 with the revised Management Plan;

**Recommend** to their Governments the following Measure for approval in accordance with paragraph 1 of Article 6 of Annex V to the Protocol on Environmental Protection to the Antarctic Treaty:

That:

1. the revised Management Plan for Antarctic Specially Managed Area No 2 (McMurdo Dry Valleys, Southern Victoria Land), which is annexed to this Measure, be approved; and

2. the Management Plan for ASMA 2 annexed to Measure 1 (2004) shall cease to be effective.

# Antarctic Historic Sites and Monuments:
## Monument to the Antarctic Treaty and Plaque

**The Representatives,**

*Recalling* the requirements of Article 8 of Annex V to the Protocol on Environmental Protection to the Antarctic Treaty to maintain a list of current Historic Sites and Monuments, and that such sites shall not be damaged, removed or destroyed;

*Recalling*

- Measure 3 (2003), which revised and updated the "List of Historic Sites and Monuments";

- Measure 3 (2007), which added Monument to the Antarctic Treaty and Plaque to the List of Historic Monuments and Sites annexed to Measure 3 (2003);

*Desiring* to modify the description of a Historic Site and Monument;

**Recommend** to their Governments the following Measure for approval in accordance with Paragraph 2 of Article 8 of Annex V to the Protocol on Environmental Protection to the Antarctic Treaty:

That the description of the Historic Monument and Site No 82 (Measure 3 (2007)) be modified in order to read as follows:

"No 82: Monument to the Antarctic Treaty and Plaque"

This Monument is located near the Frei, Bellingshausen and Escudero bases, Fildes Peninsula, King George Island. The plaque at the foot of the monument commemorates the signatories of the Antarctic Treaty. This Monument has 4 plaques in the official languages of the Antarctic Treaty. The plaques were installed in February 2011 and read as follows: "This historic monument, dedicated to the memory of the signatories of the Antarctic Treaty, Washington D.C., 1959, is also a reminder of the legacy of the First and Second International Polar Years (1882-1883 and 1932-1933) and of the International Geophysical Year (1957-1958) that preceded the Antarctic Treaty, and recalls the heritage of International Cooperation that led to the International Polar Year 2007-2008." This monument was designed and built by the American Joseph W. Pearson, who offered it to Chile. It was unveiled in 1999, on the occasion of the 40th anniversary of the signature of the Antarctic Treaty.".

# Antarctic Historic Sites and Monuments:
## No 1 Building at Great Wall Station

**The Representatives,**

*Recalling* the requirements of Article 8 of Annex V to the Protocol on Environmental Protection to the Antarctic Treaty to maintain a list of current Historic Sites and Monuments, and that such sites shall not be damaged, removed or destroyed;

*Recalling* Measure 3 (2003), which revised and updated the "List of Historic Sites and Monuments";

*Desiring* to add a further Historic Monument to the "List of Historic Sites and Monuments";

**Recommend** to their Governments the following Measure for approval in accordance with Paragraph 2 of Article 8 of Annex V to the Protocol on Environmental Protection to the Antarctic Treaty:

That the following Historic Monument be added to the "List of Historic Sites and Monuments" annexed to Measure 3 (2003):

"No 86: No 1 Building at Great Wall"

The No 1 Building, built in 1985 with a total floor space of 175 square metres, is located at the centre of the Chinese Antarctic Great Wall Station which is situated in Fildes Peninsula, King George Island, South Shetlands, West Antarctica. The Building marked the commencement of China devoting to Antarctic research in the 1980s, and thus it is of great significance in commemorating China's Antarctic expedition.

Location: 62°13'4" S, 58°57'44" W

Original proposing Party: CHINA

Party undertaking management: CHINA

# 2. Decisions

# Measures designated as no longer current

**The Representatives,**

*Recalling* Decision 3 (2002) and Decision 1 (2007), which established lists of measures* that were designated as spent or no longer current;

*Having reviewed* a number of measures on the subject of Protected Areas and General Environmental Issues;

*Recognising* that the measures listed in the Annex to this Decision are no longer current;

*Noting* that the Committee for Environmental Protection provided advice where asked;

**Decide:**

1. that the measures listed in the Annex to this Decision require no further action by the Parties; and

2. to request the Secretariat of the Antarctic Treaty to post the text of the measures that appear in the Annex to this Decision on its website in a way that makes clear that these measures are no longer current and that the Parties do not need to take any further action with respect to them.

---

*Note: measures previously adopted under Article IX of the Antarctic Treaty were described as Recommendations up to ATCM XIX (1995) and were divided into Measures, Decisions and Resolutions by Decision 1 (1995).

# 1. Management plans

- Recommendation IV-1
- Recommendation IV-2
- Recommendation IV-3
- Recommendation IV-8
- Recommendation IV-9
- Recommendation IV-13
- Recommendation VIII-2
- Recommendation VIII-4
- Recommendation X-5
- Recommendation XIII-9
- Recommendation XIII-10
- Recommendation XIII-12
- Recommendation XIII-14
- Recommendation XV-6
- Recommendation XV-7
- Recommendation XVI-4
- Recommendation XVI-5
- Recommendation XVI-8
- Measure 2 (1995)

# 2. Extension of expire dates of management plans

- Recommendation X-6
- Recommendation XII-5
- Recommendation XIII-7
- Recommendation XIV-4
- Recommendation XVI-7
- Resolution 7 (1995)
- Resolution 3 (1996)

### 3. Protected Areas general

- Recommendation VI-8
- Recommendation VII-9
- Resolution 5 (1996)

### 4. Environmental Impact Assessment

- Recommendation XII-3
- Recommendation XIV-2
- Resolution 6 (1995)
- Resolution 1 (1999)

### 5. Conservation of Antarctic fauna and flora

- Recommendation I-VIII
- Recommendation II-II
- Recommendation III-8
- Recommendation III-10
- Recommendation VI-9
- Recommendation IV-16
- Recommendation IV-17
- Recommendation IV-19
- Recommendation VII- 5

### 6. Waste disposal and management

- Recommendation XII-4
- Recommendation XIII-4
- Recommendation XV-3

### 7. Prevention of marine pollution

- Recommendation IX-6
- Recommendation X-7
- Recommendation XV-4

## 8. Precursors of the Environment Protocol

- Recommendation VIII-11
- Recommendation VIII-13
- Recommendation IX-5
- Recommendation XV-1

## 9. SCAR advice on environmental issues

- Recommendation VI-4
- Recommendation VII-1
- Recommendation X-4

## 10. Liability issues

- Decision 3 (1998)
- Decision 3 (2001)

## 11. Other environmental matters

- Resolution 4 (1995)
- Resolution 4 (1999)

# Revised Rules of Procedure for the Antarctic Treaty Consultative Meeting (2011); Revised Rules of Procedure for the Committee for Environmental Protection (2011); Guidelines for the Submission, Translation and Distribution of Documents for the ATCM and the CEP

**The Representatives,**

*Acknowledging* the value of information exchanged in official documents circulated between participants in the Antarctic Treaty Consultative Meeting ("ATCM") and the Committee on Environmental Protection ("CEP");

*Recalling*;

- Decision 1 (2008) containing the Revised Rules of Procedure of the ATCM;

- Decision 3 (2009) containing the Guidelines for the Submission and Handling of Documents for the ATCM and the CEP;

- Decision 3 (2010) containing the Revised Rules for Procedure for the CEP;

*Considering* that the efficiency of meetings could be enhanced by the establishment of a new category of official documents to allow the formal exchange of information that does not require introduction or discussion during meetings;

*Considering* that timely submission of meeting documents can enhance the effectiveness of the ATCM and CEP by ensuring that the Parties have sufficient time to develop their positions for the meeting;

*Considering* also that the Consultative Parties should be able to provide accurate, timely, substantial and up-to-date information to international organisations having a scientific or technical interest in Antarctica about their cooperation as well as the achievements and functioning of the Antarctic Treaty System;

*Noting* the need to update the ATCM and CEP Rules of Procedure and the Guidelines to reflect changes to the submission and handling of official documents;

**Decide:**

1. that the Revised Rules of Procedure of the Antarctic Treaty Consultative Meeting (2011) annexed to this Decision (Annex 1) shall replace the Revised Rules of Procedure (2008) attached to Decision 1 (2008);

2. that the Revised Rules of Procedure for the Committee for Environmental Protection (2011) annexed to this Decision (Annex 2) shall replace the Revised Rules of Procedure for the Committee for Environmental Protection (2010) attached to Decision 3 (2010);

3. that the Guidelines for the Submission, Translation and Distribution of Documents for the ATCM and the CEP appended to Decision 3 (2009) are no longer current; and

4. that Decision 1 (2008) and Decision 3 (2010) are no longer current.

# Revised Rules of Procedure (2011)

(1) Meetings held pursuant to Article IX of the Antarctic Treaty shall be known as Antarctic Treaty Consultative Meetings. Contracting Parties entitled to participate in those Meetings shall be referred to as "Consultative Parties"; other Contracting Parties which may have been invited to attend those Meetings shall be referred to as "non-Consultative Parties". The Executive Secretary of the Secretariat of the Antarctic Treaty shall be referred to as the "Executive Secretary".

(2) The Representatives of the Commission for the Conservation of Antarctic Marine Living Resources, the Scientific Committee on Antarctic Research and the Council of Managers of National Antarctic Programs, invited to attend those Meetings in accordance with Rule 31, shall be referred to as "Observers".

**Representation**

(3) Each Consultative Party shall be represented by a delegation composed of a Representative and such Alternate Representatives, Advisers and other persons as each State may deem necessary. Each non-Consultative Party which has been invited to attend a Consultative Meeting shall be represented by a delegation composed of a Representative and such other persons as it may deem necessary within such numerical limit as may from time to time be determined by the Host Government in consultation with the Consultative Parties. The Commission for the Conservation of Antarctic Marine Living Resources, the Scientific Committee on Antarctic Research and the Council of Managers of National Antarctic Programs shall be represented by their respective Chairman or President, or other persons appointed to this end. The names of members of delegations and of the observers shall be communicated to the Host Government prior to the opening of the Meeting.

(4) The order of precedence of the delegations shall be in accordance with the alphabet in the language of the Host Government, all delegations of non-Consultative Parties following after those of Consultative Parties, and all delegations of observers following after non-Consultative Parties.

**Officers**

(5) A Representative of the Host Government shall be the Temporary Chairman of the Meeting and shall preside until the Meeting elects a Chairman.

(6) At its inaugural session, a Chairman from one of the Consultative Parties shall be elected. The other Representatives of Consultative Parties shall serve as Vice-Chairmen of the Meeting in order of precedence. The Chairman normally shall preside at all plenary sessions. If he is absent from any session or part thereof, the Vice-Chairmen, rotating on the basis of the order of precedence as established by Rule 4, shall preside during each such session.

**Secretariat**

(7) The Executive Secretary shall act as Secretary to the Meeting. He or she shall be responsible, with the assistance of the Host Government, for providing secretariat services for the meeting, as provided in Article 2 of Measure 1 (2003), as provisionally applied by Decision 2 (2003) until Measure 1 becomes effective.

**Sessions**

(8) The opening plenary session shall be held in public, other sessions shall be held in private, unless the Meeting shall determine otherwise.

**Committees and Working Groups**

(9) The Meeting, to facilitate its work, may establish such committees as it may deem necessary for the performance of its functions, defining their terms of reference.

(10) The committees shall operate under the Rules of Procedure of the Meeting, except where they are inapplicable.

(11) Working Groups may be established by the Meeting or its committees to deal with various agenda items. The Chair(s) of the Working Group(s) will be appointed at the beginning of the Meeting or committee meeting. The Chair(s) will serve no more than four consecutive Meetings or committee meetings, unless otherwise decided. At the conclusion of each Meeting, the Meeting may decide as a preliminary matter which Working Group(s) are proposed for the subsequent Meeting.

**Conduct of Business**

(12) A quorum shall be constituted by two-thirds of the Representatives of Consultative Parties participating in the Meeting.

(13) The Chairman shall exercise the powers of his office in accordance with customary practice. He shall see to the observance of the Rules of Procedure and the maintenance of proper order. The Chairman, in the exercise of his functions, remains under the authority of the Meeting.

(14) Subject to Rule 28, no Representative may address the Meeting without having previously obtained the permission of the Chairman and the Chairman shall call upon speakers in the order in which they signify their desire to speak. The Chairman may call a speaker to order if his remarks are not relevant to the subject under discussion.

(15) During the discussion of any matter, a Representative of a Consultative Party may rise to a point of order and the point of order shall be decided immediately by the Chairman in accordance with the Rules of Procedure. A Representative of a Consultative Party may appeal against the ruling of the Chairman. The appeal shall be put to a vote immediately, and the Chairman's ruling shall stand unless over-ruled by a majority of the Representatives of Consultative Parties present and voting. A Representative

of a Consultative Party rising to a point of order shall not speak on the substance of the matter under discussion.

(16) The Meeting may limit the time to be allotted to each speaker, and the number of times he may speak on any subject. When the debate is thus limited and a Representative has spoken his allotted time, the Chairman shall call him to order without delay.

(17) During the discussion of any matter, a Representative of a Consultative Party may move the adjournment of the debate on the item under discussion. In addition to the proposer of the motion, Representatives of two Consultative Parties may speak in favour of, and two against, the motion, after which the motion shall be put to the vote immediately. The Chairman may limit the time to be allowed to speakers under this Rule.

(18) A Representative of a Consultative Party may at any time move the closure of the debate in the item under discussion, whether or not any other Representative has signified his wish to speak. Permission to speak on the closure of the debate shall be accorded only to Representatives of two Consultative Parties opposing the closure, after which the motion shall be put to the vote immediately. If the Meeting is in favour of the closure, the Chairman shall declare the closure of the debate. The Chairman may limit the time to be allowed to speakers under this Rule. (This Rule shall not apply to debate in committees.)

(19) During the discussion of any matter, a Representative of a Consultative Party may move the suspension or adjournment of the Meeting. Such motions shall not be debated, but shall be put to the vote immediately. The Chairman may limit the time to be allowed to the speaker moving the suspension or adjournment of the Meeting.

(20) Subject to Rule 15, the following motions shall have precedence in the following order over all other proposals or motions before the Meeting:

    (a)   to suspend the Meeting;

    (b)   to adjourn the Meeting;

    (c)   to adjourn the debate on the item under discussion;

    (d)   for the closure of the debate on the item under discussion.

(21) Decisions of the Meeting on all matters of procedure shall be taken by a majority of the Representatives of Consultative Parties participating in the Meeting, each of whom shall have one vote.

## Languages

(22) English, French, Russian and Spanish shall be the official languages of the Meeting.

(23) Any Representative may speak in a language other than the official languages. However, in such cases he shall provide for interpretation into one of the official languages.

**Measures, Decisions, and Resolutions and Final Report**

(24) Without prejudice to Rule 21, Measures, Decisions and Resolutions, as referred to in Decision 1 (1995), shall be adopted by the Representatives of all Consultative Parties present and will thereafter be subject to the provisions of Decision 1 (1995).

(25) The final report shall also contain a brief account of the proceedings of the Meeting. It will be approved by a majority of the Representatives of Consultative Parties present and shall be transmitted by the Executive Secretary to Governments of all Consultative and non-Consultative Parties which have been invited to take part in the Meeting for their consideration.

(26) Notwithstanding Rule 25, the Executive Secretary, immediately following the closure of the Consultative Meeting, shall notify all Consultative Parties of all Measures, Decisions and Resolutions taken and send them authenticated copies of the definitive texts in an appropriate language of the Meeting. In respect to a Measure adopted under the procedures of Article 6 or 8 of Annex V of the Protocol, the respective notification shall also include the time period for approval of that Measure.

**Non-Consultative Parties**

(27) Representatives of non-Consultative Parties, if invited to attend a Consultative Meeting, may be present at:

    (a)   all plenary sessions of the Meeting; and

    (b)   all formal Committees or Working Groups, comprising all Consultative Parties, unless a Representative of a Consultative Party requests otherwise in any particular case.

(28) The relevant Chairman may invite a Representative of a non-Consultative Party to address the Meeting, Committee or Working group which he is attending, unless a Representative of a Consultative Party requests otherwise. The Chairman shall at any time give priority to Representatives of Consultative Parties who signify their desire to speak and may, in inviting Representatives of non-Consultative Parties to address the Meeting, limit the time to be allotted to each speaker and the number of times he may speak on any subject.

(29) Non-Consultative Parties are not entitled to participate in the taking of decisions.

(30)

    (a)   Non-Consultative Parties may submit documents to the Secretariat for distribution to the Meeting as information documents. Such documents shall be relevant to matters under Committee consideration at the Meeting.

    (b)   Unless a Representative of a Consultative Party requests otherwise such documents shall be available only in the language or languages in which they were submitted.

## Antarctic Treaty System Observers

(31) The observers referred to in Rule 2 shall attend the Meetings for the specific purpose of reporting on:

    (a)   in the case of the Commission for the Conservation of Antarctic Marine Living Resources, developments in its area of competence.

    (b)   in the case of the Scientific Committee on Antarctic Research:

        (i) the general proceedings of SCAR;

        (ii) matters within the competence of SCAR under the Convention for the Conservation of Antarctic Seals;

        (iii) such publications and reports as may have been published or prepared in accordance with Recommendations IX-19 and VI-9 respectively.

    (c)   in the case of the Council of Managers of National Antarctic Programs, the activities within its area of competence.

(32) Observers may be present at:

    (a)   the plenary sessions of the Meeting at which the respective Report is considered;

    (b)   formal committees or working groups, comprising all Contracting Parties at which the respective Report is considered, unless a Representative of a Consultative Party requests otherwise in any particular case.

(33) Following the presentation of the pertinent Report, the relevant Chairman may invite the observer to address the Meeting at which it is being considered once again, unless a Representative of a Consultative Party requests otherwise. The Chairman may allot a time limit for such interventions.

(34) Observers are not entitled to participate in the taking of decisions.

(35) Observers may submit their Report and/or documents relevant to matters contained therein to the Secretariat, for distribution to the Meeting as working papers.

## Agenda for Consultative Meetings

(36) At the end of each Consultative Meeting, the Host Government of that Meeting shall prepare a preliminary agenda for the next Consultative Meeting. If approved by the Meeting, the preliminary agenda or the next Meeting shall be annexed to the Final Report of the Meeting.

(37) Any Contracting Party may propose supplementary items for the preliminary agenda by informing the Host Government for the forthcoming Consultative Meeting no later than 180 days before the beginning of the Meeting; each proposal shall be accompanied by an explanatory memorandum. The Host Government shall draw the attention of all Contracting Parties to this Rule no later than 210 days before the Meeting.

(38) The Host Government shall prepare a provisional agenda for the Consultative Meeting. The provisional agenda shall contain:

    (a)   all items on the preliminary agenda decided in accordance with Rule 36; and

    (b)   all items the inclusion of which has been requested by a Contracting Party pursuant to Rule 37.

Not later than 120 days before the Meeting, the Host Government shall transmit to all the Contracting Parties the provisional agenda, together with explanatory memoranda and any other papers related thereto.

### Experts from International Organisations

(39) At the end of each Consultative Meeting, the Meeting shall decide which international organisations having a scientific or technical interest in Antarctica shall be invited to designate an expert to attend the forthcoming Meeting in order to assist it in its substantive work.

(40) Any Contracting Party may thereafter propose that an invitation be extended to other international organisations having a scientific or technical interest in Antarctica to assist the Meeting in its substantive work; each such proposal shall be submitted to the Host Government for that Meeting not later than 180 days before the beginning of the Meeting and shall be accompanied by a memorandum setting out the basis for the proposal.

(41) The Host Government shall transmit these proposals to all Contracting Parties in accordance with the procedure in Rule 38. Any Consultative Party which wishes to object to a proposal shall do so not less than 90 days before the Meeting.

(42) Unless such an objection has been received, the Host Government shall extend invitations to international organisations identified in accordance with Rules 39 and 40 and shall request each international organisation to communicate the name of the designated expert to the Host Government prior to the opening of the Meeting. All such experts may attend the Meeting during consideration of all items, except for those items relating to the operation of the Antarctic Treaty System which are identified by the previous Meeting or upon adoption of the agenda.

(43) The relevant Chairman, with the agreement of all the Consultative Parties, may invite an expert to address the meeting he is attending. The Chairman shall at any time give priority to Representatives of Consultative Parties or non-Consultative Parties or Observers referred to in Rule 31 who signify their desire to speak, and may in inviting an expert to address the Meeting limit the time to be allotted to him and the number of times he may speak on any subject.

(44) Experts are not entitled to participate in the taking of decisions.

(45)

    (a)   Experts may, in respect of the relevant agenda item, submit documents to the Secretariat for distribution to the Meeting as information documents.

    (b)   Unless a Representative of a Consultative Party requests otherwise, such documents shall be available only in the language or languages in which they were submitted.

## Intersessional Consultations

(46) Intersessionally, the Executive Secretary shall, within his/her competence as established under Measure 1 (2003) and associated instruments that govern the operation of the Secretariat, consult the Consultative Parties, when legally required to do so under relevant instruments of the ATCM and when the exigencies of the circumstances require action to be taken before the opening of the next ATCM, using the following procedure:

    (a)   The Executive Secretary shall transmit the relevant information and any proposed action to all Consultative Parties through contact persons designated by them, indicating an appropriate date by which responses are requested;

    (b)   The Executive Secretary shall ensure that all Consultative Parties acknowledge the receipt of such transmission, and shall also ensure the list of contact persons is current;

    (c)   Each Consultative Party shall consider the matter and communicate their reply, if any, to the Executive Secretary through their respective contact person by the specified date;

    (d)   The Executive Secretary after informing the Consultative Parties of the result of the consultations, may proceed to take the proposed action if no Consultative Party has objected; and

    (e)   The Executive Secretary shall keep a record of the intersessional consultations, including their results and the actions taken by him/her and shall reflect these results and actions in his/her report to the ATCM for its review.

(47) Intersessionally, when a request for information about the activities of the ATCM is received from an international organisation having a scientific or technical interest in Antarctica, the Executive Secretary shall coordinate a response, using the following procedure:

    (a)   The Executive Secretary shall transmit the request and a first draft response to all Consultative Parties through contact persons designated by them, proposing to answer the request, and including an appropriate date by which Consultative Parties should *either* (1) indicate that it would not be appropriate to answer, *or* (2) provide comments to the first draft response.

        The date shall give a reasonable amount of time to provide comments, taking into account any deadlines set by the initial requests for information.

If a Consultative Party indicates that a response would not be appropriate, the Executive Secretary shall send only a formal response, acknowledging the request without going into the substance of the matter.

(b) If there is no objection to proceeding and if comments are provided before the date specified in the transmission referred to in paragraph (a) above, the Executive Secretary shall revise the response in light of the comments and transmit the revised response to all Consultative Parties, including an appropriate date by which reactions are requested;

(c) If any further comments are provided before the date specified in the transmission referred to in paragraph (b) above, the Executive Secretary shall repeat the procedure referred to in paragraph (b) above until no further comments are provided;

(d) If no comments are provided before the date specified in a transmission referred to in paragraph (a), (b) or (c) above, the Executive Secretary shall circulate a final version and shall request both an active digital "read"-confirmation and an active digital "accept"-confirmation from each Consultative Party, suggesting a date by which the "accept"-confirmation should be received. The Executive Secretary shall keep the Consultative Parties informed about the progress of received confirmations.

After receipt of "accept"-confirmations from all Consultative Parties the Executive Secretary shall sign and send the response to the international organisation concerned, on behalf of all Consultative Parties, and shall provide a copy of the signed response to all Consultative Parties.

(e) Any Consultative Party may, at any stage of this process, ask for more time for consideration.

(f) Any Consultative Party may, at any stage of this process, indicate that it would not be appropriate to respond to the request. In this case the Executive Secretary shall send only a formal response, acknowledging the request without going into the substance of the matter.

**Meeting Documents**

(48) Working Papers shall refer to papers submitted by Consultative Parties that require discussion and action at a Meeting and papers submitted by Observers referred to in Rule 2.

(49) Secretariat Papers shall refer to papers prepared by the Secretariat pursuant to a mandate established at a Meeting, or which would, in the view of the Executive Secretary, help inform the Meeting or assist in its operation.

(50) Information Papers shall refer to:

- Papers submitted by Consultative Parties or Observers that provide information in support of a Working Paper or that are relevant to discussions at a Meeting;

- Papers submitted by Non-Consultative Parties that are relevant to discussions at a Meeting; and
- Papers submitted by Experts that are relevant to discussions at a Meeting.

(51) Background Papers shall refer to papers submitted by any participant that will not be introduced in a Meeting, but that are submitted for the purpose of formally providing information.

(52) Procedures for the submission, translation and distribution of documents are annexed to these Rules of Procedure.

**Amendments**

(53) These Rules of Procedure may be amended by a two-thirds majority of the Representatives of Consultative Parties participating in the Meeting. This Rule shall not apply to Rules 24, 27, 29, 34, 39-42, 44, and 46, amendments of which shall require the approval of the Representatives of all Consultative Parties present at the Meeting.

**Annex**

## Procedures for the Submission, Translation and Distribution of Documents for the ATCM and the CEP

1. These procedures apply to the distribution and translation of official papers for the Antarctic Treaty Consultative Meeting (ATCM) and for the Committee on Environmental Protection (CEP) as defined in their respective Rules of Procedure. These papers consist of Working Papers, Secretariat Papers, Information Papers and Background Papers.

2. Documents to be translated are Working Papers, Secretariat Papers, reports submitted to the ATCM by ATCM Observers and invited Experts according to the provisions of Recommendation XIII-2, reports submitted to the ATCM in relation to Article III-2 of the Antarctic Treaty, and Information Papers that a Consultative Party requests be translated. Background Papers will not be translated.

3. Papers that are to be translated, with the exception of the reports of Intersessional Contact Groups (ICG) convened by the ATCM or CEP, Chair Reports from Antarctic Treaty Meetings of Experts, and the Secretariat's Report and Programme, should not exceed 1500 words. When calculating the length of a paper, proposed Measures, Decisions and Resolutions and their attachments are not included.

4. Papers that are to be translated should be received by the Secretariat no later than 45 days before the Consultative Meeting. If any such paper is submitted later than 45 days before the Consultative Meeting, it may only be considered if no Consultative Party objects.

5. The Secretariat should receive Information Papers for which no translation has been requested and Background Papers that participants wish to be listed in the Final Report no later than 30 days before the Meeting.

6. The Secretariat will indicate on each document submitted by a Contracting Party, an Observer, or an Expert the date it was submitted.

7. When a revised version of a Paper made after its initial submission is resubmitted to the Secretariat for translation, the revised text should indicate clearly the amendments that have been incorporated.

8. The Papers should be transmitted to the Secretariat by electronic means and will be uploaded to the ATCM website established by the Secretariat. Working Papers received before the 45 day limit should be uploaded as soon as possible and in any case not later than 30 days before the Meeting. Papers will be uploaded initially to the password protected section of the website, and moved to the non-password protected part once the Meeting has concluded.

9.   Parties may agree to present any paper for which a translation has not been requested to the Secretariat during the Meeting for translation.

10.  No paper submitted to the ATCM should be used as the basis for discussion at the ATCM or at the CEP unless it has been translated into the four official languages.

11.  Within six months of the end of the Consultative Meeting the Secretariat will circulate through diplomatic channels and also post on the ATCM website home page the Final Report of that Meeting in the four official languages.

# Revised Rules of Procedure for the Committee for Environmental Protection (2011)

*Rule 1*

Where not otherwise specified the Rules of Procedure for the Antarctic Treaty Consultative Meeting shall be applicable.

*Rule 2*

For the purposes of these Rules of Procedure:

(a)  the expression "Protocol" means the Protocol on Environmental Protection to the Antarctic Treaty, signed in Madrid on 4 October, 1991;

(b)  the expression "the Parties" means the Parties to the Protocol;

(c)  the expression "Committee" means the Committee for Environmental Protection as defined in Article 11 of the Protocol; and

(d)  the expression "Secretariat" means the Secretariat of the Antarctic Treaty.

## Part I Representatives and Experts

*Rule 3*

Each Party to the Protocol is entitled to be a member of the Committee and to appoint a representative who may be accompanied by experts and advisers with suitable scientific, environmental or technical competence.

Before each meeting of the Committee each member of the Committee shall, as early as possible, notify the Host Government of that meeting of the name and designation of each representative, and before or at the beginning of the meeting, the name and designation of each expert and adviser.

## Part II Observers and Consultation

*Rule 4*

Observer status in the Committee shall be open to:

(a)  any Contracting Party to the Antarctic Treaty which is not a Party to the Protocol;

(b)  the President of the Scientific Committee on Antarctic Research, the Chairman of the Scientific Committee for the Conservation of Antarctic Marine Living

Resources and the Chairman of the Council of Managers of National Antarctic Programmes, or their nominated Representatives;

(c) subject to the specific approval of the Antarctic Treaty Consultative Meeting, other relevant scientific, environmental and technical organisations which can contribute to the work of the Committee.

*Rule 5*

Before each meeting of the Committee each observer shall, as early as possible, notify the Host Government of that meeting of the name and designation of its representative attending the meeting.

*Rule 6*

Observers may participate in the discussions, but shall not participate in the taking of decisions.

*Rule 7*

In carrying out its functions the Committee shall, as appropriate, consult with the Scientific Committee on Antarctic Research, the Scientific Committee for the Conservation of Antarctic Marine Living Resources, the Council of Managers of National Antarctic Programmes and other relevant scientific, environmental and technical organisations.

*Rule 8*

The Committee may seek the advice of experts as required on an *ad hoc* basis.

## Part III Meetings

*Rule 9*

The Committee shall meet once a year, generally and preferably in conjunction with the Antarctic Treaty Consultative Meeting and at the same location. With the agreement of the ATCM, and in order to fulfill its functions, the Committee may also meet between annual meetings.

The Committee may establish informal open-ended contact groups to examine specific issues and report back to the Committee.

Open-ended contact groups established to undertake work during intersessional periods shall operate as follows:

(a) where appropriate, the contact group coordinator shall be agreed by the Committee during its meeting and noted in its final report;

(b)   where appropriate, the terms of reference for the contact group shall be agreed by the Committee and included in its final report;

(c)   where appropriate, the modes of communication for the contact group, such as e-mail, the online discussion forum maintained by the Secretariat and informal meetings, shall be agreed by the Committee and included in its final report;

(d)   representatives who wish to be involved in a contact group shall register their interest with the coordinator through the discussion forum, by e-mail or by other appropriate means;

(e)   the coordinator shall use appropriate means to inform all group members of the composition of the contact group;

(f)   all correspondence shall be made available to all members of the contact group in a timely manner; and

(g)   when providing comments, members of the contact group shall state for whom they are speaking.

The Committee may also agree to establish other informal sub-groups or to consider other ways of working such as, but not limited to, workshops and video-conferences.

*Rule 10*

The Committee may establish, with the approval of the Antarctic Treaty Consultative Meeting, subsidiary bodies, as appropriate.

Such subsidiary bodies shall operate on the basis of the Rules of Procedure of the Committee as applicable.

*Rule 11*

The Rules of Procedure for the preparation of the Agenda of the Antarctic Treaty Consultative Meeting shall apply with necessary changes to Committee meetings.

Before each meeting of any subsidiary body the Secretariat, in consultation with the Chairperson of both the Committee and of the subsidiary body, shall prepare and distribute a preliminary annotated Agenda.

## Part IV Submission of Documents

*Rule 12*

1. Working Papers shall refer to papers submitted by Members of the Committee that require discussion and action at a Meeting and papers submitted by Observers referred to in Rule 4(b).

2. Secretariat Papers shall refer to papers prepared by the Secretariat pursuant to a mandate established at a Meeting, or which would, in the view of the Executive Secretary, help inform the Meeting or assist in its operation.

3. Information Papers shall refer to:

- Papers submitted by Members of the Committee or Observers referred to in Rule 4(b) that provide information in support of a Working Paper or that are relevant to discussions at a Meeting;

- Papers submitted by Observers referred to in Rule 4(a) that are relevant to discussions at a Meeting; and

- Papers submitted by Observers referred to in Rule 4(c) that are relevant to discussions at a Meeting.

4. Background Papers shall refer to papers submitted by any participant that will not be introduced in a Meeting, but that are submitted for the purpose of formally providing information.

5. Procedures for the submission, translation and distribution of documents are annexed to the ATCM Rules of Procedure.


## Part V Advice and Recommendations

*Rule 13*

The Committee shall try to reach consensus on the recommendations and advice to be provided by it pursuant to the Protocol.

Where consensus cannot be achieved the Committee shall set out in its report all views advanced on the matter in question.


## Part VI Decisions

*Rule 14*

Where decisions are necessary, decisions on matters of substance shall be taken by a consensus of the members of the Committee participating in the meeting. Decisions on matters of procedure shall be taken by a simple majority of the members of the Committee present and voting. Each member of the Committee shall have one vote. Any question as to whether an issue is a procedural one shall be decided by consensus.

## Part VII Chairperson and Vice-chairs

*Rule 15*

The Committee shall elect a Chairperson and two Vice-chairs from among the Consultative Parties. The Chairperson and the Vice-chairs shall be elected for a period of two years and, where possible, their terms shall be staggered.

The Chairperson and the Vice-chairs shall not be re-elected to their post for more than one additional two-year term. The Chairperson and Vice-chairs shall not be representatives from the same Party.

The Vice-chair who has been a Vice-chair for the longer period of time (in total, counting any previous term of office) shall be first Vice-chair.

In the event that both Vice-chairs are appointed for the first time at the same meeting, the Committee shall determine which Vice-chair is elected as first Vice-chair.

*Rule 16*

Amongst other duties the Chairperson shall have the following powers and responsibilities:

(a)  convene, open, preside at and close each meeting of the Committee;

(b)  make rulings on points of order raised at each meeting of the Committee provided that each representative retains the right to request that any such decision be submitted to the Committee for approval;

(c)  approve a provisional agenda for the meeting after consultation with Representatives;

(d)  sign, on behalf of the Committee, the report of each meeting;

(e)  present the report referred to in Rule 22 on each meeting of the Committee to the Antarctic Treaty Consultative Meeting;

(f)  as required, initiate intersessional work; and

(g)  as agreed by the Committee, represent the Committee in other forums.

*Rule 17*

Whenever the Chairperson is unable to act, the first Vice-chair shall assume the powers and responsibilities of the Chairperson.

Whenever both the Chair and first Vice-chair are unable to act, the second Vice-chair shall assume the powers and responsibilities of the Chairperson.

*Rule 18*

In the event of the office of the Chairperson falling vacant between meetings, the first Vice-chair shall exercise the powers and responsibilities of the Chairperson until a new Chairperson is elected.

If the offices of both the Chairperson and first Vice-chair fall vacant between meetings, the second Vice-chair shall exercise the powers and responsibilities of the Chairperson until a new Chairperson is elected.

*Rule 19*

The Chairperson and Vice-chairs shall begin to carry out their functions on the conclusion of the meeting of the Committee at which they have been elected.

## Part VIII Administrative Facilities

*Rule 20*

As a general rule the Committee, and any subsidiary bodies, shall make use of the administrative facilities of the Government which agrees to host its meetings.

## Part IX Languages

*Rule 21*

English, French, Russian and Spanish shall be the official languages of the Committee and, as applicable, the subsidiary bodies referred to in Rule 10.

## Part X Records and Reports

*Rule 22*

The Committee shall present a report on each of its meetings to the Antarctic Treaty Consultative Meeting. The report shall cover all matters considered at the meeting of the Committee, including at its intersessional meetings and by its subsidiary bodies as appropriate, and shall reflect the views expressed. The report shall also include a comprehensive list of the officially circulated Working Papers, Information Papers and Background Papers. The report shall be presented to the Antarctic Treaty Consultative Meeting in the official languages. The report shall be circulated to the Parties, and to observers attending the meeting, and shall thereupon be made publicly available.

## Part XI Amendments

*Rule 23*

The Committee may adopt amendments to these rules of procedure, which shall be subject to approval by the Antarctic Treaty Consultative Meeting.

# Secretariat Reports, Programme and Budgets

**The Representatives,**

*Recalling* Measure 1 (2003) on the establishment of the Secretariat of the Antarctic Treaty (the Secretariat);

*Bearing in mind* the Financial Regulations for the Secretariat annexed to Decision 4 (2003);

**Decide:**

1.  to approve the audited Financial Report for 2009/10 annexed to this Decision (Annex 1);

2.  to take note of the Secretariat Report 2010/11 (SP 2 rev. 2) which includes the Estimate of Income and Expenditures 2010/11 annexed to this Decision (Annex 2); and

3.  to take note of the five year forward budget profile for 2011 to 2016 and to approve all other components of the Secretariat Programme (SP3) including the budget for 2011/12 and the Forecast Budget for 2012/13 annexed to this Decision (Annex 3).

SIGEN

## DICTAMEN DEL AUDITOR

*XXXIV Reunión Consultiva del Tratado Antártico 2011, Buenos Aires Argentina*

### 1. Informe de los Estados Financieros

Hemos auditado los Estados Financieros de la Secretaría del Tratado Antártico que se acompañan, los cuales incluyen: Estado de Ingresos y Egresos, Estado de la Posición Financiera, Estado de Evolución del Patrimonio Neto, Estado de Origen y Aplicación de Fondos y Notas aclaratorias por el período comenzado el 1° de abril de 2009 y finalizado el 31 de marzo de 2010.

### 2. Responsabilidad de la Dirección en los Estados Financieros

La Secretaría del Tratado Antártico es responsable de la preparación y razonable presentación de estos Estados Financieros de acuerdo con las Normas Internacionales de Contabilidad y normas específicas de las Reuniones Consultivas del Tratado Antártico. Esta responsabilidad incluye: diseño, implementación y mantenimiento de control interno con respecto a la preparación y presentación de los estados financieros de modo que los mismos, estén libres de tergiversación, sea por fraude o error; selección e implementación de políticas contables apropiadas, y elaboración de estimaciones contables que sean razonables a las circunstancias.

### 3. Responsabilidad del Auditor

Nuestra responsabilidad es expresar una opinión sobre estos Estados Financieros basados en la auditoría efectuada. La auditoría se realizó conforme Normas Internacionales de Auditoría y el Anexo a la Decisión 3 (2008) de la XXXI Reunión Consultiva del Tratado Antártico el cual describe las tareas a ser llevadas a cabo por la auditoría externa.

Dichas normas requieren el cumplimiento de requisitos éticos y un planeamiento y ejecución de auditoría para obtener seguridad razonable que los Estados Financieros no contienen declaraciones inexactas.

Una auditoría incluye la ejecución de procedimientos para obtener evidencias sobre los montos y exposición en los Estados Financieros. Los procedimientos seleccionados dependen del juicio del auditor, incluyendo la evaluación de los riesgos de afirmación material inexacta en los estados financieros, sea por fraude o por error. Al efectuar dicha evaluación de riesgos, el auditor considera el control interno relevante a la preparación y razonable presentación por la organización de los Estados financieros a fin de diseñar los procedimientos adecuados que resulten apropiados a las circunstancias.

**SIGEN**

Una auditoria incluye también la evaluación de lo apropiado, de los principios contables utilizados y que las estimaciones contables efectuadas por la gerencia sean razonables, así como la evaluación de la presentación general de los Estados Financieros.

Creemos que la evidencia auditada que hemos obtenido es suficiente y apropiada para proveer una base para nuestra opinión como auditores.

### 4. *Opinión*

En nuestra opinión, los Estados Financieros auditados presentan razonablemente, en todos los aspectos materiales, el estado financiero de la Secretaría del Tratado Antártico al 31 de marzo de 2010 y su desempeño financiero por el periodo entonces concluido de acuerdo con las Normas Internacionales de Contabilidad y normas específicas de las Reuniones Consultivas del Tratado Antártico.

Dr. Edgardo de Rose
Contador Público
FT82 F7195 CPCECABA

*Buenos Aires, 25 de abril de 2011*

**Sindicatura General de la Nación**
**Av. Corrientes 381, Buenos Aires**
**República Argentina**

**Annex A – Financial Report 2009/10**

1. Statement of Income and Expenditure for All Funds for the Period 1 April 2009 to 31 March 2010

| INCOME | Budget | Provisional Report | Actual |
|---|---|---|---|
| Contributions prior years (Note 1.10 & 8) | $ 32,613 | $ 32,613 | $ 32,613 |
| Contributions current year (Note 1.10 & 8) | $ 808,124 | $ 808,124 | $ 808,127 |
| Other income (Note 2) | $ 1,400 | $ 1,292 | $ (3,753) |
| **TOTAL INCOME** | **$ 842,137** | **$ 842,029** | **$ 836,987** |

| EXPENDITURES | | | |
|---|---|---|---|
| **Salaries** | | | |
| Executive Staff | $ 232,425 | $ 232,425 | $ 232,425 |
| General Staff | $ 161,905 | $ 167,876 | $ 167,876 |
| **Total Salaries** | **$ 394,330** | **$ 400,301** | **$ 400,301** |

| Goods and Services | | | |
|---|---|---|---|
| Audit | $ 7,185 | $ 7,813 | $ 9,248 |
| Data entry | $ 2,000 | $ 0 | $ 0 |
| Documentation services | $ 2,000 | $ 3,062 | $ 3,062 |
| Legal advice | $ 5,900 | $ 3,600 | $ 3,600 |
| Miscellaneous | $ 8,000 | $ 9,344 | $ 9,950 |
| Office expenses | $ 15,200 | $ 10,604 | $ 10,950 |
| Postage | $ 7,700 | $ 1,798 | $ 1,483 |
| Printing | $ 23,100 | $ 13,981 | $ 13,581 |
| Representation | $ 3,300 | $ 2,927 | $ 2,802 |
| Telecommunications | $ 10,700 | $ 11,479 | $ 11,720 |
| Training | $ 1,400 | $ 4,100 | $ 5,504 |
| Translation | $ 248,500 | $ 233,376 | $ 232,876 |
| Travel | $ 43,000 | $ 58,538 | $ 56,843 |
| **Total Goods and Services** | **$ 377,985** | **$ 360,622** | **$ 361,619** |

| Equipment | | | |
|---|---|---|---|
| Documentation | $ 1,100 | $ 1,633 | $ 1,762 |
| Furniture | $ 4,400 | $ 8,805 | $ 6,643 |
| IT Equipment | $ 21,400 | $ 20,878 | $ 23,729 |
| Development | $ 15,000 | $ 12,390 | $ 11,794 |
| **Total Equipment** | **$ 41,900** | **$ 43,706** | **$ 43,928** |

| Fund Appropriation | | | |
|---|---|---|---|
| Future Meeting Fund (Note 1.9) | $ 13,001 | $ 13,001 | $ 13,001 |
| Staff Termination Fund (Note 1.6) | $ 7,900 | $ 7,900 | $ 15,662 |
| Working Capital Fund (Note 1.8) | $ 2,475 | $ 2,475 | $ 2,475 |
| **Total Fund Appropriation** | **$ 23,376** | **$ 23,376** | **$ 31,138** |

| **TOTAL EXPENDITURES** | **$ 837,591** | **$ 828,005** | **$ 836,987** |
|---|---|---|---|

| (Deficit) / Surplus | $ 4,546 | $ 14,024 | $ 0 |
|---|---|---|---|

This statement should be read in conjunction with NOTES 1 to 9 attached

2. Statement of Financial Position as at 31 March 2010

| ASSETS | Prior Year | Actual |
|---|---|---|
| **Current assets** | | |
| Cash and cash equivalents (Note 3) | $ 959,231 | $ 876,024 |
| Contributions owed (Note 8) | $ 0 | $ 70,159 |
| Other debtors (Note 4) | $ 48,421 | $ 34,818 |
| Other current assets (Note 5) | $ 0 | $ 12,779 |
| Total | $ 1,007,652 | $ 993,781 |
| **Non-current assets** | | |
| Furniture and equipment (Note 1.5 & 6) | $ 62,196 | $ 66,297 |
| **Total non-current assets** | **$ 62,196** | **$ 66,297** |
| Total Assets | $ 1,069,848 | $ 1,060,078 |
| | | |
| **LIABILITIES** | | |
| **Current liabilities** | | |
| Payables (Note 7) | $ 91,630 | $ 31,357 |
| Unearned income (Note 1.2 & 8) | $ 379,605 | $ 407,572 |
| Salaries payable | $ 4,103 | $ 22,080 |
| Total | $ 475,339 | $ 461,008 |
| **Non-current liabilities** | | |
| Staff Termination Fund (Note 1.6) | $ 23,119 | $ 38,781 |
| Staff Replacement Fund (Note 1.7) | $ 50,000 | $ 23,421 |
| **Total non-current liabilities** | **$ 73,119** | **$ 62,203** |
| **Total Liabilities** | **$ 548,458** | **$ 523,211** |
| | | |
| **NET ASSETS** | **$ 521,390** | **$ 536,867** |

**This statement should be read in conjunction with NOTES 1 to 9 attached**

3. Statement of changes in Net Assets as at 31 March 2010

| Represented by Funds | Net Assets 01-04-2009 | Funding | Appro-priation | Net Assets 31-03-2010 |
|---|---|---|---|---|
| General Fund | $ 35,051 | $ 836,987 | ($ 836.987) | $ 35,051 |
| Working Capital Fund (Note 1.8) | $ 126,917 | | ($ 2.475) | $ 129,392 |
| Future Meeting Fund (Note 1.9) | $ 359,423 | | ($ 13.001) | $ 372,424 |
| Net Assets | $ 521,391 | ($ 836,987) | $ 852,463 | $ 536,867 |

**This statement should be read in conjunction with NOTES 1 to 9 attached**

4. Cash Flow for all Funds for the period 1 April 2009 to 31 March 2010

**Variations in cash & cash equivalents**

| | | | |
|---|---|---|---|
| - | Cash & cash equivalents at beginning of period | $ 959,231 | |
| - | Cash & cash equivalents at end of period | $ 876,024 | |
| | Net decrease of cash & cash equivalents | | ($ 83,207) |

**Causes in the variations in cash & cash equivalents**

**Operating activities**

| | | |
|---|---|---|
| - | Collection of contributions | $ 612,973 |
| - | Payment of salaries | ($ 400,301) |
| - | Payment of translation services | ($ 586,809) |
| - | Travel paid | ($ 32,171) |
| - | Printing, editing & copying paid | ($ 13,581) |
| - | Moving expenses paid | ($ 21,412) |
| - | Others payments | ($ 132,325) |

**Net cash & cash equivalents from operating activities**       ($ 573,626)

**Investment activities**

| | | |
|---|---|---|
| - | Purchase of fixed assets | ($ 12,969) |
| - | Other | 120 |

**Net cash & cash equivalents from investment activities**       ($ 12,849)

**Financing activities**

| | | |
|---|---|---|
| - | Contributions received in advance | $ 407,572 |
| - | Advance for translation services | $ 131,933 |
| - | Payment pt. 5.6 Staff Regulation | ($ 12,779) |
| - | Pre paid expenses ATCM XXXIII | ($ 18,360) |

**Net cash & cash equivalents from financing activities**       $ 508,366

**Foreign currency activities**

| | | |
|---|---|---|
| - | Net foreign exchange | ($ 5,098) |

**Net cash & cash equivalents from foreign currency activities** ($ 5,098)

**Net decrease of cash & cash equivalents**       ($ 83,207)

This statement should be read in conjunction with NOTES 1 to 9 attached

### NOTES TO AND FORMING PART OF THE FINANCIAL STATEMENTS
### 31 MARCH 2010

## NOTE 1: SUMMARY OF SIGNIFICANT ACCOUNTING PRINCIPLES AND POLICIES

### 1.1 Historical Cost
The accounts are drawn up in accordance with the convention of historical costs, except where otherwise indicated, and therefore do not reflect changes in purchasing power of money or current valuation of non-monetary assets.

### 1.2 Accrual Basis
The Secretariat Statement of Income and Expenditure, Statement of Financial Position and Statement of changes in Net Assets are prepared on an accrual basis in accordance with International Accounting Standards. See point 1.9.

### 1.3 Currency
All transactions in the financial statements are presented in United States currency.

### 1.4 Premises
The use of the Secretariat offices is provided rent-free by the Ministry of Foreign Affairs, International Trade and Worship of the Argentine Republic, as are the utilities and common area expenses of the building.

### 1.5 Furniture and Equipment
All items are shown at cost less accumulated depreciation and any recognized impairment loss. Depreciation of these assets is calculated on a straight-line basis at rates appropriate to their estimated useful life.
A full inventory with a calculation of their useful life was performed according to SIGEN's instructions. The definite composition is shown in Note 6.

### 1.6 Staff Termination Fund
The Secretariat has changed from a restrictive to a all inclusive interpretation of Regulation 10.4 of the Staff Regulations "... executive staff members shall be compensated at a rate of one month base pay for each year of service, beginning the second year...". The Fund as of March 31$^{st}$ 2010 is under funded by $ 11.531; this does not include any money owed to the prior Executive Secretary who left on August 31$^{st}$ 2009.

### 1.7 Staff Replacement Fund
This Fund is used when moving expenses occur related to relocating of the Executive Secretary.

### 1.8 Working Capital Fund
In accordance to the Financial Regulations 6.2 (a), the fund was adjusted to one-sixth (1/6) of the budget of the financial year.

### 1.9 Future Meeting Fund
In accordance to the Decision 4 (2009), the fund was increased.

### 1.10 Revenue Recognition
Starting 2009/2010 revenue from Members' annual contributions is recorded at the beginning of each year when budget contributions fall due.
Special contributions and interest income are recognized upon receipt.

**NOTES TO AND FORMING PART OF THE FINANCIAL STATEMENTS**
**31 MARCH 2010**

| | Prior year | Actual |
|---|---|---|
| **Note 2 Other Income** | | |
| Interest income | $ 2,082 | $ 1,135 |
| Exchange rate adjustment | $ 11,254 | ($ 5,098) |
| Other | $ 181 | $ 210 |
| | $ 13,517 | ($ 3,753) |
| | | |
| **Note 3 Cash and cash equivalents** | | |
| Cash US Dollar | $ 589 | $ 2,731 |
| Cash Argentine Pesos | $ 552 | $ 680 |
| BNA US Dollar account | $ 922,491 | $ 868,933 |
| BNA Argentine Peso account | $ 35,599 | $ 3,679 |
| Total | $ 959,231 | $ 876,024 |
| | | |
| **Note 4 Others debtors** | | |
| Prepayments to suppliers | $ 35,972 | $ 28,480 |
| VAT to be reimbursed | $ 11,930 | $ 6,338 |
| Salary advance | $ 500 | $ 0 |
| Turnover tax to be reimbursed | $ 19 | $ 0 |
| Total | $ 48,421 | $ 34,819 |
| | | |
| **Note 5 Other current assets** | | |
| Refund of Staff Regulation 5.6 | $ 0 | $ 12,779 |
| | $ 0 | $ 12,779 |
| | | |
| **Note 6 Furniture and Equipment** | | |
| Books & subscriptions | $ 3,240 | $ 2,877 |
| Office appliances | $ 12,133 | $ 28,307 |
| Furniture | $ 22,129 | $ 24,374 |
| IT equipment & software | $ 32,071 | $ 39,747 |
| Total original cost | $ 69,573 | $ 95,305 |
| Accumulated depreciation | ($ 7,377) | ($ 29,008) |
| Total net cost | $ 62,196 | $ 66,297 |
| | | |
| **Note 7 Payables** | | |
| Provision Staff Regulation 5.6 | $ 67,800 | $ 0 |
| Accounts payable | $ 9,120 | $ 4,160 |
| Accrued expenses | $ 14,710 | $ 27,197 |
| | $ 91,630 | $ 31,357 |

245

## NOTES TO AND FORMING PART OF THE FINANCIAL STATEMENTS
### 31 MARCH 2010

### Note 8 Contributions
The breakdowns of contributions owed and received in advance are as follows:

| Financial Year | 2008/09 | 2009/10 | | 2009/10 | |
|---|---|---|---|---|---|
| Received | Owed | Pledged | Received | Outstanding | Unearned |
| Argentina | | $ 36,404 | $ 36,404 | $ 0 | |
| Australia | | $ 36,404 | $ 36,404 | $ 0 | |
| Belgium | | $ 24,197 | $ 24,180 | $ 18 | |
| Brasil | | $ 24,197 | $ 14,640 | $ 9,557 | |
| Bulgaria | | $ 20,534 | $ 20,534 | $ 0 | $ 22,868 |
| Chile | $ 14,320 | $ 27,859 | $ 24,320 | $ 17,859 | |
| China | | $ 27,859 | $ 27,859 | $ 0 | |
| Ecuador | | $ 20,534 | $ 20,534 | $ 0 | |
| Finland | | $ 24,197 | $ 24,197 | $ 0 | |
| France | | $ 36,404 | $ 36,404 | $ 0 | $ 40,540 |
| Germany | | $ 31,521 | $ 31,491 | $ 30 | $ 35,070 |
| India | | $ 27,859 | $ 27,797 | $ 62 | |
| Italy | | $ 31,521 | $ 31,521 | $ 0 | |
| Japan | | $ 34,404 | $ 36,405 | ($ 1) | |
| Korea | | $ 24,197 | $ 24,197 | $ 0 | $ 26,946 |
| Netherlands | | $ 27,859 | $ 27,859 | $ 0 | |
| New Zealand | | $ 36,404 | $ 36,374 | $ 30 | $ 40,540 |
| Norway | | $ 36,404 | $ 36,404 | $ 0 | $ 40,510 |
| Peru | | $ 20,534 | $ 20,534 | $ 0 | |
| Poland | | $ 24,197 | $ 24,197 | $ 0 | $ 26,946 |
| Russia | | $ 27,859 | $ 27,859 | $ 0 | $ 31,024 |
| South Africa | | $ 27,859 | $ 27,859 | $ 0 | $ 31,024 |
| Spain | | $ 27,859 | $ 27,844 | $ 115 | |
| Sweden | | $ 27,859 | $ 27,859 | $ 0 | $ 31,024 |
| Ukraine | $ 18,293 | $ 24,197 | $ 0 | $ 42,490 | |
| United Kingdom | | $ 36,404 | $ 36,404 | $ 0 | $ 40,540 |
| United States | | $ 36,404 | $ 36,404 | $ 0 | $ 40,540 |
| Uruguay | | $ 24,197 | $ 24,197 | $ 0 | |
| TOTAL | $ 32,613 | $ 808,127 | $ 770,581 | $ 70,159 | $ 407,572 |

NOTES TO AND FORMING PART OF THE FINANCIAL STATEMENTS
31 MARCH 2010

**Note 9 New Statement of Income and Expenditure for all Funds for the period 1 April 2009 to 31 March 2010**

This will be the format that in future the Secretariat will show the income and expenditure.

| INCOME | Prior year | Budget | Actual |
|---|---|---|---|
| Contributions prior years | $ 138,317 | $ 32,613 | $ 32,613 |
| Contributions current year | $ 404,118 | $ 808,124 | $ 808,127 |
| Other income | $ 2,263 | $ 1,400 | $ 1,364 |
| Total income | $ 544,698 | $ 842,137 | $ 842,104 |
| | | | |
| EXPENDITURE | | | |
| Salaries | $ 371,637 | $ 399,530 | $ 403,363 |
| Translation services | $ 232,554 | $ 248,500 | $ 232,876 |
| Travel | $ 59,563 | $ 43,000 | $ 56,843 |
| Information technology | $ 41,296 | $ 36,400 | $ 35,523 |
| Printing, editing & copying | $ 37,249 | $ 23,100 | $ 13,581 |
| General services | $ 34,449 | $ 30,685 | $ 33,147 |
| Communications | $ 14,288 | $ 16,000 | $ 10,708 |
| Office expenses | $ 12,644 | $ 10,000 | $ 12,220 |
| General administration | $ 3,808 | $ 3,700 | $ 4,786 |
| Representation | $ 3,172 | $ 3,300 | $ 2,802 |
| Financing | ($ 11,472) | $ 0 | $ 5,117 |
| Total expenditure | $ 799,277 | $ 814,215 | $ 810,966 |
| | | | |
| FUNDS APPROPIATION | | | |
| Future Meeting Fund | $ 0 | $ 13,001 | $ 13,001 |
| Staff Termination Fund | $ 9,415 | $ 7,900 | $ 15,662 |
| Working Capital Fund | ($ 6,866) | $ 2,475 | $ 2,475 |
| Total funds appropriation | $ 2,549 | $ 23,376 | $ 31,138 |
| | | | |
| Total expenses & appropriation | $ 801,826 | $ 837,591 | $ 842,104 |
| | | | |
| (Deficit) / Surplus for the period | ($ 257,128) | ($ 4,546) | $ 0 |

Dr. Manfred Reinke
Executive Secretary

Roberto A. Fennell
Certified Accountant

## AUDITOR'S DECLARATION

**XXXIV** *Antarctic Treaty Consultative Meeting 2011. Buenos Aires Argentina.*

### 1. Report on Financial Statements

We have audited the attached Financial Statements of the Antarctic Treaty Secretariat, which include: Statement of Income and Expenditure, Statement of Financial Position, Statement of Net Capital Assets, Statement of Origin and Application of Funds and Explanatory Notes for the period commencing 1 April 2009 and ending 31 March 2010.

### 2. Responsibility of the Directorate for Financial Statements

The Antarctic Treaty Secretariat is responsible for the preparation and reasonable presentation of these Financial Statements according to International Accounting Standards and the specific standards for Antarctic Treaty Consultative Meetings. This responsibility includes: design, implementation and maintenance of internal control over the preparation and presentation of the financial statements such that they are free of distortion, either by fraud or error: selection and implementation of appropriate accounting policies, and preparation of accounting estimates which are reasonable under the circumstances.

### 3. Auditor's Responsibility

Our responsibility is to express an opinion on these Financial Statements based on the audit carried out. The audit was carried out in accordance with International Auditing Standards and the Annexe to Decision 3 (2008) of the XXXI Antarctic Treaty Consultative Meeting, which describes the tasks to be carried out by the external audit.

These standards require compliance with ethical requirements, and planning and execution of the audit so as to ensure reasonable certainty that the Financial Statements do not contain inaccuracies.

An audit includes the execution of procedures to obtain evidence on the amounts and the exposition given in the Financial Statements. The procedures selected depend on the auditor's judgement, including an assessment of the risks of a declaration of inaccurate material in the financial statements, either by fraud or error. When making such an assessment of risks, the auditor considers the internal control corresponding to the preparation and reasonable presentation by the organisation of the Financial statements in order to design suitable procedures which will be appropriate to the circumstances.

An audit also includes an assessment of what is appropriate, of the accounting principles used, and that the accounting estimates made by the management are reasonable, as well as an assessment of the general presentation of the Financial Statements.

We believe that the audited evidence which we have obtained is sufficient and appropriate to provide a basis for our opinion as auditors.

### 4. *Opinion*

In our opinion, the Financial Statements audited reasonably present, in all material aspects, the financial state of the Antarctic Treaty Secretariat at 31 March 2010 and its financial performance for the period concluding on that date in accordance with International Accounting Standards and the specific standards for Antarctic Treaty Consultative Meetings.

*Dr. Edgardo de Rose*
  *Public Accountant*
*Tº182 Fº195 CPEBCABA*

*Buenos Aires, 25 April 2011*

**Sindicatura General de la Nación**
**Av. Corrientes 381, Buenos Aires**
**República Argentina**

**Estimate of Income and Expenditure for all Funds for the Period
1 April 2010 to 31 March 2011**

|  | Statement 2009/10 | Budget 2010/11 | Prov. Statement 2010/11 |
|---|---|---|---|
| *INCOME* | | | |
| Previous FY contributions | $ 32,613 | $ 0 | |
| Current FY contributions | $ 808,127 | $ 899,942 | $ 899,942 |
| Other | -$ 3,753 | $ 1,000 | -$ 1,510 |
| **TOTAL** | **$ 836,987** | **$ 900,942** | **$ 898,432** |
| | | | |
| *EXPENDITURES* | | | |
| **SALARIES** | | | |
| Executive Staff | $ 232,425 | $ 247,974 | $ 250,104 |
| General Staff | $ 167,876 | $ 193,543 | $ 194,102 |
| Overtime | $ 0 | $ 8,038 | $ 7,365 |
| Auxiary Staff | $ 0 | $ 16,864 | $ 18,378 |
| **Total Salaries** | **$ 400,301** | **$ 466,419** | **$ 469,948** |
| | | | |
| *GOODS AND SERVICES* | | | |
| Audit | $ 9,248 | $ 9,360 | $ 9,299 |
| Data entry | $ 0 | $ 0 | $ 0 |
| Doc. Services | $ 3,062 | $ 0 | $ 0 |
| Legal advice | $ 3,600 | $ 4,200 | $ 4,360 |
| Miscellaneous | $ 9,950 | $ 8,500 | $ 9,976 |
| Office expenses | $ 10,950 | $ 11,700 | $ 12,141 |
| Postage | $ 1,483 | $ 2,500 | $ 1,870 |
| Printing | $ 13,581 | $ 11,500 | $ 15,964 |
| Representation | $ 2,802 | $ 2,000 | $ 3,143 |
| Telecom | $ 11,720 | $ 13,000 | $ 12,393 |
| Training | $ 5,504 | $ 4,100 | $ 8,131 |
| Translation & Interpretation | $ 232,876 | $ 585,093 | $ 531,693 |
| Travel | $ 56,843 | $ 68,800 | $ 60,583 |
| Relocation | $ 0 | $ 0 | $ 0 |
| **Total Goods & Services** | **$ 361,619** | **$ 720,753** | **$ 669,554** |
| | | | |
| *EQUIPMENT* | | | |
| Documentation | $ 1,762 | $ 1,900 | $ 1,137 |
| Furniture | $ 6,643 | $ 5,000 | $ 4,179 |
| IT Equipment | $ 23,729 | $ 23,600 | $ 21,497 |
| Development | $ 11,795 | $ 15,100 | $ 15,820 |
| **Total equipment** | **$ 43,929** | **$ 45,600** | **$ 42,632** |
| | | | |
| **Total Appropriations** | **$ 805,849** | **$ 1,232,772** | **$ 1,182,135** |
| | | | |
| Translation Contingency Fund | | | |
| (Future Meeting Fund) | $ 13,001 | $ 0 | $ 0 |
| Staff Replacement Fund | $ 0 | $ 8,333 | $ 8,333 |
| Staff Termination Fund | $ 15,662 | $ 25,974 | $ 25,974 |
| Working Capital Fund | $ 2,475 | $ 62,260 | $ 62,260 |
| **Total Funding** | **$ 31,138** | **$ 96,567** | **$ 96,567** |
| | | | |
| **EXPENDITURES** | **$ 836,987** | **$ 1,329,339** | **$ 1,278,702** |
| | | $ 0 | |
| Surplus / (deficit) | $ 0 | -$ 428,397 | -$ 380,269 |
| | | | |
| *FINANCING* | | **$ 0** | |
| General Fund | $ 0 | $ 49,076 | $ 7,845 |
| Translation Contingency Fund | | | |
| (Future Meeting Fund) | $ 0 | $ 372,424 | $ 372,424 |
| Working Capital Fund | $ 0 | $ 6,898 | $ 0 |
| | **$ 0** | **$ 428,398** | **$ 380,269** |
| | | | |
| **Summary of Funds** | 31/03/2010 | 31/03/2011 | 31/03/2011 |
| General Fund | $ 35,051 | $ 0 | $ 27,206 |
| Translation Contingency Fund | | | |
| (Future Meeting Fund) | $ 372,424 | $ 0 | $ 0 |
| Staff Replacement Fund | $ 23,421 | $ 31,754 | $ 31,754 |
| Staff Termination Fund | $ 38,781 | $ 64,755 | $ 64,755 |
| Working Capital Fund | $ 129,392 | $ 184,754 | $ 191,652 |

# Secretariat Programme 2011/12

## Introduction

This work programme outlines the activities proposed for the Secretariat in the Financial Year 2011/12 (1 April 2011 to 31 March 2012). The main areas of activity of the Secretariat are treated in the first three chapters, which are followed by a section on management and a forecast of the programme for the financial year 2011/12.

The draft budget for 2011/12, the forecast budget for 2012/13, and the accompanying contribution and salary scales are included in the appendices.

The Secretariat has developed a five-year budget profile as requested by the ACTM XXXIII (Final Report para. (113)).

The programme and the accompanying budget figures for 2011/12 are based on the Forecast Budget for 2011/12 (Decision 4 (2010), Appendix 1).

The Programme focuses on the regular activities, such as preparation of the ATCM XXXIV and ATCM XXXV, publication of Final Reports, and the various specific tasks assigned to the Secretariat under Measure 1 (2003).

*Contents:*

1. ATCM/CEP support
2. Information Exchange
3. Documentation
4. Public Information
5. Management
6. Forecast Programme 2011/12

   Appendix 1: Prov. Report 2010/11, Budget 2011/12, Forecast Budget 2012/13
   Appendix 2: Five year forward budget profile 2011 to 2016
   Appendix 3: Contribution scale 2012/13
   Appendix 4: Salaries Scale

## 1. ATCM/CEP Support

### ATCM XXXIV

The Secretariat will support the ATCM XXXIV by gathering and collating the documents for the Meeting and publishing them in a restricted section of the Secretariat website. The

Delegates section will also provide online registration for delegates and a downloadable, up-to-date list of delegates.

The Secretariat will support the functioning of the ATCM through the production of Secretariat Papers, a Manual for Delegates, and annotated agendas for the ATCM, the CEP, and the ATCM Working Groups.

The Secretariat maintains contact with the Government of Australia in connection with the preparation of the ATCM XXXV in 2012, and will maintain contact with the Government of Belgium regarding the preparation of the ATCM XXXVI.

### Review of ATCM Recommendations

The Secretariat will continue its support of the Intersessional Contact Group "Review of ATCM Recommendations".

### Coordination and contact

Aside from maintaining constant contact via email, telephone and other means with the Parties and international institutions of the Antarctic Treaty System, attendance at meetings is an important tool to maintain coordination and contact.

COMNAP XXIV will take place in Stockholm from 1 August to 5 August 2011. Attendance at the meeting will provide an opportunity to further strengthen the connections and interaction with COMNAP and brief the NAPs about the issues to be faced in the operational phase of the EIES. Another issue for which contact with COMNAP may be necessary is the review of the status of recommendations on operational matters.

The Secretariat's staff is already in close co-operation with Australian authorities as the host government secretariat of the ATCM XXXV. The staff will be strengthened during the Meeting with staff members contracted *ad hoc*.

The travelling to be undertaken is as follows:

- *COMNAP, 1 to 5 August 2011.*
- *CCAMLR, Hobart, Australia, 24 October to 4 November 2011.* The CCAMLR meeting, which takes place roughly halfway between succeeding ATCMs, provides a good opportunity for the Secretariat to brief the ATCM Representatives, many of whom attend the CCAMLR meeting, on developments in the Secretariat's work. Liaison with the CCAMLR Secretariat is also important for the Antarctic Treaty Secretariat, as many of its regulations are modelled after those of the CCAMLR Secretariat.

### Development of the Secretariat website

The new website will include some small updates to make it more concise and easier to use, and to increase the visibility of the most relevant sections and information. The reporting facilities of the website databases, especially the Antarctic Treaty database, will be further developed. The Secretariat will continue incorporating meeting documents from previous ATCMs, SATCMs, and Meetings of Experts. Because many of these documents are not available in digital form, this involves the scanning, proofreading, and data entry of printed documents. The Protected Areas Database will be enhanced by including new fields and geographical information.

### Support of intersessional activities

During recent years both the CEP and the ATCM have produced an important amount of intersessional work, mainly through Intersessional Contact Groups (ICG). The Secretariat will provide technical support for the online establishment of the ICGs agreed at the ATCM XXXIV and CEP XIV and by producing specific documents if required by the ATCM or the CEP.

The Secretariat will update the website with the measures adopted by the ATCM and with the information produced by the CEP and the ATCM.

### Printing

The Secretariat will publish and distribute the Final Report and its Annexes of the ATCM XXXIV in the four Treaty languages within six months of the end of the meeting. The text of the Final Report will be printed, while the annexes will be published as a CD attached to the printed report. The full text of the Final Report will be available in book form through the company Amazon.com (http://www.amazon.com).

## 2. Information Exchange

### General

The Secretariat will continue to assist Parties in posting their information exchange materials, as well as integrating information on EIAs in the EIA database.

### Electronic Information Exchange System

During the next operational season and depending on the decisions of the ATCM XXXIV, the Secretariat will make any adjustments necessary to facilitate the use of the electronic system for the Parties, as well as develop tools to compile and present summarised reports.

## 3. Records and Documents

### Documents of the ATCM

The Secretariat will continue its efforts to complete its archive of the Final Reports and other records of the ATCM and other meetings of the Antarctic Treaty System in the four

Treaty languages. Assistance from the Parties in searching for their archives will be essential in achieving a complete archive.

### Antarctic Treaty database

The database of the Recommendations, Measures, Decisions and Resolutions of the ATCM is at present complete in English and almost complete in Spanish and French, although the Secretariat still lacks various Final Report copies in those languages. In Russian, more Final Reports are lacking, and materials that have been received are being converted into electronic formats and proofread.

## 4. Public Information

The Secretariat and its website will continue to function as a clearinghouse for information on the Parties' activities and relevant developments in Antarctica.

## 5. Management

### Relocation of the Secretariat

The Secretariat will relocate its office from Av Leandro N. Alem 844 piso 4 to Maipú 757 piso 4 in May 2011. On 19 March 2011 the Argentine Government signed a contract for a new office space which meets the long-term requirements for the archives and employees of the Secretariat and offers improved working conditions.

The Secretariat is grateful to the Argentine Government for this offer that will safeguard the quality of the services to the Parties in the future.

### Personnel

On April 1, 2011, the Secretariat staff consisted of the following personnel:

*Executive staff*

| Name | Position | Since | Rank |
|---|---|---|---|
| Manfred Reinke | Executive Secretary | 1-09-2009 | E1 |
| José María Acero | Assistant Executive Secretary | 1-01-2005 | E3 |

*General staff*

| | | | |
|---|---|---|---|
| José Luis Agraz | Information Officer | 1-11-2004 | G1 |
| Diego Wydler | Information Technology Officer | 1-02-2006 | G1 |
| Roberto Alan Fennell | Accountant (part time) | 1-12-2008 | G2 |
| Pablo Wainschenker | Editor | 1-02-2006 | G3 |
| Ms. Violeta Antinarelli | Librarian (part time) | 1-04-2007 | G3 |

| Ms. Gloria Fontán | Office Manager | 1-12-2004 | G5 |
| Ms. Karina Gil (ill since 15-03-2010) | Data Entry Assistant (part time) | 1-04-2007 | G6 |
| Ms. Anna Balok Replacement for Ms. Karina Gil (fix term contract until 31-07-2011) | Data Entry Assistant (part time) | 1-10-2010 | G6 |

## Financial Matters

### Translation and Interpretation

In cooperation with Argentina and Australia, the hosts of the next two Meetings, the Secretariat prepared an international call for proposals for translation and interpretation services for the 34th and 35th ATCMs. The Secretariat sent this call to three international companies, all of which have known experiences with translation and interpretation of ATCMs or ATCM-related issues on 22 September 2010.

The call asked the offerers to submit both a technical proposal and a price schedule, which allowed independent assessments of their qualities and their prices. The technical proposal asked for sample translations, a proposed work plan, and a description of personnel resources. The Secretariat decided to issue a call for proposals for two years to safeguard a constant high quality of translation and interpretation at these Meetings. The General Conditions of this contract contain a clause that if Parties feel that the services provided were insufficient, the contract could be terminated after the first Meeting. The Secretariat was aware that high quality interpretation and translation services are crucial for the success of ATCMs.

The Secretariat's auditor SIGEN agreed to witness the opening of the proposals on 1 November 2010. The Secretariat received three proposals from companies in Japan, Argentina and Australia. The offers showed a considerable variance in prices. For the translation of 1000 words, the companies asked for between 110 US\$ and 220 US\$. For interpretation at the Meetings, they asked between 222,920 US\$ and 420,575 US\$ for the ATCM in Buenos Aires 2011, and between 292,771 US\$ and 489,066 US\$ for the ATCM in Hobart 2012.

Based on the submitted proposals and in coordination with Australia and Argentina, the Secretariat has decided to place ONCALL Conference Interpreters & Translators in the first position. ONCALL has been organising the language services for CCAMLR in Hobart since 2002. It is the only offerer whose workflow has been certified under the ISO 9001 quality management standards. The evaluation of the competence and reliability of these three companies shows that ONCALL is the only offerer that has presented a clear and precise overview of its financial and organizational capacities. In the cases of the two other offerers, their services are fully dependant on the owners, creating a potential risk for the meetings in case of personal unavailability due to whatever reason.

The costs for translation and interpretation are budgeted for the ATCM XXXIV at 365,825 US$ and for the ATCM XXXV at 358,002 US$. The cost at the ATCM XXXII in Baltimore amounted to 668,800 US$ and at the ATCM XXXIII in Punta del Este, 533,949 US$.

**Salaries**

Costs of living rose considerably in Argentina in the year 2010. Salaries for the Secretariat staff have been recalculated taking into account the increase of the IVS (Salary Variation Index provided by the Argentine National Office of Statistics and Census) adjusted for the devaluation of the Argentine Peso against the US$ during the same period to compensate effects of inflation. This method was explained by the ES and agreed at ATCM XXXII (Final Report p. 238).

In the year 2010 the IVS rose exceptionally by 26.3% compared to 16.7% in the previous year. The rate ARG Peso/US$ Dollar changed from $0.264 to $0.252. This caused a rise of costs of living of 19.9% for the year 2011/12 in terms of US$.

Regulation 5.10 of the Staff Regulations requires compensating general staff members in the general category when they have to work more than 40 hours during one week. Overtime is requested during the ATCM Meetings.

**Funds**

*Working Capital Fund*

According to the Financial Regulation 6.2 (a), the Working Capital Fund has to be maintained at 1/6 of the Secretariat's budget of 223,600 US$ in the upcoming years. The contributions of the Parties form the basis of the calculation of the level of the Working Capital Fund.

*Staff Termination Fund*

The Staff Termination Fund was replenished due to the results of discussions at the ATCM which were reflected in the Final Report (para. 100).

**Appropriation Lines**

The ATCM XXXIII agreed that the budget should be presented with a new set of budget lines developed in cooperation with the external auditor SIGEN to better demonstrate how the Secretariat spent the contributions.

Right now the appropriation lines reflect items on which the Secretariat spends money, but without informing exactly how it spends the contributions. The idea is to classify the Secretariat's expenditure into categories of dollar value, work programme, and specific expense. The total spent will be the same dollar amount as before the change, but it will be shown in a different manner.

The new appropriation lines are:

- *Salaries*: this would include not only the salaries approved in the budget for ATS direct staff but also for those who assist us in the Meetings and the overtime for the general staff during the ATCM
- *Translation*: all moneys for translation before, during and after the ATCM yearly meeting (includes air fares, lodging and sundry)
- *Information technology*: all investments in equipment, software development, and IT maintenance and security
- *Printing, editing and copying*: for the printed Final Report and electronic support
- *General services:* all local support services, such as legal, auditing, banking, training
- *Communications*: includes telephone, internet, WEB hosting, postage
- *Office:* stationary, books, insurance, maintenance
- *Administrative:* local transport, supplies
- *Financing:* net translation gain or loss

The Secretariat asks whether to implement these new appropriation lines for the upcoming financial years.

The Report of FY 2010/11 and budget of FY 2011/12 and the forecast budget of FY 2012/13 are presented in both schemes (Appendix 1 and 2).

**Further Details of the Draft Budget 2011/12**

The allocation to the appropriation lines has been adjusted according to the foreseen expenses of the financial year 2011/2012.

- *Category of Goods and Services*: The total budget for this category equals the total budget in the forecast budget 2010/11 but it was necessary to make some adjustments in the appropriation lines. The "*Travel*" costs for the ATCM XXXIV in Buenos Aires include costs for the supporting staff (3 Persons) and hotel costs of some of the Secretariat staff during the Meeting. Foreseen are travels to COMNAP XVI in Stockholm (31 July to 4 August 2011) and CCAMLR (October 2011) and one travel to the home country for the ES and his spouse under Staff Regulation 7.6 (December 2011). Costs of Translation and Interpretation are considerably less due to the results of the tender process. The relocation of the Secretariat to a new office space in Buenos Aires will incur a cost of approximately 50,000 US$. The Government of Argentina is considering whether it will support the associated cost of relocation through an additional financial contribution.
- *Category of Salaries:* The salaries are calculated higher to compensate the unforeseen effect of rising costs of living in Argentina.

Appendix 2 shows the draft budget in the new and the current appropriation lines. The salary scale is given in Appendix 4.

*Five-year budget profile*

The Meeting has requested "the Secretariat to produce for ATCM XXXIV a multi-year forward budget profile which aimed to flatten out the predictable elements within the budget over a five-year period" (Final Report para. 113).

Due to the savings in Translation and Interpretation, the total budget will show no real increase in the financial year 2012/13. Several major risks remain for the budget. The biggest risk is the effect of inflation. Other risks are the varying costs for travel expenditures for the ATCM and new contracts for translation and interpretation services. The Secretariat will negotiate new contracts for the FYs 2013/14 to 2016/17 in 2012.

The Secretariat anticipated an inflation adjustment of 10% in the FY 2012/13 and 5% in the following years. The travel costs will be high for the ATCM XXXV in Australia and ATCM XXXVI in Belgium. They may be lower for the ATCM XXXVII and ATCM XXXVIII in Brazil and Bulgaria.

The Working Capital Fund plays a key role. Due to Financial Regulation 6.2 (a) it has to be maintained at 1/6 of the Secretariat's budget. The Secretariat suggests filling the Working Capital Fund above this rate and using this amount to balance the varying travel costs and to buffer costs of a high local inflation rate.

In the years 2013/14, 2014/15 and 2015/16 the Secretariat calculated an adjustment of 3% of the contributions to compensate parts of the anticipated inflation.

*Contribution for the Financial Year 2012/13*

The contributions for the Financial Year 2012/13 will be the same as for the Financial Year 2011/12. Appendix 3 shows the contributions of the Parties.

## 6. Forecast Programme 2012/13 and 2013/14

It is expected that most of the ongoing activities of the Secretariat will be continued in 2012/13 and therefore, unless the programme undergoes major changes, no change in staff positions is foreseen for the following years.

The contributions in FY 2012/13 will not rise. In FY 2013/14 the Secretariat expects contributions to increase by 3% to 1,379,788 US$ (Appendix 2).

**Appendix 1**

# Provisional Report 2010/11, Budget 2011/12 and Forecast 2012/13

|  | Prov. Statement 2010/11 | Forecast 2011/12 | Budget 2011/12 | Forecast 2012/13 |
|---|---|---|---|---|
| ***INCOME*** | | | | |
| Current FY contributions | $ 899,942 | $ 1,339,600 | $ 1,339,600 | $ 1,339,600 |
| Other | -$ 1,510 | $ 1,000 | $ 1,000 | $ 1,000 |
| **TOTAL** | **$ 898,432** | **$ 1,340,600** | **$ 1,340,600** | **$ 1,340,600** |
| | | | | |
| ***EXPENDITURES*** | | | | |
| **SALARIES** | | | | |
| Executive Staff | $ 250,104 | $ 270,291 | $ 305,654 | $ 342,332 |
| General Staff | $ 194,102 | $ 210,962 | $ 241,159 | $ 277,333 |
| Overtime | $ 7,365 | $ 8,761 | $ 14,926 | $ 11,565 |
| Auxiliary Staff | $ 18,378 | $ 16,864 | $ 16,361 | $ 16,939 |
| **Total Salaries** | **$ 469,948** | **$ 506,878** | **$ 578,100** | **$ 648,169** |
| | | | | |
| **GOODS AND SERVICES** | | | | |
| Audit | $ 9,299 | $ 9,360 | $ 9,360 | $ 10,764 |
| Data entry | $ 0 | $ 0 | $ 0 | $ 0 |
| Doc. services | $ 0 | $ 0 | $ 0 | $ 0 |
| Legal advice | $ 4,360 | $ 4,490 | $ 9,000 | $ 9,900 |
| Miscellaneous | $ 9,976 | $ 8,500 | $ 9,500 | $ 10,450 |
| Office expenses | $ 12,141 | $ 12,520 | $ 14,000 | $ 15,400 |
| Postage | $ 1,870 | $ 2,680 | $ 2,680 | $ 2,814 |
| Printing | $ 15,964 | $ 12,310 | $ 14,000 | $ 15,400 |
| Representation | $ 3,143 | $ 2,000 | $ 4,500 | $ 3,500 |
| Telecom | $ 12,393 | $ 13,910 | $ 15,000 | $ 16,500 |
| Training | $ 8,131 | $ 4,100 | $ 8,000 | $ 8,400 |
| Translation & Interpretation | $ 531,693 | $ 585,093 | $ 365,825 | $ 358,002 |
| Travel | $ 60,583 | $ 42,508 | $ 52,815 | $ 110,380 |
| Relocation | $ 0 | $ 0 | $ 50,000 | $ 0 |
| **Total Goods & Services** | **$ 669,554** | **$ 697,471** | **$ 554,680** | **$ 561,510** |

**EQUIPMENT**

| | | | | |
|---|---|---|---|---|
| Documentation | $ 1,137 | $ 1,500 | $ 1,500 | $ 1,650 |
| Furniture | $ 4,179 | $ 5,000 | $ 5,000 | $ 5,500 |
| IT Equipment | $ 21,497 | $ 25,000 | $ 27,500 | $ 28,875 |
| Development | $ 15,820 | $ 16,000 | $ 16,000 | $ 17,600 |
| **Total equipment** | **$ 42,632** | **$ 47,500** | **$ 50,000** | **$ 53,625** |
| | | | | |
| **Total Appropriations** | **$ 1,182,135** | **$ 1,251,849** | **$ 1,182,780** | **$ 1,263,304** |
| | | | | |
| Translation Contingency Fund (Future Meeting Fund) | $ 0 | $ 0 | $ 30,000 | $ 0 |
| Staff Replacement Fund | $ 8,333 | $ 16,667 | $ 18,246 | $ 0 |
| Staff Termination Fund | $ 25,974 | $ 27,084 | $ 42,502 | $ 32,778 |
| Working Capital Fund | $ 62,260 | $ 45,000 | $ 67,072 | $ 44,518 |
| **Total Funding** | **$ 96,567** | **$ 88,751** | **$ 157,820** | **$ 77,296** |
| | | | | |
| **EXPENDITURES** | **$ 1,278,702** | **$ 1,340,600** | **$ 1,340,600** | **$ 1,340,600** |
| | | | | |
| Surplus / (deficit) | -$ 380,269 | $ 0 | $ 0 | $ 0 |

*FINANCING*

| | | | | |
|---|---|---|---|---|
| General Fund | $ 7,845 | $ 0 | $ 0 | $ 0 |
| Translation Contingency Fund (Future Meeting Fund) | $ 372,424 | $ 0 | $ 0 | $ 0 |
| Working Capital Fund | $ 0 | $ 0 | $ 0 | $ 0 |
| | $ 380,269 | $ 0 | $ 0 | $ 0 |

| **Summary of Funds** | **31/03/2011** | **31/03/2012** | **31/03/2012** | **31/03/2013** |
|---|---|---|---|---|
| General Fund | $ 27,206 | $ 0 | $ 0 | $ 0 |
| Translation Contingency Fund (Future Meeting Fund) | $ 0 | $ 0 | $ 30,000 | $ 30,000 |
| Staff Replacement Fund | $ 31,754 | $ 48,421 | $ 50,000 | $ 50,000 |
| Staff Termination Fund | $ 64,755 | $ 62,343 | $ 107,257 | $ 140,035 |
| Working Capital Fund | $ 191,652 | $ 263,858 | $ 285,930 | $ 330,448 |

**Appendix 2**

# Five Year Forward Budget Profile 2011 to 2016

| | Prov. Statement 2010/11 | Budget 2011/12 | Forecast 2012/13 | Estimation 2013/14 | Estimation 2014/15 | Estimation 2015/16 |
|---|---|---|---|---|---|---|
| **Account Name** | | | | | | |
| **CONTRIBUTIONS (* 1)** | -$ 899,942 | -$ 1,339,600 | -$ 1,339,600 | -$ 1,379,788 | -$ 1,421,182 | -$ 1,463,817 |
| | | | | | | |
| **OTHER INCOME** | | | | | | |
| from Future Meeting Fund | -$ 380,269 | | | | | |
| from Working Capital Fund | $ 0 | $ 0 | $ 0 | -$ 23,369 | -$ 30,797 | -$ 77,207 |
| Interest Income Bank | -$ 27 | $ 0 | $ 0 | $ 0 | $ 0 | $ 0 |
| Interest Income Investments | -$ 163 | $ 0 | $ 0 | $ 0 | $ 0 | $ 0 |
| Interest Income V.A.T. | -$ 65 | -$ 70 | -$ 70 | -$ 70 | -$ 70 | -$ 70 |
| Gain on sale of fixed assets | $ 0 | $ 0 | $ 0 | $ 0 | $ 0 | $ 0 |
| Discounts obtained | -$ 69 | $ 0 | $ 0 | $ 0 | $ 0 | $ 0 |
| RESOURCES | -$ 380,592 | -$ 70 | -$ 70 | -$ 23,439 | -$ 30,867 | -$ 77,277 |
| | | | | | | |
| **SALARIES (* 2)** | | | | | | |
| Executive | $ 250,104 | $ 305,654 | $ 342,332 | $ 366,296 | $ 391,936 | $ 419,372 |
| General Staff | $ 194,102 | $ 241,159 | $ 277,333 | $ 305,066 | $ 335,573 | $ 369,130 |
| ATCM Support Staff | $ 13,577 | $ 11,561 | $ 12,139 | $ 12,503 | $ 12,878 | $ 13,265 |
| Trainee | $ 4,800 | $ 4,800 | $ 4,800 | $ 4,800 | $ 4,800 | $ 4,800 |
| Overtime | $ 7,365 | $ 14,926 | $ 11,565 | $ 12,722 | $ 13,358 | $ 14,025 |
| | $ 469,948 | $ 578,100 | $ 648,169 | $ 701,387 | $ 758,545 | $ 820,592 |
| | | | | | | |
| **TRANSLATION AND INTERPRETATION** | | | | | | |
| Translation and Interpretation | $ 531,693 | $ 365,825 | $ 358,002 | $ 391,433 | $ 403,176 | $ 415,271 |
| | | | | | | |
| **TRAVEL** | | | | | | |
| Travel | $ 60,583 | $ 52,815 | $ 110,380 | $ 121,418 | $ 90,000 | $ 90,000 |
| | | | | | | |
| **INFORMATION TECHNO-LOGY (* 2)** | | | | | | |
| Hardware | $ 11,856 | $ 12,000 | $ 13,000 | $ 12,000 | $ 12,000 | $ 12,000 |
| Software | $ 2,322 | $ 3,500 | $ 3,500 | $ 3,500 | $ 3,850 | $ 4,235 |
| Development | $ 15,820 | $ 16,000 | $ 18,400 | $ 20,240 | $ 20,240 | $ 22,264 |
| Support | $ 7,318 | $ 11,000 | $ 10,000 | $ 11,000 | $ 12,100 | $ 13,310 |
| | $ 37,316 | $ 42,500 | $ 44,900 | $ 46,740 | $ 48,190 | $ 51,809 |
| | | | | | | |
| **PRINTING, EDITING & COPYING (* 2)** | | | | | | |
| Final report | $ 15,964 | $ 14,000 | $ 15,400 | $ 16,170 | $ 16,979 | $ 17,827 |
| Site guidelines | $ 0 | $ 0 | $ 0 | $ 0 | $ 0 | $ 0 |
| Drochure | $ 0 | $ 0 | $ 0 | $ 0 | $ 0 | $ 0 |
| | $ 15,964 | $ 14,000 | $ 15,400 | $ 16,170 | $ 16,979 | $ 17,827 |

| Account Name | Prov. Statement 2010/11 | Budget 2011/12 | Forecast 2012/13 | Estimation 2013/14 | Estimation 2014/15 | Estimation 2015/16 |
|---|---|---|---|---|---|---|
| **GENERAL SERVICES** (* 2) | | | | | | |
| Legal advice | $ 4,360 | $ 9,000 | $ 9,900 | $ 10,395 | $ 10,915 | $ 11,460 |
| External audit | $ 9,299 | $ 9,360 | $ 10,764 | $ 11,840 | $ 13,024 | $ 14,327 |
| Cleaning, maintenance & security | $ 9,240 | $ 9,900 | $ 11,385 | $ 11,954 | $ 12,552 | $ 13,180 |
| Training | $ 8,131 | $ 8,000 | $ 8,000 | $ 8,000 | $ 8,000 | $ 8,000 |
| Banking | $ 5,394 | $ 5,400 | $ 5,940 | $ 6,534 | $ 7,187 | $ 7,906 |
| Rental of equipment | $ 2,353 | $ 2,400 | $ 2,550 | $ 2,600 | $ 2,600 | $ 2,600 |
| | $ 38,778 | $ 44,060 | $ 48,539 | $ 51,324 | $ 54,279 | $ 57,473 |
| | | | | | | |
| **RELOCATION** (* 3) | | | | | | |
| Relocation | | | | | | |
| Av. Leandro Alem 884 - Maipú 757 | | $ 50,000 | | | | |
| | | $ 50,000 | | | | |
| | | | | | | |
| **COMMUNICATION** (* 2) | | | | | | |
| Telephone | $ 2,656 | $ 3,055 | $ 3,360 | $ 2,800 | $ 2,900 | $ 3,190 |
| Internet | $ 1,204 | $ 1,565 | $ 1,879 | $ 2,066 | $ 2,273 | $ 2,500 |
| Web hosting | $ 5,779 | $ 6,068 | $ 6,675 | $ 7,342 | $ 8,077 | $ 8,884 |
| Postage | $ 1,870 | $ 2,680 | $ 2,814 | $ 1,950 | $ 1,950 | $ 2,145 |
| | $ 11,509 | $ 13,368 | $ 14,728 | $ 14,159 | $ 15,200 | $ 16,720 |
| | | | | | | |
| **OFFICE** (* 2) | | | | | | |
| Stationery & supplies | $ 1,576 | $ 2,000 | $ 2,200 | $ 2,420 | $ 2,662 | $ 2,928 |
| Books & Subscriptions | $ 1,492 | $ 1,500 | $ 1,650 | $ 1,700 | $ 1,700 | $ 1,700 |
| Insurance | $ 1,325 | $ 1,900 | $ 2,280 | $ 2,622 | $ 3,015 | $ 3,468 |
| Furniture | $ 107 | $ 800 | $ 800 | $ 1,000 | $ 1,000 | $ 1,000 |
| Office equipment | $ 2,586 | $ 4,000 | $ 4,610 | $ 5,071 | $ 5,071 | $ 5,071 |
| Maintenance | $ 1,486 | $ 1,783 | $ 1,961 | $ 2,158 | $ 2,373 | $ 2,611 |
| | $ 8,572 | $ 11,983 | $ 13,501 | $ 14,971 | $ 15,822 | $ 16,777 |
| | | | | | | |
| **ADMINISTRATIVE** (* 2) | | | | | | |
| Supplies | $ 1,505 | $ 1,600 | $ 1,920 | $ 1,600 | $ 1,600 | $ 1,680 |
| Local transport | $ 779 | $ 800 | $ 800 | $ 800 | $ 800 | $ 880 |
| Miscellaneous | $ 2,134 | $ 2,298 | $ 2,534 | $ 2,200 | $ 2,420 | $ 2,662 |
| | $ 4,418 | $ 4,698 | $ 5,254 | $ 4,600 | $ 4,820 | $ 5,222 |
| | | | | | | |
| **REPRESENTATION** | | | | | | |
| Representation | $ 3,143 | $ 4,500 | $ 3,500 | $ 3,500 | $ 3,500 | $ 3,500 |
| | | | | | | |
| **FINANCING** | | | | | | |
| Exchange gain | -$ 19 | $ 0 | $ 0 | $ 0 | $ 0 | $ 0 |
| Exchange loss | $ 2,057 | $ 0 | $ 0 | $ 0 | $ 0 | $ 0 |
| Rounding | $ 6 | $ 0 | $ 0 | $ 0 | $ 0 | $ 0 |
| | $ 2,043 | $ 0 | $ 0 | $ 0 | $ 0 | $ 0 |

264

| Account Name | Prov. Statement 2010/11 | Budget 2011/12 | Forecast 2012/13 | Estimation 2013/14 | Estimation 2014/15 | Estimation 2015/16 |
|---|---|---|---|---|---|---|
| **Appropriations** | $ 1,183,967 | $ 1,181,850 | $ 1,262,374 | $ 1,365,700 | $ 1,410,509 | $ 1,495,192 |
| | | | | | | |
| **Funds Appropriations** | | | | | | |
| Working Capital Fund  (* 4) | $ 62,260 | $ 67,072 | $ 44,518 | $ 0 | $ 0 | $ 0 |
| Staff Termination Fund | $ 25,974 | $ 42,502 | $ 32,778 | $ 37,526 | $ 41,539 | $ 45,903 |
| Staff Replacement Fund | $ 8,333 | $ 18,246 | $ 0 | $ 0 | $ 0 | $ 0 |
| Translation Contingency Fund (Future Meeting Fund) | $ 0 | $ 30,000 | $ 0 | $ 0 | $ 0 | $ 0 |
| SUMA | $ 96,567 | $ 157,820 | $ 77,296 | $ 37,526 | $ 41,539 | $ 45,903 |
| | | | | | | |
| | | | | | | |
| Profit *I* (deficit) | $ 0 | $ 0 | $ 0 | $ 0 | $ 0 | ($ 0) |
| | | | | | | |
| **Summary of Funds** | | | | | | |
| General Fund | $ 27,206 | $ 0 | $ 0 | $ 0 | $ 0 | $ 0 |
| Translation Contingency Fund (Future Meeting Fund) | $ 0 | $ 30,000 | $ 30,000 | $ 30,000 | $ 30,000 | $ 30,000 |
| Staff Replacement Fund | $ 31,754 | $ 50,000 | $ 50,000 | $ 50,000 | $ 50,000 | $ 50,000 |
| Staff Termination Fund | $ 64,755 | $ 107,257 | $ 140,035 | $ 177,561 | $ 219,101 | $ 265,004 |
| Working Capital Fund  (* 4) | $ 191,652 | $ 285,930 | $ 330,448 | $ 307,079 | $ 276,282 | $ 199,075 |

**Comments:**

**1. Contributions:** Increase of Contributions in %
2012/13:  0%
2013/14:  3%
2014/15:  3%
2015/16:  3%

**2.** Estimation of increase in costs in appropriation lines with high labor content
2011/12: 19.9%
2012/13: 10%
2013/14:  5%
2014/15:  5%
2015/16:  5%

**3. Relocation:**
The Government  of Argentina is considering an extra contribution to cover parts of the relocation costs

**4. Working Capital Fund:**
Amount due to Financial Regulation 6.2

| | |
|---|---|
| 2011/12: | $ 223,267 |
| 2012/13: | $ 223,267 |
| 2013/14: | $ 229,965 |
| 2014/15: | $ 236,864 |
| 2015/16: | $ 243,970 |

## Appendix 3

# Contribution Scale 2012/13

| 2012/13 | Cat. | Mult. | Variable | Fixed | Total |
|---|---|---|---|---|---|
| Argentina | A | 3.6 | $ 36,424.17 | $ 23,921.43 | $60,346 |
| Australia | A | 3.6 | $ 36,424.17 | $ 23,921.43 | $60,346 |
| Belgium | D | 1.6 | $ 16,188.52 | $ 23,921.43 | $40,110 |
| Brazil | D | 1.6 | $ 16,188.52 | $ 23,921.43 | $40,110 |
| Bulgaria | E | 1 | $ 10,117.82 | $ 23,921.43 | $34,039 |
| Chile | C | 2.2 | $ 22,259.21 | $ 23,921.43 | $46,181 |
| China | C | 2.2 | $ 22,259.21 | $ 23,921.43 | $46,181 |
| Ecuador | E | 1 | $ 10,117.82 | $ 23,921.43 | $34,039 |
| Finland | D | 1.6 | $ 16,188.52 | $ 23,921.43 | $40,110 |
| France | A | 3.6 | $ 36,424.17 | $ 23,921.43 | $60,346 |
| Germany | B | 2.8 | $ 28,329.91 | $ 23,921.43 | $52,251 |
| India | C | 2.2 | $ 22,259.21 | $ 23,921.43 | $46,181 |
| Italy | B | 2.8 | $ 28,329.91 | $ 23,921.43 | $52,251 |
| Japan | A | 3.6 | $ 36,424.17 | $ 23,921.43 | $60,346 |
| Korea | D | 1.6 | $ 16,188.52 | $ 23,921.43 | $40,110 |
| Netherlands | C | 2.2 | $ 22,259.21 | $ 23,921.43 | $46,181 |
| New Zealand | A | 3.6 | $ 36,424.17 | $ 23,921.43 | $60,346 |
| Norway | A | 3.6 | $ 36,424.17 | $ 23,921.43 | $60,346 |
| Peru | E | 1 | $ 10,117.82 | $ 23,921.43 | $34,039 |
| Poland | D | 1.6 | $ 16,188.52 | $ 23,921.43 | $40,110 |
| Russia | C | 2.2 | $ 22,259.21 | $ 23,921.43 | $46,181 |
| South Africa | C | 2.2 | $ 22,259.21 | $ 23,921.43 | $46,181 |
| Spain | C | 2.2 | $ 22,259.21 | $ 23,921.43 | $46,181 |
| Sweden | C | 2.2 | $ 22,259.21 | $ 23,921.43 | $46,181 |
| Ukraine | D | 1.6 | $ 16,188.52 | $ 23,921.43 | $40,110 |
| United Kingdom | A | 3.6 | $ 36,424.17 | $ 23,921.43 | $60,346 |
| United States | A | 3.6 | $ 36,424.17 | $ 23,921.43 | $60,346 |
| Uruguay | D | 1.6 | $ 16,188.52 | $ 23,921.43 | $40,110 |
| | | 66.2 | $ 669,800.00 | $669,800.00 | **$1,339,600** |

| | |
|---|---|
| Budget amount | $1,339,600 |
| Base rate | $10,118 |

**Appendix 4**

# Salary Scale 2011/12

**STEPS**

| 2010/11 Level | | I | II | III | IV | V | VI | VII | VIII | IX | X | XI | XII | XIII | XIV | XV |
|---|---|---|---|---|---|---|---|---|---|---|---|---|---|---|---|---|
| 1 | A | $133,830 | $136,320 | $138,810 | $141,301 | $143,791 | $146,281 | $148,771 | $151,262 | | | | | | | |
| 1 | B | $167,287 | $170,400 | $173,512 | $176,626 | $179,739 | $182,851 | $185,964 | $189,078 | | | | | | | |
| 2 | A | $112,692 | $114,812 | $116,931 | $119,050 | $121,168 | $123,286 | $125,404 | $127,524 | $129,643 | $131,761 | $133,880 | $134,120 | $136,210 | | |
| 2 | B | $140,865 | $143,515 | $146,164 | $148,812 | $151,460 | $154,107 | $156,755 | $159,405 | $162,054 | $164,702 | $167,349 | $167,650 | $170,263 | | |
| 3 | A | $93,973 | $96,016 | $98,061 | $100,106 | $102,151 | $104,195 | $106,240 | $108,285 | $110,328 | $112,372 | $114,417 | $114,852 | $116,869 | $118,886 | $120,901 |
| 3 | B | $117,466 | $120,020 | $122,577 | $125,133 | $127,689 | $130,243 | $132,800 | $135,356 | $137,910 | $140,465 | $143,021 | $143,565 | $146,086 | $148,607 | $151,126 |
| 4 | A | $77,922 | $79,815 | $81,710 | $83,599 | $85,494 | $87,386 | $89,275 | $91,171 | $93,065 | $94,955 | $96,849 | $97,377 | $99,244 | $101,110 | $102,977 |
| 4 | B | $97,403 | $99,768 | $102,138 | $104,498 | $106,868 | $109,232 | $111,594 | $113,964 | $116,332 | $118,694 | $121,062 | $121,722 | $124,055 | $126,388 | $128,721 |
| 5 | A | $64,604 | $66,299 | $67,992 | $69,685 | $71,377 | $73,070 | $74,763 | $76,452 | $78,147 | $79,841 | $81,530 | $82,078 | | | |
| 5 | B | $80,755 | $82,874 | $84,989 | $87,106 | $89,222 | $91,337 | $93,454 | $95,565 | $97,684 | $99,801 | $101,913 | $102,597 | | | |
| 6 | A | $51,143 | $52,771 | $54,396 | $56,025 | $57,650 | $59,276 | $60,905 | $62,531 | $64,156 | $65,146 | $65,784 | | | | |
| 6 | B | $63,929 | $65,963 | $67,994 | $70,031 | $72,062 | $74,095 | $76,131 | $78,164 | $80,195 | $81,432 | $82,230 | | | | |

**STEPS**

| Level | I | II | III | IV | V | VI | VII | VIII | IX | X | XI | XII | XIII | XIV | XV |
|---|---|---|---|---|---|---|---|---|---|---|---|---|---|---|---|
| 1 | $53,015 | $55,488 | $57,962 | $60,435 | $63,013 | $65,700 | | | | | | | | | |
| 2 | $44,179 | $46,240 | $48,302 | $50,362 | $52,510 | $54,750 | | | | | | | | | |
| 3 | $36,815 | $38,532 | $40,250 | $41,968 | $43,759 | $45,627 | | | | | | | | | |
| 4 | $30,680 | $32,111 | $33,543 | $34,974 | $36,466 | $38,022 | | | | | | | | | |
| 5 | $25,344 | $26,528 | $27,710 | $28,893 | $30,128 | $31,415 | | | | | | | | | |
| 6 | $20,775 | $21,743 | $22,712 | $23,682 | $24,693 | $25,747 | | | | | | | | | |
| 7 | | | | | | | | | | | | | | | |
| 8 | | | | | | | | | | | | | | | |

# 3. Resolutions

# Strengthening Support for the Protocol on Environmental Protection to the Antarctic Treaty

**The Representatives,**

*Recalling* the Protocol on Environmental Protection to the Antarctic Treaty adopted on 4 October 1991 (the Protocol);

*Convinced* of the continuing need for comprehensive protection of the Antarctic environment and dependent and associated ecosystems;

*Reaffirming* their will to protect the Antarctic environment, in the interest of mankind as a whole and to preserve the value of Antarctica as an area for the conduct of scientific research;

*Reaffirming* the objectives and principles contained in the Antarctic Treaty and its Protocol, the Convention for the Conservation of Antarctic Marine Living Resources and the Convention for the Conservation of Antarctic Seals;

*Convinced* that the Protocol has, since its entry into force, contributed to ensuring a high level of protection of the Antarctic environment;

*Welcoming* the work of the Committee for Environmental Protection (the Committee), and noting that all Parties to the Protocol are entitled to participate in the Committee;

*Convinced* that the achievement of the objectives and principles of the Protocol will be better ensured if the Protocol is supported by a larger number of States;

**Recommend** that their Governments:

1. appeal to States that are Antarctic Treaty Parties but not yet Party to the Protocol on Environmental Protection to the Antarctic Treaty, to become Party to the Protocol;

2. accept the offer by France, Australia and Spain to coordinate with other Consultative Parties on representations to these States; and

3. invite France, Australia and Spain to report on the outcome of these representations at the Antarctic Treaty Consultative Meeting XXXV.

# Revised Guide to the Preparation of Management Plans for Antarctic Specially Protected Areas

**The Representatives,**

*Recalling* the requirements under Article 5 of Annex V to the Protocol on Environmental Protection to the Antarctic Treaty (the Protocol) to prepare and revise Management Plans for Antarctic Specially Protected Areas;

*Noting* that under Resolution 2 (1998) the Antarctic Treaty Consultative Meeting (ATCM) adopted a Guide to the Preparation of Management Plans for Antarctic Specially Protected Areas;

*Desiring* to update the Guide to reflect current best practice in the preparation of Management Plans for Antarctic Specially Protected Areas;

*Considering* the revision of the Guide by the Committee for Environmental Protection and its Subsidiary Group on Management Plans;

**Recommend** that:

1. the Guide to the Preparation of Management Plans for Antarctic Specially Protected Areas annexed to this Resolution replace the Guide adopted by Resolution 2 (1998) and be used by those engaged in the preparation or revision of Management Plans; and

2. the Antarctic Treaty Secretariat post the text of Resolution 2 (1998) on its website in a way that makes clear that it is no longer current.

# Guide to the Preparation of Management Plans for Antarctic Specially Protected Areas

## Background

### Purpose of the Guide

In 1991 the Antarctic Treaty Consultative Parties (ATCPs) adopted the Protocol on Environmental Protection to the Antarctic Treaty (Environment Protocol) to ensure comprehensive environmental protection in Antarctica. The Environment Protocol designates the whole of Antarctica as "a natural reserve" devoted to peace and science.

Annex V to the Environment Protocol, adopted subsequently at ATCM XVI under Recommendation XVI-10, provides a legal framework for the establishment of specially protected and managed areas within the overall "natural reserve". The text of Annex V is available on the ATS website at *http://www.ats.aq/documents/recatt/Att004_e.pdf*.

Annex V specifies that any area in the Antarctic Treaty area, including any marine area, may be designated as an Antarctic Specially Protected Area (ASPA) to protect outstanding environmental, scientific, historic, aesthetic or wilderness values, any combination of those values, or ongoing or planned scientific research (Article 3, Annex V).

The Annex further specifies that any Party to the Antarctic Treaty, the Committee for Environmental Protection (CEP), the Scientific Committee on Antarctic Research (SCAR) or the Commission for the Conservation of Antarctic Marine Living Resources (CCAMLR) *may propose an area for designation as an Antarctic Specially Protected Area by submitting a proposed Management Plan to the Antarctic Treaty Consultative Meeting* (Article 5, Annex V).

This Guide is a revision of the original version adopted by the Parties as an appendix to Resolution 2 (1998). It has been developed in order to assist any proponent in the process of proposing an Antarctic Specially Protected Area, with the following concrete aims:

- to assist Parties in their efforts to prepare Management Plans for proposed Antarctic Specially Protected Areas (ASPA) as required by the Protocol (Article 5, Annex V);
- to provide a framework which, when followed, enables Management Plans to meet the requirements of the Protocol; and
- to help achieve clear content, clarity, consistency (with other Management Plans) and effectiveness to expedite their review, adoption and implementation.

It is important to note that this guide is intended as no more than an aide-mémoire to the production of Management Plans for ASPAs. It has no legal status. Anyone intending to prepare a Management Plan should examine the provisions of Annex V to the Protocol carefully and seek advice from their national authority at an early stage.

**Protected areas network**

Annex V obliges Parties to seek to identify, within a *systematic environmental-geographical framework*, and to include in the series of Antarctic Specially Protected Areas:

- areas kept inviolate from human interference so that future comparisons may be possible with localities that have been affected by human activities;

- representative examples of major terrestrial, including glacial and aquatic, ecosystems and marine ecosystems;

- areas with important or unusual assemblages of species, including major colonies of breeding native birds or mammals;

- the type locality or only known habitat of any species;

- areas of particular interest to ongoing or planned scientific research;

- examples of outstanding geological, glaciological or geomorphological features;

- areas of outstanding aesthetic and wilderness value;

- sites or monuments of recognised historic value; and

- such other areas as may be appropriate to protect the outstanding environmental, scientific, historic, aesthetic or wilderness values, any combination of those values, or ongoing or planned scientific research.

This provision of the Environment Protocol provides the essential framework for an *Antarctic protected areas network*. The operationalization of what this framework entails has, however, been debated since the adoption of Annex V.

A number of analyses and evaluations of representation of the nine categories listed in Article 3(2) of Annex V have been conducted since the adoption of Annex V, first through a SCAR/IUCN Workshop on Protected Areas in 1992, then in two Protected Area workshops held in conjunction with CEP I and II in 1998 and 1999. In the analysis presented to CEP VIII in 2005 (ATCM XXVIII WP 11) it was noted that:

- there is an uneven distribution of ASPAs amongst the categories set out in Article 3(2) of Annex V, which is simply a product of history, in that a series of ad hoc designations have been made over time, rather than a systematic selection of sites within an overarching strategy or framework.

- in the absence of such a framework there is no means for assessing whether the current distribution is appropriate or not.

- in the absence of an holistic approach to management of the protected areas system (along the lines of a strategic environmental geographic framework as provided for in Article 3(2) of Annex V), the distribution of sites can be no more than simply noted.

The understanding of the term systematic environmental-geographic framework has evolved over time. However, the Environmental Domains Analysis prepared and presented in its final version to the CEP by New Zealand in 2005 constitutes the basis for our latest understanding of the concept. The Environmental Domains Analysis provides a classification of areas providing a data-derived, spatially explicit delineation of environmental variables in Antarctica, to be used for *inter alia* identification of priority sites for protection. The Domains Analysis provides a tool for an holistic and strategic designation of ASPAs, rather than assessing sites on their individual merits in isolation of other factors.

The ATCM has concurred that the Environmental Domains Analysis for the Antarctic Continent be used consistently and in conjunction with other tools agreed within the Antarctic Treaty System as a dynamic model for the identification of areas that could be designated as Antarctic Specially Protected Areas within the systematic environmental-geographical framework referred to in Article 33 of Annex V of the Protocol (Resolution 3 (2008)).

The Environmental Domains Analysis provides a useful and important measure of environmental variation across Antarctica that, in terms of the ice-free domains, can be considered essential as a first order assessment of likely systematic variation in biodiversity. For meaningful analysis at the finer spatial scales typically used in protected area designation, the EDA must nevertheless be supplemented with biodiversity data, which not only reflect current conditions but, importantly, historical processes that cannot in many instances be captured by modern environmental data.

### Identifying areas for protection

The designation of an area as a protected area provides the area with a higher level of protection beyond that achieved by other forms of planning and management measures under the Protocol in order to achieve specific protection aims and objectives.

When seeking to assess whether an area in fact needs such protection, it is necessary to be clear as to what values the area would aim to protect and as to the actual need to protect these values beyond the general protection provided by the Environment Protocol. The CEP has adopted guidelines for implementation of the Framework for Protected Areas set forth in Article 3, Annex V of the Environment Protocol that will assist any proponent in the process of such an evaluation. In such a process it would also need to consider how the designation of an ASPA would complement the existing protected areas network within the systematic environmental-geographical framework provided by the Environmental Domains Analysis and other relevant data available. Ensuring a thorough and in-depth analysis along these lines will indicate to the proponent whether designation of the area as a protected area is in fact required.

Only when a candidate area has been through such an overall assessment is it correct to initiate the process of developing a Management Plan for the area, in line with the guidance provided by this document.

### Relevant guidance material

- Annex V to the Environment Protocol *(http://www.ats.aq/documents/recatt/ Att004_e.pdf)*
- Guidelines for implementation of the Framework for Protected Areas set forth in Article 3, Annex V of the Environmental Protocol *(http://www.ats.aq/documents/ recatt/Att081_e.pdf)*
- Environmental Domains Analysis *(http://www.ats.aq/documents/recatt/Att408_e.pdf)*

## Format of Management Plans for ASPAs

Article 5 of Annex V specifies matters that each ASPA Management Plan should address. The following sections of this Guide provide guidance in addressing those requirements (summarised in Table 1).

The CEP has highlighted the benefits of promoting consistency between protected area Management Plans. The Template for Antarctic Specially Protected Area Management Plans presented at Appendix 3 is intended as a standard framework into which proponents can insert content specific to the area in question when preparing a new or revised ASPA Management Plan.

The template includes cross-reference to the relevant sections of this Guide. References to the Guide are provided in *italicised text*, and should be deleted from the Management Plan.

The template is formatted in accordance with the *Manual for the submission of documents to the Antarctic Treaty Consultative Meeting and the Committee for Environmental Protection* prepared by the Secretariat of the Antarctic Treaty. Proponents should consult the Manual for guidance on specific formatting issues, such as for tables and figures incorporated in a Management Plan.

**Table 1. Headings used in this Guide cross-referenced to Article 5 of Annex V**

| Management plan section / section of Guide | Article 5 reference |
|---|---|
| Introduction | |
| 1. Description of values to be protected | 3a |
| 2. Aims and objectives | 3b |
| 3. Management activities | 3c |
| 4. Period of designation | 3d |
| 5. Maps | 3g |
| 6. Description of the Area | 3 e (i - iv) |
| 6(v) Special zones within the Area | 3f |
| 7. Terms and conditions for entry Permits | 3 i (i - x) |
| 8. Supporting documentation | 3h |

## Guidance for the content of Management Plans

Since the development of Management Plans for ASPAs is an evolving process, preparers of Management Plans should be aware of current best practice and are strongly urged to consult examples agreed at past ATCMs. The current Management Plan for each ASPA can be accessed from the Protected Areas database on the website of the Secretariat of the Antarctic Treaty, at *http://www.ats.aq/devPH/apa/ep_protected.aspx*.

The template at Appendix 3 includes suggested standard wording for some sections. The availability of suggested standard wording is not intended to discourage proponents from developing and implementing site-specific or creative and innovative approaches to area protection and management. Suggested wording that relates directly to requirements arising from the Environment Protocol is identified with an asterisk (*). As appropriate, the suggested wording should be utilised, modified, or replaced with alternative text that adequately reflects site-specific considerations for the Area in question.

A Management Plan should provide sufficient details about the special features of the Area and any requirements for access and management to ensure that individuals planning to visit the Area and national authorities responsible for issuing permits are able to do so in a manner consistent with the purpose for designation. It should clearly identify why the Area is designated, and what additional measures (beyond the general provisions of the Environment Protocol and Annexes) apply to the Area as a result. The following sections provide guidance to proponents on the content addressed under each standard Management Plan heading.

### Introduction

An introduction to the Management Plan is not a stated requirement of Article 5 of Annex V, but can provide a useful overview. Information might include a summary of the important features of the Area, its history (e.g. initial designation, modifications, earlier Management Plans), the scientific research and other activities that have been carried out there.

Reasons why special protection is deemed necessary or desirable should also be stated in the Management Plan, preferably in the introduction. In this respect, the *Guidelines for implementation of the Framework for Protected Areas set forth in Article 3, Annex V of the Environmental Protocol* appended to Resolution 1 (2000) (*http://www.ats.aq/documents/recatt/Att081_e.pdf*) are a useful reference.

The CEP has agreed that Management Plans should include a clear statement about the primary reason for the Area's designation[1]. It is useful to include such a statement in the Introduction to the Management Plan, which serves as a summary of the Management Plan, as well as in the following section describing the values to be protected.

---

[1] CEP VIII Final Report, paragraph 187.

The CEP has also encouraged proponents to describe how the Area complements the Antarctic protected areas system as a whole[2]. For this purpose it should *inter alia* refer to the Environmental Domains Analysis of Antarctica (*http://www.ats.aq/documents/recatt/ Att408_e.pdf*), appended to Resolution 3 (2008) and to the existing suite of ASPAs. If applicable, the Introduction might also usefully describe how the Area complements others in the local vicinity or region.

## 1. Description of values to be protected

Article 3 of Annex V of the Environment Protocol states that any area, including any marine area, may be designated as an ASPA so as to protect outstanding environmental, scientific, historic, aesthetic or wilderness values and sets out a series of such values which ATCPs shall seek to incorporate into ASPAs.

In considering any new proposal for an ASPA, thought needs to be given as to how protected area status would address the values identified in Article 3 of Annex V, and whether such values are already adequately represented by protected areas in Antarctica.

This section should include a statement about the primary reason for designation, but should also describe the full range of reasons for the Area's designation. The description of the value or values of the Area should state, clearly and in detail, why it is that the site deserves special protection and how ASPA designation will strengthen protection measures. This may include a description of the actual or potential risks the values are facing. For example, if the designation of the Area is intended to prevent interference with ongoing or planned scientific investigations this section should describe the nature and value of this research.

The Antarctic environment is subject not only to natural variability in factors such as climate, ice extent and the density and spatial extent of biological populations, but also the effects of rapid regional climate warming (particularly in the Antarctic Peninsula region). Therefore this section could also, where relevant, give a description of the potential environmental changes faced by the Area in light of such rapid warming (e.g. potential thinning of glaciers; rapid retreat of ice-shelves and exposure of new ice-free terrain; impacts on sea ice-dependent penguin species by ocean warming and declining sea ice extent; the likelihood/risk of establishment of non-native species or natural colonists originating from more northerly (and therefore less climatically severe) latitudes etc.)

In cases where the intent is to protect the value of sites as reference areas or controls for long-term environmental monitoring programmes, the particular characteristics of the area relevant to long-term monitoring should be described. In cases where ASPA designation is being conferred to protect historic, geological, aesthetic, wilderness or other values, those values should be described in this section.

In all cases the description of values should provide sufficient detail to enable readers to understand precisely what the ASPA designation is intended to protect. It should not provide a full description of the Area, which is presented in Section 6.

---

[2] CEP VIII Final Report, paragraph 187.

## 2. Aims and objectives

This section should establish what is intended to be achieved by the Management Plan and how the Plan will address protection of the values described above. For example the aims of the Plan might highlight an intention to:

- avoid certain specified changes to the area;
- prevent any human interference with specified features or activities in the area;
- allow only certain types of research, management, or other activities that would not interfere with the reason for the site's designation; or
- minimise, to the maximum extent practicable, the introduction of non-native species, which could compromise the environmental and scientific values of an area.

It is important to note that the description of values and the objectives will be used by the national permitting authority to help decide activities that can, and cannot, be authorised to be conducted in the Area. Consequently the values to be protected and the objectives of the plan must be described specifically, not generally.

## 3. Management activities

Management activities outlined in this section should relate to the aims of the Management Plan and to the objectives for which the Area was designated.

There should be a clear indication of what is prohibited, what should be avoided or prevented as well as what is allowed. The Plan should make it clear when permitted activities can take place. For example some activities may only be allowed during periods that do not coincide with the breeding season of sensitive species.

This section should describe such actions as will be taken to protect the particular values of the Area (e.g. installation and maintenance of scientific instruments, establishment of marked routes or landing sites, erection of signs indicating that the site is an ASPA and that entry is prohibited except in accordance with a permit issued by an appropriate national authority, removal of abandoned equipment or materials). If the management activities require cooperative action by two or more Parties conducting or supporting research in the area, the arrangements for carrying out the required activities should be jointly developed, and described in the Management Plan.

It is important to remember and to note in the Management Plan that active management may require an environmental impact assessment, which should be undertaken in accordance with the requirements of Annex 1 of the Environment Protocol.

If no special management activities are required, this section of the Plan should state, "None required".

### 4. Period of designation

Designation of an ASPA is for an indefinite period unless the Management Plan provides otherwise. It is a requirement under Article 6(3) of Annex V that the Management Plan is reviewed at least every five years, and updated as necessary.

If the intent is to provide protection for a finite period, while a particular study or other activity is conducted, an expiry date should be included in this section.

### 5. Maps

Maps are a critical component of any Management Plan and should be clear and sufficiently detailed. If the area is particularly large a number of maps that vary in scale may be appropriate, but the minimum is likely to be two: one showing the general region in which the Area is situated, as well as the position of all nearby protected areas; and a second map illustrating the details of the Area itself.

It is essential that the maps clearly indicate the boundary of the Protected Area as described under section 6.1 below.

Guidelines for maps are given in Appendix 1 together with a checklist of features to be considered for inclusion.

### 6. Description of the Area

This section requires an accurate description of the Area and, where appropriate, its surroundings to ensure that individuals planning a visit and national authorities responsible for issuing permits are sufficiently appraised of the special features of the area.

It is important that this section describe adequately those features of the Area that are being protected, thus alerting users of the Management Plan to features of particular sensitivity. This section should preferably not duplicate the description of the values of the Area.

The section is divided into five subsections:

*6(i) Geographical coordinates, boundary markers and natural features*

The boundary of the Area should be delineated unambiguously and the important features clearly described, as the boundary delineation will form the basis of legal enforcement. The boundary of the Area should be carefully selected and described. It is preferable to describe a boundary that is identifiable at all times of the year. This is often difficult due to snow cover in winter, but at least in summer it should be possible for any visitor to determine the limits of the Area. For Areas near to sites frequented by tourists this is especially important. It is best to choose static boundary markers such as exposed rock features. Features that might be expected to vary in location throughout the year or during the five-year review period of the Management Plan, such as the edges of snow fields or wildlife colonies, are unlikely to be suitable. In some instances it may be advisable to install boundary markers where natural features are not sufficient.

284

Consideration should be given to the likely future impacts of climate change when determining or reviewing the boundaries of the Protected Area. Particular thought should be given to the designation of boundaries using features other than ice-free ground. For example, future climate change induced glacial retreat, ice shelf collapse and lake level change will have an impact on ASPAs whose boundary definitions follow these features.

Geographical coordinates included in the boundary description should be as accurate as possible. They should be given as latitude and longitude in degrees, minutes and seconds. If possible, reference should be made to published maps or charts to allow the Area boundaries to be delineated on the map. The survey and mapping methods employed should be stated if possible along with the name of the agency producing the maps or charts referred to.

The importance of GPS for fixing positions cannot be overstated. Over past years it has become clear that the original positioning of some protected areas is highly suspect. The opportunity to revise the plan for each ASPA is an opportunity to use GPS, to provide accurate locational information on boundaries. It is strongly recommended that plans are not submitted without such information.

When describing the physical features of the Area, only place names formally approved by a Consultative Party and included in the SCAR Composite Gazetteer of Antarctica should be used *(http://data.aad.gov.au/aadc/gaz/scar/)*. All names referred to in the text of the Plan should be shown on the maps. If a new place name is needed, approval will be required by the appropriate national committee and the place name submitted for inclusion in the SCAR Composite Gazetteer of Antarctica before using the new name on any maps and before submitting the plan.

The description of the natural features of the Area should include descriptions of, the local topography such as permanent snow/ice fields, the presence of any water bodies (lakes, streams, pools) and a brief summary of the local geology and geomorphology. An accurate, brief description of the biological features of the Area is also useful including notes on major plant communities; bird and seal colonies and numbers of individuals or breeding pairs of birds.

If the area contains a marine component the management plan may need to be submitted to CCAMLR for consideration – see the section below on "Approval process for ASPA Management Plans".

*6(ii) Access to the area*

This subsection should include descriptions of preferred access routes to the Area by land, sea or air. These should be clearly defined to prevent confusion and suitable alternatives provided if the preferred route is unavailable.

All access routes as well as marine anchorages and helicopter landing areas should be described and clearly marked on the accompanying map of the Area. Helicopter landing areas should usually be located well outside the ASPA boundary to ensure minimum interference with the integrity of the Area.

The subsection should also describe preferred walking and, when permitted, vehicle routes within the area.

*6(iii) Location of structures within and adjacent to the Area*

It is necessary to describe and accurately locate all structures within or adjacent to the Area. These include, for example, boundary markers, sign boards, cairns, field huts, depots and research facilities. Where possible the date the structures were erected and the country to whom they belong should be recorded, as well as the details of any HSMs in the area. If applicable the timing of the planned removal of any structures should also be noted (e.g. in the case of temporary scientific or other installations).

*6(iv) Location of other protected areas in the vicinity*

There is no specific radius to be used when describing other protected areas "in the vicinity", but a distance of approximately 50 km has been used in many plans adopted so far. All such protected areas (i.e. ASPAs, ASMAs, HSMs, CCAS Seal Reserves, CCAMLR CEMP sites etc.) in the vicinity should be given by name and, where appropriate, number. The coordinates and approximate distance and direction from the Area in question should also be provided.

*6(v) Special zones within the Area*

Article 5.3(f) of Annex V allows for the identification of zones within ASPAs and ASMAs *"in which activities are to be prohibited, restricted, or managed for the purpose of achieving the aims and objectives..."* of the management plan.

Those preparing management plans should consider whether the objectives of the plan could be achieved more effectively by designating one or more zones. Clearly demarcated zones help provide clear information to site visitors on where, when and why special management conditions apply. They can be useful to communicate the goals and requirements of management in a clear and simple manner. For example, special zones might include bird colonies to which access is restricted during the breeding season, or sites where scientific experiments should not be disturbed.

In order to help achieve greater consistency in the application of the zoning tool in Antarctica, a standard set of commonly used zones that should meet management needs in most situations has been identified and defined (Table 2).

As is the case with all guidelines, there may arise instances where exceptions are both needed and desirable. When this is the case, those preparing management plans might consider the application of alternative zones. It is important to keep in mind, however, that management plans should aim to use zones that are as simple and consistent as possible across all sites within Antarctica. This will help to ensure that plan conditions are understandable and easy to follow, and thereby assist in the practical protection and management of these special areas.

If no zones are designated within the Area, this should be specifically stated in the Management Plan.

**Table 2. Zoning Guidelines for ASPAs**

| Zone | Specific Zone Objectives |
|------|--------------------------|
| **Facilities Zone** | To ensure that science support facilities and related human activities within the Area are contained and managed within designated areas |
| **Access Zone** | To provide guidance for approach and/or landing of aircraft, boats, vehicles or pedestrians accessing the Area and by doing so protect areas with sensitive assemblages of species or scientific equipment etc and/or provide for safety |
| **Historic Zone** | To ensure those who enter the Area are aware of the areas or features within that are sites, buildings and/or artefacts of historic importance and to manage them appropriately |
| **Scientific Zone** | To ensure those who enter the Area are aware of the areas within that are sites of current or long-term scientific investigation or have sensitive scientific equipment installed |
|  | To restrict access into a particular part of the Area and/or activities within it for a range of management or scientific reasons, e.g. owing to special scientific or ecological values, because of sensitivity, presence of hazards, or to restrict emissions or constructions at a particular site. Access into Restricted Zones should normally be for compelling reasons that cannot be served elsewhere within the Area |
|  | To prohibit access into a particular part of the ASPA until such time it is agreed by the ATCM (and not individual Parties) that the Management Plan should be changed to allow access |

## 7. Terms and conditions for entry permits

*7(i) General permit conditions*

Article 3 (4) of Annex V of the Environment Protocol specifies that entry into ASPAs is prohibited except in accordance with a permit issued by an appropriate national authority.

The Management Plan should set out the conditions under which a permit might be issued. When drafting Management Plans, authors should be aware that the authorities appointed to issue permits for entry into ASPAs will use the contents of this section to determine whether, and under what conditions, permits may be issued.

Article 7(3) of Annex V of the Environment Protocol directs that each Party must require the permit holder to carry a copy of the permit whilst in the ASPA. This section of the Management Plan should note that all permits should contain a condition requiring the permit holder to carry a copy of the permit whilst in the ASPA.

Article 5 of Annex V sets out 10 separate issues that need to be addressed when considering the terms and conditions that might be attached to permits. These are set out below:

*7(ii) Access to, and movement within or over, the Area*

This section of the Management Plan should set out restrictions on the means of transport, points of access, routes and movement within the Area. It should also address the direction of approach for aircraft and the minimum height for overflying the Area. Such information should state the type of aircraft (e.g. fixed or rotary wing) on which the restrictions are based, that should be included as conditions of permits that are issued.

Where appropriate, the Management Plan should make reference to relevant guidelines adopted by the CEP, such as the *Guidelines for the Operation of Aircraft near Concentrations of Birds (http://www.ats.aq/documents/recatt/Att224_e.pdf)* appended to Resolution 2 (2004).

*7(iii) Activities which may be conducted in the Area*

This should detail what may be undertaken within the protected area and the conditions under which such activities are allowed. For example, to avoid interference with wildlife, only certain types of activity might be permitted.

If the Management Plan proposes that active management within the Area may be necessary in the future, this should also be listed here.

*7(iv) Installation, modification, or removal of structures*

It is useful to identify what, if any, structures are permitted within the Area. For example, certain scientific research equipment, markers or other structures might be allowed to be installed within the Area.

To assist with tracking the purpose of such structures, the Management Plan should explain how structures are to be identifiable. General and/or specific guidance on relevant considerations to minimise the adverse effects of installations on the values of the Area may also be useful.

If any existing structures are present (e.g. refuges) the Management Plan should also indicate action which might be authorised to modify or remove the structures. Alternatively, if no structures are to be permitted within the Area the Management Plan should make this clear.

*7(v) Location of field camps*

It is likely that field camps would not usually be permitted within the boundaries of the Area. However, it may be permissible under certain conditions such as overriding reasons of safety. If so the conditions under which field camps may be permitted should be stated. It is possible that field camps would only be acceptable in certain parts of the Area. Such campsites should be identified and recorded on the supporting maps.

*7(vi) Restrictions on materials and organisms which may be brought into the Area*

This section should set out prohibitions and give guidance on the management of any materials that are to be used or stored in the Area.

There is a complete prohibition on the deliberate introduction of non-native species and diseases to the Antarctic Treaty area under Article 4 of Annex II of the Environment Protocol, except in accordance with a separate permit issued under the Authority provided for in Annex II. Article 4 also states that (i) precautions are taken within the Treaty area to prevent accidental introductions of microorganisms, (ii) appropriate efforts are made to ensure poultry and avian products are free from contamination by diseases, (iii) deliberate introduction of non-sterile soil is prohibited and (iv) the unintentional importation of non-sterile soil is minimised to the maximum extent practicable. Therefore, recommended measures to reduce the risk of non-native species introductions applied throughout Antarctica should also apply to the Protected Area. The management should, as appropriate, include provisions relating to the cleaning of camping equipment, scientific equipment, vehicles and personal footwear and clothing to remove propagules before entering the ASPA. SCAR's "Environmental code of conduct for terrestrial scientific field research in Antarctica" may provide some useful biosecurity recommendations.

Careful consideration should be given to the risk of introducing non-native species to the Protected Area on or via foodstuffs or associated containers and packaging. Non-sterile soil, plant propagules, eggs and live insects could be introduced in association with fresh fruits and vegetables, while bird or marine mammal pathogens may be introduced to the area via poultry products. The Management Plan may state that such products should not be permitted in the area or specify measures to minimise the risk of pathogen release to the environment.

In some instances special precautions may need to be taken to prevent the introduction of non-native species. If, for example, the Area has been designated for its special microbial communities, it may be necessary to require more stringent biosecurity precautions to minimise shedding of human commensal microorganisms and redistribution of other environmental microorganism from outside the Area. The use of sterile protective over-clothing and thoroughly cleaned footwear may be appropriate.

It may be necessary, for example, to bring some chemicals into the Area for research or management purposes. If so guidance should be provided as to how they must be stored, handled and removed. It may also be necessary to bring food and fuel into the Area, and guidance about the use, storage and removal of such materials should be given. Radio isotope and/or stable isotopes should only be released into the environment within the ASPA after careful consideration of the long-term impacts of such activities on the future environmental and scientific values of the Area.

*7(vii) Taking of, or harmful interference with, native flora and fauna*

This is prohibited under Article 3 of Annex II of the Environment Protocol except in accordance with a permit issued under the provisions of Annex II; this should be stated in all permits authorising this activity in the area. The requirements under Article 3 of Annex II must be adhered to, and commonly applied guidelines such as the SCAR Code of Conduct for the Use of Animals for Scientific Purposes in Antarctica may be presented as the minimum standard.

*7(viii) The collection or removal of materials not brought into the Area by the permit holder*

It may be permissible to remove from the Area materials such as beach litter, dead or pathological fauna or flora or abandoned relics and artefacts from previous activities. What items or samples can be removed by the permit holder should be clearly stated.

*7(ix) Disposal of waste*

Annex III of the Environment Protocol deals with the management of wastes in Antarctica. This section of the plan should specify requirements for the disposal of wastes that should be included as conditions of permits. The requirements set out in Annex III must be used as the minimum standards for waste disposal in an ASPA.

As a general rule all wastes, including all human wastes, generated by visitors to an ASPA should be removed from the Area. Exceptions, which must accord with the provisions of the Environment Protocol, should be identified as appropriate in this section of the Management Plan. In particular, consideration should be given to the likely impacts of sewage waste disposal on birds and marine mammals within the Area.

*7(x) Measures that may be necessary to continue to meet the aims of the Management Plan*

When appropriate this section should establish the conditions under which the issue of a permit may be necessary so as to ensure continued protection of the Area. For example it may be necessary to issue permits to allow for monitoring of the Area; to allow for repair or replacement of boundary markers and signs; or to allow for some active management as set out in section 3 above.

Where a management plan provides that, for exceptional reasons, non-native species are introduced in accordance with a separate permit, this section should discuss the need for measures to contain the non-native species and contingency procedures to be followed should the non-native species be released unintentionally into the environment. For example, it might specify that adequate biosecurity materials should be taken into the field work location to fulfil the requirements of the biosecurity plan, and personnel undertaking the work should be trained in their use.

In Protected Areas where non-native species are known to have become established, the Management Plan may outline measures to minimise further distribution of the species or its propagules to other locations.

*7(xi) Requirements for reports*

This section should describe the requirement for reports that should be included as a condition in permits issued by an appropriate national authority. It should, as appropriate, specify the information that should be included in reports. An ASPA visit report form is presented in Appendix 2 of this guide, and is available for download from the ATS website, *www.ats.aq.*

It may be useful to give a deadline by which time reports of a visit to the Area must be made (e.g. within six months). To address instances where the Area may be visited by groups authorised by Parties other than the Party that proposed the Management Plan, it may be useful to indicate that visit reports should be exchanged to assist in managing the Area and reviewing the Management Plan.

Many reporting requirements will be generally applicable, but in some cases it may be appropriate to specify particular information that will be of assistance in managing the Area. For example, for Areas designated to protect bird colonies it may be appropriate to request visiting groups undertaking surveys to report detailed information on census data, and locations of any new colonies or nests not previously recorded.

## 8. Supporting documentation

This section should refer to any additional documents that may be relevant. These may include any scientific reports or papers describing the values of the Area in greater detail, although as a general rule the various components of the Area and the intended management activities should be explained in the various sections of the Management Plan itself. Any such papers or supporting documents should be fully cited.

## Approval process for ASPA Management Plans

Article 5 of Annex V provides that any Party, the CEP, SCAR or CCAMLR may submit a draft Management Plan for consideration by the ATCM. In practice, draft Management Plans are generally submitted by one or more Parties to the CEP for consideration.

The process by which Management Plans are handled from drafting through to acceptance is summarised by the flow chart in Figure 1. This is based on the requirements of Article 6 of Annex V, the *Guidelines for CEP Consideration of New and Revised Draft ASPA and ASMA Management Plans* (Annex 1 of Appendix 3 to the CEP XI Final Report), and other related guidelines.

The approval process for an ASPA Management Plan has many critical stages, which can take a long time to complete. However, these stages are necessary as an ASPA Management Plan requires the agreement of all Antarctic Treaty Consultative Parties at an ATCM.

### Preparing the draft Management Plan

In the initial stages of drafting the Management Plan, it is recommended that widespread consultation, both nationally and internationally, is undertaken on the scientific, environmental and logistical elements of the Plan as appropriate. This will aid the passage of the Plan through the more formal process at the ATCM.

Proponents of new Areas are strongly encouraged to consider relevant guidelines and references that will assist in assessing, selecting, defining and proposing areas that might require greater protection through designation as an ASPA, including:

- *Guidelines for Implementation of the Framework for Protected Areas set forth in Article 3, Annex V of the Environmental Protocol* – Resolution 1 (2000).
- *Environmental Domains Analysis for the Antarctic continent* – Resolution 3 (2008).

When considering the designation of a new ASPA, proponents are encouraged to inform the CEP at an early stage (e.g. even before detailing a management plan for the area) so that proposals can be discussed in the context of the protected areas system as a whole.

When revising an existing Management Plan, it may be informative to use the *Checklist to assist in the inspection of Antarctic Specially Protected Areas and Antarctic Specially Managed Areas* (Resolution 4 (2008)) as a tool to identify necessary changes and improvements.

### Submitting the draft Management Plan for consideration

The draft Management Plan should be submitted to the CEP, as an attachment to a Working Paper prepared in accordance with Resolution 1 (2008) *Guide to the presentation of Working Papers containing proposals for Antarctic Specially Protected Areas, Antarctic Specially Managed Areas or Historic Sites and Monuments*.

If the Area contains a marine component that meets the criteria outlined in Decision 9 (2005) *Marine protected areas and other areas of interest to CCAMLR*, the draft Management Plan should also be submitted to CCAMLR for consideration. The proponents should make arrangements to ensure that any feedback from CCAMLR (which holds its annual meetings in October/November) is available before the proposal is considered by the CEP.

### Consideration by the CEP and ATCM

The CEP will consider the Management Plan, if appropriate taking into account any comments from CCAMLR. The CEP may refer the Management Plan to the ATCM for consideration and adoption, or to the Subsidiary Group on Management Plans (SGMP) for intersessional review.

In accordance with its Terms of Reference (see Appendix 1 to the CEP XIII Final Report), the SGMP will consider each draft Management Plan referred to it, advise the proponent(s) on recommended changes, consider any revised version of the Management Plan prepared during the intersessional period, and report to the CEP on its review. The revised Management Plan and the CEP's report would then be considered by the CEP meeting and, if agreed, referred to the ATCM for consideration and adoption.

If the ATCM agrees on the management plan a Measure is adopted in accordance with Article IX(1) of the Antarctic Treaty. Unless the Measure specifies otherwise, the Plan is deemed to have been approved 90 days after the close of the ATCM at which it was adopted, unless one or more of the Consultative Parties notifies the Depository, within that time period, that it wishes an extension of that period or is unable to approve the Measure.

### Review and revision of Management Plans

The Management Plan shall be reviewed every five years in accordance with Article 6(3) of Annex V of the Environment Protocol and updated as required. Updated Management Plans then follow the same course of agreement as before.

When undertaking Management Plan reviews, thought should be given to the need for further or continued site protection of species whose abundance or range has increased substantially. In contrast, site protection may be deemed unnecessary in an area where a protected species is no longer present and the environmental or scientific values for which the area was designated, no longer apply.

**Figure 1. Flow chart showing the approval process for ASPA Management Plans**

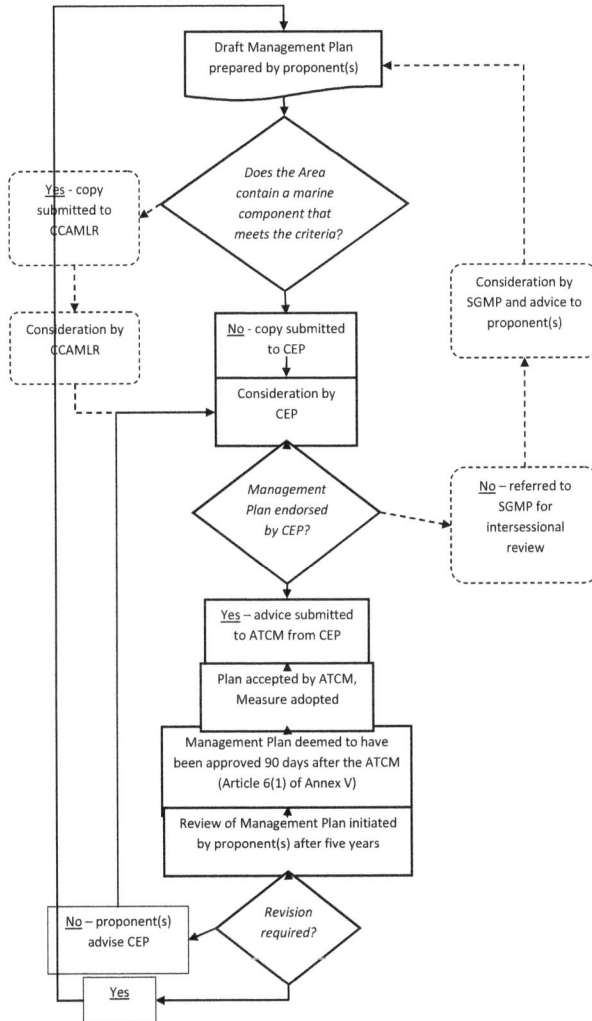

293

**Appendix 1**

# Guidance notes for producing maps for inclusion in Management Plans

Management Plans should include a general location map to show the position of the Area and the location of any other protected areas in the vicinity, and at least one detailed map of the site showing those features essential for meeting the Management plan objectives.

1.  Each map should include latitude and longitude as well as having a scale bar. Avoid statements of scale (e.g. 1:50000) because enlargement/reduction renders such statements useless. The map projection, and horizontal and vertical datums used should be indicated.

2.  It is important to use up-to-date coastline data including features such as ice shelves, ice tongues and glaciers. Ice recession and advance continues to affect many areas with consequent changes to Area boundaries. If an ice feature is used as a boundary the date of the source from which the data was acquired (e.g. survey or satellite image) should be shown.

3.  Maps should show the following features: any specified routes; any restricted zones; boat and/or helicopter landing sites and access points; campsites; installations and huts; major animal concentrations and breeding sites; any extensive areas of vegetation and should clearly delineate between ice/snow and ice-free ground. In many instances it is useful to include a geological map of the Area. It is suggested that, in most cases, it is helpful to have contouring at an appropriate interval on all maps of the Area. But contouring should not be too close as to mark other features or symbols on the map.

4.  Contours should be included on maps at an interval appropriate to the scale of the map.

5.  Be aware when preparing the map that it will be reduced to about 150 x 200 mm size to fit into the ATCM official report. This is of importance in selecting the size of symbols, the closeness of contouring and the use of shading. Reproduction is always monochrome so do not use colours to distinguish features in the original. There may well be other versions of an Area map available but as far as the legal status of the Management Plan is concerned it is the version published with the Final Report of the Antarctic Treaty Consultative Meeting that is the definitive version which will be included in national legislation.

6.  If the Area will require evaluation by CCAMLR the location of nearby CEMP sites should be indicated. CCAMLR has requested that the location of bird and seal colonies and the access routes from the sea should be indicated on a map wherever possible.

295

7.    Other figures can assist with using the Management Plan in the field:

- For photographs, good contrast prints are essential for adequate reproduction. Screening or digitising of photograph will improve reproduction when the plan is photocopied. If an image such as an aerial photograph or satellite image is used in the map the source and date of acquisition of the image should be stated.

- Some plans have already used 3-dimensional terrain models which again can provide important locational information when approaching an Area, especially by helicopter. Such drawings need careful design if they are not to become confusing when reduced.

# A checklist of features to be considered for inclusion on maps

**1.    Essential features**
 1.1   Title
 1.2   Latitude and longitude
 1.3   Scale bar with numerical scale
 1.4   Comprehensive legend
 1.5   Adequate and approved place names
 1.6   Map projection and spheroid modification
 1.7   North arrow
 1.8   Contour interval
 1.9   If image data are included, date of image collection

**2.    Essential topographical features**
 2.1   Coastline, rock and ice
 2.2   Peaks and ridge lines
 2.3   Ice margins and other glacial features
 2.4   Contours (labelled as necessary) survey points and spot heights

**3.    Natural Features**
 3.1   Lakes, ponds, streams
 3.2   Moraines, screes, cliffs, beaches
 3.3   Beach areas
 3.4   Vegetation
 3.5   Bird and seal colonies

**4.    Anthropogenic Features**
 4.1   Station
 4.2   Field huts, refuges
 4.3   Campsites
 4.4   Roads and vehicle tracks, footpaths features overlap
 4.5   Landing areas for fixed wing aeroplanes and helicopters
 4.6   Wharf, jetties
 4.7   Power supplies, cables
 4.8   Aerials. antennae
 4.9   Fuel storage areas

The same approach is obviously required of any inset maps.

At the conclusion of drafting a check should be made on cartographic quality to ensure:

- Balance between the elements.
- Appropriate shading to enhance features but which will not be confusing when photocopied and where degree should reflect importance.
- Correct and appropriate text with no features overlap.
- An appropriate legend using SCAR approved map symbols wherever possible.
- White text appropriately shadowed on all image data.

**Appendix 2**

# Antarctic Specially Protected Area (ASPA) visit report form

| |
|---|
| (1) ASPA number: |
| (2) ASPA name: |
| (3) Permit number: |
| (4) Permit period<br><br>From:<br><br>To: |
| (5) National authority issuing Permit: |
| (6) Date Report filed: |
| (7) Contact details for Principal Permit Holder:<br><br>Name:<br><br>Job Title or Position:<br><br>Phone number:<br><br>Email: |
| (8) Number of people<br><br>Permitted to enter the Area:<br><br>That actually entered the Area: |
| (9) List of all persons who entered the Area under the current Permit: |
| (10) Objectives of the visit to the Area under the current Permit: |
| (11) Date(s) and duration of visit(s) under the current Permit: |
| (12) Mode of transport to/from and within the Area: |
| (13) Summary of activities conducted in the Area: |
| (14) Descriptions and locations of samples collected (type, quantity, and details of any Permits for sample collection): |
| (15) Descriptions and locations of markers, instrumentation or equipment installed or removed, or any material released into the environment (noting how new installations are intended to remain in the Area): |
| (16) Measures taken during this visit to ensure compliance with the Management Plan: |

(17) On an attached photocopy of the map of the Area, please show (as applicable): camp site location(s), land/sea/air movements or routes, sampling sites, installations, deliberate release of materials, any impacts, and features of special significance not previously recorded. GPS coordinates should be provided for such locations wherever possible:

(18) Any other comment or information, such as:

    • Observations of human effects on the Area, distinguishing between those resulting from the visit and those due to previous visitors:

    • Evaluation of whether the values for which the Area was designated are being adequately protected:

    • Features of special significance that have not been previously recorded for the Area:

    • Recommendations on further management measures needed to protect the values of the Area, including location and appraisal of condition of structures, markers, etc.:

    • Any departures from the provisions of the Management Plan during this visit, noting dates, magnitudes and locations:

**Appendix 3**

## Template for Antarctic Specially Protected Area Management Plans

## Management Plan for Antarctic Specially Protected Area No. [XXX]

## [INSERT NAME OF PROTECTED AREA]

### Introduction

*The Guide to the Preparation of Management Plans for Antarctic Specially Protected Areas (the Guide) provides guidance for this section of Management Plans. No suggested standard wording is provided here because the content of this section will be specific to the Area in question.*

[Site-specific content should be inserted here]

### 1. Description of values to be protected

*Section 1 of the Guide provides guidance for this section of Management Plans. No suggested standard wording is provided here because the content of this section will be specific to the Area in question.*

[Site-specific content should be inserted here]

### 2. Aims and objectives

*Many existing Management Plans share similar aims and objectives. A pool of suggested standard wording has been developed and can be used, amended or deleted as appropriate for the Area in question (see below). Proponents are encouraged to identify site-specific aims and objectives, and should consider the guidance for this section of Management Plans given in Section 2 of the Guide.*

Management of [insert name of Area] aims to:

- avoid degradation of, or substantial risk to, the values of the Area by preventing unnecessary human disturbance to the Area;
- avoid degradation of, or substantial risk to, the values of the Area by preventing unnecessary human disturbance to the Area, its features and artefacts through managed access to [insert specific hut here];
- allow scientific research in the Area provided it is for compelling reasons which cannot be served elsewhere and which will not jeopardise the natural ecological system in that Area;
- prevent or minimise the introduction to the Area of alien plants, animals and microbes;
- minimise the possibility of the introduction of pathogens which may cause disease in fauna populations within the Area;
- preserve [a part of] the natural ecosystem of the Area as a reference area for future comparative studies;
- maintain the historic values of the Area through planned conservation and archaeological work programmes;
- [further site-specific content should be inserted here]

*In the case of Areas to which educational and outreach visits are permitted, the following text might be considered:*

- allow activities in the Area for educational and outreach purposes, provided that such activities are for compelling reasons which cannot be served elsewhere and which will not jeopardise the natural ecological system in that Area;
- [further site-specific content should be inserted here]

### 3. Management activities

*Many existing Management Plans share similar wording in this section. A pool of suggested standard wording has been developed and can be used, amended or deleted as appropriate for the Area in question (see below). Proponents are encouraged to identify site-specific management activities, and should consider the guidance for this section of Management Plans given in Section 3 of the Guide.*

None required.

[Insert type of information] on the location of the Area [stating special restrictions that apply] shall be displayed prominently, and a copy of this Management Plan shall be made available, at [insert location of information].

Copies of this Management Plan [and informative material] shall be made available to vessels [and aircraft] [insert: travelling/ planning to visit/visiting/operating in] the vicinity of the Area.

Signs illustrating the location and boundaries, with clear statements of entry restrictions, shall be placed at appropriate locations on the boundary of the Area [and Restricted Zone] to help avoid inadvertent entry.

Markers, signs or other structures (e.g. fences, cairns) erected within the Area for scientific or management purposes shall be secured and maintained in good condition and removed when no longer required.

In accordance with the requirements of Annex III of the Protocol on Environmental Protection to the Antarctic Treaty, abandoned equipment or materials shall be removed to the maximum extent possible provided doing so does not adversely impact on the environment and the values of the Area.*

The Area shall be visited as necessary[, and no less than once every five years,] to assess whether it continues to serve the purposes for which it was designated and to ensure that management [and maintenance] activities are adequate.

Visits shall be permitted as necessary in order to facilitate the study and monitoring of anthropogenic changes that could affect the protected values in the Area, in particular, [insert specific activity]. Impact study and monitoring should be conducted, to the maximum extent possible, by non-invasive methods.

National Antarctic Programmes operating in the Area shall consult together with a view to ensuring the above management activities are implemented.

The Management Plan shall be reviewed no less than once every five years and updated as required.*

Personnel [national programme staff, field expeditions, tourists and pilots] in the vicinity of, accessing or flying over the Area shall be specifically instructed, by their national programme [or appropriate national authority] as to the provisions and contents of the Management Plan.

All pilots operating in the region shall be informed of the location, boundaries and restrictions applying to entry and over-flight in the Area.

[Further site-specific content should be inserted here]


## 4. Period of designation

*Many existing Management Plans share similar wording in this section. Suggested wording has been developed and can be utilised as appropriate (see below) Section 4 of the Guide provides guidance for this section of Management Plans.*

Designated for an indefinite period. / Designated for a [x] year period.

## 5. Maps

*Section 5 of the Guide provides guidance for this section of Management Plans. Guidance for producing the maps themselves is given in Appendix 1 of the Guide. No suggested standard wording is provided here because the content of this section will be specific to the Area in question. However, proponents could utilise the following suggested format:*

- [Map X, Title of Map X
- Map Y, Title of Map Y
- Map Z, Title of Map Z]

## 6. Description of the Area

*Section 6 of the Guide provides general guidance for this section of Management Plans. Content should be inserted under the following sub-section headings.*

### 6(i)  Geographical coordinates, boundary markers and natural features

*Section 6(i) of the Guide provides guidance for this section of Management Plans. No suggested standard wording is provided here because the content of this section will be specific to the Area in question.*

[Site-specific content should be inserted here]

### 6(ii)  Access to the area

*Section 6(ii) of the Guide provides guidance for this section of Management Plans. No suggested standard wording is provided here because the content of this section will be specific to the Area in question.*

[Site-specific content should be inserted here]

### 6(iii) Location of structures within and adjacent to the Area

*Section 6(iii) of the Guide provides guidance for this section of Management Plans. No suggested standard wording is provided here because the content of this section will be specific to the Area in question.*

[Site-specific content should be inserted here]

### 6(iv) Location of other protected areas in the vicinity

*Section 6(iii) of the Guide provides guidance for this section of Management Plans. No suggested standard wording is provided here because the content of this section will be specific to the Area in question. However, proponents could utilise the following suggested format (e.g. ASPA 167, Hawker Island, 68°35'S, 77°50'E, 22 km to the north-east):*

304

[Other protected areas in the vicinity include (see Map XX):

- ASPA XXX, Name of Protected Area, latitude, longitude, XX km to the [direction]
- ASPA YYY, Name of Protected Area, latitude, longitude, XX km to the [direction]
- etc]

### 6(v)  Special zones within the Area

*Section 6(v) of the Guide provides guidance for this section of Management Plans, if any such zones are present. If there are no special zones, the following standard wording could be used. No other suggested standard wording is provided here because the content of this section will be specific to the Area in question.*

There are no special zones within the Area. / [Site-specific content should be inserted here]

## 7. Terms and conditions for entry permits

### 7(i) General permit conditions

*Many existing Management Plans share similar wording in this section. A pool of suggested standard wording has been developed and can be used, amended or deleted as appropriate for the Area in question (see below). Proponents are encouraged to identify site-specific permit conditions, and should consider the guidance for this section of Management Plans given in Section 7(i) of the Guide.*

Entry into the Area is prohibited except in accordance with a Permit issued by an appropriate national authority. Conditions for issuing a Permit to enter the Area are that:*

- it is issued for compelling scientific reasons which cannot be served elsewhere, or for reasons essential to the management of the Area;
- the actions permitted are in accordance with this Management Plan;*
- the activities permitted will give due consideration via the environmental impact assessment process to the continued protection of the [environmental, scientific, historic, aesthetic or wilderness] values of the Area;
- the Permit shall be issued for a finite period;
- the Permit shall be carried when in the Area;*
- [further site-specific content should be inserted here]

*In the case of Areas to which educational and outreach visits are permitted, the following text might be considered:*

- it is issued for compelling scientific, educational or outreach reasons which cannot be served elsewhere, or for reasons essential to the management of the Area;
- [further site-specific content should be inserted here]

**7(ii) Access to, and movement within or over, the Area**

*Many existing Management Plans share similar wording in this section. A pool of suggested standard wording has been developed and can be used, amended or deleted as appropriate for the Area in question (see below). Proponents are encouraged to identify site-specific content, and should consider the guidance for this section of Management Plans given in Section 7(ii) of the Guide.*

Vehicles are prohibited within the Area and all movement within the Area should be on foot.

Vehicle use in the Area should be kept to a minimum.

The operation of aircraft over the Area should be carried out, as a minimum requirement, in compliance with the "Guidelines for the Operation of Aircraft near Concentrations of Birds" contained in Resolution 2 (2004).

Pedestrian traffic should be kept to the minimum necessary to undertake permitted activities and every reasonable effort should be made to minimise trampling effects.

Movement within the Area by foot should be on designated tracks only.

Where no routes are identified, pedestrian traffic should be kept to the minimum necessary to undertake permitted activities and every reasonable effort should be made to minimise trampling effects.

Visitors should avoid areas of visible vegetation and care should be exercised walking in areas of moist ground, particularly the stream course beds, where foot traffic can easily damage sensitive soils, plant and algal communities, and degrade water quality.

[Further site-specific content should be inserted here]

**7(iii) Activities which may be conducted within the Area**

*Many existing Management Plans share similar wording in this section. A pool of suggested standard wording has been developed and can be used, amended or deleted as appropriate for the Area in question (see below). Proponents are encouraged to identify site-specific content, and should consider the guidance for this section of Management Plans given in Section 7(iii) of the Guide.*

Activities which may be conducted within the Area include:

- compelling scientific research which cannot be undertaken elsewhere;
- sampling, which should be the minimum required for approved research programmes;
- conservation and maintenance;
- essential management activities, including monitoring;

- operational activities in support of scientific research or management within or beyond the Area, including visits to assess the effectiveness of the Management Plan and management activities;
- [further site-specific content, including any requirements for active management within the site which may be necessary in the future, should be added here]

*In the case of Areas to which tourist visits are permitted (e.g. Historic Sites and Monuments designated as ASPAs) or to which educational and outreach visits are permitted, the following text might be considered:*

- tourist visits;
- activities for educational and outreach purposes;
- [further site-specific content should be inserted here]

### 7(iv) Installation, modification, or removal of structures

*Many existing Management Plans share similar wording in this section. A pool of suggested standard wording has been developed and can be used, amended or deleted as appropriate for the Area in question (see below). Proponents are encouraged to identify site-specific content, and should consider the guidance for this section of Management Plans given in Section 7(iv) of the Guide.*

No [new] structures are to be erected within the Area, or scientific equipment installed, except for compelling scientific or management reasons and for a pre-established period, as specified in a permit.

Permanent structures or installations are prohibited [with the exception of permanent survey markers and boundary signs].

No [new] structures are to be erected within the Area, or scientific equipment installed.

All markers, structures or scientific equipment installed in the Area must be clearly identified by country, name of the principal investigator or agency, year of installation and date of expected removal.

All such items should be free of organisms, propagules (e.g. seeds, eggs) and non-sterile soil, and be made of materials that can withstand the environmental conditions and pose minimal risk of contamination of the Area.

Installation (including site selection), maintenance, modification or removal of structures and equipment shall be undertaken in a manner that minimises disturbance to the values of the Area.

Existing structures must not be removed, except in accordance with a permit.

Structures and installations must be removed when they are no longer required, or on the expiry of the permit, whichever is the earlier.

Removal of specific structures or equipment for which the permit has expired shall be [the responsibility of the authority which granted the original permit and shall be] a condition of the Permit.

[Further site-specific content should be inserted here]

### 7(v) Location of field camps

*In most cases the content of this section will be specific to the Area in question. Proponents are encouraged to identify site-specific content, and should consider the guidance for this section of Management Plans given in Section 7(v) of the Guide. In the case of Areas where camping is prohibited, or where there are existing campsites, the following text might be considered:*

Camping is prohibited within the Area.

Existing campsites should be used where practicable.

[Further site-specific content should be inserted here]

### 7(vi) Restrictions on materials and organisms which may be brought into the Area

*Many existing Management Plans share similar wording in this section. A pool of suggested standard wording has been developed and can be used, amended or deleted as appropriate for the Area in question (see below). Proponents are encouraged to identify site-specific content, and should consider the guidance for this section of Management Plans given in Section 7(vi) of the Guide.*

In addition to the requirements of the Protocol on Environmental Protection to the Antarctic Treaty, restrictions on materials and organisms which may be brought into the area are:

- the deliberate introduction of animals, plant material, micro-organisms and non-sterile soil into the Area shall not be permitted. Precautions shall be taken to prevent the accidental introduction of animals, plant material, micro-organisms and non-sterile soil from other biologically distinct regions (within or beyond the Antarctic Treaty area).* Site-specific bio-security measures are listed below:

    - [site-specific measures should be inserted here];
- fuel or other chemicals shall not be stored in the Area unless specifically authorised by Permit condition. They shall be stored and handled in a way that minimises the risk of their accidental introduction into the environment;
- materials introduced into the Area shall be for a stated period only and shall be removed by the end of that stated period;
- [further site-specific conditions should be inserted here]

### 7(vii) Taking of, or harmful interference with, native flora and fauna

*Many existing Management Plans share similar wording in this section. A pool of suggested standard wording has been developed and can be used, amended or deleted as appropriate for the Area in question (see below). Proponents are encouraged to identify site-specific content, and should consider the guidance for this section of Management Plans given in Section 7(vii) of the Guide.*

Taking of, or harmful interference with, native flora and fauna is prohibited, except in accordance with a permit issued in accordance with Annex II of the Protocol on Environmental Protection to the Antarctic Treaty.*

Where taking or harmful interference with animals is involved this should, as a minimum standard, be in accordance with the SCAR Code of Conduct for the Use of Animals for Scientific Purposes in Antarctica.

[Further site-specific content should be inserted here]

### 7(viii) The collection or removal of materials not brought into the Area by the permit holder

*Many existing Management Plans share similar wording in this section. A pool of suggested standard wording has been developed and can be used, amended or deleted as appropriate for the Area in question (see below). Proponents are encouraged to identify site-specific content, and should consider the guidance for this section of Management Plans given in Section 7(viii) of the Guide.*

Unless specifically authorised by permit, visitors to the Area are prohibited from interfering with or from handling, taking or damaging any designated historic site or monument, or any anthropogenic material meeting the criteria in Resolution 5 (2001). Similarly, relocation or removal of artefacts for the purposes of preservation, protection or to re-establish historical accuracy is allowable only by permit. Any new or newly identified anthropogenic materials found should be notified to the appropriate national authority.

Other material of human origin likely to compromise the values of the Area, and which was not brought into the Area by the Permit Holder or otherwise authorised may be removed from the Area unless the environmental impact of the removal is likely to be greater than leaving the material in situ: if this is the case the appropriate national authority must be notified and approval obtained.

[Further site-specific content should be inserted here]

### 7(ix) Disposal of waste

*Many existing Management Plans share similar wording in this section. A pool of suggested standard wording has been developed and can be used, amended or deleted as appropriate for the Area in question (see below). Proponents are encouraged to identify site-specific content, and should consider the guidance for this section of Management Plans given in Section 7(ix) of the Guide.*

All wastes, including all human wastes, shall be removed from the Area.

All wastes, other than human wastes, shall be removed from the Area. [Although removal from the Area is preferable, human wastes may be disposed of into the sea]

Waste generated as a consequence of the activities developed in the Area shall be temporarily stored (insert site specific location details) in such a way as to prevent their dispersal into the environment and removed when activities have been concluded.

[Further site-specific content should be inserted here]

### 7(x) Measures that may be necessary to continue to meet the aims of the Management Plan

*Many existing Management Plans share similar wording in this section. A pool of suggested standard wording has been developed and can be used, amended or deleted as appropriate for the Area in question (see below). Proponents are encouraged to identify site-specific content, and should consider the guidance for this section of Management Plans given in Section 7(x) of the Guide.*

Permits may be granted to enter the Area to:

- carry out monitoring and Area inspection activities, which may involve the collection of a small number of samples or data for analysis or review;
- erect or maintain signposts, structures or scientific equipment;
- carry out protective measures;
- [further site-specific content should be inserted here]

Any specific sites of long-term monitoring shall be appropriately marked on site and on maps of the Area. A GPS position should be obtained for lodgement with the Antarctic Data Directory System through the appropriate national authority.

To help maintain the ecological and scientific values of the Area visitors shall take special precautions against introductions. Of particular concern are microbial, animal or vegetation introductions sourced from soils from other Antarctic sites, including stations, or from regions outside Antarctica. To the maximum extent practicable, visitors shall ensure that footwear, clothing and any equipment – particularly camping and sampling equipment – is thoroughly cleaned before entering the Area.

To avoid interference with long-term research and monitoring activities or duplication of effort, persons planning new projects within the Area should consult with established programmes and/or appropriate national authorities.

[Further site-specific content should be inserted here]

## 7(xi) Requirements for reports

*Many existing Management Plans share similar wording in this section. A pool of suggested standard wording has been developed and can be used, amended or deleted as appropriate for the Area in question (see below). Proponents are encouraged to identify site-specific content, and should consider the guidance for this section of Management Plans given in Section 7(xi) of the Guide.*

The principal permit holder for each visit to the Area shall submit a report to the appropriate national authority as soon as practicable, and no later than six months after the visit has been completed.*

Such reports should include, as appropriate, the information identified in the visit report form contained in the Guide to the Preparation of Management Plans for Antarctic Specially Protected Areas.

If appropriate, the national authority should also forward a copy of the visit report to the Party that proposed the Management Plan, to assist in managing the Area and reviewing the Management Plan.

Parties should, wherever possible, deposit originals or copies of such original visit reports in a publicly accessible archive to maintain a record of usage, for the purpose of any review of the Management Plan and in organising the scientific use of the Area.

[Further site-specific content should be inserted here]

## 8. Supporting documentation

*Section 8 of the Guide provides guidance for this section of Management Plans. No suggested standard wording is provided here because the content of this section will be specific to the Area in question.*

[Site-specific content should be inserted here]

# General Guidelines for Visitors to the Antarctic

**The Representatives,**

*Recalling* Resolution 5 (2005), Resolution 2 (2006), Resolution 1 (2007), Resolution 2 (2008), Resolution 4 (2009) and Resolution 1 (2010) which adopted lists of sites subject to Site Guidelines;

*Acknowledging* the benefits of focussing on site-specific information in Site Guidelines;

*Recalling* Recommendation XVIII-1(1994) *Guidance for those organising and conducting tourism and non-Governmental activities in the Antarctic*;

*Noting* that Recommendation XVIII-1(1994) provides guidance on both environmental and organisational matters;

*Affirming* the value of providing general environmental advice to visitors to complement site-specific information;

*Acknowledging* the work of the Committee for Environmental Protection since 1998 in enhancing the understanding of environmental impacts associated with visits to Antarctica;

*Noting* the desirability of providing contemporary advice to visitors to Antarctica to guide them in minimising their impacts at all sites;

*Believing* that the *General Guidelines for Visitors to the Antarctic* must be reviewed and revised as further information becomes available;

*Confirming* that the term "visitors" does not include scientists conducting research within such sites, or individuals engaged in official governmental activities;

**Recommend** that:

1.  their Governments endorse the annexed *General Guidelines for Visitors to the Antarctic*;

2.  the Guidelines be placed on the website of the Antarctic Treaty Secretariat;

3.  their Governments urge all those intending to visit sites in Antarctica to ensure that they are fully conversant with and adhere to the advice in these *General Guidelines for Visitors to the Antarctic*; and

4.  Parties work to make Recommendation XVIII-1 (1994) effective as soon as possible.

# General Guidelines for Visitors to the Antarctic

All visits to Antarctica should be conducted in accordance with the Antarctic Treaty, its Protocol on Environmental Protection, and relevant Measures and Resolutions adopted at Antarctic Treaty Consultative Meetings (ATCM). Visits may only occur after prior approval by a relevant national authority or if they have met all the requirements of their national authority.

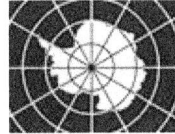

These Guidelines provide general advice for visiting any location, with the aim of ensuring visits do not have adverse impacts on the Antarctic environment, or on its scientific and aesthetic values. ATCM Site Guidelines for Visitors provide additional site-specific advice for some locations.

Read these Guidelines before you visit Antarctica and plan how to minimise your impact.

If you are part of a guided visitor group, abide by these guidelines, pay attention to your guides, and follow their instructions.

If you have organised your own visit, you are responsible for abiding by these guidelines. You are also responsible for identifying the features of the sites you visit that may be vulnerable to visitor impacts, and for complying with any site specific requirements, including Site Guidelines, Antarctic Specially Protected Area (ASPA) and Antarctic Specially Managed Area (ASMA) management plans, or station visit guidelines. Guidelines for particular activities or risks (such as aircraft use, or avoiding the introduction of non-native species) may also apply. Management plans, a list of historic sites and monuments, and other relevant information can be found at *www.ats.aq/e/ep_protected.htm*. Site Guidelines can be found at *www.ats.aq/e/ats_other_siteguidelines.htm*.

## PROTECT ANTARCTIC WILDLIFE

The taking of, or harmful interference with, Antarctic wildlife is prohibited except in accordance with a permit.

WILDLIFE

- When in the vicinity of wildlife, walk slowly and carefully and keep noise to a minimum.

- Maintain an appropriate distance from wildlife. While in many cases a greater distance may be appropriate, in general don't approach closer than 5m. Abide by any guidance on distances in site specific guidelines.

- Observe wildlife behaviour. If wildlife changes its behaviour stop moving, or slowly increase your distance.

- Animals are particularly sensitive to disturbance when they are breeding (including nesting) or moulting. Stay outside the margins of a colony and observe from a distance.

- Every situation is different. Consider the topography and the individual circumstances of the site, as these may have an impact on the vulnerability of wildlife to disturbance.

- Always give animals the right of way and do not block their access routes to the sea.

- Do not feed wildlife or leave food or scraps lying around.

- Do not use guns or explosives.

315

| VEGETATION | • Vegetation, including mosses and lichens, is fragile and very slow growing. Do not damage the vegetation by walking, driving or landing on any moss beds or lichen covered rocks. |
| | • When travelling on foot, stay on established tracks whenever possible to minimise disturbance or damage to the soil and vegetated surfaces. Where a track does not exist, take the most direct route and avoid vegetation, fragile terrain, scree slopes, and wildlife. |
| INTRODUCTION OF NON-NATIVE SPECIES | • Do not introduce any plants or animals into the Antarctic. |
| | • In order to prevent the introduction of non-native species and disease, carefully wash boots and clean all equipment including clothes, bags, tripods, tents and walking sticks before bringing them to Antarctica. Pay particular attention to boot treads, velcro fastenings and pockets which could contain soil or seeds. Vehicles and aircraft should also be cleaned. |
| | • The transfer of species and disease between locations in Antarctica is also a concern. Ensure all clothing and equipment is cleaned before moving between sites. |

## RESPECT PROTECTED AREAS

Activities in Antarctic Specially Protected Areas (ASPAs) or Antarctic Specially Managed Areas (ASMAs) must comply with the provisions of the relevant Management Plan.

Many historic sites and monuments (HSMs) have been formally designated and protected.

| SPECIALLY MANAGED AND SPECIALLY PROTECTED AREAS | • A permit from a relevant national authority is required for entry into any ASPA. Carry the permit and obey any permit conditions at all times while visiting an ASPA. |
| | • Check the locations and boundaries of ASPAs and ASMAs in advance. Refer to the provisions of the Management Plan and abide by any restrictions regarding the conduct of activities in or near these areas. |
| HISTORIC SITES AND MONUMENTS AND OTHER STRUCTURES | • Historic huts and structures can in some cases be used for tourist, recreational and educational visits. Visitors should not use them for other purposes except in emergency circumstances. |
| | • Do not interfere with, deface or vandalise any historic site, monument, or artefact, or other building or emergency refuge (whether occupied or unoccupied). |
| | • If you come across an item that may be of historic value that authorities may not be aware of, do not disturb it. Notify your expedition leader or national authorities. |
| | • Before entering any historic structure, clean your boots of snow and grit and remove snow and water from clothes, as these can cause damage to structures or artefacts. |
| | • Take care not to tread on any artefacts which may be obscured by snow when moving around historic sites. |

## RESPECT SCIENTIFIC RESEARCH

Do not interfere with scientific research, facilities or equipment.

• Obtain permission before visiting Antarctic stations.

• Reconfirm scheduled visits no less than 24-72 hours before arriving.

• Comply with any site specific rules when visiting Antarctic stations.

• Do not interfere with or remove scientific equipment or markers, and do not disturb experimental study sites, field camps or stored supplies.

## KEEP ANTARCTICA PRISTINE

Antarctica remains relatively pristine. It is the largest wilderness area on earth. Please leave no trace of your visit.

WASTE
- Do not deposit any litter or garbage on land nor discard it into the sea.
- At stations or camps smoke only at designated areas, to avoid litter and risk of fire to structures. Collect ash and litter for disposal outside Antarctica.
- Ensure that wastes are managed in accordance with Annexes III and IV of the Protocol on Environmental Protection to the Antarctic Treaty.
- Ensure that all equipment and rubbish is secured at all times in such a way as to prevent dispersal into the environment through high winds or wildlife foraging.

WILDERNESS VALUES
- Do not disturb or pollute lakes, streams, rivers or other water bodies (e.g. by walking, washing yourself or your equipment, throwing stones, etc.)
- Do not paint or engrave names or other graffiti on any man-made or natural surface in Antarctica.
- Do not take souvenirs, whether man-made, biological or geological items, including feathers, bones, eggs, vegetation, soil, rocks, meteorites or fossils.
- Place tents and equipment on snow or at previously used campsites where possible.

## BE SAFE

Be prepared for severe and changeable weather. Ensure that your equipment and clothing meet Antarctic standards. Remember that the Antarctic environment is inhospitable, unpredictable and potentially dangerous.

SAFETY PRECAUTIONS/ PREPARATIONS
- Know your capabilities, the dangers posed by the Antarctic environment, and act accordingly. Plan activities with safety in mind at all times.
- Keep a safe distance from dangerous wildlife like fur seals, both on land and at sea. Keep at least 15m away, where practicable.
- If you are travelling in a group, act on the advice and instructions of your leaders. Do not stray from your group.
- Do not walk onto glaciers or large snow fields without proper equipment and experience. There is a real danger of falling into hidden crevasses.
- Do not expect a rescue service. Self-sufficiency is increased and risks reduced by sound planning, quality equipment, and trained personnel.
- Do not enter emergency refuges (except in emergencies). If you use equipment or food from a refuge, inform the nearest research station or national authority once the emergency is over.
- Respect any smoking restrictions. Use of combustion style lanterns and naked flames in or around historic structures should be avoided. Take great care to safeguard against the danger of fire. This is a real hazard in the dry environment of Antarctica.

## LANDING AND TRANSPORT REQUIREMENTS

Act in Antarctica in such a way so as to minimise potential impacts on the environment, wildlife and associated ecosystems, or the conduct of scientific research.

**TRANSPORT**
- Do not use aircraft, vessels, small boats, hovercraft or other means of transport in ways that disturb wildlife, either at sea or on land. Avoid overflying concentrations of birds and mammals. Follow the advice in Resolution 2 (2004) *Guidelines for the operation of aircraft near concentrations of birds in Antarctica*, available from *www.ats.aq/devAS/ info_measures_list.aspx?lang=e.*

- Refilling of fuel tanks for small boats should take place in a way that ensures any spills can be contained, for example onboard a vessel.

- Small boats must be free of any soil, plants, or animals and must be checked for the presence of any soil, plants, or animals prior to the commencement of any ship-to-shore operations.

- Small boats must at all times regulate their course and speed so as to minimise disturbance to wildlife and to avoid any collisions with wildlife.

**SHIPS***
- Only one ship may visit a site at any one time.

- Vessels with more than 500 passengers shall not make landings in Antarctica.

**LANDING OF PASSENGERS FROM VESSELS**
- A maximum of 100 passengers may be ashore from a vessel at any one time, unless site specific advice requires fewer passengers.

- During landings from vessels, maintain a 1:20 guide to passenger ratio at all sites, unless site specific advice requires more guides.

* A ship is defined as a vessel which carries more than 12 passengers

# Site Guidelines for visitors

**The Representatives,**

*Recalling* Resolution 5 (2005), Resolution 2 (2006), Resolution 1 (2007), Resolution 2 (2008), Resolution 4 (2009) and Resolution 1 (2010), which adopted lists of sites subject to Site Guidelines;

*Recalling* Resolution 1 (2010), which provided that any proposed amendment to existing Site Guidelines be discussed by the Committee for Environmental Protection ("CEP"), which should advise the Antarctic Treaty Consultative Meeting ("ATCM") accordingly, and that if such advice is endorsed by the ATCM, the Antarctic Treaty Secretariat (the Secretariat) should make the necessary changes to the texts of Site Guidelines on its website;

*Believing* that Site Guidelines enhance the provisions set out in Recommendation XVIII-1 (1994) *Guidance for those organising and conducting tourism and non-Governmental activities in the Antarctic*;

*Confirming* that the term "visitors" does not include scientists conducting research within such sites, or individuals engaged in official governmental activities;

*Noting* that the Site Guidelines have been developed based on the current levels and types of visits at each specific site, and aware that the Site Guidelines would require review if there were any significant changes to the levels or types of visits to a site;

*Believing* that the Site Guidelines for each site must be reviewed and revised promptly in response to changes in the levels and types of visits, or in any demonstrable or likely environmental impacts;

*Desiring* to increase the number of Site Guidelines developed for visited sites and to keep existing Guidelines up to date;

**Recommend** that:

1.  the list of sites subject to Site Guidelines that have been adopted by the Antarctic Treaty Consultative Meeting be extended to include a further three new sites (Taylor Valley Visitor Zone, Southern Victoria Land; North-east beach of Ardley Island; Mawson's Huts and Cape Denison, East Antarctica), and that the full list of sites subject to Site Guidelines be replaced by the one annexed to this Resolution;

2.  the Site Guidelines for the Sites Whalers Bay, Deception Island, South Shetland Islands and Hannah Point be replaced by the modified Guidelines;

3.  the Antarctic Treaty Secretariat (the Secretariat) place the full list and the modified Guidelines, as adopted by the ATCM, on its website;

4.  their Governments urge all those intending to visit such sites to ensure that they are fully conversant with, and adhere to, the advice in the relevant Site Guidelines as published by the Secretariat;

5.  any proposed amendment to existing Site Guidelines be discussed by the Committee for Environmental Protection, which should advise the ATCM accordingly, and that if such advice is endorsed by the ATCM, the Secretariat should make the necessary changes to the texts of Site Guidelines on the website; and

6.  the Secretariat post the text of Resolution 1 (2010) on its website in a way that makes clear that it is no longer current.

# List of Sites subject to Site Guidelines

1.  Penguin Island (Lat. 62° 06' S, Long. 57° 54' W);
2.   Barrientos Island, Aitcho Islands (Lat. 62° 24' S, Long. 59° 47' W);
3.  Cuverville Island (Lat. 64° 41' S, Long. 62° 38' W);
4.  Jougla Point (Lat 64° 49' S, Long 63° 30' W);

5.  Goudier Island, Port Lockroy (Lat 64° 49' S, Long 63° 29' W);
6.  Hannah Point (Lat. 62° 39' S, Long. 60° 37' W);
7.  Neko Harbour (Lat. 64° 50' S, Long. 62° 33' W);
8.  Paulet Island (Lat. 63° 35' S, Long. 55° 47' W);
9.  Petermann Island (Lat. 65° 10' S, Long. 64° 10' W);
10. Pleneau Island (Lat. 65° 06' S, Long. 64° 04' W);
11. Turret Point (Lat. 62° 05' S, Long. 57° 55' W);
12. Yankee Harbour (Lat. 62° 32' S, Long. 59° 47' W);

13. Brown Bluff, Tabarin Peninsula (Lat. 63° 32' S, Long. 56° 55' W);
14. Snow Hill (Lat. 64° 22' S, Long. 56° 59' W);
15. Shingle Cove, Coronation Island (Lat. 60° 39' S, Long. 45° 34' W);
16. Devil Island, Vega Island (Lat. 63° 48' S, Long. 57° 16.7' W);
17. Whalers Bay, Deception Island, South Shetland Islands (Lat. 62° 59' S, Long. 60° 34' W);
18. Half Moon Island, South Shetland Islands (Lat. 60° 36' S, Long. 59° 55' W);

19. Baily Head, Deception Island, South Shetland Islands (Lat. 62° 58' S, Long. 60° 30' W);
20. Telefon Bay, Deception Island, South Shetland Islands (Lat. 62° 55' S, Long. 60° 40' W);
21. Cape Royds, Ross Island (Lat. 77° 33' 10.7" S, Long. 166° 10' 6.5" E);
22. Wordie House, Winter Island, Argentine Islands (Lat. 65° 15' S, Long. 64° 16' W);
23. Stonington Island, Marguerite Bay, Antarctic Peninsula (Lat. 68° 11' S, Long. 67° 00' W);
24. Horseshoe Island, Antarctic Peninsula (Lat. 67° 49' S, Long. 67° 18' W);
25. Detaille Island, Antarctic Peninsula (Lat. 66° 52' S, Long. 66° 48' W);

26. Torgersen Island, Arthur Harbour, Southwest Anvers Island (Lat. 64° 46' S, Long. 64° 04' W);

27. Danco Island, Errera Channel, Antarctic Peninsula (Lat. 64° 43' S, Long. 62° 36' W);

28. Seabee Hook, Cape Hallett, Northern Victoria Land, Ross Sea, Visitor Site A and Visitor Site B (Lat. 72° 19' S, Long. 170° 13' E);

29. Damoy Point, Wiencke Island, Antarctic Peninsula (Lat. 64° 49' S, Long. 63° 31' W);

30. Taylor Valley Visitor Zone, Southern Victoria Land (Lat. 77° 37.59' S, Long. 163° 03.42' E);

31. North-east beach of Ardley Island (Lat. 62° 13' S; Long. 58° 54' W);

32. Mawson's Huts and Cape Denison, East Antarctica (Lat. 67° 01' S; Long. 142 ° 40' E).

# Revised Guide to the Presentation of Working Papers Containing Proposals for Antarctic Specially Protected Areas, Antarctic Specially Managed Areas or Historic Sites and Monuments

**The Representatives,**

*Noting* that Annex V to the Protocol on Environmental Protection to the Antarctic Treaty (the Protocol) provides for the Antarctic Treaty Consultative Meeting ("ATCM") to adopt proposals to designate an Antarctic Specially Protected Area ("ASPA") or an Antarctic Specially Managed Area ("ASMA"), to adopt or amend a Management Plan for such an area, or to designate an Historic Site or Monument ("HSM"), by a Measure in accordance with Article IX(1) of the Antarctic Treaty;

*Conscious* of the need to ensure clarity concerning the current status of each ASPA and ASMA and its management plan, and each HSM;

*Recalling* Resolution 3 (2008), which recommended that the "Environmental Domains Analysis for the Antarctic Continent", annexed to it, be used consistently and in conjunction with other tools agreed within the Antarctic Treaty system as a dynamic model for the identification of areas that could be designated as Antarctic Specially Protected Areas within the systematic environmental-geographical framework referred to in Article 3(2) of Annex V of the Protocol;

*Recalling* also Resolution 1 (2008), which recommended that the Guide to the presentation of Working Papers containing a proposal for Antarctic Specially Protected Areas, Antarctic Specially Managed Areas or Historic Sites and Monuments, annexed to it, be used by those engaged in the preparation of such Working Papers;

*Desiring* to update the Guide appended to Resolution 1 (2008), to facilitate the collection of information to assist with the assessment and further development of the Antarctic protected areas system, specifically including the primary reason for designation of each ASPA and, where known, the main Environmental Domain represented by each ASPA and ASMA;

**Recommend** that:

1.  the *Guide to the presentation of Working Papers containing proposals for Antarctic Specially Protected Areas, Antarctic Specially Managed Areas or Historic Sites and Monuments* annexed to this Resolution replace the version appended to Resolution 1 (2008) and the updated version of the Guide be used by those engaged in the preparation of such Working Papers; and

2.  the Antarctic Treaty Secretariat post the text of Resolution 1 (2008) on its website in a way that makes clear that it is no longer current.

# Guide to the presentation of Working Papers containing proposals for Antarctic Specially Protected Areas, Antarctic Specially Managed Areas or Historic Sites and Monuments

## A. Working Papers on ASPA or ASMA

It is recommended that the Working Paper contain two parts:

(i) COVER SHEET explaining the intended effects of the proposal and the history of the ASPA/ASMA, using Template A as a guide. This cover sheet will NOT form part of the Measure adopted by the ATCM, so will not be published in the Final Report nor on the ATS website. Its sole purpose is to facilitate consideration of the proposal and the drafting of the Measures by the ATCM.

and

(ii) MANAGEMENT PLAN, written as a final version as it is intended to be published. This will be annexed to the Measure and published in the Final Report and on the ATS website.

It would be helpful if the plan is written *as final*, ready for publication. Of course, when it is first submitted to the CEP it is a draft and may be amended by the CEP or ATCM. However, the version adopted by the ATCM should be in final form for publication, and should not require further editing by the Secretariat, other than to insert cross-references to other instruments adopted at the same meeting.

For example, in its final form, the plan should not contain expressions such as:

- "this *proposed* area";
- "this *draft* plan";
- "this plan, *if adopted*, would…";
- accounts of discussions in the CEP or ATCM or details of intersessional work (unless this covers important information eg about the consultation process or activities that have occurred within the Area since the last review);
- views of individual delegations on the draft or intermediate versions of it;
- references to other protected areas using their pre-Annex V designations.

Please use the "Guide to the Preparation of Management Plans for Antarctic Specially Protected Areas" if the proposal concerns an ASPA. (The current version of this Guide is appended to Resolution 2 (1998) and is contained in the CEP Handbook).

There are several high quality management plans, including that for ASPA 109: Moe Island, that could be used as a model for the preparation of new and revised plans.

## B. Working Papers on Historic Sites and Monuments (HSM)

HSMs do not have management plans, unless they are also designated as ASPAs or ASMAs. All essential information about the HSM is included in the Measure. The rest of the Working Paper will not be annexed to the Measure; if it is desired to keep any additional background information on the record, this material may be annexed to the report of the CEP for inclusion in the Final Report of the ATCM. To ensure that all the information required for inclusion in the Measure is provided, it is recommended that Template B below is used as a guide when drafting the Working Paper.

## C. The tabling of draft Measures on ASPA, ASMA and HSM to the ATCM

When a draft Measure to give effect to the advice of the CEP on an ASPA, ASMA or HSM is submitted to the Secretariat for tabling at the ATCM, the Secretariat is requested also to provide to the ATCM copies of the cover sheet from the original Working Paper setting out the proposal, subject to any revisions made by the CEP.

The sequence of events is as follows:

- A Working Paper consisting of a draft management plan and an explanatory cover sheet is prepared and submitted by the proponent.
- The Secretariat prepares a draft Measure before the ATCM;
- Draft Management Plan is discussed by the CEP and any revisions made (by the proponent in liaison with the Secretariat);
- If the CEP recommends adoption, the Management Plan (as agreed) plus the cover sheet (as agreed) are passed from the CEP Chair to the Chair of the Legal and Institutional Working Group;
- Legal and Institutional Working Group reviews the draft Measure;
- The Secretariat formally table the draft measure plus the agreed cover sheet;
- The ATCM considers and makes a decision.

## TEMPLATE A: COVER SHEET FOR A WORKING PAPER ON AN ASPA OR ASMA

*Please ensure that the following information is provided on the cover sheet:*

(1) Is a new ASPA proposed? Yes/No

(2)   Is a new ASMA proposed? Yes/No

(3)   Does the proposal relate to an existing ASPA or ASMA?

If so, list all Recommendations, Measures, Resolutions and Decisions pertaining to this ASPA/ASMA, including any previous designations of this area as an SPA, SSSI or other type of protected area:

In particular, please include the date and relevant Recommendation/Measure for the following:

*   First designation:

*   First adoption of management plan:

*   Any revisions to management plan:

*   Current management plan:

*   Any extensions of expiry dates of management plan:

*   Renaming and renumbering as ………..... by Decision 1 (2002).

(Note: this information may be found on the ATS website in the Documents database by searching under the name of the area. While the ATS has made every effort to ensure the completeness and accuracy of the information in the database, occasional errors or omissions may occur. The proponents of any revision to a protected area are best placed to know the history of that area, and are kindly requested to contact the Secretariat if they notice any apparent discrepancy between the regulatory history as they understand it and that displayed on the ATS database.)

(1)   If the proposal contains a revision of an existing management plan, please indicate the types of amendment:

   (i)   Major or minor?

   (ii)   any changes to the boundaries or coordinates?

   (iii)   any changes to the maps? If yes, are the changes in the captions only or also in the graphics?

   (iv)   any change to the description of the area that is relevant to identifying its location or its boundaries?

   (v)   any changes that affect any other ASPA, ASMA or HSM within this area or adjacent to it? In particular, please explain any merger with, incorporation of or abolition of any existing area or site.

   (vi)   Other - brief summary of other types of changes, indicating the paragraphs of the management plan in which these are located (especially helpful if the plan is long).

(2)   If a new ASPA or ASMA is proposed, does it contain a marine area? Yes/No

(3)   If yes, does the proposal require the prior approval of CCAMLR in accordance with Decision 9 (2005)? Yes/No

(4)  If yes, has the prior approval of CCAMLR been obtained? Yes/No (If yes, the reference to the relevant paragraph of the relevant CCAMLR Final Report should be given).

(5)  If the proposal relates to an ASPA, what is the primary reason for designation (i.e. which part under Article 3.2 of Annex V)?

(6)  Have you identified the main Environmental Domain represented by the ASPA/ASMA (refer to the 'Environmental Domains Analysis for the Antarctic Continent' appended to Resolution 3 (2008))? Yes/No (If yes, the main Environmental Domain should be noted here).

The above format may be used as a template or as a checklist for the cover sheet, to ensure that all the requested information is provided.

## TEMPLATE B: COVER SHEET FOR A WORKING PAPER ON A HISTORIC SITE OR MONUMENT

*Please ensure that the following information is provided on the cover sheet:*

(1)  Has this site or monument been designated by a previous ATCM as a Historic Site or Monument? Yes/No (If yes, please list the relevant Recommendations and Measures).

(2)  If the proposal is for a new Historic Site or Monument, please include the following information, worded for inclusion in the Measure:

   (i)  Name of the proposed HSM, to be added to the list annexed to Measure 2 (2003);

   (ii)  Description of the HSM to be included in the Measure, including sufficient identifying features to enable visitors to the area to recognise it;

   (iii)  Coordinates, expressed in degrees, minutes and seconds;

   (iv)  Original proposing Party;

   (v)  Party undertaking management.

(3)  If the proposal is to revise an existing designation of an HSM, please list the relevant past Recommendations and Measures.

The above format may be used as a template or as a checklist for the cover sheet, to ensure that all the requested information is provided.

# Non-native Species

**The Representatives,**

*Recognising* that the introduction of non-native species to the Antarctic region, including the movement of species between locations in the region, presents a serious risk to biodiversity and to the intrinsic values of Antarctica;

*Recalling* the valuable discussions held at the 2006 workshop in New Zealand on Non-native Species, and the subsequent agreement by the Committee for Environmental Protection ("CEP") IX that:

- the issue of non-native species in the Antarctic should be given the highest priority consistent with the high environmental standards set out in the Protocol on Environmental Protection to the Antarctic Treaty (the Protocol);

- a set of comprehensive and standardised guidance and / or procedures should be developed, aimed at all operators in the Antarctic;

*Recalling* also the 2010 Antarctic Treaty Meeting of Experts on Implications of Climate Change for Antarctic Management and Governance, which:

- acknowledged that the greatest effort should be placed on preventing the introduction of non-native species, and on minimising the risk of human assisted introductions;

- recommended that Parties be encouraged to comprehensively and consistently implement management measures to respond to the environmental implications of climate change, particularly measures to avoid introduction and translocation of non-native species, and to report on their effectiveness;

*Welcoming* the development by the CEP of a Non-native Species Manual that Parties can apply and use, as appropriate, to assist with meeting their obligations under Annex II of the Protocol;

*Welcoming* also the CEP's advice that it will continue to develop and refine the Manual to reflect improvements in the understanding of non-native species risks and in best practice measures for prevention, surveillance and response;

**Recommend** that Parties:

1. disseminate and encourage, as appropriate, the use of the Non-native Species Manual annexed to this Resolution; and

2. encourage the Committee for Environmental Protection to continue to develop the Non-native Species Manual with the input of the Scientific Committee on Antarctic Research and the Council of Managers of National Antarctic Programs on scientific and practical matters, respectively.

# Non-native Species Manual
# July 2011

## 1. Introduction

### a. Objective

The overall objective for Parties' actions to address risks posed by non native species is:

*To conserve Antarctic biodiversity and intrinsic values by preventing the unintended introduction to the Antarctic region of species not native to that region, and the movement of species within Antarctica from one biogeographic zone to any other.*

Preventing unintended introductions is an ambitious goal, consistent with the principles of the Protocol. In practice, measures should be put in place to minimise the risk of impacts from non-native species in the Antarctic, taking all possible steps towards prevention.

### b. Purpose and background

The purpose of this manual is to provide guidance to Antarctic Treaty Parties in order to meet the objective (above), and minimise the risk of accidental or unintentional introduction of non-native species. This manual includes key guiding principles and links to recommended practical guidelines and resources that operators can apply and use, as appropriate, to assist with meeting their responsibilities under Annex II to the Protocol. The guidelines are recommendatory, not all guidelines will apply to all Parties' operations, and it is a 'living' document that will be updated and added to as new work, research and best practice develops to support further guidance. These measures are recommended as appropriate to assist Parties' efforts to prevent such accidental or unintended introductions and they should not be considered as mandatory.

This work is focussed on the unintended or accidental introduction of non-native species. The introduction of non-native species under permit (in accordance with Article 4 of Annex II to the Environmental Protocol) is not included. However, guidelines for response to unintentional introductions can be applied to responding to any dispersal of species intentionally introduced under permits. Consideration of natural pathways of introduction, human "ecosystems" (e.g. stomach flora) and human to human transfer of pathogens (e.g. illness) are also outside the scope of this work.

There is a limited understanding of the risks related to non-native species introductions and their impacts on the ecosystems. Another objective of this work is to support and encourage further work to fill in the gaps in our knowledge.

## c. Context[3]

Biological invasions are amongst the most significant threats to biodiversity worldwide, threatening species survival and being responsible for major changes to ecosystem structure and functioning. Despite Antarctica's isolation and harsh climatic conditions, invasions are now recognised as a serious risk to the region: the ice-free areas of Antarctica and the surrounding Sub-Antarctic Islands support a large proportion of the world's seabird species, and their terrestrial biotas, though species poor, include a high proportion of endemic and well-adapted taxa. Species richness in the Southern Ocean is higher than in the Antarctic terrestrial environment, and there is a high level of endemism. With rapid climate change occurring in some parts of Antarctica, increased numbers of introductions and enhanced success of colonisation by aliens are likely, with consequent increases in impacts on ecosystems, as is already visible in the Sub-Antarctic islands. In addition to introduction of species from outside Antarctica, cross-contamination between ice-free areas including isolated nunataks, or between different marine areas, also threatens the genetic diversity of the biogeographic zones and the risk must be addressed. Further development of human activity in these regions (including science, logistics, tourism, fisheries and recreation) will increase the risk of unintentional introductions of organisms which have a suite of life history traits that benefit them during transport, establishment and expansion phases of invasion, and are likely to be favored by warming conditions.

The vast majority of global alien species do not become invasive, but those that do are one of the main threats to global diversity. It is easier to fight invasiveness if the discovery of the alien species is made early. In addition, the presence of non-native species which are only "transient" or "persistent" but not yet "invasive" is also highly undesirable in terms of protecting the environmental and scientific values of Antarctica, especially as such species may become invasive. Therefore, prevention is the key. If not prevention, then early detection and rapid response will be very important.

The current environmental changes which occur in Antarctica, as in other parts of the world, will be very likely responsible for a natural alteration of the local biodiversity during the next decades or centuries. It is the responsibility of the Parties and others active in the region to minimise the chance of humans being a direct vector for change through introduction of non-native species and/or spread of diseases in the terrestrial and marine ecosystems of the Antarctic Treaty area.

The 2010 Antarctic Treaty Meeting of Experts on Implications of Climate Change for Antarctic Management emphasised the importance of preventing introductions, identifying species and environments at risk and developing measures to manage the issue. The meeting:

- Acknowledged that the greatest effort should be placed on preventing the introduction of non-native species, and on minimising the risk of human assisted introductions through national programmes and tourism activities. It stressed the

---

[3] This section was written with the contribution of several scientists involved in the IPY "Aliens in Antarctica" project (D. Bergstrom, S. Chown, P. Convey, Y. Frenot, N. Gremmen, A. Huiskes, K. Hughes, S. Imura, M. Lebouvier, J. Lee, F. Steenhuisen, M.Tsujimoto, B. van de Vijver and J. Whinam) and adapted according to the ICG Members' comments.

importance of ensuring comprehensive implementation of new measures to address this risk (Para. 111, Co-chair's report).

- Recommended that the CEP 'consider using established methods of identifying a) Antarctic environments at high risk from establishment by non-natives and b) non-native species that present a high risk of establishment in Antarctica' (Recommendation 22).

- Recommended that Parties be encouraged to comprehensively and consistently implement management measures to respond to the environmental implications of climate change, particularly measures to avoid introduction and translocation of non-native species, and to report on their effectiveness (Recommendation 23).

### d. Glossary

Terminology for non-native and invasive species has not been standardised internationally and some of the terms below are defined in the specific context of Antarctica.

- *Non-native / alien species*: an organism occurring outside its natural past or present range and dispersal potential, whose presence and dispersal in any biogeographic zone of the Antarctic Treaty area is due to unintentional human action.

- *Introduction / introduced*: direct or indirect movement by human agency, of an organism outside its natural range. This term may be applied to intercontinental or intracontinental movement of species.

- *Transient*: non-native species that have survived in small populations for a short period in Antarctica, but which have either died out naturally or have been removed by human intervention.

- *Persistent / established*: non-native species that have survived, established and reproduced for many years in a restricted locality in Antarctica, but which have not expanded their range from a specific location.

- *Invasive / invasion*: non-native species that are extending their range in the colonised Antarctic region, displacing native species and causing significant harm to biological diversity or ecosystem functioning.

- *Endemic*: Native species restricted to a specified region or locality in Antarctica.

## 2. Key Guiding Principles

In order to provide greater focus on the environmental risk related to the unintentional introduction of non-native species in Antarctica and to guide Parties' actions in accordance with the overall objective, 11 key guiding principles are proposed. They are categorised according to the three major components of a non-native species management framework: prevention, monitoring and response.

*Prevention*

Prevention is the most effective means of minimising the risks associated with the introduction of non-native species and their impacts.

### *Awareness*

(1) Raising awareness at multiple levels for different audiences is a critical component of management. All people travelling to the Antarctic should take appropriate steps to prevent the introduction of non-native species.

### *Operational procedures*

(2) The risk of non-native species introductions should be identified and addressed in the planning of all activities, including through the environmental impact assessment (EIA) process under Article 8 and Annex I to the Protocol.

(3) In the absence of sound scientific baseline data, a precautionary approach should be applied to minimise the risk of human-mediated introduction of non-native species, as well as the risk of intra-regional and local transfer of propagules to pristine regions.

(4) Preventive measures are most likely to be implemented and effective if they are:

- focused on addressing activities and areas of highest risk;
- developed to suit the particular circumstances of the activity or area in question, and at the appropriate scale;
- technically and logistically simple;
- easily applicable;
- cost effective and not unnecessarily time consuming.

(5) Prevention should focus on pre-departure measures within the logistics and supply chain,

- at the point of origin outside Antarctica (e.g. cargo, personal gear, packages),
- at gateways to Antarctica (ports, airports),
- on means of transport (ships, aircraft),
- at Antarctic stations and field camps that are departure points for activities within the continent.

(6) Particularly close attention should be given to ensuring the cleanliness of items previously used in cold climates (e.g. Arctic, Sub-Antarctic, mountainous areas) which may be a means for transporting species 'pre-adapted' to the Antarctic environment.

*Monitoring*

Monitoring can be passive observation (i.e. waiting for non-native species to appear) or targeted (i.e. an active programme of identifying potential non-native species). Having good baseline data on native fauna and flora is important to support monitoring of non-native species.

(7) Regular/periodic monitoring of high-risk sites (e.g. including, but not restricted to the area around research stations) should be encouraged.

(8) Preventive measures should be periodically reviewed and revised.

(9) Information and best practice related to non-native species should be exchanged between Parties and other stakeholders.

*Response*

The key factor will be to respond quickly and to assess the feasibility and desirability of eradicating non-native species. If eradication is not a feasible or desirable option then control and/or containment measures need to be considered.

(10) To be effective, responses to introductions should be undertaken as a priority, to prevent an increase in the species' distribution range and to make eradication simpler, cost effective and more likely to succeed.

(11) Efficacy of control or eradication programmes must be regularly assessed, including follow-up surveys.

## 3. Guidelines and resources to support prevention of the introduction of non-native species, including the transfer of species between sites in the Antarctic

In line with the objective for Parties' actions to address risks posed by non-natives species and the key guiding principles (sections 1 and 2), the following voluntary guidelines and resources have been developed that operators can apply and use, as appropriate, to assist with meeting their responsibilities under Annex II to the Protocol.

| Prevention |
|---|
| **1. Develop and deliver awareness programmes for all people travelling to and working in the Antarctic** on the risks of inter- and intra-continental movements of non-native species and on the measures required to prevent their introduction, including a standard set of key messages for awareness programmes. Education and training programmes should be tailored to the activities and risks associated with the target audience, including:<br><br>— managers of national programmes<br>— logisticians / crew / contractors<br>— tour operators<br>— scientists<br>— tourists<br>— staff on fishing vessels<br>— staff at suppliers / vendors / warehouses<br>— other visitors |

*Guidelines:*

Checklists for supply chain managers (COMNAP, SCAR 2010).
Link: *https://www.comnap.aq/nnsenvironment/*

Environmental code of conduct for terrestrial scientific field research in Antarctica (SCAR, 2009).
Link: *http://www.ats.aq/documents/ATCM32/ip/ATCM32_ip004_e.doc*

*Resources:*

Preliminary Results from the International Polar Year Programme: Aliens in Antarctica (SCAR, 2010).
Link: *http://www.ats.aq/documents/ATCM33/wp/ATCM33_wp004_e.doc*

Instructional video on cleaning (Aliens in Antarctica Project, 2010).
Link: *http://academic.sun.ac.za/cib/video/Aliens_cleaning_video%202010.wmv*

'Don't pack a pest' pamphlet (United States).
Link: *http://www.usap.gov/usapgov/travelAndDeployment/documents/PackaPest_brochure_Final.pdf*

'Don't pack a pest' pamphlet (IAATO).
Link: *http://www.iaato.org/do_not_pack_a_pest.html*

Antarctic Pre-Arrival Biosecurity Declaration (IAATO) – available from IAATO.
Boot washing guidelines (IAATO).
Link: *http://www.iaato.org/docs/Boot_Washing07.pdf*

'Know before you go' pamphlet (ASOC).
Link: *http://www.asoc.org/storage/documents/tourism/ASOC_Know_Before_You_Go_tourist_pamphlet_2009_editionv2.pdf*

---

**2. Include consideration of non-native species in future ASPA and ASMA Management Plans.**

*Guidelines:*

Guide for the Preparation of Management Plans.
Link: *http://www.ats.aq/documents/ATCM34/att/ATCM34_att004_e.doc*

---

**3. Manage ballast water in accordance with the Practical Guidelines for Ballast Water Exchange in the Antarctic Treaty Area Resolution 3 (2006).**

*Guidelines:*

Practical Guidelines for Ballast Water Exchange in the Antarctic Treaty Area Resolution 3 (2006).
Link: *http://www.ats.aq/documents/recatt/Att345_e.pdf*

---

**4. Clean vehicles in order to prevent transfer of non-native species into and around the Antarctic.**

*Guidelines:*

Procedures for vehicle cleaning to prevent transfer of non-native species into and around Antarctica (United Kingdom 2010).
Link: *http://www.ats.aq/documents/ATCM33/wp/ATCM33_wp008_e.doc*

| Monitoring |
| --- |
| **5. Record non-native species introductions and submit records to the Aliens database managed by the Australian Antarctic Data Centre, as agreed by the CEP.** <br><br> *Data base for entering records:* <br> Link: *http://data.aad.gov.au/aadc/biodiversity* <br><br> *Resource:* <br><br> Colonisation status of known non-native species in the Antarctic terrestrial environment (United Kingdom, 2010). <br> Link: *http://www.ats.aq/documents/ATCM33/ip/ATCM33_ip042_e.doc* |

| Response |
| --- |
| **6. Develop or employ assessment metrics to help determine whether a newly discovered species is likely to have arrived through natural colonisation pathways or through human means.** <br><br> *Guidelines:* <br><br> Guidance for visitors and environmental managers following the discovery of a suspected non-native species in the terrestrial and freshwater Antarctic environment (United Kingdom, 2010). <br> Links: *http://www.ats.aq/documents/ATCM33/att/ATCM33_att010_e.doc http://www.ats.aq/documents/ATCM33/att/ATCM33_att011_e.doc* <br><br> Suggested framework and considerations for scientists attempting to determine the colonisation status of newly discovered terrestrial or freshwater species within the Antarctic Treaty Area (United Kingdom, 2010). <br> Link: *http://www.ats.aq/documents/ATCM33/ip/ATCM33_ip044_e.doc* |

**Appendix**

## Guidelines and resources requiring further attention or development

In addition to the measures, guidelines and resources that have been developed (section 3) the following guidelines have been identified as appropriate for assisting Parties' work on non-native species. The use of these and the development of more detailed guidance under these items for inclusion in the Manual are encouraged.

| **Prevention** |
| --- |
| 1. Revise EIA guidelines to include a special section on non-native species. |
| 2. Improve understanding of risks and develop more specific guidelines for preventing introductions in the Antarctic marine environment. |
| 3. Reduce non-native species risks for Antarctica, including identifying regions / activities / vectors / pathways of highest risk for introduction of non-native species, providing guidance on what will constitute a gateway between Antarctic biogeographical zones (according to organism types), and developing practical measures to address risks associated with the transport of personnel and equipment between locations in Antarctica. More generally, encourage Parties to develop baseline studies. <br><br> *Resources:* <br> Current knowledge for reducing risks posed by terrestrial non-native species: towards an evidence-based approach (SCAR, Australia, 2010). <br> Link: *http://www.ats.aq/documents/ATCM33/wp/ATCM33_wp006_e.doc* <br><br> A framework for analysing and managing non-native species risks in Antarctica (New Zealand, 2009). <br> Link: *http://www.ats.aq/documents/ATCM32/ip/ATCM32_ip036_e.doc* |
| 4. Provide a list, with suitable descriptions, of the potential non-native species based on the experience of the Sub-Antarctic Islands (or other relevant environments) and the biological characteristics and adaptability of the "effective" colonisers. <br><br> *Resources:* <br> Information paper: Colonisation status of known non-native species in the Antarctic terrestrial environment (United Kingdom, 2010). <br> Link: *http://www.ats.aq/documents/ATCM33/ip/ATCM33_ip042_e.doc* |
| 5. Fresh foods and food wastes are strictly managed to prevent them entering the environment (secured from wildlife and removed from the Antarctic or incinerated). |

6. Unless new, clothing supplied for use in Antarctica is cleaned using normal laundry procedures prior to sending to Antarctica. Pre-worn footwear is cleaned thoroughly before arrival in Antarctica or between sites in Antarctica. Specific cleaning requirements may be required if there is reason to think that people, clothing, equipment or vehicles have been in contact with diseased animals, disease causing agents or have been in an area of known disease risk.

7. Equip research stations with the means to clean and maintain clothing and equipment that is to be used in the field, particularly in distinct or multiple locations.

8. Check cargo to ensure it is clean of visible contamination before loading on board the aircraft or vessels.

9. Confirm vessels as being rodent-free before departure to the Antarctic.

10. Pack, store and load cargo in an area with a clean, sealed surface (e.g. bitumen, concrete free from weedy plants, soil, rodents and areas of waste ground). These areas should be regularly cleaned and inspected.

11. Containers, including ISO containers and boxes/crates, are not moved from one Antarctic site to another, except if cleaned before arrival at the new location.

12. Intercontinental aircraft are checked and treated as necessary, where applicable, to ensure they are insect free before departure to the Antarctic.

13. Preventive measures to diminish risks of introduction of diseases to Antarctic wildlife could include, for example, specific guidance for handling field and station waste to minimise introduction of non-native species.

## Monitoring

14. Develop generally applicable monitoring guidelines, based on several workshops held on monitoring in the 1990s and in 2005, acknowledging that more detailed or site-specific monitoring may be required for particular locations; identify who will undertake the monitoring. A status report on established monitoring to be submitted regularly to the CEP.

*Resources:*
Information paper: Summary of Environmental Monitoring and Reporting Discussions (Australia, 2008). Link: *http://www.ats.aq/documents/ATCM31/ip/ATCM31_ip007_e.doc*

15. Baseline biodiversity surveys and compilation of existing biodiversity data (terrestrial - including aquatic and marine) should be carried out to assist with identifying scale and scope of current and future introductions. Because it is not practical to conduct surveys everywhere, priority should be given to sites of high human activity (stations, most frequently visited scientific field sites and tourist sites), high value and/or high sensitivity.

*Resources:*
German experience with carrying out a terrestrial survey on soil fauna organisms on highly frequented visitor sites (German IP to CEP XIV).

Existing methods from other environments, e.g. port surveys.

| **Response** |
| --- |
| 16. Expert advice should be sought as quickly as possible when a non-native species (including diseases of wildlife) is detected. A network of experts (taxonomists and specialists of eradication or control of non-native species, should be identified, including a list of names, details and e-mail available on the ATS website) in order to react as quickly as possible when a non-native species or disease event is discovered. This network should primarily 1) provide advice and 2) facilitate action by Parties. |
| 17. Consider a 'rapid response guideline', including possible guide with practical eradication tools / means. <br><br>*Resources:* <br>Eradication of a vascular plant species recently introduced to Whaler's Bay, Deception Island (United Kingdom, Spain 2010). <br>Link: *http://www.ats.aq/documents/ATCM33/ip/ATCM33_ip043_e.doc* <br><br>Mass animal mortality event response plan (British Antarctic Survey) – Available from BAS. <br><br>Unusual mortality response plan (Australia). <br>Link: referred to in: *http://www.ats.aq/documents/ATCM27/ip/ATCM27_ip071_e.doc* <br><br>Procedures for reporting a high mortality event (IAATO) – Available from IAATO. |
| 18. Develop (or formally adopt existing) guidance for responses to disease events. <br><br>*Resources:* <br>Report on the open-ended intersessional contact group on diseases of Antarctic wildlife. Report 2 – Practical measures to diminish risk (draft) (Australia, 2001). <br>Link: *http://www.ats.aq/documents/ATCM24/wp/ATCM24_wp011_e.pdf* <br>Health of Antarctic Wildlife: A Challenge for Science and Policy (Kerry and Riddle, 2009). |

**References**

(1) ATCMXXII-IP4 (Australia) 1998 - Introduction of Diseases to Antarctic Wildlife: Proposed Workshop

(2) ATCMXXIII- WP32 (Australia) 1999 - Report to ATCM XXIII on outcomes from the Workshop on Diseases of Antarctic Wildlife

(3) ATCMXII- WP6 (Australia) 2000 - Diseases of Antarctic Wildlife

(4) ATCMXXIV-WP10 (Australia) 2001 - Report on the open-ended intersessional contact group on Diseases of Antarctic Wildlife: Report 1 - Review and Risk Assessment

(5) ATCM XXIV-WP11 (Australia) 2001 - *Report on the open-ended intersessional contact group on diseases of Antarctic wildlife. Report 2 – Practical measures to diminish risk (draft)*

(6) ATCM XXV-IP62 (Australia) 2002 - Draft Response Plan in the Event that Unusual Animal Deaths are Discovered

(7) ATCMXXVII-IP71 (Australia) 2004 - *Australia's Antarctic quarantine practices*

(8) ATCMXXVIII-WP 28 (Australia) 2005 - Measures to address the unintentional introduction and spread of non-native biota and disease to the Antarctic Treaty Area

(9) ATCM XXVIII-IP97 (IAATO) 2005 - Update on Boot and Clothing Decontamination Guidelines and the Introduction and Detection of Diseases in Antarctic Wildlife: IAATO's Perspective

(10) ATCMXXIX-WP5 Rev.1 (United Kingdom) 2006 - Practical Guidelines for Ballast Water Exchange in the Antarctic Treaty Area

(11) ATCMXXIX-IP44 (Australia) 2006 - Principles underpinning Australia's approach to Antarctic quarantine management

(12) TCMXXX-IP49 (Australia, SCAR) 2007 - Aliens in Antarctica

(13) ATCMXXXI-WP 16 (Australia) - Antarctic Alien Species Database

(14) ATCMXXXI-IP07 (Australia) 2008 - Summary of Environmental Monitoring and Reporting Discussions

(15) ATCMXXXI-IP17 (Australia, China, India, Romania, Russian Federation) Measures to protect the Larsemann Hills, East Antarctica, from the introduction of non-native species

(16) ATCM XXXI-IP098 (COMNAP) - A survey on existent procedures concerning introduction of non native species in Antarctica

(17) ATCM XXXII-IP4 (SCAR) 2009 - SCAR's environmental code of conduct for terrestrial scientific field research in Antarctica.

(18) ATCM XXXII-IP012 (United-Kingdom) 2009 – ASPA and ASMA management plans: review of provisions relating to non-native species introductions

(19) ATCM XXXII-SP11 (ATS) 2009 - Topic Summary of CEP discussions on Non-native species (NNS) in Antarctica

(20) ATCM XXXII-WP5 (Australia, France, New Zealand) 2009 - *A Work Program for CEP Action on Non-native Species*

(21) ATCM XXXII-WP032 (United-Kingdom) 2009 – Procedures for vehicle cleaning to prevent transfer of non-native species into and around Antarctica

(22) ATCM XXXII-WP033 (United-Kingdom) 2009 – Review of provisions relating to non-native species introductions in ASPA and ASMA management plans

(23) ATCM XXXII-WP23 (South Africa) 2009 - Propagule transport associated with logistic operations: a South African appraisal of a regional issue

(24) ATCM XXXIII-WP4 (SCAR) 2010 - Preliminary Results from the International Polar Year Programme: Aliens in Antarctica

(25) ATCM XXXIII-WP6 (SCAR, Australia) 2010 - Current knowledge for reducing risks posed by terrestrial non-native species: towards an evidence-based approach

(26) ATCM XXXIII-WP8 (United Kingdom) 2010 - Draft procedures for vehicle cleaning to prevent transfer of non-native species into and around Antarctica

(27) ATCM XXXIII-WP9 (France) 2010 - Open-ended Intersessional Contact Group on "Non-Native Species" (NNS) - 2009-2010 Report

(28) ATCM XXXIII-WP14 (United Kingdom) 2010 - Intra-regional transfer of species in terrestrial Antarctica

(29) ATCM XXXIII-WP 15 (United Kingdom) 2010 - Guidance for visitors and environmental managers following the discovery of a suspected non-native species in the terrestrial and freshwater Antarctic environment

(30) ATCM XXXIII-IP14 (Germany) 2010 - Research Project "The role of human activities in the introduction of non-native species into Antarctica and in the distribution of organisms within the Antarctic"

(31) ATCM XXXIII-IP42 (United Kingdom) 2010 - Colonisation status of known non-native species in the Antarctic terrestrial environment

(32) ATCM XXXIII-IP43 (United Kingdom, Spain) 2010 - Eradication of a vascular plant species recently introduced to Whaler's Bay, Deception Island

(33) ATCM XXXIII-IP44 (United Kingdom) 2010 - Suggested framework and considerations for scientists attempting to determine the colonisation status of newly discovered terrestrial or freshwater species within the Antarctic Treaty Area

(34) Chown S.L., Convey P. 2007 - Spatial and temporal variability across life's hierarchies in the terrestrial Antarctic. *Phil. Trans. R. Soc. B*, **362**, 2307–2331

(35) Convey, P., Frenot, Y., Gremmen, N. & Bergstrom, D.M. 2006 – Biological Invasions. In Convey P., Huiskes A. & Bergstrom D.M. (eds) Trends in Antarctic Terrestrial and Limnetic Ecosystems. Springer, Dordrecht pp. 193-220.

(36) De Poorter M., Gilbert N., Storey B., Rogan-Finnemore M. 2006 Final Report of the Workshop on "Non-native Species in the Antarctic", Christchurch, New-Zealand, 10-12 April 2006.

(37) Falk-Petersen J., Bohn T. & Sandlund O.T. 2006. On the numerous concepts in invasion biology. Biological Invasions, 8, 1409-1424.

(38) Frenot, Y., Chown S.L., Whinam, J., Selkirk P.M., Convey, P, Skotnicki, M., Bergstrom D.M. 2005 - Biological invasions in the Antarctic: extent, impacts and implications? *Biological Reviews*, **80**, 45-72.

(39) Hughes, K. A., and Worland, M. R. 2009 - Spatial distribution, habitat preference and colonisation status of two alien terrestrial invertebrate species in Antarctica. *Antarctic Science*, in press.

(40) Hughes, K.A., and Convey, P. 2009 - The protection of Antarctic terrestrial ecosystems from inter- and intra-continental transfer of non-indigenous species by human activities: a review of current systems and practices. *Global Environmental Change*. DOI:10.1016/j.gloenvcha.2009.09.005

(41) Hughes, K. A., Convey, P., Maslen, N. R., Smith, R. I. L. 2009 - Accidental transfer of non-native soil organisms into Antarctica on construction vehicles. *Biological Invasions*. DOI: 10.1007/s10530-009-9508-2.

(42) Kerry, KR and Riddle, M. (Eds.) 2009 - Health of Antarctic Wildlife: A Challenge for Science and Policy, Springer Verlag, ISBN-13: 9783540939221.

(43) Potter S. 2006 - The Quarantine Management of Australia's Antarctic Program. Australasian. *Journal of Environmental Management*, **13**, 185-195.

(44) Potter S. 2009 - Protecting Antarctica from Non-Native Species: The Imperatives and the Impediments. In G. Alfredsson and T. Koivurova (eds), D. Leary sp. ed. The Yearbook of Polar Law, vol. 1, pp383-400.

(45) Tin T., Fleming Z.L., Hughes K.A., Ainley D.G., Convey P., Moreno C.A., Pfeiffer S., Scott J., Snape I. 2009 - Impacts of local human activities on the Antarctic environment. *Antarctic Sciences*, **21**, 3-33.

(46) Walther G.-R., Roques A., Hulme P.E., Sykes M.T., Pysek P., Kühn I. & Zobel M. 2009. Alien species in a warmer world: risks and opportunities. Trends in Ecology and Evolution 26 August 2009. doi:10.1016/j.tree.2009.06.008

(47) Whinam J. 2009 – Aliens in the Sub-Antarctic – Biosecurity and climate change. Papers and *Proceedings of the Royal Society of Tasmania*.

RCTA XXXIV ATCM
BUENOS AIRES JUNE 20TH. – JULY 1ST. 2011

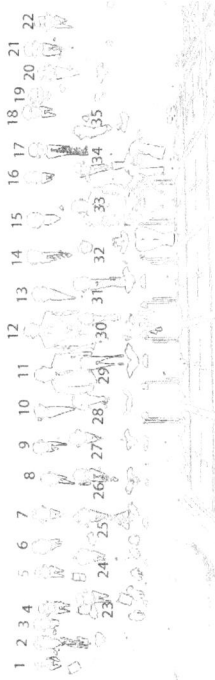

1 Christo Pimpirev (Bulgaria)
2 Jane Rumble (United Kingdom)
3 Steve Wellmeier (IAATO)
4 Fábio Vaz Pitaluga (Brazil)
5 Fausto López Crozet (Argentina)
6 Zhou Jian (China)
7 Karsten Klepsvic (Norway)
8 Serge Segura (France)
9 Ora Meres-Wuori (Finland)
10 Key Cheol Lee (Republic of Korea)
11 Evan Bloom (United States)
12 Martin Ney (Germany)
13 Oleksandr Taranenko (Ukraine)
14 Manfred Reinke (ATS)
15 Jakub Wolski (Poland)
16 Alexandre de Lichtervelde (Belgium)
17 James Barnes (ASOC)
18 Kirill Gevorgian (Russian Federation)

19 Jesús Ortega Hernández (Venezuela)
20 Luis Sandiga Cabrera (Peru)
21 Manuel Burgos (Uruguay)
22 Jorge Roballo (HCS)
23 Juan Antonio Martínez-Cattaneo (Spain)
24 Richard Rowe (Australia)
25 Suginaka Atsushi (Japan)
26 Henry Valentine (South Africa)
27 Vincent Van Zeijst (Netherlands)
28 Helena Odmark (Sweden)
29 Ariel Mansi (ATCM Chair)
30 Mercy Borbor (Ecuador)
31 Andrzej Misztal (Poland)
32 Patrizia Vigni (Italy)
33 Camilo Sanhueza (Chile)
34 Rasik Ravindra (India)
35 Carolyn Schwalger (New Zealand)

**Volume 2
(in CD and online purchased
copies)**

# PART II

**Measures, Decisions and Resolutions (cont.)**

# 4. Management Plans

# Management Plan For
## Antarctic Specially Protected Area No. 116
# NEW COLLEGE VALLEY, CAUGHLEY BEACH, CAPE BIRD, ROSS ISLAND

### 1. Description of values to be protected

In 1985, two areas at Cape Bird, Ross Island were designated as SSSI No. 10, Caughley Beach (Recommendation XIII-8 (1985)) and SPA No. 20, New College Valley (Recommendation XIII-12 (1985)), following proposals by New Zealand that these areas should be protected because they contained some of the richest stands of moss and associated microflora and fauna in the Ross Sea region of Antarctica. This is the only area on Ross Island where protection is specifically given to plant assemblages and associated ecosystems.

At that time, SPA No. 20 was enclosed within SSSI No. 10, in order to provide more stringent access conditions to that part of the Area. In 2000, SSSI No. 10 was incorporated with SPA No. 20 by Measure 1 (2000), with the former area covered by SPA No. 20 becoming a Restricted Zone within the revised SPA No. 20. The boundaries of the Area were revised from the boundaries in the original recommendations, in view of improved mapping and to follow more closely the ridges enclosing the catchment of New College Valley. Caughley Beach itself was adjacent to, but never a part of, the original Area, and for this reason the entire Area was renamed as New College Valley, which was within both of the original sites.

The Area was redesignated by Decision 1 (2002) as Antarctic Specially Protected Area (ASPA) No. 116 and a revised Management Plan was adopted through Measure 1 (2006).

The boundaries of the Area closely follow the ridges enclosing the catchment of New College Valley and cover approximately 0.33 km$^2$. Moss in this Area is restricted to localised areas of water-flushed ground, with cushions and carpets up to 20 m$^2$ in area. A diverse range of algal species also inhabit streams in the Area, and springtails, mites and nematodes are plentiful on water surfaces and underneath rocks. The absence of lichens makes the species assemblage in this Area unique on Ross Island.

The susceptibility of mosses to disturbance by trampling, sampling, pollution or introductions of non-native species is such that the Area requires long-term special protection. Designation of this Area is intended to ensure examples of this habitat type are adequately protected from visitors and overuse from scientific investigations. The ecosystem at this site remains of exceptional scientific value for ecological investigations and the Restricted Zone is valuable as a reference site for future comparative studies.

### 2. Aims and objectives

Management of New College Valley, Caughley Beach, Cape Bird aims to:

- avoid degradation of, or substantial risk to, the values of the Area by preventing unnecessary human disturbance to the Area;

- preserve a part of the natural ecosystem of the Area as a reference area for the purpose of future comparative studies;
- allow scientific research on the ecosystem, in particular on mosses, algae and invertebrates in the Area, while ensuring protection from over-sampling;
- allow other scientific research in the Area provided it is for compelling reasons which cannot be served elsewhere;
- prevent or minimise the introduction to the Area of alien plants, animals and microbes;
- allow visits for management purposes in support of the aims of the Management Plan.

## 3. Management activities

The following management activities are to be undertaken to protect the values of the Area:

- Copies of this Management Plan, including maps of the Area, shall be made available at all adjacent operational research/field stations.
- Rock cairns or signs illustrating the location and boundaries of the Area, with clear statements of entry restrictions, shall be placed at appropriate locations on the boundary of the Area and the Restricted Zone to help avoid inadvertent entry.
- Markers, signs or structures erected within the Area for scientific or management purposes shall be secured and maintained in good condition, and removed when no longer required.
- Visits shall be made as necessary (preferably at least once every five years) to assess whether the Area continues to serve the purposes for which it was designated and to ensure management and maintenance measures are adequate.
- National Antarctic Programmes operating in the Area shall consult together with a view to ensuring the above management activities are implemented.

## 4. Period of designation

Designated for an indefinite period.

## 5. Maps

Map A: New College Valley, Caughley Beach, Cape Bird, Ross Island, Regional Topographic Map. Map specifications: Projection - Lambert conformal conic. Standard parallels - 1st 76° 40' 00" S; 2nd 79° 20' 00"S. Central Meridian - 166° 30' 00" E. Latitude of Origin - 78° 01' 16. 211" S. Spheroid - WGS84.

Map B: New College Valley, Caughley Beach, Cape Bird, Ross Island, Vegetation Coverage Map. Map specification: Projection - Lambert conformal conic. Standard parallels – 1st - 76.6° S; 2nd -79.3° S.  Spheroid - WGS84. Map includes vegetation coverage and streams.

## 6. Description of the Area

*6(i) Geographical coordinates, boundary markers and natural features*
Cape Bird is at the northwest extremity of Mount Bird (1,800 m), an inactive volcanic cone which is probably the oldest on Ross Island. New College Valley is located south of Cape Bird on ice-free slopes above Caughley Beach, and lies between two Adélie penguin colonies known as the Cape Bird Northern and Middle Rookeries (Map A). The Area, comprising veneered glacial moraines at the fore of the Cape Bird Ice Cap, consists of seaward dipping olivine-augite basalts with scoriaceous tops erupted from the main Mount Bird cone.

The northwest corner of the north boundary of the Area is approximately 100 m south of the Cape Bird hut (New Zealand) and is marked by an ASPA sign post (77° 13.128'S, 166° 26.147'E) (Map B). The north boundary of the Area extends upslope and eastward toward a prominent terminal moraine ridge, approximately 20 m from the Cape Bird Ice Cap and is marked with a rock cairn (77° 13.158'S, 166° 26.702'E).

The eastern boundary follows the terminal moraine ridge from the rock cairn (77° 13.158'S, 166° 26.702'E) southeast until the ridge disappears where it joins the Cape Bird Ice Cap. The boundary continues southeast following the glacier edge to the southern boundary.

The southern boundary is a straight line crossing the broad southern flank of New College Valley, and is marked with rock cairns at the south-western corner of the Area (77° 13.471'S, 166° 25.832'E) and the south-eastern corner of the area on the hilltop 100 m from the Cape Bird Ice Cap glacier edge (77° 13.571'S, 166° 27.122'E).

The western boundary of the Area follows the top of the coastal cliffs of Caughley Beach from the south-western corner rock cairn (77° 13.471'S, 166° 25.832'E) for a distance of 650 m to the northwest corner of the Area (77° 13.128'S, 166° 26.147'E) where the ASPA signpost is located.

Based on the Environmental Domain Analysis for Antarctica (Resolution 3 (2008)), New College Valley, Caughley Beach is located within Environment S *McMurdo South Victoria Land geologic.*

Northwest-facing New College Valley drains meltwater from the Cape Bird Ice Cap during the summer. Streams in the Area are fed by melt from persistent summer snow drifts and have eroded their own shallow gullies and channels. The ground is largely covered by stones and boulders of volcanic origin which have been reworked by glacial action.

The Area contains the most extensive ephemeral stream course distributions of the moss *Hennediella heimii* on Ross Island. Surveys have shown that this moss, together with much lower occurrences of two other species – *Bryum subrotundifolium* and *Bryum pseudotriquetrum* – are confined almost entirely to the stream courses across the steep till and scoria covered slopes (Map B). The mosses are generally associated with algal growths, namely rich, red-brown oscillatorian felts and occasional reddish-black growths of *Nostoc commune*. The Area includes the full course of three stream systems that contain significant growths of algae, together with the mosses.

The Area supports a terrestrial invertebrate community including populations of springtails *Gomphiocephalus hodgsonii* (Collembola: Hypogastruridae), mites *Nanorchestes antarcticus* and *Stereotydeus mollis* (Acari: Prostigmata) and nematodes (*Panagrolaimus davidi*, *Plectus antarcticus*, *Plectus frigophilus*, *Scottnema lindsayae* and *Eudorylaimus antarcticus*) with the presence of rotifers, tardigrades, and ciliate and flagellate protozoa noted. The distribution of terrestrial invertebrates at this site is related to the abiotic environment with most arthropod species being associated with macroscopic vegetation or soil algal biomass level, although this relationship does not describe the distribution of all taxa.

Skuas (*Catharacta maccormicki*) frequently rest on Caughley Beach and overfly, land and nest within the Area. Adélie penguins (*Pygoscelis adeliae*) from the nearby rookeries do not nest in the Area, but have been observed occasionally to traverse across New College Valley.

*6(ii) Special zones within the Area*
An area of New College Valley is designated as a Restricted Zone in order to preserve part of the Area as a reference site for future comparative studies, while the remainder of the Area (which is similar in biology, features and character) is more generally available for research programmes and sample collection. The Restricted Zone encompasses ice-free slopes within New College Valley above Caughley Beach some of which are north-facing with snow drifts which provide a ready supply of melt water to foster moss and algal growth.

The northwest corner (77° 13.164'S, 166° 26.073'E) of the Restricted Zone is 60 m to the south and across a small gully from the northwest corner of the Area. The north boundary of the Restricted Zone extends 500 m upslope from the northwest corner to a cairn (77° 13.261'S, 166° 26.619'E), then following a faint but increasingly prominent ridge southeast to a point in the upper catchment of New College Valley marked by a cairn approximately 60 m from the ice terminus of the Cape Bird Ice Cap (77° 13.368'S, 166° 26.976'E). The Restricted Zone boundary extends 110 m southwest across the valley to a cairn marking the southeast corner of the Restricted Zone (77° 13.435'S, 166° 26.865'E). The south boundary of the Restricted Zone extends in a straight line from this cairn (77° 13.435'S, 166° 26.865'E) 440 m northwest down a broad and relatively featureless slope to the southwest corner of the Area (77° 13.328'S, 166° 26.006'E). A cairn is placed on the southwest boundary of the Restricted Zone to mark the lower position of the south boundary (77° 13.226'S, 166° 25.983'E).

Access to the Restricted Zone is allowed only for compelling scientific and management purposes that cannot be served by visits elsewhere in the Area.

*6(iii) Location of structures within and adjacent to the Area*
Structures known to exist within the Area include a United States Navy Astrofix marker, cairns marking the boundaries of the Area and the Restricted Zone, a signpost situated at the northwest corner of the Area and an approximately one meter square wooden frame marking the site of an experimental oil spill from 1982.

A field hut (New Zealand), stores hut and toilet are located north of the northwest corner of the Area (Map B).

*6(iv) Location of other protected areas in the vicinity*
The nearest protected areas are:
- Lewis Bay, Mount Erebus, Ross Island (ASPA No. 156), approximately 25 km SE;
- Tramway Ridge, Mount Erebus, Ross Island (ASPA No. 130) 30 km SSE;
- Cape Crozier, Ross Island (ASPA No. 124) 75 km SE;

- Cape Royds, Ross Island (ASPA No. 121 and No. 157) and Cape Evans, Ross Island (ASPA No. 155) 35 km and 45 km south on Ross Island respectively; and
- Beaufort Island, McMurdo Sound, Ross Sea (ASPA No. 105) 40 km to the north.

## 7. Terms and conditions for entry Permits

Entry into the Area is prohibited except in accordance with a Permit issued by an appropriate national authority. Conditions for issuing a Permit to enter the Area are that:

- outside of the Restricted Zone, it is issued only for scientific study of the ecosystem, or for compelling scientific reasons that cannot be served elsewhere, or for essential management purposes consistent with the Management Plan objectives such as inspection or review;
- access to the Restricted Zone is allowed only for compelling scientific or management reasons that cannot be served elsewhere in the Area;
- the actions permitted are not likely to jeopardise the ecological or scientific values of the Area or other permitted activities;
- any management activities are in support of the objectives of the Management Plan;
- the actions permitted are in accordance with the Management Plan;
- the Permit, or a copy, shall be carried within the Area;
- a visit report shall be supplied to the authority named in the Permit;
- the Permit shall be issued for a stated period.

*7(i) Access to and movement within or over the Area*
Helicopters are prohibited from landing within the Area. Two helicopter landing sites are located outside the Area. Between October to February, the preferred landing site is below the cliffs on Caughley Beach, 100 m west of the west boundary of the Area (Maps A and B). Between March and September, an alternative helicopter landing site is located adjacent to the Cape Bird field hut (New Zealand), above Caughley Beach (Map B).

Between October and February the preferred flight path is an approach from the south upslope from Middle Rookery (Map A). Under certain wind conditions, flights north of the helicopter pad may be necessary, and in this case should follow the recommended aircraft approach and departure routes, and be in accordance with the 'Guidelines for the Operation of Aircraft Near Concentrations of Bird in Antarctica' (Resolution 2, 2004) to the maximum extent possible. See Map A for the recommended aircraft approach routes into and out of Cape Bird.

Overflight of the Area lower than 50 m (~150 ft) above ground level is prohibited. Hovering over the Area is not permitted lower than 100 m (~300 ft) above ground level. Use of helicopter smoke grenades within the Area is prohibited.

Vehicles are prohibited within the Area and all movement within the Area should be on foot. Access into the Area should preferably follow the track from the Cape Bird Hut (New Zealand). Visitors should avoid areas of visible vegetation and care should be exercised walking in areas of moist ground, particularly the stream course beds, where foot traffic can easily damage sensitive soils, plant and algal communities, and degrade water quality. Visitors should avoid walking on such areas by walking on ice or rocky ground. Pedestrian traffic should be kept to the minimum necessary consistent with the objectives of any permitted activities and every reasonable effort should be made to minimise effects.

Access to regions south of the Area from the Cape Bird Hut should be made by a route below the cliffs along Caughley Beach.

*7(ii) Activities which may be conducted in the Area*
- Compelling scientific research which cannot be undertaken elsewhere and which will not jeopardise the ecosystem or values of the Area or interfere with existing scientific studies;
- Essential management activities, including monitoring and inspection.

*7(iii) Installation, modification or removal of structures*
No structures are to be erected within the Area, or scientific equipment installed, except for compelling scientific or management reasons, as specified in a Permit. All markers, structures or scientific equipment installed in the Area must be authorised by Permit and clearly identified by country, name of the principal investigator or agency, year of installation and date of expected removal. All such items should be free of organisms, propagules (e.g. seeds, eggs) and non-sterile soil, and be made of materials that pose minimal risk of contamination of the Area. Removal of specific structures or equipment for which the Permit has expired shall be a condition of the Permit.

*7(iv) Location of field camps*
Camping within the Area is prohibited. A field hut (New Zealand), stores hut and toilet are located north of the northwest corner of the Area (Map B).

*7(v) Restrictions on materials and organisms which may be brought into the Area*
No living animals, plant material or microorganisms shall be deliberately introduced into the Area and precautions listed in 7(ix) shall be taken against accidental introductions. No poultry products shall be brought into the Area. No herbicides or pesticides shall be brought into the Area. Any other chemicals, including radio-nuclides or stable isotopes, which may be introduced for scientific or management purposes specified in the Permit, shall be removed from the Area at or before the conclusion of the activity for which the Permit was granted. Fuel or other chemicals shall not be stored in the Area, unless required for essential purposes connected with the activity for which the Permit has been granted, and must be contained within an emergency cache authorized by an appropriate authority. All materials introduced shall be for a stated period only, shall be removed at or before the conclusion of that stated period, and shall be stored and handled so that risk of their introduction into the environment is minimised.

*7(vi) Taking or harmful interference with native flora or fauna*
Taking of, or harmful interference with native flora or fauna is prohibited, except in accordance with a separate Permit issued in accordance with Annex II of the Protocol on Environmental Protection to the Antarctic Treaty. Where taking or harmful interference with animals is involved this should, as a minimum standard, be in accordance with the SCAR Code of Conduct for the Use of Animals for Scientific Purposes in Antarctica.

*7(vii) The collection or removal of materials not imported by the Permit holder*
Material may be collected or removed from the Area only in accordance with a permit and should be limited to the minimum necessary to meet scientific or management needs.

Similarly, sampling is to be carried out using techniques which minimise disturbance to the Area, as well as duplication. Material of human origin likely to compromise the values of the Area, which was not brought into the Area by the Permit holder or otherwise authorised and which is not an historical artefact or abandoned relic, may be removed from any part of the Area, including the Restricted Zone, unless the environmental impact of removal is likely to be greater than leaving the material *in situ*. Where the environmental impact of removal is likely to be greater than leaving the material *in situ*, the appropriate national authority must be notified and approval obtained.

*7(viii) Disposal of waste*
All wastes, including all human wastes, shall be removed from the Area.

*7(ix) Measures that may be necessary to continue to meet the aims and objectives of the Management Plan*
Permits may be granted to enter the Area to:
- carry out biological monitoring and Area inspection activities, which may involve the collection of a small number of samples or data for analysis or review;
- erect or maintain signposts, structures or scientific equipment; or
- carry out management activities.

Any specific sites of long-term monitoring shall be appropriately marked on site and on maps of the Area. A GPS position should be obtained for sites of long-term monitoring and scientific sampling for lodgement with the Antarctic Master Directory system through the appropriate national authority. If appropriate, metadata should also be provided for the Antarctic Master Directory system through the appropriate national authority.

To help maintain the ecological and scientific values of the isolation and relatively low level of human impact at the Area, visitors shall take special precautions against introductions. Of particular concern are microbial or vegetation introductions sourced from soils at other Antarctic sites, including stations, or from regions outside Antarctica. To minimise the risk of introductions, visitors shall thoroughly clean footwear and any equipment to be used in the area particularly sampling equipment and markers before entering the Area.

*7(x) Requirements for reports*

The principal permit holder for each visit to the Area shall submit a report to the appropriate national authority as soon as practicable, and no later than six months after the visit has been completed. Such reports should include, as appropriate, the information identified in the visit report form contained in the Guide to the Preparation of Management Plans for Antarctic Specially Protected Areas.

If appropriate, the national authority should also forward a copy of the visit report to the Party that proposed the Management Plan, to assist in managing the Area and reviewing the Management Plan. Parties should maintain a record of activities and report them in the Annual Exchange of Information. Parties should, wherever possible, deposit originals or copies of such original visit reports in a publicly accessible archive to maintain a record of usage, for the purposes of any review of the management plan and in organising the scientific use of the Area.

## 8. Bibliography

Ainley, D.G., Ballard, G., Barton, K.J., Karl, B.J., Rau, G.H., Ribic, C.A. and Wilson, P.R. 2003. Spatial and temporal variation of diet within a presumed metapopulation of Adelie penguins. Condor 105: 95-106.

Ainley, D.G., Ribic, C.A., Ballard, G., Heath, S., Gaffney, I., Karl, B.J., Barton, K.J., Wilson, P.R. and Webb, S. 2004. Geographic structure of Adelie penguin populations: overlap in colony-specific foraging areas. Ecological monographs 74(1): 159- 178.

Block, W. 1985. Ecological and physiological studies of terrestrial arthropods in the Ross Dependency 1984-85. British Antarctic Survey Bulletin 68: 115-122.

Broady, P.A. 1981. Non-marine algae of Cape Bird, Ross Island and Taylor Valley, Victoria Land, Antarctica. Report of the Melbourne University Programme in Antarctic Studies No. 37.

Broady, P.A. 1983. Botanical studies at Ross Island, Antarctica, in 1982-83; preliminary report. Report of the Melbourne University Programme in Antarctic Studies.

Broady, P.A. 1985. The vegetation of Cape Bird, Ross Island, Antarctica. Melbourne University Programme in Antarctic Studies, No. 62.

Broady, P.A. 1985. A preliminary report of phycological studies in northern Victoria Land and on Ross Island during 1984-85. Report of the Melbourne University Programme in Antarctic Studies, Report No. 66.

Broady, P.A. 1989. Broadscale patterns in the distribution of aquatic and terrestrial vegetation at three ice-free regions on Ross Island, Antarctica. Hydrobiologia 172: 77-95.

Butler, E.R.T. 2001. Beaches in McMurdo Sound, Antarctica. Unpublished PhD, Victoria University of Wellington, New Zealand. (pg 219)

Cole, J.W. and Ewart, A. 1968. Contributions to the volcanic geology of the Black Island, Brown Peninsula, and Cape Bird areas, McMurdo Sound, Antarctica. New Zealand Journal of Geology and Geophysics 11(4): 793-823.

Dochat, T.M., Marchant, D.R. and Denton, G.H. 2000. Glacial geology of Cape Bird, Ross Island, Antarctica. Geografiska Annaler 82A (2-3): 237-247.

Duncan, K.W. 1979. A note on the distribution and abundance of the endemic collembolan Gomphiocephalus hodgsonii Carpenter 1908 at Cape Bird, Antarctica. Mauri Ora 7: 19-24.

Hall, B.L., Denton, G.H. and Hendy, C.H. 2000. Evidence from Taylor Valley for a Grounded Ice Sheet in the Ross Sea, Antarctica. Geografiska annaler 82A(2-3): 275-304.

Konlechner, J.C. 1985. An investigation of the fate and effects of a paraffin-based crude oil in an Antarctic terrestrial ecosystem. New Zealand Antarctic Record 6(3): 40-46.

Lambert, D.M., Ritchie, P.A., Millar, C.D., Holland, B., Drummond, A.J. and Baroni, C. 2002. Rates of evolution in ancient DNA from Adélie penguins. Science 295: 2270-2273.

McGaughran, A., Hogg, I.D. and Stevens, M.I. 2008. Patterns of population genetic structure for springtails and mites in southern Victoria Land, Antarctica. Molecular phylogenetics and evolution 46: 606-618.

McGaughran, A., Redding, G.P., Stevens, M.I. and Convey, P. 2009. Temporal metabolic rate variation in a continental Antarctica springtail. Journal of Insect Physiology 55: 130-135.

Nakagawa, S., Möstl, E. and Waas, J.R. 2003. Validation of an enzyme immunoassay to measure faecal glucocorticoid metabolites from Adelie penguins (*Pygoscelis adeliae*): a non-invasive tool for estimating stress? Polar biology 26: 491-493.

Peterson, A.J. 1971. Population studies on the Antarctic Collembolan *Gomphiocephalus hodgsonii* Carpenter. Pacific Insects Monograph 25: 75-98.

Ritchie, P.A., Millar, C.D., Gibb, G.C., Baroni, C., Lambert, D.M. 2004. Ancient DNA enables timing of the Pleistocene origin and Holocene expansion of two Adelie penguin lineages in Antarctica. Molecular biology and evolution 21(2): 240-248.

Roeder, A.D., Marshall, R.K., Mitchelson, A.J., Visagathilagar, T., Ritchie, P.A., Love, D.R., Pakai, T.J., McPartlan, H.C., Murray, N.D., Robinson, N.A., Kerry, K.R. and Lambert, D.M. 2001. Gene flow on the ice: genetic differentiation among Adélie penguin colonies around Antarctica. Molecular Ecology 10: 1645-1656.

Seppelt, R.D. and Green, T.G.A. 1998. A bryophyte flora for Southern Victoria Land, Antarctica. New Zealand Journal of Botany 36: 617-635.

Sinclair, B.J. 2000. The ecology and physiology of New Zealand Alpine and Antarctic arthropods. Unpublished PhD, University of Otago, New Zealand. (pg 231)

Sinclair, B. J. 2001. On the distribution of terrestrial invertebrates at Cape Bird, Ross Island, Antarctica. Polar Biology 24(6): 394-400.

Sinclair, B. J. and Sjursen, H. 2001. Cold tolerance of the Antarctic springtail *Gomphiocephalus hodgsonii* (Collembola, Hypogastruridae). Antarctic Science 13(3): 271-279.

Sinclair, B.J. and Sjursen, H. 2001. Terrestrial invertebrate abundance across a habitat transect in Keble Valley, Ross Island, Antarctica. Pedobiologia 45: 134-145.

Smith, D.J. 1970. The ecology of *Gomphiocephalus hodgsonii* Carpenter (Collembola, Hypogastuidae) at Cape Bird, Antarctica. Unpublished MSc Thesis, University of Canterbury, Christchurch, New Zealand.

Stevens, M.I. and Hogg, I.D. 2003. Long-term isolation and recent expansion from glacial refugia revealed for the endemic springtail *Gomphiocephalus hodgsonii* from Victoria Land, Antarctica. Molecular ecology 12: 2357-2369.

Wilson, P.R., Ainley, D.G., Nur, N., Jacobs, S.S., Barton, K.J., Ballard, G. and Comisco, J.C. 2001. Adélie penguin population change in the Pacific sector of Antarctica: relation to sea-ice extent and the Antarctic Circumpolar Current. Marine ecology progress series 213: 301-309.

Wharton, D.A. and Brown, I.M. 1989. A survey of terrestrial nematodes from the McMurdo Sound region, Antarctica. New Zealand Journal of Zoology 16: 467-470.

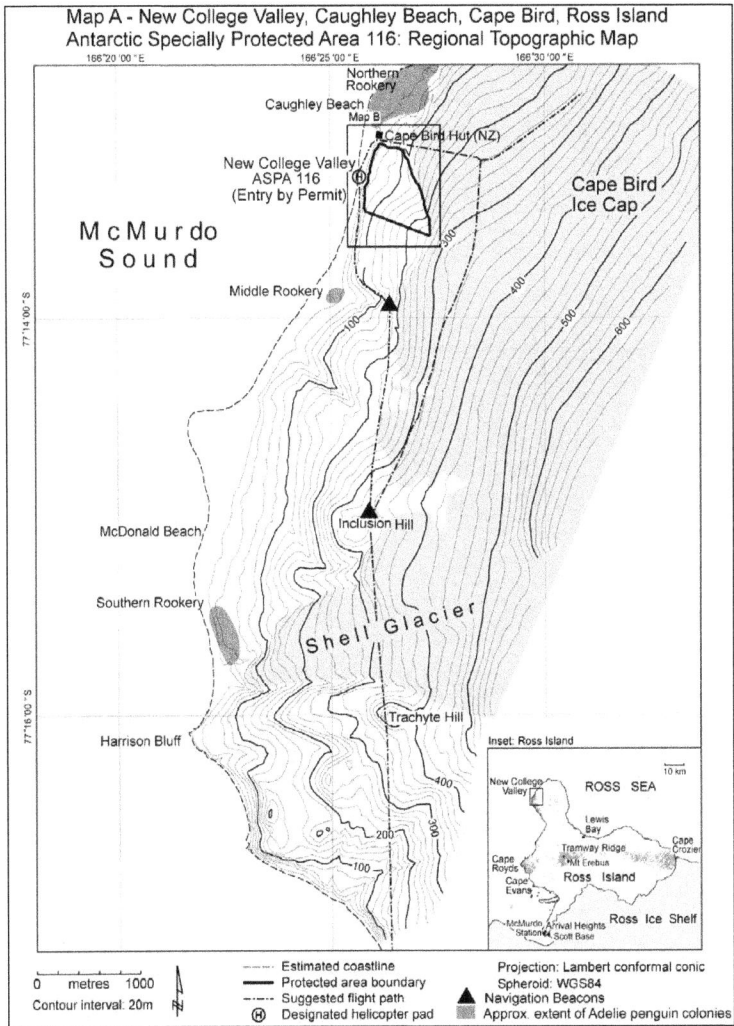

Map A - New College Valley, Caughley Beach, Cape Bird, Ross Island
Antarctic Specially Protected Area 116: Regional Topographic Map

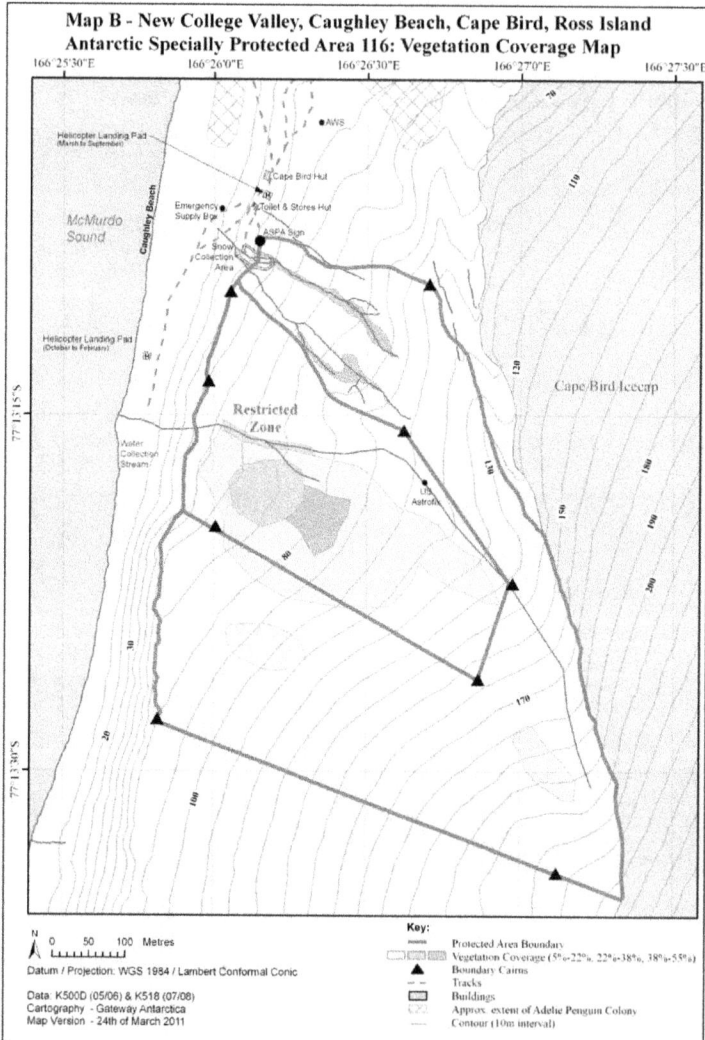

Map B - New College Valley, Caughley Beach, Cape Bird, Ross Island
Antarctic Specially Protected Area 116: Vegetation Coverage Map

# Management Plan for Antarctic Specially Protected Area No. 120

# POINTE-GÉOLOGIE ARCHIPELAGO, TERRE ADÉLIE

# Jean Rostand, Le Mauguen (former Alexis Carrel), Lamarck and Claude Bernard Islands, The Good Doctor's Nunatak and breeding site of Emperor Penguins

## 1. Description of values to be protected

In 1995, four islands, a nunatak and a breeding ground for emperor penguins were classified as an Antarctic Specially Protected Area (Measure 3 (1995), ATCM XIX, Seoul) because they were a representative example of terrestrial Antarctic ecosystems from a biological, geological and aesthetics perspective. A species of marine mammal, the Weddell seal (*Leptonychotes weddelli*) and various species of birds breed in the area: emperor penguin (*Aptenodytes forsteri*); Antarctic skua (*Catharacta maccormicki*); Adélie penguins (*Pygoscelis adeliae*); Wilson's petrel (*Oceanites oceanicus*); giant petrel (*Macronectes giganteus*); snow petrel (*Pagodroma nivea*), cape petrel (*Daption capense*).

Well-marked hills display asymmetrical transverse profiles with gently dipping northern slopes compared to the steeper southern ones. The terrain is affected by numerous cracks and fractures leading to very rough surfaces. The basement rocks consist mainly of sillimanite, cordierite and garnet-rich gneisses which are intruded by abundant dikes of pink anatexites. The lowest parts of the islands are covered by morainic boulders with a heterogeneous granulometry (from a few cm to more than a m across).

Long-term research and monitoring programs of birds and marine mammals have been going on for a long time already (since 1952 or 1964 according to the species), currently supported by the French Polar Institute Paul Émile Victor (IPEV) and the French National Centre for Scientific Research (CNRS). This has enabled the implementation of a population database which is particularly useful in view of the long timescale of the observations. It is maintained and used by the Centre d'Etudes Biologiques de Chize (CEBC-CNRS). Within this context, human scientific presence in the protected area is currently estimated at four people for a few hours, three times a month between the 1st November and the 15th February, and, inside the emperor penguin colony itself, at two people for a few hours between the 1st April and the 1st November.

Among the approximately thirty emperor penguin breeding sites on record, this is the only one located adjacent to a permanent station. It is therefore a providential spot to study this species and its environment.

## 2. Aims and objectives

Management of the Cape Géologie Archipelago Specially Protected Area aims at:

- preventing disturbance in the area due to the proximity of the Dumont d'Urville Station;
- avoiding any major changes to the structure and composition of flora and fauna and the association of different species of vertebrates harbored in the area, which is one of the most representative for both faunistic and scientific interest on Adélie Coast;
- permitting scientific research in the field of marine and terrestrial biology, i.e., ethology, ecology, physiology and biochemistry, demographic monitoring of marine birds and mammals, and environmental impact assessment of surrounding human activities;

- permitting scientific or technological research programmes in areas other than those previously mentioned (e.g. geology) or management programmes, with particular attention to the scheduling of visits in order to minimise the impacts on the flora and fauna.
- controlling the logistic operations related to the activities of the nearby Dumont d'Urville station, which may require temporary access to the ASPA.

### 3. Management activities

The following management activities will be undertaken to protect the values of the Area:

The present management plan is kept under periodical review to ensure that the values of the ASPA are monitored. Any activity carried out in the area undergoes an environmental impact assessment before being undertaken.

All members of staff staying at or in transit at the Dumont d'Urville base will be duly informed of the existence of the ASPA, of its geographical boundaries, of the entry restrictions in place and of the current management plan. To ensure this, a sign displaying a map of the area and listing the restrictions and relevant management measures shall be displayed prominently at the Dumont d'Urville station.

Copies of this management plan shall also be available in each of the four Treaty languages at the Dumont d'Urville station.

Information related to each incursion into the ASPA, namely a minima: activity undertaken or reason for presence, number of people involved, duration of stay, is recorded by the head of the Dumont d'Urville station.

### 4. Period of Designation

The Area is designated as an Antarctic Specially Protected Area (ASPA) for an indefinite period.

### 5. Maps

Map 1 shows the geographical location of Terre Adélie in the Antarctic and the location of the Cape Geology Archipelago on the Terre Adélie coast.

On Map 2 of the Cape Geology Archipelago, the dotted line indicates the boundary of the ASPA within the archipelago.

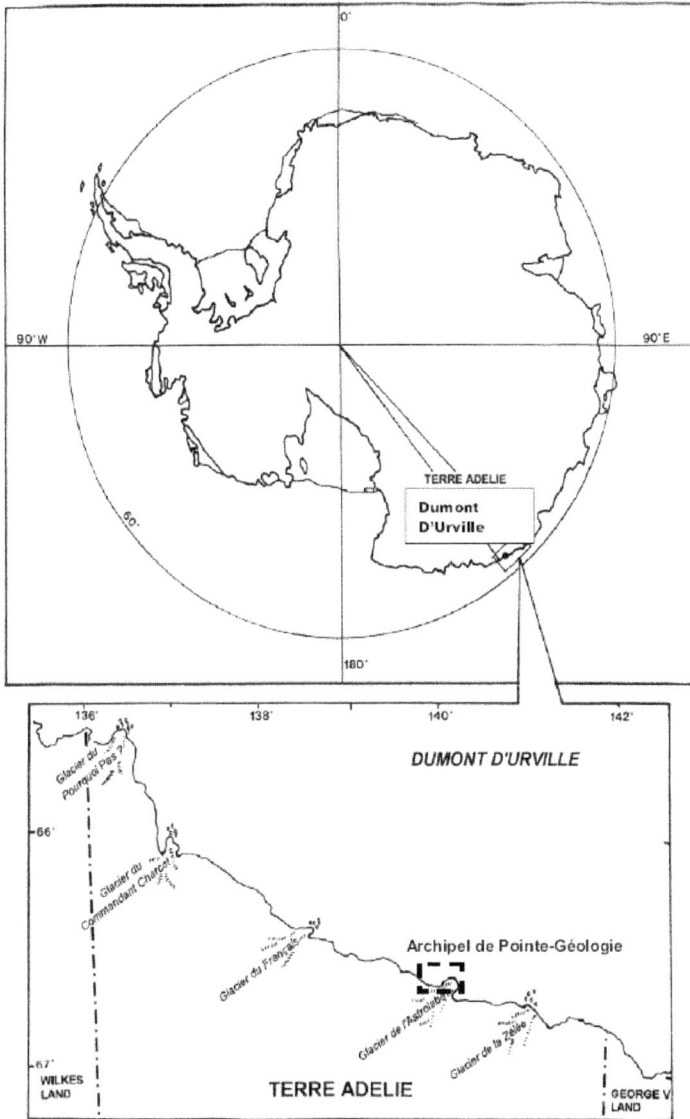

Map 1 - Location of the Cape Geology Archipelago, Terre Adélie (Antarctica).

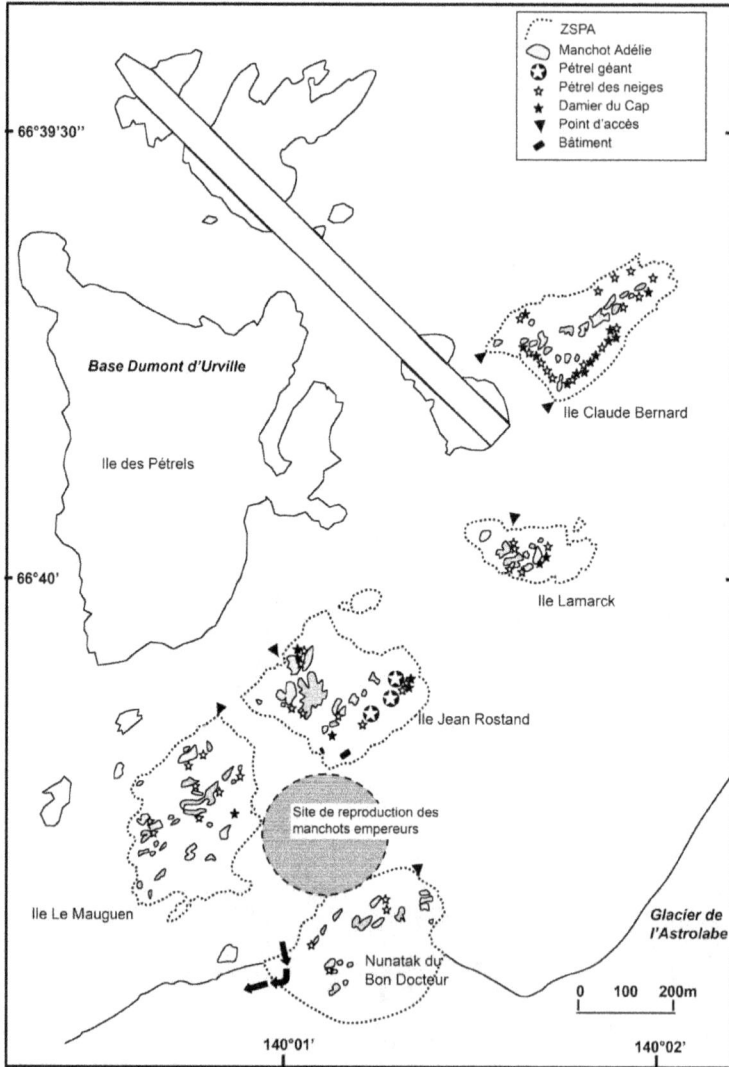

Map 2 - Location of bird colonies (except skua territories and Wilson's petrels nests) within the Cape Geology Archipelago ASPA. The dotted lines show the ASPA boundary. Possible access of land vehicles to the continent via the Good Doctor's Nunatak is shown by means of arrows.

## 6. Description of the Area and Identification of Sectors

*6(i) Geographic coordinates, boundary markers and natural features*

The ASPA 120 is located along the Terre Adélie coast, in the heart of the Cape Geology Archipelago, coastal area of Adélie Coast (140° - 140°02'E ; 66°39'30'' à 66°40'30'' S). It comprises the following territories:

-    Jean Rostand Island,
-    Le Mauguen (formerly Alexis Carrel) Island,
-    Lamarck Island,
-    Claude Bernard Island,
-    the 'Bon Docteur' Nunatak,
-    and the Emperor penguins breeding grounds, on the pack ice which surrounds the islands in winter.

As a whole, the surface of the rock outcrops does not exceed 2 km². The highest points are distributed along North-East-South-West ridges (C. Bernard Island: 47.6 m; J.Rostand Island 36.39 m; Le Mauguen (formerly Alexis Carrel) Island: 28.24 m Nunatak: 28.50 m).

During the summer, the pack ice between the islands disappears, and only the Southern flanks of the islands are still covered by firns. The area is then clearly limited by natural markers (island outlines and rocky outcrops).

No tracks or roads exist in the area.

*6(ii) Identification of restricted or prohibited zones*

Access to any part of the area is prohibited unless authorized by a permit.

Entry restrictions to different sites within the ASPA are determined according to the distribution of bird species (Table 1), the timing of their presence on breeding grounds (Table 2) and their specific sensitivity (Table 3). Location of breeding colonies is shown on the map. Birds are mainly present during the austral summer, except for the emperor penguins, which breed in winter.

Among the bird species present on the Cape Geology Archipelago, the emperor penguin and the southern giant petrel only breed inside the ASPA. Since the ASPA was established in 1995, the populations of those two species are now stable or slightly increasing (Table 3). However, long-term forecasts suggest that the high protection status should be maintained through the current management plan.

**The case of Rostand Island**

The establishment of the Dumont d'Urville station has resulted in a drastic decrease of the populations of emperor penguins and southern giant petrels in the Cape Geology Archipelago. The breeding colony on Petrel Island disappeared completely during the first years when the base was being set up in close proximity to this colony (building extensions, intensification of helicopter flights, installation and replacement of fuel storage tanks). Currently, 100% of the population breeds inside the ASPA, in the South-Eastern part of Rostand Island. The birds are present in an area defined by the NE-SW ridge going through the 33.10 metre and the 36.39 metre marks North West of the colony, marked on the floor with stakes. Access to this breeding area is strictly prohibited, except to ornithologists holding a Permit allowing access once a year when southern giant petrel chicks are being banded. Access to the rest of Rostand Island is authorised throughout the year to Permit Holders.

**The case of the emperor penguin colony**

The significant decrease of emperor penguins by the end of the 1970s seems to have been due to long weather anomalies between 1976 and 1982 causing a significant decrease in the surface area of the pack ice. For the last fifteen years, the emperor penguin breeding population has been slightly increasing in parallel with an increase in pack ice surface area in the Terre Adélie sector. No one, except Permit Holders, is allowed to approach or to disturb the emperor penguin colony in any manner during the period when they are present at the breeding grounds, from March to mid-December when the chicks fledge. It is recommended that the minimum distance between authorised observers and the colony should be 20 m.

The emperor penguin colony is not always at the same site and moves about on the pack ice during winter. The protection zone for these animals is therefore defined by the sites where birds are present (colony or groups of individuals), with an additional 40 m buffer zone.

*6(iii) Location of structures in the Area*

Prévost hut and a shelter are located on Rostand Island. There are no other buildings anywhere else in the Area.

There is no other protected area within 50 km of the Pointe-Géologie ASPA No. 120.

**Table 1.** Number of seabird breeding pairs within ASPA No. 120 (count done during the 2010/2011 breeding cycle). The population breeding within the ASPA compared to that of the Cape Geology (PG) population as a whole is also mentioned (Source: unpublished data CEBC-CNRS on the breeding cycle 2010/2011 except for Wilson's storm petrels, data Micol & Jouventin 2001[1])

| Site | Emperor penguin | Adélie penguin | South Polar skua | Snow petrel | Cape petrel | Wilson's storm petrel | Southern giant petrel |
|---|---|---|---|---|---|---|---|
| C. Bernard | -- | 3360 | 7 | 214 | 238 | 178 | -- |
| Lamarck | -- | 1160 | 1 | 38 | 36 | 45 | -- |
| J. Rostand | -- | 3994 | 7 | 61 | 46 | 35 | 15-18 |
| Le Mauguen (formerly Alexis Carrel) | -- | 3478 | 15 | 21 | 2 | 72 | -- |
| Nunatak | --- | 1831 | 1 | 5 | -- | 41 | -- |
| Winter pack ice between islands | 2838 | -- | -- | -- | -- | -- | -- |
| ASPA TOTAL | 2838 | 13823 | 31 | 369 | 322 | 371 | 15-18 |
| PG TOTAL | 2838 | 32746 | 67 | 1066 | 516 | 1200 | 15-18 |
| % ASPA/PG | 100 | 42 | 46 | 32 | 62 | 31 | 100 |

[1] Micol T. et Jouventin P 2001, Long-term population trends in seven Antarctic seabirds at Pointe Géologie (Terre Adélie) *Polar Biology* **24** :175-185.

**Table 2.** Presence of birds on breeding grounds

|  | Emperor penguin | Adelie penguin | South Polar skua | Snow petrel | Cape petrel | Wilson's storm petrel | Southern giant petrel |
|---|---|---|---|---|---|---|---|
| First arrival | March | October | October | September | October | November | July |
| First egg laying | May | November | November | November | November | December | October |
| Last departure | Mid-December | March | March | March | March | March | April |

**Table 3.** Sensitivity to disturbance caused by human beings and changes in populations of the Cape Geology Archipelago (Sources : unpublished data CEBC-CNRS, Thomas 1986[2], and Micol & Jouventin 2001 for data on Wilson's storm petrel)

|  | Emperor penguin | Adelie penguin | South Polar skua | Snow petrel | Cape petrel | Wilson's storm petrel * | Southern giant petrel |
|---|---|---|---|---|---|---|---|
| Sensitivity [2] | High | Medium | Medium | Medium | High | High | High |
| Trend 1952-1984 | Diminishing | Stable | Stable | ? | ? | ? | Diminishing |
| Trend 1984-2000 | Stable | Increasing | Increasing | Stable | Stable | ? | Stable |
| Trend 2000-2011 | Slightly increasing | Increasing | Increasing | Increasing | Stable | ? | Stable |
| Trend 1952-2011 | Diminishing | Increasing | Increasing | Stable | Stable | ? | Diminishing |

## 7. Permit Conditions

- Entry into the Area is subject to obtaining a Permit issued by an appropriate national authority.
- Permits may be granted to carry out various scientific research, site monitoring or inspection activities, or one-off logistical operations. For each single entry, permits will authorize the scope of the tasks to be undertaken, their time-span and the maximum number of people commissioned to enter the Area (Permit Holders and any accompanying persons who may be needed for professional or safety reasons).

*7(i) Access to and movement within the Area*

- No helicopters or terrestrial vehicles are authorized within the Area. No overflights over the Area, either by helicopters or other aircraft are authorized. Access to the Area is only permitted by foot or by light watercraft (in summer).
- The transit traffic of land vehicles between the Dumont d'Urville station, on Petrel Island, and the Cap Prudhomme station on the continent, will normally take place in winter, following a straight line across the pack ice. During the very rare occasions when sea-ice conditions do not allow these transits to be made safely, a route along the western edge of the 'Bon Docteur' Nunatak can be permitted exceptionally, as indicated on Map 2. The vehicles will then follow the distance instructions regarding emperor penguins as mentioned in Section 6(ii).
- The movement of authorised persons within the Area shall, in any case, be limited, in order to avoid unnecessary disturbance to birds, and to ensure that breeding areas or their access are not damaged or endangered.

---

[2] Thomas T., 1986 L'effectif des oiseaux nicheurs de l'archipel de Pointe Géologie (Terre Adélie) et son évolution au cours des trente dernières années. *L'oiseau RFO* **56** :349-368.

*7(ii) Activities which are or may be conducted within the Area, including restrictions on time and place*
- Compelling scientific activities which cannot be conducted elsewhere.
- Essential management and logistical activities
- Educational and scientific outreach activities (filming, photography, sound recording...)

*7(iii) Installation, modification or removal of structures*
- No structures are to be erected or scientific equipment installed in the Area except for compelling scientific reasons or management activities as authorized by an appropriate national authority.
- The possible modification or dismantling of installations currently on Rostand Island can only proceed after authorisation.

*7(iv) Location of field camps*

Only safety tents should be erected when security reasons so require it provided all precautions have been taken in order to avoid damaging or disturbing the fauna.

*7(v) Restriction on materials and organisms which may be brought into the Area*
- According to the provisions set forth in Annex II to the Madrid Protocol, no living animals or plant materials, poultry products, including dried eggs, shall be introduced into the Area.
- No chemicals shall be brought into the Area, except chemicals which may be introduced for a compelling scientific purpose as specified n the Permit. Any chemical introduced shall be removed from the Area at or before the conclusion of the activity for which the Permit was granted.
- Fuel, food and other materials are not to be stored in the Area, unless required for compelling purposes connected with the activity for which the Permit has been granted. Such materials are to be removed when no longer required. Permanent storage is not permitted.

*7(vi) The taking of or harmful interference with flora and fauna*
- Taking of or harmful interference with native flora and fauna is prohibited except in accordance with a specific Permit. In the case of authorised taking or interference, the requirements of article 3 of Annex II of the Protocol will be used as the minimum standard.

*7 (vii) The collection or removal of anything not brought into the Area by the Permit Holder*
- Collection or removal of anything not brought into the Area by a Permit Holder is prohibited unless specifically mentioned in the Permit.
- Debris of man-made origin may be removed from the Area and dead or pathological specimens of fauna or flora cannot be removed unless explicitly mentioned in the Permit.

*7(viii) Disposal of waste*
- All waste produced must be removed from the Area after each visit.

*7(ix) Measures that may be necessary to ensure that the aims and objectives of the Management Plan can continue to be met*
- Visits to the Area shall be restricted to scientific, logistic and management objectives only.

*7(x) Requirements for reports of visits to the Area*

Parties should ensure that the principal Holder of each Permit issued submits to the appropriate authority a report describing the activities undertaken. Such reports should include, as appropriate, the information identified in the visit report form contained in the Guide to the Preparation of Management Plans for Antarctic Specially Protected Areas.

Parties should maintain a record of such activities and, in the Annual Exchange of Information, should provide summary descriptions of activities conducted by persons subject to their jurisdiction, in sufficient detail to allow evaluation of the effectiveness of the Management Plan. Parties should, wherever possible, deposit original or copies of such original reports in a publicly accessible archive to maintain a record of usage, to be taken into consideration both when reviewing the Management Plan and when organizing the scientific manipulation of the Area.

# Management Plan for
# Antarctic Specially Protected Area No. 122

# ARRIVAL HEIGHTS, HUT POINT PENINSULA, ROSS ISLAND

## Introduction

The Arrival Heights Antarctic Specially Protected Area (ASPA) is situated near the south-western extremity of Hut Point Peninsula, Ross Island, at 77° 49' 41.2" S, 166° 40' 2.8" E, with an approximate area 0.73 km². The primary reason for designation of the Area is its value as an electromagnetically 'quiet' site for the study of the upper atmosphere and its close proximity to logistical support. The Area is used for a number of other scientific studies, including trace gas monitoring, auroral and geomagnetic studies and air quality surveys. As an example, the longevity and quality of the numerous atmospheric datasets makes the Area of high scientific value. Since its designation in 1975, numerous projects have been located in or near the Area with a potential to degrade the electromagnetically quiet conditions at Arrival Heights. The interference generated by these activities appears to have an acceptably low impact on scientific experiments, although a detailed review of the level of interference is currently being undertaken. The continued use of the Area is favored by its geographical characteristics, its proximity to logistical support and high costs associated with relocation. The Area was proposed by the United States of America and adopted through Recommendation VIII-4 [1975, Site of Special Scientific Interest (SSSI) No. 2]; date of expiry was extended through Recommendations X-6 (1979), XII-5 (1983), XIII-7 (1985), and XIV-4 (1987) and Resolution 3 (1996). The Area was renamed and renumbered through Decision 1 (2002); a revised management plan was provided through Measure 2 (2004). The degradation of electromagnetically 'quiet' conditions within the Area was recognized by SCAR Recommendation XXIII-6 (1994). Minor corrections to the boundaries of the Area have been made to ensure consistency between the text and the updated and more accurate maps provided in the current management plan.

## 1. Description of values to be protected

An area at Arrival Heights was originally designated in Recommendation VIII-4 (1975, SSSI No. 2), after a proposal by the United States of America on the grounds that it was "an electromagnetic and natural 'quiet site' offering ideal conditions for the installation of sensitive instruments for recording minute signals associated with upper atmosphere programs." For example, electromagnetic recordings have been carried out at Arrival Heights as part of long term scientific studies, yielding data of outstanding quality because of the unique characteristics of the geographic location with respect to the geomagnetic field combined with relatively low levels of electromagnetic interference. The electromagnetically quiet conditions and the longevity of data collection at Arrival Heights make the data obtained of particularly high scientific value.

In recent years, however, increases in science and support operations associated with Scott Base and McMurdo Station have raised the levels of locally generated electromagnetic noise at Arrival Heights and it has been recognized that the electromagnetically 'quiet' conditions have to some degree been degraded by these activities, as identified in SCAR Recommendation XXIII-6 (1994).

Scientific research within the Area appears to operate within an acceptably low level of electromagnetic interference (EMI) from other activities in the vicinity and the aims and objectives set out in the management plan for Arrival Heights therefore remain relevant. However, recent site visits and deployment of new instruments have shown that there is some elevated very-low frequency (VLF) noise in the 50 Hz – 12 kHz range from sources located outside of the Area (most likely wind turbines installed ~1 km from the Area). There is also evidence of increased VLF noise in the 12 - 50 KHz frequency range, which probably arises inside of the Area from, for example, the electrical power grid configuration and grounding, and the proliferation of units such as uninterruptable power supplies (UPS). The US and NZ scientific communities that run projects at Arrival Heights are currently undertaking a detailed analysis of the possible causes of EMI with the goal of providing practical recommendations for mitigating potential effects.

Notwithstanding these observations, the original geographical characteristics of the site, such as its elevated position and thus broad viewing horizon, the volcanic crater morphology, and the close proximity to the full logistic support of nearby McMurdo Station (US) 1.5 km south and Scott Base (NZ) 2.7 km SE, continue to render the Area valuable for upper atmospheric studies and boundary layer air sampling studies. Moreover, there are scientific, financial and practical constraints associated with any proposed relocation of the Area and the associated facilities. Thus, the current preferred option for management is to minimize sources of EMI to the maximum extent practicable, and to monitor these levels routinely so that any significant threat to the values of the site can be identified and addressed as appropriate.

Since original designation the site has been used for several other scientific programs that benefit from the restrictions on access in place within the Area. In particular, the broad viewing horizon and relative isolation from activities (e.g.

vehicle movements, engine exhausts) has been valuable for measurement of trace gases, particularly ozone, spectroscopic and air particulate investigations, pollution surveys, and auroral and geomagnetic studies. In addition, the protected status of Arrival Heights has also had the effect of limiting the extent and magnitude of physical disturbance within the Area. As a result, soils and landscape features are much less disturbed than is the case in the surrounding areas of Hut Point where station developments have taken place. In particular, sand-wedge polygons are far more extensive than elsewhere in the Hut Point vicinity, covering an area of approximately $0.5$ km$^2$. The relatively undisturbed nature of the environment at Arrival Heights makes the Area valuable for comparative studies of impacts associated with station developments, and valuable as a reference against which to consider changes. These additional values are also important reasons for special protection at Arrival Heights.

The Area continues to be of high scientific value for a variety of high quality and long-term atmospheric data sets that have been collected at this site. Despite the acknowledged potential for interference from local and surrounding sources, the long-term data series, the accessibility of the site for year-round observations, its geographical characteristics, and the high cost of relocation, warrant that the site receive ongoing and strengthened protection. The vulnerability of this research to disturbance through chemical and noise pollution, in particular electromagnetic interference, is such that this Area requires continued special protection.

## 2. Aims and objectives

Management at Arrival Heights aims to:

- avoid degradation of, or substantial risk to, the values of the Area by preventing unnecessary human disturbance to the Area;
- allow scientific research in the Area, in particular atmospheric research, while ensuring protection from incompatible uses and uncontrolled equipment installation that may jeopardize such research;
- minimize the possibility of generation of excessive electromagnetic noise interference within the Area through regulating the types, quantity and use of equipment that can be installed and operated in the Area;
- encourage the consideration of the values of the Area in the management of surrounding activities and land uses, in particular to monitor the levels, and encourage the minimization of sources of electromagnetic radiation that may potentially compromise the values of the Area;
- allow access for maintenance, upgrade and management of communications and scientific equipment located within the Area;
- allow visits for management purposes in support of the aims of the management plan; and
- allow visits for education or public awareness purposes associated with the scientific studies being conducted in the Area that cannot be fulfilled elsewhere.

## 3. Management activities

The following management activities are to be undertaken to protect the values of the Area:

- Signs showing the location and boundaries of the Area with clear statements of entry restrictions shall be placed at appropriate locations at the boundaries of the Area to help avoid inadvertent entry.
- Signs showing the location of the Area (stating the special restrictions that apply) shall be displayed prominently, and a copy of this management plan shall be kept available, in the principal research hut facilities within the Area and at McMurdo Station and Scott Base.
- Markers, signs or structures erected within or near the boundary of the Area for scientific or management purposes shall be secured and maintained in good condition, and removed when no longer necessary.
- Visits shall be made as necessary (no less than once every five years) to assess whether the Area continues to serve the purposes for which it was designated and to ensure management and maintenance measures are adequate.
- Electromagnetic noise surveys shall be undertaken within the Area bi-annually to detect equipment faults and to monitor levels of interference that may have potential to compromise the values of the Area unacceptably, for the purposes of identification and mitigation of their sources.
- Potentially disruptive activities that are planned to be conducted outside of but close to the Area, such as blasting or drilling, or the operation of transmitters or other equipment with the potential to cause significant electromagnetic interference within the Area, should be notified in advance to the appropriate representative(s) of national authorities operating in the region, with a view to coordinating activities and / or undertaking mitigating actions in order to avoid or minimize disruption to scientific programs.
- National Antarctic Programs operating in the region shall appoint an Activity Coordinator who will be responsible for inter-program consultation regarding all activities within the Area.

- National Antarctic Programs operating in the region shall consult together with a view to ensuring the conditions in this management plan are implemented, and take appropriate measures to detect and enforce compliance where the conditions are not being followed.

### 4. Period of designation

Designated for an indefinite period.

### 5. Maps and photographs

**Map 1:** Arrival Heights, ASPA No. 122 in relation to Hut Point Peninsula, showing the location of nearby stations (McMurdo Station, US; and Scott Base, NZ), installations (SuperDARN, satellite receptors and wind turbines) and routes (roads and recreational trails). Projection Lambert Conformal Conic: Standard parallels: 1st 77° 40' S; 2nd 78° 00' S; Central Meridian: 166° 45' E; Latitude of Origin: 77° 50' S; Spheroid WGS84; Datum McMurdo Sound Geodetic Control Network. Data sources: Topography: contours (10 m interval) derived from digital orthophoto and DEM from aerial imagery (Nov 1993); Permanent ice extent digitized from orthorectified Quickbird satellite image (15 Oct 05) (Imagery © 2005 Digital Globe, provided through the NGA Commercial Imagery Program); Infrastructure: station layout CAD data USAP (Feb 09 / Mar 11), ERA (Nov 09) and USAP (Jan 11) field survey; Recreational trails PGC field survey (Jan 09 / Jan 11).

**Inset 1:** The location of Ross Island in the Ross Sea. **Inset 2:** The location of Map 1 on Ross Island and key topographic features.

**Map 2:** Arrival Heights, ASPA No. 122 topographic map, showing protected area boundaries, site facilities, nearby installations (SuperDARN, satellite receptors) and routes (access roads and recreational trails). Projection details and data sources are the same as for Map 1.

### 6. Description of the Area

*6(i) Geographical coordinates, boundary markers and natural features*

*Boundaries and coordinates*

Arrival Heights (77° 49' 41.2" S, 166° 40' 2.8" E; Area: 0.73 km$^2$) is a small range of low hills located near the southwestern extremity of Hut Point Peninsula, Ross Island. Hut Point Peninsula is composed of a series of volcanic craters extending from Mount Erebus, two of which, namely First Crater and Second Crater, respectively form part of the southern and northern boundaries of the Area. The Area is predominantly ice-free and elevations range from 150 m to a maximum of 280 m at Second Crater. Arrival Heights is located approximately 1.5 km north of McMurdo Station and 2.7 km northwest of Scott Base. The Area has a broad viewing horizon and is comparatively isolated from activities at McMurdo Station and Scott Base, with the majority of McMurdo Station being hidden from view.

The southeastern boundary corner of the Area is defined by Trig T510 No.2, the center of which is located at 77° 50' 08.4" S, 166° 40' 16.4" E at an elevation of 157.3 m. Trig T510 No.2 replaced, and is 0.7 m from, the former boundary survey marker (T510) which no longer exists. The replacement T510 No.2 marker is an iron rod (painted orange) installed into the ground approximately 7.3 m west of the access road to Arrival Heights, and is surrounded by a small circle of rocks. The boundary of the Area extends from Trig T510 No.2 in a straight line 656.0 m northwest over First Crater to a point located at 77° 49' 53.8" S, 166° 39' 03.9" E at 150 m elevation. The boundary thence follows the 150 m contour northward for 1186 m to a point (77° 49' 18.6" S, 166° 39' 56.1" E) due west of the northern rim of Second Crater. The boundary thence extends 398 m due east to Second Crater, and around the crater rim to a US Hydrographic Survey marker (a stamped brass disk) which is installed near ground level at 77° 49' 23.4" S, 166° 40' 59.0" E and 282 m elevation, forming the northeastern boundary of the Area. The boundary thence extends from the US Hydrographic Survey marker southward for 1423 m in a straight line directly to Trig T510 No.2.

*Geology, geomorphology and soils*

Hut Point Peninsula is 20 km long and is formed by a line of craters that extend south from the flanks of Mt. Erebus (Kyle 1981). The basaltic rocks of Hut Point Peninsula constitute part of the Erebus volcanic province and the dominant rock types are alkali basanite lavas and pyroclastics, with small amounts of phonolite and occasional outcrops of intermediate lavas (Kyle 1981). Aeromagnetic data and magnetic models indicate that the magnetic volcanic rocks underlying Hut Point Peninsula are likely to be <2 km in thickness (Behrendt *et al.* 1996) and dating studies suggest that the majority of basaltic rocks are younger than ~ 750 ka (Tauxe *et al.* 2004).

The soils at Arrival Heights consist mostly of volcanic scoria deposited from the eruptions of Mount Erebus, with particle size ranging from silt to boulders. The thickness of surface deposits ranges from a few centimetres to tens of metres, with permafrost underlying the active layer (Stefano, 1992). Surface material at Arrival Heights also includes magma flows from Mount Erebus, which have been weathered and reworked over time. Sand-wedge polygons cover an area of approximately 0.5 km$^2$ at Arrival Heights and, because physical disturbance has been limited by the protected status of the Area, are far more extensive than elsewhere in the southern Hut Point Peninsula vicinity (Klein *et al.* 2004).

*Climate*

Arrival Heights is exposed to frequent strong winds and conditions are generally colder and windier than at nearby McMurdo Station and Scott Base (Mazzera *et al.* 2001). During the period February 1999 to April 2009, the maximum temperature recorded within the Area was 7.1°C (30 Dec 2001) and the minimum was -49.8°C (21 July 2004). During this period, December was the warmest month, with mean monthly air temperatures of -5.1°C, and August was the coolest month, averaging –28.8°C (data sourced from National Institute of Water and Atmospheric Research, New Zealand, http://www.niwa.cri.nz, 21 May 2009).

The mean annual wind speed recorded at Arrival Heights between 1999 and 2009 was 6.96 ms-1, with June and September being the windiest months (data sourced from National Institute of Water and Atmospheric Research, New Zealand, http://www.niwa.cri.nz, 21 May 2009). The highest recorded gust at Arrival Heights between 1999-2011 was 51 m/s (~184 km/h) on 16 May 2004. The prevailing wind direction at Arrival Heights is north-easterly, as southern air masses are deflected by the surrounding topography (Sinclair 1988). Hut Point Peninsula lies at the confluence of three dissimilar air masses, predisposing the area to rapid onset of severe weather (Monaghan *et al.* 2005).

*Scientific research*

Numerous long-term scientific investigations are conducted at Arrival Heights, with the majority of research focusing on the earth's atmosphere and magnetosphere. Research areas include extremely low and very low radio frequencies, auroral events, geomagnetic storms, meteorological phenomena and variations in trace gas levels, particularly ozone. The Area has good access and logistical support from nearby McMurdo Station and Scott Base, which helps to facilitate research within the Area.

The extremely-low-frequency and very-low-frequency (ELF/VLF) data have been continuously collected at Arrival Heights since the austral summer of 1984-1985 (Fraser-Smith *et al.* 1991). The ELF/VLF noise data are unique in both length and continuity for the Antarctic and were recorded concurrently with ELF/VLF data at Stanford University, allowing for comparison between polar and mid-latitude time series. The lack of electromagnetic interference and remote location of Arrival Heights allow researchers to measure background ELF/VLF noise spectra and weak ELF signals, such as Schumann resonances, which are associated changes in the magnetosphere and ionosphere (Füllerkrug & Fraser-Smith 1996). ELF/VLF and Schumann resonance data collected within the Area have been studied in relation to fluctuations in sun spots, solar particle precipitation events, and planetary-scale meteorological phenomenon (Anyamba *et al.* 2000; Schlegel & Füllerkrug 1999; Fraser-Smith & Turtle 1993). Furthermore, ELF data have been used as a proxy measure of global cloud-to-ground lightning activity and thunderstorm activity (Füllerkrug *et al.* 1999) and VLF data provide input to global networks which monitor lightning activity and conditions in the ionosphere (Clilverd *et al.* 2009; Rodger *et al.* 2009). High quality electromagnetic data from Arrival Heights has enabled determination of an upper limit for the photon rest mass of ~10$^{-52}$ kg (Füllerkrug 2004) based on detection of minute global ionospheric reflection height measurements (Füllerkrug *et al.* 2002), and it has also provided a critical link between lightning at mid- and tropical latitudes and surface temperature variations in moderate and tropical climates (Füllerkrug & Fraser-Smith 1997). Recent research has developed novel measurement technologies with a sensitivity of µV/m over the broad frequency range from ~4 Hz to ~400 kHz (Füllerkrug 2010), which has promising scientific potential requiring conditions of electromagnetic quiescence such as are present at Arrival Heights.

The southerly location of Arrival Heights results in several weeks of total darkness during the austral winter, allowing low intensity auroral events and dayside emissions to be observed (Wright *et al.* 1998). Data recorded at Arrival Heights have been used to track the motion of polar cap arcs, a form of polar aurora, and results have been related to solar wind and interplanetary magnetic field conditions. Auroral observations made at Arrival Heights by researchers for the University of Washington have also been used to calculate the velocity and temperature of high altitude winds by analyzing the Doppler shift of auroral light emissions. In addition to auroral research, optical data collected within the Area have been used to monitor the response of the thermosphere to geomagnetic storms (Hernandez & Roble 2003) and medium frequency radar has been used to measure middle atmospheric (70-100 km) wind velocities (McDonald *et al.* 2007).

A range of trace gas species are measured at Arrival Heights, including ozone, bromine, methane, nitrogen oxides, hydrogen chloride and carbon monoxide, with records commencing as early as 1982 (Connor *et al.* 2005). Arrival Heights represents a key site in the Network of the Detection of Atmospheric Composition (NDACC), with data being used to monitor changes in the stratosphere, including long-term evolution of the ozone layer and changes in overall atmospheric composition. Ozone levels have been recorded at Arrival Heights since 1988 and are used to monitor both long-term and seasonal variations in ozone (Oltmans *et al.* 2008; Nichol *et al.* 1991), as well as in estimations of Antarctic ozone loss (Kuttippurath *et al.* 2010). In addition to longer-term trends, sudden and substantial ozone depletion events have been recorded during spring-time at Arrival Heights, which occur over a period of hours and thought to result from the release of bromine compounds from sea salt (Riedel *et al.* 2006; Hay *et al.* 2007).

Tropospheric bromine levels have been continuously recorded since 1995 within the Area and have been studied in relation to ozone depletion, stratospheric warming and changes in the polar vortex, as well as being used in validation of satellite measurements (Schofield *et al.* 2006). Nitrogen oxide ($NO_2$) data collected at Arrival Heights have also been used to investigate variations in ozone levels and results show substantial variations in $NO_2$ at daily to interannual timescales, potentially resulting from changes in atmospheric circulation, temperature and chemical forcing (Struthers *et al.* 2004, Wood et al., 2004). In addition, ground-based Fourier transform spectroscopy has been used at Arrival Heights to monitor atmospheric carbonyl sulfide levels and to record HCL fluxes from Mount Erebus (Deutscher *et al.* 2006; Keys *et al.* 1998).

*Vegetation*

Lichens at Arrival Heights were surveyed in 1957 by C.W. Dodge and G.E. Baker, with species recorded including: *Buellia alboradians, B. frigida, B. grisea, B. pernigra, Caloplaca citrine, Candelariella flava, Lecanora expectans, L. fuscobrunnea, Lecidella siplei, Parmelia griseola, P. leucoblephara* and *Physcia caesia*. Moss species recorded at Arrival Heights include *Sarconeurum glaciale* and *Syntrichia sarconeurum* (BAS Plant Database, 2009), with *S. glaciale* documented within drainage channels and disused vehicle tracks (Skotnicki *et al.* 1999).

*Human activities and impact*

The Arrival Heights facilities are used year-round by personnel from McMurdo Station (US) and Scott Base (NZ). In addition to two laboratory buildings, numerous antenna arrays, aerials, communications equipment, and scientific instruments are located throughout the Area, along with associated cabling.

The scientific instruments used for atmospheric research in the Area are sensitive to electromagnetic noise and interference, with potential local noise sources including VLF radio transmissions, powerlines, vehicle emission systems and also laboratory equipment. Noise sources generated outside of the Area that may also affect electromagnetic conditions at Arrival Heights include radio communications, entertainment broadcast systems, ship, aircraft, or satellite radio transmissions, or aircraft surveillance radars. A site visit report from 2006 suggested that levels of interference at that time were acceptably low, despite activities operating out of McMurdo Station and Scott Base. In order to provide some degree of protection from local radio transmissions and station noise, some of the VLF antennas at Arrival Heights are located within Second Crater.

Unauthorised access to the Area, both by vehicle and on foot, is thought to have resulted in damage to cabling and scientific instruments, although the extent of damage and impact upon scientific results is unknown. A camera was installed at the USAP building in early 2010 to monitor traffic entering the Area via the road leading to the laboratories.

Recent installations within and close to the Area include an FE-Boltzmann LiDAR in the New Zealand Arrival Heights Research Laboratory in 2010, the Super Dual Auroral RADAR Network (SuperDARN) Antenna Array (2009-10) and two satellite earth station receptors (Map 2). The SuperDARN Antenna Array transmits at low frequencies (8 – 20 MHz), with the main transmission direction to the southwest of the Area, and its location was selected in part to minimize interference with experiments at Arrival Heights. Two satellite earth station receptors (Joint Polar Satellite System (JPSS) and MG2) are located nearby. One of the receptors has the ability to transmit (frequency range 2025 – 2120 Hz) and measures have been taken to ensure that any irradiation of the Area is minimal.

Three wind turbines were constructed approximately 1.5 km east of the Area and close to Crater Hill during austral summer 2009-10 (Map 1). EMI emissions from the turbines should comply with accepted standards for electrical machinery and utilities. However, EMI originating from the new wind turbines has been detected in very low frequency datasets at Arrival Heights, with potential sources of EMI including turbine transformers, generators and power lines.

A detailed analysis of EMI is currently being carried out, with particular attention being paid to determining possible impacts arising from operation of the nearby wind turbines and the LiDAR and power systems installed in laboratories within the Area. Results are anticipated in late 2011.

Air quality monitoring has been regularly carried out at Arrival Heights since 1992 and recent studies suggest that air quality has been reduced, most likely due to emissions originating from McMurdo or Scott Base (Mazzera *et al.* 2001), for example from construction and vehicle operations. Investigations found that air quality samples contained higher concentrations of pollution derived species (EC, SO2, Pb, Zn) and PM10 (particles with aerodynamic diameters less than 10 μm) aerosols than other coastal and Antarctic sites.

*6(ii) Access to the Area*

Access to the Area may be made over land by vehicle or on foot. The access road to the Area enters at the south-east and extends to the research laboratories. Several vehicle trails are present within the Area and run from the Satellite Earth Station in First Crater to the foot of Second Crater. Pedestrian access may be made from the access road.

Access by air and overflight of the Area are prohibited, except when specifically authorized by permit, in which case the appropriate authority supporting research programs within the Area must be notified prior to entry.

*6(iii) Restricted and managed zones within the Area*

None.

*6(iv) Structures within and near the Area*

Both the New Zealand and United States programs have research and living facilities within the Area. New Zealand opened a new research laboratory at Arrival Heights on 20 January 2007, replacing an old building which has been removed from the Area. The US maintains one laboratory within the Area. A range of antenna arrays and aerials designed to meet scientific needs are located throughout the Area (Map 2), and a new VLF antenna was installed at Arrival Heights during December 2008. A Satellite Earth Station (SES) is located several meters inside the boundary of the Area on First Crater (Map 2).

The SuperDARN Antenna Array is located approximately 270 m SW of the Area, while two satellite earth station receptors are installed approximately 150 m SW of the Area (Map 2).

*6(v) Location of other protected areas within close proximity of the Area*

The nearest protected areas to Arrival Heights are on Ross Island: Cape Evans (ASPA No. 155) is the closest at 22 km north; Backdoor Bay (ASPA No. 157) is 32 km north, Cape Royds (ASPA No. 121) is 35 km NNW; Tramway Ridge (ASPA No. 130) near the summit of Mt. Erebus is 40 km north; Lewis Bay (ASPA No. 156) the site of the 1979 DC-10 passenger aircraft crash is 50 km NE; New College Valley (ASPA No. 116) is 65 km north at Cape Bird; and Cape Crozier (ASPA No. 124) is 70 km to the NE. NW White Island (ASPA No. 137) is 35 km to the south across the Ross Ice Shelf. Antarctic Specially Managed Area No. 2 McMurdo Dry Valleys is located approximately 50 km to the west of the Area.

### 7. Permit conditions

Entry into the Area is prohibited except in accordance with a permit issued by an appropriate national authority. Conditions for issuing a permit to enter the Area are that:

- it is issued only for scientific study of the atmosphere and magnetosphere, or for other scientific purposes that cannot be served elsewhere; or
- it is issued for operation, management and maintenance of science support facilities (including safe operations), on the condition that movement within the Area be restricted to that necessary to access those facilities; or
- it is issued for educational or public awareness activities that cannot be fulfilled elsewhere and which are associated with the scientific studies being conducted in the Area, on the condition that visitors are accompanied by permitted personnel responsible for the facilities visited; or
- it is issued for essential management purposes consistent with plan objectives such as inspection or review;
- the actions permitted will not jeopardize the scientific or educational values of the Area;
- any management activities are in support of the objectives of the Management Plan;
- the actions permitted are in accordance with the Management Plan;
- the Permit, or a copy, shall be carried within the Area;
- a visit report shall be supplied to the authority or authorities named in the Permit;
- permits shall be valid for a stated period.

*7(i) Access to and movement within the Area*

Access to the Area is permitted by vehicle and on foot. Landing of aircraft and overflight within the Area is prohibited unless specifically authorized by permit. Prior written notification must be given to the appropriate authority or authorities supporting scientific research being conducted in the Area at the time of the proposed aircraft activity. The location and timing of the aircraft activity should be coordinated as appropriate in order to avoid or minimize disruption to scientific programs.

Vehicle and pedestrian traffic should be kept to the minimum necessary to fulfil the objectives of permitted activities and every reasonable effort should be made to minimize potential impacts on scientific research: e.g. personnel entering the Area by vehicle should coordinate travel so vehicle use is kept to a minimum.

Vehicles shall keep to the established vehicle tracks as shown on Map 2, unless specifically authorized by permit otherwise. Pedestrians should also keep to established tracks wherever possible. Care should be taken to avoid cables and other instruments when moving around the Area, as they are susceptible to damage from both foot and vehicle traffic. During hours of darkness, vehicle headlights should be switched off when approaching the facilities, in order to prevent damage to light-sensitive instruments within the Area.

*7(ii) Activities that are or may be conducted in the Area, including restrictions on time or place*

Activities that may be conducted within the Area include:

- scientific research that will not jeopardize the scientific values of the Area;
- essential management activities, including the installation of new facilities to support scientific research;
- Activities with educational aims (such as documentary reporting (photographic, audio or written) or the production of educational resources or services) that cannot be served elsewhere;
- use of hand-held and vehicle radios by visitors entering the Area is allowed; however, their use should be minimized and shall be restricted to communications for scientific, management or safety purposes;
- surveys of electromagnetic noise to help ensure that scientific research is not significantly compromised.

*7(iii) Installation, modification or removal of structures*

- No structures are to be erected within the Area except as specified in a permit.
- All structures, scientific equipment or markers installed within the Area, outside of research hut facilities, must be authorized by permit and clearly identified by country, name of the principal investigator and year of installation. Removal of such structures, equipment or markers upon expiration of the permit shall be the responsibility of the authority which granted the original permit, and shall be a condition of the permit.
- 
- Installation (including site selection), maintenance, modification or removal of structures shall be undertaken in a manner that minimizes environmental disturbance and installations should not jeopardize the values of the Area, particularly the electromagnetically 'quiet' conditions. Installations should be made of materials that pose minimal risk of environmental contamination of the Area. The time period for removal of equipment shall be specified in the permit.
- No new Radio Frequency (RF) transmitting equipment other than low power transceivers for essential local communications may be installed within the Area. Electromagnetic radiation produced by equipment introduced to the Area shall not have significant adverse effects on any on-going investigations unless specifically authorized. Precautions shall be taken to ensure that electrical equipment used within the Area is adequately shielded to keep electromagnetic noise to a minimum.
- Installation or modification of structures or equipment within the Area is subject to an assessment of the likely impacts of the proposed installations or modifications on the values of the Area, as required according to national procedures. Details of proposals and the accompanying assessment of impacts shall, in addition to any other procedures that may be required by appropriate authorities, be submitted by investigators to the activity coordinator for their national program, who will exchange documents received with other activity coordinators for the Area. Activity coordinators will assess the proposals in consultation with national program managers and relevant investigators for the potential impacts on the scientific or natural environmental values of the Area. Activity coordinators shall confer with each other and make recommendations (to proceed as proposed, to proceed with revisions, to trial for further assessment, or not to proceed) to their national program within 60 days of receiving a proposal. National programs shall be responsible for notifying investigators whether or not they may proceed with their proposals and under what conditions.
- The planning, installation or modification of nearby structures or equipment outside the Area that emit EMR should take into account their potential to affect the values of the Area.

*7(iv) Location of field camps*

Camping within the Area is prohibited. Overnight visits are permitted in buildings equipped for such purposes.

*7(v) Restrictions on materials and organisms that can be brought into the Area*

There are no specific restrictions on materials and organisms that can be brought into the Area.

*7(vi) Taking or harmful interference with native flora or fauna*

Taking or harmful interference with native flora and fauna is prohibited, except in accordance with a separate permit issued by the appropriate national authority specifically for that purpose under Article 3 of Annex II to the Protocol.

*7(vii) Collection or removal of anything not brought into the Area by the permit holder*

- Material may be collected or removed from the Area only in accordance with a permit and should be limited to the minimum necessary to meet scientific or management needs.
- Material of human origin likely to compromise the values of the Area, which was not brought into the Area by the permit holder or otherwise authorized, may be removed from any part of the Area unless the

impact of removal is likely to be greater than leaving the material *in situ*. If this is the case the appropriate authority should be notified.

- The appropriate national authority should be notified of any items removed from the Area that were not introduced by the permit holder.

*7(viii) Disposal of waste*

All wastes, including human wastes, shall be removed from the Area.

*7(ix) Measures that are necessary to ensure that the aims and objectives of the management plan can continue to be met*

1) Permits may be granted to enter the Area to carry out scientific monitoring and site inspection activities, which may involve the collection of data for analysis or review, or for protective measures.

2) Any specific sites of long-term monitoring shall be appropriately marked.

3) Electromagnetic bands of particular scientific interest and that warrant special protection from interference should be identified by parties active within the Area. As far as practically possible, the generation of electromagnetic noise should be limited to frequencies outside of these bands.

4) The intentional generation of electromagnetic noise within the Area is prohibited, apart from within agreed frequency bands and power levels or in accordance with a permit.

*7(x) Requirements for reports*

- Parties should ensure that the principal holder for each permit issued submits to the appropriate authority a report describing the activities undertaken. Such reports should include, as appropriate, the information identified in the visit report form contained in the Guide to the Preparation of Management Plans for Antarctic Specially Protected Areas.

- Parties should maintain a record of such activities and, in the annual Exchange of Information, should provide summary descriptions of activities conducted by persons subject to their jurisdiction, which should be in sufficient detail to allow evaluation of the effectiveness of the Management Plan. Parties should, wherever possible, deposit originals or copies of such original reports in a publicly accessible archive to maintain a record of usage, to be used both for review of the management plan and in organizing the scientific use of the Area.

- The appropriate authority should be notified of any activities / measures undertaken, and / or of any materials released and not removed, that were not included in the authorized permit. All spills shall be reported to the appropriate authority.

## References

Anyamba, E., Williams, E., Susskind, J., Fraser-Smith, A. & Fullerkrug, M. 2000. The Manifestation of the Madden-Julian Oscillation in Global Deep Convection and in the Schumann Resonance Intensity. *American Meteorology Society* **57**(8): 1029–44.

Behrendt, J. C., Saltus, R., Damaske, D., McCafferty, A., Finn, C., Blankenship, D. D. & Bell, R. E. 1996. Patterns of Late Cenozoic volcanic tectonic activity in the West Antarctic rift system revealed by aeromagnetic surveys. *Tectonics* **15**: 660–76.

Clilverd, M. A., C. J. Rodger, N. R. Thomson, J. B. Brundell, Th. Ulich, J. Lichtenberger, N. Cobbett, A. B. Collier, F. W. Menk, A. Seppl, P. T. Verronen, and E. Turunen. 2009. Remote sensing space weather events: the AARDDVARK network. *Space Weather* **7** (S04001). DOI: 10.1029/2008SW000412.

Connor, B. J., Bodeker, G., Johnston, P. V., Kreher, K., Liley, J. B., Matthews, W. A., McKenzie, R. L., Struthers, H. & Wood, S. W. 2005. Overview of long-term stratospheric measurements at Lauder, New Zealand, and Arrival Heights, Antartica. *American Geophysical Union, Spring Meeting 2005.*

Deutscher, N. M., Jones, N. B., Griffith, D. W. T., Wood, S. W. and Murcray, F. J. 2006. Atmospheric carbonyl sulfide (OCS) variation from 1992-2004 by ground-based solar FTIR spectrometry. *Atmospheric Chemistry and Physics Discussions* **6**: 1619–36.

Fraser-Smith, A. C., McGill, P. R., Bernardi, A., Helliwell, R. A. & Ladd, M. E. 1991. Global Measurements of Low-Frequency Radio Noise *in* Environmental and Space Electromagnetics (Ed. H. Kikuchi). Springer-Verlad, Tokyo.

Fraser-Smith, A. C. & Turtle, J. P.1993. ELF/VLF Radio Noise Measurements at High Latitudes during Solar Particle Events. Paper presented at the 51st AGARD-EPP Specialists meeting on *ELF/VLF/LF Radio Propagation and Systems Aspects*. Brussels, Belgium; 28 Sep – 2 Oct, 1992.

M. Füllekrug, M. 2004. Probing the speed of light with radio waves at extremely low frequencies. *Physical Review Letters* **93**(4), 043901: 1-3.

Füllekrug, M. 2010. Wideband digital low-frequency radio receiver. *Measurement Science and Technology*, **21**, 015901: 1-9. doi:10.1088/0957-0233/21/1/015901.

Füllekrug , M. & Fraser-Smith, A. C.1996. Further evidence for a global correlation of the Earth-ionosphere cavity resonances. *General Assembly of the International Union of Geodesy and Geophysics No. 21, Boulder, Colorado, USA.*

Füllekrug, M. & Fraser-Smith, A.C. 1997. Global lightning and climate variability inferred from ELF magnetic field variations. *Geophysical Research Letters* **24**(19), 2411

Füllekrug, M., Fraser-Smith, A. C., Bering, E. A. & Few, A. A. 1999. On the hourly contribution of global cloud-to-ground lightning activity to the atmospheric electric field in the Antarctic during December 1992. *Journal of Atmospheric and Solar-Terrestrial Physics* **61**: 745-50.

Füllekrug, M., Fraser-Smith, A.C. & Schlegel, K. 2002. Global ionospheric D-layer height monitoring. *Europhysics Letters* **59**(4): 626.

Hay, T., Kreher, K., Riedel, K., Johnston, P., Thomas, A. & McDonald, A. 2007. Investigation of Bromine Explosion Events in McMurdo Sound, Antarctica. *Geophysical Research Abstracts.* Vol. 7.

Hernandez, G. & Roble, R. G. 2003. Simultaneous thermospheric observations during the geomagnetic storm of April 2002 from South Pole and Arrival Heights, Antarctica. *Geophysical Research Letters* **30** (10): 1511.

Keys, J. G., Wood, S. W., Jones, N. B. & Murcray. 1998. Spectral Measurements of HCl in the Plume of the Antarctic Volcano Mount Erebus. *Geophysical Research Letters* **25** (13): 2421–24.

Klein, A. G., Kennicutt, M. C., Wolff, G. A., Sweet, S. T., Gielstra, D. A. & Bloxom, T. 2004. Disruption of Sand-Wedge Polygons at McMurdo Station Antarctica: An Indication of Physical Disturbance. *61st Eastern Snow Conference*, Portland, Maine, USA.

Kyle, P. 1981. Mineralogy and Geochemistry of a Basanite to Phonolite Sequence at Hut Point Peninsula, Antarctica, based on Core from Dry Valley Drilling Project Drillholes 1,2 and 3. *Journal of Petrology.* **22** (4): 451 – 500.

Kuttippurath, J., Goutail, F., Pommereau, J.-P., Lefèvre, F., Roscoe, H. K., Pazmi̇no A., Feng, W., Chipperfield, M. P., & Godin-Beekmann, S. 2010. Estimation of Antarctic ozone loss from ground-based total column measurements. *Atmospheric Chemistry and Physics* **10**: 6569–81.

Mazzera, D. M., Lowenthal, D. H., Chow, J, C. & Watson, J. G. 2001. Sources of $PM_{10}$ and sulfate aerosol at McMurdo station, Antarctica. *Chemosphere* **45**: 347–56.

McDonald, A. J., Baumgaertner, A. J. G., Fraser, G. J., George, S. E. & Marsh, S. 2007. Empirical Mode Decomposition of the atmospheric wave field. *Annals of Geophysics* **25**: 375–84.

Monaghan, A. J. & Bromwich, D. H. 2005. The Climate of the McMurdo, Antarctica, Region as Represented by One Year Forecasts from the Antarctic Mesoscale Prediction System. *Journal of Climate.* 18, pp. 1174–89.

Nichol, S. E., Coulmann, S. & Clarkson, T. S. 1991. Relationship of springtime ozone depletion at Arrival Heights, Antarctica, to the 70 HPA temperatures. *Geophysical Research Letters* **18** (10): 1865–68.

Oltmans, S. J., Johnson, B. J. & Helmig, D. 2008. Episodes of high surface-ozone amounts at South Pole during summer and their impact on the long-term surface-ozone variation. *Atmospheric Environment* **42**: 2804–16.

Riedel, K., Kreher, K., Nichol, S. & Oltmans, S. J. 2006. Air mass origin during tropospheric ozone depletion events at Arrival Heights, Antarctica. *Geophysical Research Abstracts* **8**.

Rodger, C. J., J. B. Brundell, R. H. Holzworth, and E. H. Lay. 2009. Growing detection efficiency of the World Wide Lightning Location Network. American Institute of Physics Conference Proceedings **1118**: 15-20. DOI:10.1063/1.3137706.
Schlegel, K. & Fullekrug, M. 1999. Schumann resonance parameter changes during high-energy particle precipitation. *Journal of Geophysical Research* **104** (A5): 10111-18.

Schofield, R., Johnston, P. V., Thomas, A., Kreher, K., Connor, B. J., Wood, S., Shooter, D., Chipperfield, M. P., Richter, A., von Glasow, R. & Rodgers, C. D. 2006. Tropospheric and stratospheric BrO columns over Arrival Heights, Antarctica, 2002. *Journal of Geophysical Research* **111**: 1–14.

Sinclair, M. R. 1988. Local topographic influence on low-level wind at Scott Base, Antarctica. *New Zealand Journal of Geology and Geophysics.* **31**: 237–45.

Skotnicki, M. L., Ninham, J. A. & Selkirk P. M. 1999. Genetic diversity and dispersal of the moss Sarconeurum glaciale on Ross Island, East Antarctica. *Molecular Ecology* **8**: 753-62.

Stefano, J. E. 1992. Application of Ground-Penetrating Radar at McMurdo Station, Antarctica. Presented at the Hazardous Materials Control Research Institute federal environment restoration conference, Vienna, USA, 15-17 April 1992.

Struthers, H., Kreher, K., Austin, J., Schofield, R., Bodeker, G., Johnston, P., Shiona, H. & Thomas, A. 2004. Past and future simulations of $NO_2$ from a coupled chemistry-climate model in comparison with observations. *Atmospheric Chemistry and Physics Discussions* **4**: 4545–79.

Tauxe, L., Gans, P. B. & Mankinen, E. A. 2004. Paleomagnetic and 40Ar/39Ar ages from Matuyama/Brunhes aged volcanics near McMurdo Sound, Antarctica. *Geochemical Geophysical Geosystems* **5** (10): 1029.

Wood, S. W., Batchelor, R. L., Goldman, A., Rinsland, C. P., Connor, B. J., Murcray, F. J., Stephan, T. M. & Heuff, D. N. 2004. Ground-based nitric acid measurements at Arrival Heights, Antarctica, using solar and lunar Fourier transform infrared observations. *Journal of Geophysical Research* **109**: D18307.

Wright, I. M., Fraser, B. J., & Menk F.W. 1998. Observations of polar cap arc drift motion from Scott Base S-RAMP Proceedings of the AIP Congress, Perth, September 1998.

ASPA No. 122 - Arrival Heights
Map 1: Regional overview

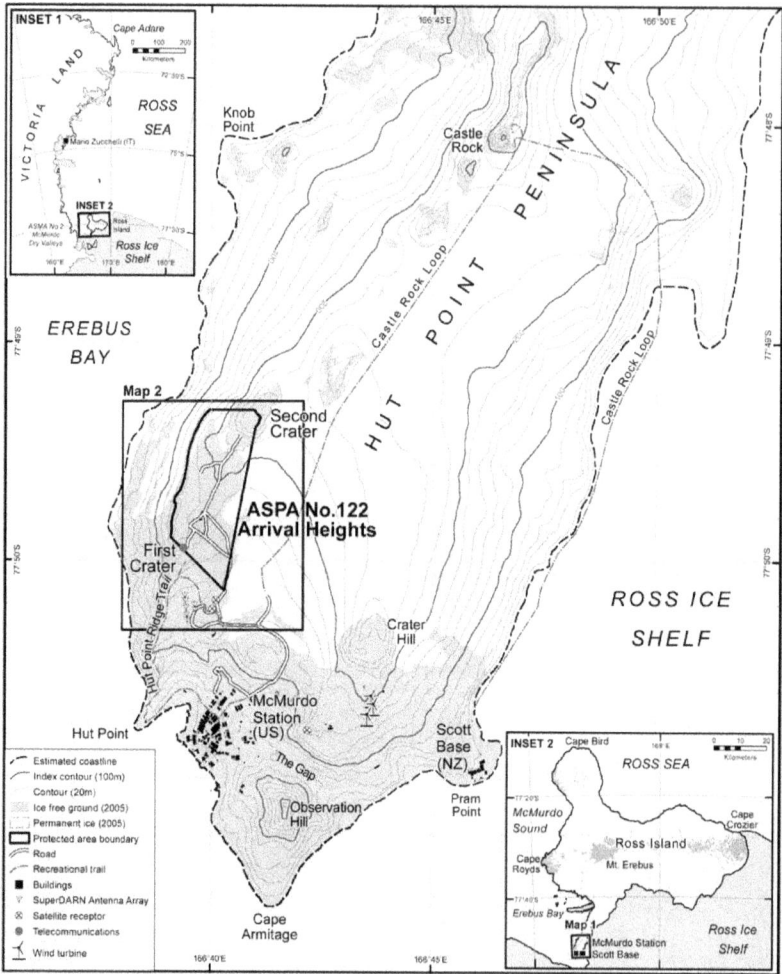

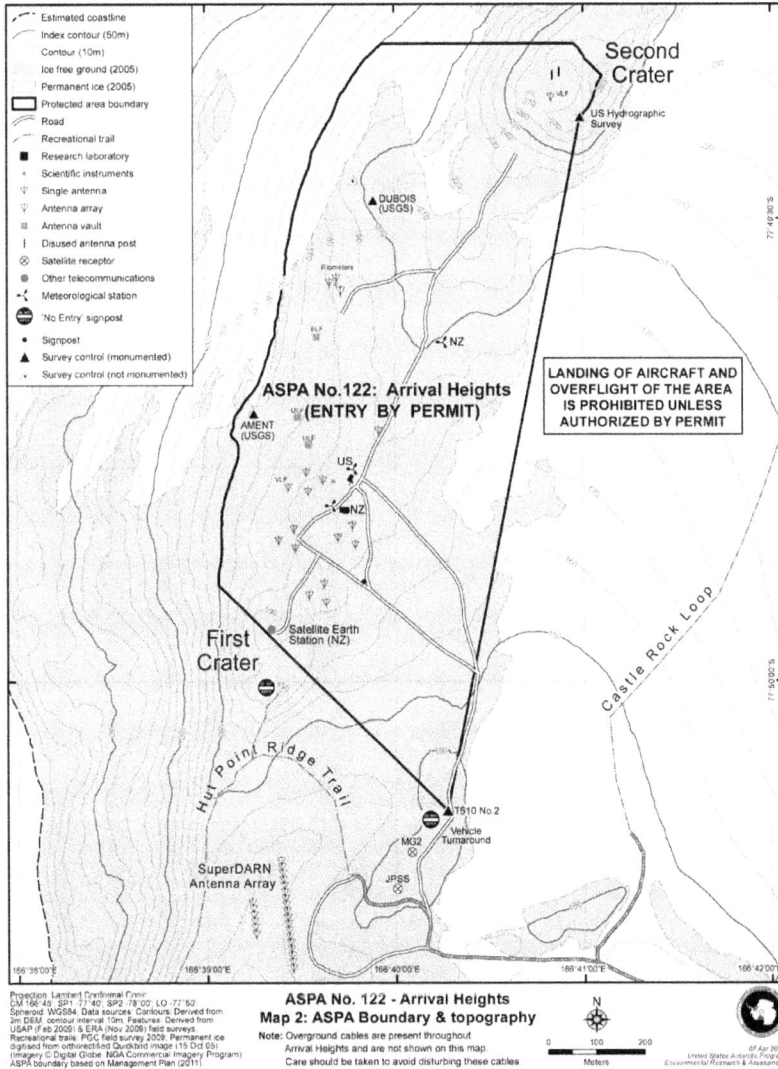

ASPA No. 122 - Arrival Heights
Map 2: ASPA Boundary & topography

# Management Plan for
# Antarctic Specially Protected Area No. 126
# BYERS PENINSULA, LIVINGSTON ISLAND,
# SOUTH SHETLAND ISLANDS

## Introduction

The primary reason for the designation of Byers Peninsula (latitude 62°34'35" S, longitude 61°13'07" W), Livingston Island, South Shetland Islands, as an Antarctic Specially Protected Area (ASPA) is to protect the terrestrial and lacustrine habitats within the Area.

Byers Peninsula was originally designated as Specially Protected Area (SPA) No. 10 through Recommendation IV-10 in 1966. This area included the ice-free ground west of the western margin of the permanent ice sheet on Livingston Island, below Rotch Dome, as well as Window Island about 500 m off the northwest coast and five small ice-free areas on the south coast immediately to the east of Byers Peninsula. Values protected under the original designation included the diversity of plant and animal life, many invertebrates, a substantial population of southern elephant seals (*Mirounga leonina*), small colonies of Antarctic fur seals (*Arctocephalus gazella*), and the outstanding scientific values associated with such a large variety of plants and animals within a relatively small area.

Designation as an SPA was terminated through Recommendation VIII-2 and redesignation as a Site of Special Scientific Interest (SSSI) was made through Recommendation VIII-4 (1975, SSSI No. 6). The new designation as an SSSI more specifically sought to protect four smaller ice-free sites on the peninsula of Jurassic and Cretaceous sedimentary and fossiliferous strata, considered of outstanding scientific value for study of the former link between Antarctica and other southern continents. Following a proposal by Chile and the United Kingdom, the SSSI was subsequently extended through Recommendation XVI-5 (1991) to include boundaries similar to those of the original SPA: i.e. the entire ice-free ground of Byers Peninsula west of the margin of the permanent Livingston Island ice sheet, including the littoral zone, but excluding Window Island and the five southern coastal sites originally included, as well as excluding all offshore islets and rocks. Recommendation XVI-5 noted that in addition to the special geological value, the Area was also of considerable biological and archaeological importance.

While the particular status of designation and boundaries have changed from time to time, Byers Peninsula has in effect been under special protection for most of the modern era of scientific activity in the region. Recent activities within the Area have been almost exclusively for scientific research. Most visits and sampling within the Area, since original designation in 1966, have been subject to Permit conditions, and some areas (e.g. Ray Promontory) have been rarely visited. During the International Polar Year, Byers Peninsula was established as an 'International Antarctic Reference Site for Terrestrial, Freshwater and Coastal Ecosystems' (Quesada et al 2009). During this period baseline data relating to terrestrial, limnetic and coastal ecosystems was established, including permafrost characteristics, geomorphology, vegetation extent, limnetic diversity and functioning, marine mammal and bird diversity, microbiology, and coastal marine invertebrate diversity. The archaeological values of Byers Peninsula have been described as unique in possessing the greatest concentration of historical sites in Antarctica, namely the remains of refuges, together with contemporary artefacts and shipwrecks of early nineteenth century sealing expeditions (see Map 2).

Byers Peninsula makes a substantial contribution to the Antarctic protected areas system as it (a) contains a particularly wide diversity of species, (b) is distinct from other areas due to its numerous lakes, freshwater ponds and streams, (c) is of great ecological importance and represents the most significant limnological site in the region, (d) is vulnerable to human interference, in particular, due to the oligotrophic nature of the lakes which are highly sensitive to pollution and (e) is of great scientific interest across a range of disciplines. While some of these quality criteria are represented in other ASPAs in the region, Byers Peninsula is unique in possessing a high number of different criteria within one area. While Byers Peninsula is protected primarily for its outstanding environmental values (specifically its biological diversity and terrestrial and lake ecosystems) the Area contains a combination of other values including scientific (i.e. for terrestrial biology, limnology, ornithology, palaeolimnology, geomorphology and geology), historic (artefacts and refuge remains of early sealers), wilderness (e.g. Ray Promontory) and on-going scientific values that may benefit from the Area's protection.

The ice-free ground of Byers Peninsula is surrounded on three sides by ocean and the Rotch Dome glacier to the east. The Area has been designated to protect values found within the ice-free ground on Byers Peninsula. To fulfil this objective a portion of Rotch Dome has been included within the ASPA to ensure newly exposed ice-free ground, (resulting from any retreat of Rotch Dome), will be within the boundaries of the ASPA. In addition, the northwestern Rotch Dome including adjacent de-glaciated ground and Ray Promontory have been designated as restricted zones to allow microbiological studies that required higher quarantine standards than considered necessary within the rest of the Area. The Area (84.7 km$^2$) is considered to be of sufficient size to provide adequate protection of the values described below.

## 1. Description of values to be protected

The Management Plan attached to Measure 1 (2002) noted values considered important as reasons for special protection of the Area. The values recorded in the original Management Plans are reaffirmed. These values are set out as follows:

- The described terrestrial flora and fauna is of exceptional diversity, with one of the broadest representations of species known in the maritime Antarctic. For example, sparse but diverse flora of calcicolous and calcifuge plants and cyanobacteria are associated with the lavas and basalts, respectively, and several rare cryptogams and the two native vascular plants (*Deschampsia antarctica* and *Colobanthus quitensis*) occur at several sites.

- With over 60 lakes, numerous freshwater pools and a great variety of often extensive streams, it is the most significant limnological site in the South Shetland Islands – and perhaps the Antarctica Peninsula region – and also one which has not been subjected to significant levels of human disturbance.

- *Parochlus steinenii* (the only native winged insect in Antarctica) is of limited distribution in the South Shetland Islands. The only other native dipteral, the wingless midge *Belgica antarctica,* has a very restricted distribution on the Antarctic Peninsula. Both species are abundant at several of the lakes and pools on Byers Peninsula.

- Unusually extensive cyanobacterial mats dominated by *Phormidium* sp.and other species, particularly on the upper levels of the central Byers Peninsula plateau, are the best examples so far described in the maritime Antarctic.

- The breeding avifauna within the Area is diverse, including two species of penguin [chinstrap (*Pygoscelis antarctica)* and gentoo (*P. papua*)], Antarctic tern (*Sterna vittata*), Wilson's storm petrels (*Oceanites oceanicus*), cape petrels (*Daption capense*), kelp gulls (*Larus dominicanus*), southern giant petrels (*Macronectes giganteus*), black-bellied storm petrels (*Fregetta tropica*), blue-eyed cormorants (*Phalacrocorax atriceps*), brown skuas (*Catharacta loennbergi*), and sheathbills (*Chionis alba*).

- The lakes and their sediments constitute one of the most important archives for study of the Holocene palaeoenvironment in the Antarctic Peninsula region, as well as for establishing a regional Holocene tephrachronology.

- Well-preserved sub-fossil whale bones are present in raised beaches, which are important for radiocarbon dating of beach deposits.

- The ice-free sites on the peninsula with exposed Jurassic and Cretaceous sedimentary and fossiliferous strata, are considered of outstanding scientific value for study of the former link between Antarctica and other southern continents.

## 2. Aims and objectives

Management at Byers Peninsula aims to:

- avoid degradation of, or substantial risk to, the values of the Area by preventing unnecessary human disturbance;

- allow scientific research on the terrestrial and lacustrine ecosystems, marine mammals, avifauna, coastal ecosystems and geology;

- allow other scientific research within the Area provided it is for compelling reasons which cannot be served elsewhere;

- allow archaeological research and measures for artefact protection, while protecting historic artefacts present within the Area from unnecessary destruction, disturbance, or removal;

- prevent or minimise the introduction to the Area of alien plants, animals and microbes;
- minimise the possibility of the introduction of pathogens which may cause disease in fauna within the Area; and
- allow visits for management purposes in support of the aims of the management plan.

### 3. Management activities

The following management activities shall be undertaken to protect the values of the Area:

- A map showing the location of the Area and stating the special restrictions that apply, shall be displayed prominently at Base Juan Carlos I (Spain) and St. Kliment Ochridski Station (Bulgaria) on Hurd Peninsula, where copies of this management plan shall be made available.
- Markers, signs, fences or other structures erected within the Area for scientific or management purposes shall be secured and maintained in good condition.
- Visits shall be made as necessary to assess whether the Area continues to serve the purposes for which it was designated and to ensure management and maintenance measures are adequate.

Byers Peninsula has been described as extremely sensitive to human impact (Tejedo et al 2009). The Area was designated as an ASPA to protect a diverse range of values present within the Area. As a result, it attracts scientists (representing a diverse range of disciplines) and archaeologists from a number of Treaty nations. The high number of people present in the Area at peak times (mid-summer) means there is potential for the environmental values of the area to be negatively impacted upon by human activities, for example by potentially increasing (i) the size and number of camping location, (ii) the trampling of vegetation, (iii) the disturbance of native wildlife (iv) the generation of waste and (v) the need for fuel storage. Consequently, when making plans for field work within the Area, Parties are **strongly encouraged** to liaise with other nations likely to be operating in the Area that season and co-ordinate activities to keep environmental impacts, including cumulative impacts, to an absolute minimum (e.g. fewer than c. 12 people in the International Field Camp at any one time).

　　All Parties are strongly encouraged to use the established International Field Camp (located on South Beaches, 62°39'49.7" S, 61°05'59.8' W), to reduce the creation of new camping sites that would increase levels of human impacts within the Area. Two melon huts are found within the camp (one set up for scientific research, the other for domestic activities; both huts are managed by Spain). The melon huts are available to all Treaty Parties, should they wish to use them. Parties should liaise with Spain to co-ordinate access to the melon huts.

### 4. Period of designation

Designated for an indefinite period.

### 5. Maps and photographs

Map 1: Byers Peninsula ASPA No. 126 in relation to the South Shetland Islands, showing the location of Base Juan Carlos I (Spain) and St. Kliment Ochridski Station (Bulgaria), and showing the location of protected areas within 75 km of the Area. Inset: the location of Livingston Island along the Antarctica Peninsula.

Map 2: Byers Peninsula ASPA No. 126 topographic map. Map specifications: Projection UTM Zone 20S; Spheroid: WGS 1984; Datum: Mean Sea Level. Horizontal accuracy of control: ±0.05 m. Vertical contour interval 50 m.

### 6. Description of the Area

*6(i) Geographical coordinates, boundary markers and natural features*

BOUNDARIES

The Area encompasses:

- Byers Peninsula and all ice-free ground and ice sheet west of longitude 60°53'45'' W, including Clark Nunatak and Rowe Point;
- the near-shore marine environment extending 10 m offshore from the low tide water line; and
- Demon Island and Sprite Island, adjacent to the southern shoreline of Devils Point, but excluding all other offshore islets, including Rugged Island, and rocks (Map 2).

The linear eastern boundary follows longitude 60°53'45'' W to ensure newly exposed ice-free ground resulting from the retreat of Rotch Dome, which may contain scientifically useful opportunities and new habitats for colonization studies, will be within the boundaries of the ASPA.

No boundary markers are in place.

## GENERAL DESCRIPTION

Byers Peninsula (between latitudes 62°34'35" and 62°40'35" S and longitudes 60°53'45''" and 61°13'07" W, 84.7 km$^2$) is situated at the west end of Livingston Island, the second-largest of the South Shetland Islands (Map 1). The ice-free area on the peninsula has a central west-east extent of about 9 km and a NW-SE extent of 18.2 km, and is the largest ice-free area in the South Shetland Islands. The peninsula is generally of low, gently rolling relief, although there are a number of prominent hills ranging in altitude between 80 – 265 m (Map 2). The interior is dominated by a series of extensive platforms at altitudes of up to 105 m, interrupted by isolated volcanic plugs such as Chester Cone (188 m) and Negro Hill (143 m) (Thomson and López-Martínez 1996). There is an abundance of rounded, flat landforms resulting from marine, glacial and periglacial erosional processes. The most rugged terrain occurs on Ray Promontory, a ridge forming the northwest-trending axis of the roughly 'Y'-shaped peninsula. Precipitous cliffs surround the coastline at the northern end of Ray Promontory with Start Hill (265 m) at the NW extremity being the highest point on the peninsula.

The coast of Byers Peninsula has a total length of 71 km (Map 2). Although of generally low relief, the coast is irregular and often rugged, with numerous headlands, cliffs, offshore islets, rocks and shoals. Byers Peninsula is also notable for its broad beaches, prominent features on all three coasts (Robbery Beaches in the north, President Beaches in the west, and South Beaches). The South Beaches are the most extensive; extending 12 km along the coast and up to almost 0.9 km in width, these are the largest in the South Shetland Islands (Thomson and López-Martínez 1996). For a detailed description of the geology and biology of the Area see Annex 1.

Resolution 3 (2008) recommended that the "Environmental Domains Analysis for the Antarctic Continent", be used as a dynamic model for the identification of Antarctic Specially Protected Areas within the systematic environmental-geographical framework referred to in Article 3(2) of Annex V of the Protocol. Using this model, Byers Peninsula is predominantly Environment Domain G (Antarctic Peninsula off-shore islands geologic), which is described as "*a very small terrestrial environment focused around the Antarctic Peninsula and associated offshore islands such as Deception Island. At 966 km$^2$ it is by far the smallest environment within the classification. The environment consists entirely of ice-free land cover and contains a combination of three geological units - sedimentary (2%), intrusive (24%), and volcanic (28%). Climatically the environment is the warmest in the classification with an average air temperature of only -3.29°C, has the smallest seasonal range at -8.82°C, and receives the highest level of solar radiation at 10.64 MJ/m2/day. The average wind speed within the environment is moderate, at 13.86 m/sec. The environment is moderately sloping with an average slope of 13.41°. Well-known locations the environment covers include parts of ice free areas on South Shetland Islands such as Fildes Peninsula on King George Island, and small points on the Antarctic Peninsula along Davis Coast'*. The scarcity of Environment G, relative to the other environmental domain areas, means that substantial efforts have been made to conserve the values found within this environment type elsewhere: other protected areas containing Domain G include ASPAs 109, 111, 112, 114, 125, 128, 140, 145, 149, 150, and 152 and ASMAs 1 and 4.

The permanent ice of Rotch Dome comes under Environment Domain E, which is described as "*a moderately sized ice sheet environment focussed around the Antarctic Peninsula as far south as latitude 73°S. The size of the environment (173,130 km$^2$) is moderate when compared with other environments. The environment consists entirely of ice sheet and contains no mapped geology. Climatically the environment is warm when compared across the continent and is the warmest of the environments that contain only ice sheet. Environment E is ranked ninth warmest in average air temperature (-14.06 °C), fourth smallest in seasonal range (-15.04 °C), and seventh in the amount of solar radiation (9.85 MJ/m$^2$/day). The average* *wind speed within the environment is low ranking, 17th out of 21 environments (10.28 m/s). The environment is a moderately sloping environment with an average slope of 15.01°. Well-known locations the environment covers include the glacierised parts of South Orkney, South Shetland (including Deception), Snow Hill, Brabant, Anvers, Adelaide and Alexander Islands as well as the Antarctic Peninsula north of 73°S'.* Other protected areas containing Domain E include ASPAs 113, 114, 117, 126, 128, 129, 133, 134, 139, 147, 149, 152 and ASMAs 1 and 4.

*6(ii) Access to the Area*

- Access shall be by helicopter or small boat.
- There are no special restrictions on boat landings from the sea, or that apply to the sea routes used to move to and from the Area. Due to the large extent of accessible beach around the Area, landing is possible at many locations. Nevertheless, if possible, landing of cargo and scientific equipment should be close to the International Field Camp located at Southern Beaches (62°39'49.7" S, 61°05'59.8' W; see 6(*iii*) for further details).
- A designated helicopter landing site is located at 62°39'36.4" S, 61°05'48.5' W, to the east of the International Field Camp.
- Under exceptional circumstances necessary for purposes consistent with the objectives of the Management Plan, helicopters may land elsewhere within the Area, although landings should, where practicable, be made on ridge and raised beach crests.
- No helicopter lands shall be made within the restricted zones [see section 6(*v*)].
- Helicopters should avoid sites where there are concentrations of birds (e.g. Devils Point, Lair Point and Robbery Beaches) or well-developed vegetation (e.g. large stands of mosses near President and South Beaches).
- To avoid disturbance of wildlife, aircraft should avoid landing within an over-flight restriction zone extending ¼ nautical mile (c. 460 m) inland from the coast during the period 1 October – 30 April inclusive (see Map 2). The only exception to this is the designated helicopter landing site at 62°39'36.4" S, 61°05'48.5'W.
- Within the over-flight restriction zone the operation of aircraft should be carried out, as a minimum requirement, in compliance with the 'Guidelines for the Operation of Aircraft near Concentrations of Birds' contained in Resolution 2 (2004). In particular, aircraft should maintain a vertical height of 2000 ft (~ 610 m) AGL and cross the coastline at right angles where possible. When conditions require aircraft to fly at lower elevations than recommended in the guidelines, aircraft should maintain the maximum elevation possible and minimise the time taken to transit the coastal zone.
- Use of helicopter smoke grenades is prohibited within the Area unless absolutely necessary for safety. If used all smoke grenades should be retrieved.

*6(iii) Location of structures within and adjacent to the Area*

An International Field Camp is located at South Beaches, at 62°39'49.7" S, 61°05'59.8' W. It is comprised of two fibreglass 'melon huts'. It is maintained by the Spanish Polar Programme and is available for use by all Parties. The locations of 19th Century sealers remains, including refuges and caves used for shelter are given in Smith and Simpson (1987) (see Map 2). Several cairns marking sites used for topographical survey are also present within the Area, predominantly on high points.

The nearest scientific research stations are 30 km east at Hurd Peninsula, Livingston Island [Base Juan Carlos I (Spain) and St Kliment Ochridski (Bulgaria)].

*6(iv) Location of other protected areas within close proximity of the Area*

The nearest protected areas to Byers Peninsula are: Cape Shirreff (ASPA No. 149) which lies about 20 km to the northeast, Deception Island (ASMA No. 4), Port Foster and other parts of Deception Island (ASPAs No. 140, 145) which are approximately 40 km SSE and 'Chile Bay' (Discovery Bay) (ASPA No. 144), which is about 70 km to the east at Greenwich Island (Map 1).

*6(v)  Restricted and managed zones within the Area*

Some zones on Byers Peninsula are thought to have been visited only very rarely, or never.  New metagenomic techniques are predicted to allow future identification of microbial biodiversity (bacteria, fungi and viruses) to an unprecedented level, allowing many fundamental questions regarding microbial dispersal and distribution to be answered.  Restricted zones have been designated that are of scientific importance to Antarctic microbiology and greater restriction is placed on access with the aim of preventing microbial or other contamination by human activity:

- In keeping with this aim, within the restricted zones sterile protective over-clothing shall be worn. The protective clothing shall be put on immediately prior to entering the restricted zones. Spare boots, previously cleaned using a biocide then sealed in plastic bags, shall be unwrapped and put on just before entering the restricted zones.  If accessing the restricted zones by boat, protective clothing shall be put on immediately upon landing.

- To the greatest extent possible, all sampling equipment, scientific apparatus and markers brought into the restricted zones shall have been sterilized, and maintained in a sterile condition, before being used within the Area. Sterilization should be by an accepted method, including UV radiation, autoclaving or by surface sterilisation using 70% ethanol or a commercially available biocide (e.g. Virkon®).

- General equipment includes harnesses, crampons, climbing equipment, ice axes, walking poles, ski equipment, temporary route markers, pulks, sledges, camera and video equipment, rucksacks, sledge boxes and all other personal equipment.  To the maximum extent practicable, all equipment used or brought into the restricted zones shall have been thoroughly cleaned and sterilized at the originating Antarctic station or ship. Equipment shall have been maintained in this condition before entering the restricted zones, preferably by sealing in sterile plastic bags or other clean containers.

- Scientists from disciplines other than microbiology are permitted to enter the restricted areas, but shall adhere to the quarantine measures detailed above.

- Camping within the restricted zones is not permitted.

- Helicopter landings within the restricted zones are not permitted.

- If access to the restricted zones is required for research or for emergency reasons, a detailed record of where visitation occurred (preferably using GPS technology) and the specific activities, should be submitted to the appropriate national authority and included in the Exchange of Information Annual Report, preferably through the Electronic Information Exchange System (EIES).

The restricted zones are:

1. North-western Rotch Dome and adjacent deglaciated ground.  The restricted zone includes all land and ice sheet within an area bordered to the east by longitude 60°53'45"W, to the west by longitude 60°58'48" W, to the south by latitude 62°38'30"S, and the northern boundary follows the coastline (see Map 2).
2. Ray Promontory.  The restricted zone includes all land and permanent ice northwest of a straight line crossing the Promontory from 62°37'S, 61°08'W (marked by a small coastal lake) to 62°36'S, 61°06'W.  Within the Ray Promontory restricted zone, access to archaeological remains located on the coast is permitted without the need for quarantine precautions required elsewhere within the restricted zone. Access to inland areas beyond the coastal archaeological remains is not permitted without quarantine measures, detailed in this section, in place.  Preferably, access to the archaeological remains shall be from the sea using small boats.  Access to the archaeological remains on foot is also permitted without the need for the additional quarantine measures, by following the coastline from the unrestricted area of the Byers Peninsula ASPA to the southeast. Access to the archaeological remains shall be solely for archaeological investigations, authorised by the appropriate national authority.

## 7.    Terms and conditions for entry permits

Entry into the Area is prohibited except in accordance with a Permit issued by an appropriate national authority.

*7(i)  General permit conditions*

Conditions for issuing a Permit to enter the Area are that:

- it is issued only for scientific study of the ecosystem, geology, palaeontology or archaeology of the Area, or for compelling scientific reasons that cannot be served elsewhere; or
- it is issued for essential management purposes consistent with management plan objectives such as inspection, maintenance or review;
- the actions permitted will not jeopardise the ecological, geological, historical or scientific values of the Area;
- the sampling proposed will not take, remove or damage such quantities of soil, rock, native flora or fauna that their distribution or abundance on Byers Peninsula would be significantly affected;
- any management activities are in support of the objectives of the management plan;
- the actions permitted are in accordance with the management plan;
- the Permit, or an authorised copy, shall be carried within the Area;
- a visit report shall be supplied to the authority named in the Permit;
- permits shall be issued for a stated period; and
- the appropriate authority should be notified of any activities/measures undertaken that were not included in the authorised Permit.

*7(ii)  Access to and movement within or over the Area*

- Land vehicles are prohibited within the Area.
- Movement within the Area shall be on foot unless under exceptional circumstances when helicopter may be used.
- All movement shall be undertaken carefully so as to minimise disturbance to archaeological remains, animals, soils, geomorphological features and vegetated surfaces, walking on rocky terrain or ridges if practical to avoid damage to sensitive plants, patterned ground and waterlogged soils.
- Pedestrian traffic should be kept to the minimum consistent with the objectives of any permitted activities and every reasonable effort should be made to minimise trampling effects.  Where possible, existing tracks should be used to transit the area (Map 2).  If no track exists, care should be taken to avoid creation of new tracks.  Research has shown that vegetation on Byers Peninsula can recover if fewer than 200 transits are made over it in a single season (Tejedo et al 2009). Pedestrian routes over vegetated ground should therefore be chosen depending on the forecasted number of transits (i.e. number of people × transits per day × number of days).  When the number of transits on the same track is expected to be less than 200 in the same season, the track should be clearly identified and transits always made along the track. When the number is expected to be larger than 200 in a season, then the route should not be fixed along a single track, but transits should be done across a wide belt (i.e. multiple tracks, each with fewer than 200 transits), to diffuse the impact and allow quicker recovery of trampled vegetation.
- Conditions for use of helicopters within the Area are described in section 6(*ii*)
- Pilots, air and boat crew, or other people on aircraft or boats, are prohibited from moving on foot beyond the immediate vicinity of their landing site unless specifically authorised by Permit.
- Restrictions on access and movement within the restricted zones are described in section 6(*v*)

*7(iii)  Activities which may be conducted in the Area*

- Compelling scientific research which cannot be undertaken elsewhere and that will not jeopardise the ecosystem or values of the Area or interfere with existing scientific studies.
- Archaeological research.
- Essential management activities, including monitoring.

*7(iv)  Installation, modification or removal of structures*

No new structures are to be erected within the Area, or scientific equipment installed, except for compelling scientific or management reasons and for a pre-established period, as specified in a permit. Installation (including site selection), maintenance, modification or removal of structures and equipment shall be undertaken in a manner that minimises disturbance to the values of the Area. All structures or scientific equipment installed in the Area shall be clearly identified by country, name of the principal investigator and year of installation. All such items should be free of organisms, propagules (e.g. seeds, eggs) and non-sterile soil, and be made of materials that can withstand the environmental conditions and pose minimal risk of contamination of the Area. Removal of specific structures or equipment for which the Permit has expired shall be a condition of the Permit. Permanent structures or installations are prohibited.

### 7(v)  Location of field camps

In order to minimise the area of ground within the ASPA impacted by camping activities, camps should be within the immediate vicinity of the International Field Camp (62°39'49.7" S, 61°05'59.8" W). When necessary for purposes specified in the Permit, temporary camping beyond the International Field Camp is allowed within the Area. Camps should be located on non-vegetated sites, such as on the drier parts of the raised beaches, or on thick (>0.5 m) snow-cover when practicable, and should avoid concentrations of breeding birds or mammals. Camping within 50 m of any sealers' refuge or shelter is prohibited. Previously used campsites should be re-used where practical, unless the guidance above suggests that they were inappropriately located. Camping within the restricted zones is not permitted.

### 7(vi) Restrictions on materials and organisms which can be brought into the Area

The deliberate introduction of animals, plant material, microorganisms and non-sterile soil into the Area shall not be permitted. Precautions shall be taken to prevent the accidental introduction of animals, plant material, micro-organisms and non-sterile soil from other biologically distinct regions (within or beyond the Antarctic Treaty area). In view of the presence of breeding bird colonies on Byers Peninsula, no poultry products, including wastes from such products and products containing uncooked dried eggs, shall be released into the Area or into the adjacent sea.

No herbicides or pesticides shall be brought into the Area. Any other chemicals, including radio-nuclides or stable isotopes, which may be introduced for scientific or management purposes specified in the Permit, shall be removed from the Area at or before the conclusion of the activity for which the Permit was granted. Release of radio-nuclides or stable isotopes directly into the environment in a way that renders them unrecoverable should be avoided. Fuel or other chemicals shall not be stored in the Area unless specifically authorised by Permit condition. They shall be stored and handled in a way that minimises the risk of their accidental introduction into the environment. Materials introduced into the Area shall be for a stated period only and shall be removed by the end of that stated period. If release occurs which is likely to compromise the values of the Area, removal is encouraged only where the impact of removal is not likely to be greater than that of leaving the material *in situ*. The appropriate authority should be notified of anything released and not removed that was not included in the authorised Permit.

### 7(vii) Taking of, or harmful interference with, native flora or fauna

Taking of or harmful interference with native flora or fauna is prohibited, except by Permit issued in accordance with Annex II to the Protocol on Environmental Protection to the Antarctic Treaty. Where taking of or harmful interference with animals is involved, the *SCAR Code of Conduct for the Use of Animals for Scientific Purposes in Antarctica* should be used as a minimum standard.

### 7(viii) The collection or removal of materials not brought into the Area by the Permit holder

Collection or removal of anything not brought into the Area by the permit holder shall only be in accordance with a Permit and should be limited to the minimum necessary to meet scientific, archaeological or management needs.

Unless specifically authorized by permit, visitors to the Area are prohibited from interfering with or from handling, taking or damaging any historic anthropogenic material meeting the criteria in Resolution 5 (2001). Similarly, relocation or removal of artefacts for the purposes of preservation, protection or to re-establish historical accuracy is allowable only by permit. The appropriate national authority shall be informed of the location and nature of any newly identified anthropogenic materials.

Other material of human origin likely to compromise the values of the Area which was not brought into the Area by the permit holder or otherwise authorised, may be removed from the Area unless the environmental impact of the removal is likely to be greater than leaving the material in situ; if this is the case the appropriate Authority must be notified and approval obtained.

### 7(ix) Disposal of waste

As a minimum standard all waste shall be disposed of in accordance with Annex III to the Protocol on Environmental Protection to the Antarctic Treaty. In addition, all wastes, including all solid human waste, shall be removed from the Area. Liquid human wastes may be disposed of into the sea. Solid human waste should not be disposed of to the sea as the near-shore reefs will prevent dispersal, but shall be removed from the Area. No human waste shall be disposed of inland as the oligotrophic characteristics of the lakes and other water-bodies on the plateau can be compromised by even a small quantity of human waste, including urine.

### 7(x) Measures that are necessary to ensure that the aims and objectives of the management plan can continue to be met

Permits may be granted to enter the Area to:

- carry out monitoring and site inspection activities, which may involve the collection of data and/or a small number of samples for analysis or review;
- erect or maintain signposts, structures or scientific equipment; or
- carry out protective measures.

Any specific sites of long-term monitoring shall be appropriately marked on site and on maps of the Area. A GPS position should be obtained for lodgement with the Antarctic Data Directory System through the appropriate national authority.

To help maintain the ecological and scientific values of the Area, visitors shall take special precautions against introductions. Of particular concern are microbial, animal or vegetation introductions sourced from soils from other Antarctic sites, including stations, or from regions outside Antarctica. To the maximum extent practicable, visitors shall ensure that footwear, clothing and any equipment – particularly camping and sampling equipment – is thoroughly cleaned before entering the Area. Poultry products and other introduced avian products, which may be a vector of avian diseases, shall not be released into the Area.

### 7(xi) Requirements for reports

The principal permit holder for each visit to the Area shall submit a report to the appropriate national authority as soon as practicable, and no later than six months after the visit has been completed. Such reports should include, as appropriate, the information identified in the visit report form contained in the Guide to the Preparation of Management Plans for Antarctic Specially Protected Areas. If appropriate, the national authority should also forward a copy of the visit report to the Party that proposed the Management Plan, to assist in managing the Area and reviewing the Management Plan. Wherever possible, Parties should deposit the original or copies of the original visit reports, in a publicly accessible archive to maintain a record of usage, for the purpose of any review of the Management Plan and in organising the scientific use of the Area.

*8. Supporting documentation*

Bañón, M., Justel M. A., Quesada, A. 2006. Análisis del microclima de la península Byers, isla Livingston, Antártida, en el marco del proyecto LIMNOPOLAR. In: *Aplicaciones meteorológicas*. Asociación Meteorológica Española.

Birnie, R.V., Gordon, J.E. 1980. Drainage systems associated with snow melt, South Shetland Islands, Antarctica. *Geografiska Annaler* **62A**: 57-62.

Björck, S., Hakansson, H, Zale, R., Karlén, W., Jönsson, B.L. 1991. A late Holocene lake sediment sequence from Livingston Island, South Shetland Islands, with palaeoclimatic implications. *Antarctic Science* **3**: 61-72.

Björck, S., Sandgren, P., Zale, R. 1991. Late Holocene tephrochronology of the Northern Antarctic Peninsula. *Quaternary Research* **36**: 322-28.

Björck, S., Hjort, C, Ingólfsson, O., Skog, G. 1991. Radiocarbon dates from the Antarctic Peninsula - problems and potential. In: Lowe, J.J. (ed.), *Radiocarbon dating: recent applications and future potential*. *Quaternary Proceedings* 1, Quaternary Research Association, Cambridge. pp 55-65.

Björck, S., Håkansson, H., Olsson, S., Barnekow, L., Janssens, J. 1993. Palaeoclimatic studies in South Shetland Islands, Antarctica, based on numerous stratigraphic variables in lake sediments. *Journal of Paleolimnology* **8**: 233-72.

Björck, S., Zale, R. 1996. Late Holocene tephrochronology and palaeoclimate, based on lake sediment studies. In: López-Martínez, J., Thomson, M. R. A., Thomson, J.W. (eds.) *Geomorphological map of Byers Peninsula, Livingston Island*. BAS GEOMAP Series Sheet 5-A, 43-48. British Antarctic Survey, Cambridge.

Björck, S., Hjort, C., Ingólfsson, O., Zale, R., Ising, J. 1996. Holocene deglaciation chronology from lake sediments. In: López-Martínez, J., Thomson, M. R. A., Thomson, J.W. (eds.) *Geomorphological map of Byers Peninsula, Livingston Island*. BAS GEOMAP Series Sheet 5-A, 49-51. British Antarctic Survey, Cambridge.

Block, W., Starý, J. 1996. Oribatid mites (Acari: Oribatida) of the maritime Antarctic and Antarctic Peninsula. *Journal of Natural History* **30**: 1059-67.

Bonner, W.N., Smith, R.I.L. (Eds) 1985. *Conservation areas in the Antarctic*. SCAR, Cambridge: 147-56.

Booth, R.G., Edwards, M., Usher, M.B. 1985. Mites of the genus Eupodes (Acari, Prostigmata) from maritime Antarctica: a biometrical and taxonomic study. *Journal of the Zoological Society of London (A)* **207**: 381-406.

Carlini, A.R., Coria, N.R., Santos, M.M., Negrete, J., Juares, M.A., Daneri, G.A. 2009. Responses of *Pygoscelis adeliae* and *P. papua* populations to environmental changes at Isla 25 de Mayo (King George Island). *Polar Biology* **32**: 1427-1433.

Convey, P., Greenslade, P. Richard, K.J., Block, W. 1996. The terrestrial arthropod fauna of the Byers Peninsula, Livingston Island, South Shetland Islands - Collembola. *Polar Biology* **16**: 257-59.

Covacevich, V.C. 1976. Fauna valanginiana de Peninsula Byers, Isla Livingston, Antartica. *Revista Geologica de Chile* **3**: 25-56.

Crame, J.A. 1984. Preliminary bivalve zonation of the Jurassic-Cretaceous boundary in Antarctica. In: Perrilliat, M. de C. (Ed.) *Memoria, III Congreso Latinamerico de Paleontologia, Mexico, 1984. Mexico City*, Universidad Nacional Autonoma de Mexico, Instituto de Geologia. pp 242-54.

Crame, J.A. 1985. New Late Jurassic Oxytomid bivalves from the Antarctic Peninsula region. *British Antarctic Survey Bulletin* **69**: 35-55.

Crame, J.A. 1995. Occurrence of the bivalve genus Manticula in the Early Cretaceous of Antarctica. *Palaeontology* **38** Pt. 2: 299-312.

Crame, J.A. 1995. A new Oxytomid bivalve from the Upper Jurassic–Lower Cretaceous of Antarctica. *Palaeontology* **39** Pt. 3: 615-28.

Crame, J.A. 1996. Early Cretaceous bivalves from the South Shetland Islands, Antarctica. *Mitt. Geol-Palaont. Inst. Univ. Hamburg* **77**: 125-127.

Crame, J.A., Kelly, S.R.A. 1995. Composition and distribution of the Inoceramid bivalve genus *Anopaea*. *Palaeontology* **38** Pt. 1: 87-103.

Crame, J.A., Pirrie, D., Crampton, J.S., Duane, A.M. 1993. Stratigraphy and regional significance of the Upper Jurassic - Lower Cretaceous Byers Group, Livingston Island, Antarctica. *Journal of the Geological Society* **150** Pt. 6: 1075-87.

Croxall, J.P., Kirkwood, E.D. 1979. *The distribution of penguins on the Antarctic Peninsula and the islands of the Scotia Sea.* British Antarctic Survey, Cambridge.

Davey, M.C. 1993. Carbon and nitrogen dynamics in a maritime Antarctic stream. *Freshwater Biology* **30**: 319-30.

Davey, M.C. 1993. Carbon and nitrogen dynamics in a small pond in the maritime Antarctic. *Hydrobiologia* **257**: 165-75.

Duane, A.M. 1994. Preliminary palynological investigation of the Byers Group (Late Jurassic-Early Cretaceous), Livingston Island, Antarctic Peninsula. *Review of Palaeobotany and Palynology* **84**: 113-120.

Duane, A.M. 1996. Palynology of the Byers Group (Late Jurassic-Early Cretaceous) Livingston and Snow Islands, Antarctic Peninsula: its biostratigraphical and palaeoenvironmental significance. *Review of Palaeobotany and Palynology* **91**: 241-81.

Duane, A.M. 1997. Taxonomic investigations of Palynomorphs from the Byers Group (Upper Jurassic-Lower Cretaceous), Livingston and Snow Islands, Antarctic Peninsula. *Palynology* **21**: 123-144.

Ellis-Evans, J.C. 1996. Biological and chemical features of lakes and streams. In: López-Martínez, J., Thomson, M. R. A., Thomson, J.W. (eds.) *Geomorphological map of Byers Peninsula, Livingston Island.* BAS GEOMAP Series Sheet 5-A, 20-22. British Antarctic Survey, Cambridge.

Fernández-Valiente, E., Camacho, A., Rochera, C., Rico, E., Vincent, W. F., Quesada, A. 2007 Community structure and physiological characterization of microbial mats in Byers Peninsula, Livingston Island (South Shetland islands, Antarctica). *FEMS Microbiology Ecology* **59**: 377- 385

Gil-Delgado, J.A., Villaescusa, J.A., Diazmacip, M.E., Velazquez, D., Rico, E., Toro, M., Quesada, A., Camacho, A. Is the southern elephant seal *mirounga leonina* population on the Byers Peninsula (Livingston Island, South Shetland Islands) increasing? *Polar Biology* (submitted)

Gil-Delgado, J.A., González-Solis, J., Barbosa, A. 2010. Breeding birds populations in Byers Peninsula (Livingston Is., South Shetlands Islands. 18th International Conference of the European Bird Census Council. 22-26 March. Caceres. Spain.

González-Ferrán, O., Katsui, Y., Tavera, J. 1970. Contribución al conocimiento geológico de la Península Byers, Isla Livingston, Islas Shetland del Sur, Antártica. *Publ. INACH Serie. Cientifica* **1**: 41-54.

Gray, N.F., Smith, R.I. L. 1984. The distribution of nematophagous fungi in the maritime Antarctic. *Mycopathologia* **85**: 81-92.

Harris, C.M. 2001. *Revision of management plans for Antarctic protected areas originally proposed by the United States of America and the United Kingdom: Field visit report.* Internal report for the National Science Foundation, US, and the Foreign and Commonwealth Office, UK. Environmental Research and Assessment, Cambridge.

Hansom, J.D. 1979. Radiocarbon dating of a raised beach at 10 m in the South Shetland Islands. *British Antarctic Survey Bulletin* **49**: 287-288.

Hathway, B. 1997. Non-marine sedimentation in an Early Cretaceous extensional continental-margin arc, Byers Peninsula, Livingston Island, South Shetland Islands. *Journal of Sedimentary Research* **67**: 686-697.

Hathway, B., Lomas, S.A. 1998. The Upper Jurassic-Lower cretaceous Byers Group, South Shetland Islands, Antarctica: revised stratigraphy and regional correlations. *Cretaceous Research* **19**: 43-67.

Hernandez, P.J., Azcarate, V. 1971. Estudio paleobotanico preliminar sobre restos de una tafoflora de la Peninsula Byers (Cerro Negro), Isla Livingston, Islas Shetland del Sur, Antartica. *Publ. INACH Serie. Cientifica* **2**: 15-50.

Hjort, C., Ingólfsson, O., Björck, S. 1992. The last major deglaciation in the Antarctic Peninsula region - a review of recent Swedish Quaternary research. In: Y. Yoshida *et al.* (eds.) *Recent Progress in Antarctic Science.* Terra Scientific Publishing Company (TERRAPUB), Tokyo: 741-743.

Hjort, C., Björck, S., Ingólfsson, Ó., Möller, P. 1998. Holocene deglaciation and climate history of the northern Antarctic Peninsula region: a discussion of correlations between the Southern and Northern Hemispheres. *Annals of Glaciology* **27**: 110-112.

Hodgson, D.A., Dyson, C.L., Jones, V.J., Smellie, J.L. 1998. Tephra analysis of sediments from Midge Lake (South Shetland Islands) and Sombre Lake (South Orkney Islands), Antarctica. *Antarctic Science* **10**: 13-20.

John, B.S., Sugden, D.E. 1971. Raised marine features and phases of glaciation in the South Shetland Islands. *British Antarctic Survey Bulletin* **24**: 45-111.

Jones, V.J., Juggins, S., Ellis-Evans, J.C. 1993. The relationship between water chemistry and surface sediment diatom assemblages in maritime Antarctic lakes. *Antarctic Science* **5**: 339-48.

Kelly, S.R.A. 1995. New Trigonioid bivalves from the Early Jurassic to Earliest Cretaceous of the Antarctic Peninsula region: systematics and austral paleobiogeography. *Journal of Paleontology* **69**: 66-84.

Lindsay, D.C. 1971. Vegetation of the South Shetland Islands. *British Antarctic Survey Bulletin* **25**: 59-83.

López-Bueno, A., Tamames, J. Velazquez, D., Moya, A., Quesada, A., Alcami, A. 2009. Viral Metagenome of an Antarctic lake: high diversity and seasonal variations. *Science* **326**: 858-861.

Lopez-Martinez, J., Serrano, E., Martinez de Pison, E. 1996. Geomorphological features of the drainage system. In: López-Martínez, J., Thomson, M. R. A., Thomson, J.W. (eds.) *Geomorphological map of Byers Peninsula, Livingston Island.* BAS GEOMAP Series Sheet 5-A, 15-19. British Antarctic Survey, Cambridge.

Lopez-Martínez, J., Martínez de Pisón, E., Serrano, E., Arche, A. 1996 *Geomorphological map of Byers Peninsula, Livingston Island.* BAS GEOMAP Series, Sheet 5-A, Scale 1:25 000. Cambridge, British Antarctic Survey,.

Martínez De Pisón, E., Serrano, E., Arche, A., Lopez-Martinez, J. 1996. Glacial geomorphology. In: López-Martínez, J., Thomson, M. R. A., Thomson, J.W. (eds.) *Geomorphological map of Byers Peninsula, Livingston Island.* BAS GEOMAP Series Sheet 5-A, 23-27. British Antarctic Survey, Cambridge.

Pankhurst, R.J., Weaver, S.D., Brook, M., Saunders, A.D. 1979. K-Ar chronology of Byers Peninsula, Livingston Island, South Shetland Islands. *British Antarctic Survey Bulletin* **49**: 277-282.

Petz, W., Valbonesi, A., Schiftner, U., Quesada, A., Ellis-Evans, C.J. 2007. Ciliate biogeography in Antarctic and Arctic freshwater ecosystems: endemism or global distribution of species? *FEMS Microbiology Ecology* **59**: 396-408.

Quesada, A., Fernández Valiente, E., Hawes, I., Howard.Williams, C. 2008. Benthic primary production in polar lakes and rivers. In: Vincent, W., Leybourn-Parry J. (eds). *Polar Lakes and Rivers – Arctic and Antarctic Aquatic Ecosystems.* Springer. pp 179-196.

Quesada, A., Camacho, A. Rochera, C., Velazquez, D. 2009. Byers Peninsula: a reference site for coastal, terrestrial and limnetic ecosystems studies in maritime Antarctica. *Polar Science* **3**: 181-187.

Richard, K.J., Convey, P., Block, W. 1994. The terrestrial arthropod fauna of the Byers Peninsula, Livingston Island, South Shetland Islands. *Polar Biology* **14**: 371-79.

Rodríguez, P., Rico, E. 2008. A new freshwater oligochaete species (Clitellata: Enchytraeidae) from Livingston Island, Antarctica. *Polar Biology* **31**: 1267-1279.

SGE, WAM and BAS. 1993. *Byers Peninsula, Livingston Island.* Topographic map, Scale 1:25 000. Cartografia Antartica. Madrid, Servicio Geografia del Ejercito.

Serrano, E., Martínez De Pisón, E., Lopez-Martínez, J. 1996. Periglacial and nival landforms and deposits. In: López-Martínez, J., Thomson, M. R. A., Thomson, J.W. (eds.) *Geomorphological map of Byers Peninsula, Livingston Island.* BAS GEOMAP Series Sheet 5-A, 28-34. British Antarctic Survey, Cambridge.

Smellie J.L., Davies, R.E.S., Thomson, M.R.A. 1980. Geology of a Mesozoic intra-arc sequence on Byers Peninsula, Livingston Island, South Shetland Islands. *British Antarctic Survey Bulletin* **50**: 55-76.

Smith, R.I.L., Simpson, H.W. 1987. Early Nineteeth Century sealers' refuges on Livingston Island, South Shetland Islands. *British Antarctic Survey Bulletin* **74**: 49-72.

Starý, J., Block, W. 1998. Distribution and biogeography of oribatid mites (Acari: Oribatida) in Antarctica, the sub-Antarctic and nearby land areas. *Journal of Natural History* **32**: 861-94.

Sugden, D.E., John, B.S. 1973. The ages of glacier fluctuations in the South Shetland Islands, Antarctica. In: van Zinderen Bakker, E.M. (ed.) *Paleoecology of Africa and of the surrounding islands and Antarctica*. Balkema, Cape Town, pp. 141-159.

Tejedo, P., Justel, A., Benayas, J., Rico, E., Convey, P., Quesada, A. 2009. Soil trampling in an Antarctic Specially Protected Area: tools to assess levels of human impact. *Antarctic Science* **21**: 229-236.

Thom, G. 1978. Disruption of bedrock by the growth and collapse of ice lenses. *Journal of Glaciology* **20**: 571-75.

Thomson, M.R.A., López-Martínez, J. 1996. Introduction. In: López-Martínez, J., Thomson, M. R. A., Thomson, J.W. (eds.) *Geomorphological map of Byers Peninsula, Livingston Island*. BAS GEOMAP Series Sheet 5-A, 1-4. British Antarctic Survey, Cambridge.

Toro, M., Camacho, A., Rochera, C., Rico, E., Bañón, M., Fernández, E., Marco, E., Avendaño, C., Ariosa, Y., Quesada, A. 2007. Limnology of freshwater ecosystems of Byers Peninsula (Livingston Island, South Shetland Islands, Antarctica. *Polar Biology* **30**: 635-649.

Torres, D., Cattan, P., Yanez, J. 1981. Post-breeding preferences of the Southern Elephant seal *Mirounga leonina* in Livingston Island (South Shetlands). *Publ. INACH Serie. Cientifica* **27**: 13-18.

Torres, D., Jorquera, D. 1994. Marine debris analysis collected at cape Shirreff, Livingston Island, South Shetland, Antarctica. *Ser. Cient. INACH* **44**: 81-86.

Usher, M.B., Edwards, M. 1986. The selection of conservation areas in Antarctica: an example using the arthropod fauna of Antarctic islands. *Environmental Conservation* **13**: 115-22.

Van der Vijver, J., Agius, T., Gibson, J., Quesada, A. 2009. An unusual spine-bearing Pinnularia species from the Antarctic Livingston Island. *Diatom Research* **24**: 431-441.

White, M.G. Preliminary report on field studies in the South Shetland Islands 1965/66. Unpublished field report in BAS Archives AD6/2H1966/N6.

Woehler, E.J. (Ed.) 1993. *The distribution and abundance of Antarctic and sub-Antarctic penguins*. SCAR, Cambridge.

Zidarova, E., Van de Vijver, B., Quesada, A., de Haan, M. 2010. Revision of the genus Hantzschia (Bacillariophyceae) on Livingston Island (South Shetland Islands, Southern Atlantic Ocean). *Plant Ecology and Evolution*. In press.

**Annex 1**

*Supporting information*

CLIMATE

No extended meteorological records are available for Byers Peninsula before 2001, but the climate is expected to be similar to that at Base Juan Carlos I, Hurd Peninsula (recorded since 1988). Conditions there indicate a mean annual temperature of below 0 °C, with temperatures less than 0 °C for at least several months each summer and a relatively high precipitation rate estimated at about 800 mm yr$^{-1}$, much of which falls as rain in summer (Ellis-Evans 1996). The peninsula is snow-covered for much of the year, but is usually completely snow-free by the end of the summer. The peninsula is exposed to weather from the Drake Passage in the north and northwest, the directions from which winds prevail, and Bransfield Strait to the south. The climate is polar maritime, with a permanently high relative humidity (about 90%), cloud covered skies for most of the time, frequent fogs and regular precipitation events. Mean temperature in summer is 1.1 ° C, but occasionally can be higher than 5 °C. Exceptionally summer temperature has reached 9 °C. Minimum average temperature is close to 0 °C. In winter, temperatures can be lower than -26 °C, although the average value is -6 °C and maximum temperatures in winter can be close to 0 °C. Mean radiation in summer is 14,000 KJ m$^{-2}$, reaching 30,000 KJ m$^{-2}$ on sunny days close to the solstice. Winds are high and average speed is 24 km h$^{-1}$, with frequent storms with winds over 140 Km h$^{-1}$. The predominant winds are from SW and NE.

GEOLOGY

The bedrock of Byers Peninsula is composed of Upper Jurassic to Lower Cretaceous marine sedimentary, volcanic and volcaniclastic rocks, intruded by igneous bodies (see Smellie *et al* 1980; Crame *et al* 1993, Hathway and Lomas 1998). The rocks represent part of a Mesozoic-Cenozoic magmatic arc complex which is exposed throughout the whole of the Antarctic Peninsula region, although most extensively on the Byers Peninsula (Hathway and Lomas 1998). The elevated interior region of the eastern half of the peninsula – surrounded to the north and south by Holocene beach deposits – is dominated by Lower Cretaceous non-marine tuffs, volcanic breccias, conglomerates, sandstones and minor mudstones, with intrusions in several places by volcanic plugs and sills. The western half of the peninsula, and extending NW half-way along Ray Promontory, is predominantly Upper Jurassic-Lower Cretaceous marine mudstones, with sandstones and conglomerates, with frequent intrusions of volcanic sills, plugs and other igneous bodies. The NW half of Ray Promontory comprises mainly volcanic breccias of the same age. Mudstones, sandstones, conglomerates and pyroclastic rocks are the most common lithologies found on the peninsula. Expanses of Holocene beach gravels and alluvium are found in coastal areas, particularly on South Beaches and the eastern half of Robbery Beaches, with less-extensive deposits on President Beaches.

The Area is of high geological value because "the sedimentary and igneous rocks exposed at Byers Peninsula constitute the most complete record of the Jurassic-Early Cretaceous period in the northern part of the Pacific flank of the magmatic arc complex, and they have proved a key succession for the study of marine molluscan faunas (e.g. Crame 1984, 1995, Crame and Kelly 1995) and non-marine floras (e.g. Hernandez and Azcárte 1971, Philippe *et al* 1995)" (Hathway and Lomas 1998).

GEOMORPHOLOGY AND SOILS

Much of the terrain consists of lithosols, essentially a layer of shattered rock, with permafrost widespread below an active layer of 30-70 cm depth (Thom 1978, Ellis-Evans 1996, Serrano *et al* 1996). Stone fields (consisting of silty fines with dispersed boulders and surficial clasts), gelifluction lobes, polygonal ground (both in flooded and dry areas), stone stripes and circles and other periglacial landforms dominate the surface morphology of the upper platforms where bedrock outcrop is absent (Serrano at al 1996). Debris and mud-flows are observed in several localities. Beneath some of the moss and grass communities there is a 10-20 cm deep layer of organic matter although, because vegetation is sparse over most of Byers Peninsula, there are no deep accumulations of peat (Bonner and Smith 1985). Ornithogenic soils are present especially in the Devils Point vicinity and on a number of knolls along President Beaches (Ellis-Evans 1996).

Parts of the interior of the peninsula have been shaped by coastal processes with a series of raised beaches ranging from 3 to 54 m in altitude, some of which are over 1 km wide. A radiocarbon date for the highest beach deposits suggests that Byers Peninsula was largely free of permanent ice by 9700 yr B.P., while the lowest beach deposits are dated at 300 yr B.P (John and Sugden 1971, Sugden and John 1973). Lake sediment analyses, however, suggest a more recent general deglaciation of central Byers Peninsula of around 4000-5000 yr B.P. and radiocarbon dates in the locality need to be interpreted cautiously (Björck *et al* 1991a, b). In several places sub-fossil whalebones are embedded in the raised beaches, occasionally as almost entire skeletons. Radiocarbon dates of skeletal material from about 10 m a.s.l. on South Beaches suggest an age of between 2000 and 2400 yr B.P. (Hansom 1979). Pre-Holocene surfaces of Byers Peninsula exhibit clear evidence of a glacial landscape, despite the gentle landforms. Today only three small residual glaciers (comprising less then 0.5 km$^2$) remain on Ray Promontory. The pre-existing glacially modified landforms, have been subsequently overprinted by fluvial and periglacial processes, and moraines and other glacial deposits are scarce (Martinez de Pison *et al* 1996).

## STREAMS AND LAKES

Byers Peninsula is perhaps the most significant limnological site in the South Shetland Islands/Antarctic Peninsula region, with over 60 lakes, numerous freshwater pools (differentiated from lakes in that they freeze to the bottom in winter) and a dense and varied stream network. The gentle terrain favours water retention and waterlogged soils are common in the summer. The water capacity of the thin soils is limited, however, and many of the channels are frequently dry, with flow often intermittent except during periods of substantial snow melt or where they drain glaciers (Lopez-Martinez *et al* 1996). Most of the streams drain seasonal snowfields and are often no more than 5-10 cm in depth (Ellis-Evans 1996) although snow accumulation in some narrow gorges can reach over 2 m height, and result in ice dams blocking the lake outlet. The larger streams are up to 4.5 km in length, up to 20 m in width and 30-50 cm in depth in the lower reaches during periods of flow. Streams that drain to the west often have sizeable gorges (Lopez-Martinez *et al* 1996) and gullies up to 30 m in depth have been cut into the uppermost, and largest, of the raised marine platforms (Ellis-Evans 1996). Above the Holocene raised beaches the valleys are gentle, with widths of up to several hundred metres.

Lakes are especially abundant on the higher platforms (i.e. at the heads of basins) and on the Holocene raised beaches near the coast. Midge Lake is the largest at 587 × 112 m, and deepest with a maximum depth of 9.0 m. The inland lakes are all nutrient-poor and highly transparent, with extensive sediments in deeper water overlain by a dense aquatic moss carpet [*Drepanocladus longifolius (=D. aduncus)*]. In some lakes, such as Chester Cone Lake about 500 m to the south of Midge Lake, or Limnopolar Lake, stands of aquatic moss are found growing at one to several metres in depth and cover most of the lake bottom, which is the habitat for *Parochlus* larvae (Bonner and Smith 1985). Large masses of this moss are sometimes washed up along parts of the shoreline. The lakes are generally frozen to a depth of 1.0 - 1.5 m for 9 - 11 months of the year and overlain by snow, although surfaces of some of the higher lakes remain frozen year-round (Ellis-Evans 1996, Lopez-Martinez *et al* 1996). On the upper levels of the central plateau many small, shallow, slow-flowing streams flow between lakes and drain onto large flat areas of saturated lithosol covered with thick cyanobacterial mats of *Phormidium* sp. These mats are more extensive than in any other maritime Antarctic site thus far described and reflect the unique geomorphology and relatively high annual precipitation of the Area. With spring melt there is considerable flush through most lakes, but outflow from many lakes may cease late in the season as seasonal snowmelt decreases. Most lakes contain some crustaceans such as the copepods *Boeckella poppei* and the fairy shrimp *Branchinecta gainii*. Some of the streams also contain substantial growths of cyanobacterial and green filamentous algae, along with diatoms and copepods. A number of relatively saline lakes of lagoonal origin occur close to the shore, particularly on President Beaches. Where these are used as southern elephant seal (*Mirounga leonina*) wallows these lakes have been highly organically enriched. Those coastal shallow lakes and pools located behind the first raised beach often have abundant algal mats and crustaceans, including the copepods *B. poppei* and *Parabroteas sorsi*, and occasionally the fairy shrimp *Br. gainii*. Some of these water bodies have high biological diversity, with newly described species of diatoms (van der Vijver 2010), oligochaete (Rodriguez and Rico, 2009) and ciliate protozoa (Petz et al 2008).

## VEGETATION

Although much of Byers Peninsula lacks abundant vegetation, especially inland (see Lindsay 1971), the sparse communities contain a diverse flora, with at least 56 lichen species, 29 mosses, 5 hepatics and 2 phanerogams having been identified as present within the Area. Numerous unidentified lichens and mosses have also been collected. This suggests the Area contains one of the most diverse representations of terrestrial flora known in the maritime Antarctic. A number of the species are rare in this part of the maritime Antarctic. For example, of the bryophytes, *Anthelia juratzkana*, *Brachythecium austroglareosum*, *Chorisodontium aciphyllum*, *Ditrichum hyalinum*, *Herzogobryum teres*, *Hypnum revolutum*, *Notoligotrichum trichodon*, *Pachyglossa dissitifolia*, *Platydictya jungermannioides*, *Sanionia* cf. *plicata*, *Schistidium occultum*, *Syntrichia filaris* and *Syntrichia saxicola* are considered rare. For *A. juratzkana*, *D. hyalinum*, *N. trichodon* and *S. plicata*, their furthest-south record is on Byers Peninsula. Of the lichen flora, *Himantormia lugubris*, *Ochrolechia parella*, *Peltigera didactyla* and *Pleopsidium chlorophanum* are considered rare.

Vegetation development is much greater on the south coast than on the north. Commonly found on the higher, drier raised beaches in the south is an open community dominated by abundant *Polytrichastrum alpinum* (=*Polytrichum alpinum*), *Polytrichum piliferum* (=*Polytrichum antarcticum*), *P. juniperinum*, *Ceratodon purpureus*, and the moss *Pohlia nutans* and several crustose lichens are frequent. Some large stands of mosses occur near President and South Beaches, where extensive snowdrifts often accumulate at the base of slopes rising behind the raised beaches, providing an ample source of melt water in the summer. These moss stands are dominated mainly by *Sanionia uncinata* (=*Drepanocladus uncinatus*), which locally forms continuous carpets of several hectares. The vegetation composition is more diverse than on the higher, drier areas. Inland, wet valley floors have stands of *Brachythecium austro-salebrosum*, *Campylium polygamum*, *Sanionia uncinata*, *Warnstorfia laculosa* (=*Calliergidium austro-stramineum*), and *W. sarmentosa* (=*Calliergon sarmentosum*). In contrast, moss carpets are almost non-existent within 250 m of the northern coast, replaced by scant growth of *Sanionia* in hollows between raised beaches of up to 12 m in altitude. Lichens, principally of the genera *Acarospora*, *Buellia*, *Caloplaca*, *Verrucaria* and *Xanthoria*, are present on the lower (2-5 m) raised beach crests, with *Sphaerophorus*, *Stereocaulon* and *Usnea* becoming the more dominant lichens with increasing altitude (Lindsay 1971).

On better drained ash slopes *Bryum* spp., *Dicranoweisia* spp., *Ditrichum* spp., *Pohlia* spp., *Schistidium* spp., and *Tortula* spp. are common as isolated cushions and turves with various liverworts, lichens (notably the pink *Placopsis contortuplicata* and black foliose *Leptogium puberulum*), and the cyanobacterium *Nostoc commune*. *P. contortuplicata* occurs in inland and upland habitats lacking in nitrogen, and is typical of substrata with some degree of disturbance such as solifluction; it is often the only plant to colonise the small rock fragments of stone stripes and frost-heave polygons (Lindsay 1971). It is usually found growing alone, though rarely with species of *Andreaea* and *Usnea*. *N. commune* covers extensive saturated areas on level or gently sloping, gravelly boulder clay from altitudes of between 60-150 m, forming discrete rosettes of about 5 cm in diameter 10-20 cm apart (Lindsay 1971). Scattered, almost spherical, cushions of *Andreaea*, *Dicranoweisia*, and *Ditrichum* are found on the driest soils. In wet, bird- and seal-influenced areas the green foliose alga *Prasiola crispa* is sometimes abundant.

Rock surfaces on Byers Peninsula are mostly friable, but locally colonised by lichens, especially near the coast. Volcanic plugs are composed of harder, more stable rock and are densely covered by lichens and occasional mosses. Usnea Plug is remarkable for its luxuriant growth of *Himantormia lugubris* and *Usnea aurantiaco-atra* (=*U. fasciata*). More generally, *H. lugubris* and *U. aurantiaco-atra* are the dominant lichen species on inland exposed montane surfaces, growing with the moss *Andreaea gainii* over much of the exposed rock with up to 80% cover of the substratum (Lindsay 1971). In sheltered pockets harbouring small accumulations of mineral soil, the liverworts *Barbilophozia hatcheri* and *Cephaloziella varians* (= *C. exiliflora*) are often found, but more frequently intermixed with cushions of *Bryum*, *Ceratodon*, *Dicranoweisia*, *Pohlia*, *Sanionia*, *Schistidium*, and *Tortula*. *Sanionia* and *Warnstorfia* form small stands, possibly correlated with the absence of large snow patches and associated melt streams. *Polytrichastrum alpinum* forms small inconspicuous cushions in hollows, but it may merge with *Andreaea gainii* cushions in favourable situations (Lindsay 1971).

Crustose lichens are mainly species of *Buellia*, *Lecanora*, *Lecidella*, *Lecidea*, *Placopsis* and *Rhizocarpon* growing on rock, with species of *Cladonia* and *Stereocaulon* growing on mosses, particularly *Andreaea* (Lindsay 1971). On the south coast moss carpets are commonly colonised by epiphytic lichens, such as *Leptogium puberulum*, *Peltigera rufescens*, *Psoroma* spp., together with *Coelocaulon aculeata* and *C. epiphorella*. On sea cliffs *Caloplaca* and *Verrucaria* spp. dominate on lower surfaces exposed to salt spray up to about 5 m, with nitrophilous species, such as *Caloplaca regalis*, *Haematomma erythromma*, and

*Xanthoria elegans* often dominant at higher altitudes where seabirds are frequently nesting. Elsewhere on dry cliff surfaces a *Ramalina terebrata* - crustose lichen community is common. A variety of ornithocoprophilous lichens, such as *Catillaria corymbosa, Lecania brialmontii*, and species of *Buellia, Haematomma, Lecanora*, and *Physcia* occur on rocks near concentrations of breeding birds, along with the foliose lichens *Mastodia tessellata, Xanthoria elegans* and *X. candelaria* which are usually dominant on dry boulders.

Antarctic hairgrass (*Deschampsia antarctica*) is common in several localities, mainly on the south coast, and occasionally forms closed swards (e.g. at Sealer Hill); Antarctic pearlwort (*Colobanthus quitensis*) is sometimes associated. Both plants are quite abundant in southern gullies with a steep north-facing slope, forming large, occasionally pure stands with thick carpets of *Brachythecium* and *Sanionia*, although they are rarely found above 50 m in altitude (Lindsay 1971). An open community of predominantly *Deschampsia* and *Polytrichum piliferum* extends for several kilometres on the sandy, dry, flat raised beaches on South Beaches. A unique growth-form of the grass, forming isolated mounds 25 cm high and up to 2 m across, occurs on the beach near Sealer Hill. *Deschampsia* has been reported at only one locality on the north coast (Lair Point), where it forms small stunted tufts (Lindsay 1971).

INVERTEBRATES

The microinvertebrate fauna on Byers Peninsula thus far described comprises 25 taxa (Usher and Edwards 1986, Richard *et al* 1994, Block and Stary 1996, Convey *et al* 1996, Rodriguez and Rico, 2008): six Collembola (*Cryptopygus antarcticus, Cryptopygus badasa, Friesea grisea, Friesea woyciechowskii, Isotoma (Folsomotoma) octooculata (=Parisotoma octooculata)* and *Tullbergia mixta*; one mesostigmatid mite (*Gamasellus racovitzai*), five cryptostigmatid mites (*Alaskozetes antarcticus, Edwardzetes dentifer, Globoppia loxolineata (=Oppia loxolineata), Halozetes belgicae* and *Magellozetes antarcticus*); nine prostigmatid mites (*Bakerdania antarcticus, Ereynetes macquariensis, Eupodes minutus, Eupodes parvus grahamensis, Nanorchestes berryi, Nanorchestes nivalis, Pretriophtydeus tilbrooki, Rhagidia gerlachei, Rhagidia leechi*, and *Stereotydeus villosus*); two Dipterans (*Belgica antarctica* and *Parochlus steinenii*), and two oligochaetes (*Lumbricillus healyae* and *Lumbricillus sp.*).

Larvae of the wingless midge *Belgica antarctica* occur in limited numbers in moist moss, especially carpets of *Sanionia*, although it is of very restricted distribution on Byers Peninsula (found especially near Cerro Negro) and may be near its northern geographical limit. The winged midge *Parochlus steinenii* and its larvae inhabit the margins of inland lakes and pools, notably Midge Lake and another near Usnea Plug, and are also found amongst the stones of many stream beds (Bonner and Smith 1985, Richard *et al* 1994, Ellis-Evans pers comm 1999). During warm calm weather, swarms of adults may be seen above lake margins.

The diversity of the arthropod community described at Byers Peninsula is greater than at any other documented Antarctic site (Convey *et al* 1996). Various studies (Usher and Edwards 1986, Richard *et al* 1994, Convey *et al* 1996) have demonstrated that the arthropod population composition on Byers Peninsula varies significantly with habitat over a small area. *Tullbergia mixta* has been observed in relatively large numbers; it appears to be limited in Antarctic distribution to the South Shetland Islands (Usher and Edwards 1986). Locally, the greatest diversity is likely to be observed in communities dominated by moss cushions such as *Andreaea* spp. (Usher and Edwards 1986). Further sampling is required to establish populations and diversities with greater reliability. While further sampling at other sites may yet reveal the communities described at Byers Peninsula to be typical of similar habitats in the region, available data on the microfauna confirm the biological importance of the Area.

MICROORGANISMS

An analysis of soil samples collected from Byers Peninsula yielded several nematophagous fungi: in soil colonised by *Deschampsia* were found *Acrostalagmus goniodes, A. obovatus, Cephalosporium balanoides* and *Dactylaria gracilis*, while in *Colobanthus*-dominated soil was found *Cephalosporium balanoides* and *Dactylella gephyropaga* (Gray and Smith 1984). The basidiomycete *Omphalina antarctica* is often abundant on moist stands of the moss *Sanionia uncinata* (Bonner and Smith 1985).

Some of the water bodies have high microbial biodiversity including the largest viral genetic diversity found in Antarctic lakes (López-Bueno et al 2009)

BREEDING BIRDS

The avifauna of Byers Peninsula is diverse, although breeding colonies are generally not large. Two species of penguin, the chinstrap (*Pygoscelis antarctica*) and the gentoo (*P. papua*), breed in the Area.

Adélie penguins (*P. adeliae*) have not been observed to breed on Byers Peninsula or its offshore islets. In the South Shetlands Islands, Adélie penguins only breeds on King George Island where the populations are declining (Carlini et al. 2009).

The principal chinstrap penguin colony is at Devils Point, where a rough estimate of about 3000 pairs was made in 1987; a more accurate count made in 1965 indicated about 5300 pairs in four discrete colonies, of which almost 95% were nesting on Demon Island, 100 m to the south of Devils Point (Croxall and Kirkwood 1979; Woehler 1993). Two colonies of about 25 chinstrap penguin pairs surrounded by a colony of gentoo penguins can be found on the President Beaches close to Devils Point. Small chinstrap penguin colonies have been reported on the northern coast, e.g. on Robbery Beaches (50 pairs in 1958; Woehler 1993), but no breeding pairs were reported there in a 1987 survey. In other locations, Lair Point contained 156 pairs in 1966, declining to 25 pairs in 1987 (Woehler 1993). In a recent visit to the area (January 2009) 20 pairs were counted (Barbosa pers.com).

Gentoo penguins breed at several colonies on Devils Point, with approximately 750 pairs recorded in 1965 (Croxall and Kirkwood 1979, Woehler 1993). Currently three colonies of about 3000 pairs in total can be found (Barbosa pers.com). On the northern coast, a rookery of three colonies with 900 pairs in total is located in Robbery Beaches (Woehler 1993). In a visit to Lair Point in January 2009, about 1200 pairs were counted. Woehler (1993) gives no data on gentoo penguins at this location.

Recent estimations of population size for some species of flying birds were obtained from a survey conducted in December 2008 and January 2009 (Gil-Delgado et al. 2010). The Antarctic tern (*Sterna vittata*) population was estimated at 1873 breeding pairs. Two hundred and thirty eight pairs of southern giant petrels *(Macronectes giganticus)* and 15 pairs of brown skua (*Catharacta lonnbergi*) nest locally. A detailed survey of other breeding birds was conducted in 1965 (White 1965). The most populous breeding species recorded then, with approximately 1760 pairs, was the Antarctic tern (*Sterna vittata*), followed by 1315 pairs of Wilson's storm petrels (*Oceanites oceanicus*), approximately 570 pairs of cape petrels (*Daption capense*), 449 pairs of kelp gulls (*Larus dominicanus*), 216 pairs of southern giant petrels, 95 pairs of black-bellied storm petrels (*Fregetta tropica*), 47 pairs of blue-eyed cormorants (*Phalacrocorax atriceps*) (including those on nearshore islets), 39 pairs of brown skuas, and 3 pairs of sheathbills (*Chionis alba*). In addition, prions (*Pachytilla* sp.) and snow petrels (*Pagodroma nivea*) have been seen on the peninsula but their breeding presence has not been confirmed. The census of burrowing and scree-nesting birds is considered an underestimate (White pers. comm. 1999). The majority of the birds nest in close proximity to the coast, principally in the west and south.

Recently some vagrant waders, probably white-rumped sandpipers (*Calidris fuscicollis*) have been seen frequently foraging in some streams in the southern beaches (Quesada pers. comm. 2009).

## BREEDING MAMMALS

Large groups of southern elephant seals (*Mirounga leonina*) breed on the Byers Peninsula coast, with a total of over 2500 individuals reported on South Beaches (Torres *et al.* 1981), which is one of the largest populations of this species recorded in the South Shetland Islands. A estimation made in 2008-2009 showed a population ranging from 4700 to 6300 individuals (Gil-Delgado et al. 2010). Large numbers haul out in wallows and along beaches in summer. Weddell (*Leptonychotes weddellii*), crabeater (*Lobodon carcinophagous*) and leopard (*Hydrurga leptonyx*) seals may be seen around the shorelines. Antarctic fur seals (*Arctocephalus gazella*) were once very abundant on Byers Peninsula (see below), but have not substantially recolonised the Area in high numbers in spite of the recent rapid population expansion in other parts of the maritime Antarctic.

## HISTORICAL FEATURES

Following discovery of the South Shetland Islands in 1819, intensive sealing at Byers Peninsula between 1820 and 1824 exterminated almost all local Antarctic fur seals and southern elephant seals (Smith and Simpson 1987). During this period there was a summer population of up to 200 American and British sealers living ashore in dry-stone refuges and caves around Byers Peninsula (Smith and Simpson 1987). Evidence of their occupation remains in their many refuges, some of which still contain artefacts (clothing, implements, structural materials, etc.). Several sealing vessels were wrecked near Byers Peninsula and timbers from these ships may be found along the shores. Byers Peninsula has the greatest concentration of early 19th Century sealers' refuges and associated relics in the Antarctic and these are vulnerable to disturbance and/or removal.

Elephant seal numbers, and to some extent fur seal numbers, recovered after 1860, but were again decimated by a second sealing cycle extending to the first decade of the twentieth century.

## HUMAN ACTIVITIES/IMPACTS

The modern era of human activity at Byers Peninsula has been largely confined to science. The impacts of these activities have not been described, but are believed to be minor and limited to items such as campsites, footprints, markers of various kinds, sea-borne litter washed onto beaches (e.g. from fishing vessels) and from human wastes and scientific sampling. Several wooden stake markers and a plastic fishing float were observed in the southwest of the Area in a brief visit made in February 2001 (Harris 2001). In summer 2009-2010, a beach litter survey was undertaken (Rodriguez-Pertierra pers. comm.). The highest proportion of litter on beaches (averaged over beach length) was found in Robbery Beach (64%) followed by President Beach (28%) and beaches to the southwest of the Area (8%). This is likely to be related to their exposure to the Drake Passage (Torres and Jorquera, 1994). The majority of the litter found on the three beaches was wood (78% by number of items) and plastic (19%) whereas metal, glass and cloth were found more rarely (less than 1%). Several pieces of timber were found, some of them quite large (several meters in length). The plastic items were highly diverse, with bottles, ropes and tape the most numerous items. Floats and glass bottles were also found on the beaches.

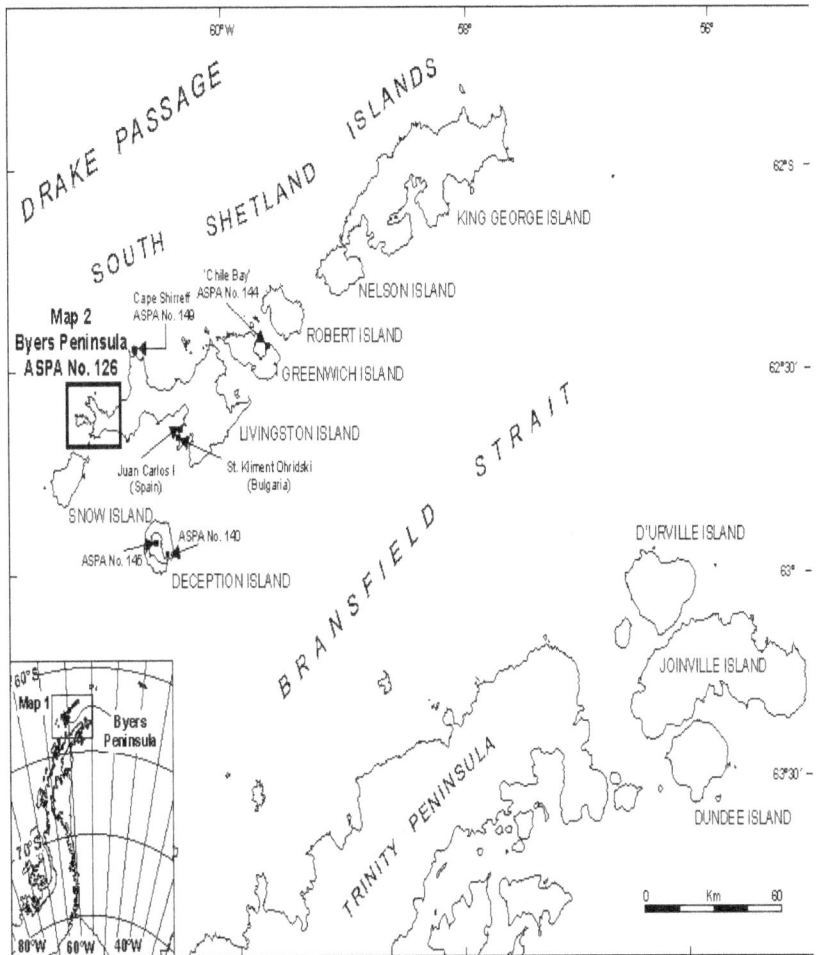

**Map 1.** Byers Peninsula, ASPA No. 126, Livingston Island, South Shetland Islands, location map. Inset: location of Byers Peninsula on the Antarctic Peninsula

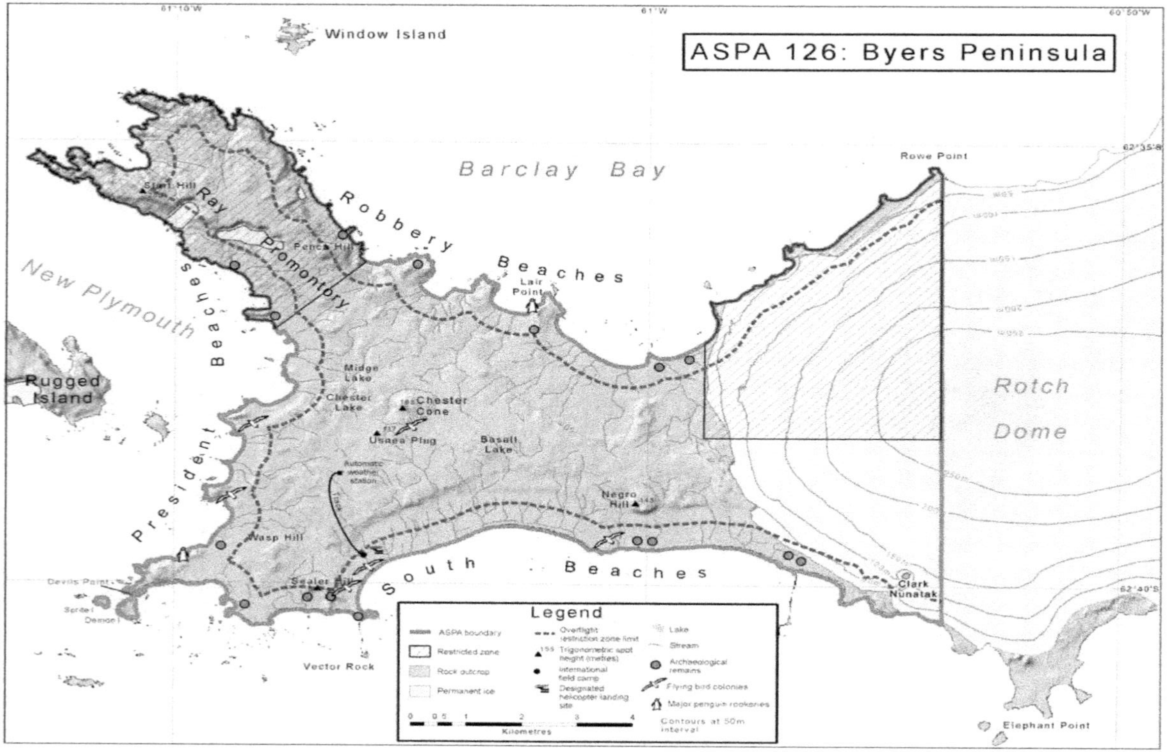

Map 2.  ASPA 126: Byers Peninsula topographic map.

# Management Plan for

# Antarctic Specially Protected Area No. 127

# HASWELL ISLAND

# (Haswell Island and Adjacent Emperor Penguin Rookery on Fast Ice)

**Revised Management Plan**

## 1. Description of values to be protected

Haswell Island is a unique breeding site for almost all breeding bird species in East Antarctica including the: Antarctic petrel (*Talassoica antarctica*), Antarctic fulmar (*Fulmarus glacioloides*), Cape petrel (*Daption capense*), Snow petrel (*Pagodroma nivea*), Wilson's storm petrel (*Oceanites oceanicus*), South polar skua (*Catharacta maccormicki*), and Adelie penguin (*Pygoscelis adeliae*). The Area supports five species of pinnipeds, including the Ross seal (*Ommatophoca rossii*) which is a protected species.

South-east of the island, there is a large colony of Emperor penguins (*Aptenodytes forsteri*) on fast ice.

The Area consists of Haswell Island (66°31'S, 93°00'E), about 1 km² in area, the largest of a group of islands lying close to Mirny station, together with its littoral zone and the area of fast ice, when present. ATCM VIII (Oslo, 1975) approved its designation as SSSI 7 on the aforementioned grounds after a proposal by the USSR. Map 1 shows the location of the Haswell Islands (except Vkhodnoy Island), Mirny station, and logistic activity sites. It was renamed and renumbered as ASPA No. 127 by Measure 1 (2002).

Currently it is proposed to detail the boundaries of the Antarctic Specially Protected Area, Haswell Island (66°31'S, 93°00'E), about 1 km2 in area and the adjacent section of Davis Sea fast ice of approximately 5 km2 (when present), that supports a colony of Emperor penguins (Map 2). It is one of a few Emperor penguin colonies in the vicinity of a permanent Antarctic station, and therefore it has advantages for the study of the species and its habitat.

Described by biologists during the first Soviet expeditions, the Area was studied in the 1970s and recent years, providing valuable materials for comparative analyses and monitoring of the long-term long environmental impact of a large Antarctic station.

## 2. Aims and Objectives

Research in the ASPA is conducted to provide a better understanding of how natural and anthropogenic environmental changes affect the status and dynamics of local populations of flora and fauna, and how these changes affect the interaction between key species of the Antarctic ecosystem.

Management at Haswell Island aims to:

- Avoid direct impact of logistic activities on the Area;
- Regulate access to the Area;
- Avoid anthropogenic changes in the structure and abundance of local populations of flora and fauna;
- Allow scientific research, provided it is for compelling scientific reasons that cannot be served elsewhere;
- Facilitate scientific research on the environment in the context of monitoring and assessment of human impact on populations:
- Encourage environmental education and awareness.

### 3. Management Activities

The following management activities shall be undertaken to protect the values of the Area:

- When the vessel is approaching Mirny station and upon arrival at the station, all persons arriving shall be informed of the existence and location of the ASPA and the relevant provisions of the Management Plan.
- Copies of the Management Plan and maps of the Area showing its location shall be available at all units engaged in logistic and scientific activities on the Haswell Islands.
- A sign showing directions of the Area boundaries, with clear statements of entry restrictions ("No entry! Antarctic Specially Protected Area"), shall be placed at the crossing point of lines Gorev Island – Fulmar Island and Cape Mabus – eastern extremity of Haswell Island to help avoid inadvertent entry into the Area following the formation of fast ice which is safe for pedestrian and vehicle traffic. Information signs shall be installed at the top of Cape Mabus slope, and at station activity sites in the direct vicinity of the Area.
- Markers and signs erected within the Area shall be secured, maintained in good condition, and have no impact on the environment.
- Overflight shall only be allowed under those conditions as set out under *7. Permit Conditions*

The Management Plan shall be revised periodically to ensure that the values of the Antarctic Specially Protected Area are adequately protected. Any activity in the Area shall be preceded by the environmental impact assessment.

### 4. Period of Designation

Designated for an indefinite period.

### 5. Maps

Map 1: Location of the Haswell Islands, Mirny Station, and logistic activity sites.
Map 2: Boundaries of Antarctic Specially Protected Area 127, Haswell Island.
Map 3: Location of breeding seabird colonies.
Map 4: Topographic map of Haswell Island.

### 6. Description of the Area

#### 6(i) Geographical co-ordinates, boundary markers and natural features

The Area occupies a territory inside polygon ABFEDC (66° 31'10" S, 92° 59'20" E; 66° 31'10" S, 93° 03' E; 66° 32'30" S, 93° 03' E; 66° 32'30" S, 93° 01'E; 66° 31'45" S, 93° 01'E; 66° 31'45" S, 92° 59'20'' E) (Map 2). The marked section of fast ice in the Davis Sea encompasses the most likely routes taken by Emperor penguins during the breeding season.

*Topography*

The Area boundaries on fast ice closer to the station can be broadly (visually) identified on site as directions EF (Vkhodnoy Island – Fulmar Island) and ED (Cape Mabus – eastern extremity of Haswell Island). A sign showing the directions of the Area boundaries, with clear statements of entry restrictions ("No entry! Antarctic Specially Protected Area"), shall be placed in point E. Information signs showing distance to the Area boundary shall be installed at station activity sites in the direct vicinity of the Area (at the top of Cape Mabus slope, and on Buromsky, Zykov, Fulmar, and Tokarev Islands).

It is highly unlikely that the outlying marine boundaries of the Area will be crossed inadvertently, as there is presently no activity this far away from the station. These boundaries have no visual features and shall be identified by the map.

There are no paths or roads within the Area.

*Ice conditions*

The Area comprises Haswell Island (the largest island in the archipelago), its littoral zone, and the adjacent section of fast ice in the Davis Sea. Russia's Mirny Observatory on Mirny Peninsula located in coastal nunataks south of the ASPA has been operational since 1956.

For the larger part of the year, the sea within the Area is covered with fast ice, whose width reaches 30-40 km by the end of winter. Fast ice breaks up between December 17 and March 9 (February 3, on average) and freezes between March 18 and May 5 (April 6, on average). The probability that the ice-free period off Mirny will last more than 1 month is 85%, more than 2 months 45%, and more than 3 months 25%. The Area is always full of icebergs frozen in the ice. In summer, when fast ice disappears, icebergs drift westward along the coast. Seawater temperature is always below zero. The tide has an irregular daily pattern.

*Environmental domains analysis*

Based on the Environmental Domains Analysis for Antarctica (Resolution 3(2008)) Haswell Island is located within Environment L *Continental coastal-zone ice sheet*.

*Biological Features*

Coastal waters support a rich benthic fauna. Fish fauna in the Area is dominated by various icefish species, while Antarctic toothfish (*Dissostichus mawsoni*) and Antarctic silverfish (*Pleuragramma antarcticum*) are less abundant. An ample forage base and the availability of suitable nesting sites create a favorable environment for numerous seabirds. According to records, there are 12 bird species in the vicinity of Mirny (Table 1).

The coastal fauna is mainly represented by pinnipeds, among which Weddell seals (*Leptonychotes weddelli*) are most abundant. Other Antarctic seal species can be seen occasionally in very small numbers. Minke whales (*Balaenoptera acutorostrata*) and killer whales (*Orcinus orca*) have frequently been observed near Mirny.

Table 1: The avifauna of the Haswell Islands (ASPA 127).

| 1 | Emperor penguin (*Aptenodytes forsteri*) | B, M |
|---|---|---|
| 2 | Adelie penguin (*Pygoscelis adeliae* ) | B, M |
| 3 | Chinstrap penguin (*Pygoscelis antarctica*) | V |
| 4 | Macaroni penguin (*Eudyptes chrysolophus*) | V |
| 5 | Southern fulmar (*Fulmarus glacioloides*) | B |
| 6 | Antarctic petrel (*Thalassoica antarctica*) | B |
| 7 | Cape petrel (*Daption capense*) | B |
| 8 | Snow petrel (*Pagodroma nivea*) | B |
| 9 | Southern giant petrel (Macronectes giganteus) | V |
| 10 | Wilson's storm petrel (Oceanites oceanicus) | B |
| 11 | Pomarine skua (Stercorarius pomarinus) | V |
| 12 | South-polar skua (Catharacta maccormicki) | B |
| 13 | Lonnberg skua Catharacta (Antarctica lonnbergi) | V |
| 14 | Kelp gull (*Larus dominicanus*) | V |

Notes: B – breeding species; M – molting sites in the vicinity of the station; V – vagrant species.

At present, seabirds nest on six out of seventeen archipelago islands. Seven species breed directly on the islands, and one species – the Emperor penguin (Aptenodytes forsteri) – on fast ice. A few vagrant species have also been observed in the Area. In general, core species composition of the aviafauna remains stable during past 60 years, and is characteristic of the East Antarctica coastal areas. Recent updates to the species list (Table 1, added Southern giant petrel Macronectes giganteus and Lonnberg skua Catharacta Antarctica lonnbergi) are explained by more extensive ornithological observations at the Mirny station during last decade. All new species are recorded as vagrants only. At the same time, the Southern giant petrel observed in 2006 for the first time at Mirny, seems to become rare but regular visitor to the Area.

Emperor penguin (*Aptenodytes forsteri*)

The Emperor penguin colony of the Haswell Islands is located on fast ice in the Davis Sea 2 to 3 km north-east of the Mirny Observatory and usually within 1 km of Haswell Island. The colony was discovered and described by the Western Party of the Australasian Antarctic Expedition on November 25, 1912. However, a detailed study of the colony was initiated only after the establishment of the Mirny Observatory. Since its foundation in 1956, the Observatory has been conducting periodic monitoring of the size of the breeding population. The first round-the-year observation of the colony was initiated by E.S. Korotkevich in 1956 (Korotkevich, 1958), continued until 1962 (Makushok, 1959; Korotkevich, 1960; Prior, 1968), and was then resumed by V.M. Kamenev in the late 1960s-early 1970s (Kamenev, 1977). After a long break, observations of the avifauna were resumed at the area in 1999-2011 (Gavrilo, Mizin, 2007, Gavrilo, Mizin, 2011, Neelov et al., 2007).

Table 2 shows a schedule of various phenological events in the Emperor penguin colony of the Haswell Islands.

Table 2: Dates of phenological events in the Emperor penguin colony, Haswell Islands.

| Penguins arrive at the colony site | Last 10 days in March |
|---|---|
| Peak of the mating period | Late April – first ten days in May |
| Commencement of egg laying | First 5 days in May |
| Commencement of hatching | July 5–15 |
| Chicks start leaving brood pouches | Last 10 days in August |
| Chicks start getting together in creches | First 10 days in September |
| Chicks start molting | Late October – early November |
| Adult birds start molting | Last 10 days in November – first 5 days in December |
| The colony starts disintegrating | Last 10 days in November – mid-December |
| Birds abandon the colony site | Last 5 days in December – first 10 days in January |

The most recent data on the colony status were obtained during 2010-2011 when the colony initially consisted of two sub-colonies 400 m apart. Single adult birds and those with eggs and chicks migrated between the subcolonies. Later, the third subcolony separated. All subcolonies were located and moved within the same area as in previous years, i.e. east andsouth-east off the Haswell Island.

During last decade, the Haswell colony of the emperor penguins should be considered rather stable and even slightly increasing . Highest population numbers as observed during egg laying period in 2010/2011 season reached ca. 13,000 adults, which is the maximal counts for the last 12years (RAE, unpublished data). According to estimates and censuses conducted in 1956–1966, the total population varied from 14,000 to 20,000 birds (Korotkevich, 1958, Makushok, 1959, Prior, 1964, Kamenev, 1977). After that, during 1970-s – 1980-s population declined at ca. 30%, but later, in 2000-s, a recovery process is observed.

Comparative analysis of the emperor penguin population dynamics in two colonies located in the same ecoregion (80°E - 140°E), i.e. Haswell and Pointe Géologie, revealed similar trends during past 60 years (Barbraud et al., 2011). Before 1970-s penguin population at Pointe-Geologie Archipelago,Terre Adelie (ASPA 120) was stable, and at Haswell it was also stable or slightly decreasing. Population growth rate notably decreased and population numbers declined in both colonies during climatic regime shift in 1970-1980. Magnitude of decline was similar as well, and the numbers of breeding pairs correlated. Given that, one could suggest common large-scale environmental/climatic changes and related ecosystem shifts observed widely over the Southern Ocean might affect penguin populations. The same string negative factor is likely to impact both populations. The ice cover, which is known to effect emperor penguin ecology, is suggested to be such a factor. In particular, decrease in iced cover and earlier onset of the fast-ice break-up dates negatively impacted penguin survival and further breeding population numbers via changes in food availability as shown previously Barbraud, Weimerskirch, 2001, Jenouvrier et al., 2009). During past 20 years both colonies demonstrated positive population dynamics under conditions of increasing extent of the ice cover and shift of fast-ice break-up onset to the later dates.

Table 3: Factors affecting the population of Emperor penguins on the Haswell Islands and relevant mitigation actions.

| | Actions to mitigate the impact of anthropogenic factors |
|---|---|

| Anthropogenic factors | Disturbance by visitors | Visits to the colony should be strictly regulated |
| --- | --- | --- |
| | Collection of eggs | The collection of eggs is prohibited, except in accordance with a permit for research issued by a national authority. |
| | Disturbance by flights | Flight route and height should be selected in accordance with this Management Plan |
| Natural factors | | Climate changes and related changes in food resources. Ice conditions affect food availability and survival of adults and chicks. (Decrease in sea ice extent in April – June leads to decline in population growth rate and population numbers decline. An early break-up of fast ice increases chick mortality). |

Data on changes in the size of other populations are less complete (Table 4). Long-term changes may show a negative trend. However, it's not possible to make well-grounded conclusions based just on the three surveys with not full coverage of the populations and which are several decades apart.

Table 4: Long-term changes in the size of bird populations on the Haswell Islands. Trend: 0 = uncertain, -1 = negative, ? = supposed.

| Species | 1960s-1970s, adults in individuals | 1999/2001 | 2009/10, adults in individuals | Trend |
| --- | --- | --- | --- | --- |
| Adelie penguin | 41,000-44,500 | Ca. 31,000 adults | Ca. 27,000 | -1 |
| Southern fulmar | 9,500-10000 | 2300 nests with clutches | Ca. 5,000 | -1 |
| Antarctic petrel | 900-1050 | 150-200 nests with clutches | Ca. 500 | -1 |
| Cape petrel | 750 | 150 nests with clutches | Ca. 300 | -1 |
| Snow petrel | 600-700 | 60-75 nests with clutches | No data | -1 ? |
| Wilson's storm-petrel | 400-500 | Min 30 occupied nests | Over 80 | -1 ? |
| South-polar skua | 48 (24 pairs) | Min. 38 (19 pairs) | 134 (62 pairs) | 1 |

The data from Haswell Island area show possible long-term negative trends in different seabird species including both penguins and flying birds. It is possible that large-scaled climate changes may be responsible for the negative population dynamics in the Haswell Island area, not only in emperor penguin populations but also in other seabird populations except for the south-polar skua.

More research and further monitoring are needed to reveal population trends in the birds of Haswell Island and to understand their causes.

**6(ii) Definition of seasons; restricted and prohibited zones within the Area**

Entry into any part of the Area is allowed only for holders of a Permit issued by an appropriate National Authority.

Activity in the Area shall be subject to special restrictions during the bird breeding season:

- From mid-April to December in the vicinity of the Emperor penguin colony; and
- From October to March in the vicinity of the nesting sites on Haswell Island.

The location of the breeding colonies is shown in Map 3. Emperor penguins, which are especially sensitive to disturbance, shall also be protected outside the designated breeding site as the breeding site may vary in location.

### 6(iii) Structures within the Area

A beacon – a metal pole whose base is secured by stones – is located on Haswell Island. There are no other structures on the island.

A heated shack containing an emergency food supply may be located on one of the neighboring islands (but not on Haswell Island).

### 6(iv) Location of other protected areas within close proximity

HSM No 9 Cemetery on Buromskiy Island is located in 200 m to boundary of the Area.

## 7. Permit Conditions

### 7(i) Permit conditions

Entry into the Area is prohibited unless in accordance with a Permit issued by an appropriate national authority. Issue of a Permit to enter the Area must satisfy the following conditions:

- A Permit is issued only for purposes specified in para. 2 of the Management Plan;

- Permits shall be issued for a stated period;

- The actions permitted will not jeopardize the ecosystems of the Area or interfere with existing scientific research;

- Visits to the Area under a Permit shall be allowed to organized groups accompanied by a authorized person. Relevant information shall be entered in the Visit Logbook specifying the date and purpose of the visit and the number of visitors. The leader of the Mirny station keeps the Logbook. The authorized person is appointed in accordance with national procedure; and

- A visit report shall be supplied to the authority named in the Permit by the end of stated period or annually.

Permits shall be issued for scientific research, monitoring studies, or inspections that do not require collection of biological materials or fauna samples, or that require collecting in small quantities. A Permit for a visit to or stay in the Area shall specify the scope of tasks to be implemented, the implementation period, and the maximum number of staff allowed to visit the Area.

### 7(ii) Access to and movement within the Area

Vehicles other than skidoos are prohibited within the Area.

When approaching or moving within the Area, care shall be taken to avoid any disturbance to birds and seals, especially during the breeding season. Deterioration of the conditions of or approaches to the bird nesting sites, or seal haulouts shall be prohibited at all times.

*Haswell Island.* The western or south-western slopes are most suitable for access (Map 4). Movement shall only be on foot.

*Fast ice section.* During the formation of fast ice which provides pedestrian and vehicle safety, entry into the section shall be at any suitable place from the Mirny station. The use of any vehicles in the Area shall be prohibited during the nest sitting season (May-July). When using skidoos, visitors shall not approach the Emperor penguin colony closer than 500 m (irrespective of its location).

Overflight of the Area is prohibited during the most sensitive period of the Emperor penguin breeding cycle, from April 15 to August 31.

During the remainder of the year, overflight of the Area shall be conducted according to the following restrictions (Table 5). Direct overflights of the seabird breeding colonies should be avoided whenever it is possible.

Table 5: Minimum overflight heights within the Area according to aircraft type.

| Aircraft type | Number of engines | Minimum height above ground | |
| --- | --- | --- | --- |
| | | Feet | Meters |
| Helicopter | 1 | 2,460 | 750 |
| Helicopter | 2 | 3,300 | 1,000 |
| Fixed-wing | 1 or 2 | 2,460 | 750 |
| Fixed-wing | 4 | 3,300 | 1,000 |

### 7(iii) Activities that are or may be conducted in the Area, including restrictions on time or place

- Research on avifauna and other environmental studies that cannot be conducted elsewhere;
- Management activities, including monitoring.
- Education visits to the Emperor penguins colony except of the early nesting period (May – July)

### 7(iv) Installation, modification, or removal of structures

Structures or scientific equipment may be installed in the Area only for compelling scientific or management purposes approved by an appropriate authority pursuant to the effective regulations.

### 7(v) Location of field camps

Camping shall be allowed only for safety reasons, and every precaution shall be taken to avoid damage to the local ecosystem and disturbance to the local fauna.

### 7(vi) Restrictions on materials and organisms which can be brought into the Area

No living organisms or chemicals other than chemicals required for scientific purposes specified in the Permit shall be introduced into the Area (chemicals introduced for scientific purposes shall be removed from the Area before the Permit expiry).

Fuel is not to be stored in the Area unless it is required for essential needs relating to the permitted activity. Anything introduced shall be for a stated period only, handled so that the risk to the ecosystem is minimized, and removed at the conclusion of the stated period. No permanent storage facilities shall be established in the Area.

### 7(vii) Taking of or harmful interference with native flora or fauna

Taking of or harmful interference with native flora or fauna is prohibited, except by Permit. In the case the activity is determined to have less than a minor or transitory impact, it should be conducted in accordance with the *SCAR Code of Conduct for the Use of Animals for Scientific Purposes in Antarctica,* to be used as a minimum standard.

### 7(viii) Collection or removal of anything not brought into the Area by the Permit holder

Collection or removal of anything not brought into the Area by the Permit holder shall only be for scientific or management purposes specified in the Permit.

However, human waste may be removed from the Area, and dead or pathological samples of fauna and flora may be removed for laboratory analysis.

### 7(ix) Disposal of waste

All waste shall be removed from the Area.

**7(x) Measures that are necessary to ensure that the aims and objectives of the Management Plan continue to be met**

Permits to enter the Area may be granted to carry out scientific observation, monitoring, and site inspection activities, which may involve limited collection of fauna samples, eggs, and other biological materials for scientific purposes. To help maintain the environmental and scientific values of the Area, visitors shall take every precaution against the introduction of alien materials and organisms.

Any long-term monitoring sites shall be appropriately marked on a map and on site. A map showing the boundary of the ASPA shall be displayed at Mirny station. A copy of the Management Plan shall be displayed at Mirny station. A copy of the Management Plan shall be freely available at Mirny station.

Visits to the Area shall be limited to scientific, management and educational purposes.

**7(xi) Requirements for reports**

Parties should ensure that the principal holder of each Permit issued submits to the appropriate authority a report describing the activities undertaken. Such reports should include, as appropriate, the information identified in the visit report form contained in the Guide to the Preparation of Management Plans for Antarctic Specially Protected Areas. Parties should maintain a record of such activities, and, in the Annual Exchange of Information, should provide summary descriptions of activities conducted by persons subject to their jurisdiction, which should be in sufficient detail to allow evaluation of the effectiveness of the management plan. Parties should, wherever possible, deposit originals or copies of such original reports in a publicly accessible archive to maintain a record of usage, to be used both in any review of the management plan and in organizing the scientific use of the Area.

## 8. References

Androsova, E.I.. Antarctic and Subantarctic bryozoans // Soviet Antarctic Expedition Newsletter.-1973.-No. 87.-P.65-69. (in Russian)

Averintsev, V.G. Ecology of sublittoral polychaetes in the Davis Sea // Animal Morphology, Systematics and Evolution.-L.,1978.-P.41-42. (in Russian)

Averintsev, V.G. Seasonal variations of sublittoral polychaetes in the Davis Sea // Marine Fauna Studies.-L.,1982.-Vol.. 28(36).-P.4-70. (in Russian)

Barbroud C. & Weimerskirch H. 2001 Emperor Penguins and climate change. Nature, 411: 183 – 185.

Barbroud C., Gavrilo M., Mizin Yu., Weimerskirch H. Comparison of emperor penguin declines between Pointe Géologie and Haswell Island over the past 50 years. Antarctic Science. 2011. (Accepted)

Budylenko, G.A., and Pervushin, A.S. The migration of finwhales, sei whales and Minke whales in the Southern Hemisphere // Marine Mammals: Proceedings of VI All-Union Meeting.-Kiev, 1975.-Part.1.-P.57-59. (in Russian)

Bushueva, I.V. A new Acanthonotozommella species in the Davis Sea (East Antarctica) // Zool. Zhurn.-1978.-Vol.57, issue 3.-P.450-453. (in Russian)

Bushueva, I.V. A new Pseudharpinia (Amphipoda) species in the Davis Sea (Antarctica) // Zool. Zhurn.-1982.-Vol.61, issue.8.-P.1262-1265.

Bushueva, I.V. Some peculiarities of off-shore amphipod (Gammaridea) distribution in the Davis Sea (East Antarctica) // Hydrobiology and Biogeography of Cold and Moderate World Ocean Waters in the Off-shore Zone: Report Abstracts.-L.,1974.-P.48-49. (in Russian)

Bushueva, I.V. Some peculiarities of Paramola walkeri ecology in the Davis Sea (East Antarctica) // Off-shore Biology: Abstracts of Reports Presented at the All-Union Conference. - Vladivostok,1975.-P.21-22. (in Russian)

Chernov, A., Mizin, Yu. 2001 Avifauna observations at Mirny Station during RAE 44 (1999-2000) — The State of the Antarctic Environment as Shown by Real-time Data from Russia's Antarctic Stations. — SPb: AARI. (in Russian)

Doroshenko, N.V. The distribution of Minke whales (Balaenoptera acutorostrata Lac) in the Southern Hemisphere // V All-Union Meeting on Marine Mammal Research: Report Abstracts. - Makhachkala, 1972.-Part1.-P.181-185. (in Russian)

Egorova, E.N. Biogeographic composition and possible development of gastropods and bivalves in the Davis Sea, // Soviet Antarctic Expedition Newsletter.-1972.-No. 83.-P.70-76. (in Russian)

Egorova, E.N. Mollusks of the Davis Sea (East Antarctica).- L.:Nauka, 1982.-144 pp. - (Marine Fauna Research; No. 26(34). (in Russian)

Egorova, E.N. Zoogeographic composition of the mollusk fauna in the Davis Sea (East Antarctica) // Mollusks. Major Results of the Study: VI All-Union Mollusk Research Meeting.- L.,1979.-Vol.6.-P..78-79. (in Russian)

Gavrilo, M.V., Chupin, I.I., Mizin, Yu.A., and Chernov A.S. 2002. Study of the Biological Diversity of Antarctic Seabirds and Mammals. – Report on Antarctic Studies and Research under the World Ocean Federal Targeted Program. SPb: AARI (unpublished). (in Russian)

Gavrilo M., Mizin Yu. 2007. Penguin population dynamics in Haswell Archipelago area, ASPA № 127, East Antarctica. – p. 92 in Wohler E.j. (ed.) 2007. Abstracts of oral and poster presentations, 6th International Penguin Conference. Hobart, Australia, 3-7 September 2007

Gavrilo M., Mizin I. Current zoological researches in the area of Mirny station.Russian Polar Researches. Iss. 3. AARI, 2011.

Gruzov, E.N. Echinoderms in coastal biocenoses of the Davis Sea (Antarctica) // Systematics, Evolution, Biology, and Distribution of Modern and Extinct Echinoderms.-L.,1977.-P.21-23. (in Russian)

Kamenev, V.M. Adaptive peculiarities of the reproduction cycle of some Antarctic birds. - Body Adaptation to Far North Conditions: Abstracts of Reports Presented at the All-Union Meeting. Tallinn, 1984. P. 72-76. (in Russian)

Kamenev, V.M. Antarctic petrels of Haswell Island // Soviet Antarctic Expedition Newsletter.-1979.-No. 99.-P.78-84. (in Russian)

Kamenev, V.M. Ecology of Adelie penguins of the Haswell Islands // Soviet Antarctic Expedition Newsletter. 1971. No. 82. P. 67-71. (in Russian)

Kamenev, V.M. Ecology of Cape and snow petrels. - Soviet Antarctic Expedition Newsletter. 1988. No. 110. P. 117-129. (in Russian)

Kamenev, V.M. Ecology of Emperor penguins of the Haswell Islands. – The Adaptation of Penguins. M., 1977. P. 141-156. (in Russian)

Kamenev, V.M. Ecology of Wilson's storm petrels (Oceanites oceanicus Kuhl) on the Haswell Islands // Soviet Antarctic Expedition Newsletter. 1977. No. 94. P. 49-57. (in Russian)

Kamenev, V.M. Protected Antarctica. – Lecturer's Aid. L.: Znanie RSFSR, 1986. P. 1-17. (in Russian)

Kamenev, V.M. The Antarctic fulmar (Fulmarus glacialoides) of the Haswell Islands // Soviet Antarctic Expedition Newsletter. - 1978. No. 98. P. 76-82. (in Russian)

Korotkevish, E.P. 1959 The bids of East Antarctica. – Arctic and Antarctic Issues. – No. 1. (in Russian)

Korotkevish, E.P. 1960 By radio from Antarctica. — Soviet Antarctic Expedition Newsletter. - № 20-24. (in Russian)

Krylov, V.I., Medvedev, L.P. The distribution of the Ceteans in the Atlantic and South Oceans // Soviet Antarctic Expedition Newsletter.-1971.-No. 82.-P.64-66. (in Russian)

Makushok, V.M. 1959 Biological takings and observations at the Mirny Observatory in 1958. — Soviet Antarctic Expedition Newsletter. – No. 6. (in Russian)

Minichev, Yu.R. Opisthobranchia (Gastropoda, Opisthobranchia) of the Davis Sea // Marine Fauna Research.-L.,1972.-Vol.11(19).-P.358-382. (in Russian)

Mizin, Yu.V. 2004 Report on the Ecological and Environmental Research Program Conducted by RAE 48 at the Mirny Observatory – SPb: AARI, unpublished. (in Russian)

Neelov A.V., Smirnov I.S., Gavrilo M.V. 2007 50 years of the Russian studies of antarctic ecosystems. – Problemy Arktiki I Antarktiki. – № 76. – Pp. 113 – 130

Popov, L.A., Studenetskaya, I.R. Ice-based Antarctic seals // The Use of the World Ocean Resources for Fishery Needs. An overview by the Central Research Institute of Fishery Information and Technical Studies. Series. 1.- M., 1971. Issue 5.-P.3-42. (in Russian)

Prior, M.E. 1964 Observations of Emperor penguins (Aptenodytes forsteri Gray) in the Mirny area in 1962. Soviet Antarctic Expedition Newsletter. – No. 47. (in Russian)

Pushkin, A.F. Some ecological and zoogeographic peculiarities of the Pantopoda fauna in the Davis Sea // Hydrobiology and Biogeography of Cold and Moderate World Ocean Waters in the Off-shore Zone: Report Abstracts.- L.,1974.-P.43-45. (in Russian)

Splettstoesser J.F., Maria Gavrilo, Carmen Field, Conrad Field, Peter Harrison, M. Messicl, P. Oxford, F. Todd 2000 Notes on Antarctic wildlife: Ross seals Ommatophoca rossii and Emperor penguins Aptenodytes forsteri. New Zealand Journal of Zoology, 27: 137-142.

Stepaniants, R.D. Coastal hydrozoans of the Davis Sea (materials of the 11th Soviet Antarctic Expedition, 1965/66) // Marine Fauna Research.- L.,1972.-Vol.11(19).-P.56-79. (in Russian)

ASPA No 127 - Haswell Island

The Final Report of the Twenty Second Antarctic Treaty Consultative Meeting (Tromse, Norway, May 25 – June 5, 1998). [Oslo, Royal Ministry of Foreign Affairs], P. – 93 – 130. (in Russian).

Map 1: Location of the Haswell Islands, Mirny Station, and logistic activity sites.

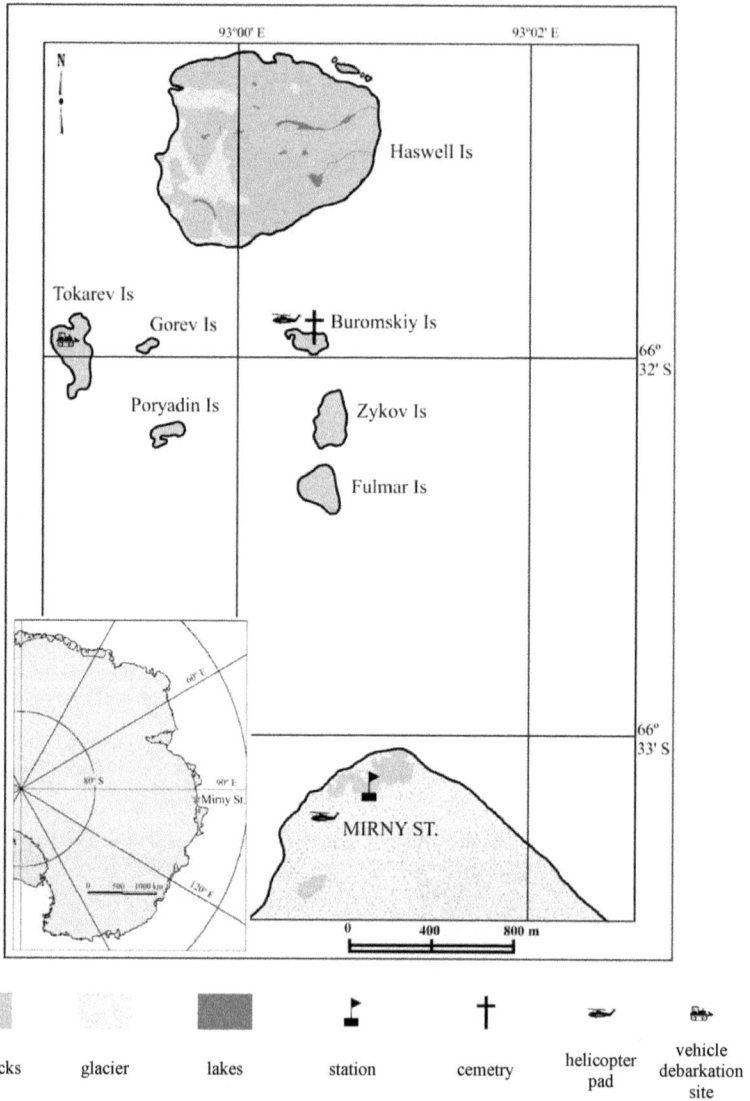

| soil, rocks | glacier | lakes | station | cemetry | helicopter pad | vehicle debarkation site |

Map 2: Boundaries of Antarctic Specially Protected Area 127, Haswell Island.

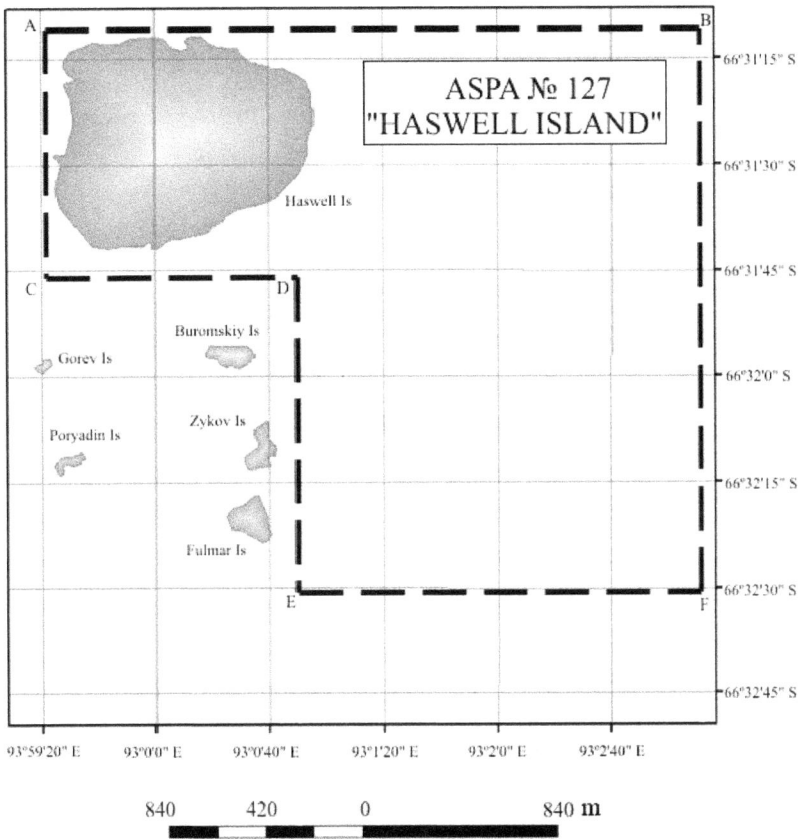

ASPA № 127
"HASWELL ISLAND"

Haswell Is

Buromskiy Is

Gorev Is

Zykov Is

Poryadin Is

Fulmar Is

A  B
C  D
E  F

66°31'15" S
66°31'30" S
66°31'45" S
66°32'0" S
66°32'15" S
66°32'30" S
66°32'45" S

93°59'20" E    93°0'0" E    93°0'40" E    93°1'20" E    93°2'0" E    93°2'40" E

840        420        0        840 m

Map 3: Location of breeding seabird colonies.

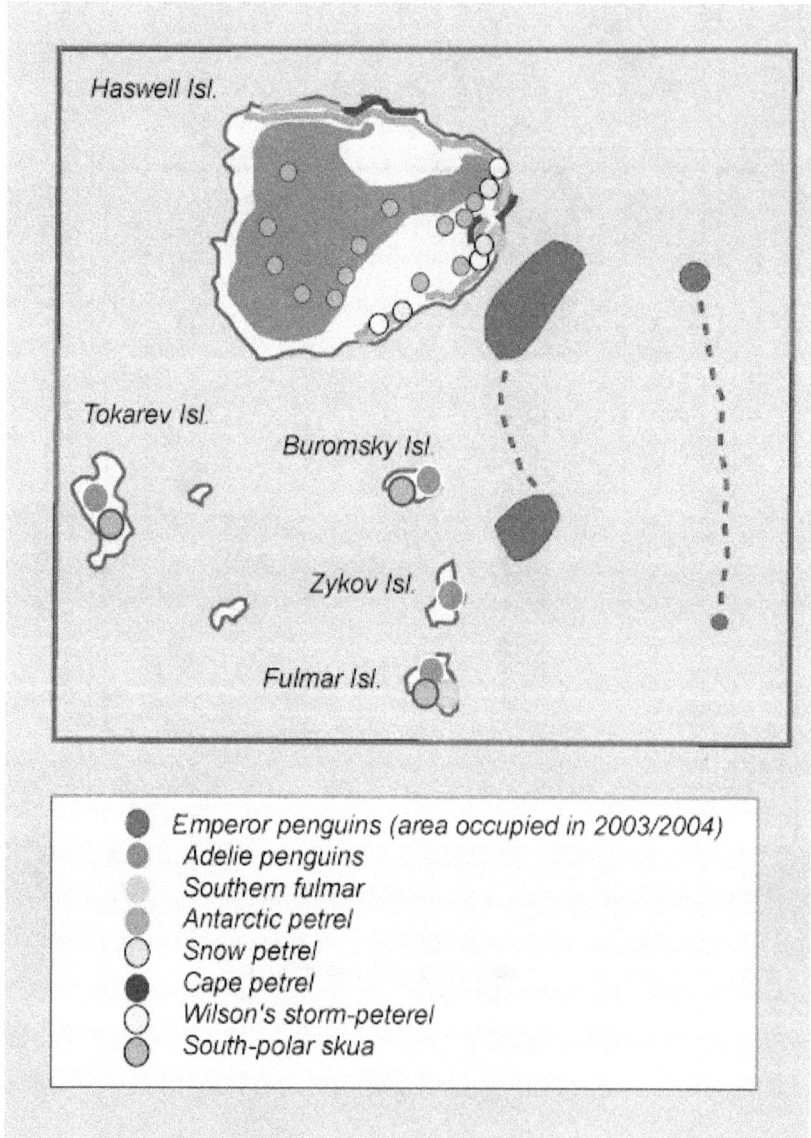

Haswell Isl.

Tokarev Isl.

Buromsky Isl.

Zykov Isl.

Fulmar Isl.

- Emperor penguins (area occupied in 2003/2004)
- Adelie penguins
- Southern fulmar
- Antarctic petrel
- Snow petrel
- Cape petrel
- Wilson's storm-peterel
- South-polar skua

Map 4: Topographic map of Haswell Island.

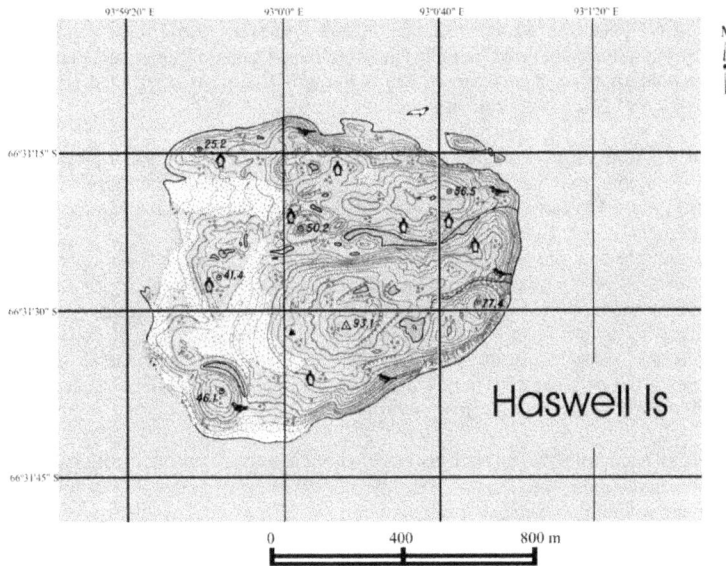

# Management Plan For
# Antarctic Specially Protected Area No. 131
# CANADA GLACIER, LAKE FRYXELL, TAYLOR VALLEY, VICTORIA LAND

## 1. Description of values to be protected

In 1985, an area of approximately 1 km² between the east side of Canada Glacier and Lake Fryxell was designated in Recommendation XIII-8 (1985) as SSSI No. 12, following a proposal by New Zealand on the grounds that it contained some of the richest plant growth (bryophytes and algae) in the McMurdo Dry Valleys. The Area is designated primarily to protect the site's scientific and ecological values.

The boundaries of the Area were increased by Measure 3 (1997) to include biologically rich areas that were previously excluded. The Area was redesignated by Decision 1 (2002) as Antarctic Specially Protected Area (ASPA) No. 131. and a revised Management Plan was adopted through Measure 1 (2006).

The Area comprises sloping ice-free ground with summer ponds and small meltwater streams draining from Canada Glacier towards Lake Fryxell. Most of the plant growth occurs in a wet area (referred to as 'the flush') close to the glacier in the central part of the Area. The composition and distribution of the moss, lichen, cyanobacteria, bacteria and algae communities in the Area are correlated closely with the water regime. Thus, hydrology and water quality are important to the values of the site.

The Area has been well-studied and documented, which adds to its scientific value. The vegetation communities, particularly the bryophytes, are vulnerable to disturbance by trampling and sampling. Damaged areas may be slow to recover. Sites damaged at known times in the past have been identified, which are valuable in that they provide one of the few areas in the McMurdo Dry Valleys where the long-term effects of disturbance, and recovery rates, can be measured.

The Area is of regional significance and remains of exceptional scientific value for ecological investigations. Increasing pressure from scientific, logistic and tourist activities in the region coupled with the vulnerability of the Area to disturbance through trampling, sampling, pollution or introduction of non-native species mean the values of the Area continue to require on-going protection.

## 2. Aims and objectives

Management of Canada Glacier aims to:

- avoid degradation of, or substantial risk to, the values of the Area by preventing unnecessary human disturbance to the Area;
- allow scientific research on the ecosystem and elements of the ecosystem while ensuring protection from over-sampling;

- allow other scientific research in the Area provided it is for compelling reasons which cannot be served elsewhere;
- prevent or minimise the introduction to the Area of alien plants, animals and microbes; and
- allow visits for management purposes in support of the aims of the management plan.

## 3. Management activities

The following management activities are to be undertaken to protect the values of the Area:

- Copies of this Management Plan, including maps of the Area, shall be made available at adjacent operational research stations and all of the research hut facilities located in the Taylor Valley that are within 20 km of the Area.
- Signs illustrating the location and boundaries of the Area, with clear statements of entry restrictions, shall be placed at appropriate locations on the boundary of the Area to help avoid inadvertent entry.
- Markers, signs or other structures erected within the Area for scientific or management purposes shall be secured and maintained in good condition and removed when no longer required.
- The Area shall be visited as necessary, and no less than once every five years, to assess whether it continues to serve the purposes for which it was designated and to ensure that management activities are adequate.
- National Antarctic Programmes operating in the Area shall consult together with a view to ensuring the above management activities are implemented.

## 4. Period of designation

Designated for an indefinite period.

## 5. Maps

Map A: Canada Glacier, Lake Fryxell, Taylor Valley, Regional Topographic Map.
Map specifications: Projection - Lambert conformal conic. Standard parallels - 1st 79° 18' 00" S; 2nd 76° 42' 00"S. Central Meridian - 162° 30' 00" E. Latitude of Origin - 78° 01' 16.2106" S. Spheroid - WGS84.

Map B: Canada Glacier, Lake Fryxell, Taylor Valley, Vegetation Density Map.
Map specifications are the same as those for Map A. Contours are derived from combining orthophotograph and Landsat images. Precise areas of moist ground associated with the flush are subject to variation seasonally and inter-annually.

**6. Description of the Area**

*6(i) Geographical coordinates, boundary markers and natural features*
Canada Glacier is situated in the Taylor Valley, in the McMurdo Dry Valleys. The designated Area encompasses most of the glacier forefront area on the east side of the lower Canada Glacier, on the north shore of Lake Fryxell (77° 37' S, 163° 03' E: Map A). It comprises gently to moderately sloping ice-free ground at an elevation of 20 m to 220 m with seasonal melt water ponds and streams draining Canada Glacier into Lake Fryxell.

The southern boundary of the Area is defined as the shoreline of Lake Fryxell, to the water's edge. This boundary extends northeast for approximately 1 km along the shoreline from where Canada Glacier meets Lake Fryxell (77° 37.20' S, 163° 3.64' E) to the southeast corner of the boundary which is marked with a cairn (77° 36.83' S, 163° 4.88' E) adjacent to a small island in Lake Fryxell. The island was once a part of a small peninsula extending into Lake Fryxell but recent lake level rise has turned it into an island (Map B). The peninsula was once marked by a large split rock surrounded by a circle of rocks which was a benchmark for the 1985 NZ survey of the original SSSI, but is no longer visible. A wooden post marking the Dry Valley Drilling Project Site 7 (1973) is still visible on the island.

A moraine ridge extending upslope from the southeast corner of the boundary in a northerly direction defines the eastern boundary of the Area. A cairn (77° 36.68' S, 163° 4.40' E) is located on a knoll on this ridge 450 m from the southeast corner of the boundary. The ridge dips sharply before joining the featureless slope of the main Taylor Valley wall. The northeast boundary corner of the Area is in this dip and is marked by a cairn (77° 36.43' S, 163° 3.73' E).

From the northeast boundary cairn, the northern boundary slopes gently upwards and west for 1.7 km to Canada Glacier, to the point where the stream flows from the glacier and snow field, through a conspicuously narrow gap in the moraine (77° 36.42' S, 162° 59.69' E).

The western boundary follows the glacier edge for about 1 km, down a slope of lateral moraine of fairly even gradient to the southwest corner of the boundary where the glacier meets the lake shore (77° 37.20' S, 163° 3.64' E).

The flush area at Canada Glacier is believed to be the largest high density area of vegetation in the McMurdo Dry Valleys (Map B). The summer water flow, in conjunction with the microtopography, has the greatest influence in determining where mosses, lichens, cyanobacteria, bacteria and algae grow. The glacier face also provides protection from destructive winds which could blow the mosses away in their freeze dry state and from abrasion from wind borne dust.

The flush is located close to the glacier edge. There are two main vegetated areas, separated to the north and south by a small, shallow pond (Map B). The flush area is gently sloping and very moist in summer with areas of wet ground, numerous small ponds and rivulets. The slopes above this area are drier, but vegetation colonises several small stream channels which extend parallel to the glacier from the upper boundary of the Area down to the flush. Undulating moraines assist accumulation of persistent snow patches on this slope, which may also provide moisture for plant growth. Stream channels, and associated vegetation, become less obvious with distance from the glacier (Map B). These slopes and the central flush are drained to the southeast by Canada Stream. Hydrological data collected from this stream measured the average discharge rate of Canada Stream when it was flowing as 26.41 L/s [min = 0.0 L/s and max = 190.4 L/s] from November 2009 to February 2010. The average water temperature over this time was 3.96 °C [min = -0.1 °C and max = 11.73 °C] (http://www.mcmlter.org/).

Four moss species have been identified from the flush area: *Bryum argenteum* (previously referred to as *Bryum subrotundifolium)* and *Hennediella heimii* (previously referred to as *Pottia heimii)* dominate, with rare occurrences of *Bryum pseudotriquetrum* and *Syntrichia sarconeurum* (formerly known as *Sarconeurum glaciale)*. *B. argenteum* occurs mainly in areas of flowing water and seepage. Where water is flowing, a high proportion of this moss has epiphytic *Nostoc* communities associated with it. Towards the edges of the flowing water zones or on higher ground, *Hennediella heimii* dominates. Sporophytes of *Hennediella heimii* are found at this location and may be the most southerly recorded fruiting location for a moss.

Lichen growth in the Area is inconspicuous, but the epilithic lichens, *Carbonea vorticosa, Sarcogyne privigna, Lecanora expectans, Rhizoplaca melanophthalma* and *Caloplaca citrina* may be found in a small area near the outflow of the pond near Canada Glacier. Chasmoendolithic lichens also occur in many boulders throughout the flush area.

Over 37 species of freshwater algae and cyanobacteria have been described at the site. The upper part of Canada Stream superficially appears sparse but encrusting communities dominated by cyanobacterium grow on the sides and undersides of stones and boulders. The green alga *Prasiola calophylla* and cyanobacterium *Chamaesiphon subglobosus* have been observed only in this upper part of the stream. *Prasiola calophylla,* growing in dense green ribbons beneath stones in the stream, is generally only apparent when stones are overturned. Cyanobacterial mats, comprising a diverse assemblage of species (including *Oscillatoria, Pseudanabaena, Leptolyngbya, Phormidium, Gloeocapsa, Calothrix* and *Nostoc*) are extensive in the middle and lower reaches of the stream and more diverse than those in the upper stream. Mucilaginous colonies of *Nostoc commune* dominate standing water in the central flush and grow epiphytically on mosses in the wetted margins of water courses, while cyanobacterial mats cover much of the mineral fines and gravels in flowing sections. The filamentous green alga *Binuclearia* is found streaming out in the flow in the middle reaches of the stream. The lower stream is similar in floral composition to the upper, although the algae *Tribonema elegans* and *Binuclearia* have been reported as abundant, but *Prasiola calophylla* is absent. *Tribonema elegans* is rarely encountered in this region of Antarctica.

Invertebrates from six phyla have been described in the Area: the three main groups are Rotifera, Nematoda and Tardigrada, with Protozoa, Platyhelminthes, and Arthropoda also present.

The Canada flush vegetation has been described as profuse but lacking in diversity, when compared to other botanically rich sites in Antarctica. This may be attributable at least in part to the oligotrophic nature of the site. Water flowing through the stream is similar to glacial ice melt, with conductivity in December 2010 of close to 30 µS cm$^{-1}$ from the point where it left the glacier to the delta where it enters the lake. The prevalence of nitrogen fixing cyanobacteria (*Nostoc* and *Calothrix* species) further supports the view of a low nutrient status.

Based on the Environmental Domain Analysis for Antarctica (Resolution 3 (2008)), Canada Glacier is located within Environment S *McMurdo South Victoria Land geologic.*

Evidence of past human activity is noticeable within the Area. Within the flush area, damage to the vegetation including paths and footprints and sites of experimental removal of core samples and larger clumps from moss turfs are visible. A number of old markers are also present in the flush area.

A plastic greenhouse was erected within the Area close to the flush from 1979 to 1983 for research and experimental growth of garden vegetables. The structure was removed at the end of each season. In 1983 it was destroyed by a winter storm. Remains of the greenhouse found in the Area have since been removed.

Near the flush area, the first site of the New Zealand hut at Canada Glacier consisted of paths marked by lines of rocks, areas cleared for use as campsites, an old helicopter pad, and several low rock structures. A series of at least four shallow pits (~1 m in depth) were also dug close to the site. This site was relocated to a second site in 1989 and the first hut site was remediated. The second hut site comprised two small buildings, several new campsites, and a helicopter pad. The buildings were removed completely in the 1995–96 season. However, the helicopter pad remains and is the only helicopter landing site in the Area. This camp site area is still the preferred camping site in the Area (Map B).

A weir is present on Canada Stream (see Section 6(iii)). A path from the Lake Fryxell Camp Facilities Zone is located between the lake shore and the weir on Canada Stream (Map B). Another path exists between the designated camp site and the Canada Glacier edge, crossing a moist area of plant growth, but is not indicated on the map. An access route is also located between Lake Hoare Camp Facilities Zone and Lake Fryxell Camp Facilities Zone running just above the northern boundary (Maps A and B).

*6(ii) Special zones within the Area*
None.

*6(iii) Location of structures within and adjacent to the Area*
A rock weir was constructed in the constricted part of Canada Stream in the 1981/1982 season and was fully removed at the end of the season. In 1990 a more substantial weir and 9-inch Parshall flume were installed nearby (Maps B). The flume is made of black fibreglass. The weir consists of polyester sandbags filled with alluvium from near the stream channel. Areas disturbed during construction were restored and after one season were not evident. The upstream side of the weir is lined with vinyl-coated nylon. A notch has been built into the weir for relief in case of high flow. Clearance of seasonal snow from the channel has been necessary to prevent water from backing up at the weir. Data logging instrumentation and batteries are stored in a plywood crate located nearby on the north side of the stream. The weir is maintained by the McMurdo Dry Valleys Long Term Ecological Research project.

Three cairns mark the Area boundaries.

The Lake Fryxell Camp Facilities Zone (USA) is located 1.5 km to the east of the Area (20 m asl) midway along Lake Fryxell on the north side of the lake. The F6 Camp Facilities Zone is located approximately 10 km to the east of the Area on the south side of Lake Fryxell. The Lake Hoare Camp Facilities Zone (USA) is located 3 km to the west of the Area (65 m asl) on the western side of Canada Glacier at the base of the glacier on the north side of Lake

Hoare. The Taylor Valley Visitor Zone is located to the south of the Area at the terminus of Canada Glacier (Map A).

*6(iv) Location of other protected areas in the vicinity*
The nearest protected areas to Canada Glacier are:

- Linnaeus Terrace, Asgard Range (ASPA No. 138) 47 km west in the Wright Valley; and
- Barwick and Balham Valleys, Southern Victoria Land (ASPA No. 123) 50 km to the northwest (Map A, Inset).

## 7. Terms and conditions for entry Permits

Entry into the Area is prohibited except in accordance with a Permit issued by an appropriate national authority. Conditions for issuing a Permit to enter the Area are that:
- it is issued for compelling scientific reasons that cannot be served elsewhere, or for reasons essential to the management of the Area;
- the actions permitted will not jeopardise the ecological or scientific values of the Area;
- access·to any zone marked as possessing medium or higher vegetation density (Map B) should be carefully considered and special conditions to access such areas should be attached to the Permit;
- any management activities are in support of the aims of the Management Plan;
- the actions permitted are in accordance with the Management Plan;
- the Permit, or an authorized copy, shall be carried within the Area;
- a visit report shall be supplied to the authority named in the Permit; and
- the Permit shall be issued for a stated period.

*7(i) Access to and movement within or over the Area*
Access to the Area shall be by foot or by helicopter. Vehicles are prohibited within the Area and all movement within the Area should be on foot.

Pedestrians travelling up or down the valley shall not enter the Area without a Permit. Permitted visitors entering the Area are encouraged to keep to established paths where possible. Visitors should avoid walking on visible vegetation or through stream beds. Care should be exercised when walking in areas of moist ground, where foot traffic can easily damage sensitive soils, plant, algal and bacteria communities, and degrade water quality: walk around such areas, on ice or rocky ground, and step on larger stones when stream crossing is unavoidable. Care should also be taken around salt-encrusted vegetation in drier areas, which can be inconspicuous. Pedestrian traffic should be kept to the minimum necessary consistent with the objectives of any permitted activities and every reasonable effort should be made to minimise effects.

Where possible, helicopters should land at existing landing sites in nearby Facilities Zones and the Visitor Zone. Helicopter access to the Area should be approached from south of the line marked on Map B. Helicopters shall land only at the designated landing site (163° 02.88' E, 77° 36.97' S: Map B). Over flight of the Area should generally be avoided. Within the Area overflights less than 100 m Above Ground Level (AGL) north of the line indicated on

Map B are prohibited. Exceptions to these flight restrictions will only be granted for an exceptional scientific or management purpose and must be specifically authorised by Permit. Use of helicopter smoke grenades within the Area is prohibited unless absolutely necessary for safety, and then these should be retrieved. Visitors, pilots, air crew, or passengers en route elsewhere on helicopters, are prohibited from moving on foot beyond the immediate vicinity of the designated landing and camping site unless specifically authorised by a Permit.

*7(ii) Activities which may be conducted in the Area*
- Scientific research that will not jeopardise the ecosystem of the Area;
- Essential management activities, including monitoring and inspection.

In view of the importance of the water regime to the ecosystem, activities should be conducted so that disturbance to water courses and water quality is minimised. Activities occurring outside of the Area (e.g. on the Canada Glacier) which may have the potential to affect water quantity and quality should be planned and conducted taking possible downstream effects into account. Those conducting activities within the Area should also be mindful of any downstream effects within the Area and on endorheic Lake Fryxell.

*7(iii) Installation, modification or removal of structures*
No structures are to be erected within the Area, or scientific equipment installed, except for compelling scientific or management reasons as specified in a permit. All markers, structures or scientific equipment installed in the Area must be authorised by a Permit and clearly identified by country, name of the principal investigator, year of installation and date of expected removal. All such items should be free of organisms, propagules (e.g. seeds, eggs) and non-sterile soil, and be made of materials that pose minimal risk of contamination of the Area. Removal of specific structures or equipment for which the Permit has expired shall be a condition of the Permit. Permanent structures or installations are prohibited.

*7(iv) Location of field camps*
Nearby Facilities Zones outside of the Area should be used as a base for work in the Area (Map A). Camping at the designated campsite (Map B) may be permitted to meet specific essential scientific or management needs.

*7(v) Restrictions on materials and organisms which may be brought into the Area*
No living animals, plant material or microorganisms shall be deliberately introduced into the Area and precautions listed in paragraph 7(ix) below shall be taken against accidental introductions. No herbicides or pesticides shall be brought into the Area. Any other chemicals, including radio-nuclides or stable isotopes, which may be introduced for scientific or management purposes specified in the Permit, shall be removed from the Area at or before the conclusion of the activity for which the Permit was granted. Fuel or other chemicals shall not be stored in the Area, unless required for essential purposes connected with the activity for which the Permit has been granted, and must be contained within an emergency cache authorized by an appropriate authority. All materials introduced shall be for a stated period only, be removed at or before the conclusion of that stated period, and be stored and handled so that risk of their introduction into the environment is minimised.

*7(vi) Taking or harmful interference with native flora or fauna*
Taking of, or harmful interference with, native flora and fauna is prohibited, except in accordance with a separate permit issued in accordance with Annex II to the Protocol on Environmental Protection to the Antarctic Treaty. Where taking or harmful interference with

animals is involved this should, as a minimum standard, be in accordance with the SCAR Code of Conduct for the Use of Animals for Scientific Purposes in Antarctica.

*7(vii) The collection or removal of materials not imported by the Permit holder*
Material may be collected or removed from the Area only in accordance with a Permit and should be limited to the minimum necessary to meet scientific or management needs. Similarly, sampling is to be carried out using techniques which minimise disturbance to the Area as well as duplication. Material of human origin likely to compromise the values of the Area, and which was not brought into the Area by the Permit holder or otherwise authorised, may be removed unless the impact of removal is likely to be greater than leaving the material in situ: if the impact of removal is likely to be greater than leaving the material in situ the appropriate authority should be notified and approval obtained.

*7(viii) Disposal of waste*
All wastes, including all human wastes, shall be removed from the Area.

*7(ix) Measures that may be necessary to continue to meet the aims and objectives of the Management Plan*
Permits may be granted to enter the Area to:
- carry out biological monitoring and Area inspection activities, which may involve the collection of a small number of samples or data for analysis or review;
- erect or maintain signposts, structures or scientific equipment;
- carry out protective measures;

Any specific sites of long-term monitoring shall be appropriately marked on site and on maps of the Area. A GPS position should be obtained for sites of long-term monitoring and scientific sampling for lodgement with the Antarctic Master Directory system through the appropriate national authority. If appropriate, metadata should also be provided for the Antarctic Master Directory system through the appropriate national authority.

To help maintain the ecological and scientific values of the plant communities found at the Area visitors shall take special precautions against introductions. Of particular concern are microbial or vegetation introductions sourced from soils at other Antarctic sites, including stations, or from regions outside Antarctica. To minimise the risk of introductions, visitors shall thoroughly clean footwear and any equipment to be used in the area particularly camping and sampling equipment and markers before entering the Area.

*7(x) Requirements for reports*
The principal permit holder for each visit to the Area shall submit a report to the appropriate national authority as soon as practicable, and no later than six months after the visit has been completed. Such reports should include, as appropriate, the information identified in the visit report form contained in the Guide to the Preparation of Management Plans for Antarctic Specially Protected Areas.

If appropriate, the national authority should also forward a copy of the visit report to the Party that proposed the Management Plan, to assist in managing the Area and reviewing the Management Plan. Parties should maintain a record of such activities and report them in the Annual Exchange of Information. Parties should, wherever possible, deposit originals or copies of such original visit reports in a publicly accessible archive to maintain a record of usage, for the purpose of any review of the management plan and in organising the scientific use of the Area.

## 8. Bibliography

Broady, P.A. 1982. Taxonomy and ecology of algae in a freshwater stream in Taylor Valley, Victoria Land, Antarctica. Archivs fur Hydrobiologia 32 (Supplement 63 (3), Algological Studies): 331-349.

Conovitz, P.A., McKnight, D.M., MacDonald, L.H., Fountain, A.G. and House, H.R. 1998. Hydrologic processes influencing stream flow variation in Fryxell Basin, Antarctica. Ecosystem Processes in a Polar Desert: The McMurdo Dry Valleys, Antarctica. Antarctic Research Series 72: 93-108.

Green, T.G.A., Seppelt, R.D. and Schwarz, A-M.J. 1992. Epilithic lichens on the floor of the Taylor Valley, Ross Dependency, Antarctica. Lichenologist 24(1): 57-61.

Lewis, K.J., Fountain, A.G. and Dana, G.L. 1999. How important is terminus cliff melt? A study of the Canada Glacier terminus, Taylor Valley, Antarctica. Global and Planetary Change 22(1-4): 105-115.

Lewis, K.J., Fountain, A.G. and Dana, G.L. 1998. Surface energy balance and meltwater production for a Dry Valley glacier, Taylor Valley, Antarctica. International Symposium on Antarctica and Global Change: Interactions and Impacts, Hobart, Tasmania, Australia, July 13-18, 1997. Papers. Edited by W.F. Budd, et al; Annals of glaciology, Vol.27, p.603-609. United Kingdom.

McKnight, D.M. and Tate, C.M. 1997. Canada Stream: A glacial meltwater stream in Taylor Valley, South Victoria Land, Antarctica. Journal of the North American Benthological Society 16(1): 14-17.

Pannewitz, S., Green, T.G.A., Scheiddegger, C., Schlensog, M. and Schroeter, B. 2003. Activity pattern of the moss *Hennediella heimii* (Hedw.) Zand. in the Dry Valleys, Southern Victoria Land, Antarctica during the mid-austral summer. Polar Biology 26(8): 545-551.

Seppelt, R.D. and Green, T.G.A. 1998. A bryophyte flora for Southern Victoria Land, Antarctica. New Zealand Journal of Botany 36: 617-635.

Seppelt, R.D., Green, T.G.A., Schwarz, A-M.J. and Frost, A. 1992. Extreme southern locations for moss sporophytes in Antarctica. Antarctic Science 4: 37-39.

Seppelt, R.D., Turk, R., Green, T.G.A., Moser, G., Pannewitz, S., Sancho, L.G. and Schroeter, B. 2010. Lichen and moss communities of Botany Bay, Granite Harbour, Ross Sea, Antarctica. Antarctic Science 22(6): 691-702.

Schwarz, A.-M. J., Green, J.D., Green, T.G.A. and Seppelt, R.D. 1993. Invertebrates associated with moss communities at Canada Glacier, southern Victoria Land, Antarctica. Polar Biology 13(3): 157-162.

Schwarz, A-M. J., Green, T.G.A. and Seppelt, R.D. 1992. Terrestrial vegetation at Canada Glacier, South Victoria Land, Antarctica. Polar Biology 12: 397-404.

Sjoling, S. and Cowan, D.A. 2000. Detecting human bacterial contamination in Antarctic soils. Polar Biology 23(9): 644-650.

Skotnicki, M.L., Ninham, J.A. and Selkirk, P.M. 1999. Genetic diversity and dispersal of the moss *Sarconeurum glaciale* on Ross Island, East Antarctica. Molecular Ecology 8(5): 753-762.

Strandtmann, R.W. and George, J.E. 1973. Distribution of the Antarctic mite *Stereotydeus mollis* Womersley and Strandtmann in South Victoria Land. Antarctic Journal of the USA 8:209-211.

Vandal, G.M., Mason, R.P., McKnight, D.M. and Fitzgerald, W. 1998. Mercury speciation and distribution in a polar desert lake (Lake Hoare, Antarctica) and two glacial meltwater streams. Science of the Total Environment 213(1-3): 229-237.

Map A - Canada Glacier, Lake Fryxell, Taylor Valley, Antarctic Specially Protected Area 131: Regional Topographic Map

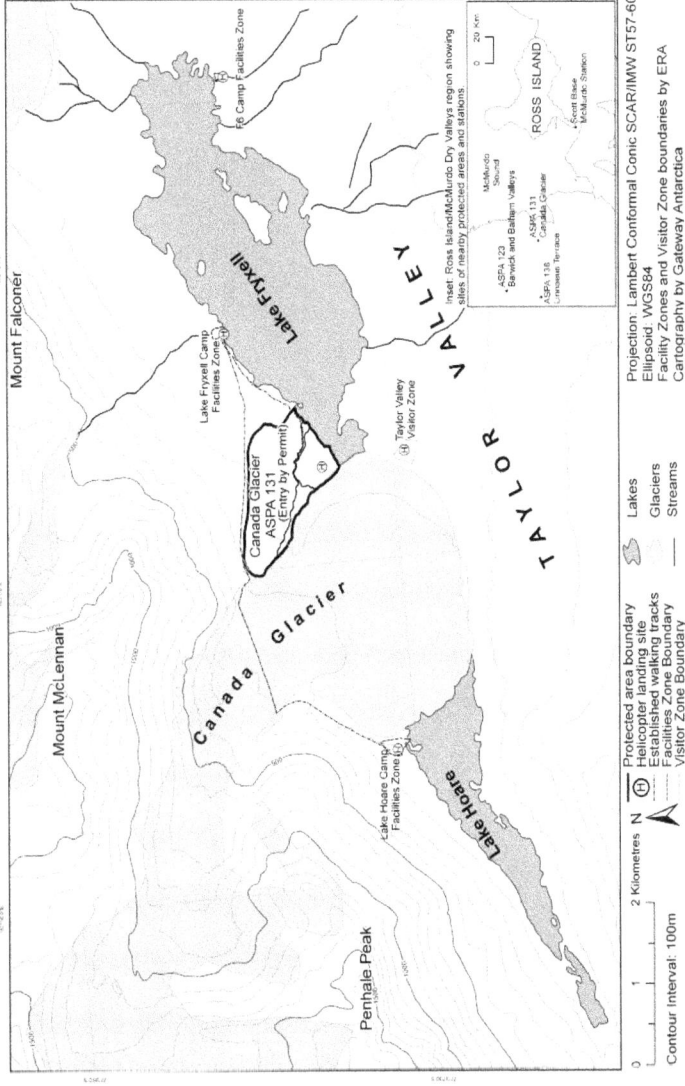

Inset: Ross Island/McMurdo Dry Valleys region showing sites of nearby protected areas and stations.

ROSS ISLAND

McMurdo Sound

ASPA 123
Barwick and Balham Valleys

ASPA 131
Canada Glacier

ASPA 138
Linnaeus Terrace

Scott Base
McMurdo Station

0          20 Km

Projection: Lambert Conformal Conic SCAR/IMW ST57-60
Ellipsoid: WGS84
Facility Zones and Visitor Zone boundaries by ERA
Cartography by Gateway Antarctica

Mount Falconer

F6 Camp Facilities Zone

Lake Fryxell

Lake Fryxell Camp
Facilities Zone

Canada Glacier
ASPA 131
(Entry by Permit)

Taylor Valley
Visitor Zone

T A Y L O R   V A L L E Y

Mount McLennan

C a n a d a     G l a c i e r

Lake Hoare Camp
Facilities Zone

Lake Hoare

Penhale Peak

N

0          1          2 Kilometres

Contour Interval: 100m

Lakes
Glaciers
Streams

Protected area boundary
Helicopter landing site
Established walking tracks
Facilities Zone Boundary
Visitor Zone Boundary

# ASPA No 131 - Canada Glacier

Map B - Canada Glacier, Lake Fryxell, Taylor Valley, Antarctic Specially Protected Area 131: Vegetation Density Map

**Vegetation Density**
(within ASPA only)

- Dense > 25%
- Medium 1-25%
- Scattered 0.01-1%
- Very Low / Bare <0.01%
- Ice
- Pond or Lake

**Legend**

- Preferred walking routes
- Protected Area Boundary
- Designated helicopter pad
- Designated camp site (see text)
- Mummified Seals
- Cairn

Canada Glacier ASPA 131
(Entry by Permit)

Lake Fryxell

LTER Weir

Former First
Hut Site

Former Second
Hut Site

Canada Glacier

Overflight prohibited below 100m (328ft)
above ground level north of the line

0    500
Metres

Contour interval: 5m

Projection: Lambert conformal conic   Spheroid: WGS84

Vegetation Survey: Dept of Biological Sciences, University of Waikato   Cartography: Gateway Antarctica

# Management Plan for

# Antarctic Specially Protected Area (ASPA) No. 149

# CAPE SHIRREFF AND SAN TELMO ISLAND, LIVINGSTON ISLAND, SOUTH SHETLAND ISLANDS

**Introduction**

The Cape Shirreff Antarctic Specially Protected Area (ASPA) is situated on the northern coast of Livingston Island, South Shetland Islands, at 62°27'30"S, 60°47'17"W, and is approximately 9.7 km² in area. The primary reason for designation of the Area is to protect the biota present within the Area, in particular the large and diverse seabird and pinniped populations which are the subject of long term scientific monitoring. Krill fishing is carried out within the foraging range of these species. Cape Shirreff is thus a key site for ecosystem monitoring, which helps to meet the objectives of the Convention on the Conservation of Antarctic Marine Living Resources (CCAMLR). The Area contains the largest Antarctic fur seal (*Arctocephalus gazella*) breeding colony in the Antarctic Peninsula region and is the most southerly colony where fur seal reproduction, demography and diet can be monitored. Palynoflora discovered within the Area are of significant scientific interest. The Area also contains numerous items of historical and archaeological value, mostly associated with sealing activities in the 19th Century. The Area was originally designated following proposals by Chile and the United States of America and adopted through Recommendation IV-11 [1966, Specially Protected Area (SPA) No. 11]. The Area was re-designated as Site of Special Scientific Interest (SSSI) No. 32 through Recommendation XV-7 (1989). The Area was designated as CCAMLR Ecosystem Monitoring Program (CEMP) Site No. 2 through CCAMLR Conservation Measure 82/XIII (1994); protection was continued by Conservation Measure (CM) 91/02 (2004) and boundaries were extended through Measure 2 (2005) to include a larger marine component and to incorporate plant fossil sites. Conservation Measure 91-02 was lapsed in November 2009 and protection of Cape Shirreff continues as ASPA No. 149 (SC-CCAMLR-XXVIII, Annex 4, para 5.29).

## 1. Description of values to be protected

Cape Shirreff (62°27'30" S, 60°47'17" W, a peninsula of approximately 3.1 km²), Livingston Island, South Shetland Islands, was originally designated as Specially Protected Area (SPA) No. 11 through Recommendation IV-11 (1966). In the light of results from the first census of Pinnipedia carried out in the South Shetland Islands (Aguayo and Torres, 1966), Chile considered special protection for the site was needed. Formal proposal of the SPA was made by the United States (US). The Area included the ice-free ground of the Cape Shirreff peninsula north of the Livingston Island ice cap margin. Values protected under the original designation included the diversity of plant and animal life, many invertebrates, a substantial population of southern elephant seals (*Mirounga leonina*) and a small colony of Antarctic fur seals (*Arctocephalus gazella*).

Following designation, the size of the Cape Shirreff Antarctic fur seal colony increased to a level at which biological research could be undertaken without threatening continued colony growth. A survey of the South Shetland Islands and the Antarctic Peninsula identified Cape Shirreff – San Telmo Island as the most suitable site to monitor Antarctic fur seal colonies potentially affected by fisheries around the South Shetland Islands. In order to accommodate the monitoring program, the SPA was redesignated as Site of Special Scientific Interest (SSSI) No. 32 through Recommendation XV-7 (1989) following a joint proposal by Chile, the United Kingdom and the US. Designation was on the grounds that the "presence of both Antarctic fur seal and penguin colonies, and of krill fisheries within the foraging range of these species, make this a critical site for inclusion in the ecosystem monitoring network being established to help meet the objectives of the Convention on the Conservation of Antarctic Marine Living Resources (CCAMLR). The purpose of the designation is to allow planned research and monitoring to proceed, while avoiding or reducing, to the greatest extent possible, other activities which could interfere with or affect the results of the research and monitoring program or alter the natural features of the Site". The boundaries were enlarged to include San

Telmo Island and associated nearby islets. Following a proposal prepared by Chile and the US, the Area was subsequently designated as CCAMLR Ecosystem Monitoring Program (CEMP) Site No. 2 through CCAMLR Conservation Measure 82/XIII (1994), with boundaries identical to SSSI No. 32. Protection of Cape Shirreff as a CCAMLR Ecosystem Monitoring Program (CEMP) was continued by Conservation Measure (CM) 91/02 (2004).

The boundaries of the Area were further enlarged through Measure 2 (2005) to include a larger marine component and to incorporate two new sites where plant fossils were discovered in 2001 (Maps 1 and 2). The designated Area (9.7 km$^2$) comprises the entire Cape Shirreff peninsula north of the Livingston Island permanent ice cap, the adjacent part of the Livingston Island permanent ice cap where the fossil discoveries were made in 2001, the San Telmo Island group, and the surrounding and intervening marine area enclosed within 100 m of the coast of the Cape Shirreff peninsula and of the outer islets of the San Telmo Island group. The boundary extends from the San Telmo Island group to the south of Mercury Bluff.

Conservation Measure 91-02 lapsed in November 2009, with the protection of Cape Shirreff continuing under the management plan for ASPA No. 149 (SC-CCAMLR-XXVIII, Annex 4, para 5.29). The change was made with the aim of harmonizing protection under both CCAMLR and the Protocol on Environmental Protection to the Antarctic Treaty (The Protocol) and to eliminate any potential duplication in management requirements and procedures.

The current Management Plan reaffirms the exceptional scientific and monitoring values associated with the large and diverse populations of seabirds and pinnipeds which breed within the Area, and in particular those of the Antarctic fur seal colony. The Antarctic fur seal colony is the largest in the Antarctic Peninsula region and is the most southerly that is large enough to study growth, survival, diet, and reproduction parameters: it numbered around 21,000 individuals in 2002 (Hucke-Gaete *et al.* 2004). Monitoring of the Antarctic fur seal colony began in 1965 (Aguayo and Torres 1966, 1967) and seasonal data are available from 1991, making this one of the longest continuous Antarctic fur seal monitoring programs. As part of the CCAMLR Ecosystem Monitoring Program (CEMP), monitoring was established to detect and avoid possible adverse effects of fisheries on dependant species such as pinnipeds and seabirds, as well as target species such as Antarctic krill (*Euphausia superba*). Long-term studies are assessing and monitoring the survival, feeding ecology, growth, condition, reproduction, behavior, vital rates, and abundance of pinnipeds and seabirds that breed within the Area. Data from these studies will be evaluated in context with environmental and other biological data and fisheries statistics to help identify possible cause-effect relationships between fisheries and pinniped and seabird populations.

In 2001-02 imprints of megaflora were discovered in rocks incorporated within moraines of the Livingston Island glacier (Palma-Heldt *et al.* 2004, 2007) (Map 2). The fossiliferous rocks were found to contain two distinct palynological assemblages, indicative of different time periods and climatic conditions, and formed part of a study into the geological history of Antarctica and Gondwana. Studies of microbial research were carried out within the Area in 2009-10, to assess the influence of microhabitats on microbial diversity and metabolic capacity (INACH 2010).

The original values of the protected area associated with the plant and invertebrate communities cannot be confirmed as primary reasons for special protection of the Area because there is a lack of data available describing the communities.

The Area contains a number of pre -1958 human artifacts. HSM No.59, a rock cairn commemorating those who died when the Spanish ship San Telmo sank in the Drake Passage in 1819, lies within the Area. Remnants of a 19th Century sealing community also can be found within the Area.

## 2. Aims and objectives

Management at Cape Shirreff aims to:

- avoid degradation of, or substantial risk to, the values of the Area by preventing unnecessary human disturbance;

- avoid activities that would harm or interfere with CEMP research and monitoring activities;

- allow scientific research on the ecosystem and physical environment in the Area associated with the CEMP;

- allow other scientific research within the Area provided it is for compelling reasons which cannot be served elsewhere and provided it will not compromise the values for which the Area is protected;
- allow archaeological and historical research and measures for artifact protection, while protecting the historic artifacts present within the Area from unnecessary destruction, disturbance, or removal;
- minimize the possibility of introduction of alien plants, animals and microbes to the Area; and
- allow visits for management purposes in support of the aims of the management plan.

### 3. Management activities

The following management activities shall be undertaken to protect the values of the Area:

- Copies of this management plan, including maps of the Area, shall be made available at the following locations:

  1. accommodation facilities at Cape Shirreff;
  2. Saint Kliment Ohridski Station (Bulgaria), Hurd Peninsula, Livingston Island;
  3. Arturo Prat Station (Chile), Discovery Bay/Chile Bay, Greenwich Island; and
  4. Base Juan Carlos I (Spain), Hurd Peninsula, Livingston Island.

- A sign showing the location and boundaries of the Area with clear statements of entry restrictions should be placed at Módulo Beach, Cape Shirreff, to help avoid inadvertent entry;
- Markers, signs or other structures erected within the Area for scientific or management purposes shall be secured and maintained in good condition;
- National Antarctic programs operating within the Area should maintain a record of all new markers, signs and structures erected within the Area;
- Visits shall be made as necessary (no less than once every five years) to assess whether the Area continues to serve the purposes for which it was designated and to ensure management and maintenance measures are adequate;
- National Antarctic programs operating in the region shall consult together for the purpose of ensuring that the above provisions are implemented.

### 4. Period of designation

Designated for an indefinite period.

### 5. Maps and photographs

**Map 1:** Cape Shirreff and San Telmo Island, ASPA No. 149, in relation to Livingston Island, showing the location of Base Juan Carlos I (Spain) and Saint Kliment Ohridiski Station (Bulgaria), and the location of the closest protected area, Byers Peninsula (ASPA No. 126), also on Livingston Island. Map specifications: Projection: Lambert Conformal Conic; Standard parallels: 1st 60°00' S; 2nd 64°00' S; Central Meridian: 60°45' W; Latitude of Origin: 62°00' S; Spheroid: WGS84; Horizontal accuracy: < ±200 m. Bathymetric contour interval 50 m and 500 m; vertical accuracy unknown. Data sources: land features from SCAR Antarctic Digital Database v. 4.1 (2007); bathymetry supplied by the Antarctic Marine Living Resources (AMLR) Program, NOAA, US (2002).

Inset: the location of Map 1 in relation to the South Shetland Islands and the Antarctic Peninsula.

**Map 2:** Cape Shirreff and San Telmo Island, ASPA No. 149, protected area boundary and access guidelines. Map specifications as per Map 1, except the vertical contour interval is 10 m and the horizontal accuracy is expected to be greater than ±5 m. Data source: from digital data supplied by Instituto Antártico Chileno (INACH) (2002) (Torres *et al.* 2001).

**Map 3:** Cape Shirreff, ASPA No. 149: breeding wildlife and human features. Map specifications and data source as per Map 2 with the exception of the vertical contour interval, which is 5 m.

### 6. Description of the Area

*6(i) Geographical coordinates, boundary markers and natural features*

*Boundaries and coordinates*

Cape Shirreff (62°27'30" S, 60°47'17" W) is situated on the northern coast of Livingston Island, the second largest of the South Shetland Islands, between Barclay Bay and Hero Bay (Map 1). The cape lies at the northern extremity of an ice-free peninsula of low-lying, hilly relief. To the west of the peninsula lies Shirreff Cove, to the east Black Point, and to the south lies the permanent ice cap of Livingston Island. The peninsula has an area of approximately 3.1 $km^2$, being 2.6 km from north to south and ranging from 0.5 to 1.5 km from east to west. The interior of the peninsula comprises a series of raised beaches and both rounded and steep-sided hills, rising to a high point at Toqui Hill (82 m) in the central northern part of the peninsula. The western coast is formed by almost continuous cliffs 10 to 15 m high, while the eastern coast has extensive sand and gravel beaches.

A small group of low-lying, rocky islets lie approximately 1200 m west of the Cape Shirreff peninsula, forming the western enclosure of Shirreff Cove. San Telmo Island, the largest of the group, is 950 m in length, up to 200 m in width, and of approximately 0.1 $km^2$ in area. There is a sand and pebble beach on the southeastern coast of San Telmo Island, separated from a sand beach to the north by two irregular cliffs and narrow pebble beaches.

The designated Area comprises the entire Cape Shirreff peninsula north of the permanent Livingston Island ice cap, the San Telmo Island group, and the surrounding and intervening marine area (Map 2). The marine boundary encloses an area that extends 100 m from, and parallel to, the outer coastline of the Cape Shirreff peninsula and the San Telmo Island group. In the north, the marine boundary extends from the northwestern extremity of the Cape Shirreff peninsula to the southwest for 1.4 km to the San Telmo Island group, enclosing the intervening sea within Shirreff Cove. The western boundary extends southwards for 1.8 km from 62°28' S to a small island near 62°29' S, passing around the western shore of this small island and proceeding a further 1.2 km south-east to the shore of Livingston Island at 62°29'30" S, which is approximately 300 m south of Mercury Bluff. From this point on the coast, the southern boundary extends approximately 300 m due east to 60°49' W, from where it proceeds in a northeasterly direction parallel to the coast for approximately 2 km to the ice sheet margin at 60°47' W. The southern boundary then extends due east for 600 m to the eastern coast. The eastern boundary is marine, following the eastern coastline 100 m from the shore. The boundary encompasses an area of 9.7 $km^2$ (Map 2).

*Climate*

Meteorological records for Cape Shirreff have been collected for a number of years by Chilean and US scientists and are currently recorded by instruments mounted on the Cape Shirreff Field Station buildings. During recent summer seasons (Nov – Feb inclusive, 2005-06 to 2009-10) the mean air temperature recorded at Cape Shirreff was 1.84°C (AMLR Program data, 2005-2010). The maximum air temperature recorded during this period was 19.9°C and the minimum was -8.1°C. Wind speed averaged 5.36 m/s and the maximum recorded wind speed reached 20.1 m/s. Wind direction over the data collection period was predominantly from the west, followed by WNW and ENE. Meteorological data are available for two recent winters, with mean daily temperature for Jun-Aug 2007 of -6.7°C with a minimum of -20.6°C and a maximum of +0.9°C, and a mean daily temperature for Jun-Sep 2009 of -5.8°C with a minimum of -15.2°C and a maximum of +1.9°C.

Precipitation recorded in summer seasons (21 Dec – 24 Feb, 1998-2001) ranged from 56.0 mm (recorded on 36 days in 2000-01) to 59.6 mm (recorded on 43 days in 1998-99) (Goebel *et al.* 2000; 2001). The peninsula is snow-covered for much of the year, but is mostly snow-free by the end of the summer.

*Geology, geomorphology and soils*

Cape Shirreff is composed of porphyritic basaltic lavas and minor volcanic breccias of approximately 450 m in thickness (Smellie *et al.* 1996). The rocks at Cape Shirreff are deformed into open folds, which trend in a NW-SE direction, and subvertical axial surfaces that are intruded by numerous dykes. A rock sample obtained from the southern side of Cape Shirreff was identified as fresh olivine basalt and was composed of approximately 4% olivine and 10% plagioclase phenocrysts in a groundmass of plagioclase, clinopyroxene and opaque oxide. Rock samples at Cape Shirreff have been K-Ar dated as of late Cretaceous age with a minimum age of 90.2± 5.6 million years old (Smellie *et al.* 1996). The volcanic sequences at Cape Shirreff form part of a broader group of relatively fresh basalt and andesite lavas covering eastern-central Livingston Island that are similar to basalts found on Byers Peninsula.

The Cape Shirreff peninsula is predominantly a raised marine platform, 46 to 53 m above sea level, (Bonner and Smith 1985). The bedrock is largely covered by weathered rock and glacial deposits. Two lower platforms, covered with rounded water-worn pebbles, occur at elevations of approximately 7-9 m and 12-15 m above Mean Sea Level (MSL) (Hobbs 1968).

There is little information on the soils of Cape Shirreff. They are mainly fine, highly porous, ash and scoria. The soils support a sparse vegetation and are enriched by bird and seal colonies which inhabit the Area.

*Palaeonotology*

A fossilized wood specimen belonging to the Araucariaceae family (*Araucarioxylon* sp.) was recorded from Cape Shirreff (Torres, 1993). It is similar to fossils found at Byers Peninsula (ASPA No. 126), a site with rich fossil flora and fauna 20 km to the southwest. Several fossil specimens have also been found at the northern extremity of the Cape Shirreff peninsula. In 2001-02 fossiliferous rocks of two different ages were discovered incorporated within frontal and lateral moraines of the Livingston Island permanent ice cap (Map 2). Study of the palynomorphs found within the moraines identified two distinct palynological assemblages, arbitrarily named 'Type A' and 'B' (Palma-Held *et al.* 2004, 2007). The 'Type A' association was dominated by Pteridophyta, mainly Cyatheaceae and Gleicheniaceae, and by *Podocarpidites* spp. and also contained *Myrtaceidites eugenioides* and epiphyllous fungal spores. The assemblage is believed to be indicative of warm and humid conditions of Early Cretaceous in age (Palma-Heldt *et al.* 2007). The 'Type B' assemblage was characterized by a subantarctic flora with *Nothofagidites*, *Araucariacites australis*, *Podocarpidites otagoensis*, *P. marwickii*, *Proteacidites parvus* and also epiphyllous fungal spores, which indicate a cold and humid temperate climate (Palma-Heldt *et al.* 2007). The age of the assemblage is estimated to be Late Cretaceous-Paleogene (Palma-Heldt *et al.* 2004; Leppe *et al.* 2003). Palynological investigations were undertaken at Cape Shirreff in order to investigate the evolution of the southern Pacific margin of Gondwana and to develop a model of the Mesozoic-Cenozoic evolution of the Antarctic Peninsula. It has been noted that other fossils may be revealed by further recession of the Livingston Island permanent ice cap (D. Torres, A. Aguayo and J. Acevedo, pers. comm. 2010).

*Streams and lakes*

There is one permanent lake on Cape Shirreff, located north and at the base of Toqui Hill (Map 3). The lake is approximately 2-3 m deep and 12 m long at full capacity, diminishing in size after February (Torres 1995). Moss banks grow on surrounding slopes. There are also several ephemeral ponds and streams on the peninsula, fed by snow-melt, especially in January and February. The largest of the streams is found draining southwestern slopes toward the coast at Yamana Beach.

*Vegetation and invertebrates*

Although a comprehensive survey of the vegetation communities at Cape Shirreff has not been undertaken, Cape Shirreff appears to be less well vegetated than many other sites in the South Shetland Islands. Observations to date have recorded one grass, five species of moss, six of lichen, one fungi and one nitrophilous macroalgae (Torres 1995).

Patches of Antarctic hairgrass (*Deschampsia antarctica*) can be found in some valleys, often growing with mosses. Mosses are predominantly found inland from the coast. In a valley running northwest from Half Moon Beach, there is a moderately well-developed wet moss carpet of *Warnstorfia laculosa* (=*Calliergidium austro-stramineum*, also =*Calliergon sarmentosum*) (Bonner 1989, in Heap 1994). In areas with better drainage, *Sanionia uncinata* (=*Drepanocladus uncinatus*) and *Polytrichastrum alpinum* (=*Polytrichum alpinum*) are found. The raised beach areas and some higher plateaus have extensive stands of the foliose nitrophilous macroalga *Prasiola crispa*, which is characteristic of areas enriched by animal excreta and has been observed to replace moss-lichen associations damaged by fur seals (Bonner 1989, in Heap 1994).

The six lichen species thus far described at Cape Shirreff are *Caloplaca spp, Umbilicaria antarctica, Usnea antarctica, U. fasciata, Xanthoria candelaria* and *X. elegans*. The fruticose species *Umbilicaria antarctica, Usnea antarctica* and *U. fasciata* form dense growths on cliff faces and on the tops of steep rocks (Bonner 1989, in Heap 1994). The bright yellow and orange crustose lichens *Caloplaca spp, Xanthoria candelaria* and *X. elegans* are common beneath bird colonies and are also present with the fruticose species. The identity of the single recorded fungal species is unknown.

The invertebrate fauna at Cape Shirreff has not been described.

*Microbial ecology*

Field studies of the microbial ecology at Cape Shirreff were carried out 11-21 January 2010 and results were compared with the bacterial communities present at Fildes Peninsula, King George Island. The study aimed to evaluate the influence of the different microhabitats on the biodiversity and metabolic capacities of bacterial communities found at Cape Shirreff and Fildes Peninsula (INACH, 2010).

*Breeding birds*

The avifauna of Cape Shirreff is diverse, with ten species known to breed within the Area, and several non-breeding species present. Chinstrap (*Pygoscelis antarctica*) and Gentoo (*P. papua*) penguins breed within the Area; Adélie penguins (*P. adeliae*) have not been observed to breed on Cape Shirreff or San Telmo Island, although are widely distributed throughout the region. Both Chinstrap and Gentoo penguins are found in small colonies on the northeastern and northwestern coasts of Cape Shirreff peninsula (Map 3). Data have been collected on the Chinstrap and Gentoo penguin colonies every summer season since 1996-97, including reproductive success, demography, diet, foraging and diving behaviour (e.g. Hinke *et al.* 2007; Pietrzak *et al.* 2009). During the 2009-10 summer season, Chinstrap and Gentoo penguins at Cape Shirreff were tagged with satellite transmitters, in order to study their over-winter behaviour.

In 2008-09 there were 19 active breeding sub-colonies at Cape Shirreff, with a total of 879 Gentoo and 4026 Chinstrap penguin nests (Pietrzak *et al.* 2009), although the number of the sub-colonies and their composition show some inter-annual variation. From the late 1990's to 2004, the numbers of Chinstrap penguins at Cape Shirreff declined significantly, whilst Gentoo populations showed no discernible trend. (Hinke *et al.* 2007). The negative trend in Chinstrap numbers has continued and nest counts for both penguin species reached their lowest for 11 years in 2007-08, due to poor weather conditions (Chisholm *et al.* 2008; Miller and Trivelpiece 2008). In 2008-09 the population and reproductive success of both Gentoos and Chinstraps at Cape Shirreff increased significantly in comparison to the previous season but numbers of Chinstrap nests remained 30% below average for the site (Pietrzak *et al.* 2009). The differing trends in Chinstrap and Gentoo populations at Cape Shirreff have been attributed to the higher winter juvenile mortality rate experienced by Chinstraps (Hinke *et al.* 2007) and a greater flexibility in feeding patterns exhibited by Gentoos (Miller *et al.* 2009).

In general, the Chinstrap penguins nest on higher escarpments at Cape Shirreff, although they are also found breeding on small promontories near the shore. Gentoo penguins tend to breed on more gentle slopes and rounded promontories. During the period of chick rearing, foraging by both species of penguin is confined to the shelf region, approximately 20 to 30km offshore of Cape Shirreff (Miller and Trivelpiece 2007).Data available on penguin numbers are presented in Table 1.

Several other species breed within the Area (Map 3), although data on numbers are patchy. Kelp gulls (*Larus domincanus)* and Brown skuas (*Catharacta loennbergi*) nest in abundance along the entire coastline of the Area. In 2000 there were 25 and 22 breeding pairs of these species respectively (AMLR, pers. comm. 2000). In 2007-08, 24 pairs of skuas were identified at Cape Shirreff and Punta Oeste, of which 23 were Brown skuas (*Catharacta loennbergi*) and one pair was a hybrid of Brown-South Polar skuas (*C. maccormicki*). Fifty-six Kelp gull nests were observed at Cape Shirreff during the 2006-07 season. Reproductive success of skuas and kelp gulls has been regularly monitored during recent summer seasons at nesting sites around Cape Shirreff (Chisholm *et al.* 2008; Pietrzak *et al.* 2009).

Sheathbills (*Chionis alba*) nest in two places: one pair has been recorded nesting on the western coast of the Cape Shirreff peninsula; a second pair has been observed breeding among rocks at the northern beach on San Telmo Island, near an Antarctic fur seal breeding site (Torres, pers. comm. 2002). Antarctic terns (*Sterna vittata*) breed in several locations, which have been observed to vary from year to year. Since 1990-91 a small colony of approximately 11 pairs of Antarctic shag (*Phalacrocorax* [atriceps] *bransfieldensis*) has been observed breeding on Yeco Rocks, on the western coast of the peninsula (Torres, 1995). Cape petrels (*Daption capense*) breed on cliffs on the western coast of the Area; 14 pairs were recorded in January 1993, nine in January 1994, three in January 1995 and eight in 1999. Wilson's storm petrel (*Oceanites oceanicus*) also breed on the western coast of the Area. Black-bellied storm petrel (*Fregetta tropica*) have been observed to breed near the field camp on the eastern coast. A large number of non-breeding Southern Giant petrels (*Macronectes giganteus*) frequent the Area in the summer, and a report of a breeding colony on the peninsula (Bonner 1989, in Heap 1994) is incorrect (Torres, pers. comm. 2002). Other bird species recorded but not breeding within the Area include Macaroni penguin (*Eudyptes chrysolophus*), King penguin (*Aptenodytes patagonicus*), Emperor penguin (*Aptenodytes forsteri*), Snow petrel (*Pagadroma nivea*), White-rumped sandpiper (*Calidris fuscicollis*), Black-necked swan (*Cygnus melanocoryphus*), and the Cattle egret *Bubulcus ibis* (Torres 1995; Olavarría *et al.* 1999). Additional bird species recorded as foraging close to Cape Shirreff include the Black-browed albatross (*Thalassarche melanophris*) and Gray-headed albatross (*T. chrysostoma*), although neither species has yet been recorded within the Area (Cox *et al.* 2009).

**Table 1:** Chinstrap (*Pygoscelis antarctica)* and Gentoo (*P. papua*) penguin numbers at Cape Shirreff.

| Year | Chinstrap (pairs) | Gentoo (pairs) | Source |
|------|------|------|------|
| 1958 | 2000 (N3[1]) | 200-500 (N1[1]) | Croxall and Kirkwood, 1979 |
| 1981 | 2164 (A4) | 843 (A4) | Sallaberry and Schlatter, 1983 [2] |
| 1987 | 5200 (A3) | 300 (N4) | Woehler, 1993 |
| 1997 | 6907 (N1) | 682 (N1) | Hucke-Gaete *et al.* 1997a |
| 1999-00 | 7744 (N1) | 922 (N1) | AMLR data, Carten *et al.* 2001 |
| 2000-01 | 7212 (N1) | 1043 (N1) | AMLR data, Taft *et al.* 2001 |
| 2001-02 | 6606 | 907 | AMLR data, Saxer *et al.* 2003 |
| 2002-03 | 5868 (A3) | 778 (A3) | AMLR data, Shill *et al.* 2003 |
| 2003-04 | 5636 (N1) | 751 (N1) | AMLR data, Antolos *et al.* 2004 |
| 2004-05 | 4907 (N1) | 818 (N1) | AMLR data, Miller *et al.* 2005 |
| 2005-06 | 4849 (N1) | 807 (N1) | AMLR data, Leung *et al.* 2006 |
| 2006-07 | 4544 (N1) | 781 (N1) | AMLR data, Orben *et al.* 2007 |
| 2007-08 | 3032 (N1) | 610 (N1) | AMLR data, Chisholm *et al.* 2008 |
| 2008-09 | 4026 (N1) | 879 (N1) | AMLR data, Pietrzak *et al.* 2009 |

1. Alphanumeric code refers to the type of count, as in Woehler (1993).
2. Reported data did not specify species. It has been assumed that the higher number referred to Chinstrap penguins. Data were reported as individuals, which have been halved to derive 'pairs' in the table.

*Breeding mammals*

Cape Shirreff (including San Telmo Island) is presently the site of the largest known breeding colony of the Antarctic fur seal in the Antarctic Peninsula region. Antarctic fur seals were once abundant throughout the South Shetland Islands but were hunted to local extinction between 1820 and 1824. The next observation of Antarctic fur seals at Cape Shirreff was on 14 January 1958, when 27 animals were recorded, including seven juveniles (Tufft 1958). The following season, on 31 January 1959, a group of seven adult males, one female and one male pup were recorded, along with one dead male pup (O'Gorman, 1961). A second female arrived three days later, and by mid-March 32 Antarctic fur seals were present. By 2002, the estimated Antarctic fur seal population at Cape Shirreff (excluding San Telmo Island) increased to 14,842 animals (including 6,453 pups), with the total population (including San Telmo Island) being 21,190 animals (including 8577 pups) (Hucke-Gaete *et al.* 2004). More recent data on Antarctic fur seal numbers have yet to be published. However, the present number of Antarctic fur seals at Cape Shirreff remain an order of magnitude lower than pre-exploitation populations, and it is unclear whether numbers will recover to their previous levels (Hucke-Gaete *et al.* 2004).

Antarctic fur seal breeding sites at Cape Shirreff are concentrated around the coastline of the northern half of the peninsula (Map 3). At San Telmo Island, breeding is concentrated at both ends of the island, with juveniles commonly found near the middle (Torres 1995). Long term monitoring of Antarctic fur seals has been carried at Cape Shirreff since 1991, with the primary objective of studying breeding success in relation to prey availability, environmental variability and human impacts (Osman *et al.* 2004). Researchers have studied various aspects of the fur seal colony, including pup production, predation and growth, female attendance behavior, seal diet and diving and foraging. During the 2009-10 summer season, researchers tagged Antarctic fur seals, along with Weddell seals and Leopard seals, to monitor their behavior over the winter period.

During the 2008-09 season, the AMLR program reported a 13.3% reduction in pup production from the previous summer season (Goebel *et al.* 2009). Pup production at Cape Shirreff was particularly low during both the 2007-08 and 2008-09 seasons, most likely as a result unfavorable winter conditions (Goebel *et al.* 2008; 2009). During recent seasons, growth rates of fur seal pups within the Area have been studied in relation to sex, breeding season and maternal foraging and attendance (Vargas *et al.* 2009) and a number of extremely rare color patterns in fur seal pups have been recorded within the Area. Antarctic fur seals with pie-bald or light colorings were documented for the first time and an albino Weddell seal represented the first confirmed case of albinism in Weddell, Leopard, Ross or Crabeater seals (Acevedo *et al.* 2009a, 2009b).

A small number of Southern Elephant seals breed in October on several eastern beaches (AMLR, pers. comm. 2000; Torres, pers. comm. 2002). On 2 Nov 1999 34 pups were counted on beaches south of Condor Hill (AMLR, unpublished data). During the 2008-09 season, a total of 34 Southern Elephant seal pups were born at Cape Shirreff and an additional six were born on a small sandy point between Cape Shirreff and Punta Oeste (Goebel *et al.* 2009). Groups of non-breeding Southern Elephant seals are also present, while isolated animals, mainly juveniles, may be found on various beaches. The foraging behavior of Southern Elephant seals has been studied using satellite tracking of animals tagged at Cape Shirreff and analyzed in relation to the physical properties of the water column (Huckstadt *et al.* 2006; Goebel *et al.* 2009). Seals were found to forage as far afield as the Amundsen Sea and one animal was observed travelling 4700 km due west of the Antarctic Peninsula.

Weddell seals, Leopard seals and Crabeater seals have been observed on the Cape Shirreff peninsula and are the subject of monitoring programs (O'Gorman 1961; Bengtson *et al.* 1990; Oliva *et al.* 1988; Torres 1995; Goebel, pers. comm. 2010). Monitoring of leopard seal predation on the Antarctic fur seal pup population was initiated in 2001-02 and was recorded during the 2003-04 Antarctic season (Vera *et al.* 2004). Leopard seals hauling out at Cape Shirreff have been fitted with satellite trackers to monitor their foraging range and dispersal. Observations of leopard seal feeding behaviour and pup survival studies suggest that they consume up to half of all Antarctic fur seal pups born within the Area each year (Goebel *et al.* 2008, 2009,). During the 2008-09 field season, DNA samples were collected from four seal species at Cape Shirreff and stored in the Southwest Fisheries Science Center DNA archives (Goebel *et al.* 2009). Humpback whales (*Megaptera novaeangliae*) have been observed in the offshore area immediately to the north-east of the Area (Cox *et al.* 2009).

*Marine environment and ecosystem*

The seafloor surrounding the Cape Shirreff peninsula slopes relatively gently from the coast, reaching depths of 50 m approximately 2-3 km from the shore and 100 m at about 6-11 km (Map 1). This relatively shallow and broad submarine ridge extends to the NW for about 24 km before dropping more steeply at the continental shelf edge. The ridge is about 20 km in width and flanked either side by canyons reaching depths of around 300-400 m. There is abundant macroalgae present in the intertidal zone. The limpet *Nacella concinna* is common, as elsewhere in the South Shetland Islands.

The waters offshore from Cape Shirreff have been identified as one of three areas of consistently high krill biomass density in the South Shetland Islands area, although absolute krill populations fluctuate significantly over time (Hewitt *et al.* 2004; Reiss *et al.* 2008). The spatial distribution, demography, density and size of krill and krill swarms have been studied in the nearshore region at Cape Shirreff, primarily using acoustic surveys and also using an Autonomous Underwater Vehicle (AUV) (Reiss *et al.* 2008; Warren *et al.* 2005). Acoustic surveys of the nearshore environment indicate that krill in this area are most abundant in to the south and SE of Cape Shirreff and at the margins of the two submarine canyons, which are believed to be a source of nutrient rich water that may increase productivity in the nearshore area surrounding Cape Shirreff (Warren *et al.* 2006, 2007). Nearshore net tows indicated that the organisms identified in acoustic surveys were primarily the euphausiids, *Euphausia superba*, *Thysanoessa macrura* and *Euphausia frigida*, and may also include chaetognaths, salps, siphonophores, laval fish, myctophids and amphipods (Warren *et al.* 2007).

The nearshore environment surrounding Cape Shirreff has been identified as a primary feeding ground for penguins resident at the site, particularly during the breeding season when chick provisioning limits foraging range (Cox *et al.* 2009). Fur seals and penguins at Cape Shirreff depend strongly upon krill for prey, particularly when juvenile. Predator foraging ranges are known to overlap with areas of commercial krill fisheries and changes in the abundance of both predators and krill have been linked to climatic change. Research at Cape Shirreff therefore aims to monitor krill abundance in combination with predator populations and breeding success, in order to assess the potential effects of commercial fishing, as well as environmental variability and climatic change on the ecosystem.

Numerous studies of the marine environment have been conducted in the region offshore from Cape Shirreff as part of research carried out within the AMLR survey grid. These studies include investigations into various aspects of the marine environment, including physical oceanography, environmental conditions, phytoplankton distribution and productivity, krill distribution and biomass and the distribution and density of seabirds and marine mammals (AMLR 2008, 2009).

*Historical features*

Following discovery of the South Shetland Islands in 1819, intensive sealing at Cape Shirreff between 1820 and 1824 exterminated almost the entire local populations of Antarctic fur seals and Southern Elephant seals (Smith and Simpson 1987). In January 1821 60–75 British sealers were recorded living ashore at Cape Shirreff and 95,000 skins were taken during the 1821-22 season (O'Gorman 1963). Evidence of the sealers' occupation remains, with ruins of at least one sealers' hut in the northwestern region of the peninsula and remains of sealer's settlements recorded on a number of the beaches (D. Torres, A. Aquayo and J. Acevedo, pers. comm. 2010). The shoreline of several bays is also littered with timbers and sections of wrecked sealers' vessels. Other evidence of sealing activity includes the remains of stoves, pieces of glass bottles, a wooden harpoon, and a handcrafted bone figure (Torres and Aguayo 1993). Fildes (1821) reported that sealers found spars and an anchor stock from the Spanish ship San Telmo on Half Moon Beach around the time she was lost. The ship sank in the Drake Passage at around 62°S on 4 September 1819, with 644 persons aboard (Headland 1989; Pinochet de la Barra 1991). These were possibly the first people to die in Antarctica, and the event remains the greatest single loss of life yet to occur south of 60°S. A cairn has been erected on the northwestern coast of Cape Shirreff peninsula to commemorate the loss, which is designated as Historic Monument No. 59 (Map 3).

The remains of a camp were found close to the site of present camp facilities (Torres and Aguayo 1993). On the evidence of the script on items found at the site, the camp is believed to be of Russian origin and date from the 1940-50s, although its exact origins have yet to be determined. Items found include parts of an antenna, electrical wires, tools, boots, nails, battery cells, canned food, and a wooden box covered by a pyramid of stones. Several notes in Russian, dating from later visits, were found in this box.

In January 1985 a human skull was found at Yamana Beach (Torres 1992), determined to be that of a young woman (Constantinescu and Torres 1995). In January 1987 part of a human femur was found on the ground surface nearby, inland from Yamana Beach. After a careful surface survey, no other remains were evident at that time. However, in January 1991, another part of a femur was found in close proximity to the site of the earlier (1987) find. In January 1993 an archaeological survey was carried out in the area, although no further human remains were found. The original samples were dated as from approximately 175 years BP, and it was hypothesised they belong to a single individual (Torres 1999).

*Human activities / impacts*

The modern era of human activity at Cape Shirreff has been largely confined to science. During the past three decades, the population of Antarctic fur seals in the South Shetland Islands grew to a level at which tagging and other research could be undertaken without threatening the existence and growth of the local population. Chilean studies on Cape Shirreff began in 1965 (Aguayo and Torres 1966, 1967), with a more intensive program initiated by Chilean scientists in 1982, including an ongoing Antarctic fur seal tagging program (Cattan *et al.* 1982; Torres 1984; Oliva *et al.* 1987). United States investigators have conducted pinniped and seabird surveys at Cape Shirreff and San Telmo Island since 1986-87 (Bengtson *et al.* 1990).

CEMP studies at Cape Shirreff began in the mid-1980s, initiated by Chilean and US scientists. Cape Shirreff was designated as a CEMP Site in 1994 to protect the site from damage or disturbance that could adversely affect long-term CEMP monitoring. As part of the CEMP, long-term studies are assessing and monitoring the feeding ecology, growth and condition, reproductive success, behavior, vital rates, and abundance of pinnipeds and seabirds that breed in the Area. The results of these studies will be evaluated in context with environmental data, offshore sampling data, and fishery statistics to identify possible cause-effect relationships between krill fisheries and pinniped and seabird populations.

Brucella and herpes virus antibodies were detected in tissue samples taken from Antarctic fur seals at Cape Shirreff over summer seasons from 1998-2001, and Brucella antibodies were also detected in Weddell seal tissue (Blank *et al.* 1999; Blank *et al.* 2001a & b). Studies on the mortality of Antarctic fur seal pups from diseases began in the 2003-04 Antarctic season (Torres and Valdenegro 2004). Enteropathogenic *Escherichia coli* (EPEC) has been recorded in swabs from Antarctic fur seals at Cape Shirreff, with two out of 33 pups sampled testing positive for the pathogen. The findings were the first reports of EPEC in Antarctic wildlife and in pinipeds, and the effects of the pathogen on Antarctic wildlife is unknown (Hernandez *et al.* 2007).

Plastic rubbish was first reported at Cape Shirreff by Torres and Gajardo (1985), and marine debris monitoring studies have been carried out regularly since 1992 (Torres and Jorquera 1995). Debris remains an ongoing problem at the site, with over 1.5 tons of material removed from the area by Chilean scientists to date (D. Torres, A. Aquayo and J. Acevedo, pers. comm., 2010). Recent surveys have yielded large numbers of articles, mostly made of plastic, but have also included vegetable waste from ships, metal oil drums, rifle shells and an antenna on beaches. For example, the 2000-01 season survey recorded a total of 1,774 articles, almost 98% of which were made of plastic and the remainder made of glass, metal and paper. It is significant that 34% of the plastic items found in 2000-01 were packing bands, representing approximately 589 bands. Of these, 40 were uncut and another 48 had been knotted into a loop. Several articles found in this survey were oiled, and some plastic articles were partially burnt. Antarctic fur seal entanglement in marine debris has been recorded frequently at Cape Shirreff (Torres 1990; Hucke-Gaete *et al.* 1997c; Goebel *et al.* 2008, 2009), primarily in fishing equipment such as nylon ropes, net fragments and packing bands. Between 1987-1997 a total of 20 Antarctic fur seals were recorded with 'neck collars' from such debris. Plastic fibers are also found in Kelp gull and Chinstrap penguin nests (Torres and Jorquera 1992), as well as those of Sheathbills (Torres and Jorquera 1994).

The waters surrounding Cape Shirreff represent an important krill fishing area. Catch data specifically for Cape Shirreff are unavailable, but fishing statistics are published for CCAMLR Statistical Subarea 48.1, within which the Area lies. In 2008-09, 33970 tons of Antarctic krill (*Euphausia superba*) were caught in Subarea 48.1 compared with an average of 32993 tons per year caught during the period 1999-00 to 2008-09 (CCAMLR 2010). On 10 October 2010, the krill fishery in Subarea 48.1 was closed for the remainder of the 2009-10 fishing season (1 December 2009- 30 November 2010) because the catch reached 99.9% of the annual limit for the Subarea (155,000 tonnes). Nations recorded as fishing for krill within the Subarea during the recent past included Japan, Korea, Norway, Poland, Ukraine, Uruguay, the United States and Vanuatu. Krill fishing generally occurred between December and August, with the highest catches usually occurring between March and May. Catches of other species occurred in very much smaller quantities and included *Champsocephalus gunnari*, *Champsocephalus gunnari*, *Nototheniops nybelini*, *Notothenia coriiceps*, *Notolepis* spp, *Notothenia gibberifrons*, *Notothenia neglecta*, *Notothenia rossii*, *Pseudochaenichthys georgianus* and *Chaenocephalus aceratus* (CCAMLR 2010).

*6(ii) Access to the Area*

Access to the Area may be made by small boat, by aircraft or across sea ice by vehicle or on foot. Historically seasonal sea ice formation in the South Shetlands area generally began in early April and persisted until early December, although more recently the South Shetland Islands can be ice-free year round as a result of regional warming.

Air access restrictions apply for the period 01 November – 31 March inclusive. During this time, helicopters may land at either of the two helicopter landing sites (Map 2), but landing at site A is preferred under most circumstances. Landing site A is located approximately 150m north-west of the summit of Condor Hill on the eastern side of the peninsula (62°46'27"S, 60°28'17"W). Landing site B is situated on a wide area of flat ground on Ancho Pass, approximately 300m east of Selknam Hill (62°46'48"S, 60°28'16"W). To the maximum extent practicable, aircraft should follow the Helicopter Access Zone when accessing the Area and should approach from the south, across the Livingston Island permanent ice cap. Air access is prohibited within the Restricted Zone, unless authorised by permit. The zone is situated north of 62°28' S (Map 2), or north of 62°29' S and west of 60°48' W and is designated because it contains the highest concentrations of wildlife in the Area. Due to the presence of wildlife, aircraft are encouraged to maintain a horizontal and vertical separation of 2000 ft (~610 m) from the protected area boundary, unless accessing the designated landing sites or otherwise authorized by permit.

When access to the Area is made from the sea, small boats should land at one of the following locations: the eastern coast of the peninsula at El Módulo Beach, where a deep channel enables relatively easy access; the northern end of Half Moon Beach; the northern end of Yámana Beach, on the western coast (suitable at high tide only);or the southern end of the northern beach on San Telmo Island. Small boats may land at any other location within the Area, provided that this is consistent with the purposes for which a permit has been granted and where practicable, visitors should avoid landing where wildlife colonies are present. Two anchorages have been identified close to the Area; 1600 m north-east of the main camp facilities and approximately 800 m north of San Telmo Island. Sea states are generally between 1 and 4 m, decreasing closer to shore or in lea of Cape Shirreff (Warren *et al.* 2006, 2007).

When sea ice conditions allow, the Area may be accessed over sea ice on foot or by vehicle. However, vehicle use within the Area is restricted to the coastal zone between Módulo Beach and the Chilean / US camp facilities only. Persons entering the Area may not move beyond the immediate vicinity of their landing site unless authorised by Permit.

*6(iii) Restricted and managed zones within the Area*

A zone in the north and west of the Area is designated as a Restricted Zone, due to its high concentrations of wildlife. Restrictions apply to air access only and prohibit overflight below 2000 ft (~610m), unless specifically authorized by permit. The Restricted Zone is defined as the area north of 62°28' S (Map 2), and north of 62°29' S and west of 60°48' W.

A Helicopter Access Zone (Map 2) has been defined which applies to aircraft entering the Area and accessing the designated landing sites. The Helicopter Access Zone extends from the Livingston Island permanent ice cap northward following the main ridgeline of the peninsula for 1200 m (~ 0.65 n. mi.) towards Selknam Hill. The Helicopter Access Zone then extends east by 300 m (~0.15 n. mi) (to helicopter landing site B at Ancho Pass and a further 400 m (~0.23 n. mi) east to the summit of Condor Hill close to helicopter landing site. The southern boundary of the Helicopter Access Zone is coincident with the southern boundary of the Area.

*6(iv) Structures within and near the Area*

A semi-permanent summer-only research camp has been established on the eastern coast of the Cape Shirreff peninsula, located at the base of Condor Hill (62°28'12" S, 60°46'17" W) (Map 3). Buildings for the camp remain *in situ* year-round. In 2010, the field camp known as Cape Shirreff Field Station (US), consisted of four small buildings and an outhouse. The camp 'Dr Guillermo Mann-Fischer' (Chile) is located around 50 m from the US station and comprised of a main hut, laboratory, store house, a fiberglass igloo, an outhouse and a wind-powered generator in 2010 (Goebel pers. comm. 2010, D. Torres, A. Aquayo and J. Acevedo, pers. comm., 2010)). The Chilean fiberglass igloo was originally installed in 1990-91, while the US camp was established in 1996-97. Storage areas are also present, and tents are erected seasonally nearby as required. During the 2009-10 season, an All Terrain Vehicle (ATV) shed, with secondary containment for summer use and winter storage of ATVs, was constructed at the US camp. The site was selected to remain within the existing station footprint and to avoid interference with seal traffic. A 'Weatherport' is stored at Cape Shirreff as additional accommodation for visiting scientists and is erected within 10 m of the south side of the US station when needed.

Two automatic weather stations are mounted on the exterior of existing buildings at Cape Shirreff. A remote receiving station used for seal tracking studies is stored within a box (90x60x100cm) located on a small ridge to the southeast of Mansa Bay.

A boundary marker is located at Módulo Beach, close to the Chilean and US stations. The marker states that the Area is protected and that access is prohibited. In 2009-10 season, the marker was weathered but legible (Goebel, pers. comm. 2010). The boundaries of the protected area are not otherwise marked.

The remains of a camp, believed to be of Russian origin, are present near the Chilean and US camps. In other parts of the peninsula, sparse evidence may be found of 19th Century sealers' camps (Smith and Simpson 1987; Torres 1993; Stehberg and Lucero 1996). A cairn (Historic Monument No. 59) has been erected on

Gaviota Hill on the northwestern coast to commemorate the loss of those aboard the San Telmo in 1819 (Map 3). In 1998-99 a 5x7 m bird observation / emergency hut (62°27'41" S, 60°47'28" W) was installed by US scientists on the northern slopes of Enrique Hill above Bahamonde Beach, close to the penguin colonies (Map 3).

*6(v) Location of other protected areas within close proximity of the Area*

The nearest protected areas to Cape Shirreff are Byers Peninsula (ASPA No. 126), which lies about 20 km to the southwest; Port Foster (ASPA No. 145, Deception Island) and other parts of Deception Island (ASPA No. 140), which are approximately 30 km to the south; and 'Chile Bay' (Discovery Bay) (ASPA No. 144), which lies about 30 km to the east at Greenwich Island (Map 1).

## 7.    Permit conditions

Entry into the Area is prohibited except in accordance with a Permit issued by an appropriate national authority. Conditions for issuing a Permit to enter the Area are that:

- it is issued only for scientific study associated with the CEMP, or for compelling scientific, educational, archaeological or historic purposes that cannot be served elsewhere; or
- it is issued for essential management purposes consistent with plan objectives such as inspection, maintenance or review;
- the actions permitted will not jeopardize the ecological, scientific, educational archaeological or historic values of the Area;
- any management activities are in support of the objectives of the Management Plan;
- the actions permitted are in accordance with the Management Plan;
- the Permit, or a copy, shall be carried within the Area;
- a visit report shall be supplied to the authority named in the Permit;
- permits shall be issued for a stated period.

*7(i) Access to and movement within the Area*

Access to the Area shall be by small boat, by helicopter, on foot or by vehicle.

*Boat access*

Access by small boats should be at one of the following locations (Map 2):

1. the eastern coast of the peninsula at El Módulo Beach, 300 m north of the camp facilities, where a deep channel enables relatively easy access;
2. the northern end of Half Moon Beach, on the eastern coast of the peninsula;
3. the northern end of Yámana Beach, on the western coast (suitable at high tide only);
4. the southern end of the northern beach on San Telmo Island.

Access by small boat at other locations around the coast is allowed, provided this is consistent with the purposes for which a Permit has been granted. Two anchorages have been identified close to the Area; 1600 m north-east of the main camp facilities and approximately 800 m north of San Telmo Island. Visitors should, where practicable, avoid landing where pinniped or seabird colonies are present on or near the coast.

*Aircraft access and overflight*

Due to the widespread presence of pinnipeds and seabirds over the Cape Shirreff peninsula during the breeding season (01 November – 31 March), access to the Area by aircraft in this period is strongly discouraged. Where possible and by preference, access should be by small boat. All restrictions on aircraft access and overflight apply between 01 November – 31 March inclusive, when aircraft shall operate and land within the Area according to strict observance of the following conditions:

1) It is recommended that aircraft maintain a horizontal and vertical separation distance 2000 ft (~610 m) from the Antarctic Specially Protected Area boundary (Map 2), unless accessing the designated landing sites through the Helicopter Access Zone or otherwise authorized by permit;

2) Overflight of the Restricted Zone is prohibited below 2000 ft (~610 m) unless authorized by permit. The Restricted Zone is defined as the area north of 62°28' S, or north of 62°29' S and west of 60°48' W (Map 2), and includes the areas of greatest wildlife concentration;

3) Helicopter landing is permitted at two designated sites (Map 2). The landing sites with their coordinates are described as follows:

   **(A)** on a small area of flat ground, ~150 m northwest of the summit of Condor Hill (50 m, or ~150 ft) (62°46'27"S, 60°28'17"W), which is the preferred landing site for most purposes; and

   **(B)** on the wide flat area on Ancho Pass (25 m), situated between Condor Hill and Selknam Hill (62°46'48"S, 60°28'16"W).

4) Aircraft accessing the Area should follow the Helicopter Access Zone to the maximum extent practicable. The Helicopter Access Zone allows access from the south across the Livingston Island permanent ice cap and extends along the main ridgeline of the peninsula for 1200 m (~ 0.65 n. mi.) towards Selknam Hill (elevation = 50 m, or ~150 ft). The Helicopter Access Zone then extends east by 300m (~ 0.15 n. mi) to Ancho Pass, where helicopter landing site B is situated, and a further 400m (~0.23 n. mi) east to the summit of Condor Hill (elevation -= 50 m, or ~150 ft), close to helicopter landing site A. Aircraft should avoid overflight of the hut and beach areas on the eastern side of Condor Hill.

5) The preferred approaches to the Helicopter Access Zone are from the south across the Livingston Island permanent ice cap, from the southwest from the direction of Barclay Bay, and from the southeast from the direction of Hero Bay (Maps 1 and 2).

6) Weather with a low cloud ceiling often prevails at Cape Shirreff, particularly in the vicinity of the permanent ice cap, which can make snow/ice ground definition difficult to discern from the air. On-site personnel who may be advising on local conditions before aircraft approaches should be aware that a minimum cloud base of 150 m (500 ft) AMSL over the approach zone of the Livingston Island ice cap is necessary in order for access guidelines to be followed;

7) Use of smoke grenades to indicate wind direction is prohibited within the Area unless absolutely necessary for safety, and any grenades used should be retrieved.

*Vehicle access and use*

Access by vehicle over land may be made to the boundary to the Area. Access by vehicle over sea ice may be made to the shore within the Area. Vehicles are permitted to operate on land only in the coastal zone between Módulo Beach and the Chilean / US camp facilities (Map 3). The use of vehicles elsewhere within the Area is prohibited.

*Foot access and movement within the Area*

With the exception of the restricted use of vehicles described above, movement on land within the Area shall be on foot. Pilots, air, boat or vehicle crew, or other people in aircraft, boats, or vehicles are prohibited from moving on foot beyond the immediate vicinity of their landing site or the hut facilities unless specifically authorised by Permit. Visitors should move carefully so as to minimize disturbance to flora, fauna, and soils, and should walk on snow or rocky terrain if practical, but taking care not to damage lichens. Pedestrian traffic should be kept to the minimum consistent with the objectives of any permitted activities and every reasonable effort should be made to minimize effects.

*7(ii) Activities that are or may be conducted in the Area, including restrictions on time or place*

- Scientific research that will not jeopardize the values of the Area, in particular those associated with the CEMP;
- Essential management activities, including monitoring;
- Activities with educational aims (such as documentary reporting (photographic, audio or written) or the production of educational resources or services) that cannot be served elsewhere.

- Activities with the aim of preserving or protecting historic resources within the Area.
- Archaeological research that will not threaten the values of the Area.

### 7(iii) Installation, modification or removal of structures

- No structures are to be erected within the Area except as specified in a permit;
- The principal camp facilities shall be limited to the area within 200 m of the existing Chilean and US field camps (Map 3). Small temporary hides, blinds or screens may be constructed for the purpose of facilitating scientific study of the fauna;
- All structures, scientific equipment or markers installed in the Area must be authorized by permit and clearly identified by country, name of the principal investigator and year of installation. All such items should be made of materials that pose minimal risk of harm to fauna or of contamination of the Area;
- Installation (including site selection), maintenance, modification or removal of structures shall be undertaken in a manner that minimizes disturbance to flora and fauna, preferably avoiding the main breeding season (1 November – 31 March);
- Removal of structures, equipment, hides or markers for which the permit has expired shall be the responsibility of the authority which granted the original Permit, and shall be a condition of the Permit;

### 7(iv) Location of field camps

Camping is permitted within 200 m of the facilities of the Chilean and US field camps, on the eastern coast of the Cape Shirreff peninsula (Map 3). Temporary camping is permitted at the northern extremity of Yamana beach to support fieldwork on the San Telmo Islets (Map 3). The US bird observation hut on the northern slopes of Enrique Hill (62°27'41" S, 60°47'28" W) may be used for temporary overnight camping for research purposes, although should not be used as a semi-permanent camp. Camping is permitted on San Telmo Island when necessary for purposes consistent with plan objectives. The preferred camping location is at the southern end of the northern beach on the island. Camping is prohibited elsewhere within the Area.

### 7(v) Restrictions on materials and organisms which can be brought into the Area

- No living animals, plant material, microorganisms or soils shall be deliberately introduced into the Area and the precautions listed below shall be taken against accidental introductions;
- To help maintain the ecological and scientific values at Cape Shirreff and San Telmo Island visitors shall take special precautions against introductions. Of concern are pathogenic, microbial, invertebrate or plant introductions sourced from other Antarctic sites, including stations, or from regions outside Antarctica. Visitors shall ensure that sampling equipment and markers brought into the Area are clean. To the maximum extent practicable, footwear and other equipment used or brought into the area (including backpacks, carry-bags and tents) shall be thoroughly cleaned before entering the Area;
- Dressed poultry should be free of disease or infection before shipment to the Area and, if introduced to the Area for food, all parts and wastes of poultry shall be completely removed from the Area or incinerated or boiled long enough to kill any potentially infective bacteria or viruses;
- No herbicides or pesticides shall be brought into the Area;
- Any other chemicals, including radio-nuclides or stable isotopes, which may be introduced for scientific or management purposes specified in the Permit, shall be removed from the Area at or before the conclusion of the activity for which the Permit was granted;
- Fuel, food, and other materials are not to be stored in the Area, unless required for essential purposes connected with the activities for which a permit has been granted;
- All materials introduced shall be for a stated period only, shall be removed at or before the conclusion of that stated period, and shall be stored and handled so that risk of their introduction into the environment is minimized;
- If release occurs which is likely to compromise the values of the Area, removal is encouraged only where the impact of removal is not likely to be greater than that of leaving the material in situ.

### 7(vi) Taking or harmful interference with native flora or fauna

Taking or harmful interference with native flora or fauna is prohibited, except in accordance with a separate permit issued under Article 3 of Annex II by the appropriate national authority specifically for that purpose. CEMP research programs in progress within the Area should be consulted before other Permits for taking or harmful interference with animals are granted.

### 7(vii) Collection or removal of anything not brought into the Area by the Permit holder

- Material may be collected or removed from the Area only in accordance with a Permit and should be limited to the minimum necessary to meet scientific or management needs.

- Material of human origin likely to compromise the values of the Area, which was not brought into the Area by the Permit Holder, and is clearly of no historic value or otherwise authorized, may be removed unless the impact of removal is likely to be greater than leaving the material in situ: if this is the case the appropriate authority should be notified.

- Material found that is likely to possess important archaeological, historic or heritage values should not be disturbed, damaged, removed or destroyed. Any such artifacts should be recorded and referred to the appropriate authority for a decision on conservation or removal. Relocation or removal of artifacts for the purposes of preservation, protection, or to re-establish historical accuracy is allowable by permit;

- The appropriate national authority should be notified of any items removed from the Area that were not introduced by the permit holder.

### 7(viii) Disposal of waste

All wastes shall be removed from the Area, except human wastes and domestic liquid wastes, which may be removed from the Area or disposed of into the sea.

### 7(ix) Measures that are necessary to ensure that the aims and objectives of the Management Plan can continue to be met

1) Permits may be granted to enter the Area to carry out biological monitoring and site inspection activities, which may involve the collection of limited samples for analysis or review, or for protective measures.

2) Any specific sites of long-term monitoring should be appropriately marked.

3) To avoid interference with long-term research and monitoring activities or possible duplication of effort, persons planning new projects within the Area should consult with established programs working at Cape Shirreff, such as those of Chile and the US, before initiating the work.

4) In view of the fact that geological sampling is both permanent and of cumulative impact, visitors removing geological samples from the Area shall complete a record describing the geological type, quantity and location of samples taken, which should, at a minimum, be deposited with their National Antarctic Data Centre or with the Antarctic Master Directory.

### 7(x) Requirements for reports

- Parties should ensure that the principal holder for each Permit issued submits to the appropriate authority a report describing the activities undertaken. Such reports should include, as appropriate, the information identified in the visit report form contained in the Guide to the Preparation of Management Plans for Antarctic Specially Protected Areas.

- Parties should maintain a record of such activities and, in the Annual Exchange of Information, should provide summary descriptions of activities conducted by persons subject to their jurisdiction, in sufficient detail to allow evaluation of the effectiveness of the Management Plan. Parties should, wherever possible, deposit originals or copies of such original reports in a publicly accessible archive to maintain a record of usage, to be used both in any review of the management plan and in organizing the scientific use of the Area.

- The appropriate authority should be notified of any activities/measures undertaken, and / or of any materials released and not removed, that were not included in the authorized permit.

**References**

Acevedo, J., Vallejos, V., Vargas, R., Torres, J.P. & Torres, D. 2002. Informe científico. ECA XXXVIII (2001/2002). Proyecto INACH 018 "Estuios ecológicos sobre el lobo fino antásrtico, Arctocephalus gazella", cabo Shirreff, isla Livingston, Shetland del Sur, Antártica. Ministerio de Relaciones Exteriores, Instituto Antártico Chileno. N° Ingreso 642/710, 11.ABR.2002.

Acevedo, J., Aguayo-Lobo, A. & Torres, D. 2009a. Albino Weddell seal at Cape ShirreV, Livingston Island, Antarctica. *Polar Biology* **32** (8):1239–43.

Acevedo, J., Aguayo-Lobo, A. & Torres, D. 2009b. Rare piebald and partially leucistic Antarctic fur seals, Arctocephalus gazella, at Cape Shirreff, Livingston Island, Antarctica. *Polar Biology* **32** (1): 41–45.

Agnew, A.J. 1997. Review: the CCAMLR Ecosystem Monitoring Programme. *Antarctic Science* **9** (3): 235-242.

Aguayo, A. 1978. The present status of the Antarctic fur seal *Arctocephalus gazella* at the South Shetland Islands. *Polar Record* **19**: 167-176.

Aguayo, A. & Torres, D. 1966. A first census of Pinnipedia in the South Shetland Islands and other observations on marine mammals. In: SCAR / SCOR / IAPO / IUBS Symposium on Antarctic Oceanography, Santiago, Chile, 13-16 September 1966, Section 4: Coastal Waters: 166-168.

Aguayo, A. & Torres, D. 1967. Observaciones sobre mamiferos marinos durante la Vigésima Comisión Antártica Chilena. Primer censo de pinípedos en las Islas Shetland del Sur. Revta. Biol. Mar., **13**(1): 1-57.

Aguayo, A. & Torres, D. 1993. Análisis de los censos de *Arctocephalus gazella* efectuados en el Sitio de Especial Interés Científico No. 32, isla Livingston, Antártica. *Serie Científica Instituto Antártico Chileno* **43**: 87-91.

AMLR 2008. AMLR 2007-2008 field season report. Objectives, Accomplishments and Tentative Conclusions. Southwest Fisheries Science Center Antarctic Ecosystem Research Group. October 2008.

AMLR 2009. AMLR 2008-2009 field season report. Objectives, Accomplishments and Tentative Conclusions. Southwest Fisheries Science Center Antarctic Ecosystem Research Group. May 2009.

Antolos, M.,Miller, A.K. & Trivelpiece, W.Z. 2004. Seabird research at Cape Shirreff, Livingston Island, Antarctica 2003-2004. In Lipsky, J. (ed) AMLR (Antarctic Marine Living Resources) 2003-2004 Field Season Report, Ch. 7. Antarctic Ecosystem Research Division, Southwest Fisheries Science Center, La Jolla, California.

Bengston, J.L., Ferm, L.M., Härkönen, T.J. & Stewart, B.S. 1990. Abundance of Antarctic fur seals in the South Shetland Islands, Antarctica, during the 1986/87 austral summer. In: Kerry, K. and Hempel, G. (Eds). *Antarctic Ecosystems, Proceedings of the Fifth SCAR Symposium on Antarctic Biology.* Springer-Verlag, Berlin: 265-270.

Blank, O., Retamal, P., Torres D. & Abalos, P. 1999. First record of *Brucella* spp. antibodies in *Arctocephalus gazella* and *Leptonychotes weddelli* from Cape Shirreff, Livingston Island, Antarctica. (SC-CAMLR-XVIII/BG/17.) *CCAMLR Scientific Abstracts* 5.

Blank, O., Retamal, P., Abalos P. & Torres, D. 2001a. Additional data on anti-*Brucella* antibodies in *Arctocephalus gazella* from Cape Shirreff, Livingston Island, Antarctica. *CCAMLR Science* **8**: 147-154.

Blank, O., Montt, J.M., Celedón M. & Torres, D. 2001b. Herpes virus antobodies in *Arctocephalus gazella* from Cape Shirreff, Livingston Island, Antarctica. WG-EMM- 01/59.

Bonner, W.N. & Smith, R.I.L. (Eds) 1985. *Conservation areas in the Antarctic.* SCAR, Cambridge: 59-63.

Carten, T.M., Taft, M., Trivelpiece W.Z. & Holt, R.S. 2001. Seabird research at Cape Shirreff, Livingston Island, Antarctica, 1999/2000. In Lipsky, J. (ed) AMLR (Antarctic Marine Living Resources) 1999-2000 Field Season Report, Ch. 7. Antarctic Ecosystem Research Division, Southwest Fisheries Science Center, La Jolla, California.

Cattan, P., Yánez, J., Torres, D., Gajardo, M. & Cárdenas, J. 1982. Censo, marcaje y estructura poblacional del lobo fino antártico *Arctocephalus gazella* (Peters, 1875) en las islas Shetland del Sur, Chile. *Serie Científica Instituto Antártico Chileno* **29**: 31-38.

CCAMLR 1997. Management plan for the protection of Cape Shirreff and the San Telmo Islands, South Shetland Islands, as a site included in the CCAMLR Ecosystem Monitoring Program. In: *Schedule of Conservation Measures in Force 1996/97*: 51-64.

CCAMLR 2010. *CCAMLR Statistical Bulletin* **22** (2000–2009). CCAMLR, Hobart, Australia.

Chisholm, S.E., Pietrzak, K.W., Miller, A.K. & Trivelpiece, W.Z. 2008. Seabird research at Cape Shirreff, Livingston Island, Antarctica 2007-2008. In Van Cise, A.M. (ed) AMLR (Antarctic Marine Living Resources) 2007-2008 Field Season Report, Ch. 5. Antarctic Ecosystem Research Division, Southwest Fisheries Science Center, La Jolla, California.

Constantinescu, F. & Torres, D. 1995. Análisis bioantropológico de un cráneo humano hallado en cabo Shirreff, isla Livingston, Antártica. Ser. Cient. INACH **45**: 89-99.

Cox, M.J., Demer, D.A., Warren, J.D., Cutter, G.R. & Brierley, A.S. 2009. Multibeam echosounder observations reveal interactions between Antarctic krill and air-breathing predators. *Marine Ecology Progress Series* **378**: 199–209.

Croxall, J.P. & Kirkwood, E.D. 1979. *The distribution of penguins on the Antarctic Peninsula and the islands of the Scotia Sea.* British Antarctic Survey, Cambridge.

Everett, K.R. 1971. Observations on the glacial history of Livingston Island. *Arctic* **24** (1): 41-50.

Fildes, R. 1821. A journal of a voyage from Liverpool towards New South Shetland on a sealing and sea elephant adventure kept on board Brig Robert of Liverpool, Robert Fildes, 13 August - 26 December 1821. MS 101/1, Scott Polar Research Institute, Cambridge.

Goebel, M.E., Rutishauser, M., Parker, B., Banks, A., Costa, D.P., Gales, N. & Holt, R.S. 2001a. Pinniped research at Cape Shirreff, Livingston Island, Antarctica, 1999/2000. In Lipsky, J. (ed) AMLR (Antarctic Marine Living Resources) 1999-2000 Field Season Report, Ch. 8. Antarctic Ecosystem Research Division, Southwest Fisheries Science Center, La Jolla, California.

Goebel, M.E., Parker, B., Banks, A., Costa, D.P., Pister, B. & Holt, R.S. 2001b. Pinniped research at Cape Shirreff, Livingston Island, Antarctica, 2000/2001. In Lipsky, J. (ed) AMLR (Antarctic Marine Living Resources) 2000-01 Field Season Report, Ch. 8. Antarctic Ecosystem Research Division, Southwest Fisheries Science Center, La Jolla, California.

Goebel, M.E., McDonald, B.I., Freeman, S., Haner, R., Spear, N. & Sexton, S. 2008. Pinniped Research at Cape Shirreff, Livingston Island, 2008/09. In AMLR 2007-2008 field season report. Objectives, Accomplishments and Tentative Conclusions. Southwest Fisheries Science Center Antarctic Ecosystem Research Group. La Jolla, California.

Goebel, M.E., Krause, D., Freeman, S., Burner, R., Bonin, C., Vasquez del Mercado, R., Van Cise, A.M. & Gafney, J. 2009. Pinniped Research at Cape Shirreff, Livingston Island, Antarctica, 2008/09. In AMLR 2008-2009 field season report. Objectives, Accomplishments and Tentative Conclusions. Southwest Fisheries Science Center Antarctic Ecosystem Research Group. La Jolla, California.

Garcia, M., Aguayo, A. & Torres, D. 1995. Aspectos conductuales de los machos de lobo fino antartico, *Arctocephalus gazella* en Cabo Shirreff, isla Livingston, Antártica, durante la fase de apareamiento. *Serie Científica Instituto Antártico Chileno* **45**: 101-112.

Harris, C.M. 2001. Revision of management plans for Antarctic protected areas originally proposed by the United States of America and the United Kingdom: Field visit report. Internal report for the National Science Foundation, US, and the Foreign and Commonwealth Office, UK. *Environmental Research & Assessment*, Cambridge.

Headland, R. 1989. *Chronological list of Antarctic expeditions and related historical events.* Cambridge University Press, Cambridge.

Heap, J. (ed) 1994. *Handbook of the Antarctic Treaty System.* 8th Edn. U.S. Department of State, Washington.

Hobbs, G.J. 1968. The geology of the South Shetland Islands. IV. The geology of Livingston Island. *British Antarctic Survey Scientific Reports* **47**.

Henadez, J., Prado, V., Torres, D., Waldenström, J., Haemig, P.D. & Olsen, B. 2007. Enteropathogenic *Escherichia coli* (EPEC) in Antarctic fur seals *Arctocephalus gazella*. *Polar Biology* **30** (10):1227–29.

Hewitt, R.P., Kim, S., Naganobu, M., Gutierrez, M., Kang, D., Taka, Y., Quinones, J., Lee Y.-H., Shin, H.-C., Kawaguchi, S., Emery, J.H., Demer, D.A. & Loeb, V.J. 2004. Variation in the biomass density and demography of Antarctic krill in the vicinity ofthe South Shetland Islands during the 1999/2000 austral summer. *Deep-Sea Research* II **51** 1411–1419.

Hinke, J.T., Salwicka, K., Trivelpiece, S.G., Watters, S.G., & Trivelpiece, W.Z. 2007. Divergent responses of *Pygoscelis* penguins reveal a common environmental driver. *Oecologia* **153**:845–855.

Hucke-Gaete, R., Acevedo, J., Osman, L., Vargas, R., Blank, O. & Torres, D. 2001. Informe científico. ECA XXXVII (2000/2001). Proyecto 018 "Estudios ecológicos sobre el lobo fino antártico, Arctocephalus gazella", cabo Shirreff, isla Livingston, Shetland del Sur, Antártica.

Hucke-Gaete, R., Torres, D., Aguayo, A. & Vallejos, V. 1998. Decline of Arctocephalus gazella population at SSSI No. 32, South Shetlands, Antarctica (1997/98 season): a discussion of possible causes. WG-EMM-98/17. August 1998. Kochin. 10: 16–19

Hucke-Gaete, R, Torres, D. & Vallejos, V. 1997a. Population size and distribution of *Pygoscelis antarctica* and *P. papua* at Cape Shirreff, Livingston Island, Antarctica (1996/97 Season). CCAMLR WG-EMM-97/62.

Hucke-Gaete, R, Torres, D., Vallejos, V. & Aguayo, A. 1997b. Population size and distribution of *Arctocephalus gazella* at SSSI No. 32, Livingston Island, Antarctica (1996/97 Season). CCAMLR WG-EMM-97/62.

Hucke-Gaete, R, Torres, D. & Vallejos, V. 1997c. Entanglement of Antarctic fur seals, *Arctocephalus gazella*, by marine debris at Cape Shirreff and San Telmo Islets, Livingston Island, Antarctica:1998-1997. *Serie Científica Instituto Antártico Chileno* **47**: 123-135.

Hucke-Gaete, R., Osman, L.P., Moreno, C.A. & Torres, D. 2004. Examining natural population growth from near extinction: the case of the Antarctic fur seal at the South Shetlands, Antarctica. *Polar Biology* **27** (5): 304–311

Huckstadt, L., Costa, D. P., McDonald, B. I., Tremblay, Y., Crocker, D. E., Goebel, M. E. & Fedak, M. E. 2006. Habitat Selection and Foraging Behavior of Southern Elephant Seals in the Western Antarctic Peninsula. American Geophysical Union, Fall Meeting 2006, abstract #OS33A-1684.

INACH (Instituto Antártico Chileno) 2010. Chilean Antarctic Program of Scientific Research 2009-2010. Chilean Antarctic Institute Research Projects Department. Santiago, Chile.

Kawaguchi, S., Nicol, S., Taki, K. & Naganobu, M. 2006. Fishing ground selection in the Antarctic krill fishery: Trends in patterns across years, seasons and nations. *CCAMLR Science*, **13** : 117–141.

Leppe, M., Fernandoy, F., Palma-Heldt, S. & Moisan, P 2004. Flora mesozoica en los depósitos morrénicos de Cabo Shirreff, Isla Livingston, Shetland del Sur, Península Antártica, in Actas del 10° Congreso Geológico Chileno. CD-ROM. Resumen Expandido, 4pp. Universidad de Concepción. Concepción. Chile.

Leung, E.S.W., Orben, R.A. & Trivelpiece, W.Z. 2006. Seabird research at Cape Shirreff, Livingston Island, Antarctica 2005-2006. In Lipsky, J. (ed) AMLR (Antarctic Marine Living Resources) 2005-2006 Field Season Report, Ch. 9. Antarctic Ecosystem Research Division, Southwest Fisheries Science Center, La Jolla, California.

Miller, A.K., Leung, E.S.W. & Trivelpiece, W.Z. 2005. Seabird research at Cape Shirreff, Livingston Island, Antarctica 2004-2005. In Lipsky, J. (ed) AMLR (Antarctic Marine Living Resources) 2004-2005 Field Season Report, Ch. 7. Antarctic Ecosystem Research Division, Southwest Fisheries Science Center, La Jolla, California.

Miller, A.K. & Trivelpiece, W.Z. 2007. Cycles of *Euphausia superba* recruitment evident in the diet of Pygoscelid penguins and net trawls in the South Shetland Islands, Antarctica. *Polar Biology* **30** (12):1615–1623.

Miller, A.K. & Trivelpiece, W.Z. 2008. Chinstrap penguins alter foraging and diving behavior in response to the size of their principle prey, Antarctic krill. *Marine Biology* **154**: 201-208.

Miller, A.K., Karnovsky, N.J. & Trivelpiece, W.Z. 2008. Flexible foraging strategies of gentoo penguins *Pygoscelis papua* over 5 years in the South Shetland Islands, Antarctica. *Marine Biology* **156**: 2527-2537.

O'Gorman, F.A. 1961. Fur seals breeding in the Falkland Islands Dependencies. *Nature* **192**: 914-16.

O'Gorman, F.A. 1963. The return of the Antarctic fur seal. *New Scientist* **20**: 374-76.

Olavarría, C., Coria, N., Schlatter, R., Hucke-Gaete, R., Vallejos, V., Godoy, C., Torres D. & Aguayo, A. 1999. Cisnes de cuello negro, *Cygnus melanocoripha* (Molina, 1782) en el área de las islas Shetland del Sur y península Antártica. *Serie Científica Instituto Antártico Chileno* **49**: 79-87.

Oliva, D., Durán, R, Gajardo, M. & Torres, D. 1987. Numerical changes in the population of the Antarctic fur seal *Arctocephalus gazella* at two localities of the South Shetland Islands. *Serie Científica Instituto Antártico Chileno* **36**: 135-144.

Oliva, D., Durán, R, Gajardo, M. & Torres, D. 1988. Population structure and harem size groups of the Antarctic fur seal *Arctocephalus gazella* Cape Shirreff, Livingston Island, South Shetland Islands. Meeting of the SCAR Group of Specialists on Seals, Hobart, Tasmania, Australia. *Biomass Report Series* **59**: 39.

Orben, R.A., Chisholm, S.E., Miller, S.K. & Trivelpiece, W.Z. 2007. Seabird research at Cape Shirreff, Livingston Island, Antarctica 2006-2007. In Lipsky, J. (ed) AMLR (Antarctic Marine Living Resources) 2006-2007 Field Season Report, Ch. 7. Antarctic Ecosystem Research Division, Southwest Fisheries Science Center, La Jolla, California.

Osman, L.P., Hucke-Gaete, R., Moreno, C.A., & Torress, D. 2004. Feeding ecology of Antarctic fur seals at Cape Shirreff, South Shetlands,Antarctica. *Polar Biology* **27**(2): 92–98.

Palma-Heldt, S., Fernandoy, F., Quezada, I. & Leppe, M 2004. Registro Palinológico de Cabo Shirreff, Isla Livingston, nueva localidad para el Mesozoico de Las Shetland del Sur, in V Simposio Argentino y I Latinoamericano sobre Investigaciones Antárticas CD-ROM. Resumen Expandido N° 104GP. Buenos Aires, Argentina.

Palma-Heldt, S., Fernandoy, F., Henríquez, G. & Leppe, M 2007. Palynoflora of Livingston Island, South Shetland Islands : Contribution to the understanding of the evolution of the southern Pacific Gondwana margin. U.S. Geological Survey and The National Academies; USGS OF-2007-1047, Extended Abstract 100.

Pietrzak, K.W., Breeden, J.H, Miller, A.K. & Trivelpiece, W.Z. 2009. Seabird research at Cape Shirreff, Livingston Island, Antarctica 2008-2009. In Van Cise, A.M. (ed) AMLR (Antarctic Marine Living Resources) 2008-2008 Field Season Report, Ch. 6. Antarctic Ecosystem Research Division, Southwest Fisheries Science Center, La Jolla, California.

Pinochet de la Barra, O. 1991. El misterio del "San Telmo". ¿Náufragos españoles pisaron por primera vez la Antártida? *Revista Historia* (Madrid), **16** (18): 31-36.

Reid, K., Jessop, M.J., Barrett, M.S., Kawagucji, S., Siegel, V. & Goebel, M.E. 2004. Widening the net: spatio-temporal variability in the krill population structure across the Scotia Sea. *Deep-Sea Research* II **51**: 1275–1287

Reiss, C. S., Cossio, A. M., Loeb, V. & Demer, D. A. 2008. Variations in the biomass of Antarctic krill (Euphausia superba) around the South Shetland Islands, 1996–2006. *ICES Journal of Marine Science* **65**: 497–508.

Sallaberry, M. & Schlatter, R. 1983. Estimacíon del número de pingüinos en el Archipiélago de las Shetland del Sur. *Serie Científica Instituto Antártico Chileno* **30**: 87-91.

Saxer, I.M., Scheffler, D.A. & Trivelpiece, W.Z. 2003. Seabird research at Cape Shirreff, Livingston Island, Antarctica 2001-2002. In Lipsky, J. (ed) AMLR (Antarctic Marine Living Resources) 2001-2002 Field Season Report, Ch. 6. Antarctic Ecosystem Research Division, Southwest Fisheries Science Center, La Jolla, California.

Shill, L.F., Antolos, M. & Trivelpiece, W.Z. 2003. Seabird research at Cape Shirreff, Livingston Island, Antarctica 2002-2003. In Lipsky, J. (ed) AMLR (Antarctic Marine Living Resources) 2002-2003 Field Season Report, Ch. 8. Antarctic Ecosystem Research Division, Southwest Fisheries Science Center, La Jolla, California.

Smellie, J.L., Pallàs, R.M., Sàbata, F. & Zheng, X. 1996. Age and correlation of volcanism in central Livingston Island, South Shetland Islands: K-Ar and geochemical constraints. *Jounral of South American Earth Sciences* **9** (3/4): 265-272.

Smith, R.I.L. & Simpson, H.W. 1987. Early Nineteeth Century sealers' refuges on Livingston Island, South Shetland Islands. *British Antarctic Survey Bulletin* **74**: 49-72.

Stehberg, R. & V. Lucero, 1996. Excavaciones arqueológicas en playa Yámana, cabo Shirreff, isla Livingston, Shetland del Sur, Antártica. *Serie Científica Instituto Antártico Chileno* 46: 59-81.

Taft, M.R., Saxer, I.M. & Trivelpiece W.Z 2001. Seabird research at Cape Shirreff, Livingston Island, Antarctica, 2000/2001. In Lipsky, J. (ed) AMLR (Antarctic Marine Living Resources) 2000-01 Field Season Report, Ch. 7. Antarctic Ecosystem Research Division, Southwest Fisheries Science Center, La Jolla, California.

Torres, D. 1984. Síntesis de actividades, resultados y proyecciones de las investigaciones chilenas sobre pinípedos antarcticos. *Boletín Antártico Chileno* **4**(1): 33-34.

Torres, D. 1990. Collares plásticos en lobos finos antárticos: Otra evidencia de contaminación. *Boletín Antártico Chileno* **10** (1): 20-22 .

Torres, D. 1992. ¿Cráneo indígena en cabo Shirreff? Un estudio en desarrollo. *Boletín Antártico Chileno* **11** (2): 2-6.

Torres, D. 1994. Synthesis of CEMP activities carried out at Cape Shirreff. Report to CCAMLR WG-CEMP 94/28.

Torres, D. 1995. Antecedentes y proyecciones científicas de los estudios en el SEIC No. 32 y Sitio CEMP «Cabo Shirreff e islotes San Telmo», isla Livingston, Antártica. *Serie Científica Instituto Antártico Chileno* **45**: 143-169.

Torres, D. 1999. Observations on ca. 175-Year Old Human Remains from Antarctica (Cape Shirreff, Livingston Island, South Shetlands). *International Journal of Circumpolar Health* **58**: 72-83.

Torres, D. & Aguayo, A. 1993. Impacto antrópico en cabo Shirreff, isla Livingston, Antártica. *Serie Científica Instituto Antártico Chileno* **43**: 93-108.

Torres, D. & Gajardo, M. 1985. Información preliminar sobre desechos plásticos hallados en cabo Shirreff, isla Livingston, Shetland del Sur, Chile. *Boletín Antártico Chileno* **5**(2): 12-13.

Torres, D. & Jorquera, D. 1992. Analysis of Marine Debris found at Cape Shirreff, Livingston Island, South Shetlands, Antarctica. SC-CAMLR/BG/7, 12 pp. CCAMLR, Hobart, Australia.

Torres, D. & Jorquera, D. 1994. Marine Debris Collected at Cape Shirreff, Livinston Island, during the Antarctic Season 1993/94. CCMALR-XIII/BG/17, 10 pp. 18 October 1994. Hobart, Australia.

Torres, D. & Jorquera, D. 1995. Línea de base para el seguimiento de los desechos marinos en cabo Shirreff, isla Livingston, Antártica. *Serie Científica Instituto Antártico Chileno* **45**: 131-141.

Torres, D., Jaña, R., Encina, L. & Vicuña, P. 2001. Cartografía digital de cabo Shirreff, isla Livingston, Antártica: un avance importante. *Boletín Antártico Chileno* **20** (2): 4-6.

Torres, D.E. & Valdenegro V. 2004. Nuevos registros de mortalidad y necropsias de cachorros de lobo fino antártico, Arctocephalus gazella, en cabo Shirreff, sila Livingston, Antártica. *Boletín Antártico Chileno* **23** (1).

Torres, D., Vallejos, V., Acevedo, J., Hucke-Gaete, R. & Zarate, S. 1998. Registros biologicos atípico en cabo Shirreff, isla Livingston, Antártica. *Boletín Antártico Chileno* **17** (1): 17-19.

Torres, D., Vallejos, V., Acevedo, J., Blank, O., Hucke-Gaete, R. & Tirado, S. 1999. Actividades realizadas en cabo Shirreff, isla Livingston, en temporada 1998/99. *Boletín Antártico Chileno* **18** (1): 29-32.

Torres, T. 1993. Primer hallazgo de madera fósil en Cabo Shirreff, isla Livingston, Antártica. *Serie Científica Instituto Antártico Chileno* **43**: 31-39.

Tufft, R. 1958. Preliminary biology report Livingston Island summer survey. Unpublished British Antarctic Survey report, BAS Archives Ref. AD6/2D/1957/N2.

Vargas, R., Osman, L.P. & Torres, D. 2009. Inter-sexual diVerences in Antarctic fur seal pup growth rates: evidence of environmental regulation? Polar Biology **32** (8):1177–86

Vallejos, V., Acevedo, J., Blank, O., Osman, L. & Torres, D. 2000. Informe científico - logístico. ECA XXXVI (1999/2000). Proyecto 018 "Estudios ecológicos sobre el lobo fino antártico, Arctocephalus gazella", cabo Shirreff, archipiélago de las Shetland del Sur, Antártica. Ministerio de Relaciones Exteriores, Instituto Antártico Chileno. Nº Ingreso 642/712, 19 ABR.2000.

Vallejos, V., Osman, L., Vargas, R., Vera, C. & Torres, D. 2003. Informe científico. ECA XXXIX (2002/2003). Proyecto INACH 018 "Estudios ecológicos sobre el lobo fino antártico, Arctocephalus gazella", cabo Shirreff, isla Livingston, Shetland del Sur, Antártica. Ministerio de Relaciones Exteriores, Instituto Antártico Chileno.

Vera, C., Vargas, R. & Torres, D. 2004. El impacto de la foca leopardo en la población de cachorros de lobo fino antártico en cabo Shirreff, Antártica, durante la temporada 2003/2004. *Boletín Antártico Chileno* **23** (1).

Warren, J., Sessions, S., Patterson, M. Jenkins, A., Needham, D. & Demer, D. 2005. Nearshore Survey. In AMLR 2004-2005 field season report. Objectives, Accomplishments and Tentative Conclusions. Southwest Fisheries Science Center Antarctic Ecosystem Research Group. La Jolla, California.

Warren, J., Cox, M., Sessions, S. Jenkins, A., Needham, D. & Demer, D. 2006. Nearshore acoustical survey near Cape Shirreff, Livingston Island. In AMLR 2005-2006 field season report. Objectives, Accomplishments and Tentative Conclusions. Southwest Fisheries Science Center Antarctic Ecosystem Research Group. La Jolla, California.

Warren, J., Cox, M., Sessions, S. Jenkins, A., Needham, D. & Demer, D. 2007. Nearshore acoustical survey near Cape Shirreff, Livingston Island. In AMLR 2006-2007 field season report. Objectives, Accomplishments and Tentative Conclusions. Southwest Fisheries Science Center Antarctic Ecosystem Research Group. La Jolla, California.

Woehler, E.J. (ed) 1993. *The distribution and abundance of Antarctic and sub-Antarctic penguins.* SCAR, Cambridge.

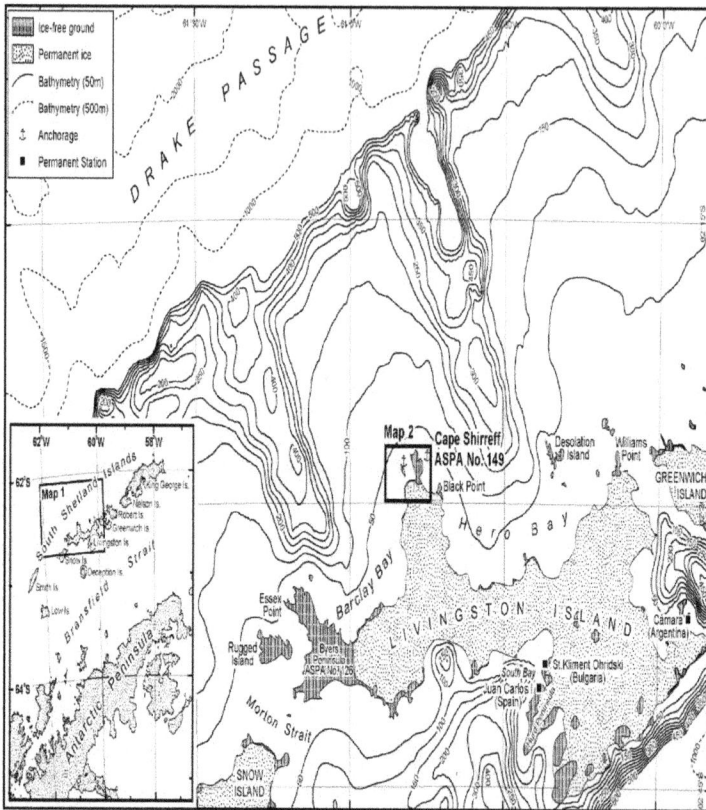

ASPA No. 149
Cape Shirreff & San Telmo Island
Map 1: Regional overview

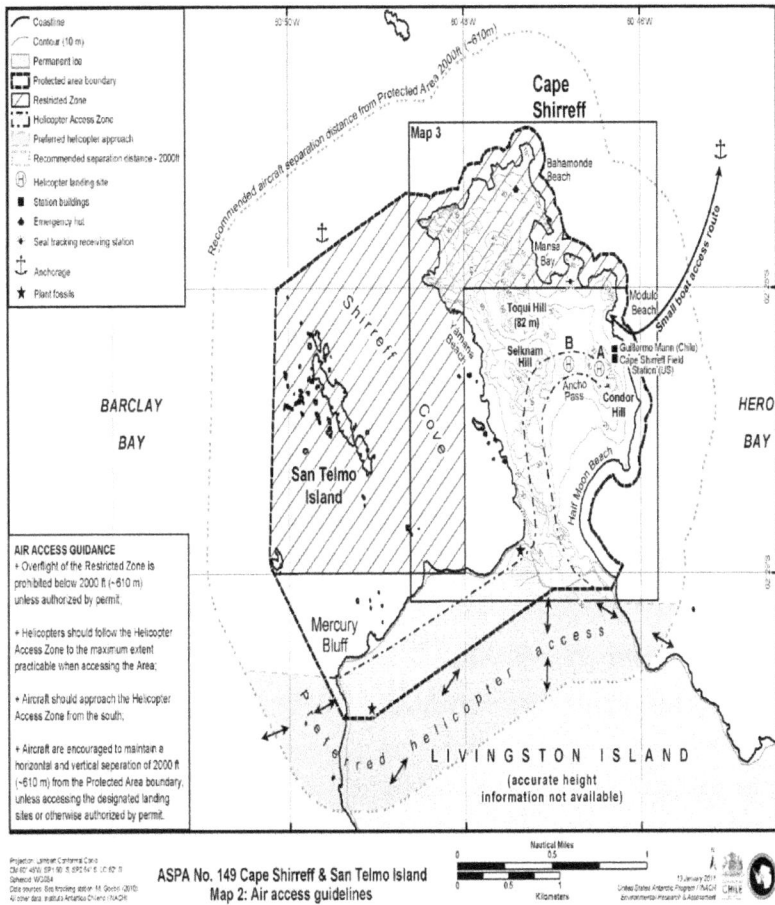

ASPA No. 149 Cape Shirreff & San Telmo Island
Map 2: Air access guidelines

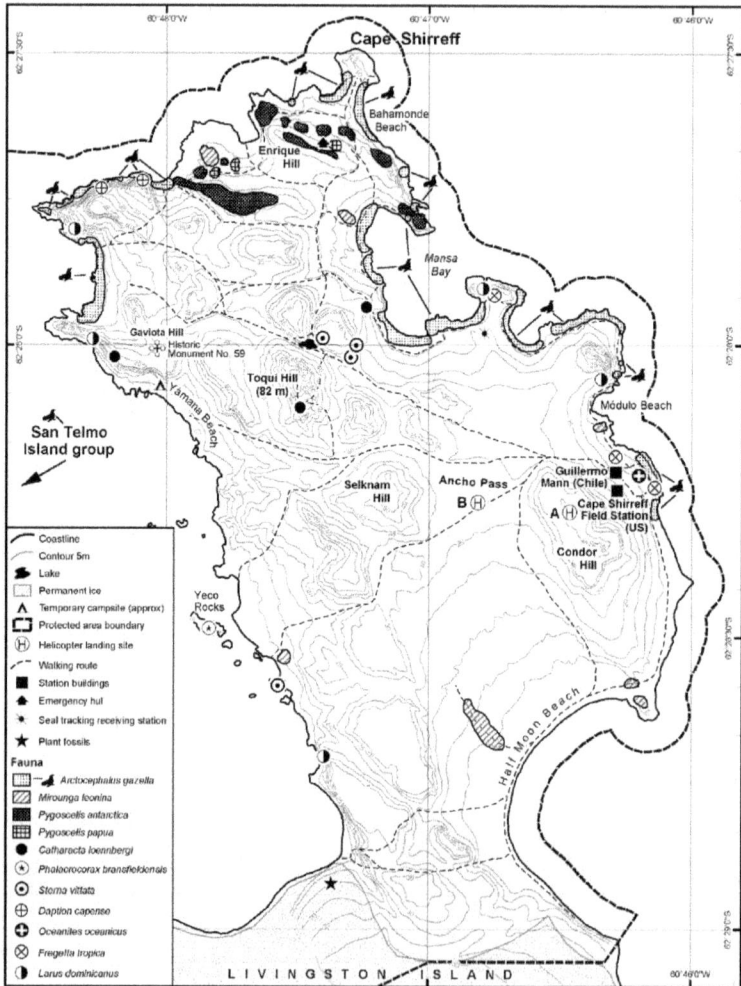

Cape Shirreff

Bahamonde Beach

Enrique Hill

Mansa Bay

Gaviota Hill
Historic Monument No. 59

Toqui Hill (82 m)

Módulo Beach

San Telmo Island group

Guillermo Mann (Chile)

Selknam Hill

Ancho Pass

Cape Shirreff Field Station (US)

Condor Hill

Yeco Rocks

Hall Moon Beach

Coastline
Contour 5m
Lake
Permanent Ice
Temporary campsite (approx)
Protected area boundary
Helicopter landing site
Walking route
Station buildings
Emergency hut
Seal tracking receiving station
Plant fossils

Fauna
Arctocephalus gazella
Mirounga leonina
Pygoscelis antarctica
Pygoscelis papua
Catharacta loennbergi
Phalacrocorax bransfieldensis
Sterna vittata
Daption capense
Oceanites oceanicus
Fregetta tropica
Larus dominicanus

LIVINGSTON ISLAND

**ASPA No. 149**
**Cape Shirreff & San Telmo Island**
**Map 3: Breeding colonies & human features**

0   100   200   300
Meters

# Management Plan for
# Antarctic Specially Protected Area No. 165

# EDMONSON POINT, WOOD BAY, VICTORIA LAND, ROSS SEA

## 1.    Description of values to be protected

Edmonson Point (74°20' S, 165°08' E, 5.49 km²), Wood Bay, Victoria Land, Ross Sea, is proposed as an Antarctic Specially Protected Area (ASPA) by Italy on the grounds that it has outstanding ecological and scientific values which require protection from possible interference that might arise from unregulated access. The Area includes ice-free ground and a small area of adjacent sea at the foot of the eastern slopes of Mount Melbourne (2732 m), which is of limited extent and is the subject of ongoing and long-term scientific research.

The terrestrial and freshwater ecosystem at Edmonson Point is one of the most outstanding in northern Victoria Land. An exceptional diversity of freshwater habitats is present, with numerous streams, lakes, ponds and seepage areas, exhibiting nutrient conditions ranging from eutrophic to oligotrophic.  Such a range of freshwater habitats is rare in Victoria Land. Consequently, these habitats support a high diversity of algal and cyanobacterial species, with over 120 species so far recorded, and the stream network is the most extensive and substantial in northern Victoria Land. The volcanic lithology and locally nutrient-enriched (by birds) substrata, together with a localised abundance of water, provides a habitat for relatively extensive bryophyte development. Plant communities are highly sensitive to changes in the hydrological regime, and environmental gradients produce sharply defined community boundaries.  Thus, the range of vegetation is diverse, and includes epilithic lichen communities, some of which are dependent on high nitrogen input from birds, communities associated with late-lying snow patches, and moss-dominated communities that favour continually moist or wet habitats.  The site represents one of the best examples of the latter community-type in Victoria Land.  Invertebrates are unusually abundant and extensively distributed for this part of Antarctica.

The nature and diversity of the terrestrial and freshwater habitats offer outstanding scientific opportunities, especially for studies of biological variation and processes along moisture and nutrient gradients. The site is considered one of the best in Antarctica for studies of algal ecology. These features were among those that led to the selection of Edmonson Point as a key site in the Scientific Committee on Antarctic Research's Biological Investigations of Terrestrial Antarctic Systems (BIOTAS) programme in 1995-96. A coordinated multinational research programme, known as BIOTEX-1, established study sites and made extensive collections of soil, rock, water, snow, guano, bacteria, vegetation (cyanobacterial mats, fungi, algae, lichens, bryophytes) and of terrestrial invertebrates.

The scientific value of Edmonson Point is also considered exceptional for studies on the impact of climate change on terrestrial ecosystems.  Its location at approximately the mid-point in a north-south latitudinal gradient extending along Victoria Land is complementary to other sites protected for their important terrestrial ecological values, such as Cape Hallett (ASPA No. 106) and Botany Bay, Cape Geology (ASPA No. 154), which are about 300 km to the north and south respectively. This geographical position is recognised as important in a continent-wide ecological research network (e.g. the Scientific Committee on Antarctic Research 'RiSCC' programme).  In addition, the lakes are among the best in northern Victoria Land for studies of biogeochemical processes with short- and long-term variations.  Together with the unique properties of the permafrost active layer, which is unusually thick in this location, these features are considered particularly useful as sensitive indicators of ecological change in response to levels of UV radiation and in shifting climate.

A colony of approximately 2000 pairs of Adélie penguins (*Pygoscelis adeliae*) has been a focus of ongoing research since 1994-95 together with a colony of approximately 120 pairs of south polar skuas (*Catharacta maccormicki*). The Edmonson Point Adélie penguin colony is included in the ecosystem monitoring network of the Commission for the Conservation of Antarctic Marine Living Resources (CCAMLR). The site is considered a good example of this species assemblage, which is representative of those found elsewhere. It is unusual, however, for the diverse range of breeding habitat available for south polar skuas, and also because of the unusually high skua to penguin ratio (1:20). The geographical position, the size of the colonies, the terrain and habitat features of the site, the natural protection given by the summer fast ice extension and the distance from Mario Zucchelli Station at Terra Nova Bay (which isolates the colony from research station disturbance but allows for logistic support) make Edmonson Point particularly suitable for the research being undertaken on these birds. The research contributes to the CCAMLR Ecosystem Monitoring Programme (CEMP), focusing on population monitoring, reproductive success, feeding and foraging strategies, migration, and behaviour. This research is important to broader studies of how natural and human-induced variations in the Antarctic ecosystem may affect the breeding success of Adélie penguins, and to understand the potential impact of harvesting of Antarctic krill (*Euphausia superba*).

The near-shore marine environment is a good and representative example of the sea-ice habitat used by breeding Weddell seals to give birth and wean pups early in the summer season. Only one other ASPA in the Ross Sea region has been designated to protect Weddell seals (ASPA No. 137 Northwest White Island, McMurdo Sound), although this site is designated because the small breeding group of seals in that locality is highly unusual; in contrast, inclusion here is as a representative example similar to breeding sites throughout the region.

In addition to the outstanding biological values, a diversity of geomorphic features is present, including a series of ice-cored moraines incorporating marine deposits, raised beaches, patterned ground, a cuspate foreland, and fossil penguin colonies. The cuspate foreland at Edmonson Point is a rare feature in Victoria Land, and is one of the best examples of its kind. It is unusual in that it is not occupied by a breeding colony of penguins, as is the case at Cape Hallett and Cape Adare. The glacial moraines that incorporate marine deposits, including seal bones and shells of the bivalves *Laternula elliptica* and *Adamussium colbecki*, are particularly valuable for dating regional glacier fluctuations. Sedimentary sequences in the north-west of Edmonson Point contain fossils from former penguin colonies. These are useful for dating the persistence of bird breeding at the site, which contributes to reconstructions of Holocene glacial phases and palaeoclimate.

The wide representation and the quality of phenomena at Edmonson Point have attracted interest from a variety of disciplines and research has been carried out at the site for more than 20 years. Over this period, substantial scientific databases have been established, which adds to the value of Edmonson Point for current, on-going and future research. It is important that pressures from human activities in the Area are managed so that the investments made in these long-term data sets are not inadvertently compromised. These factors also make the site of exceptional scientific value for multi-disciplinary studies.

Given the duration and range of past activities, Edmonson Point cannot be considered pristine. Some environmental impacts have been observed, such as occasional damage to soils and moss communities by trampling, dispersal of materials from scientific equipment by wind, and alteration of habitat by construction of facilities. In contrast, the ice-free area at Colline Ippolito (Ippolito Hills) (1.67 km$^2$) approximately 1.5 km to the north-west, has received relatively little visitation and human disturbance at this site is believed to be minimal. As such, Colline Ippolito is considered particularly valuable as a potential reference area for comparative studies to the main Edmonson Point, and it is important that this potential scientific value is maintained. While the precise effects of scientific research and human presence at both sites are uncertain, because detailed studies on human impact have not yet been undertaken, contaminants in the local marine ecosystem remain very low and human impacts on the ecosystem as a whole, particularly at Colline Ippolito, are considered to be generally minor.

The biological and scientific values at Edmonson Point and Colline Ippolito are vulnerable to human disturbance. The vegetation, water-saturated soils and freshwater environments are susceptible to damage from trampling, sampling and pollution. Scientific studies could be compromised by disturbance to phenomena or to installed equipment. It is important that human activities are managed so that the risks of impacts on the outstanding values of the Area are minimised.

The total Area of 5.49 km$^2$ comprises the ice-free area of Edmonson Point (1.79 km$^2$), the smaller but similar ice-free area at Colline Ippolito (1.12 km$^2$) approximately 1.5 km to its north which is designated a Restricted Zone, and the adjacent marine environment (2.58 km$^2$) extending 200 m offshore from Edmonson Point and Colline Ippolito and including Baia Siena (Siena Bay) (Map 1).

## 2. Aims and objectives

Management at Edmonson Point aims to:

- avoid degradation of, or substantial risk to, the values of the Area by preventing unnecessary human disturbance;
- allow scientific research while ensuring protection from mutual interference and/or over-sampling;
- allow scientific research provided it is for reasons which cannot reasonably be served elsewhere;
- protect sites of long-term scientific studies from disturbance;
- preserve a part of the natural ecosystem as a potential reference area for the purpose of future comparative studies;
- minimise the possibility of introduction of alien plants, animals and microbes to the Area;
- allow visits for management purposes in support of the aims of the Management Plan.

## 3. Management activities

The following management activities shall be undertaken to protect the values of the Area:

- Copies of this management plan, including maps of the Area, shall be made available at Mario Zucchelli Station at Terra Nova Bay (Italy), Gondwana Station (Germany), and at any other permanent stations established within 100 km of the Area;
- Structures, markers, signs, fences or other equipment erected within the Area for scientific or management purposes shall be secured and maintained in good condition and removed when no longer necessary;
- Durable wind direction indicators should be erected close to the designated helicopter landing sites whenever it is anticipated there will be a number of landings in a given season;
- Markers, which should be clearly visible from the air and pose no significant risk to the environment, should be placed to mark the designated helicopter landing sites;
- Markers, such as a series of durable sticks, should be placed to mark the preferred inland walking routes between the Adélie penguin colony and the designated helicopter landing sites;
- Visits shall be made as necessary (no less than once every five years) to assess whether the Area continues to serve the purposes for which it was designated and to ensure management and maintenance measures are adequate;
- National Antarctic Programmes operating in the region shall consult together with a view to ensuring these steps are carried out.

**4.     Period of designation**

Designated for an indefinite period.

**5.     Maps and photographs**

Map 1: Edmonson Point ASPA No. 165, Wood Bay, Victoria Land, Ross Sea. Map specifications: Projection: UTM Zone 58S; Spheroid: WGS84; Ice-free areas and coastline derived from rectified Quickbird satellite image with a ground pixel resolution of 70 cm, acquired 04/01/04 by Programma Nazionale di Ricerche in Antartide (PNRA), Italy. Horizontal accuracy approx ±10 m; elevation information unavailable. Inset 1: the location of Wood Bay in Antarctica. Inset 2. The location of Map 1 in relation to Wood Bay and Terra Nova Bay. The location of Mario Zucchelli Station (Italy), Gondwana Station (Germany), and the nearest protected areas are shown.

Map 2: Edmonson Point, ASPA No. 165, Physical / human features and access guidelines. Map derived from digital orthophotograph with ground pixel resolution of 25 cm, from ground GPS surveys and observations, and from Quickbird satellite image (04/01/04).

Map specifications: Projection: Lambert Conformal Conic; Standard parallels: 1st 72° 40' 00" S; 2nd 75° 20' 00"S;     Central Meridian: 165° 07' 00" E; Latitude of Origin: 74° 20' 00" S; Spheroid: WGS84; Vertical datum: Mean Sea Level. Vertical contour interval 10 m. Horizontal accuracy: ±1 m; vertical accuracy expected to be better than ±1 m.

Map 3: Restricted Zone, Colline Ippolito: Edmonson Point ASPA No. 165. Map derived from Quickbird satellite image (04/01/04). Map specifications as for Map 2, except for horizontal accuracy which is approx ±10 m, and elevation information is not available. Sea level is approximated from coastline evident in satellite image.

Map 4: Edmonson Point ASPA No. 165, topography, wildlife and vegetation. Map specifications as for Map 2, except for contour interval which is 2 m.

Map data and preparation: PNRA, Dipartimento di Scienze Ambientali (Università di Siena), Environmental Research & Assessment (Cambridge), Gateway Antarctica (Christchurch).

**6.     Description of the Area**

*6(i)  Geographical coordinates, boundary markers and natural features*

GENERAL DESCRIPTION

Edmonson Point (74°20' S, 165°08' E) is a coastal ice-free area of 1.79 km$^2$ situated at Wood Bay, 50 km north of Terra Nova Bay, and 13 km east of the summit and at the foot of Mount Melbourne (2732 m), Victoria Land. The Area comprises a total of 5.49 km$^2$, including the entire ice-free ground of Edmonson Point (1.79 km$^2$), the separate ice-free area of Colline Ippolito (Ippolito Hills) (1.12 km$^2$) approximately 1.5 km north-west of Edmonson Point, and the nearshore marine environment and intervening sea of Baia Siena (Siena Bay) between these ice-free areas (2.58 km$^2$), which lie east and at the foot of the permanent ice sheet extending from Mount Melbourne (Map 1). Part of the glacier from Mount Melbourne separates the two ice-free areas on land. A broad pebbly beach extends the length of the coastline of Edmonson Point, above which cliffs rise up to 128 m towards the south of the Area. The topography of the Area is rugged, with several hills of volcanic origin of up to 134 m in height, and ice-free slopes rising to around 300 m adjacent to the ice sheet, although accurate elevation information in these areas is not currently available. Undulating ice-cored moraines, boulder fields and rock outcrops are separated by small ash plains and shallow valleys. The Area is dissected by numerous valleys and melt streams, with several small lakes, and seepage areas being common features throughout the Area. In the central region of Edmonson Point are several wide shallow basins, at about 25 m elevation, covered by fine scoria and coarse sand, mixed with extensive carpets of vegetation and areas of patterned ground. The northern coast of Edmonson Point is a cuspate foreland comprising several raised beaches.

The environmental character of Colline Ippolito is similar to that of Edmonson Point. This area has a narrow boulder beach backed by a ridge running parallel to the coast. Small meltwater streams run through shallow gullies and across flats into two lakes behind the coastal ridge in the north. Ridges and cones rise to about 200 m before merging with the snow fields and glaciers of Mount Melbourne in the south.

BOUNDARIES

The margin of the permanent ice sheet extending from Mount Melbourne is defined as the boundary in the west, north and south of the Area (Maps 1-3). The eastern boundary is marine, which in the southern half of the Area follows the coastline 200 m offshore from the southern to northern extremities of the ice-free area of Edmonson Point. From the northern extremity of Edmonson Point, the eastern boundary extends NW across Baia Siena for a distance of 2 km to a position 200 m due east from the coast of the northern extremity of Colline Ippolito. Baia Siena is thus enclosed within the Area. Boundary markers have not been installed because the ice sheet margin and the coast are obvious boundary references.

CLIMATE

No extended meteorological records are available for Edmonson Point, although annual data for McMurdo Station, Scott Base and Cape Hallett suggest the average mean temperature in the Edmonson Point vicinity would be around -16° C, and the mean annual snow accumulation about 20-50 cm, equivalent to 10-20 cm of water (Bargagli *et al.*, 1997). Short-term data are available for December 1995 – January 1996, collected during the BIOTEX 1 expedition. During this period temperatures ranged from -7° C to 10° C, with 0° C exceeded every day. Relative humidity was low (15-40% day, 50-80% night), precipitation occasional as light snow and wind speeds mostly low. From late January weather conditions deteriorated, with frequent subzero daytime temperatures, snow-fall and high winds. Data available for summer seasons in 1998-99 and 1999-00 from a weather station installed near the penguin colony suggest prevailing summer winds at Edmonson Point come from the east, southeast and south. Daily average wind speeds were generally in the range of 3-6 knots, with daily maximums usually being of 6-10 knots, occasionally reaching up to 25-35 knots. Daily average air temperatures ranged from around -15°C in October, -6°C in November, -2.5°C in December to -1°C in January, decreasing to -3.5°C again in February (Olmastroni, pers. comm., 2000). The highest daily maximum in the two summer periods was recorded as 2.6°C on 25 December 1998. The average air temperature recorded over both summers was approximately -4°C, while the average wind speed was 4.5 knots. Average daily relative humidity generally ranged between 40-60%.

GEOLOGY AND SOILS

The geology at Edmonson Point is derived from Cenozoic eruptive activity of Mount Melbourne (Melbourne Volcanic Province), part of the McMurdo Volcanic Group (Kyle, 1990), combined with glacial deposits from the marine-based ice sheet that covered much of the Victoria Land coastline during the last glacial maximum (7500 to 25000 years B.P) (Baroni and Orombelli, 1994). The volcanic complex at Edmonson Point is composed of a large subaerial tuff ring, scoria cones, lava flows, and subaquatic megapillow lava sequences (Wörner and Viereck, 1990). The rocks are mainly of basaltic and/or trachytic composition, and include various additional volcanic products, such as accumulations of tuffs, pumices and debris deposits (Simeoni *et al.*, 1989; Bargagli *et al.*, 1997). The ground surface is composed mainly of dry, coarse-textured volcanic materials with a low proportion of silt and clay (Bargagli *et al.*, 1997). These exposed surfaces, as well as beneath the surfaces of stones and boulders, are often coated with white encrustations or efflorescences of soluble salts. Most of the ground is dark-coloured, with brownish or yellowish patches of scoria and tuffite. Unstable scree is common on hill slopes, which are dry and mostly unvegetated. Valley and basin floors are covered by fine scoria and coarse sand (Bargagli *et al.*, 1999).

GEOMORPHOLOGY

A series of marine deposits are visible on the cuspate foreland at the northern extremity of Edmonson Point. The gently sloping raised beaches of the foreland are composed of differing ratios of sands, pebbles and boulders distributed over lava flows (Simeoni *et al.*, 1989). Numerous small crater-like pits, many containing melt-water or ice, can be observed just above the high tide mark in this locality; these are thought to have been formed by extreme tides and the melting of coastal ice accumulations. South of the cuspate foreland, volcanic bedrock exposures are common over much of the ground extending up to about 800 m inland from the coast, most evident in the prominent hills of about 120 m in height in the central northern part of Edmonson Point. A series of late-Pleistocene moraines and related tills lie on the western side of these exposures, with bands of Holocene ice-cored moraine, talus and debris slopes adjacent to the glacier ice which extends from Mount Melbourne (Baroni and Orombelli, 1994).

STREAMS AND LAKES

There are six lakes on Edmonson Point, ranging in length up to 350 m, and in area from approximately 1600 m$^2$ up to 15,000 m$^2$ (Map 2). Two further lakes occur behind the coastal ridge at Colline Ippolito, the largest of which is approximately 12,500 m$^2$ (Map 3). In addition, on Edmonson Point there are approximately 22 smaller ponds of diameters of less than 30 m (Broady, 1987). The larger ponds are permanently ice-covered, with peripheral moats forming during the summer. Detailed physico-chemical characteristics and limnology of the lakes of Edmonson Point are reported in Guilizzoni *et al.* (1991). There are numerous streams throughout the Area, some of which are supplied with meltwater from the adjacent ice sheet, while others are fed by lakes and general ice / snow melt. Several stream beds have flood terraces of fine soil covered by pumice-like pebbles of 5-10 mm diameter. Many of the streams and pools are transient, drying up shortly after the late snow patches in their catchments disappear.

PLANT BIOLOGY

Compared to several other sites in central Victoria Land, Edmonson Point does not have a particularly diverse flora, and there are only a few extensive closed stands of vegetation. Six moss species, one liverwort, and at least 30 lichen species have been recorded within the Area (Broady, 1987; Lewis Smith, 1996, 1999; Lewis Smith pers. comm., 2004; Castello, 2004). Cavacini (pers. comm., 2003) noted that recent analyses have identified at least 120 alga and cyanobacteria species present at Edmonson Point. These are present in a range of forms including algal mats on soil and as epiphytes on mosses, and in a range of habitats such as in lakes, streams and snow, and on moist ornithogenic and raw mineral soils. At the onset of summer, snow melt reveals small stands of algae and moss on valley floors, although much of these lie buried by up to 5 cm of wind-blown and melt-washed fine mineral particles. This community is capable of rapid growth during December, when moisture is available and soil temperatures are relatively high, bringing shoot apices up to a centimetre above the surface as the surface accumulation of sand is washed or blown away. Increased water flow or strong winds can quickly bury these stands, although sufficient light for growth can penetrate 1-2 cm below the surface (Bargagli *et al.*, 1999).The principal moss communities occur on more stable substrata which are not subjected to burial by sand, for example in sheltered depressions or along the margins of ponds and meltwater streams, and seepage areas below late snow beds where moisture is available for several weeks. Some of these are among the most extensive stands found in continental Antarctica, being of up to 3000 m$^2$, most notably the stand of *Bryum subrotundifolium* (= *B. argenteum*) several hundred metres west of the main Adélie colony (Map 4). Other, less extensive, notable stands occur near the lake adjacent to the Adélie colony (Map 4), and smaller localized stands of *Ceratodon purpureus* (with relatively thick deposits of dead organic material) being found in a valley in the north of Edmonson Point and in the upper area of the principal stream in the northern ice-free area. Greenfield *et. al.* (1985) suggested that, apart from Cape Hallett, no area in the Ross Sea has a comparable abundance of plants, although in 1996 a similarly extensive area colonised almost exclusively by *Bryum subrotundifolium* (= *B. argenteum*) was discovered on Beaufort Island (ASPA No. 105), approximately 280 km to the south of Edmonson Point.

The moss-dominated communities comprise up to seven bryophyte species, several algae and cyanobacteria and, at the drier end of the moisture gradient, several lichens encrusting moribund moss (Lewis Smith, 1999; Bargagli *et al.*, 1999). There are mixed communities or zones of *Bryum subrotundifolium* (= *B. argenteum*), *B. pseudotriquetrum* and *Ceratodon purpureus*. In some wetter sites the liverwort *Cephaloziella varians* occurs amongst *C. purpureus*. Dry, very open, often lichen-encrusted moss communities usually contain *Hennediella heimii*, and often occur in hollows which hold small late snow patches. *Sarconeurum glaciale* occurs in a stable scree above the large lake in the south of the Area (Lewis Smith, 1996). The upper portions of moss colonies are often coated with white encrustations of soluble salts (Bargagli *et al.*, 1999).

The lichen communities are relatively diverse, with 24 species identified and at least six crustose species so far unidentified, although few are abundant (Castello, 2004; Lewis Smith, pers. comm. 2004). Epilithic lichens are generally sparse and not widespread, being mainly crustose and microfoliose species restricted to rocks used as skua perches and occasionally on stable boulders in scree, moist gullies and temporary seepage areas. Macrolichens are scarce, with *Umbilicaria aprina* and *Usnea sphacelata* found in a few places. The former species is more abundant on the gently sloping intermittently inundated outwash channels of Colline Ippolito, together with *Physcia* spp. and associated with small cushions of *Bryum subrotundifolium* (= *B. argenteum*) (Given, 1985, 1989), *B. pseudotriquetrum* and *Ceratodon purpureus* (Lewis Smith, pers comm. 2004). *Buellia frigida* is the most widespread crustose lichen on the hard lavas, but a distinct community of nitrophilous species occurs on rocks used as skua perches (*Caloplaca, Candelariella, Rhizoplaca, Xanthoria*). In gravelly depressions below late snow beds, moss turves are often colonised by encrusting cyanobacteria and ornithocoprophilic lichens (*Candelaria, Candelariella, Lecanora, Xanthoria*) and, where there is no bird influence, by the white *Leproloma cacuminum* (Lewis Smith, 1996).

Early work on the algal flora at Edmonson Point identified 17 species as Cyanophyta, 10 as Chrysophyta and 15 as Chlorophyta (Broady, 1987). More recent analyses (Cavacini, pers. comm., 2003) have identified 120 alga and cyanobacteria species, which is considerably more than the numbers of species of Cyanophyta (28), Chlorophyta (27), Bacillariophyta (25) and Xanthophyta (5) recorded previously (Cavacini, 1997, 2001; Fumanti *et al.*, 1993, 1994a, 1994b; Alfinito *et al.*, 1998). Broady (1987) observed few areas of algal vegetation on ground surfaces; the most extensive were oscillatoriacean mats in moist depressions in areas of beach sand, which may have been temporary melt ponds prior to when the survey was undertaken. Similar mats were found adjacent to an area of moss with a *Gloeocapsa* sp. as an abundant associate. *Prasiococcus calcarius* was observed in the vicinity of the Adélie penguin colony, both as a small area of rich green crusts on soil and growing on an area of moribund moss cushions. Other epiphytic algae include Oscillatoriaceae, *Nostoc* sp., unicellular chlorophytes including *Pseudococcomyxa simplex*, and the desmid *Actinotaenium cucurbita*. Substantial stream algae were observed with waters containing oscillatoriacean mats over the stream beds, wefts of green filaments attached to the surface of stones (mainly *Binuclearia tectorum* and *Prasiola* spp.), small ribbons of *Prasiola calophylla* on the under-surfaces of stones, and dark brown epilithic crusts of cyanophytes (dominated by *Chamaesiphon subglobosus* and *Nostoc* sp.) coating boulders. Ponds present in beach sand contained *Chlamydomonas* sp. and cf. *Ulothrix* sp., while ponds fertilized by penguin and skua guano contained *Chlamydomonas* sp. and black benthic oscillatoriacean mats. Other ponds also contained rich benthic growths of Oscillatoriaceae, frequently associated with *Nostoc sphaericum*. Other abundant algae were *Aphanothece castagnei, Binuclearia tectorum, Chamaesiphon subglobosus, Chroococcus minutus, C. turgidus, Luticola muticopsis, Pinnularia cymatopleura, Prasiola crispa* (particularly associated with penguin colonies and other nitrogen-enriched habitats),

*Stauroneis anceps*, various unicellular chlorophytes, and – in the highest conductivity pond in beach sand – cf. *Ulothrix* sp.

Algae and cyanobacteria are locally abundant in moist soils, and filaments and foliose mats of *Phormidium* spp. (dominant on patches of wet ground and in shallow lake bottoms), aggregates of *Nostoc commune* and a population of diatoms have been identified (Wynn-Williams, 1996; Lewis Smith pers. comm., 2004). The fungal species *Arthrobotrys ferox* has been isolated from moss species *Bryum pseudotriquetrum* (= *B. algens*) and *Ceratodon purpureus*. *A. ferox* produces an adhesive secretion which has been observed to capture springtails of the species *Gressittacantha terranova* (about 1.2 mm in length) (Onofri and Tosi, 1992).

## 7. Scientific values

### 7(i) Invertebrate

There is a high diversity of soil nematodes in the moist soils at Edmonson Point when compared to other areas described in Victoria Land. Nematodes found at Edmonson Point include *Eudorylaimus antarcticus, Monhysteridae* sp., *Panagrolaimus* sp., *Plectus antarcticus, P. frigophilus,* and *Scottnema lyndsayea* (Frati, 1997; Wall pers. comm., 2000). The latter species, previously only known from the McMurdo Dry Valleys, was found at Edmonson Point in 1995-96 (Frati, 1997). Less abundant are the springtails, most commonly *Gressittacantha terranova*, which was found under rocks and on soil and mosses in a number of moist microhabitats (Frati, 1997). Red mites (likely to be either *Stereotydeus* sp. or *Nanorchestes*, although species not identified) are common in aggregations beneath stones in moist habitats, and Collembola, rotifers, tardigrades and a variety of protozoans are also found (Frati *et al.,* 1996; Lewis Smith, 1996; Wall pers. comm., 2000; Convey pers. comm., 2003).

### 7(ii) Breeding birds

Adélie penguins (*Pygoscelis adeliae*) breed in two groups near the coast in the central and eastern-most part of Edmonson Point, occupying an area of about 9000 m$^2$ (Map 4). The number of breeding pairs recorded between 1981-2005 is summarised in Table 1, the average number in this period being 2080. In 1994-95 the majority of birds were recorded to arrive around 30-31 October, while the majority of the season's chicks had fledged by 12 February, with fledging complete by 21 February (Franchi *et al.,* 1997). An abandoned nesting site, occupied approximately 2600-3000 years ago, lies about 1 km to the northwest of the current colony, on bedrock adjacent to the cuspate foreland (Baroni and Orombelli, 1994).

**Table 1.** Adélie penguins (breeding pairs) at Edmonson Point 1981-2005 (data Woehler, 1993; Olmastroni, 2005, *pers. comm.*).

| Year | No. of breeding pairs | Year | No. of breeding pairs |
|------|------------------------|------|------------------------|
| 1981 | 1300 | 1995 | 1935 |
| 1984 | 1802 | 1996 | 1824 |
| 1987 | 2491 | 1997 | 1961 |
| 1989 | 1792 | 1999 | 2005 |
| 1991 | 1316 | 2001 | 1988 |
| 1994 | 1960 | 2003 | 2588 |
|      |      | 2005 | 2385 |

Between 2005 and 2010 according to CEMP procedures, three population counts were made at Edmonson Point, the colony consisting of 2385, 2303 and 2112 occupied nests in 2005, 2007 and 2010 respectively.

The average number since the beginning of the research program being 2112. Thus total population seem stable with respect to the average value 2080 from 1994 to 2005.

The ratio between skua and penguin remained high (1:20) as previously reported by Pezzo *et al*, (2001). Edmonson Point's skua population nearby Adélie penguin colony remained stable through years consisting of about 130 breeding pairs in 2010 summer season. Also at Edmonson Point North and South 55 and 61 breeding pairs respectively , were counted in 2010 summer season.

A breeding colony of south polar skuas (*Catharacta maccormicki*) within the Area is one of the most numerous in Victoria Land, with over 120 pairs, of which 36 pairs occupy Colline Ippolito (CCAMLR, 1999; Pezzo *et al*., 2001; Volpi pers. comm. 2005). . Furthermore the Area includes two "club sites", nearby large freshwater ponds, used throughout the breeding seasons by groups of non-breeders ranging between 50 and 70 individuals (Pezzo 2001; Volpi 2005 pers. comm.). Flocks of snow petrels (*Pagodroma nivea*) have been observed flying over the Area, and Wilson's storm petrels (*Oceanites oceanicus*) have been sighted regularly. Neither of these latter two species is known to breed within the Area.

*7(iii)    Breeding mammals*

At Edmonson Point numerous (>50) Weddell seals (Leptonychotes weddellii) regularly breed in the near shore marine environment (on fast ice) within the Area. Females use this area to give birth and raise pups on the fast ice along the coastline of the whole Area.  Later in the summer Weddell seals frequently haul out on beaches within the Area.

## 8.    Scientific Research

*8(i)    CCAMLR Ecosystem Monitoring Programme (CEMP) Studies*

1. The presence at Edmonson Point of breeding penguin colonies and the absence of krill fisheries within their foraging range make this a critical site for comparative studies and inclusion with other CEMP sites in the ecosystem monitoring network established to meet the objectives of CCAMLR. The purpose of protected area designation is to allow planned research and monitoring to proceed, while avoiding or reducing, to the greatest extent possible, other activities which could interfere with or affect the results of the research and monitoring programme of alter the natural features of the site.

2. The Adélie penguin is a species of particular interest for CEMP routine monitoring and directed research at this site. For this purpose the Adélie Penguin Monitoring Program, a joint research project between Italian and Australian biologists, has been ongoing at Edmonson Point since 1994-95. An Automated Penguin Monitoring System (APMS) along with on-site observations by researchers, forms the basis of a study of at least 500-600 nests within the northern sector of the colony as part of the CEMP (CCAMLR, 1999; Olmastroni *et al*., 2000). Fences have been installed to direct penguins over a bridge which registers their weight, identity and crossing direction as they move between the sea and their breeding colony.

3. Parameters routinely monitored include trends in population size (A3), demography (A4), duration of foraging trips (A5), breeding success (A6), chick fledging weight (A7), chick diet (A8) and breeding chronology (A9).

4. The studies on Adélie penguin also involve population monitoring, experiments with satellite transmitters and temperature-depth recorders to investigate foraging location and duration. Combined with stomach flushing to record the diet of monitored penguins, this programme is

developing comprehensive observations of Adélie penguin feeding ecology (Olmastroni, 2002). Diet data (Olmastroni *et al.*, 2004) confirmed the results of studies from krill distribution in the Ross Sea (Azzali and Kalinowski, 2000; Azzali *et al.*, 2000) and indicate that this colony is located at a transition point in the availability of *E. superba* between northern and more southerly colonies where this species is absent or rare in the diet of penguins (Emison, 1968; Ainley, 2002). These studies also highlighted the importance of fish to the diet of the Adélie penguin, which represented up to 50% of stomach contents in some years.

Local sea ice and weather data contribute to the understanding of possible factors affecting the breeding biology of this species (Olmastroni *et al.*, 2004). Moreover behavioural studies are also part of the research (Pilastro *et al.*, 2001).

Research on the south polar skua colony focuses on breeding biology (Pezzo *et al.*, 2001), population dynamics, biometry, reproductive biology and migratory patterns. Since 1998/99 more than 300 south polar skuas have been banded by metal and coloured rings, which facilitate field research that requires the recognition of individual birds and will allow for identification of birds migrating from the Area.

*8(ii)    Scientific Research after 2005*

Ecology of marine birds and CCAMLR Ecosystem Monitoring Programme (CEMP) Studies.

The studies on Adélie penguin population involved demographic parameters that were estimated in relation to individual characteristics (sex and age) and to large scale (Ross Sea winter ice extent anomalies and SOI) and local scale (food availability) environmental variables. While large-scale environmental factors affected adult survival, breeding success varied principally according to local variables. Breeding success was particularly low when local stochastic events (storms) occurred at sensitive times of the breeding cycle (immediately after the hatching) (Olmastroni et al. 2004; Pezzo et al, 2007; Ballerini et al., 2009). Also changes in fast-ice extent in front of the breeding area influenced the adult breeders transit times between colony and foraging grounds, and females conducted longer foraging trips, dived for longer periods and made more dives than males. The diving parameters were affected neither by the sex nor by the year, but differed between the breeding stages (Nesti et al, 2010). Annual adult survival probability at Edmonson Point (0.85, range 0.76– 0.94) was similar to that estimated from other Adélie penguin populations in which individuals were marked with passive transponders. An annual average survival rate of 0.85 seems to be typical of the species and is consistent with an expected average lifespan of about 11 years (6.6 years after adulthood) (Ballerini et al., 2009).

Some aspects of the breeding biology of the south polar skua, during five seasons are under investigation being the subject of a doctoral thesis that is being carried out at University of Siena (A. Franceschi, Aspetti della Biologia riproduttiva dello Stercorario di McCormick, *Stercorarius maccormicki*).

*8(iii)    Other Scientific Activities*

Studies of terrestrial ecology at Edmonson Point were initiated in the 1980s, although this type of research and other forms of science increased in the 1990s, in particular by Italian scientists. Edmonson Point was the location of BIOTEX 1, the first SCAR Biological Investigation of Antarctic Terrestrial Ecosystems (BIOTAS) research expedition, during December 1995 and January 1996. Ten researchers from three countries participated in a variety of scientific projects which included: taxonomic, ecological, physiological and biogeographical studies on cyanobacteria, algae, bryophytes, lichens (including chasmolithic and endolithic communities), nematodes, springtails and mites; studies of soil and freshwater biogeochemistry; microbial metabolic activity and colonisation studies; and investigations into the photosynthetic responses to ambient and controlled conditions of mosses, lichens and plant pigments that may act as photoprotectants

(Bargagli, 1999). While the BIOTAS programme has now formally concluded, it is expected that further studies of this type will be on-going at Edmonson Point.

## 9.    Human Activities/Impacts

Edmonson Point was probably first visited on 6 February 1900 when Carsten Borchgrevink landed just north of Mount Melbourne on "a promontory almost free of snow .... about 100 acres in extent" and climbed about 200 m up the slopes (Borchgrevink, 1901: 261). The Wood Bay region was rarely mentioned during the following 70 years, and presumably was visited only infrequently. Activity in the area increased in the 1980s, first with visits by the GANOVEX expeditions (Germany). Botanical research was undertaken in December 1984 (Given, 1985; Greenfield *et. al.*, 1985; Broady, 1987) and in January 1989, at which time the first proposals for special protection of the site were made (Given pers. comm. 2003). Italy established a station in close proximity at Terra Nova Bay in 1986-87 and increased research interest in the site followed.

The modern era of human activity at Edmonson Point has been largely confined to science. The impacts of these activities have not been described, but are believed to be minor and limited to items such as campsites, footprints, markers of various kinds, human wastes, scientific sampling, handling of limited numbers of birds (e.g. installation of devices to track birds, stomach lavage, biometric measurements, etc), and potentially some impacts associated with helicopter access and installation and operation of camp and research facilities at the penguin colony and on the northern cuspate foreland. At least one fuel spill of around 500 ml, and other smaller spills, were reported in 1996 as a result of refuelling operations at the generator and fuel store located at the penguin colony (see disturbed sites marked on Map 4). In addition, seaborne litter is occasionally washed onto beaches within the Area. The Restricted Zone at Colline Ippolito has received less human activity than Edmonson Point and impacts in this area are expected to be negligible.

### 9(i)   Restricted and managed zones within the Area

#### Restricted Zone

The ice-free area of Colline Ippolito (1.12 km$^2$) approximately 1.5 km north-west of Edmonson Point is designated as a Restricted Zone in order to preserve part of the Area as a reference site for future comparative studies, while the remainder of the terrestrial Area (which is similar in biology, features and character) is more generally available for research programmes and sample collection. The northern, western and southern boundaries of the Restricted Zone are defined as the margins of the permanent ice extending from Mount Melbourne, and are coincident with the boundary of the Area (Maps 1 and 3). The eastern boundary of the Restricted Zone is the mean low water level along the coastline of this ice-free area.

Access to the Restricted Zone is allowed only for compelling scientific reasons or management purposes (such as inspection or review) that cannot be served elsewhere within the Area.

### 9(ii)  Structures within and near the Area

*CEMP Site:* A fibreglass cabin for field observation, containing instrumentation and APMS panel, and two Nunsen huts  for 4 people were installed by PNRA in 1994/95 to support CEMP research. These structures are located on a rocky knoll at an elevation of 16 m, 80 m from the coast and 40 m south of the northern sub-colony of penguins (Maps 2 and 4). At the beginning of each field season a generator and a number of fuel drums are temporarily stored about 20 m from the camp and removed at the end of  each season. Adjacent to the northern penguin sub-colony, fences of metal net (30-50 cm) have been installed to direct penguins over the APMS weigh bridge.

*Other activities:* Approximately 50 plastic cloches were installed at 10 locations throughout the Area in 1995-96 as part of BIOTEX-1 (Maps 2 and 4). A number of additional cloches were installed the previous year at four locations (Wynn-Williams, 1996). It is not precisely known how many of these cloches remain within the area. Temporary camp facilities were installed at the location of the designated camp site for the duration of the BIOTEX-1 programme, which have now been removed.

The nearest permanent stations are Mario Zucchelli Station at Terra Nova Bay (Italy) and Gondwana Station (Germany), which lie approximately 50 km and 45 km south respectively.

*9(iii)  Location of other protected areas within close proximity of the Area*

The nearest protected areas to Edmonson Point are the summit of Mount Melbourne (ASPA No. 118), which lies 13 km to the west, and a marine area at Terra Nova Bay (ASPA No. 161), which lies approximately 52 km to the south (Map 1, Inset 2).

## 10.  Permit conditions

Entry into the Area is prohibited except in accordance with a Permit issued by an appropriate national authority.  Conditions for issuing a Permit to enter the Area are that:

- it is issued only for scientific research on the Area, or for compelling scientific reasons that cannot be served elsewhere; or
- it is issued for essential management purposes consistent with plan objectives such as inspection, maintenance or review;
- access to the Restricted Zone is allowed only for compelling scientific reasons or management purposes (such as inspection or review) that cannot be served elsewhere within the Area;
- the actions permitted will not jeopardise the ecological or scientific values of the Area;
- any management activities are in support of the objectives of the Management Plan;
- the actions permitted are in accordance with the Management Plan;
- the Permit, or an authorised copy, shall be carried within the Area;
- a visit report shall be supplied to the authority named in the Permit;
- Permits shall be issued for a stated period.
- The appropriate authority should be notified of any activities/measures undertaken that were not included in the authorised Permit.

*10(i)  Access to and movement within the Area*

Access to the Area shall be by small boat, on foot or by helicopter. Movement over land within the Area shall be on foot or by helicopter. Access to the Area by vehicle is restricted according to the conditions described below.

*Small boat access*

The Edmonson Point part of the Area may be entered at any point where pinnipeds or seabird colonies are not present on or near the beach. Access for purposes other than CEMP research should avoid disturbing pinnipeds and seabirds (Map 1 and 2). There are no special restrictions on landings from the sea, although when accessing the main ice-free area of Edmonson Point visitors shall land at the northern cuspate foreland and avoid landing at breeding bird colonies (Map 2).

*Restricted conditions of vehicle access*

Use of vehicles within the Area is prohibited, except at the southern boundary of the Area where they may be used on sea ice to gain access to the shore, from where visitors shall proceed on foot. Thus, vehicle use shall avoid interference with animal feeding routes and the Adélie penguin colony. When using vehicles on sea ice care should be exercised to avoid Weddell seals which may be present: speed should be kept low and seals shall not be approached by vehicle closer than 50 m.

Access over land by vehicles is allowed to the boundary of the Area. Vehicle traffic shall be kept to the minimum necessary for the conduct of permitted activities.

*Aircraft access and overflight*

All restrictions on aircraft access and overflight stipulated in this plan shall apply during the period 15 October – 20 February inclusive. Aircraft may operate and land within the Area according to strict observance of the following conditions:

(i)     All overflight of the Area for purposes other than access shall be conducted according to the height restrictions imposed in the following table:

**Minimum overflight heights within the Area according to aircraft type**

| Aircraft type | Number of Engines | Minimum height above ground | |
|---|---|---|---|
| | | Feet | Metres |
| Helicopter | 1 | 2461 | 750 |
| Helicopter | 2 | 3281 | 1000 |
| Fixed-wing | 1 or 2 | 1476 | 450 |
| Fixed-wing | 4 | 3281 | 1000 |

(ii)    Helicopter landing is normally allowed at only three designated sites (Maps 1-4). The landing sites with their coordinates are described as follows:

(A) shall be used for most purposes, located on the northern cuspate foreland of Edmonson Point (Map 2) (74°19'24"S, 165°07'12"E);

(B) is allowed in support of the Adélie Penguin Monitoring Programme when necessary for transport of heavy equipment / supplies (Map 2) (74°19'43"S, 165°07'57"E); and

(C) is allowed for access to the Restricted Zone, located at the northern ice-free area (Colline Ippolito, Map 3) (74°18'50"S, 165°04'29"E).

(iii)   In exceptional circumstances, helicopter access may be specifically authorised elsewhere within the Area for the purpose of supporting science or management according to conditions imposed by the Permit on access location(s) and timing. Landing of helicopters at sites of mammals and seabird sites and significant vegetation shall be avoided at all times (Maps 2-4).

(iv)    The designated aircraft approach route is from the west of the Area, from over the lower eastern ice slopes of Mount Melbourne (Maps 1-3). Aircraft shall approach the main designated landing site (A) on the cuspate foreland from the north-west over or near Baia Siena (Siena Bay). When appropriate, access to landing site (B) should follow the same route and proceed a further 700 m SE. The departure route is identical in reverse.

(v)     When appropriate, access to landing site (C) should be from the lower eastern ice slopes of Mount Melbourne and proceed directly to the landing site from the south over the land or where this is not feasible over Baia Siena (Siena Bay), avoiding skuas nesting to the north of the landing site;

(vi)    Use of smoke grenades to indicate wind direction is prohibited within the Area unless absolutely necessary for safety, and any grenades used should be retrieved.

*Foot access and movement within the Area*

Movement on land within the Area shall be on foot. Visitors should move carefully so as to minimise disturbance to the breeding birds, soil, geomorphological features and vegetated surfaces, and should walk on rocky terrain or ridges if practical to avoid damage to sensitive plants and the often waterlogged soils. Pedestrian traffic should be kept to the minimum consistent with the objectives of any permitted activities and every reasonable effort should be made to minimise trampling effects. Pedestrians that are not undertaking research or management related to the penguins shall not enter the colonies and should maintain a separation distance from the breeding birds of at least 15 m at all times. Care should be exercised to ensure monitoring equipment, fences and other scientific installations are not disturbed.

Pedestrians moving between the helicopter landing sites (A) or (B) to the Adélie colony shall follow the preferred walking routes marked on Maps 2 and 4 or follow a route along the beach.

*10(ii) Activities that are or may be conducted in the Area, including restrictions on time or place*

- The research programme associated with the CCAMLR CEMP
- Scientific research that will not jeopardise the ecosystem of the Area;
- Essential management activities, including monitoring.

*10(iii) Installation, modification or removal of structures*

No structures are to be erected within the Area except as specified in a Permit. All scientific equipment installed in the Area must be approved by Permit and clearly identified by country, name of the principal investigator and year of installation. All such items should be made of materials that pose minimal risk of contamination to the Area. Removal of specific equipment for which the Permit has expired shall be a condition of the Permit. Permanent structures are prohibited.

*10(iv) Location of field camps*

Semi-permanent camps and temporary camping is permitted within the Area at the primary designated site on the cuspate foreland of Edmonson Point (Map 2). Camping at the CEMP Research camp (Maps 2 & 4) is permitted only for purposes of the Adélie Penguin Monitoring Programme. When necessary within the Restricted Zone for purposes specified in the Permit, temporary camping is permitted at the designated site (C) (74°18'51"S, 165°04'16"E) approximately 100 m west of helicopter landing site (Map 3).

*10(v) Restrictions on materials and organisms which can be brought into the Area*

No living animals, plant material or microorganisms shall be deliberately introduced into the Area and the precautions listed in 7(ix) below shall be taken against accidental introductions. In view of the presence of breeding bird colonies at Edmonson Point, no poultry products, including products containing uncooked dried eggs, including wastes from such products, shall be released into the Area. No herbicides or pesticides shall be brought into the Area. Any other chemicals, including radio-nuclides or stable isotopes, which may be introduced for scientific or management purposes specified in the Permit, shall be removed from the Area at or before the conclusion of the activity for which the Permit was granted. Fuel is not to be stored in the Area, unless authorised by Permit for specific scientific or management purposes. Fuel spill clean-up equipment should be made available for use at locations where fuel is being regularly handled. Anything introduced shall be for a stated period only, shall be removed at or before the conclusion of that stated period, and shall be stored and handled so that risk of any introduction into the environment is minimised. If release occurs which is likely to compromise the values of the Area, removal is encouraged only where the impact of removal is not likely to be greater than that of leaving the material in situ. The appropriate authority should be notified of anything released or not removed that was not included in the authorised Permit.

*10(vi) Taking or harmful interference with native flora or fauna*

Taking or harmful interference with native flora or fauna is prohibited, except by Permit issued in accordance with Annex II to the Protocol on Environmental Protection to the Antarctic Treaty. Where taking or harmful interference with animals is involved, the *SCAR Code of Conduct for the Use of Animals for Scientific Purposes in Antarctica* should be used as a minimum standard.

*10(vii) Collection or removal of anything not brought into the Area by the Permit holder*

Collection or removal of anything not brought into the Area by the Permit holder shall only be in accordance with a Permit and should be limited to the minimum necessary to meet scientific or management needs. Permits shall not be granted if there is a reasonable concern that the sampling proposed would take, remove or damage such quantities of rock, soil, native flora or fauna that their distribution or abundance on Edmonson Point would be significantly affected. Anything of human origin likely to compromise the values of the Area, which was not brought into the Area by the Permit Holder or otherwise authorised, may be removed unless the impact of removal is likely to be greater than leaving the material *in situ*: if this is the case the appropriate authority should be notified.

*10(viii) Disposal of waste*

All wastes, except human wastes, shall be removed from the Area. Human wastes shall either be removed from the Area, or incinerated using purpose-designed technologies such as a propane-burning toilet, or in the case of liquid human wastes may be disposed of into the sea.

*10(ix) Measures that are necessary to ensure that the aims and objectives of the Management Plan can continue to be met*

1. Permits may be granted to enter the Area to carry out monitoring and site inspection activities, which may involve the small-scale collection of samples for analysis or review, or for protective measures.

2. Any specific long-term monitoring sites shall be appropriately marked.

3. To help maintain the ecological and scientific values of Edmonson Point special precautions shall be taken against introductions. Of concern are microbial, invertebrate or plant introductions from other Antarctic sites, including stations, or from regions outside Antarctica. All sampling equipment or markers brought into the Area shall be thoroughly cleaned. To the maximum extent practicable, footwear and other equipment used or brought into the Area (including backpacks, carry-bags and tents) shall be thoroughly cleaned before entering the Area.

*10(x) Requirements for reports*

Parties should ensure that the principal holder for each Permit issued submits to the appropriate authority a report describing the activities undertaken. Such reports should include, as appropriate, the information identified in the visit report form contained in the Guide to the Preparation of Management Plans for Antarctic Specially Protected Areas. Parties should maintain a record of such activities and, in the Annual Exchange of Information, should provide summary descriptions of activities conducted by persons subject to their jurisdiction, which should be in sufficient detail to allow evaluation of the effectiveness of the Management Plan. Parties should, wherever possible, deposit originals or copies of such original reports in a publicly accessible archive to maintain a record of usage, to be used both in any review of the Management Plan and in organising the scientific use of the Area.

## Bibliography

Ainley, D.G. 2002. *The Adélie Penguin. Bellwether of climate change.* Columbia University Press, New York.

Alfinito, S., Fumanti, B. and Cavacini, P. 1998. Epiphytic algae on mosses from northern Victoria Land (Antarctica). *Nova Hedwigia* **66** (3-4): 473-80.

Ancora, S., Volpi, V., Olmastroni, S., Leonzio, C. and Focardi, S. 2002. Assumption and elimination of trace elements in Adélie penguins from Antarctica: a preliminary study. *Marine Environmental Research* **54**: 341-44.

Azzali M. and J. Kalinowski. 2000. Spatial and temporal distribution of krill *Euphausia superba* biomass in the Ross Sea. In: Ianora A. (ed). *Ross Sea Ecology.* Springer, Berlin, 433-455.

Azzali M., J. Kalinowski, G. Lanciani and G. Cosimi. 2000. Characteristic Properties and dynamic aspects of krill swarms from the Ross Sea. In: Faranda F. G.L., Ianora A. (Ed). *Ross Sea Ecology.* Springer, Berlin, 413-431.

Bargagli, R., Martella, L. and Sanchez-Hernandez, J.C. 1997. The environment and biota at EdmonsonPoint (BIOTEX 1): preliminary results on environmental biogeochemistry. In di Prisco, G., Focardi, S. and Luporini, P. (eds) *Proceed. Third Meet. Antarctic Biology,* Santa Margherita Ligure, 13-15 December 1996. Camerino University Press: 261-71.

Bargagli, R. 1999. Report on Italian activities. *BIOTAS Newsletter* No. 13. Austral Summer 1998/99. A.H.L. Huiskes (ed) Netherlands Institute of Ecology: 16-17.

Bargagli, R., Sanchez-Hernandez, J.C., Martella, L. and Monaci, F. 1998. Mercury, cadmium and lead accumulation in Antarctic mosses growing along nutrient and moisture gradients. *Polar Biology* 19: 316-322.

Bargagli, R., Smith, R.I.L., Martella, L., Monaci, F., Sanchez-Hernandez, J.C. and Ugolini, F.C. 1999. Solution geochemistry and behaviour of major and trace elements during summer in a moss community at Edmonson Point, Victoria Land, Antarctica. *Antarctic Science* 11(1): 3-12.

Bargagli, R., Wynn-Williams, D., Bersan, F., Cavacini, P., Ertz, S., Freckman, D. Lewis Smith, R., Russell, N. and Smith, A. 1997. Field Report – BIOTEX 1: First BIOTAS Expedition (Edmonson Point – Baia Terra Nova, Dec 10 1995 – Feb 6 1996). *Newsletter of the Italian Biological Research in Antarctica* 1 (Austral summer 1995-96): 42-58.

Baroni, C. and Orombelli, G. 1994. Holocene glacier variations in the Terra Nova Bay area (Victoria Land, Antarctica). *Antarctic Science* 6(4):497-505.

Broady, P.A. 1987. A floristic survey of algae at four locations in northern Victoria Land. *New Zealand Antarctic Record* 7(3): 8-19.

Borchgrevink, C. 1901. *First on the Antarctic Continent: Being an Account of the British Antarctic Expedition 1898-1900.* G. Newnes. Ltd, London.

Cannone, N. and Guglielmin, M. 2003. Vegetation and permafrost: sensitive systems for the development of a monitoring program of climate change along an Antarctic transect. In: Huiskes, A.H.L., Gieskes, W.W.C., Rozema, J., Schorno, R.M.L., Van der Vies, S.M., Wolff, W.J. (Editors) *Antarctic biology in a global context.* Backhuys, Leiden: 31-36

Cannone, N., Guglielmin, M., Ellis Evans J.C., and Strachan R. in prep. Interactions between climate, vegetation and active layer in Maritime Antarctica. (submitted to *Journal of Applied Ecology*)

Cannone, N., Guglielmin, M., Gerdol, R., and Dramis, F. 2001. La vegetazione delle aree con permafrost per il monitoraggio del Global Change nelle regioni polari ed alpine. Abstract and Oral Presentation, 96à Congresso della Societa Botanica Italiana, Varese, 26-28 Settembre 2001.Castello, M. 2004. Lichens of the Terra Nova Bay area, northern Victoria Land (continental Antarctica). *Studia Geobotanica* **22**: 3-54.

Cavacini, P. 1997. La microflora algale non marina della northern Victoria Land (Antartide). Ph.D. Thesis. Università "La Sapienza" di Roma. 234 pp.

Cavacini, P. 2001. Soil algae from northern Victoria Land (Antarctica). *Polar Bioscience* **14**: 46-61.

CCAMLR. 1999. Report of member's activities in the Convention Area 1998/99: Italy. CCAMLR-XVIII/MA/14.

Clarke, J., Manly, B., Kerry, K., Gardner, H., Franchi, E. and Focardi, S. 1998. Sex differences in Adélie penguin foraging strategies. *Polar Biology* **20**: 248-58.

Corsolini, S. and Trémont, R. 1997. Australia-Italy cooperation in Antarctica: Adélie Penguin monitoring program, Edmonson Point, Ross Sea Region. *Newsletter of the Italian Biological Research in Antarctica* 1 (Austral summer 1995-96): 59-64.

Corsolini, S., Ademollo, N., Romeo, T., Olmastroni, S. and Focardi, S. 2003. Persistent organic pollutants in some species of a Ross Sea pelagic trophic web. *Antarctic Science* **15**(1): 95-104.

Corsolini, S., Kannan, K., Imagawa, T., Focardi, S. and Giesy J.P. 2002. Polychloronaphthalenes and other dioxin-like compounds in Arctic and Antarctic marine food webs. *Environmental Science and Technolology* **36**: 3490-96.

Corsolini, S., Olmastroni, S., Ademollo, N. and Focardi, S. 1999. Concentration and toxic evaluation of polychlorobiphenyls (PCBs) in Adélie Penguin (*Pygoscelis adeliae*) from Edmonson Point (Ross Sea, Antarctica). Tokyo 2-3 December 1999.

Emison, W. B. 1968. Feeding preferences of the Adélie penguin at Cape Crozier, Ross Island. Antarctic Research Series 12: 191-212.

Ertz, S. 1996. BIOTEX field report: December 1995 – February 1996. Strategies of Antarctic terrestrial organisms to protect against ultra-violet radiation. Unpublished field report in BAS Archives AD6/2/1995/NT3.

Fenice M., Selbmann L., Zucconi L. and Onofri S. 1997. Production of extracellular enzymes by Antarctic fungal strains. *Polar Biology* 17:275-280.

Franchi, E., Corsolini, S., Clarke, J.C., Lawless R. and Tremont, R. 1996. The three dimensional foraging patterns of Adélie penguins at Edmonson Point, Antarctica. Third International Penguin Conference, Cape Town, South Africa, 2-6 September 1996.

Franchi, E., Corsolini, S., Focardi, S., Clarke, J.C., Trémont, R. and Kerry, K.K. 1997. Biological research on Adélie penguin (*Pygoscelis adeliae*) associated with the CCAMLR Ecosystem Monitoring Program (CEMP). In di Prisco, G., Focardi, S. and Luporini, P. (eds) *Proceed. Third Meet. Antarctic Biology*, Santa Margherita Ligure, 13-15 December 1996. Camerino University Press: 209-19.

Frati, F. 1997. Collembola of the north Victoria Land: distribution, population structure and preliminary data for the reconstruction of a molecular phylogeny of Antarctic collembola. *Newsletter of the Italian Biological Research in Antarctica* 1 (Austral summer 1995-96): 30-38.

Frati F. 1999. Distribution and ecophysiology of terrestrial microarthropods in the Victoria Land. *Newsletter of the Italian Biological Research in Antarctica* 3: 13-19.

Frati F., Fanciulli P.P., Carapelli A. and Dallai R. 1997. The Collembola of northern Victoria Land (Antarctica): distribution and ecological remarks. *Pedobiologia* 41: 50-55.

Frati F., Fanciulli P.P., Carapelli A., De Carlo L. and Dallai R. 1996. Collembola of northern Victoria Land: distribution, population structure and preliminary molecular data to study origin and evolution of Antarctic Collembola. Proceedings of the 3rd Meeting on Antarctic Biology, G. di Prisco, S. Focardi and P. Luporini eds., Camerino Univ. Press: 321-330.

Fumanti, B., Alfinito, S. and Cavacini, P. 1993. Freshwater algae of Northern Victoria Land (Antarctica). *Giorn. Bot. Ital.,* **127** (3): 497.

Fumanti, B., Alfinito, S. and Cavacini, P. 1994a. Freshwater diatoms of Northern Victoria Land (Antarctica). 13th International Diatom Symposium, 1-7 September 1994, Acquafredda di Maratea (PZ), Italy, Abstract book: 226.

Fumanti, B., Alfinito, S. and Cavacini, P. 1994b. Floristic survey of the freshwater algae of Northern Victoria Land (Antarctica). Proceedings of the 2nd meeting on Antarctic Biology, Padova, 26-28 Feb. 1992. Edizioni Universitarie Patavine: 47-53.

Guilizzoni P., Libera V., Mosello R., Tartagli G., Ruggiu D., Manca M., Nocentini A, Contesini M., Panzani P., Beltrami M. 1991. Indagine per una caratterizzazione limnologica di ambienti lacustri antartici. Atti del 1° Convegno di Biologia Antartica. Roma CNR, 22-23 giu. 1989. Ed. Univ. Patavine: 377-408.Given, D.R. 1985. Fieldwork in Antarctica, November – December 1984. Report 511b. Botany Division, DSIR, New Zealand.

Given, D.R. 1989. A proposal for SSSI status for Edmonson Point, north Victoria Land. Unpublished paper held in PNRA Archives.

Greenfield, L.G., Broady, P.A., Given, D.R., Codley, E.G. and Thompson, K. 1985. Immediate science report of NZARP Expedition K053 to RDRC. Botanical and biological studies in Victoria Land and Ross Island, during 1984–85.

Harris, C.M. and Grant, S.M. 2003. Science and management at Edmonson Point, Wood Bay, Victoria Land, Ross Sea: Report of the Workshop held in Siena, 8 June 2003. Includes Science Reviews by R. Bargagli, N. Cannone & M. Guglielmin, and S. Focardi. Cambridge, *Environmental Research and Assessment.*

Keys, J.R., Dingwall, P.R. and Freegard, J. (eds) 1988. *Improving the Protected Area system in the Ross Sea region, Antarctica*: Central Office Technical Report Series No. 2. Wellington, NZ Department of Conservation.

Kyle, P.R. 1990. A.II. Melbourne Volcanic Province. In LeMasurier, W.E. and Thomson, J.W. (eds) Volcanoes of the Antarctic Plate and Southern Oceans. *Antarctic Research Series* 48: 48-52.

La Rocca N., Moro I. and Andreoli, C. 1996. Survey on a microalga collected from an Edmonson Point pond (Victoria Land, Antarctica). *Giornale Botanico Italiano,* 130:960-962.

Lewis Smith, R.I. 1996. BIOTEX 1 field report: December 1995 – January 1996: plant ecology, colonisation and diversity at Edmonson Point and in the surrounding region of Victoria Land, Antarctica. Unpublished field report in BAS Archives AD6/2/1995/NT1.

Lewis Smith, R.I. 1999. Biological and environmental characteristics of three cosmopolitan mosses dominant in continental Antarctica. *Journal of Vegetation Science* 10: 231-242.

Melick D.R. and Seppelt R.D. 1997. Vegetation patterns in relation to climatic and endogenous changes in Wilkes Land, continetal Antarctica. *Journal of Ecology* **85**: 43-56.

Meurk, C.D., Given, D.R. and Foggo, M. N. 1989. Botanical investigations at Terra Nova Bay and Wood Bay, north Victoria Land. 1988–89 NZARP Event K271 science report.

Olmastroni S, Pezzo F, Bisogno I., Focardi S, 2004b. Interannual variation in the summer diet of Adélie penguin *Pygoscelis adeliae* at Edmonson Point . WG-EMM04/ 38.

Olmastroni S, Pezzo F, Volpi V, Corsolini S, Focardi S, Kerry K. 2001b. Foraging ecology of chick rearing of Adélie penguins in two colonies of the Ross Sea; 27/8-1/9 2001; Amsterdam, The Netherlands. SCAR.

Olmastroni, S. 2002. Factors affecting the foraging strategies of Adélie penguin (*Pygoscelis adeliae*) at Edmonson Point, Ross Sea, Antarctica. PhD Thesis, Università di Siena.

Olmastroni, S., Corsolini, S., Franchi, E., Focardi, S., Clarke, J., Kerry, K., Lawless, R. and Tremont, R. 1998. Adélie penguin colony at Edmonson Point (Ross Sea, Antarctica): a long term monitoring study. 31 August-September 1998; Christchurch, New Zealand. SCAR. p 143.

Olmastroni, S., Corsolini, S., Pezzo, F., Focardi, S. and Kerry, K. 2000. The first five years of the Italian-Australian Joint Programme on the Adélie Penguin: an overview. *Italian Journal of Zoology Supplement* **1**: 141-45.

Onofri, S. and Tofi, S. 1992. *Arthrobotrys ferox* sp. nov., a springtail-capturing hyphomycete from continental Antarctica. *Mycotaxon* 44(2):445-451.Orombelli, G. 1988. Le spiagge emerse oloceniche di Baia Terra Nova (Terra Vittoria, Antartide). Rend. Acc. Naz. Lincei.

Pezzo, F., Olmastroni, S., Corsolini, S., and Focardi, S. 2001. Factors affecting the breeding success of the south polar skua *Catharacta maccormicki* at Edmonson Point, Victoria Land, Antarctica. *Polar Biology* **24**:389-93.

Pilastro, A., Pezzo, F., Olmastroni, S., Callegarin, C., Corsolini, S. and Focardi, S. 2001. Extrapair paternity in the Adélie penguin *Pygoscelis adeliae*. *Ibis* **143**: 681-84.

Ricelli A., Fabbri A.A., Fumanti B., Cavacini P., Fanelli C. 1997. Analyses of effects of ultraviolet radiation on fatty acids and α-tocopherol composition of some microalgae isolated from Antarctica. In di Prisco, G., Focardi, S., and Luporini P. (eds.), Proceedings of the 3rd meeting on "Antarctic Biology", S. Margherita Ligure, December 13-15, 1996. Camerino University Press: 239-247.

Simeoni, U., Baroni, C., Meccheri, M., Taviani, M. and Zanon, G. 1989. Coastal studies in northern Victoria Land (Antarctica): Holocene beaches of Inexpressible Island, Tethys Bay and Edmonson Point. *Bollettino di Oceanologia Teorica ed Applicata* 7(1-2): 5-17.

Taylor, R.H., Wilson, P.R. and Thomas, B.W. 1990. Status and trends of Adélie Penguin populations in the Ross Sea region. *Polar Record* 26:293-304.

Woehler, E.J. (ed) 1993. *The distribution and abundance of Antarctic and sub-Antarctic penguins.* SCAR, Cambridge.

Wörner, G. and Viereck, L. 1990. A.I0. Mount Melbourne. In Le Masurier, W.E. and Thomson, J.W. (eds) Volcanoes of the Antarctic Plate and Southern Oceans. *Antarctic Research Series* 48: 72-78.

Wynn-Williams, D.D. 1996. BIOTEX 1, first BIOTAS expedition: field report: Taylor Valley LTER Dec 1995, Terra Nova Bay Dec 1995 – Jan 1996: microbial colonisation, propagule banks and survival processes. Unpublished field report in BAS Archives AD6/2/1995/NT2.

Zucconi L., Pagano S., Fenice M., Selbmann L., Tosi S., and Onofri S. 1996. Growth temperature preference of fungal strains from Victoria Land. *Polar Biology* **16**: 53-61.

**Appendix 1**

**Recent bibliography and other publications of interest for the research activity at Edmonson Point (Ross Sea)**

D. Ainley, V. Toniolo, G. Ballard, K. Barton, J. Eastman, B. Karl, S. Focardi, G. Kooyman, P. Lyver, S. Olmastroni, B.S. Stewart, J. W. Testa, P. Wilson, 2006. Managing ecosystem uncertainty: critical habitat and dietary overlap of top-predators in the Ross Sea. WG-EMM 06/29

Tosca Ballerini, Giacomo Tavecchia, Silvia Olmastroni, Francesco Pezzo, Silvano Focardi 2009. Nonlinear effects of winter sea ice on the survival probabilities of Adélie penguins. *Oecologia* 161:253–265.

F. Borghini, A. Colacevich, S. Olmastroni 2010. Studi di ecologia e paleolimnologia nell'area protetta di Edmonson Point (Terra Vittoria, Antartide). *Etruria Natura* Anno VII: 77-86.

Cincinelli A., Martellini T. and Corsolini S., 2011. Hexachlorocyclohexanes in Arctic and Antarctic Marine Ecosystems, Pesticides - Formulations, Effects, Fate, Edited by: Margarita Stoytcheva, ISBN: 978-953-307-532-7, Publisher: InTech, Publishing, Janeza Trdine 9, 51000 Rijeka, Croatia, January 2011,453-476, available at http://www.intechopen.com/articles/show/title/hexachlorocyclohexanes-in-arctic-and-antarctic-marine-ecosystems.

Corsolini S., 2011. Contamination Profile and Temporal Trend of POPs in Antarctic Biota. In Global contamination trends of persistent organic chemicals. Ed. B. Loganathan, P.K.S. Lam, Taylor & Francis, Boca Raton, FL, USA, in press.

Corsolini S., 2011. Antarctic: Persistent Organic Pollutants and Environmental Health in the Region. In: Nriagu JO (ed.) *Encyclopedia of Environmental Health*, volume 1, pp. 83–96 Burlington: Elsevier, NVRN/978-0-444-52273-3.

Corsolini S., Ademollo N., Mariottini M., Focardi S., 2004. Poly-brominated diphenyl-ethers (PBDEs) and other Persistent Organic Pollutants in blood of penguins from the Ross Sea (Antarctica). *Organohalogen Compd.*, 66: 1695-1701.

Corsolini S, Covaci A, Ademollo N, Focardi S, Schepens P., 2005. Occurrence of organochlorine pesticides (OCPs) and their enantiomeric signatures, and concentrations of polybrominated diphenyl ethers (PBDEs) in the Adelie penguin food web, Antarctica. *Environ Pollut.*, 140(2): 371-382.

Corsolini S., Olmastroni S., Ademollo N., Minucci G., Focardi S., 2003. Persistent organic pollutants in stomach contents of Adélie penguins from Edmonson Point (Victoria Land, Antarctica). In: Antarctic Biology in a global context, Ed. A.H.L. Huiskes, W.W.C. Gieskes, J. Rozema, R.M.L. Schorno, S.M. van der Vies, W.J. Wolff. Backhuys Publishers, Leiden, The Netherlands. pp. 296-300

Fuoco, R.; Bengtson Nash, S. M.; Corsolini, S.; Gambaro, A.; Cincinelli, A. *POPs in Antarctica; A Report to the Antarctic Treaty in Kiev 2-13 June, 2008*; Environmental Contamination in Antarctica (ECA) Pisa, 2008.

Sandra Lorenzini, Silvia Olmastroni, Francesco Pezzo, Maria Cristina Salvatore, Carlo Baroni 2009. Holocene Adélie penguin diet in Victoria Land, Antarctica. *Polar Biology* 32:1077–1086.

Irene Nesti, Yan Ropert-Coudert, Akiko Kato, Michael Beaulieu, Silvano Focardi, Silvia Olmastroni 2010. Diving behaviour of chick-rearing Adélie Penguins at Edmonson Point, Ross Sea. *Polar Biology* 33:969–978.

S. Olmastroni, F. Pezzo, V. Volpi, S. Focardi 2004a. Effects of weather and sea ice on Adélie penguin reproductive performance. *CCAMLR Science* 11:99-109

F. Pezzo, **S.** Olmastroni, V. Volpi, S. Focardi 2007. Annual variation in reproductive parameters of Adélie penguins at Edmonson Point, Victoria Land, Antarctica. *Polar Biology* **31**:39-45.

## Appendix 2   Permits issued

During 2006-2011 Italian Antarctic Campaign have been issued the permits for the Interference or sampling of following living organisms into the Edmonson Point ASPA N° 165:

**2006/2007 campaign**

| Organism denomination | Amount N° or Kg | Sampling System |
|---|---|---|
| Pygoscelis adeliae | 2000 | visual census |
| "      "      " | 10 | tagging |
| "      "      " | 10 | feathers sampling |
| Stercorarius  maccormicki | 200 | visual census |

Have been carried out water sampling from lakes. Permit for entry in ASPA 165 have been performed for 40 days in the field camp.

**2007/2008 campaign**

| Organism denomination | Amount N° or Kg | Sampling System |
|---|---|---|

Have been issued permits for entry in ASPA 165 only for meteo station control for 2 times,  3hours each time

**2008/2009 campaign**

| Organism denomination | Amount N° or  Kg | Sampling System |
|---|---|---|

No activity has been performed at Edmonson Point ASPA 165 during 2007/2008 campaign

**2009/2010 campaign**

| Organism denomination | Amount N° or  Kg | | Sampling System |
|---|---|---|---|
| Pygoscelis adeliae | 2000 | | visual census |
| "      "      " | 18 | | feathers and blood sampling |
| Stercorarius maccormicki | 120 | | visual census |
| "      "      " | 10 | | feathers and blood sampling |
| Mosses | | 200 g | manual sampling |
| Algae | | 200 g | manual sampling |

Have been carried out water sampling, mosses and algae from lakes. Permit for entry in ASPA 165 have been performed during 31 days in the field camp and for 3 hours  for other sampling.

**2010/2011 campaign**

| Organism denomination | Amount N° or   Kg | Sampling System |
|---|---|---|

ASPA No 165 - Edmonson Point

| | | |
|---|---|---|
| Mosses | 600 g | manual sampling |
| Algae | 400 g | manual sampling |
| Lichens on rocks and soils | 600 g | manual sampling |
| Colonized rocks and soils by microorganisms and lichens | 2 Kg | manual sampling |

Sampling and studies activities into the ASPA area have been carried out in 12 different times for a total of 28 hours of work.

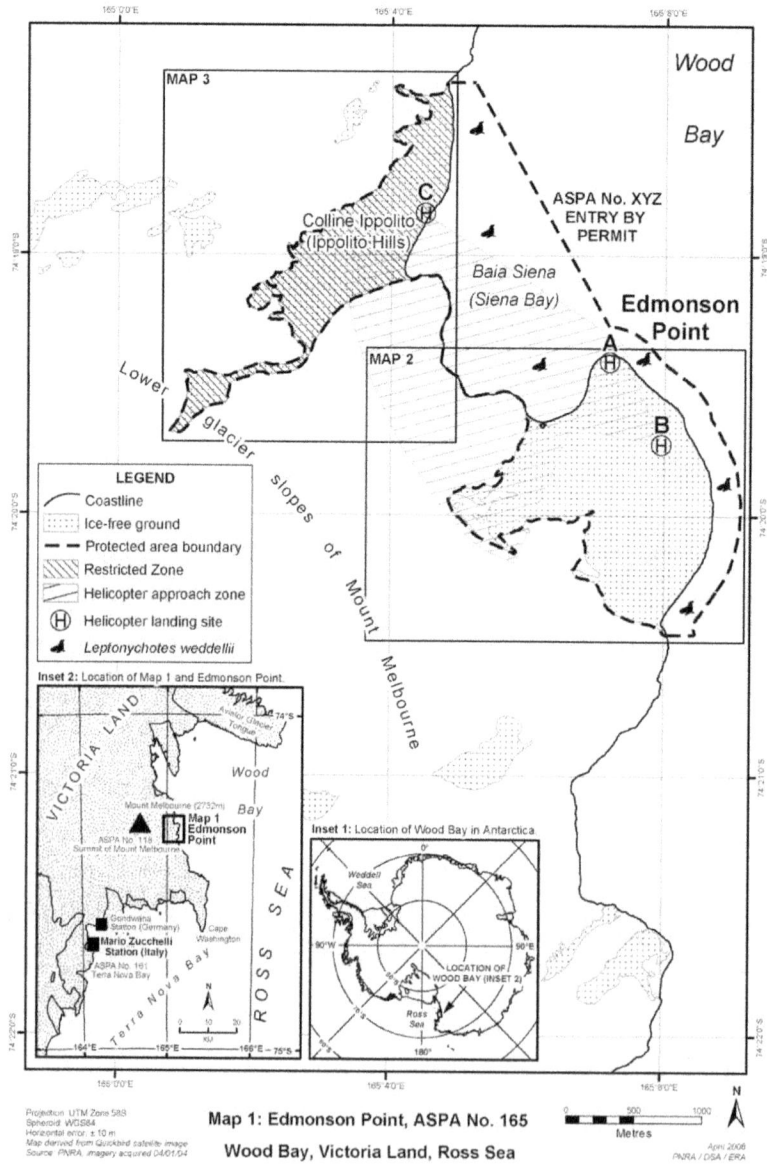

**Map 1: Edmonson Point, ASPA No. 165**

**Wood Bay, Victoria Land, Ross Sea**

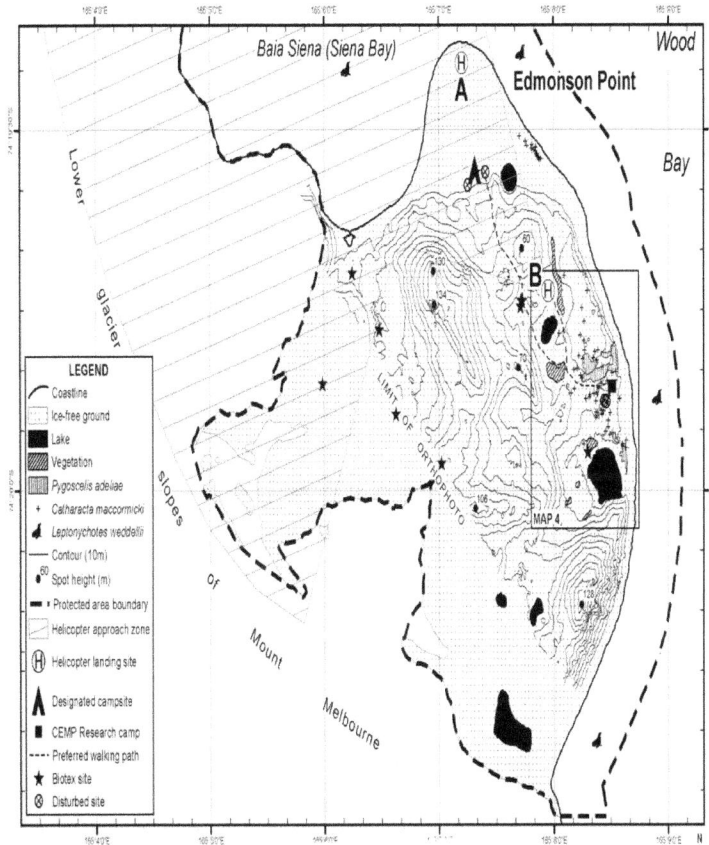

Map 2: Edmonson Point, ASPA No 165
Physical / human features and access guidelines

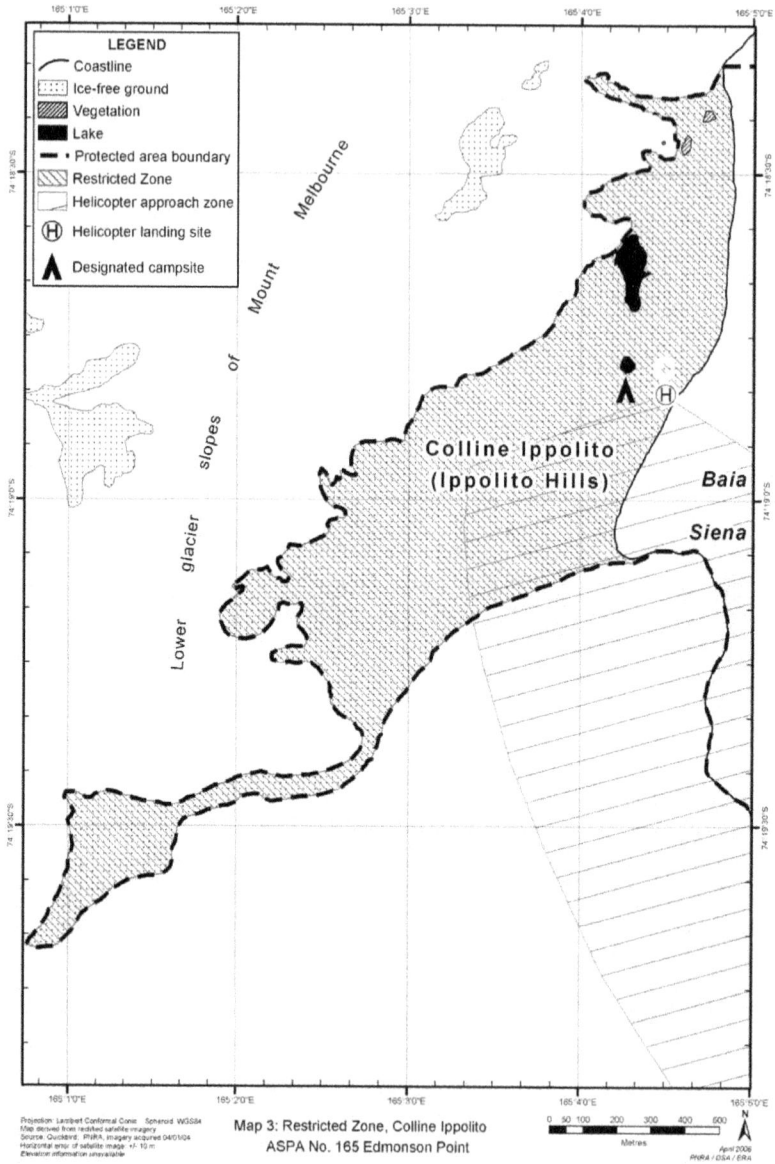

Map 3: Restricted Zone, Colline Ippolito
ASPA No. 165 Edmonson Point

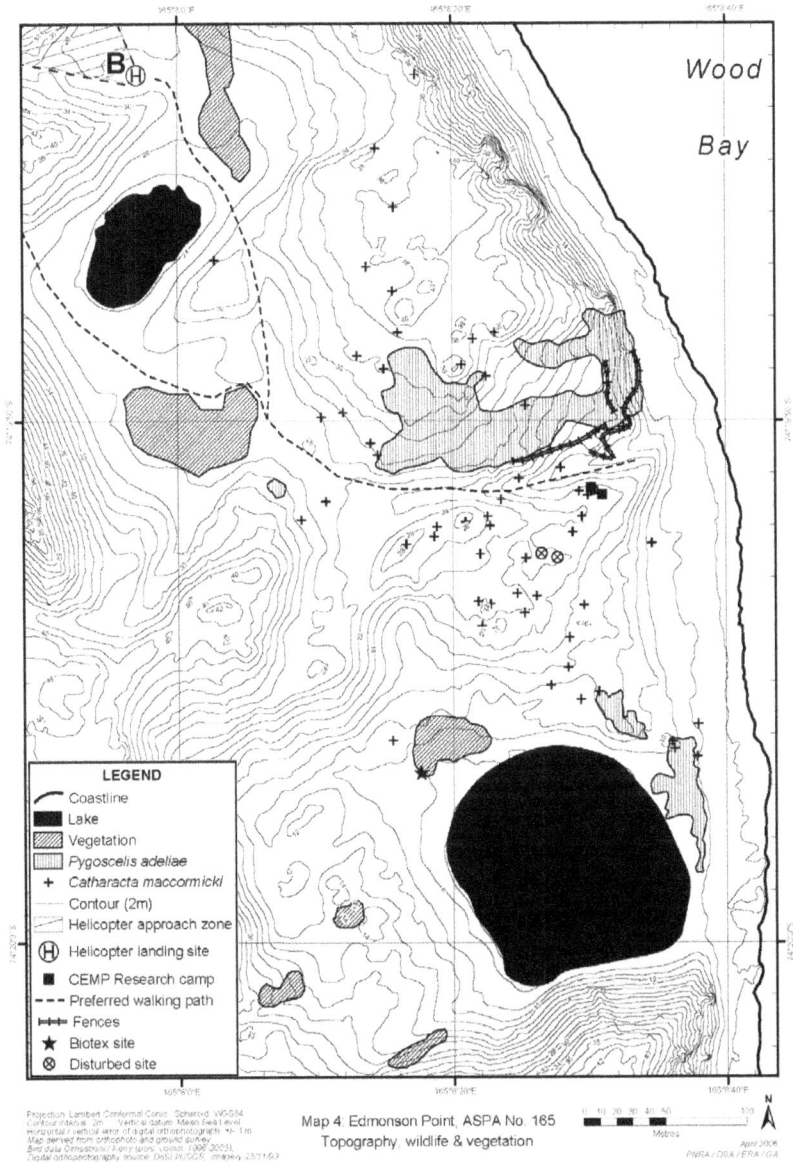

Map 4: Edmonson Point, ASPA No. 165
Topography, wildlife & vegetation

# Management Plan for
# Antarctic Specially Protected Area No. 167

# Hawker Island, Princess Elizabeth Land

## Introduction

Hawker Island (68°38'S, 77°51'E, Map A) is located 7 km south-west from Davis station off the Vestfold Hills on the Ingrid Christensen Coast, Princess Elizabeth Land, East Antarctica. The island was designated as Antarctic Specially Protected Area (ASPA) No. 167 under Measure 1 (2006), following a proposal by Australia, primarily to protect the southernmost breeding colony of southern giant petrels (*Macronectes giganteus*) (Map B). The Area is one of only four known breeding locations for southern giant petrels on the coast of East Antarctica, all of which have been designated as ASPAs: ASPA 102, Rookery Islands, Holme Bay, Mac.Robertson Land (67°36'S, 62°53'E) – near Mawson Station; ASPA 160, Frazier Islands, Wilkes Land (66°13'S, 110°11'E) – near Casey station; and ASPA 120, Pointe Géologie, Terre Adélie (66°40'S, 140°01'E) – near Dumont d'Urville. Hawker Island also supports breeding colonies of Adélie penguins (*Pygocelis adeliae*), south polar skuas (*Catharacta maccormicki*), Cape petrels (*Daption capense*) and occasionally Weddell seals (*Leptonychotes weddellii*).

## 1. Description of values to be protected

The total population of southern giant petrels in East Antarctica represents less than 1% of the global breeding population. It is currently estimated at approximately 300 pairs, comprising approximately 45 pairs on Hawker Island (2010), 2-4 pairs on Giganteus Island (Rookery Islands group) (2007), approximately 250 pairs on the Frazier Islands (2001) and 8-9 pairs at Pointe Géologie (2005). Southern giant petrels also breed on other islands in the southern Indian and Atlantic Oceans and at the Antarctic Peninsula.

The southern giant petrel colony at Hawker Island was discovered in December 1963; at that time there were 40-50 nests present, "some with eggs" but it is unclear how many nests were occupied. Between 1963 and 2007, intermittent counts of adults, eggs or chicks were undertaken at various stages of the breeding cycle. Because of the variability in the timing of counts and the inconsistency of count units it is not possible to establish a long term trend for this population. Low numbers were previously reported for this colony because only the numbers of chicks banded in a given year rather than total chick numbers. The Area also supports a breeding colony of Adélie penguins, a limited number of flying birds and southern elephant seal haul out areas.

Southern giant petrels breeding in East Antarctica are sensitive to disturbance at the nest. Restrictions in activities permitted at breeding sites near Australian stations, including a prohibition of banding, were introduced in the mid-1980s.

At the South Shetland Islands and South Orkney Islands, the incidental bycatch of southern giant petrels in longline fisheries operating in the Southern Ocean is likely to have contributed to observed population decreases. Similar observations have not been made in East Antarctica. Until recently, southern giant petrels were listed as Vulnerable by the International Union for the Conservation of Nature (IUCN). However, a re-analysis of all data available for the global population indicated that the best case scenario over the past three generations or 64 years was a 17% increase of the total population, and the worst case scenario a 7.2% decrease. These figures are below the threshold set by the IUCN to be classified as Vulnerable. The conservation status for southern giant petrels has consequently been downgraded from Near Threatened to Least Concern.Hawker Island also supports breeding colonies of Adélie penguins (*Pygocelis adeliae*), south polar skuas (*Catharacta maccormicki*), Cape petrels (*Daption capense*) and occasionally Weddell seals (*Leptonychotes weddellii*).

## 2. Aims and objectives

Management of the Hawker Island ASPA aims to:

- protect the breeding colony of southern giant petrels and other wildlife colonies;

- avoid human disturbance or other adverse impacts on the values of the Area, while still allowing research or other activities consistent with this Plan;

- protect the values of Hawker Island as a reference area for future comparative studies with other breeding populations of southern giant petrels; and

- minimise the possibility of the introduction of alien plants, animals and microbes to Hawker Island.

## 3. Management activities

The following management activities will be undertaken to protect the values of the Area:

- research visits to assess population levels and trends of the southern giant petrel colony and/or other wildlife shall be permitted. Wherever feasible, preference shall be given to activities and methodologies which minimise disturbance to the breeding colony (e.g. use of automated cameras);

- where practicable the Area shall be visited outside the breeding season of southern giant petrels (i.e. during the period mid-April to mid-September) as necessary, to assess whether it continues to serve the purposes for which it was designated and to ensure that management activities are adequate;

- information on the location of Hawker Island ASPA (stating the restrictions that apply) shall be produced and copies of this management plan shall be available at nearby stations. Informative material and the management plan should be provided to ships visiting the vicinity; and

- the management plan shall be reviewed at least every five years and updated/modified as required.

## 4. Period of designation

Designation is for an indefinite period.

## 5. Maps

Map A: Hawker Island Antarctic Specially Protected Area, Vestfold Hills, Ingrid Christensen Coast, Princess Elizabeth Land, East Antarctica.

Map B: Hawker Island, Antarctic Specially Protected Area, Vestfold Hills, Ingrid Christensen Coast, Princess Elizabeth Land, East Antarctica, Biota, Topography and Physical Features.

Specifications for maps:

        Projection: UTM Zone 49
        Horizontal Datum: WGS84

## 6. Description of the Area

### 6(i) Geographical co-ordinates, boundary markers and natural features

Hawker Island is located at 68°38'S, 77°51'E, approximately 300 m offshore from the Vestfold Hills. The Vestfold Hills are roughly triangular ice-free area of approximately 512 km$^2$ of bedrock, glacial debris, lakes and ponds. The Vestfold Hills are bound by the ice plateau to the east, the Sørsdal Glacier to the south, and Prydz Bay to the west and contain low hills (maximum height 158 m at Boulder Hill) and valleys, and are penetrated deeply by fjords and lakes. Numerous islands fringe the coast of the Vestfold Hills, and Hawker Island lies in the south-west, between Mule Island and Mule Peninsula.

Hawker Island is an irregularly shaped island of low elevation (maximum elevation of nearly 40 m), with two parallel ranges of hills running in a north south direction terminating in two small southern peninsulas. A third peninsula lies directly west and terminates with a 40 m hill with steep cliffs to the sea on the western and southerly aspects. A number of small freshwater lakes lie between the ranges of hills on the northern part of the island, with a number of small lakes lying on the flatter terrain on the eastern sector of the island. At its maximum extent the island is 2 km north to south and 1.7 km east to west.

The Hawker Island ASPA comprises the entire terrestrial area of Hawker Island, with the seaward boundary at the low water mark (Map B). The total area of the Hawker Island ASPA is approximately 1.9 km$^2$. There are no boundary markers.

*Environmental domains analysis*

Based on the Environmental Domains Analysis for Antarctica (Resolution 3 (2008)) Hawker Island is located within Environment T Inland continental geologic.

*Human History*

The first recorded sighting of the Vestfold Hills was by Douglas Mawson on the BANZARE voyage of the *'Discovery'* on 9 February 1931. Four years later, on 20 February 1935, Captain Klarius Mikkelsen of the tanker *Thorshavn* (Lars Christensen Company), sighted and landed in the area. He named many features in the area and in the Vestfold Hills after his home province in Norway. The Vestfold Hills were again visited by Mikkelsen in early 1937, while undertaking an aerial survey of the coast.

In January 1939, the American explorer, Lincoln Ellsworth, and his Australian adviser, Sir Hubert Wilkins were the next recorded visitors to the area in the motor ship *Wyatt Earp*. Ellsworth flew some 400 km inland. In early 1947, the *USS Currituck* visited the Ingrid Christensen Coast as part of Operation Highjump. Photographic flights were conducted to survey the coastline.

The first Australian National Antarctic Research Expeditions (ANARE) to the area was led by Dr Phillip Law on *Kista Dan* and reached the Vestfold Hills on 1 March 1954. During January 1956, members of the Soviet Antarctic Expedition landed on the Ingrid Christensen Coast in preparation for the International Geophysical Year and established Mirny Station 595 km to the east. Australia established Davis station in the Vestfold Hills in 1957. Hawker Island was named for A.C. Hawker, radio supervisor at Davis station in 1957.

*Climate*

Meteorological data for the Area are confined almost entirely to observations at Davis station, 7 km northwest of Hawker Island. The Vestfold Hills area has a polar maritime climate that is cold, dry and windy. Summer days are typically sunny, with a midday temperature from -1°C to +2.9°C and a summer maximum of +5°C, but temperatures are below 0°C for most of the year falling to as low as −40.7°C in winter. The maximum temperature recorded at Davis station from 1957 to 2001 was +13°C. Long periods of relatively calm, fine conditions occur throughout the year. Winds are generally light. The yearly average is around 20 km/h. Violent winds and blizzards can commence with little warning, and gusts of over 200 km/h have been recorded. Snowfall averages 78 mm/yr, with the greater proportion of annual accumulation resulting from windblown drift. Apart from several permanent ice banks, the Vestfold Hills are virtually snow free in summer and lightly covered in winter. The record illustrates the seasonal climate expected for high latitudes, but on average Davis station is warmer than other Antarctic stations at similar latitudes. This has been attributed to the "rocky oasis" which results from the lower albedo of rock surfaces compared to ice, hence more solar energy is absorbed and re-radiated.

*Geology*

The Vestfold Hills consist of Archaean gneiss, upon which thin and often fossiliferous Pliocene and Quaternary sediments occupy depressions. The oldest known Cenozoic strata in the Vestfold Hills are the mid-Pliocene Sørsdal Formation, which contains a diverse marine fossil flora and fauna. Other younger Cenozoic strata attest to repeated glaciation, and several marine transgressions and regressions. The three major lithologies forming the Vestfold Hills are (in order of age) Chelnock Paragneiss, Mossel Gneiss and Crooked Lake Gneiss. This is repeated in units from east-north-east to west-south-west. Intruded into these, are groups of mafic dykes in a rough north-south orientation. The dykes are a major feature of the Vestfold Hills. Hawker Island comprises an extension of the Crooked Lake Gneiss of the northern portion of Mule Peninsula above Laternula Inlet. In common with the Archaean gneisses in the Vestfold Hills, the Hawker Island Crooked Lake Gneiss is cut by very distinctive, middle to early Proterozoic dolerite dykes.

*Southern Giant Petrels*

The Hawker Island southern giant petrel colony is situated on level ground about 20 m above sea-level at the northern end of the island (Map B). The same area has been used for breeding since the first records were made in 1963/64. The eastern side of the breeding area forms a slight ridge with the ground dropping away below, providing a good area for take-off into the prevailing north-easterly winds.

The breeding season for southern giant petrels on Hawker Island commences in late September/early October and eggs are laid during the second half of October. Following an incubation period of about 60 days, hatching starts in the second half of December. Hatching continues over a period of three to four weeks until mid-January. About 14 – 16 weeks after hatching, the fledglings leave the colony from late March to early May. From the analysis of year round automated cameras and visits during recent winters, it is known that a small number of birds are present outside the breeding season; hence the requirement that visits to the Area at any time of the year be conducted in a manner that ensures minimal disturbance.

In the mid 1980s, a management strategy was implemented for all three southern giant petrels breeding localities in the vicinity of the Australian stations, to minimise human disturbance. Previously the Australian Antarctic Division restricted census visits to one in every three to five year period and implemented tight administrative controls over all other visits. At this time, this level of visitation was considered an appropriate compromise between the risk of disturbing the birds and the need to obtain meaningful population data. However, this management regime impacted on the level of visitation needed to assess population levels (and trends) and did not appear to significantly benefit the breeding success of the southern giant petrels. With the development of new technology (such as automated cameras), detailed information can now be obtained with little or no human presence during the breeding period.

In March 2011, 23 chicks and 64 adults were observed in the Area. Of these, four banded birds were sighted consisting of two birds banded in the Casey region (dated 1985) and two birds banded at Hawker Island (dated 1986). The two Casey banded birds were observed remaining near the same chicks and appeared to be breeding.

*Other Birds*

Adélie penguins breed along the Vestfold Hills coastline and on at least 17 offshore islands, including Hawker Island. The total number of Adélie penguins in the Vestfold Hills has been estimated at 130000 pairs. The Hawker Island colony is located in the vicinity of a small hill midway on the western side of the island and has been estimated at 2500 to 7500 pairs. There is evidence that the colony or some of the breeding groups within the colony have moved location periodically. The deserted areas are marked by deep deposits of guano, frozen eggs and the dehydrated carcasses of chicks. The first Adélie penguins usually appear in the area by the middle of October and eggs are laid about four weeks later. The interval between laying of the first and second egg is 2½ to 4½ days, and the incubation period is ranges from 32 to 35 days. The last moulted adults depart Hawker Island by the end of March.

A small colony of Cape petrels has been recorded on Hawker Island on the southern tip of the south western peninsula. Cape petrels are absent from the Area in winter; they return to their nesting sites during October, lay eggs from late November to early December and chicks fledge in late February and early March.

*Seals*

Weddell seals *(Leptonychotes weddellii)* breed in the Vestfold Hills and occasionally on the south-east part of Hawker Island. The seals start to appear inshore in late September and early October, and pupping occurs from mid-October until late November. Throughout summer, moulting Weddell seals continue to frequent firm sea-ice and haul out onto land. Most of the local population remains in the Vestfold Hills throughout the summer. Non-breeding groups of southern elephant seals (*Mirounga leonina*) haul out during the summer months in the vicinity of the south-western peninsula on Hawker Island. Their moulting areas contain deposits of hair and excrement that have accumulated over several thousand years, and could be considered as unique and sensitive areas.

*Vegetation*

The flora of the Vestfold Hills comprises at least 82 species of terrestrial algae, six moss species and at least 23 lichen species. The lichens and mosses are distributed chiefly in the eastern or inland sector and their distribution patterns reflect the availability of drift snow, time since exposure of the substrate from the ice plateau, time since the last glaciation, elevation and proximity to saline waters. Very few occurrences of lichens or mosses have been noted towards the salt-affected coastal margin including Hawker Island where the low terrain is densely covered with extensive sand and moraine deposits.

Terrestrial algae are widespread and are major primary producers in the Vestfold Hills. Sublithic (or hypolithic) algae have been reported from Hawker Island, developing on the undersurfaces of translucent quartz stones that are partially buried in soil. The dominant algae, Cyanobacteria, particularly oscillatoriacean species, *Chroococidiopsis sp.*, and *Aphanothece sp.* occur with the greatest frequency together with the Chlorophyta species, *cf. Desmococcus sp. A* and *Prasiococcus calcarius*. The endaphic alga *Prasiola crispa* occurs as green crumpled sheet-like strands at melt flushes, usually associated with the diatom *Navicula muticopsis* and oscillatoriacean algae. The ornithocophilous lichen *Candelariella flava* has been reported from Hawker Island, associated with seabird nesting sites.

*Invertebrates*

An extensive survey of terrestrial tardigrades was undertaken in the Vestfold Hills in 1981 from which four genera and four species of tardigrade were recovered. Although no tardigrades were recovered from the Hawker Island sample site it has been suggested that, as two species of tardigrade, *Hypsibius allisonii* and *Macrobiotus fuciger (?)* were recovered from Walkabout Rocks, they may be found in other coastal areas of similar ecology, associated with *Prasiola crispa*. The mite, *Tydeus erebus* is associated with breeding sites of Adélie penguins on the island.

### 6(ii) Access to the Area

Depending on sea ice conditions, the Area can be accessed by vehicle, small boat or aircraft, all of which must remain outside the Area. There are no designated landing sites.

### 6(iii) Location of structures within and adjacent to the Area

There are no permanent structures within or adjacent to the Area. At the time of writing a number of automatic cameras were temporarily located in proximity to the southern giant petrel colony, for the purposes of ongoing population monitoring.

### 6(iv) Location of other protected areas in the vicinity

The following Protected Area is located near Hawker Island:

Marine Plain, Antarctic Specially Protected Area No. 143 (68°36'S, 78°07'E).

### 6(v) Special zones within the Area

There are no special zones within the Area.

## 7. Terms and conditions for entry permits

### 7(i)    General conditions

Visits to Hawker Island ASPA are prohibited except in accordance with a permit issued by an appropriate national authority. Permits to enter the Area may only be issued for compelling scientific research that cannot be undertaken elsewhere, or for essential management purposes consistent with the objectives and provisions of the management plan. Permits are only to be issued for research that will not jeopardise the ecological or scientific values of the Area, or interfere with existing scientific studies.

Permits shall include a condition that the permit or a copy shall be carried at all times when within the Area. Additional conditions, consistent with the objectives and provisions of the management plan, may be included by the issuing authority. The principal permit holder for each permit issued is required to submit to the permit issuing authority a visit report detailing all activities undertaken within the Area, and all census data obtained during the visit.

Collaboration with other national programs is encouraged to reduce duplication of research and minimise disturbance of the southern giant petrels. National Antarctic programs planning research in this Area are encouraged to contact the Australian Antarctic Division, which maintains a regular population monitoring program on the island, to ascertain other projects that may be undertaken that season.

### 7(ii) Access to, and movement within or over the Area

- Vehicles are prohibited within the Area.

- Access to the Hawker Island ASPA boundary may be by watercraft or vehicle depending upon seasonal conditions. Boats used to visit the islands must be left at the shoreline. Movement within the Area is by foot only. Only personnel who are required to carry out scientific/management work in the Area are to leave the landing/parking site. Quad-bikes or other land vehicles used to visit the Area shall not be taken into the Area. Vehicles shall remain on the sea-ice at least 150 m (quad-bike) or 250 m (other land-vehicles) from the edge of the southern giant petrel colony (see Table 1);

- The minimum (closest) approach distances to wildlife are set out in Table 1. If disturbance of wildlife if observed, separation distance should be increased or the activity modified until there is no visible disturbance, unless a closer approach distance is authorised in a permit.

- Persons authorised in a permit to approach southern giant petrels to obtain census data or biological data, should maintain the greatest practical separation distance;

- To reduce disturbance to wildlife, noise levels, including verbal communication are to be kept to a minimum. The use of motor-driven tools and any other activity likely to generate significant noise (thereby cause disturbance to nesting southern giant petrels and other nesting birds) is prohibited within the Area during the breeding period for southern giant petrels (mid-September to mid-April);

- Overflights of the island during the breeding season are prohibited, except where essential for scientific or management purposes and authorised in a permit. Such overflights are to be at an altitude of no less than 930 m (3050 ft) for single-engined helicopters and fixed-wing aircraft, and no less than 1500 m (5000 ft) for twin-engined helicopters; and

- Landing of aircraft within 930 m for single-engined helicopters and fixed-wing aircraft and 1500 m (5000 ft) for twin-engined helicopters of a wildlife concentration is prohibited at any time other than an emergency.

**Table 1: Minimum distances to maintain when approaching wildlife at Hawker Island**

| Species | Distances (m) | | | |
|---|---|---|---|---|
| | People on foot / ski (unless a closer approach distance is authorised in a permit) | Quad/ Skidoo | Hagglunds, etc. | Small watercraft |
| Giant petrels | 100 m | Not permitted inside the Area. Parking shall be on the sea-ice and no closer than 150 m from wildlife colonies. | Not permitted inside the Area. Parking shall be on the sea-ice and no closer than 250 m from wildlife colonies. | Watercraft should not be landed within 50 m of wildlife; in particular, the Adelie penguin colony on the eastern shore. Care shall be taken when in close proximity to the island. |
| Adelie penguins in colonies | 30 m | | | |
| Moulting penguins | | | | |
| Seals with pups | | | | |
| Seal pups on their own | | | | |
| South polar skua on nest | | | | |
| Penguins on sea ice | 5 m | | | |
| Non breeding adult seals | | | | |

**7(iii) Activities which are or may be conducted within the Area, including restrictions on time and place**

The following activities may be conducted within the Area from 15 April to 15 September (southern giant petrel non-breeding period) as authorised in a permit:

- scientific research consistent with the provisions of this management plan which cannot be undertaken elsewhere or in the Area outside that period and which will not jeopardise the values for which the Area has been designated or the ecosystems of the Area;

- essential management activities, including monitoring; and

- sampling which should be the minimum required for approved research programs.

Activities undertaken within the breeding period of the southern giant petrel shall only be permitted if the activity is non-invasive and cannot reasonably be undertaken during the non-breeding period.

**7(iv) Installation, modification, or removal of structures**

- Permanent structures or installations are prohibited.

- Temporary structures or equipment, including cameras, shall only be erected within the Area in accordance with in a permit.

- Small temporary refuges, hides, blinds or screens may be constructed for the purpose of scientific study.

- Installation (including site selection), removal, modification or maintenance of structures or equipment shall be undertaken in a manner that minimises disturbance to breeding birds and the surrounding environment.

- All scientific equipment or markers installed within the Area must be clearly identified by country, name of the principal investigator and year of installation.

- Markers, signs or other structures erected within the Area for scientific or management purposes shall be secured and maintained in good condition and removed under permit when no longer required. All such items should be made of materials that pose minimal risk of harm to wildlife or of contamination of the Area.

**7(v) Location of field camps**

- Camping is prohibited within the Area except in an emergency. Any emergency camp should avoid areas of wildlife concentrations, if feasible.

**7(vi) Restrictions on materials and organisms that may be brought into the Area**

- Fuel is not to be stored in the Area. Boat refuelling is permitted at landing sites. A small amount of fuel may be taken into the Area for an emergency stove.

- No poultry products, including dried food containing egg powder, are to be taken into the Area.

- No herbicides or pesticides are to be brought into the Area.

- Any chemical which may be introduced for compelling scientific purposes as authorised in a permit shall be removed from the Area, at or before the conclusion of the activity for which the permit was granted. The use of radio-nuclides or stable isotopes is prohibited.

- No animals, plant material or microorganisms shall be deliberately introduced into the Area and precautions shall be taken against accidental introductions; all equipment and clothing (particularly footwear) should be thoroughly cleaned before entering the Area.

- All material introduced shall be for a stated period only, shall be removed at or before the conclusion of that stated period, and shall be stored and handled so as to minimise the risk of environmental impact.

**7(vii) Taking of or harmful interference with native flora and fauna**

- Taking of, or harmful interference with, native flora and fauna is prohibited unless specifically authorised by permit issued in accordance with Article 3 of Annex II to the Protocol on Environmental Protection to the Antarctic Treaty. Any such permit shall clearly state the limits and conditions for such activities which, except in an emergency, shall only occur following approval by an appropriate animal ethics committee.

- Ornithological research shall be limited to activities that are non-invasive and non-disruptive to the breeding seabirds present within the Area.

- Disturbance of southern giant petrels or other wildlife should be avoided or minimised.

### 7(viii) Collection or removal of anything not brought into the Area by the permit holder

- Material may only be collected or removed from the Area as authorised in a permit and should be limited to the minimum necessary to meet scientific or management needs.

- Material of human origin likely to compromise the values of the Area, which was not brought into the Area by the permit holder or otherwise authorised, may be removed unless the impact of the removal is likely to be greater than leaving the material *in situ*. If such material is found the appropriate National Authority must be notified.

### 7(ix) Disposal of Waste

- All wastes, including human wastes, shall be removed from the Area.

### 7(x) Measures that may be necessary to continue to meet the aims of the management plan

- GPS data shall be obtained for specific sites of long-term monitoring for lodgement with the Antarctic Master Directory through the appropriate national authority.

- Permits may be granted to enter the Area to carry out biological monitoring and management activities, which may involve the collection of samples for analysis or review; the erection or maintenance of temporary scientific equipment and structures, and signposts; or for other protective measures. Any specific sites of long-term monitoring shall be appropriately marked and a GPS position obtained for lodgement with the Antarctic Data Directory System through the appropriate national authority.

- To help maintain the ecological and scientific values of the Area, visitors shall take special precautions against introductions of non-indigenous organisms. Of particular concern are pathogenic, microbial or vegetation introductions sourced from soils, flora and fauna at other Antarctic sites, including research stations, or from regions outside Antarctica. To minimise the risk of introductions, before entering the Area visitors shall thoroughly clean footwear and any equipment, particularly sampling equipment and markers to be used in the Area.

### 7(xi) Requirement for reports

Parties shall ensure that the principal permit holder for each permit submits to the appropriate National Authority a report on activities undertaken. Such reports should include, as appropriate, the information identified in the visit report form contained in the Guide to the Preparation of Management Plans for Antarctic Specially Protected Areas.

Parties shall maintain a record of such activities and, in the annual exchange of information, shall provide summary descriptions of activities conducted by persons subject to their jurisdiction, which shall be in sufficient detail to allow evaluation of the effectiveness of this management plan.

Parties shall, wherever possible, deposit originals or copies of such original reports in a publicly accessible archive to maintain a record of usage, to be used both in any review of the plan of management and in organising the scientific use of the Area.

A copy of the report shall be forwarded to the national authority responsible for development of the management plan to assist in management of the Area, and monitoring of bird and other wildlife populations. Additionally visit reports shall provide detailed information such as census data, locations of any new colonies or nests not previously recorded, a brief summary of research findings and copies of photographs taken of the Area.

**7(xii) Emergency provisions**

Exceptions to restrictions outlined in the management plan are in emergency as specified in Article 11 of Annex V to the Protocol on Environmental Protection to the Antarctic Treaty (the Madrid Protocol). A report of any such actions shall be provided to the relevant national authority.

## 8. Supporting documentation

Some or all of the data used within this paper were obtained from the Australian Antarctic Data Centre (IDN Node AMD/AU), a part of the Australian Antarctic Division (Commonwealth of Australia).

Adamson, D.A. and Pickard, J. (1986), Cainozoic history of the Vestfold Hills, In Pickard, J., ed. *Antarctic Oasis, Terrestrial environments and history of the Vestfold Hills*. Sydney, Academic Press, 63–97.

Adamson, D.A. and Pickard, J. (1986), Physiology and geomorphology of the Vestfold Hills, In Pickard, J., ed. *Antarctic oasis: terrestrial environments and history of the Vestfold Hills*. Sydney, Academic Press, 99–139.

Agreement on the Conservation of Albatrosses and Petrels (ACAP) (2010), ACAP Species assessment Southern Giant Petrels *Macronectes giganteus*.

ANARE (1968), Unpublished data.

Australian Antarctic Division (2010), Environmental Code of Conduct for Australian Field Activities, Territories, Environment and Treaties Section, Australian Antarctic Division.

Birdlife International (2000), *Threatened birds of the world*. Barcelona and Cambridge U. K, Lynx Edicions and Birdlife International.

BirdLife International (2011), *Macronectes giganteus*, In: IUCN 2011, 2011 IUCN Red List of Threatened Species, <http://www.iucnredlist.org/>, Downloaded on 17 January2011.

BirdLife International (2011), Species fact sheet: *Macronectes giganteus*, <http://www.birdlife.org/> Downloaded on 17 January 2011.

Cooper, J., Woehler, E., Belbin, L. (2000), Guest editorial, Selecting Antarctic Specially Protected Areas: Important Bird Areas can help, *Antarctic Science* 12: 129.

Environment Australia (2001), *Recovery Plan for Albatrosses and Giant Petrels*, Canberra.

Department of Sustainability, Environment, Water, Population and Communities (2011), *Draft National recovery plan for threatened albatrosses and giant petrels 2011-2016*, Commonwealth of Australia, Hobart.

Department of Sustainability, Environment, Water, Population and Communities (2011), *Background Paper, Population Status and Threats to Albatrosses and Giant Petrels Listed as Threatened under the Environment Protection and Biodiversity Conservation Act 1999*, Commonwealth of Australia, Hobart.

Fabel, D., Stone, J., Fifield, L.K. and Cresswell, R.G. (1997), Deglaciation of the Vestfold Hills, East Antarctica; preliminary evidence from exposure dating of three subglacial erratics. In RICCI, C.A., ed. *The Antarctic region: geological evolution and processes*, Siena: Museo Nazionale dell'Antartide, 829–834.

Garnett, S.T., Crowley, G.M. (2000), *The Action Plan for Australian Birds 2000*. Commonwealth of Australia, Environment Australia, Canberra

Gore, D.B. (1997), Last glaciation of Vestfold Hills; extension of the East Antarctic ice sheet or lateral expansion of Sørsdal Glacier. *Polar Record*, 33: 5–12.

Hirvas, H., Nenonen, K. and Quilty, P. (1993), Till stratigraphy and glacial history of the Vestfold Hills area, East Antarctica, *Quaternary International*, 18: 81–95.

IUCN (2001), *IUCN Red List Categories: Version 3.1*, IUCN Species Survival Commission, IUCN, Gland, Switzerland and Cambridge, UK.

Jouventin, P., Weimerskirch, H. (1991), Changes in the population size and demography of southern seabirds: management implications, in: Perrins, C.M., Lebreton, J.D. and Hirons, G.J.M. *Bird population studies: Relevance to conservation and management*. Oxford University Press: 297-314.

Johnstone, Gavin W.; Lugg, Desmond J., and Brown, D.A. (1973), The biology of the Vestfold Hills, Antarctica. Melbourne, Department of Science, Antarctic Division, *ANARE Scientific Reports*, Series B(1) Zoology, Publication No. 123.

Law P. (1958), Australian Coastal Exploration in Antarctica, *The Geographical Journal CXXIV*, 151-162.

Leishman, M.R. and Wild, C. (2001), Vegetation abundance and diversity in relation to soil nutrients and soil water content in Vestfold Hills, East, *Antarctic Science*, 13(2): 126-134

Micol, T., Jouventin, P. (2001), Long-term population trends in seven Antarctic seabirds at Point Géologie (Terre Adélie), Human impact compared with environmental change, *Polar Biology* 24: 175-185.

Miller, J.D. et al. (1984), A survey of the terrestrial Tardigrada of the Vestfold Hills, Antarctica, In Pickard, J., ed. *Antarctic Oasis, Terrestrial environments and history of the Vestfold Hills.* Sydney, Academic Press, 197-208.

Orton, M.N. (1963), Movements of young Giant Petrels bred in Antarctica, *Emu* 63: 260.

Patterson D.L., Woehler, E.J., Croxall, J.P., Cooper, J., Poncet, S., Fraser, W.R. (2008), Breeding distribution and population status of the Northern Giant Petrel *Macronectes halli* and the southern giant petrel *M. Giganteus, Marine Ornithology* 36: 115-124.

Pickard, J. ed., 1986, *Antarctic oasis: terrestrial environments and history of the Vestfold Hills.* Sydney, Academic Press.

Puddicombe, R.A.; and Johnstone, G.W. (1988), Breeding season diet of Adélie penguins at Vestfold Hills, East Antarctica, In *Biology of the Vestfold Hills*, Antarctica, edited by J.M. Ferris, H.R. Burton, G.W. Johnstone, and I.A.E. Bayly.

Rounsevell, D.E., and Horne, P.A. (1986), Terrestrial, parasitic and introduced invertebrates of the Vestfold Hills. *Antarctic oasis; terrestrial environments and history of the Vestfold Hills*, Sydney: Academic Press, 309-331.

Stattersfield, A.J., Capper, D.R. (2000), Threatened Birds of the World. *Birdlife International*, Lynx Publications.

Wienecke, B., Leaper, R., Hay, I., van den Hoff, J. (2009), Retrofitting historical data in population studies: southern giant petrels in the Australian Antarctic Territory, *Endangered Species Research* Vol. 8: 157-164.

Woehler, E.J., Cooper, J., Croxall, J.P., Fraser, W.R., Kooyman, G.L., Miller, G.D., Nel, D.C., Patterson, D.L., Peter, H-U, Ribic, C.A., Salwicka, K., Trivelpiece, W.Z., Wiemerskirch, H. (2001), *A Statistical Assessment of the Status and Trends of Antarctic and Subantarctic Seabirds*, SCAR/CCAMLR/NSF, 43 pp.

Woehler, E. (2001), Breeding populations of Southern Giant Petrels at Heard Island, the McDonald Islands and within the AAT, Australian Antarctic Data Centre, SnoWhite Metadata <http://aadc-maps.aad.gov.au/aadc/metadata/metadata_redirect.cfm?md=AMD/AU/SOE_seabird_candidate_sp_SGP>, Downloaded on 17 January 2011.

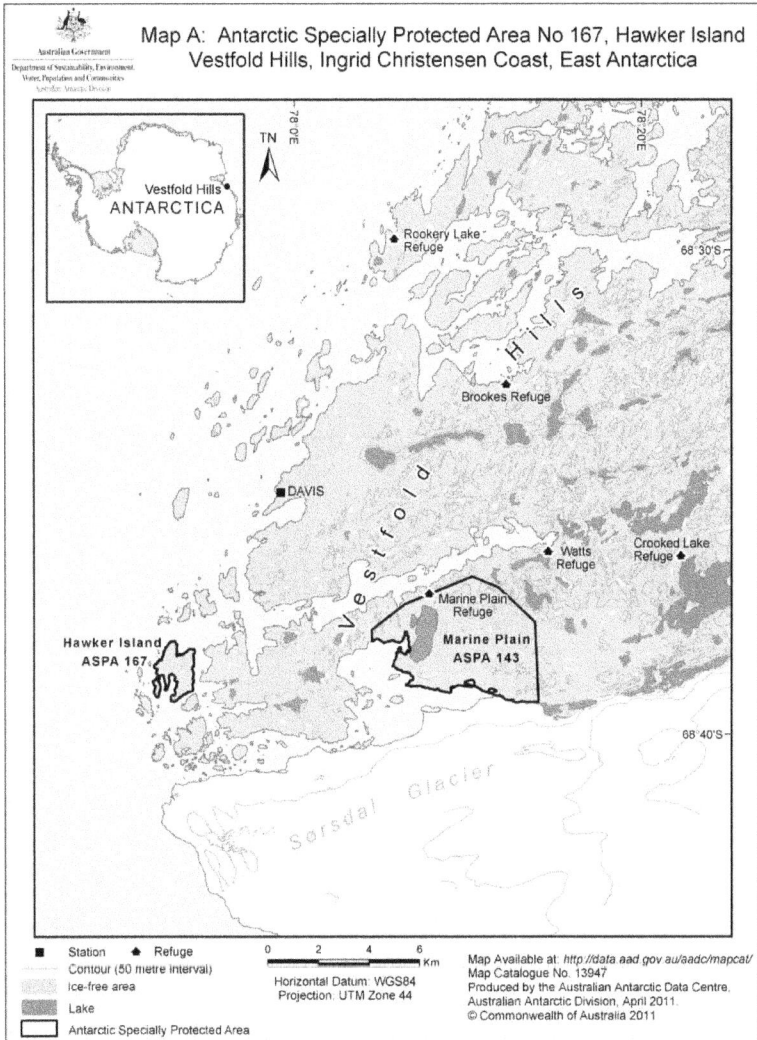

Map A: Antarctic Specially Protected Area No 167, Hawker Island Vestfold Hills, Ingrid Christensen Coast, East Antarctica

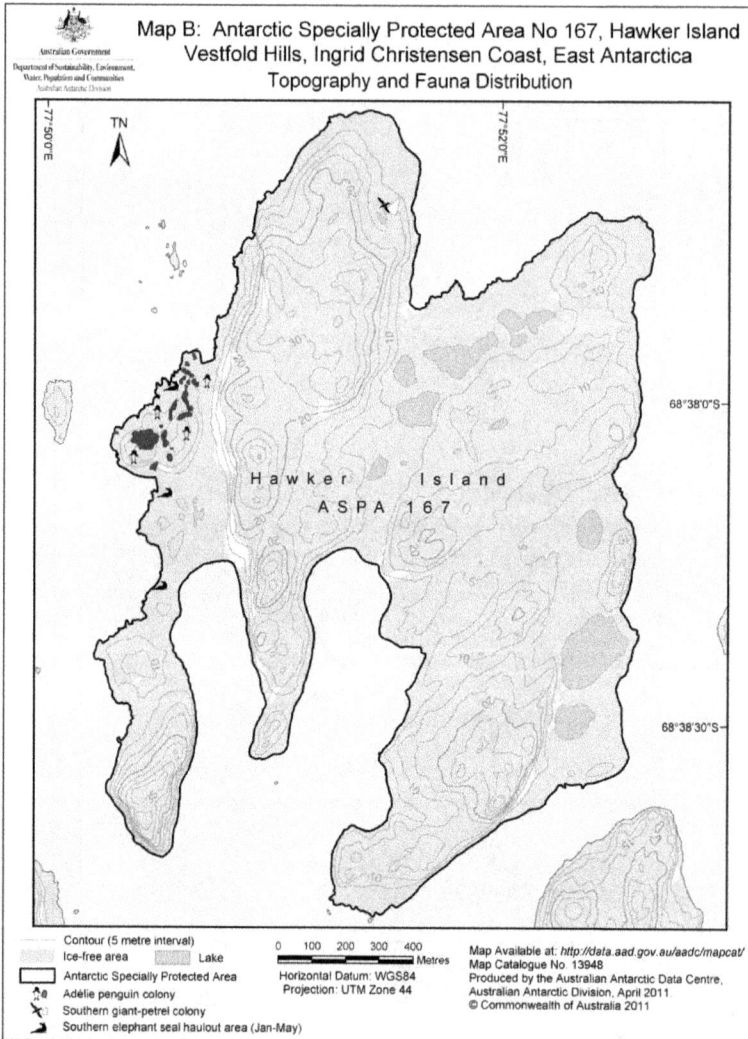

Map B: Antarctic Specially Protected Area No 167, Hawker Island
Vestfold Hills, Ingrid Christensen Coast, East Antarctica
Topography and Fauna Distribution

**Management Plan for**
**Antarctic Specially Managed Area No. 2**
**MCMURDO DRY VALLEYS, SOUTHERN VICTORIA LAND**

## Introduction

The McMurdo Dry Valleys are the largest relatively ice-free region in Antarctica with approximately thirty percent of the ground surface largely free of snow and ice. The region encompasses a cold desert ecosystem, whose climate is not only cold and extremely arid (in the Wright Valley the mean annual temperature is –19.8°C and annual precipitation is less than 100 mm water equivalent), but also windy. The landscape of the Area contains mountain ranges, nunataks, glaciers, ice-free valleys, coastline, ice-covered lakes, ponds, meltwater streams, arid patterned soils and permafrost, sand dunes, and interconnected watershed systems. These watersheds have a regional influence on the McMurdo Sound marine ecosystem. The Area's location, where large-scale seasonal shifts in the water phase occur, is of great importance to the study of climate change. Through shifts in the ice-water balance over time, resulting in contraction and expansion of hydrological features and the accumulations of trace gases in ancient snow, the McMurdo Dry Valley terrain also contains records of past climate change. The extreme climate of the region serves as an important analogue for the conditions of ancient Earth and contemporary Mars, where such climate may have dominated the evolution of landscape and biota.

The Area was jointly proposed by the United States and New Zealand and adopted through Measure 1 (2004). This Management Plan aims to ensure the long-term protection of this unique environment, and to safeguard its values for the conduct of scientific research, education, and more general forms of appreciation. The Management Plan sets out the values, objectives and general rules for conduct within the region, and includes a number of maps and appendices that provide more specific guidelines for particular activities and designated zones within the Area, arranged according to the following structure:

## Contents

APPENDIX A: General Environmental Guidelines for the McMurdo Dry Valleys

APPENDIX B: Environmental Guidelines for Scientific Research

APPENDIX C: List for Facilities Zones

APPENDIX D: Guidelines for Scientific Zones

APPENDIX E: Guidelines for Restricted Zones

APPENDIX F: Guidelines for Visitor Zones

## 1. Values to be protected and activities to be managed

The McMurdo Dry Valleys are characterized by unique ecosystems of generally low macrobiotic biodiversity and reduced food web complexity, although recent research has shown evidence of highly diverse microbial communities across relatively small areas, as well as between valleys. Moreover, as the largest ice-free region in Antarctica, the McMurdo Dry Valleys also contain relatively diverse habitats compared with other ice-free areas. The Area contains unusual microhabitats and biological communities (such as endolithic and cryoconite systems) as well as rare glaciological and geological features (for example, a brine-rich sub-glacial lake, hyper-saline surface lakes, unique marine deposits and undisturbed desert pavements). These glaciological and geological features are of value because they contain an extremely long record of natural events. The McMurdo Dry Valleys contain indicators of past and present regional climate change, as well as features that play a role in influencing local climate change. A Long Term Ecological Research (LTER) site was established in the Taylor Valley in 1993, and substantial research has been conducted by the program every season for almost twenty years, not only in the Taylor Valley but also more generally across the McMurdo Dry Valleys. The long-term environmental data sets that have been collected through this program, and through a range of other research initiatives in the McMurdo Dry Valleys, are some of the longest in Antarctica. These scientific values are of global and regional importance.

The Area is a valuable resource for understanding landscape processes and the stability of Antarctic ice sheets. The McMurdo Dry Valleys contain unique surface deposits including glacially deposited and modified sediments, sand dunes, desert pavement, glacio-lacustrine sediments, and marine fjord sediments containing valuable records of planetary change. The soil, rock, water, and ice environments and their associated biota are of scientific value as model ecosystems that allow deep insights into natural processes operating throughout the biosphere. Finally, the species that reside in the McMurdo Dry Valleys provide a biological resource for understanding adaptation to extreme environments, and are true end members of ecological continua.

The isolation of the McMurdo Dry Valleys and the extreme environment has generally protected it from human introductions of species from outside of Antarctica. Many parts of the Area are only rarely visited, and one (the Barwick and Balham Valleys protected area) has been set aside as a reference area where entry has been very strictly controlled for almost 40 years and overflight is prohibited. The relatively pristine condition of the McMurdo Dry Valleys, and the relative lack of introduced species established within the Area, are rarely observed elsewhere in the world and have both high scientific and ecological value, especially for comparative studies.

Sites of historic value originating from early exploration of the Area have also been noted, such as 'Granite House' at Botany Bay, Granite Harbor, which was constructed by members of the 1910-1913 British Antarctic Expedition and is designated as Historic Site No. 67.

The McMurdo Dry Valleys are also valued for their aesthetic and wilderness qualities. They represent a relatively pristine environment largely undisturbed and uncontaminated by humans. The dramatic landscape, composed of precipitous mountains, high ridges and sweeping valleys, imposing layered geological formations of dark dolerite set against pale sandstones, and contrasts of ice-free and glacier-covered terrain creates unique vistas with high aesthetic value.

Activities conducted in the area include a variety of scientific research, operations in support of science, media, arts, education and other official National Program visitors, and tourism.

The Area requires special management to ensure that its scientific, environmental, ecological, historic, aesthetic and wilderness values are protected, including that data sets collected over the last 100 years will continue to be of high value. Increasing human activity and potentially conflicting interests have made it necessary to manage and coordinate activities more effectively within the Area.

## 2. Aims and objectives

The aim of this Management Plan is to conserve and protect the unique and outstanding environment of the McMurdo Dry Valleys by managing and coordinating human activities in the Area such that the values of the McMurdo Dry Valleys are protected and sustained in the long term, especially the value of the extensive scientific datasets that have been collected.

The specific objectives of management in the Area are to:

- Facilitate scientific research while maintaining stewardship of the environment;
- Assist with the planning and coordination of human activities in the McMurdo Dry Valleys to manage actual or potential conflicts among different values (including those of different scientific disciplines), activities and operators;
- Ensure the long-term protection of scientific, ecological, aesthetic, wilderness and other values of the Area by minimizing disturbance to or degradation of these values, including disturbance to natural features and fauna and flora, and by minimizing the cumulative environmental impacts of human activities;
- Prevent the unintended introduction of species not native to the Area, and minimize as far as practicable the unintended transfer of native species within the Area;
- Minimize the footprint of all facilities and scientific experiments established in the Area, including the proliferation of field camps;
- Minimize any physical disturbance, contamination and wastes produced within the Area, and take all practical steps to contain, treat, remove or remediate these whether produced in the course of normal activities or by accident;
- Promote use of energy systems and modes of transport within the Area that have the least environmental impact, and minimize as far as practicable the use of fossil fuels for the conduct of activities within the Area;
- Improve the understanding of natural processes and human impacts in the Area, including through the conduct of monitoring programs; and
- Encourage communication and co-operation between users of the Area, in particular through dissemination of information on the Area and the provisions that apply.

### 3. Management activities

To achieve the aims and objectives of this Management Plan, the following management activities are to be undertaken:

- National Programs operating within the Area should convene as required, and at least annually, a McMurdo Dry Valleys Management Group (hereafter the Management Group) to oversee coordination of activities in the Area, including to:
    - facilitate and ensure effective communication among those working in or visiting the Area;
    - provide a forum to resolve any actual or potential conflicts in use;
    - help minimize the duplication of activities;
    - maintain a record of activities and, where practical, impacts in the Area;
    - develop strategies to detect and address cumulative impacts;
    - disseminate information on the Area, in particular on the activities occurring and the management measures that apply within the Area, including through maintaining this information electronically at http://www.mcmurdodryvalleys.aq/;
    - review past, existing, and future activities and evaluate the effectiveness of management measures; and
    - make recommendations on the implementation of this Management Plan.

- National Programs operating within the Area shall maintain copies of the current version of the management plan and supporting documentation in appropriate stations and research hut facilities and make these available to all persons in the Area, as well as electronically at http://www.mcmurdodryvalleys.aq/;

- National Programs operating within the Area and tour operators visiting should ensure that their personnel (including staff, crew, passengers, scientists and any other visitors) are briefed on, and are aware of, the requirements of this Management Plan, and in particular the *General Environmental Guidelines* (Appendix A) that applies within the Area;

- Tour operators and any other group or person responsible for planning and / or conducting non-governmental activities within the Area should coordinate their activities with National Programs operating in the Area in advance to ensure they do not pose risks to the values of the Area and that they comply with the requirements of the Management Plan;

- National Programs operating within the Area should seek to develop best practices with a view to achieving the objectives of the Management Plan, and to exchange freely such knowledge and information;

- Signs and / or markers should be erected where necessary and appropriate to show the location or boundaries of zones, research sites, landing sites or campsites within the Area. Signs and markers shall be secured and maintained in good condition, and removed when no longer necessary;

- Visits shall be made as necessary (no less than once every five years) to evaluate whether the Management Plan is effective and to ensure management measures are adequate. The Management Plan, Code of Conduct and Guidelines shall be revised and updated as necessary; and

- National Programs operating within the Area shall take such steps as are necessary and practical to ensure the requirements of the Management Plan are observed.

## 4. Period of designation

Designated for an indefinite period.

## 5. Maps and photographs

**Table 1:** List of maps included in the Management Plan

| Map | Title | Source Scale | Estimated Error (+/- m) |
|---|---|---|---|
| *Overviews* | | | |
| Map 1 | Overview-ASMA No.2 McMurdo Dry Valleys: boundary and zones | 1:900,000 | 200 |
| Map 2 | Overview-Central Dry Valleys | 1:400,000 | 200 |
| *Facilities Zones* | | | |
| Map 3 | Explorers Cove, New Harbor | 1:25,000 | 2 |
| Inset: | New Harbor Camp Facilities Zone | 1:3000 | 2 |
| Map 4 | Lake Fryxell – Commonwealth Glacier | 1:25,000 | 2 |
| Inset: | F-6 Camp Facilities Zone | 1:3000 | 2 |
| Map 5 | Lake Fryxell – Canada Glacier | 1:25,000 | 2 |
| Inset: | Lake Fryxell Camp Facilities Zone | 1:3000 | 2 |
| Map 6 | Lake Hoare, Canada Glacier | 1:25,000 | 2 |
| Map 7 | Lake Hoare Camp Facilities Zone | 1:3000 | 2 |
| Map 8 | Lake Bonney, Taylor Valley | 1:25,000 | 2 |
| Inset: | Lake Bonney Camp Facilities Zone | 1:3000 | 2 |
| Map 9 | Mount Newall, Asgard Range | 1:25,000 | 50 |
| Inset: | Mount Newall Radio Repeater Facilities Zone | 1:3000 | 2 |
| Map 10 | Marble Point, McMurdo Sound | 1:35,000 | 5 |
| Inset: | Marble Point Refueling Station Facilities Zone | 1:5000 | 2 |
| Map 11 | Lower Wright Valley | 1:25,000 | 50 |
| Inset: | Lower Wright Hut Facilities Zone | 1:3000 | 2 |
| Map 12 | Lake Vanda, Wright Valley | 1:25,000 | 50 |
| Inset 1: | Lake Vanda Hut Facilities Zone | 1:3000 | 2 |
| Inset 2: | Bull Pass Hut Facilities Zone | 1:3000 | 2 |
| Map 13 | Cape Roberts, Granite Harbor | 1:10,000 | 10 |
| Inset: | Cape Roberts Hut Facilities Zone | 1:3000 | 10 |
| *Scientific Zones* | | | |
| Map 14 | Explorers Cove Scientific Zone | 1:3000 | 2 |
| Map 15 | Boulder Pavement, Wright Valley | 1:30,000 | 50 |
| Inset: | Boulder Pavement Scientific Zone | 1:10,000 | 50 |
| *Restricted Zones* | | | |
| Map 16 | Trough Lake Catchment Restricted Zone | 1:70,000 | 10 |
| Map 17 | Mount Feather – Beacon Valley | 1:130,000 | 50 |
| Inset: | Mount Feather Sirius Deposit Restricted Zone | 1:25,000 | 50 |
| Map 18 | Don Juan Pond, Wright Valley | 1:50,000 | 50 |
| Inset: | Don Juan Pond Restricted Zone | 1:12,500 | 50 |
| Map 19 | Argo Gully, Wright Valley | 1:30,000 | 50 |
| Inset: | Argo Gully Restricted Zone | 1:3000 | 15 |
| Map 20 | Prospect Mesa, Wright Valley | 1:30,000 | 50 |
| Inset: | Prospect Mesa Restricted Zone | 1:5000 | 50 |
| Map 21 | Hart Glacier, Wright Valley | 1:25,000 | 50 |
| Inset: | Hart Ash Deposit Restricted Zone | 1:3000 | 50 |

| Map | Title | Source Scale | Estimated Error (+/- m) |
|---|---|---|---|
| Map 22 | Victoria Valley Sand Dunes Restricted Zone | 1:50,000 | 50 |
| Map 23 | Battleship Promontory Restricted Zone | 1:50,000 | 50 |

| *Visitor Zones* | | | |
|---|---|---|---|
| Map 24 | Taylor Valley, Lake Fryxell | 1:25,000 | 2 |
| Inset: | Taylor Valley Visitor Zone | 1:5000 | 2 |

## 6. Description of the Area

The McMurdo Dry Valleys are located in southern Victoria Land along the western coast of McMurdo Sound, southern Ross Sea, at approximately 77°30'S, 162°00'E. An area of approximately 17,500 km$^2$ is designated as an Antarctic Specially Managed Area (hereafter referred to as the 'Area') to manage human activities in the region for the protection of scientific, environmental, ecological, historic, aesthetic and wilderness values.

Based on the Environmental Domains Analysis for Antarctica (Resolution 3(2008)) the McMurdo Dry Valleys are located within Environment S – McMurdo – South Victoria Land geologic.

*6(i) Geographical coordinates, boundary markers, and natural features*

All geographic coordinates in this Management Plan are given in degrees and decimal minutes (dd mm.mm) format.

The Area boundaries have been defined primarily on the basis of the hydrological catchments in the McMurdo Dry Valleys, including all of the ice-free ground and adjacent areas within these catchments, all of the Convoy Range in the north, and bounded by the Koettlitz Glacier in the south (Map 1). Offshore islands, except Tripp Island in the north and Heald Island in the south, are not included within the Area. Proceeding clockwise from the northeast, the boundary of the Area is defined as follows:

From the northeastern extremity of Tripp Island (76°38.09'S, 162°42.90'E) the boundary extends southward following the coastline at the mean low tide level to DeMaster Point (situated east of Marshall Valley at 78°04.20'S, 164°25.43'E), a distance of approximately 170 km. The boundary thence follows the northwestern margin of the Koettlitz Glacier in a southwesterly direction for approximately 25 km to Walcott Bay and Trough Lake, including within the Area all of the streams and lakes along the glacier margin (Map 16). The boundary thence follows the approximate southern grounding line of the Koettlitz Glacier margin in Walcott Bay, extending east towards The Bulwark and encompassing all of Trough Lake. The boundary thence continues east following Bulwark Stream for approximately 1.5 km to the northern extremity of The Bulwark. The boundary thence extends 3 km in a straight line northeast to the northwestern coastline of Heald Island, following around the northern coastline to the eastern extremity of the island at 78°15.00'S, 163°57.80'E.

The boundary extends from Heald Island approximately 14.8 km southwest to the summit of The Pyramid (854 m) (78°20.64'S, 163°29.95'E). The boundary thence continues southwest approximately 13.3 km to the foot of Highway Ridge (78°23.97'S, 162°58.57'E), from where it follows up the ridgeline in a northwesterly direction approximately 3.8 km to the summit of Shark Fin (2242 m) (78°22.11'S, 162°54.66'E). The boundary extends from Shark Fin northwest approximately 6.7 km to the summit of Mount Kempe (3004 m) (78°19.35'S, 162°43.18'E). The boundary continues northwest in a straight line from the summit of Mount Kempe approximately 83 km to the summit of Mount Wisneski (2320 m) (77°57.65'S, 159°33.73'E), which is the most southerly peak of the Lashley Mountains.

From Mount Wisneski, the boundary extends northwards for approximately 8.7 km to Mount Crean (2550 m) (77°53.00'S, 159°30.66'E), the highest peak in the Lashley Mountains. The boundary continues 5.6 km northward to the summit of Mount Koger (2450 m) (77°50.05'S, 159°33.09'E), the most northerly peak in the Lashley Mountains.

The boundary thence extends northeast approximately 15.3 km to Depot Nunatak (1980 m) (77°44.88'S, 160°03.19'E), and thence northwest approximately 19.6 km to the western extremity of the ice-free ground at Horseshoe Mountain (77°34.52'S, 159°53.72'E). The boundary continues north approximately 40 km to the summit of Mount DeWitt (2190 m) (77°13.05'S, 159°50.30'E), thence extends northwest approximately 38.4 km to the summit of Carapace Nunatak (2321 m) (76°53.31'S, 159°23.76'E), and continues a further 39 km north to the summit of Battlements Nunatak (2128 m) (76°32.27'S, 159°21.41'E).

The boundary extends east from Battlements Nunatak approximately 51 km to the summit of Mount Douglas (1750 m) (76°31.25'S, 161°18.64'E), and thence approximately 18 km in a southeasterly direction to the summit of Mount Endeavour (1870 m) (76°32.49'S, 161°59.97'E). The boundary extends southeast from Mount Endeavour approximately 21.3 km to the northeastern extremity of Tripp Island.

The principal basis for the coordinates given above is the USGS / LINZ 1:50,000 digital base map prepared for the McMurdo Dry Valleys, which has an estimated maximum error of +/- 50 m. Because this map does not extend to cover the western boundary, coordinates in these areas are from the USGS 1:250,000 map, with an estimated maximum error of +/- 200 m. Accurate mapping with a maximum error of +/- 2 m is available for a limited number of sites within the Area (see Table 1), mostly in the Taylor Valley, and accurate GPS coordinates are available to describe only parts of the boundaries. The 1:50,000 series was selected as the primary map base for boundary coordinates to ensure that these are given using a map datum that is defined to a consistent standard over most of the Area. For these reasons, GPS coordinates for the boundaries are likely to differ from the coordinates given above by up to 50 m, or in the west by up to ~200 m.

### 6(ii) Restricted and managed zones within the Area

This Management Plan establishes four types of zones within the Area: Facilities, Scientific, Restricted and Visitor. The management objectives of the different types of zones are set out in Table 2. Maps 1 and 2 show the location of the different types of zones, and Maps 3-24 (which appear in the relevant appendices) show each zone in its context of surrounding geography and the detailed features or infrastructure present at each site (usually shown within an inset). A new zone or zone type may be considered by the Management Group as the need arises, and those no longer needed may be delisted. Zoning updates should be given particular consideration at the time of Management Plan reviews.

**Table 2**: Management Zones designated within the Area and their specific objectives.

| Management Zones | Specific Zone Objectives | Plan Appendix |
|---|---|---|
| Facilities Zone | To ensure that science support facilities and related human activities within the Area are contained and managed within designated areas. | C |
| Scientific Zone | To ensure those planning science or logistics within the Area, and all visitors to the Area, are aware of sites of current or long-term scientific investigation that may be sensitive to disturbance or have sensitive scientific equipment installed, so these may be taken into account during the planning and conduct of activities within the Area. | D |
| Restricted Zone | To restrict access into a particular part of the Area and/or activities within it for a range of reasons, e.g. owing to special | E |

| Management Zones | Specific Zone Objectives | Plan Appendix |
|---|---|---|
| | scientific or ecological values, because of sensitivity, presence of hazards, or to restrict emissions or constructions at a particular site. Access into Restricted Zones should normally be for compelling reasons that cannot be served elsewhere within the Area. | |
| Visitor Zone | To provide a means of managing the activities of visitors, including program personnel and/or tourists, so their impacts may be contained and, as appropriate, monitored and managed. | F |

The overall policies applying within the zones are outlined in the sections below, while site-specific guidelines for the conduct of activities at each zone are found in Appendices D to F.

*Facilities Zones*

Facilities Zones have been established to contain temporary and semi-permanent facilities within pre-defined areas and thereby control their distribution and footprint. Facilities Zones may be areas where human presence is intended to be semi-permanent or for a defined period of time in which significant activity is occurring. They may also be areas where human presence is expected to have regular occupation and/or repetitive activity such as field camps. The establishment of new Facilities Zones should be designed to minimize the footprint of facilities and associated materials.

The following provisions should be observed for Facilities Zones:

- Substantial and repeatedly used facilities, camping sites, helicopter pads, and materials / supplies stores should be located within the boundaries of the Facilities Zones;
- Existing infrastructure, camping and storage sites within the Facilities Zones should be re-used where practicable;
- Provisions for fuel storage and handling within the Facilities Zones should take account of the requirements set out in the *General Environmental Guidelines for the McMurdo Dry Valleys* (Appendix A) by providing secondary containment, appropriate equipment for refilling, decanting or servicing operations, secure storage and appropriate spill response materials;
- Alternative energy sources and energy efficiency should be considered in the planning and maintenance of activities within the Facilities Zones;
- Waste minimization and management should be considered in the planning and maintenance of activities within the Facilities Zone and all waste should be stored securely and then be removed; and
- Contingency plans for emergencies should be developed as appropriate, to take into account the special needs of specific Facilities Zones.

Facilities Zones should not be located within Restricted Zones or Antarctic Specially Protected Areas (ASPAs), or at sites that could otherwise jeopardize the values of the Area.

Facilities Zones are listed in Appendix C with locations, boundary and infrastructure descriptions, designated landing sites, and maps.

*Scientific Zones*

The Scientific Zones listed in Appendix D have been designated to raise visitor awareness of specific sites of current and on-going scientific research in order to help ensure important scientific values or experiments are not disturbed. There are no general access restrictions that apply within Scientific Zones, although visitors should familiarize themselves with the provisions set out in Appendix D prior to visiting or planning work at these zones.

*Restricted Zones*

Restricted Zones have been designated at sites of high scientific value and which are particularly sensitive to human disturbance. Restricted Zones are outlined in Appendix E with a brief description of the boundaries, site features, impacts, and any specific guidelines for access and activities. Access to Restricted Zones should be for compelling reasons that cannot be served elsewhere within the Area, and any additional measures to ensure their protection as specified in Appendix E should be strictly observed when visits are made.

*Visitor Zones*

The Taylor Valley Visitor Zone is designated in order to manage visits by tourists or non-governmental expeditions to the Area within a defined area where the exceptional aesthetic and wilderness values of the McMurdo Dry Valleys can be appreciated at the same time as ensuring that potential impacts by tourist visits on other values present within the Area, particularly scientific and environmental values, are minimized.

The Taylor Valley Visitor Zone is located in the Taylor Valley near the Canada Glacier terminus (Map 24), at a site where safe and relatively easy access and movement can be reasonably assured with minimal impact to science activities or the environment. This site was selected following consultation among the National Programs operating in the Area, tour operators and International Association of Antarctic Tour Operators (IAATO). Specific guidelines for the conduct of activities within the Visitor Zone are included in Appendix F as the Antarctic Treaty Visitor Site Guide: Taylor Valley, Southern Victoria Land, Ross Sea.

*6(iii) Structures within and near the Area*

The main structures within the Area are located in the Facilities Zones designated within the central McMurdo Dry Valleys (Maps 2 and 13). The Taylor Valley has five semi-permanent field camps (Maps 3-8), and three semi-permanent field camps are present in the Wright Valley (Maps 11 and 12). The most substantial structures are located at the Marble Point Refueling Facility (Map 10), and buildings are also located at Mount Newall (Map 9) and at Cape Roberts (Map 13).

There are a number of sites of scientific and operational instrumentation located throughout the Area outside of Facilities Zones, the most substantial of which are listed in Table 3. Other structures not listed include several Automatic Weather Stations (AWS), radio repeater sites (Mount Cerverus, Mount JJ Thompson), stream weirs and glacier mass balance devices.

**Table 3**: Structures within the Area outside of Facilities Zones.

| Name | MP[1] | Location[2] | Location Description | Structures |
|---|---|---|---|---|
| Mount Coates Radio Repeater | US | 77° 47.16'S 161° 58.23'E | Near summit of Mount Coates (1894 m), Kukri Hills. ~14 km from Lake Bonney Facilities Zone, Taylor Valley. | Radio repeater and associated equipment contained in two orange plastic cases. There is one antenna at the site. |
| Hjorth Hill Radio Repeater | US | 77° 30.97'S 163° 37.22'E | Near summit of Hjorth Hill (790 m) ~ 6 km from Cape Bernacchi, northeast of Explorers Cove and the Taylor | Radio repeater and associated equipment at small hut (2.4m x 2.6m). The antenna is installed on the hut. |

| Name | MP[1] | Location[2] | Location Description | Structures |
|------|-------|-------------|---------------------|------------|
|      |       |             | Valley.             |            |

1. Maintaining Party
2. Coordinates approximate

There are also several sites in the McMurdo Dry Valleys where semi-permanent camps have been decommissioned and removed (Table 4).

**Table 4**: Known sites of decommissioned semi-permanent camps in the Area.

| Decommissioned site | RP[1] | Geographic coordinates[2] |
|---------------------|-------|---------------------------|
| Asgard Hut | NZ | 77° 35'S, 161° 36'E |
| Brownworth Hut | NZ | 77° 27'S, 162° 53'E |
| Bull Pass Hut (US structures at Bull Pass Hut Facilities Zone remain) | NZ | 77° 31.01'S, 161° 51.08'E |
| Meserve Glacier Camp | US | 77° 30.8'S, 162° 17'E |
| Miers Valley Hut | NZ | 78° 08'S, 163° 50'E |
| Old Lake Bonney Hut | US | 77° 42.2'S, 162° 30.6'E |
| Lake Fryxell Hut | NZ | 77° 37'S, 163° 03'E |
| Vanda Station (some structures relocated to Lake Vanda Hut Facilities Zone) | NZ | 77° 31.6'S, 161° 40.1'E |
| Commonwealth Glacier Camp | NZ | 77° 34.94'S, 163° 35.81'E |
| Old New Harbor Camp | US | 77° 34.5'S, 163° 29.9'E |
| Odell Glacier Camp | US | 76° 40.86'S, 159° 54.8'E |

1. Responsible Party
2. Coordinates approximate

Eight sites within the Area were drilled, several with multiple boreholes, as a part of the McMurdo Dry Valley Drilling Project (DVDP) carried out between 1971 and 1975. Drill sites for the project are located at Lake Vanda (DVDP 4) (drilled 85.8 m below ice surface), Don Juan Pond (DVDP 5, 3.4 m; DVDP 13, 75 m),Wright Valley North Fork basin (DVDP 14, 78 m), Lake Vida (DVDP 6, 305.8 m; permanently capped and closed by the US Program in 2006-07 and now several meters below the lake surface), Lake Fryxell (DVDP 7, 11.1 m), New Harbor (DVDP 8, 157.5 m; DVDP 9, 38.3 m; DVDP 10, 187 m), Commonwealth Glacier (DVDP 11, 328 m), and Lake Hoare (DVDP 12, 185 m).

*6(iv) Location of other protected areas within the Area*

Entry to an Antarctic Specially Protected Area (ASPA) is prohibited unless a permit for entry has been issued by a national authority. Four ASPAs are designated within the Area (Maps 1 and 2):

ASPA No. 123 Barwick and BalhamValleys, Southern Victoria Land (Maps 1, 2);

ASPA No. 131 Canada Glacier, Lake Fryxell, Taylor Valley, Victoria Land (Maps 2, 5, 24);

ASPA No. 138 Linnaeus Terrace, Asgard Range, Victoria Land (Maps 2, 18);

ASPA No. 154 Botany Bay, Cape Geology, Victoria Land  (Map 1).

**7. Code of Conduct**

The Code of Conduct in this section is the main instrument for the management of activities in the Area.  It outlines the overall management and operational principles for the Area.

In addition, further guidance is provided in the *General Environmental Guidelines for the McMurdo Dry Valleys* (Appendix A), *Environmental Guidelines for Scientific Research*

(Appendix B), and in the List of Facilities Zone (Appendix C), Scientific Zones (Appendix D), Restricted Zones (Appendix E), and the Visitor Zone (Appendix F). All visitors to the McMurdo Dry Valleys should be aware of the *General Environmental Guidelines* in Appendix A, as a minimum, before entering the Area.

### 7(i) Access to and movement within the Area

The Area is large and has numerous potential access points. Access to the Area is normally made by helicopter from Ross Island, or over sea ice via New Harbor or Marble Point. Where practical, designated helicopter landing sites should be used: these are listed and shown on maps in Appendices C-F describing the management zones. Designated landing sites within ASPAs are defined and mapped in their relevant Management Plans. Where designated landing sites are unavailable, previously used landing sites should be selected when possible. Where it is expected that helicopters will be used for repetitive access to a particular location, consideration should be given to establishing a designated site for landing. Such suggestions should be referred to the Management Group. Overflight restrictions apply over ASPA No. 123 in the Barwick and Balham Valleys, ASPA No. 131 at Canada Glacier, ASPA No. 154 at Botany Bay, and over the Don Juan Pond and Victoria Valley Sand Dunes Restricted Zones.

All pedestrian access routes and movement within the Area should be undertaken so as to minimize disturbance to the soil and vegetated surfaces. There are a number of walking routes in the Area. In the Taylor Valley, these include routes between F-6 Camp and Lake Fryxell Camp, F-6 Camp and Lake Hoare Camp, Lake Hoare Camp and Lake Fryxell Camp, and Lake Hoare Camp and Lake Bonney Camp. There is a route from the edge of Lake Fryxell to the weir at Canada Stream. There are also routes outside the immediate vicinity of F-6, Lake Fryxell, Lake Bonney, and Lake Hoare camps. A route is defined to manage pedestrian movements within the Taylor Valley Visitor Zone (Appendix F). In the Wright Valley, there is a route between the Vanda Weir and the Vanda Huts. A loosely defined route exists along the Onyx River between Lake Vanda and Lake Brownworth, and tracks from overland vehicles moving along this route in the 1970's remain in evidence.

In some places where there has been sustained activity, foot tracks have developed in loose moraine soils, forming well-defined routes such as may be found near Facilities Zones and at field sites such as along the northern margin of the lower Taylor Glacier. In such cases, pedestrians should by preference use the existing tracks, unless it becomes evident that to do so would be either unsafe or result in greater impact than following an alternative route.

The use of vehicles within the Area should be restricted to lake ice or sea ice except where specifically authorized to operate on land at Marble Point (Map 11), New Harbor (Maps 3 and 14), and Cape Roberts (Map 13), where vehicles should use existing vehicle tracks.

Access into Restricted Zones should be avoided unless required for compelling reasons, and should be coordinated with National Programs operating within the Area.

Access by tourists and non-governmental expeditions should only be made to the Taylor Valley Visitor Zone in accordance with the guidelines adopted in Appendix F, and shall be coordinated in advance with National Programs operating within the Area.

### 7(ii) Activities that may be conducted in the Area

Activities which may be conducted in the area include scientific research; operations in support of science; media, arts, education or other official national program visitors; management activities including maintenance or removal of facilities; and tourism visits within the Visitor Zone, where these activities do not jeopardize the values of the Area.

All activities in the McMurdo Dry Valleys should be conducted in such a manner as to minimize impacts on the environment. Alternative energy sources (e.g. solar, wind, fuel cells) should be used wherever practicable in order to minimize fossil fuel usage. Specific guidelines for the conduct of activities in the Area are provided in Appendices A-E.

Tourism and non-governmental expeditions should additionally ensure their activities have minimal impact on the scientific activities being conducted within the Area, and are carried out in accordance with the Antarctic Treaty Visitor Site Guide: Taylor Valley (Appendix F).

*7(iii) Installation, modification, or removal of structures*

Care should be exercised when locating and establishing installations to minimize their impact on the environment. Consideration should be given to maximizing the use of existing facilities or sharing those of other programs before new facilities are constructed, and the footprint of all installations should be kept to the minimum practicable. Past installation sites should be re-used where possible and appropriate. In general, permanent or semi-permanent structures should not be installed outside of Facilities Zones, unless they are small in size and pose no significant threat to the values of the Area (e.g. an Automatic Weather Station (AWS) or a small solar- and battery-powered radio repeater with minimal associated infrastructure).

All installations should be maintained while operational and removed when no longer necessary. Installations should be identified by the National Program responsible, name of the principal investigator and year of installation. The types of installations and their coordinates should be recorded, with information provided to the responsible National Program and then shared by the Management Group.

National Programs should exchange information though the Management Group on proposals for new installations in advance of their construction, with the aim of coordinating activities and minimizing the need for new or potentially disruptive or duplicative installations.

*7(iv) Field camps*

In the McMurdo Dry Valleys, a field camp is considered to be a small temporary camp set up for research in a field season, and generally may comprise a number of tents and include temporary shelters for laboratory work or cooking. Field camps should generally only be established when the work they are intended to support cannot be accomplished practically by access from within one of the Facilities Zones.

Care should be exercised when locating and establishing field camps to minimize their impact on the environment. Consideration should be given to maximizing the use of past or existing field camp sites, or sharing those of other programs before new field camps are established, and the footprint of all field camps should be kept to the minimum practicable.

All field camps should be maintained while operational and removed when no longer necessary. Special care should be taken to secure camp equipment from dispersal by wind.

The coordinates of field camp sites should be recorded, with information provided to the responsible National Program and then shared by the Management Group.

Designated field camp sites outside of Facilities Zones or other zones within the Area are listed in Table 5.

**Table 5**: Designated field camp sites outside of Facilities Zones or other zones within the Area.

| Name | MP[1] | Location | Location Description | Field camp description |
|---|---|---|---|---|
| Blood Falls field camp site | US | 77°43.24' S 162°16.29' E 1 helicopter landing site at above location | Northwestern shore of Lake Bonney ~100 m from the terminus of Taylor Glacier and Blood Falls. | Slopes extending ~100 m upslope above the lake shoreline and for ~200 m northeast from Lawson Creek to a permanent survey benchmark (TP02) ~20 m from the lake shore. Tent sites are marked by stone circles. The designated helicopter landing site is located close to a cluster of tent sites in the southwest part of the field camp site. |

1. Maintaining Party

*7(v) Taking or harmful interference with native flora or fauna*

Taking or harmful interference with native flora or fauna is prohibited, except in accordance with a permit issued under Article 3 of Annex II to the Protocol by the appropriate national authority specifically for that purpose. Where animal taking or harmful interference is involved, this should, as a minimum standard, be in accordance with the Scientific Committee on Antarctic Research (SCAR) Code of Conduct for the Use of Animals for Scientific Purposes in Antarctica.

To help maintain the ecological and scientific values of the Area visitors should take special precautions against the introduction of non-native species. Of particular concern are introductions from other Antarctic sites, including stations, or from regions outside Antarctica. Visitors should ensure that sampling equipment and markers brought into the Area are clean. Visitors should thoroughly clean all equipment (including backpacks, carry-bags and tents), clothing and footwear before entering the Area. Visitors should also be aware of the risk of transfer of species from one part of the Dry Valleys to another, which may also affect the values of the Area. In particular, visitors should aim to minimize the movement of soils from one site to another within the Dry Valleys by cleaning their equipment (e.g. camping and sampling equipment, vehicles, footwear) before transfer to another site.

### 7(vi) Collection or removal of material found in the Area

Material not covered by 7(v) above should only be collected or removed from the Area for scientific and associated educational purposes or essential management purposes and should be limited to the minimum necessary for those needs. Any meteorites taken are to be collected and curated according to accepted scientific standards, and made available for scientific purposes. Material of human origin likely to compromise the values of the Area should be removed unless the impact of removal is likely to be greater than leaving the material in place. If this is the case the appropriate authority should be notified.

### 7(vii) Waste management

All materials taken into the Area should, to the maximum extent practicable, be collected and removed from the Area when no longer required. Water used for any human purposes, including scientific purposes, should be removed and/or treated in a gray water evaporator (and residuals removed). All human wastes should be removed from the Area, including residues from incineration.

In accordance with Article 4 of Annex III to the Protocol, wastes shall not be disposed of onto ice-free areas, into freshwater systems or onto snow or in deep ice pits in ice which terminates in ice free areas or in areas of high ablation.

### 7(viii) Requirements for reports

Reports of activities in the Area should be maintained by the Management Group to the maximum extent practicable, and made available to all Parties.

In accordance with Article 10 of Annex V to the Protocol, arrangements shall be made for collection and exchange of reports of inspection visits and on any significant changes or damage within the Area.

Tour operators should record their visits to the Area, including the number of visitors, dates, and incidents in the Area, and submit these data in accordance with the procedures for reporting on expeditions adopted by the Antarctic Treaty Parties and IAATO.

## 8. Provisions for the exchange of information in advance of proposed activities

In addition to the normal exchange of information by means of the annual, national reports to the Parties of the Antarctic Treaty, and to SCAR and Council of Managers of National Antarctic Programs (COMNAP), Parties operating in the Area should exchange information through the Management Group.

## 9. Supporting documentation

### Electronic information

National Programs operating within the Area have established a website for the purpose of providing additional information and supporting documentation on the McMurdo Dry Valleys, including up-to-date management documents, protected area management plans, maps, descriptions and policies. This information may be accessed at http://www.mcmurdodryvalleys.aq

### Management Plans

Management Plan for Antarctic Specially Protected Area No. 123 Barwick and Balham Valleys, South Victoria Land.

Management Plan for Antarctic Specially Protected Area No. 131 Canada Glacier, Taylor Valley, Victoria Land.

Management Plan for Antarctic Specially Protected Area No. 138 Linnaeus Terrace, Asgard Range, Victoria Land.

Management Plan for Antarctic Specially Protected Area No. 154 Botany Bay, Cape Geology, Victoria Land.

## APPENDIX A:

### General Environmental Guidelines for the McMurdo Dry Valleys

*Why are the McMurdo Dry Valleys considered to be so important? The McMurdo Dry Valleys ecosystem contains geological and biological features that date back thousands to millions of years. Many of these ancient features could be easily and irreversibly damaged by human actions. Unusual communities of microscopic life forms, low biodiversity, simple food webs with limited trophic competition, severe temperature stress, aridity and nutrient limitations are other characteristics that make the McMurdo Dry Valleys unique. This ancient desert landscape and its biological communities have very little natural ability to recover from disturbance. Research in such systems must aim to minimize impacts to protect the environment for future generations.*

**Before you travel to the Area:**

- Ensure that your planned activities follow the requirements of the Code of Conduct in the Management Plan, the Environmental Guidelines in Appendices A and B, and any specific guidelines that apply within management zones (Appendices C-F).

- Plan all activities such as travel, camp set up, fuel handling and secondary containment, and waste management (and minimisation), with the aim of minimizing environmental impacts. Individuals or groups should ensure sufficient equipment and survival gear is brought into the Area or available on-site for safety.

- To help prevent the unintended introduction of non-native species to the McMurdo Dry Valleys, thoroughly clean all equipment (including backpacks, carry-bags and tents), clothing and footwear before travel to the Area.

**Travel and activities within the Area:**

- To reduce the risk of transfer of species from one part of the Dry Valleys to another, clean equipment, vehicles, clothing and footwear before travel to another site.

- Be aware of the site-specific guidelines in Appendices C-F, and avoid Restricted Zones unless access is required for a compelling reason that cannot be served elsewhere within the Area.

- Stream crossings should be avoided; when it is necessary to cross streams, designated crossing points should be used whenever possible.

- Avoid swimming or diving in lakes, unless authorized by a National Program for scientific purposes.

- Avoid disturbing mummified seals or birds.

- Cairns should not be built in the Area unless authorized by a National Program.

- Do not leave any travel equipment behind (e.g. ice screws, pitons).

  **Pedestrian travel:**

  - Some biological communities and geological formations are especially fragile, even when concealed by snow; be alert and avoid such features when travelling within the Area. For example, avoid walking on vegetated areas, in streams or on stream bank sides, on dunes, through long-term soil experiments, on raised delta surfaces, on delicate rock formations, or over other sensitive features.

  - Where practicable, keep to designated or established tracks. Please refer to site-specific guidelines for Zones (Appendices C-F) for further guidance.

  **Vehicle use:**

- Vehicle use should be restricted to ice surfaces unless specifically authorized to do otherwise, or at Marble Point, Cape Roberts, and New Harbor.
- Vehicles should keep to established tracks wherever these are present.
- Vehicles should always be parked over a secondary containment unit or a drip tray.
- Vehicles should be used on lake ice only when essential, and they should be parked on permanent lake ice rather than moat ice during the period of summer melt.

### Helicopter use:

- Designated helicopter pads should be used for helicopter landings where available. Otherwise, known previous landing sites should be used when possible. Designated helicopter pads are listed in Appendices C-F and are shown on Maps 3-24.
- Designated helicopter pads should be marked so they are clearly visible from the air and markers used should be well-secured and durable.
- Helicopter landings on lakes should be avoided as far as practicable.
- Helicopter operations should not use smoke bombs, except for essential safety purposes.
- Care should be taken to ensure that helicopter sling loads are properly secured. Trained personnel should supervise these operations.

### Field camps:  location and set up

- Before new campsites are established, use designated, former or existing campsites, or share those of other programs to the maximum extent practicable.
- Minimize the footprint of all campsites.
- Campsites should be located as far as practical from lakeshores, streambeds, and long-term experiments to avoid damage or contamination.  Do not camp in streambeds, even if they are dry.
- Rocks moved for new campsites or other activities in areas not previously disturbed should be replaced after the activity in their original footprint, if possible, and at a minimum should be placed with the salt-encrusted side faced-down. If the campsite is intended for multi-year activity additional guidance should be sought from the supporting National Program.
- The location of field camps should be recorded and submitted to the supporting National Program.
- Ensure that equipment and supplies are properly secured at all times to avoid dispersion by high winds.

### Energy use:

- As far as practicable use energy systems and modes of travel within the Area that have the least environmental impact and minimize the use of fossil fuels.

### Use of Materials:

- Everything taken into the Area should be removed and returned to the appropriate National Program station for proper handling.
- Activities that could result in the dispersal of foreign materials should be avoided  (e.g. do not use spray paint to mark rocks) or should be conducted inside a hut or tent (e.g. all cutting, sawing and unpacking).
- Explosives should not be used within the Area, unless approved by a National Program for use in support of essential scientific or management purposes.

- Where possible, ensure that nothing is left frozen into glaciers, snow or lake ice that may ablate out and cause later contamination.

**Fuel and chemicals:**
- Avoid all fuel and chemical spills as far as possible.
- Steps should be taken to prevent the accidental release of chemicals including laboratory reagents and isotopes (stable or radioactive). Chemicals of all kinds should be dispensed over drip trays or other forms of containment. When permitted to use radioisotopes, safety and handling instructions should be followed precisely.
- When using chemicals or fuels, ensure that spill kits and secondary containment units appropriate to the volume of the substance are available. Those working with chemicals and fuels should be familiar with their use and with appropriate spill response procedures.
- Chemical and fuel containers should be securely positioned and capped, particularly on lake ice.
- All fuel drums should be stored with secondary containment.
- Fuel cans with spouts should be used when refueling generators.
- Generators and vehicles should be refueled over drip trays with absorbent spill pads.
- Vehicle oil should not be changed except over a drip tray.

**Waste and spills:**
- Water used for ANY human purpose should be removed and/or treated in a gray water evaporator (and residuals removed).
- All human waste should be collected and removed.
- Individuals or groups should always carry proper containers for human waste and gray water so that they may be properly and safely transported for disposal.
- Clean up any spills and/or releases to the maximum extent possible and report the location(s) including coordinates, to the appropriate National Program.

## APPENDIX B:

### Environmental Guidelines for Scientific Research

*Scientific activities in the McMurdo Dry Valleys include research on climate, glaciers, streams, lakes, soils, and local geology and geomorphology. The following environmental guidelines for scientific research seek to reduce the impact of research activities specific to key environments in the Area. These guidelines are based on the report McMurdo Dry Valley Lakes: Impacts of Research Activities (Wharton, R.A. and Doran, P.T., 1998), the product of an international workshop of scientists conducting research in the Area.*

**General requirements**

- Do not displace or collect specimens of any kind, including fossils, except under permit for scientific and associated educational purposes.
- The location of sampling (including biological transects), drilling and soil excavation sites, and of any installations (e.g. stream control structures and instrumentation) should be recorded, and the coordinates submitted to the supporting National Program.
- Installations and equipment should pose minimal risk of harmful emissions to the environment (e.g. use gel cells or other non-spill batteries).
- Ensure all installations, materials and equipment are securely stored when not in use and are removed when no longer required.
- Any markers installed should be durable and fastened securely.
- Metadata records describing data collected should be submitted to the supporting National Program and included within the Antarctic Master Directory.

**Sampling and experimental sites**

- All scientific equipment, particularly equipment used for sampling and drilling, should be clean before being brought into the Area, and cleaned before being transferred to other sites for re-use within the Area.
- Securely tether all sampling equipment where there is a reasonable risk that it could be irretrievably lost.
- Sample sizes of all biomass and non-biological materials should be limited to the minimum required for effective completion of the planned analyses and archiving.
- Sampling sites (e.g. in lake ice, on glaciers or in soils) should be kept clean.
- Minimize, and where possible avoid, the use of drilling fluids.
- Experimental or monitoring sites intended to be used for more than one season should be clearly identified by country, name of the principal investigator and year of installation.

**Scientific installations**

For scientific installations, including meteorological stations, geographic monuments, communication repeaters, lake monitoring systems, and level recorders:

- Installations should be sited carefully, should be easily retrievable when required, and properly secured at all times to avoid dispersal by high winds.
- All installations in the Area should be clearly identified by country, name of the principal investigator and year of installation.
- Installations should be as energy-efficient as possible and use renewable energy sources wherever practicable.

- Installations should pose minimal risk of harmful emissions to the environment (e.g. use gel cells or other non-spill batteries).
- Installations should be periodically evaluated for deterioration, usefulness, and potential removal. The frequency of evaluation may depend on installation characteristics and the site, although in general this is likely to be needed at least once every 3-5 years.
- Installations should be designed and constructed so they can be decommissioned and removed at the end of their use.

### Scientific equipment, fuels and materials

- Minimize the use of fossil-fuel-powered equipment; use solar-powered and hand devices when possible.
- Properly tune generators to minimize emissions and use only when necessary. Always place generators and fuel cans in drip pans.
- Carefully manage fuels, glycol, chemical waste, and all other liquids to avoid spills.
- Always refuel using drip pans.
- Ensure spill kits are always available on-site where liquid fuels or wastes (including chemicals and water extracted from lakes) are present.
- Materials liable to shatter at low temperatures, for example many polyethylene based plastics, should be avoided. Wooden and fabric components in semi-permanent structures should be avoided as these are subject to wind abrasion and occasional failure.

### Streams

- Use flumes rather than weirs.
- To the extent practicable, use local materials to construct water measuring and control structures.
- Limit the number of tracer and manipulative experiments. Whenever possible, use modeling approaches to extend the application of experimental results to other streams and lake basins.
- Use only naturally occurring tracers and document tracer use.
- Design tracer experiments to limit the movement of tracers in lakes. The incremental flux from the experiment should be appropriately small in proportion to the average annual total flux for that solute from streams. Choose an experimental site with a long enough reach such that reactions will be completed by the end of the reach.
- Establish specific sites for biomass sampling and document geographic locations, sampling extent, and frequency.
- Develop and apply methods (e.g. spectral analysis) that do not rely on removal of samples for quantifying changes in biomass in streams.

### Lakes

- Minimize the duration and extent to which structures are placed on the ice. When placing structures on the ice near shore, place them on the perennial ice rather than the moat (the moat is highly susceptible to rapid melting). Document the geographic location of the placement of structures on the ice.
- Use barriers (e.g. drip pans) between equipment (e.g. motors, tools) and ice to minimize the potential for hydrocarbon introduction into the ice as well as the physical melting of the ice surface.
- Document the area and the extent to which lake ice has been excavated, taking geographic coordinates. Areas that have been used for sampling or accessing the lake should be reused to the greatest extent possible.

- Minimize the use of motorized vehicles. All-terrain vehicles with four-stroke engines are preferable to snowmobiles with two-stroke engines (less efficient combustion in two-stroke engines causes an increase in the release of hydrocarbons and particulates).
- Use extreme caution when driving motorized vehicles to avoid rolling the vehicle or breaking through the ice cover.
- Remove materials brought up from beneath the ice. Do not dump or deposit water and sediment samples on the lake ice.
- Reduce helicopter overflights after the ice surfaces begin to melt and keep landings on lakes to a minimum.
- Avoid storage of materials on the lake ice surface.
- Use separate samplers (e.g. water collectors, plankton nets) and instruments, if feasible, for each lake to avoid cross contamination. Samplers or instruments used in more than one lake should be thoroughly cleaned (sterilize if possible) prior to reuse in a different lake.
- Carefully manage gray water extracted from lakes to avoid spills.
- Consider laboratory-based alternatives to *in situ* experiments involving any radioisotope, stable isotope, or other tracer in view of the future integrity of the biological and chemical properties of the lakes. Complete preliminary calculations to ascertain the potential impact of isotope experiments. Document and record any introductions.
- Incorporate metal-free haul lines and sampling containers such as "go-flow" bottles into sampling protocols to minimize metal contamination of the lakes.
- Promote use of an environmentally friendly substitute for glycol for use in melting access holes (e.g. a biodegradable antifreeze).
- Minimize the amount of gray water waste by collecting the least volume of water and sediment needed for research purposes.
- Train individuals working on the lake ice to take steps to reduce the loss of equipment through ice holes.
- Provide adequate training for research divers and support teams so that impacts to the lake environment are minimized.
- Prior to conducting diving or ROV operations in a particular lake, consider previous diving history at the proposed research site, the proximity of other areas of interest, and the vulnerability of the water column and benthos to disturbance. These considerations should also be applied to other sampling and measuring activities.
- Assemble and maintain records of diving and ROV activities, including timing, intensity, and duration.
- Use technological developments (e.g. rebreather apparatus, push-pull systems) that mitigate the environmental impacts of diving.

**Soils**
- Minimize surface and subsurface disturbance to the maximum extent practicable
- Restore disturbed surfaces as close as possible to their natural state upon completion of the work. For larger-scale excavations (greater than 1 m$^2$), take photographs prior to breaking ground to provide a basis for restoration. Record the location of the remediated site.
- Place excavated soil on mats or groundsheets during soil sampling.
- Backfill all excavations to approximate original contour and replace desert pavement where possible. The desert pavement can be skimmed from the surface prior to digging and kept aside for replacement.

- Conduct thorough environmental assessment of proposed exogenous amendment experiments.
- Limit use of mechanical equipment (e.g. Cobra drills, soil augers).

**Glaciers**
- Minimize the use of liquid water (e.g. with hot water drills).
- Avoid the use of chemicals and chemical solutions on the ice.
- If stakes or other markers are placed on a glacier, use the minimum number of stakes required to meet research needs; where possible, label these with event number and project duration.
- Use electric chainsaws powered by a four-stroke generator whenever possible for large-scale sawing operations (less contamination than from two-stroke engines). Avoid the use of chainsaw blade lubricants when cutting cold ice.
- Upon completion of a research project, remove all materials – wood, metal, and sensors – embedded in the ice to minimize contamination.

## APPENDIX C:

### Guidelines for Facilities Zones

Facilities Zones include a designated area around the following facilities operated by National Programs in the Area:

- New Harbor Camp, Taylor Valley;
- F-6 Camp, Taylor Valley;
- Lake Fryxell Camp, Taylor Valley;
- Lake Hoare Camp, Taylor Valley;
- Lake Bonney Camp, Taylor Valley;
- Mount Newall Radio Repeater, Asgard Range;
- Marble Point Refueling Station, Marble Point;
- Lower Wright Camp, Wright Valley;
- Lake Vanda Hut, Wright Valley;
- Bull Pass Hut, Wright Valley;
- Cape Roberts Camp, Granite Harbor.

The locations, boundaries, helicopter landings sites, and infrastructure at Facilities Zones, together with an identification of the Maintaining Party are listed in Table C-1, which is followed by maps of the Facilities Zones and their local geographical context (Maps 3-13).

Table C-1: Description of Facilities Zones within the McMurdo Dry Valleys.

| Facilities Zone | Map No. | Boundary Description | Boundary Coordinates | Helicopter Landing Site Coordinates | MP[1] | Structures in Zone |
|---|---|---|---|---|---|---|
| New Harbor Camp | 3 | The boundary goes from a point northwest of the generator shed (on the bank edge), southwest beyond the sling load area, east to a point south of the helicopter pad, northeast to a point east of the main Jamesways, northwest to a point north of the lab building, southwest to a point just north of the old bore hole, and southwest along the bank edge back to the point by the generator shed. | 77° 34.66'S, 163° 31.05'E 77° 34.71'S, 163° 30.98'E 77° 34.70'S, 163° 31.19'E 77° 34.67'S, 163° 31.34'E 77° 34.63'S, 163° 31.19'E 77° 34.64'S, 163° 31.11'E | 77° 34.692'S, 163° 31.165'E 1 helicopter landing pad plus sling load area. | US | Main building consists of two Jamesways connected by a wooden passageway, one 42 m$^2$ (448 sq. ft.) and the other 30 m$^2$ (320 sq. ft.). Adjacent to the main building are a 3 m$^{2S}$ (32 sq. ft.) storage shed and a 1.5 m$^2$ (16 sq. ft.) outhouse. The camp also includes a 21 m$^2$ (224 sq. ft.) James ways that serves as a laboratory, an 8.9 m$^2$ (96 sq. ft.) generator shack, and a 1.5 m$^2$ (16 sq. ft.) diving equipment storage box. One survival cache box and one wind generator tower. |
| F-6 Camp | 4 | The boundary goes from a point southwest of the helicopter pad, northeast to a point just east of the emergency cache (survival box), north around the northern-easternmost tent site, west to a point northwest of the tent sites (by the lake), south around the stream weir, and southeast to the original point by the helicopter pad. | 77° 36.53'S, 163° 15.32'E 77° 36.50'S, 163° 15.43'E 77° 36.46'S, 163° 15.46'E 77° 36.46'S, 163° 15.40'E 77° 36.46'S, 163° 15.21'E 77° 36.50'S, 163° 15.19'E | 77° 6.514'S, 163° 15.343'E 1 helicopter landing pad. | US | A 42 m$^2$ (448 sq. ft.) main building with outhouse adjacent. Emergency cache. |
| Lake Fryxell Camp | 5 | The boundary follows the lake edge in the southeast corner to a point southwest of the helicopter pad, up to the small plateau below a hill, behind the farthest tent site in the northwest | 77° 36.38'S, 163° 07.60'E 77° 36.40'S, 163° 07.37'E 77° 36.34'S, 163° 07.31'E | 77° 36.383'S, 163° 07.430'E 2 helicopter landing pads plus sling load | US | A 62.7 m$^2$ (675 sq. ft.) Jamesway (main building), four 13.9 m$^2$ (150 sq. ft.) laboratories, and one 13.9 m$^2$ (150 sq. ft.) generator |

Table C-1: Description of Facilities Zones within the McMurdo Dry Valleys.

| Facilities Zone | Map No. | Boundary Description | Boundary Coordinates | Helicopter Landing Site Coordinates | MP[1] | Structures in Zone |
|---|---|---|---|---|---|---|
| | | corner, east to the stream, southeast along the stream bank to the eastern most tent and south back to original point by the lake. | 77° 36.34'S, 163° 07.26'E<br><br>77° 36.29'S, 163° 07.27'E<br><br>77° 36.29'S, 163° 07.51'E<br><br>77° 36.31'S, 163° 07.59'E<br><br>77° 36.38'S, 163° 07.60'E | area.<br><br>Secondary pad is 32 m NW of the main pad. | | building. Wind generator tower, solar panel and one outhouse. Emergency cache. |
| Lake Hoare Camp | 6 & 7 | The boundary goes from the rocky area southeast of the helicopter pads, north around the emergency cache, northeast to a rock northwest of the westernmost tent site, northeast to a point north of another tent site, northeast again to the northeastern most tent site, south along the stream/glacier to a point east of the old Lake Hoare facilities (shower and dive storage buildings), southwest to the end of the spit, northwest to the beach below the main building, and northwest to the original point by the helicopter pads. | 77° 37.40'S, 162° 53.87'E<br><br>77° 37.39'S, 162° 53.86'E<br><br>77° 37.35'S, 162° 53.87'E<br><br>77° 37.31'S, 162° 53.96'E<br><br>77° 37.26'S, 162° 54.28'E<br><br>77° 37.26'S, 162° 54.35'E<br><br>77° 37.39'S, 162° 54.40'E<br><br>77° 37.47'S, 162° 54.34'E<br><br>77° 37.41'S, 162° 54.05'E | 77° 373.72'S, 162° 53.989'E<br><br>2 helicopter landing pads plus sling load area.<br><br>Secondary pad is 46 m SW of the main pad. | US | A 55.7 m$^2$ (600 sq. ft.) main building, three 13.9 m$^2$ (150 sq. ft.) labs, a generator building (96 sq. ft.), a tool shed (96 sq. ft.), and three outhouses: two 2.2 m$^2$ (24 sq. ft.) and one 1.7 m$^2$ (18 sq. ft.). Below the active camp are the old Lake Hoare Camp buildings, which are still in use. These include a 37 m$^2$ (400 sq. ft.) Jamesway used primarily for storage, a 6 m$^2$ (64 sq. ft.) generator shed, and a 7.5 m$^2$ (81 sq. ft.) old laboratory used as a shower room. Emergency cache. |
| Lake Bonney Camp | 8 | The boundary goes from a point west of the generator shed by the lake, southeast up to a boulder behind a tent site, northeast to a hill above a tent site, northeast to a point northeast of the easternmost tent site, | 77° 42.96'S, 162° 27.37'E<br><br>77° 42.99'S, 162° 27.56'E<br><br>77° 42.97'S, 162° 27.79'E<br><br>77° 42.95'S, 162° 27.93'E | 77° 42.95'S, 162° 27.65'E<br><br>1 helicopter landing pad. | US | A 55.7 m$^2$ (600 sq. ft.) Jamesway, a 2.2 m$^2$ (24 sq. ft.) outhouse, an 8.9 m$^2$ (96 sq. ft.) generator building, and three 8.9 m$^2$ (96 sq. ft.) laboratories. |

1. Maintaining Party

Table C-1: Description of Facilities Zones within the McMurdo Dry Valleys.

| Facilities Zone | Map No. | Boundary Description | Boundary Coordinates | Helicopter Landing Site Coordinates | MP[1] | Structures in Zone |
|---|---|---|---|---|---|---|
| | | west to the shoreline, southwest along the shoreline passing north of the helicopter landing pad, continuing southwest along the lake shore to a point northwest of the meteorological station and back to the original point below the generator shed. | 77° 42.90'S, 162° 27.73'E<br><br>77° 42.92'S, 162° 27.61'E | | | Emergency cache.<br><br>For 2010 - Two outhouses (5.6 m$^2$). |
| Mount Newall Radio Repeater | 9 | The boundary goes from the northeastern most point northeast of the green equipment shelter, southwest along the southeastern side of the ridge around the green equipment shelter, the NZ Repeater, the wind turbine, the AFTEC Hut, the antenna, the survival camp hut, the survival cache, around the helicopter landing pad, northeast along the north western side of the ridge around the camp hut, the antenna, the AFTEC Hut, the wind turbine, the NZ Repeater, and the green equipment shelter back to the original point. | 77° 30.23'S, 162° 37.60'E<br><br>77° 30.25'S, 162° 37.60'E<br><br>77° 30.26'S, 162° 37.55'E<br><br>77° 30.27'S, 162° 37.52'E<br><br>77° 30.27'S, 162° 37.52'E<br><br>77° 30.29'S, 162° 37.46'E<br><br>77° 30.31'S, 162° 37.33'E<br><br>77° 30.29'S, 162° 37.28'E<br><br>77° 30.28'S, 162° 37.40'E<br><br>77° 30.26'S, 162° 37.49'E<br><br>77° 30.23'S, 162° 37.56'E | 77° 30.295'S, 162° 37.340'E<br><br>1 helicopter landing pad. | US / NZ | The site includes both a US and a NZ radio repeater. There are three huts on Mt. Newall, including an 8.9 m$^2$ (96 sq. ft.) survival hut, a 22.3 m$^2$ (240 sq. ft.) shed encompassing a hybrid power system (both US), and a green equipment shelter 2.2 m$^2$ (24 m$^2$.) housing the NZ repeater. US repeater equipment contained in two orange plastic cases. There are two antennae (one US, one NZ) and a wind turbine (US) at the site. |
| Marble Point Refueling Station | 10 | The boundary goes from the easternmost point (east of soil pits), northwest around the main facilities area, northwest around the fuel storage tanks and pipe, northwest along the road, southwest around the end of the road and staging area, southeast along the road and around the | 77° 24.86'S, 163° 41.41'E<br><br>77° 24.82'S, 163° 41.22'E<br><br>77° 24.81'S, 163° 41.02'E<br><br>77° 24.80'S, 163° 40.81'E<br><br>77° 24.71'S, 163° 40.25'E<br><br>77° 24.74'S, | 77° 24.82'S, 163° 40.76'E<br><br>4 helicopter landing pads.<br><br>The four pads are in close proximity (~25 m – 30 m apart). Coordinates are given for | US | A 69.7 m$^2$ (750 sq. ft.) main building, a 41.8 m$^2$ (450 sq. ft.) bunkhouse, a 55.7 m$^2$ (600 sq. ft.) bunkhouse, a 7.4 m$^2$ (80 sq. ft.) fuel shack, 6 fuel storage tanks (25,000 gallons each), a 2.2 m$^2$ (24 sq. ft.) |

Table C-1: Description of Facilities Zones within the McMurdo Dry Valleys.

| Facilities Zone | Map No. | Boundary Description | Boundary Coordinates | Helicopter Landing Site Coordinates | MP[1] | Structures in Zone |
|---|---|---|---|---|---|---|
| | | helicopter pads, southeast around the pond, and northeast back to the point east of the soil pits. | 163° 40.15'E 77° 24.86'S, 163° 40.74'E 77° 24.89'S, 163° 41.27'E | the central pad (second from main fuel tanks). | | outhouse and incinerator for solid waste, a 1.9 $m^2$ (20 sq. ft.) storage shed, a 21 $m^2$ (224 sq. ft.) generator shed, a 27 $m^2$ (288 sq. ft.) workshop and storage building, and a 7 $m^2$ (76 sq. ft.) ASOS weather station. Fuel shed and outhouse at refuelling station. |
| Lower Wright Hut | 11 | The boundary encompasses the hut, a marked helicopter landing site, and an emergency box and is bounded by rising slopes on the western and eastern sides, a large pavement crack at the southern end and rocky areas at the northern end. A met screen and weir are outside the zone within walking distance of the site. | 77° 26.56'S, 162° 39.04'E 77° 26.53'S, 162° 39.02'E 77° 26.53'S, 162° 39.13'E 77° 26.55'S, 162° 39.15'E | 77° 26.537'S, 161° 39.070'E 1 helicopter landing pad. | NZ | One small hut with accommodation for 2 people with a floor area of 6 $m^2$ (65 sq. ft.). Emergency cache. |
| Lake Vanda Hut | 12 Inset 1 | The boundary follows the edge of the flat area on which the huts, AWS, marked helicopter landing site and tent sites are located. | 77° 31.42'S, 161° 41.15'E 77° 31.40'S, 161° 41.17'E 77° 31.34'S, 161° 41.45'E 77° 31.34'S, 161° 41.51'E 77° 31.36'S, 161° 41.51'E 77° 31.41'S, 161° 41.25'E | 77° 31.361'S, 161° 41.442'E 1 helicopter landing pad. | NZ | Three interconnected huts with a total floor area of 30 $m^2$ (323 sq. ft.). Automatic Weather Station (AWS). |
| Bull Pass Hut | 12 Inset 2 | The boundary encompasses the pebbly flat ground on which the huts and tent sites are situated, and is bounded by a large boulder to the north, small rocky ridges | 77° 31.09'S, 161° 51.23'E 77° 31.07'S, 161° 50.96'E 77° 30.98'S, | 77° 31.056'S, 161° 51.048'E 1 helicopter landing pad. | US | Two shelters located at this site, an equipment shelter and an environmental shelter approximately |

1. Maintaining Party

Table C-1: Description of Facilities Zones within the McMurdo Dry Valleys.

| Facilities Zone | Map No. | Boundary Description | Boundary Coordinates | Helicopter Landing Site Coordinates | MP[1] | Structures in Zone |
|---|---|---|---|---|---|---|
| | | to the east and west, and a line between ridge ends to the south. An AWS is established well to the west of the zone boundary. | 161° 51.11'E<br>77° 31.00'S, 161° 51.35'E | | | 28.7 m² (290 sq. ft.) which houses a hybrid power system. |
| Cape Roberts Camp | 13 | The boundary encompasses all of the flat area between north and south beaches on Cape Roberts, including the two huts and fuel rack. The southeast corner of the zone is at the fuel rack, and the boundary continues north along the edge of a bouldery slope, west along the edge of a rocky area, and south behind the huts along the edge another rocky slope. The zone is bounded to the south by the shoreline of a small bay. | 77° 2.08'S, 163° 10.73'E<br>77° 2.08'S, 163° 10.79'E<br>77° 2.09'S, 163° 10.84'E<br>77° 2.16'S, 163° 10.79'E | No helicopter landing pads. | NZ | Two huts on the ice-free area of Cape Roberts with accommodation for four people (approximately 10 m².) as well a living hut 19 m² (205 sq. ft.). A storage rack for drummed fuel is also at the site. |

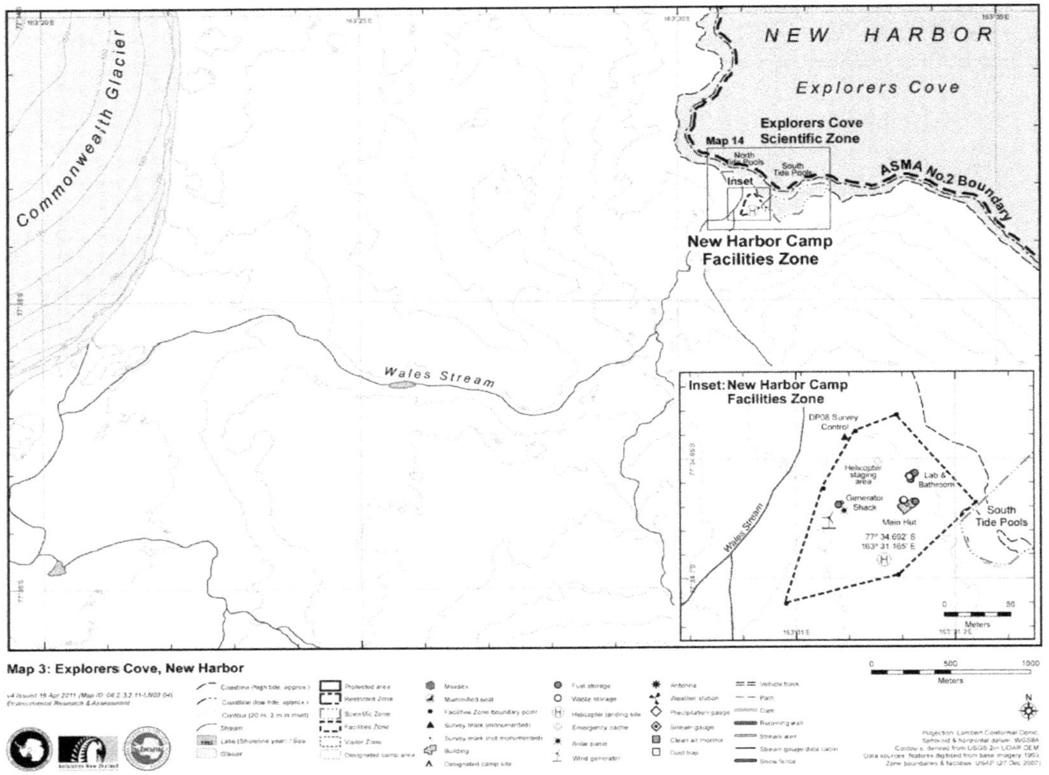
NEW HARBOR
Explorers Cove
Explorers Cove Scientific Zone
Map 14
North Tide Pools
South Tide Pools
Inset
ASMA No.2 Boundary
New Harbor Camp Facilities Zone
Commonwealth Glacier
Wales Stream
Inset: New Harbor Camp Facilities Zone
DP08 Survey Control
Helicopter staging area
Lab & Bathroom
Generator Shack
Main Hut
77° 34.692' S
163° 31.165' E
South Tide Pools
Meters
Map 3: Explorers Cove, New Harbor
Meters

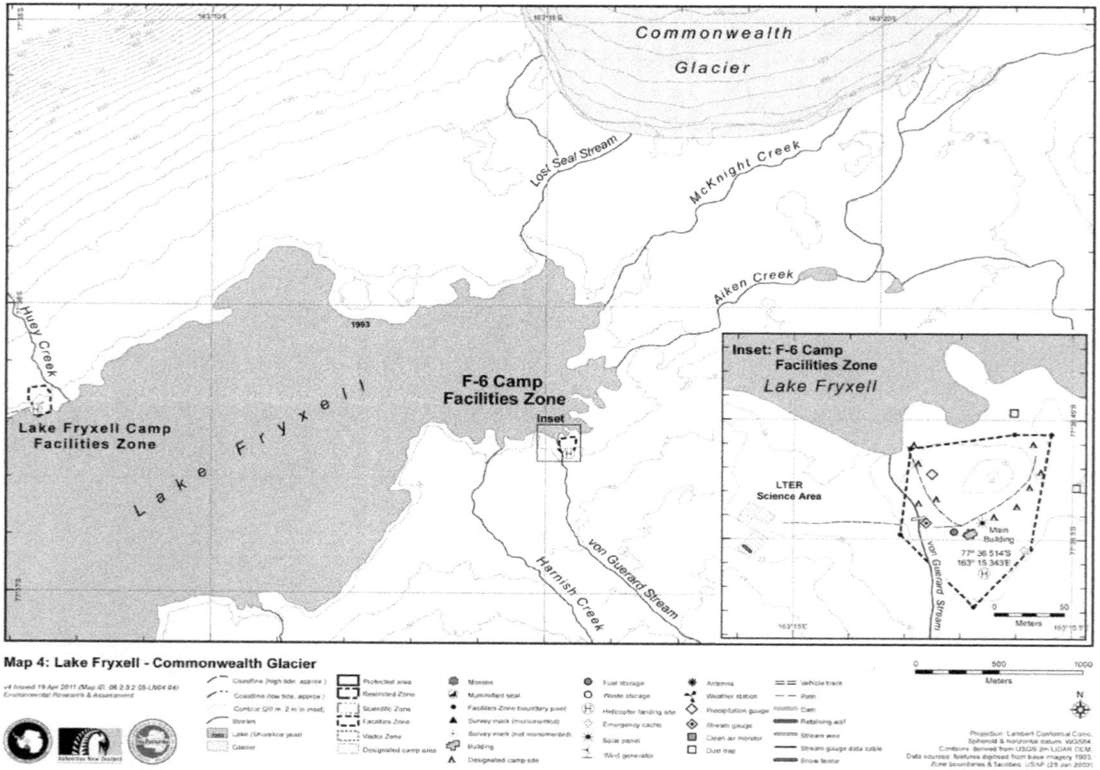

Map 4: Lake Fryxell - Commonwealth Glacier

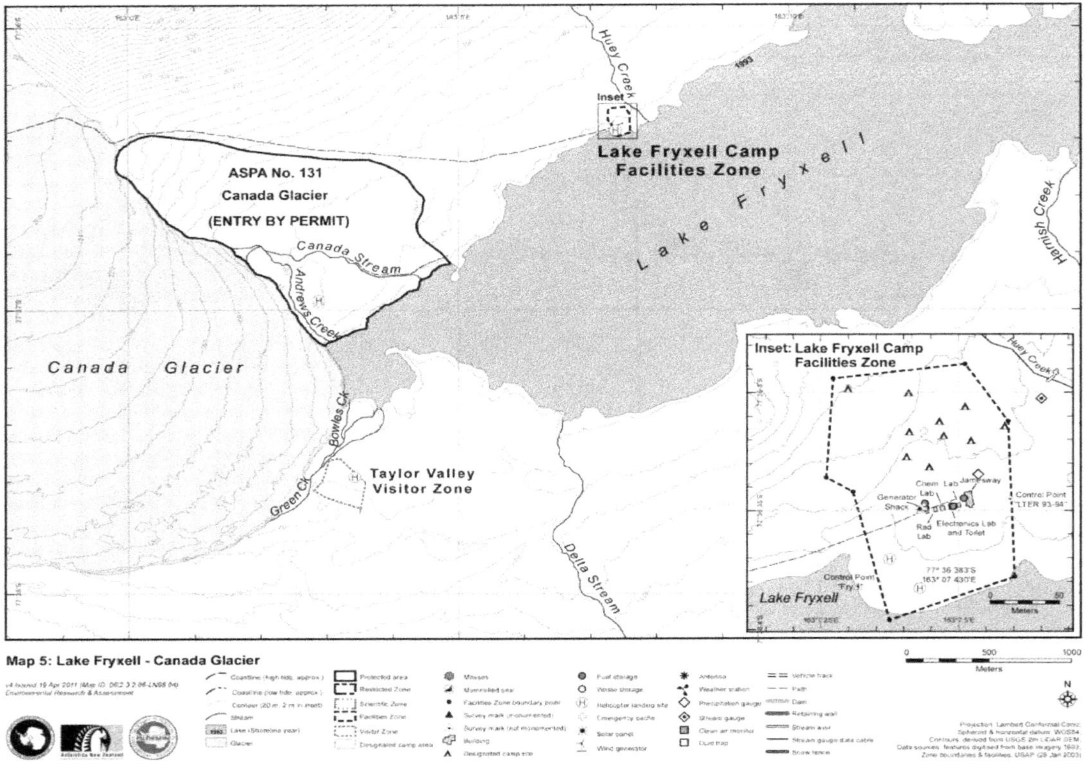

**Map 5: Lake Fryxell - Canada Glacier**

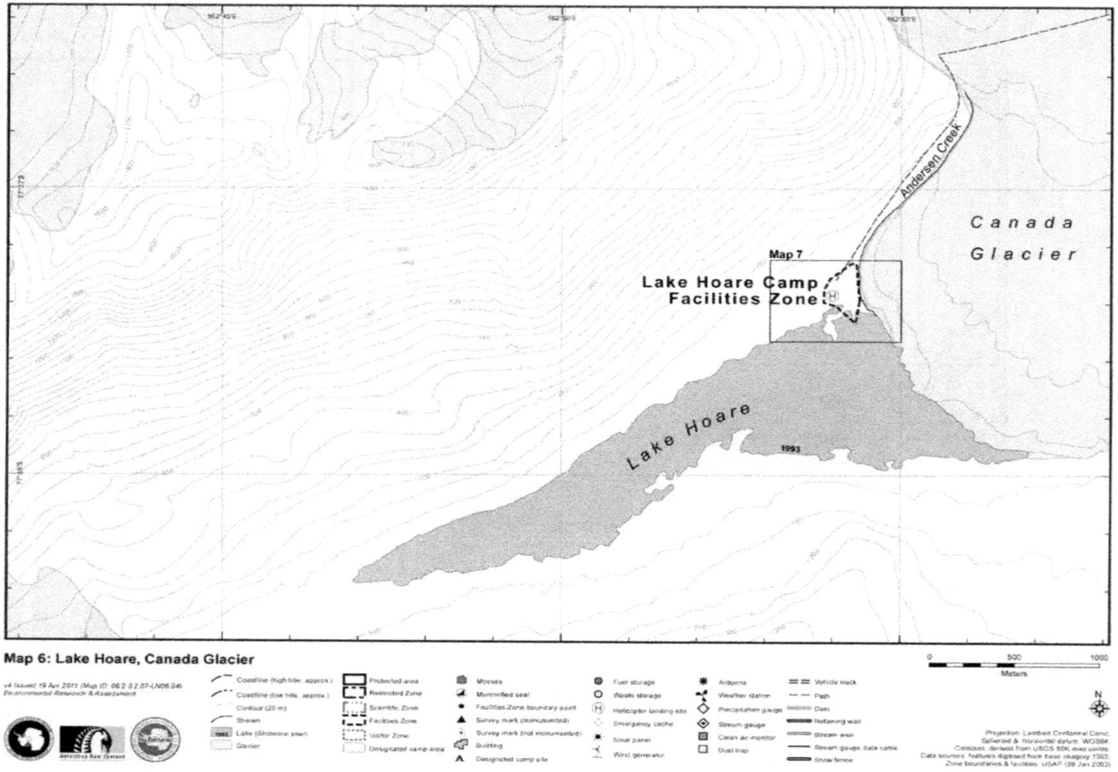

**Map 6: Lake Hoare, Canada Glacier**

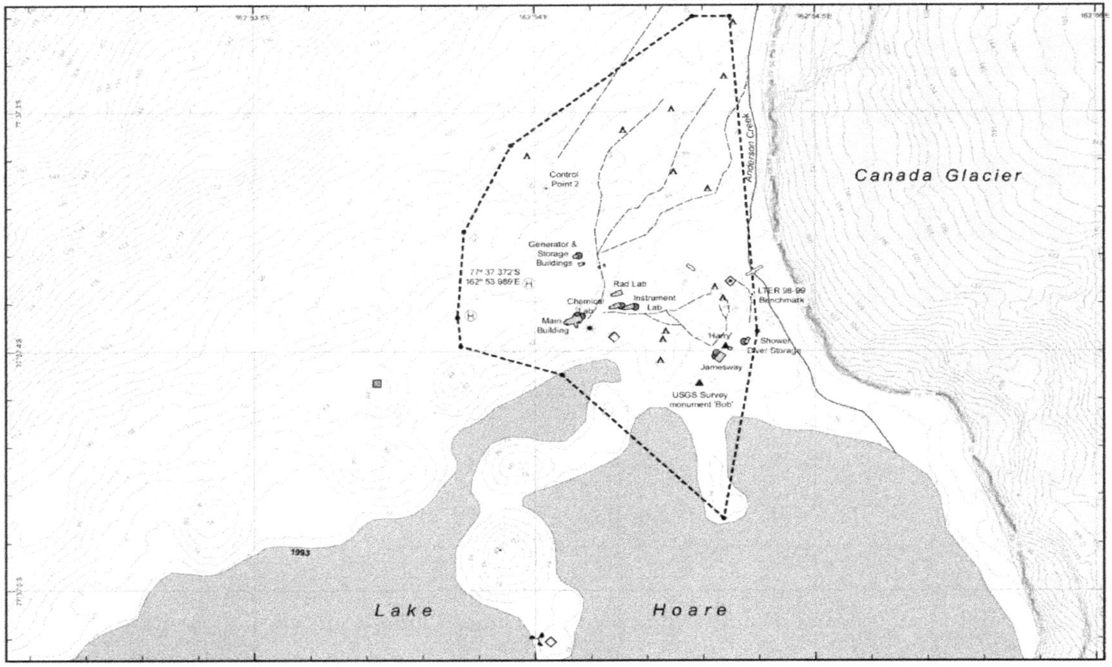

Map 7: Lake Hoare Camp Facilities Zone

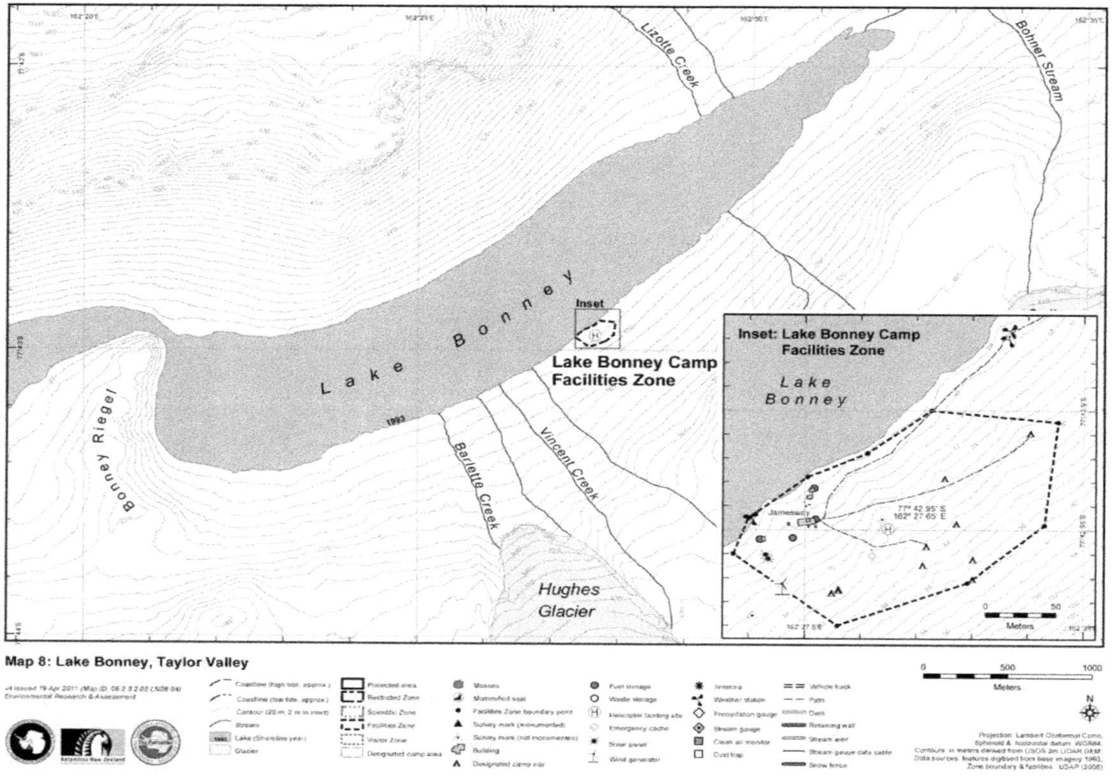

**Map 8: Lake Bonney, Taylor Valley**

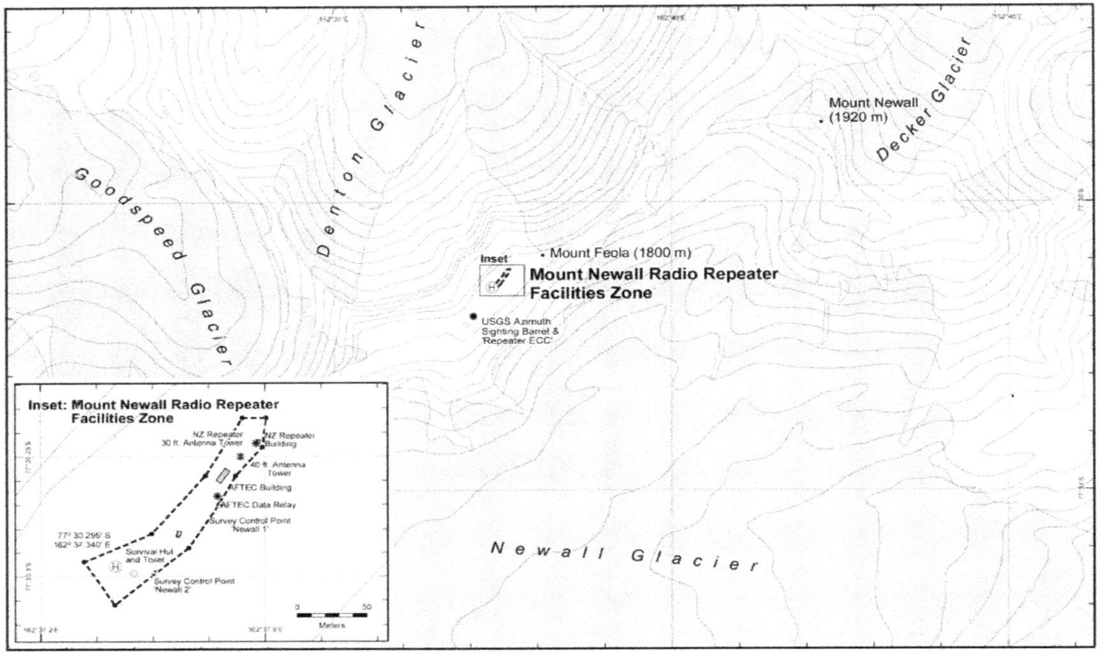

Map 9: Mount Newall, Asgard Range

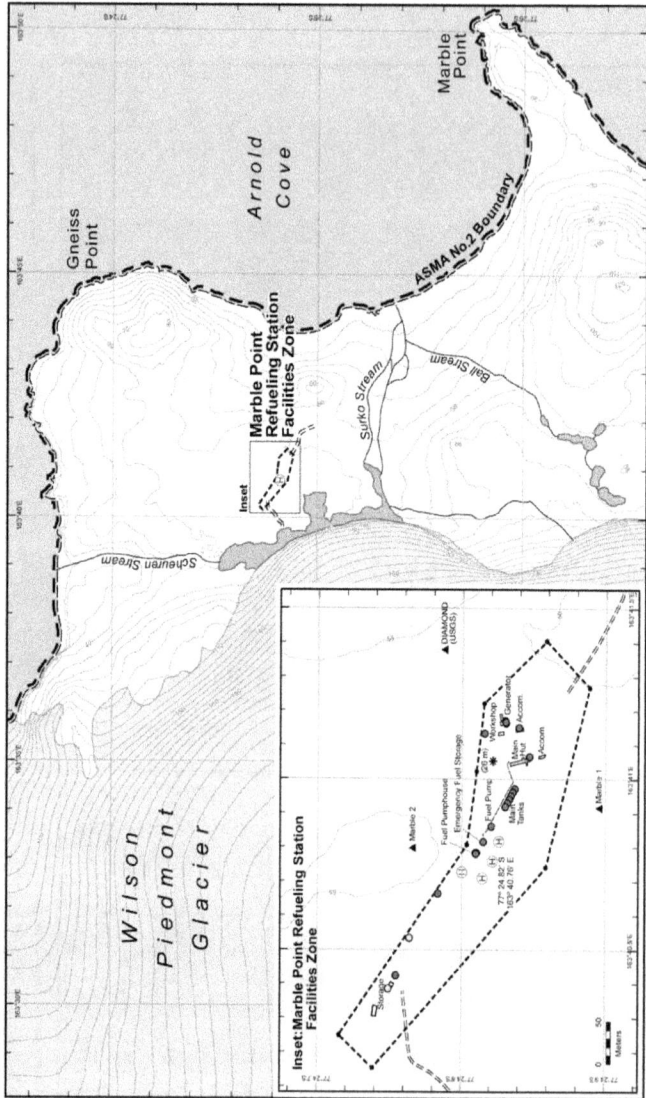

Map 10: Marble Point, McMurdo Sound

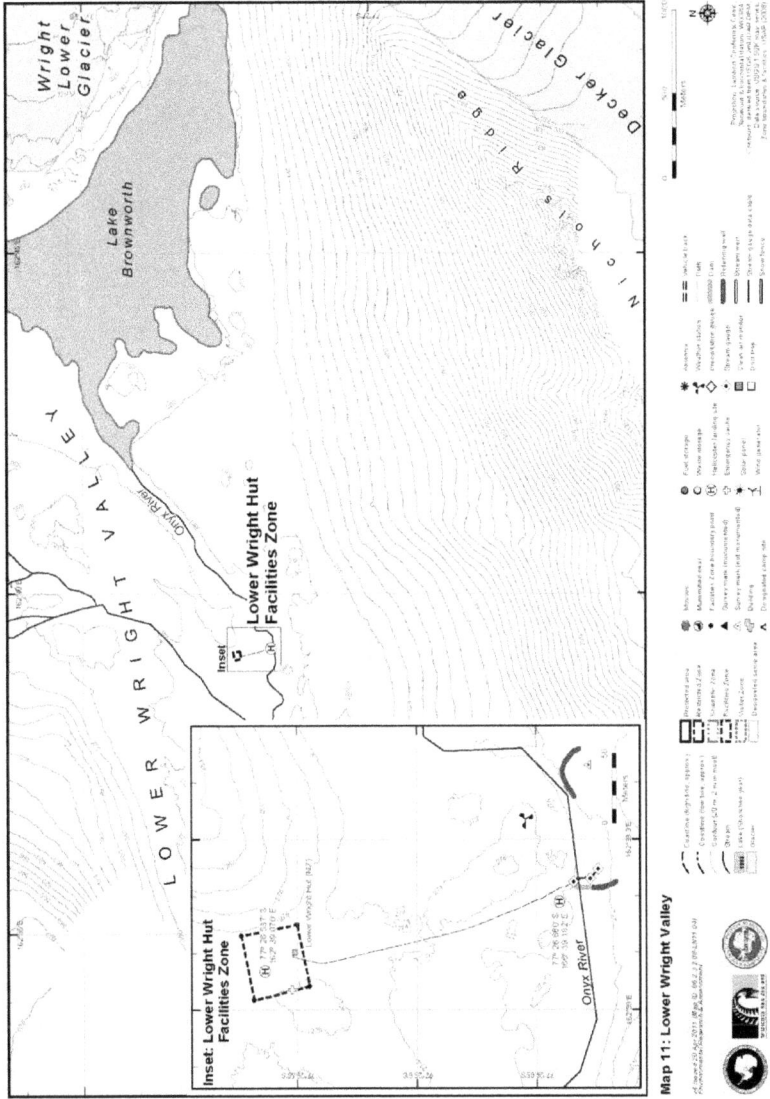

Map 11: Lower Wright Valley

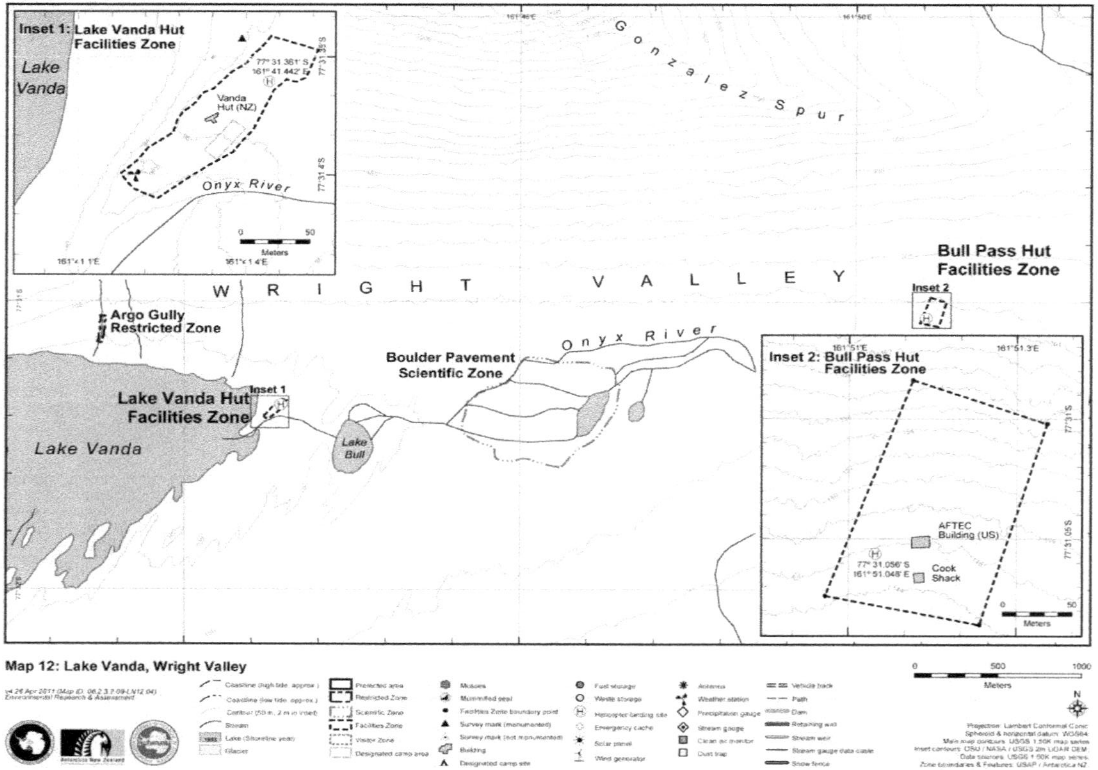

Map 12: Lake Vanda, Wright Valley

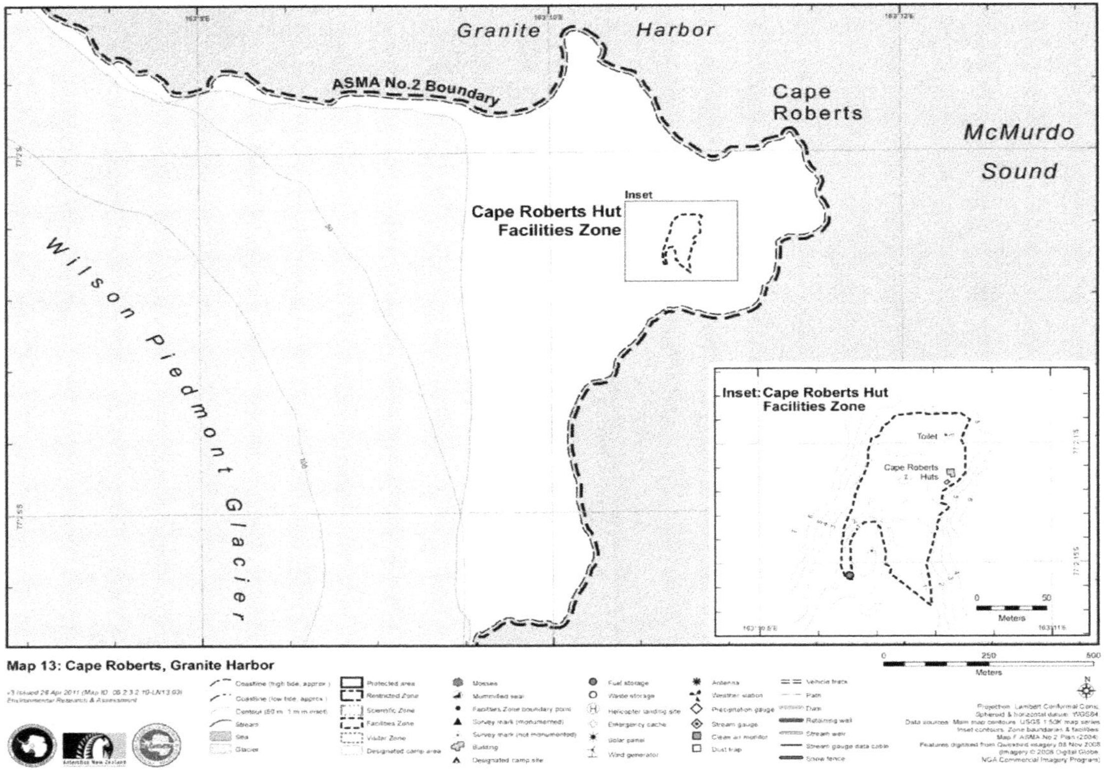

Map 13: Cape Roberts, Granite Harbor

## APPENDIX D:

### Guidelines for Scientific Zones

The following sites within the Area are designated Scientific Zones:
- Explorers Cove, New Harbor, Taylor Valley;
- Boulder Pavement, Wright Valley.

Brief site descriptions, guidelines for activities within each Scientific Zone, and Maps 14 and 15 showing the zone boundaries are attached.

# Scientific Zone

## Explorers Cove

**Location:** New Harbor, Taylor Valley
Two components centered on:
North tide pools (490 m$^2$):
77° 34.57' S, 163° 30.79' E; and
South tide pools (4360 m$^2$):
77° 34.66' S, 163° 31.82' E.

### Purpose

**To avoid disturbance to local marine environment and ecology which are the subject of long-term scientific studies.**

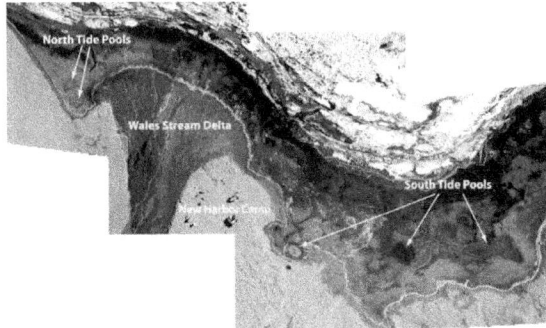

*Photo montage: S. Bowser, USAP (28 Jan 2005)*

### Description

**Zone area:** 4850 m$^2$

The Scientific Zone comprises two tide pool systems on the coast of Explorers Cove, both located close to the New Harbor Camp Facilities Zone and extending ~ 75 – 100 m offshore (Map 14). The southern component lies immediately east of New Harbor Camp, extending along the coast for ~ 500 m. The smaller northern component lies ~ 200 m northwest of New Harbor Camp, immediately west of the Wales Stream delta, and extends along the coast for ~ 100 m. These tidally inundated sand flats are characterized by tide pools containing benthic mats of diatoms and cyanobacteria, a significant source of nutrients for the Explorers Cove near-shore marine ecosystem.

### Boundaries

The coastline boundary of both tide pools follows the mean high water mark, while the seaward boundary extends parallel to the coast following the approximate grounding line of sea ice pressure ridges (when present), which occur ~ 75 – 100 m offshore (see Map 14).

**South Tide Pools:** The western boundary extends 100 m NE from the coast at the NE corner of the New Harbor Camp Facilities Zone. The eastern extent of the Scientific Zone is marked on the shore of a small coastal promontory ~ 500 m east of the Facilities Zone by a small rock cairn, from which the eastern boundary extends due north ~ 30 m offshore.

**North Tide Pools:** The western boundary extends 100 m along the coast from a small embayment west of the Wales Stream delta. The northern boundary thence extends ~ 80 m due east from the coast, while the eastern boundary extends 70 m due north from the coast at the edge of the Wales Stream delta.

### Impacts

KNOWN IMPACTS        None.

POTENTIAL IMPACTS    Shoreline sediments are soft and easily disturbed when not frozen.

### Access requirements

HELICOPTER ACCESS    Use designated helicopter landing site at New Harbor Facilities Zone: 77° 34.692' S, 163° 31.165' E

SURFACE ACCESS       Access to the New Harbor Facilities Zone over sea ice may pass through the southern component of the Scientific Zone.

### Special site guidance

- Avoid walking in the zone unless conducting scientific research, especially when the ice has thawed.

- Sterilize all sampling equipment before sampling at the site to avoid introducing non-native species.

### Key references

Gooday, A.J., Bowser, S.S. & Bernhard, J.M. 1996. Benthic foraminiferal assemblages in Explorers Cove, Antarctica: A shallow-water site with deep-sea characteristics. *Progress in Oceanography* **37**: 117-66.

**Site Map** – Map 14.

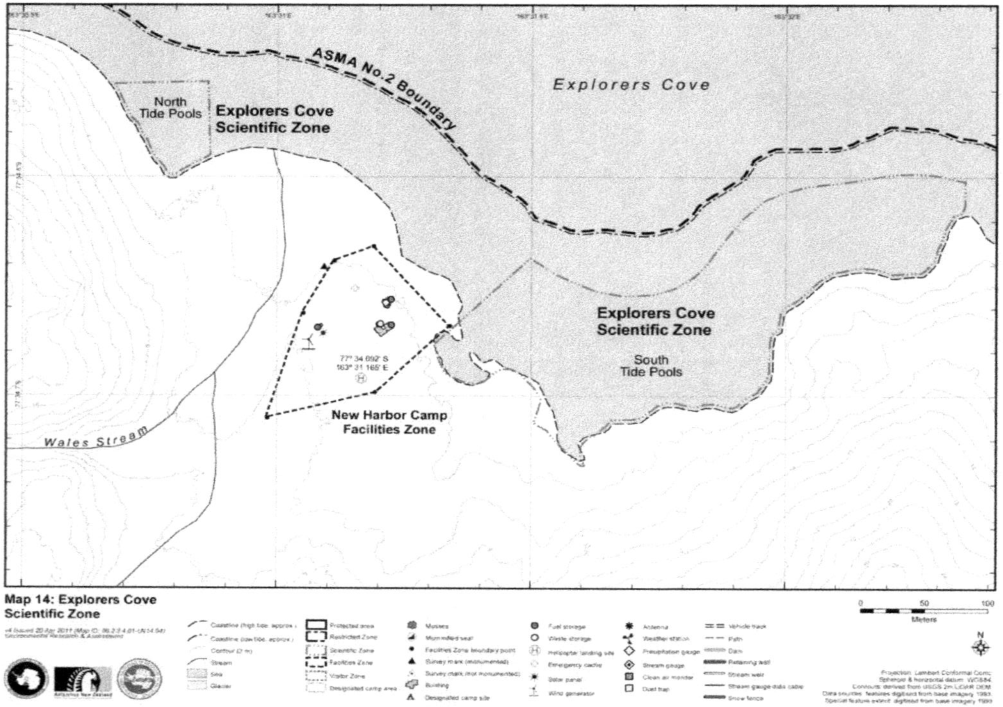
ASMA No.2 Boundary
Explorers Cove
North Tide Pools
Explorers Cove Scientific Zone
Explorers Cove Scientific Zone
South Tide Pools
77° 34.092' S
163° 31.165' E
New Harbor Camp Facilities Zone
Wales Stream
Map 14: Explorers Cove Scientific Zone
0
50
100
Meters
N

# Scientific Zone
## Boulder Pavement
**Location:** Onyx River, central Wright Valley, 4 km east and upstream from Lake Vanda: 77° 31.33' S; 161° 54.58' E

## Purpose
**To avoid disturbance to extensive microbial mats and ecology which are the subject of long-term scientific studies.**

## Description     Zone area: 0.47 km²

*Boulder Pavement: N. Biletnikoff, USAP (29 Jan 2009)*

The Scientific Zone comprises a part of the Onyx River which fans out and flows slowly through an extensive and relatively flat area of boulders, where conditions are favorable for the growth of algae and cyanobacteria, forming the most extensive microbial mats in the Wright Valley and a biofilter for Lake Vanda.

## Boundaries
The Scientific Zone extends to the perimeter of the extensive flat boulder pavement that is typically inundated by the Onyx River, which comprises an area ~ 0.8 km wide and 1.5 km long (Map 15).

## Impacts
KNOWN IMPACTS     None.

POTENTIAL IMPACTS     Trampling may damage the microbial mats. The mats may be difficult to identify when the site is frozen. Activities within the zone increase the risk of the introduction of non-native species.

## Access requirements
HELICOPTER ACCESS     Helicopter landings within the Scientific Zone should be avoided. Where practicable, visitors should use the designated helicopter landing sites at Lake Vanda Hut Facilities Zone (77° 31.361' S; 161° 41.442' E) or Bull Pass Hut Facilities Zone (77° 31.056' S 161° 51.048' E) (Maps 12 & 15).

SURFACE ACCESS     The zone should be accessed on foot. Avoid walking in this area unless necessary for scientific or management purposes.

## Special site guidance
- Avoid crossing the Scientific Zone unless necessary for scientific purposes, such as sampling.
- Walk only on the rocks and avoid trampling the microbial mats.
- Avoid the introduction of non-native species by sterilizing all sampling equipment before use at this site.

## Key references
Howard-Williams, C., Vincent, C.L., Broady, P.A. & Vincent, W.F. 1986. Antarctic stream ecosystems: variability in environmental properties and algal community structure. *International Revue der gesamten Hydrobiologie und Hydrographie* **71**(4): 511-44.

Howard-Williams, C., Hawes, I., Schwarz, A.M. & Hall, J.A. 1997. Sources and sinks of nutrients in a polar desert stream, the Onyx River, Antarctica. In: Lyons, W.B., Howard-Williams, C. & Hawes, I. (Eds) *Ecosystem processes in Antarctic ice-free landscapes*. Proceedings of an International Workshop on Polar Desert Ecosystems, Christchurch, New Zealand: 155-70.

Green, W.J., Stage, B.R., Preston, A., Wagers, S., Shacat, J. & Newell, S. 2005. Geochemical processes in the Onyx River, Wright Valley, Antarctica: major ions, nutrients, trace metals. *Geochimica et Cosmochimica Acta* **69**(4): 839-50.

**Site Map** – Map 15.

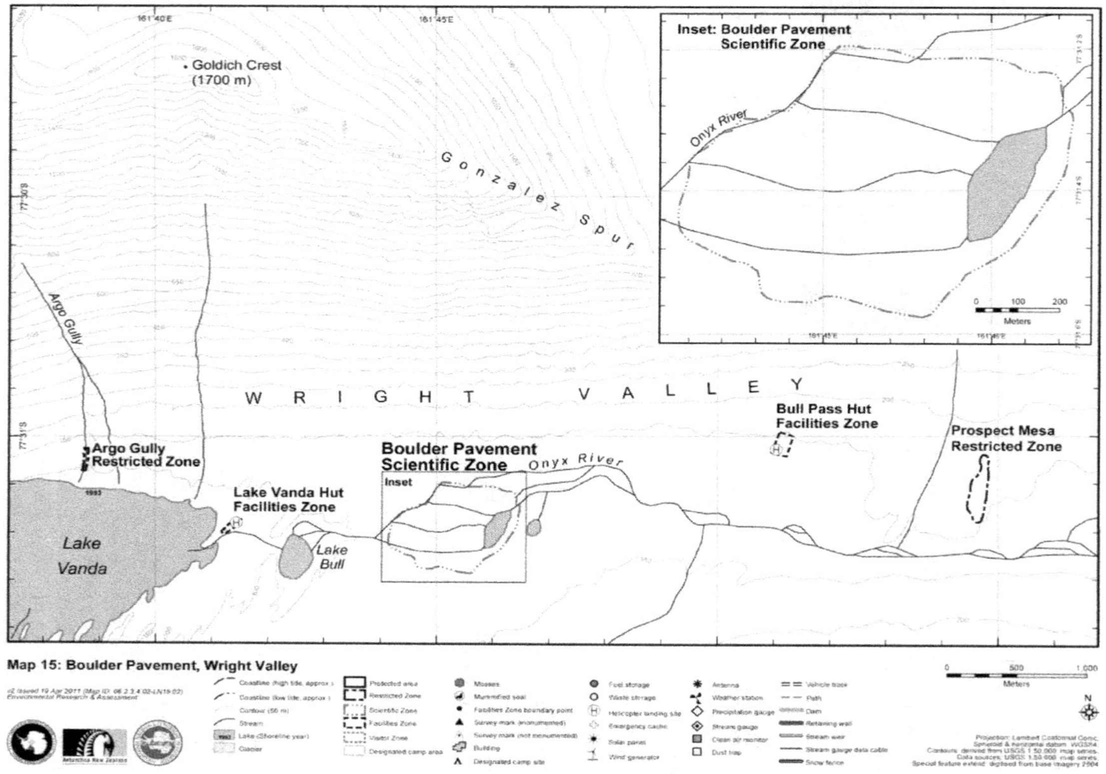

**Map 15: Boulder Pavement, Wright Valley**

## APPENDIX E:

### Guidelines for Restricted Zones

The following sites within the Area are designated Restricted Zones:
- Trough Lake catchment, Pyramid Trough, Royal Society Range;
- Mount Feather Sirius Deposit, Mount Feather;
- Don Juan Pond, South Fork, Wright Valley
- Argo Gully, Lake Vanda, Wright Valley;
- Prospect Mesa, Wright Valley;
- Hart Ash Deposit, Wright Valley;
- Victoria Valley sand dunes, Victoria Valley;
- Battleship Promontory, Alatna Valley, Convoy Range.

Brief site descriptions, guidelines for activities within each Restricted Zone, and maps showing the zone boundaries (Maps 16 – 23) are attached.

# Restricted Zone
## Trough Lake Catchment

*Pyramid Trough: C. Harris, ERA / USAP (09 Dec 2009)*

### Location
Trough Lake catchment, Royal Society Range, several km northwest of the Koettlitz Glacier and southwest of Walcott Bay: 78° 18.17' S, 163° 20.57' E

### Purpose
To avoid disturbance to a pristine hydrological catchment and its ecology, and to ensure the aesthetic and wilderness values of the zone are maintained.

### Description          Zone area: 79.8 km²
The Trough Lake catchment is enclosed by Mount Dromedary (2485 m), The Pyramid (854 m), The Bulwark (~ 600 m) and Seahorse (1008 m), and comprises a network of four main drainage systems feeding into Trough Lake (Map 16). The valley floor of Pyramid Trough contains a significant wetland system comprising a variety of pond and stream habitats in a confined area that support a range of rich biological communities that are representative of the region. Sparse communities of bryophytes and lichens are present. The catchment also contains some unique features, most notable of which are the presence of groups of cyanobacteria that are rare in other wetland systems in the region. Specifically, in addition to the common oscillatorian cyanobacteria, microbial mats in ponds and streams contain *Dichothrix* and *Schizothrix*, and a range of coccoid taxa. Trough Lake catchment has been visited infrequently compared to the other Dry Valleys, and the ecosystem is considered to be almost pristine.

### Boundaries
The Restricted Zone boundary is defined by the Trough Lake catchment. Clockwise from The Pyramid, the boundary crosses a small tongue of the Koettlitz Glacier extending into the catchment, thence follows Backdrop Ridge to an unnamed peak (1618 m) at the top of West Aisle Ridge, thence northwest following the ridge to Mount Dromedary, from where it follows a ridge northeast to Seahorse. The boundary thence follows a ridge eastward and descends to Walcott Bay. The boundary proceeds due east ~800 m from the shoreline of Walcott Bay to the approximate grounding line of the Koettlitz Glacier, and thence follows the ASMA boundary to Bulwark Stream to the foot of the northeast ridge of The Bulwark. The boundary proceeds southward following The Bulwark ridge crest, crosses the head of the Upper Alph River, and follows the Koettlitz Glacier margin to ascend the northeastern ridge of The Pyramid.

### Impacts
| | |
|---|---|
| KNOWN IMPACTS | Rocks have been moved at the campsite, where an iron survey marker is installed on a small knoll at: 78° 17.17' S, 163° 27.83' E (18 m). Sampling has been undertaken at a number of lakes in the catchment. |
| POTENTIAL IMPACTS | Disturbance to water bodies, terrestrial ecology and sensitive soils by sampling or trampling. Introduction of non-native species. |

### Access requirements
| | |
|---|---|
| HELICOPTER ACCESS | Helicopters should land at the designated site at: 78° 17.16' S, 163° 27.84' E (11 m). |
| SURFACE ACCESS | Movement within the zone should generally be on foot. Helicopters may be used for essential travel to sites that would be impracticable to access on foot from the campsite. |

### Special site guidance
- Visits to this catchment should be minimized and semi-permanent structures should not be installed within the zone.
- Avoid the introduction of non-native species by sterilizing all sampling equipment before visiting this site.
- Camping within the Restricted Zone should be at the site previously used (adjacent to the designated helicopter landing site) at: 78° 17.15' S, 163° 27.79' E (11 m).

### Key references
Chinn, T.J.H. 1993. Physical hydrology of Dry Valleys lakes. *Antarctic Research Series* **59**: 1 –51.

Hendy, C.H. & Hall, B.L. 2006. The radiocarbon reservoir effect in proglacial lakes: examples from Antarctica. *Earth and Planetary Science Letters* **241**: 413-21.

Hawes, I., Webster-Brown, J., Wood, S. & Jungblut, A. 2010. A brief survey of aquatic habitats in the Pyramid Trough region, Antarctica. Unpublished report prepared for USAP on the aquatic ecology of the Trough Lake catchment.

**Site Map** – Map 16

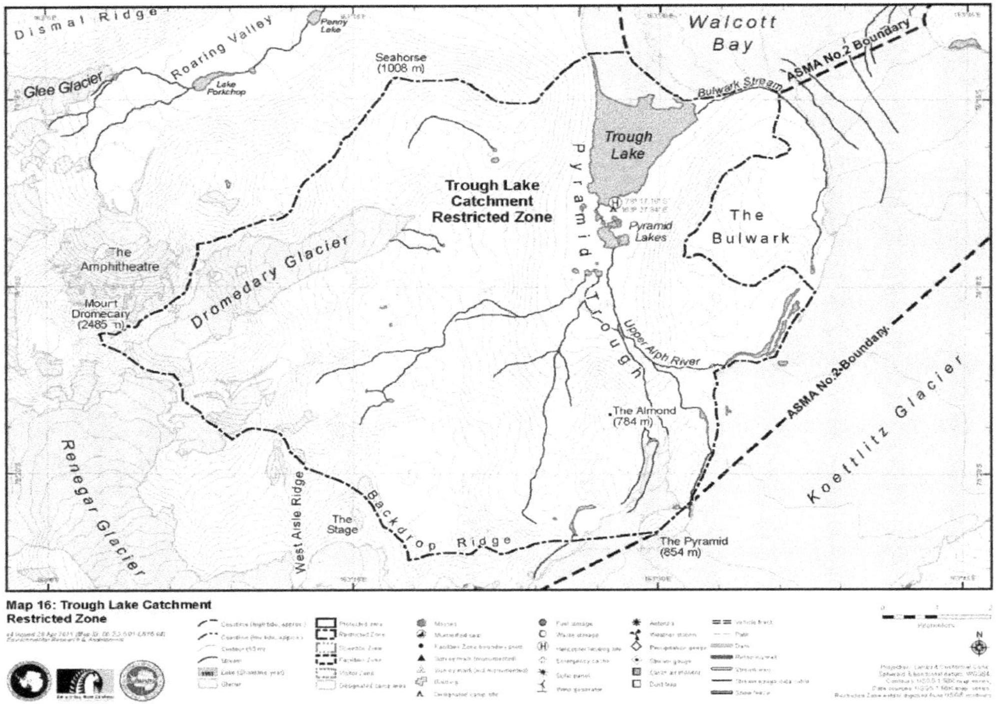

**Map 16: Trough Lake Catchment Restricted Zone**

# Restricted Zone
## Mount Feather Sirius Deposit

**Location**

Northeast flank of Mount Feather (3011 m) between Lashley Glacier and the upper Ferrar Glacier:

77° 56.05' S, 160° 26.30' E

**Purpose**

To avoid disturbance or damage to an area of Sirius Deposits, which are of high scientific value.

*Mount Feather: C. Harris, ERA / USAP (11 Dec 2009)*

**Description**          **Zone area:** 0.57 km²

The Mount Feather Diamicton is an area of semi-lithified glacigenic deposits that have been included within the Sirius Group at the upper Ferrar Glacier, ~3 km NE of Mount Feather (3011 m) (Map 17). The deposits lie at an elevation of between ~2400-2650 m, extending over ground of relatively gentle slope near the ridge crest and also outcropping on the steep eastern cliffs of the Mount Feather massif above Friedmann Valley and the Ferrar Glacier. The diamicton surface has distinct melt-water runnels near its perimeter and on steeper slopes. The deposits, which extend over an area of ~1.5 km x 1 km, contain microfossils and other evidence of high scientific importance for interpretation of the Neogene glacial history of the Dry Valleys and of the East Antarctic ice sheet as a whole.

**Boundaries**

The boundary of the Restricted Zone (Map 17) is defined based on the extent of the Mount Feather Diamicton as mapped by Wilson *et al.* (2002: Fig.1). Owing to limitations in the accuracy of available mapping in the region, the boundary is considered approximate, with an estimated accuracy of at least +/- 100 m.

**Impacts**

| | |
|---|---|
| KNOWN IMPACTS | Rock samples have been collected. At least four shallow drill cores (of 3.2 m in depth or less) have been recovered from the site, although drilling fluids were not employed. |
| POTENTIAL IMPACTS | Drilling operations, especially those employing drilling fluids. Sampling and disturbance to sedimentary sequences. |

**Access requirements**

| | |
|---|---|
| HELICOPTER ACCESS | Helicopter operations in this location can be difficult owing to altitude and winds, and no specific landing site has yet been designated. |
| SURFACE ACCESS | Movement within the Restricted Zone should be on foot. |

**Special site guidance**

- Do not move sediments, rocks and boulders, unless necessary for scientific purposes, and avoid disturbance to or alteration of the sedimentary sequences and melt-water runnels.
- Camping should be at the site previously used on adjacent snow surfaces at: 77° 55.93' S, 160° 25.66' E.

**Key references**

Wilson, G.S., Barron, J.A., Ashworth, A.C., Askin, R.A., Carter, J.A., Curren, M.G., Dalhuisen, D.H., Friedmann, E.I., Fyodorov-Davidov, D.G., Gilichinsky, D.A., Harper, M.A., Harwood, D.M., Hiemstra, J.F., Janecek, T.R, Licht, K.J., Ostroumov, V.E., Powell, R.D., Rivkina, E.M., Rose, S.A., Stroeven, A.P., Stroeven, P., van der Meer, J.J.M., and Wizevich M.C. 2002. The Mount Feather Diamicton of the Sirius Group: an accumulation of indicators of Neogene Antarctic glacial and climatic history. *Palaeogeography, Palaeoclimatology, Palaeoecology* **182**: 117-31.

**Site Map** – Map 17

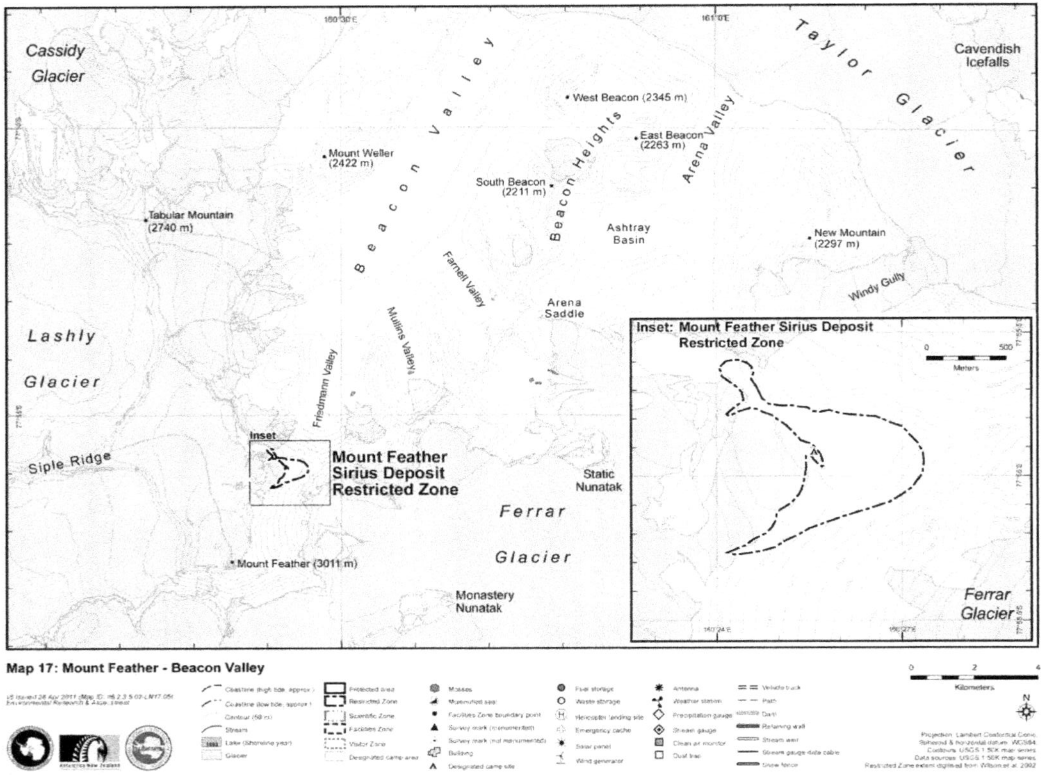

Map 17: Mount Feather - Beacon Valley

Inset: Mount Feather Sirius Deposit Restricted Zone

# Restricted Zone
## Don Juan Pond

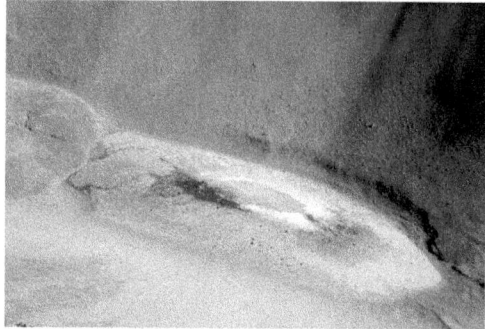

Don Juan Pond: C. Harris, ERA / USAP (14 Dec 2009)

### Location
At the foot of a rock glacier in South Fork, Wright Valley, in a closed basin at 118 m elevation below the Dais, ~ 7.5 km from Lake Vanda:
77° 33.77' S, 161° 11.32' E

### Purpose
To protect a rare and sensitive hypersaline ecosystem of high scientific value from disturbance and damage.

### Description                    Zone area: 20 ha
Don Juan Pond is a small hypersaline lake currently of ~400 x 150 m containing a calcium-chloride-rich brine with a salinity level of ~40%, making it the most saline natural water body known on Earth. Water levels have fluctuated over time, although recently the pond has been ~10 cm in depth. While water levels vary, the Restricted Zone extends to the perimeter of the pond floor salt deposits (Map 18). Microbial life, including numerous heterotrophic bacteria and a yeast, are found in the pond. A mat of mineral material and detritus cemented together by organic matter, referred to as the Don Juan Pond Salt Deposits, is found at the edge of the pond where the calcium chloride concentrations are reduced. Don Juan Pond is also the site where Antarcticite ($CaCl_2$ 6H20), a hygroscopic colorless mineral, was first identified forming naturally.

### Boundaries
The Restricted Zone boundary is defined by the outer extent of the Don Juan Pond Salt Deposits, which extend to the edge of the basin pond floor, occupying an area of ~720 x 300 m (Map 18).

### Impacts
KNOWN IMPACTS        The Dry Valleys Drilling Project drilled two boreholes at Don Juan Pond: DVDP 5 (3.5 m depth) and DVDP 13 (75 m depth), situated within the salt deposit area ~60 m and ~110 m respectively east of the rock glacier. DVDP 13 remains in evidence as an iron tube (capped) protruding ~ 1 m above the dry pond floor (Map 18). Small quantities of waste (e.g. rusted cans) were observed  in soils ~50-100 m south and east of the Restricted Zone in Dec 2009, most likely originating from early camps established near the site.

POTENTIAL IMPACTS    Disturbance to water body, salt deposits and sensitive soils by sampling or trampling.

### Access requirements
HELICOPTER ACCESS    Helicopters should avoid landing in the Restricted Zone and avoid overflight below 50 m above ground level. Helicopters should land at the designated site ~250 m east of Don Juan Pond at: 77° 33.784' S, 161° 12.948' E.

SURFACE ACCESS    Access to and movement within the Restricted Zone should be on foot.

### Special site guidance
- Avoid walking through the pond and adjacent salt deposits unless necessary for scientific or management purposes.
- Walk carefully to minimize disturbance to the salt deposits and surrounding soft soils and sensitive slopes.
- Do not move any boulders.
- Camping is not permitted within the Restricted Zone.

### Key references
Harris, H.J.H. & Cartwright, K. 1981. Hydrology of the Don Juan Basin, Wright Valley, Antarctica. *Antarctic Research Series* **33**: 161-84.

Chinn, T.J. 1993. Physical hydrology of the Dry Valley lakes. *Antarctic Research Series* **59**: 1-51.

Samarkin, V.A., Madigan, M.T., Bowles, M.W., Casciotti, K.L., Priscu, J.C., McKay, C.P. & Joye, S.B. 2010. Abiotic nitrous oxide emission from the hypersaline Don Juan Pond in Antarctica. *Nature Geoscience* Online: 25 April 2010. DOI: 10.1038/NGEO847.

**Site Map** – Map 18

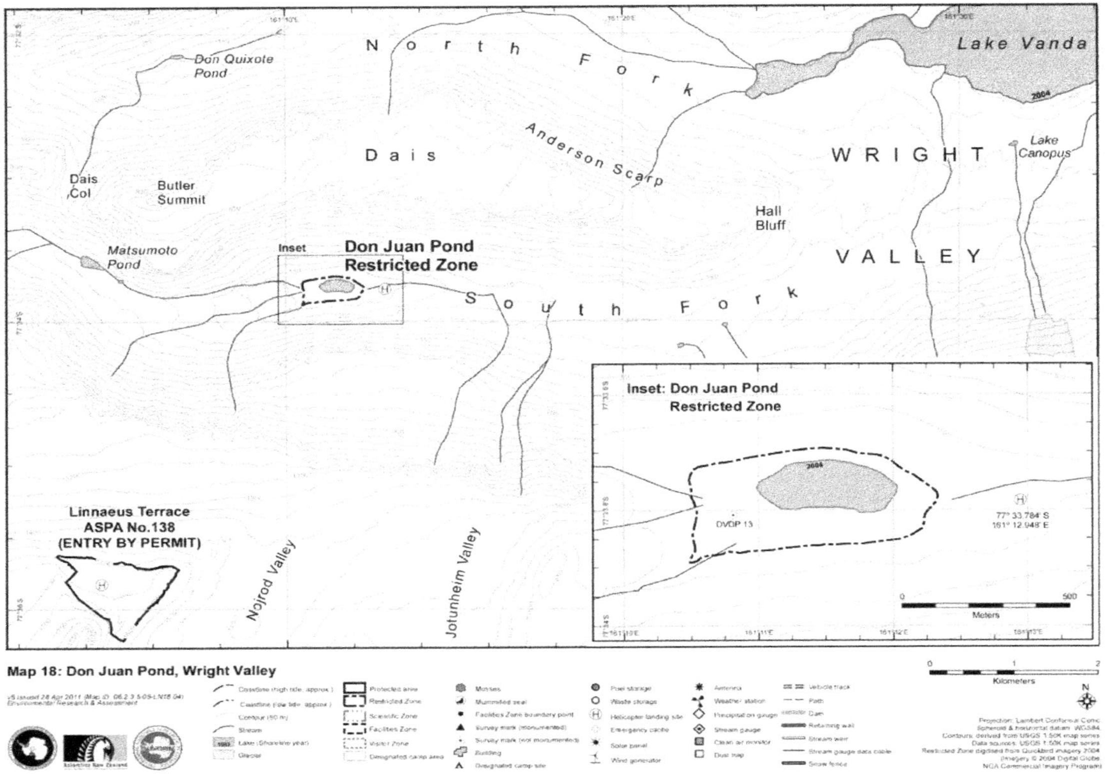

**Map 18: Don Juan Pond, Wright Valley**

# Restricted Zone
## Argo Gully

### Location
Northeastern shore of Lake Vanda, Wright Valley, below Mount Jason, at an elevation between 104 m and 235 m:
77° 31.09' S, 161° 38.77' E

### Purpose
To avoid damage to exposed stratified marine fossiliferous deposits within the gully, which are of high scientific value.

*Argo Gully: K. Pettway, USAP (31 Jan 2011)*

### Description          Zone area: 4800 m²
Part of the lower reach of a prominent stream channel in Argo Gully, below Mount Jason (1920 m), Olympus Range (Map 19), contains exposed beds (up to 2.8 meters thick) of massive glacial silts containing abundant marine diatom and silicoflagellate material overlying sediment. Pecten shell fragments have reportedly been found in the upper few centimeters of the deposit. The beds are horizontally stratified, which is in contrast to the underlying sediments. The deposits are overlain by deltaic sands, silts and gravels, deposited by the stream in Argo Gully. The deposits are indicative that the Wright Valley was formerly a shallow marine fjord, and have been dated as Middle Miocene. The full extent of the deposits below the overlying sediment is unknown, and the intermittent exposures along the channel change over time as a result of natural erosion.

### Boundaries
The Restricted Zone extends from the first prominent raised beach (elevation 104 m) above, and ~140 meters from, the shore of Lake Vanda, for 175 meters up the stream channel to an elevation of ~135 m. The zone extends 25 meters either side of the stream channel (Map 19).

### Impacts
KNOWN IMPACTS          None.

POTENTIAL IMPACTS      The deposit is within the permafrost but the surface continually slumps when the permafrost melts. The surface of the deposit if friable when touched.

### Access requirements
HELICOPTER ACCESS      Helicopters should land at the designated site at Lake Vanda Hut Facilities Zone ~1.2 km to the east at: 77° 31.361' S, 161° 41.442' E.

SURFACE ACCESS         Access to and movement within the Restricted Zone should be on foot.

### Special site guidance
- Avoid walking on the edges of the gully or above the exposed outcrops.
- Minimize disturbance to the sediments surrounding the deposits.
- Avoid touching the exposed outcrops unless conducting scientific research.

### Key references
Brady, H.T. 1980. Palaeoenvironmental and biostratigraphic studies in the McMurdo and Ross Sea regions, Antarctica. Unpublished PhD thesis, Macquarie University, Australia.

Brady, H.T. 1979. A diatom report on DVDP cores 3, 4a, 12, 14, 15 and other related surface sections. In: Nagatta, T. (Ed) *Proceedings of the Seminar III on Dry Valley Drilling Project, 1978.* Memoirs of National Institute of Polar Research, Special Issue 13: 165-75.

**Site Map** – Map 19.

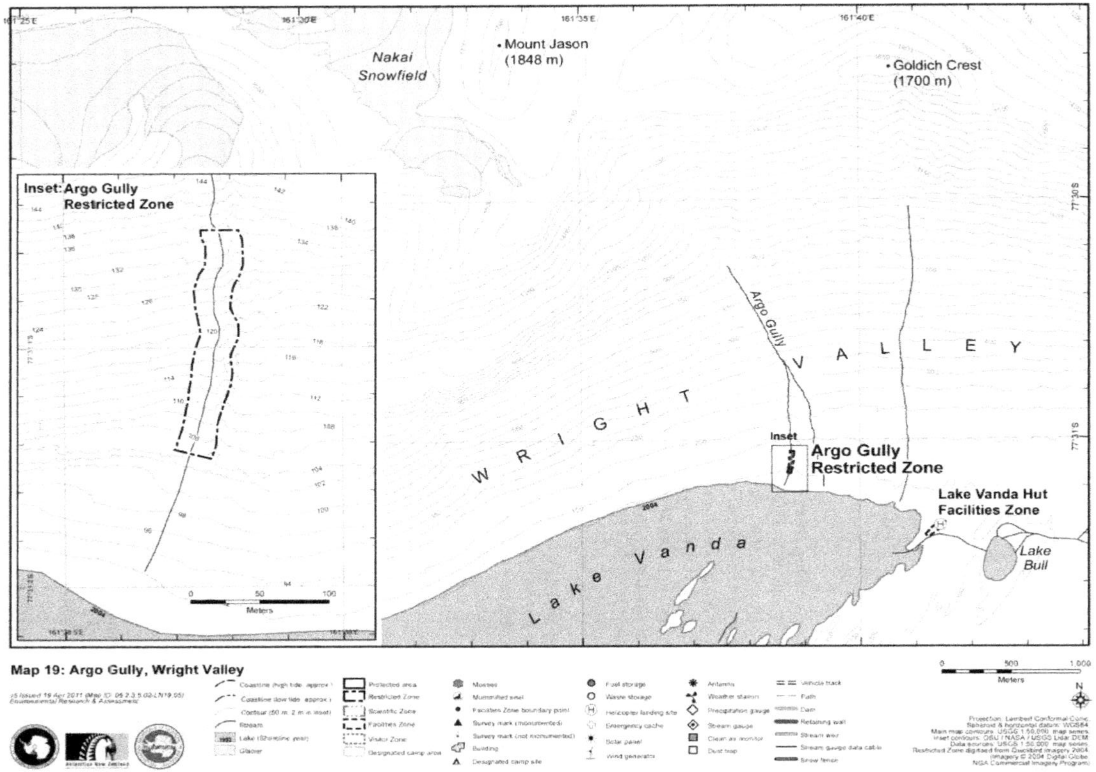

Map 19: Argo Gully, Wright Valley

# Restricted Zone

## Prospect Mesa

**Location**

Below Bull Pass ~250 m north of the Onyx River, Wright Valley:

77° 31.33′ S; 161° 54.58′ E

**Purpose**

To avoid damage to a fragile deposit of fossilized extinct marine pecten (scallop) shells of a single species.

*Prospect Mesa: C. Harris, ERA / USAP (15 Dec 2009)*

**Description**     **Zone area:** 4.76 ha

Prospect Mesa is a deposit of fossiliferous gravels overlying till containing a high density of well-preserved extinct marine pecten (scallop) shells of a single species, *Chlamys (Zygochlamys) tuftsensi*, of the Family Pectinidae. This is the only known site where this species is found. A stratified layer of sand and gravel overlying till is exposed in a gully cut by a stream flowing from Bull Pass a few hundred meters from its junction with the Onyx River (Map 20). The precise age of the deposit is unknown, although the presence of articulated shells, the abundance of complete shells, the lack of abrasion, the similarity of internal and external matrix, the lack of good size segregation and a generally very poor sorting of the clasts suggest that the fossils were deposited *in situ* in a marine fjord. Sponge spicules, radiolarian and a few ostracod fragments are also present but foraminifera are the most abundant and diverse microfossil group present.

**Boundaries**

The Restricted Zone boundary is defined around two adjacent mesa features, the smaller of the two being ~100 m north of the main feature. The boundary follows the well-defined NE bank of the stream descending from Bull Pass in the SW of the zone, and then follows around the base of the slopes that define the two features (Map 20).

**Impacts**

KNOWN IMPACTS     An excavation from early research exists on the southwest slope of the mesa (see photo), which is marked by a pole at the base.

POTENTIAL IMPACTS     Isolation of unbroken pecten fragments is extremely difficult. Disturbance or damage to the sediments may cause damage to the fossils.

**Access requirements**

HELICOPTER ACCESS     Helicopters should not land within the Restricted Zone. Use the designated helicopter landing site at Bull Pass Hut Facility Zone: 77° 31.056′S, 161° 51.048′E

SURFACE ACCESS     Access to and movement within the Restricted Zone should be on foot.

**Special site guidance**

- Avoid walking on top of the mesa.
- Pedestrians should walk carefully to minimize disturbance to fragile sedimentary structures, deposits and slopes.
- Camping is not permitted within the Restricted Zone.

**Key references**

Turner, R.D. 1967. A new species of fossil Chlamys from Wright Valley, McMurdo Sound, Antarctica. *New Zealand Journal of Geology and Geophysics* **10**: 446-55.

Vucetich, C.G. & Topping, W.W. 1972. A fjord origin for the pecten deposits, Wright Valley, Antarctica. *New Zealand Journal of Geology and Geophysics* **15**(4): 660-73.

Webb, P.N. 1972. Wright fjord, Pliocene marine invasion of an Antarctic Dry Valley. *Antarctic Journal of the United States* **7**: 227-34.

Prentice, M.L., Bockheim, J.G., Wilson, S.C., Burckle, L.H., Jodell, D.A., Schluchter, C. & Kellogg, D.E. 1993. Late Neogene Antarctic glacial history: evidence from central Wright Valley. *Antarctic Research Series* **60**: 207-50.

**Site Map** – Map 20

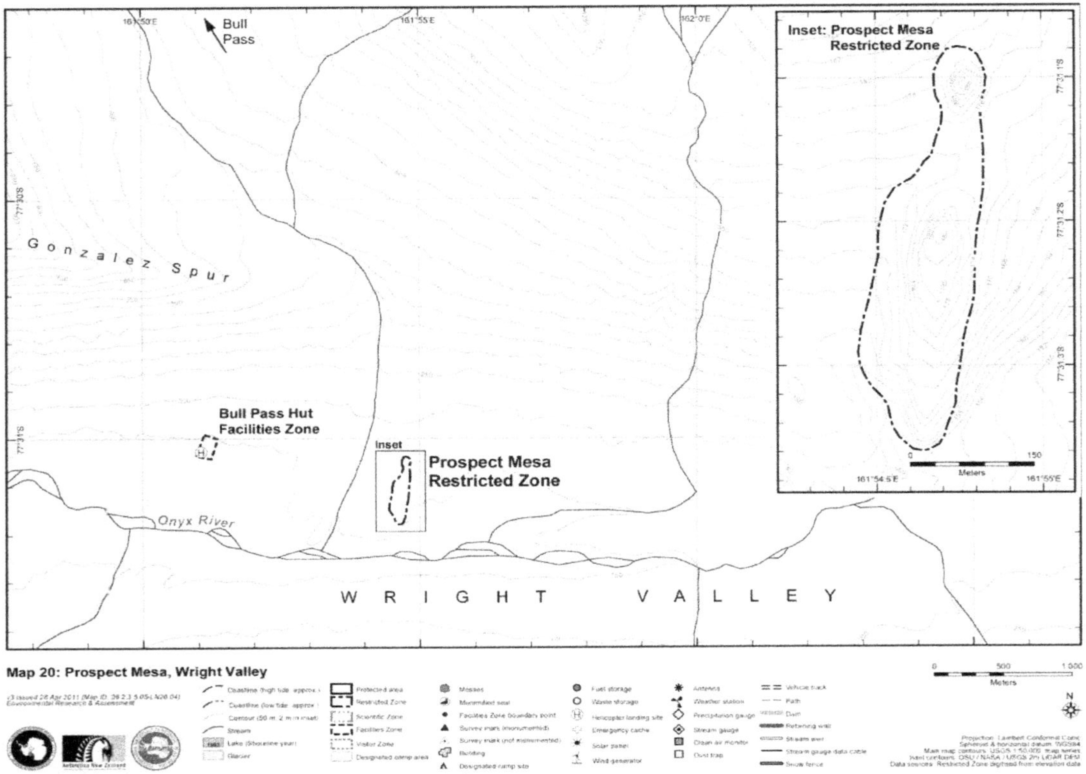
Bull
Pass
Gonzalez Spur
Bull Pass Hut
Facilities Zone
Inset
Prospect Mesa
Restricted Zone
Onyx River
WRIGHT VALLEY
Inset: Prospect Mesa
Restricted Zone
Map 20: Prospect Mesa, Wright Valley

# Restricted Zone
## Hart Ash Deposit

**Location**

On a relatively featureless slope between the Goodspeed and Hart Glaciers, Wright Valley, at an elevation of ~400 m:

77° 29.76' S, 162° 22.35' E

**Purpose**

To avoid damage to an *in situ* deposit of volcanic ash airfall tephra that is of high scientific value.

*Hart Ash deposit: J. Aislabie*
*Antarctica NZ Pictorial Collection (2005)*

**Description**          **Zone area:** 1.8 ha

The Hart Ash deposit is an *in situ* preserved deposit of volcanic ash airfall tephra protected by a surface layer of gravel. The surface gravel protecting the ash layer has a wide spatial extent and the Hart Ash is not immediately visible unless the surface gravel is removed, making field identification difficult. The full extent of the Hart Ash deposit is thus unknown, although its maximum extent has been estimated as ~100 x 100 m (Map 21). The Hart Ash deposit, dated 3.9 ± 0.3 million years old, is of high scientific importance for interpreting the paleoclimate of the McMurdo Dry Valleys.

**Boundaries**

Owing to a lack of prominent surface landmarks, the boundary of the Restricted Zone is defined as an area of 150 m x 120 m following lines of latitude and longitude (Map 21) extending from the coordinates:

Upper Left: 77°29.72' S, 162°22.2' E

Lower Right: 77 29.8' S, 162 22.5' E

**Impacts**

| | |
|---|---|
| KNOWN IMPACTS | None. |
| POTENTIAL IMPACTS | The deposit is covered by a thin gravel desert pavement which is easily disturbed by walking. Wind erosion of the ash deposits would be rapid if the desert pavement is disturbed. |

**Access requirements**

| | |
|---|---|
| HELICOPTER ACCESS | Helicopters should avoid landings and overflight below 50 m above ground level within the Restricted Zone. Helicopter landings should be made at least 100 m from the boundary. |
| SURFACE ACCESS | Access to and movement within the Restricted Zone should be on foot. |

**Special site guidance**

- Avoid walking on the desert pavement overlying the ash deposits unless necessary for essential scientific or management purposes, and then walk carefully to minimize disturbance.
- Should the desert pavement be removed for essential scientific purposes, ensure the material is replaced to protect the feature.
- Camping is not permitted within the Restricted Zone.

**Key references**

Hall, B.L., Denton, G.H., Lux, D.R. & Bockheim, J. 1993. Late tertiary Antarctic paleoclimate and ice-sheet dynamics inferred from surficial deposits in Wright Valley. *Geografiska Annaler* **75A**(4): 239-67.

Morgan, D.J., Putkonen, J., Balco, G. & Stone, J. 2008. Colluvium erosion rates in the McMurdo Dry Valleys, Antarctica. Proceedings of the American Geophysical Union, Fall Meeting, 2008.

Schiller, M., Dickinson, W., Ditchburn, R.G., Graham, I.J. & Zondervan, A. 2009. Atmospheric 10Be in an Antarctic soil: implications for climate change. *Journal of Geophysical Research* **114**, FO1033.

**Site Map** – Map 21

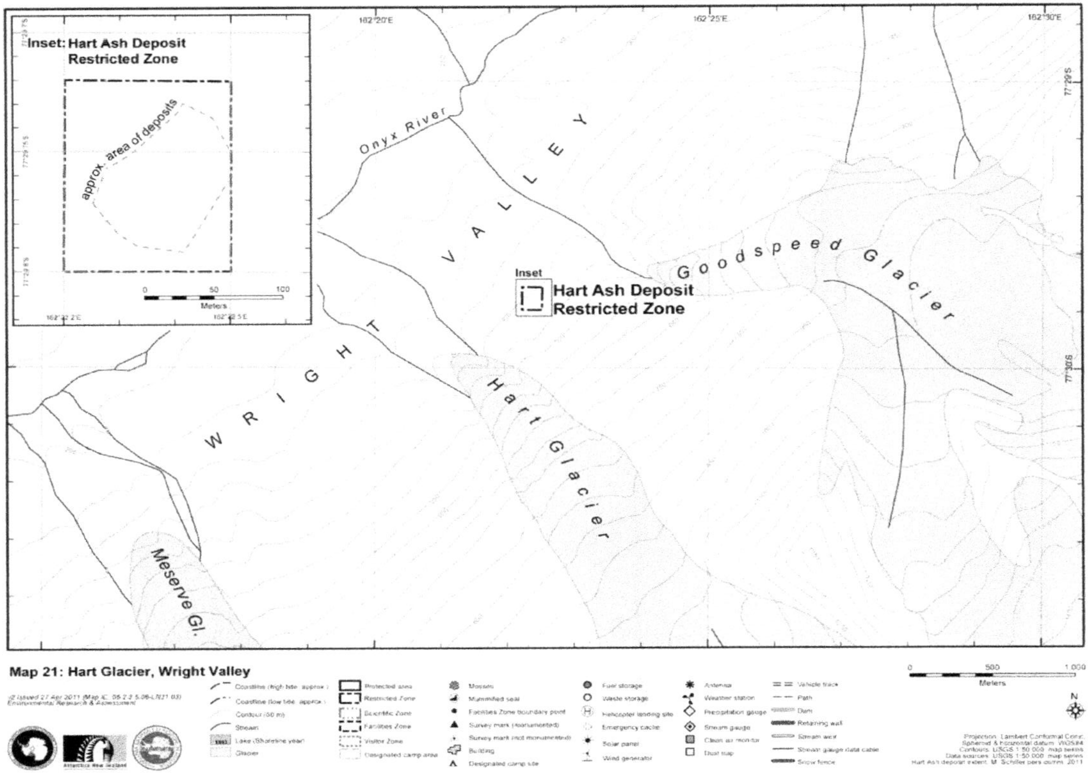
Inset: Hart Ash Deposit
Restricted Zone
approx. area of deposits
Meters
162°20'E
162°25'E
162°30'E
77°29'S
77°30'S
Onyx River
WRIGHT VALLEY
Inset
Hart Ash Deposit
Restricted Zone
Goodspeed Glacier
Hart Glacier
Meserve Gl.
Meters
N

**Map 21: Hart Glacier, Wright Valley**

# Restricted Zone
## Victoria Valley Sand Dunes
### Location
In two main groups between Lake Vida and Victoria Lower Glacier, ~ 1 km south from the Packard Glacier terminus, Victoria Valley:
77° 22.19' S, 162° 12.45' E

### Purpose
To avoid damage to the sand dune system, which is fragile and of high scientific value.

*Victoria Valley sand dunes (eastern group below Packard Glacier) H. McGowan, Antarctica NZ Pictorial Collection (Dec 2004).*

### Description   Zone area: 3.16 km²

The extensive Victoria Valley sand dune system is comprised of two distinctive areas made up of crescent-, transverse- and whaleback-shaped dunes and numerous sand mounds (Map 22). The largest group of dunes in the west extends over ~6 km and ranges between 200 to 800 m wide, with a total area of ~1.9 km². The smaller group of dunes in the east, which is bisected by Packard Stream and bounded to the south by Kite Stream, extends over ~3 km and ranges between 300 to 600 m wide with a total area of ~1.3 km². The source of sediment is from the surface and margins of the Victoria Lower Glacier and from ground moraine, which are transported west toward Lake Vida by the dominant easterly wind and meltwater streams. It is the only area where major eolian sand depositional forms occur in Antarctica. The dunes differ from the usual desert and coastal formations because the sand in the dunes is interbedded with compacted snow and contains permafrost.

### Boundaries
The Restricted Zone boundary is defined by the outer extent of the main sand dune system in Victoria Valley, which extends in two groups for a distance of ~9 km with a width from varying from 200 to 800 m (Map 22).

### Impacts
| | |
|---|---|
| KNOWN IMPACTS | None |
| POTENTIAL IMPACTS | A thin surface layer of the sand dunes is mobile and dynamic. Damage or disruption to the internal permafrost of the dunes, can affect the integrity of the sand dune structure. |

### Access requirements
| | |
|---|---|
| HELICOPTER ACCESS | Helicopters should avoid landing within the Restricted Zone and avoid overflight below 50 m above ground level. |
| SURFACE ACCESS | Access to and movement within the Restricted Zone should be on foot. |

### Special site guidance
- Avoid walking through the dunes unless necessary for scientific or management purposes.
- Walk carefully to minimize disturbance to the sensitive dune surfaces and slopes. Avoid disturbing the internal permafrost and structure of the sand dunes.
- Camping is not permitted within the Restricted Zone.

### Key references
Lindsay, J.F. 1973. Reversing barchans dunes in Lower Victoria Valley, Antarctica. *Geological Society of America Bulletin* **84**: 1799-1806.

Calkin, P.E. & Rutford, R.H. 1974. The sand dunes of Victoria Valley, Antarctica. *The Geographical Review* **64**(2): 189-216.

Selby, M.J., Rains, R.B. & Palmer, R.W.P. 1974. Eolian deposits of the ice-free Victoria Valley, Southern Victoria Land, Antarctica. *New Zealand Journal of Geology and Geophysics* **17**(3): 543-62.

Speirs, H.C., McGowan, J.A. & Neil, D.T. 2008. Meteorological controls on sand transport and dune morphology in a polar-desert: Victoria Valley, Antarctica. *Earth Surface Processes and Landforms* **33**: 1875-91.

### Site Map – Map 22

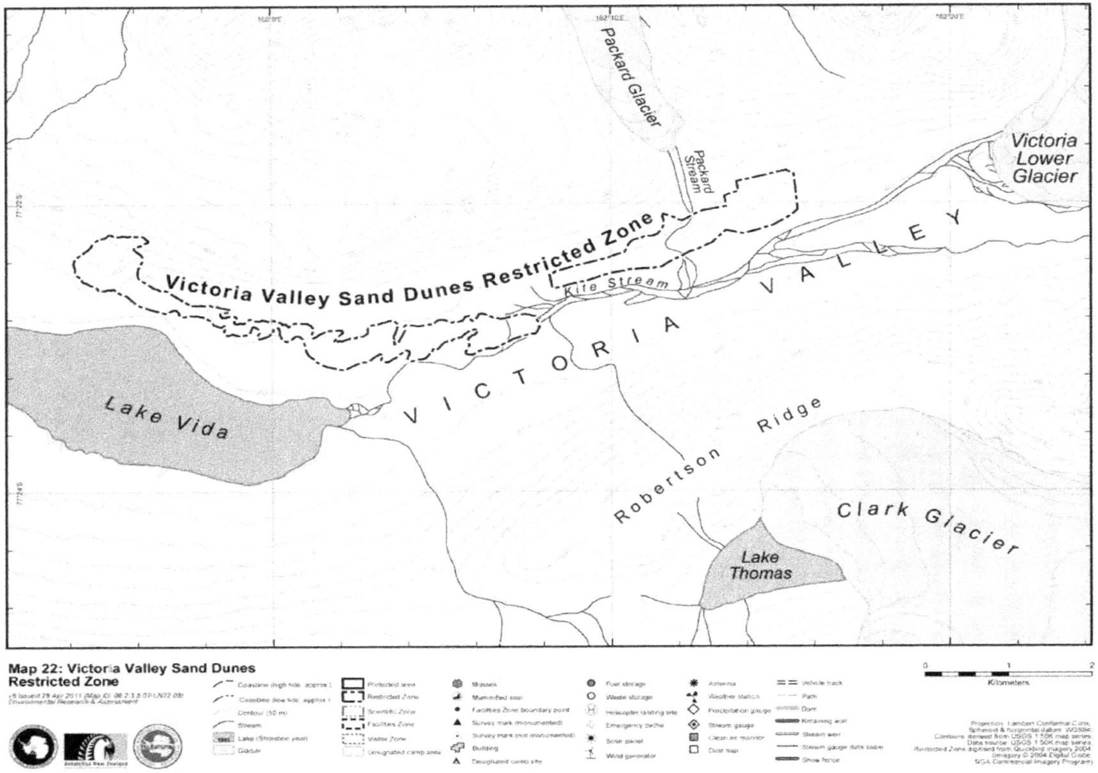

**Map 22: Victoria Valley Sand Dunes Restricted Zone**

# Restricted Zone
## Battleship Promontory

**Location**
Southwest Alatna Valley, Convoy Range,
~1 km west of Benson Glacier:
76° 55.17' S, 161° 02.77' E

**Purpose**
To avoid damage to the fragile sandstone rock formations that host microbial communities, and to ensure aesthetic and wilderness values of the site are maintained.

*a) Aerial from Alatna Valley. b) from Cargo Pond.*
*C. Harris, ERA / USAP (16 Dec 2009)*

**Description**     **Zone area:** 4.31 km²

Battleship Promontory is an area of dramatic Beacon Sandstone outcrops rising from the southwestern floor of Alatna Valley, near Cargo Pond (Map 23). The cliff formation is ~5 km in length, and extends over an area of between 0.4 – 1.2 km in width. The promontory stands ~300 m in height at an elevation of between ~900-1200 m in the west and ~1050-1350 m in the east. The russet and white sandstone outcrops are deeply weathered into striking spires, ledges and eroded gully formations, into which dark boulders and sediments have accumulated from the overlying dolerite as it weathers from above. The environment hosts rich microbial communities, including lichens, cyanobacteria, non-photosynthetic bacteria, and fungi, with the highest microbial biodiversity yet recorded in the Dry Valleys. Cryptoendolithic microbial communities live in pore spaces within the sandstone rock, and comprise lichens and cyanobacteria growing to depths of up to 10 mm beneath the surface. These communities are extremely slow-growing, and the rocks in which they live are susceptible to breakage.

**Boundaries**
The Restricted Zone boundaries encompass the main area of sandstone outcrops at Battleship Promontory, extending from and including several small lakes present the foot of the formation, to its maximum upper extent (Map 23).

**Impacts**

KNOWN IMPACTS           Small instruments have previously been installed in rocks for *in situ* measurements, and a small quantity of rock samples collected. The designated helicopter landing site is marked by cloth flags weighed down by rocks, some of which were selected to ensure they were not used by subsequent scientists because they were modified by an early experiment (E. Friedmann, pers. comm. 1994). Air safety smoke canisters have been released at the site, causing localized contamination, a practice discontinued in the 1990s.

POTENTIAL IMPACTS       Breakage of fragile rock formations, over-sampling, introduction of non-native species.

**Access requirements**

HELICOPTER ACCESS       Helicopters should land at the designated site at: 76° 55.35' S, 161° 04.80' E (1296 m). If access is required to the base of the cliffs, or parts of the zone that are impractical to reach on foot, helicopters should avoid landing on sandstone surfaces or on lakes / ponds.

SURFACE ACCESS          Movement within the Restricted Zone should be on foot.

**Special site guidance**

- Walk carefully to minimize disturbance, avoid moving rocks and boulders, and do not break the fragile sandstone rock formations.
- Camping within the Restricted Zone should be at the site previously used, which is adjacent to the designated helicopter landing site at 76° 55.31' S, 161° 04.80' E (1294 m).

**Key references**

Friedmann, E.I., Hua, M.S., Ocampo-Friedmann, R. 1988. Cryptoendolithic lichen and cyanobacterial communities of the Ross Desert, Antarctica. *Polarforschung* **58**: 251-59.

Johnston, C.G. & Vestal, J.R. 1991. Photosynthetic carbon incorporation and turnover in Antarctic cryptoendolithic microbial communities: are they the slowest-growing communities on Earth? *Applied & Environmental Microbiology* **57**(8): 2308-11.

**Site Map** – Map 23

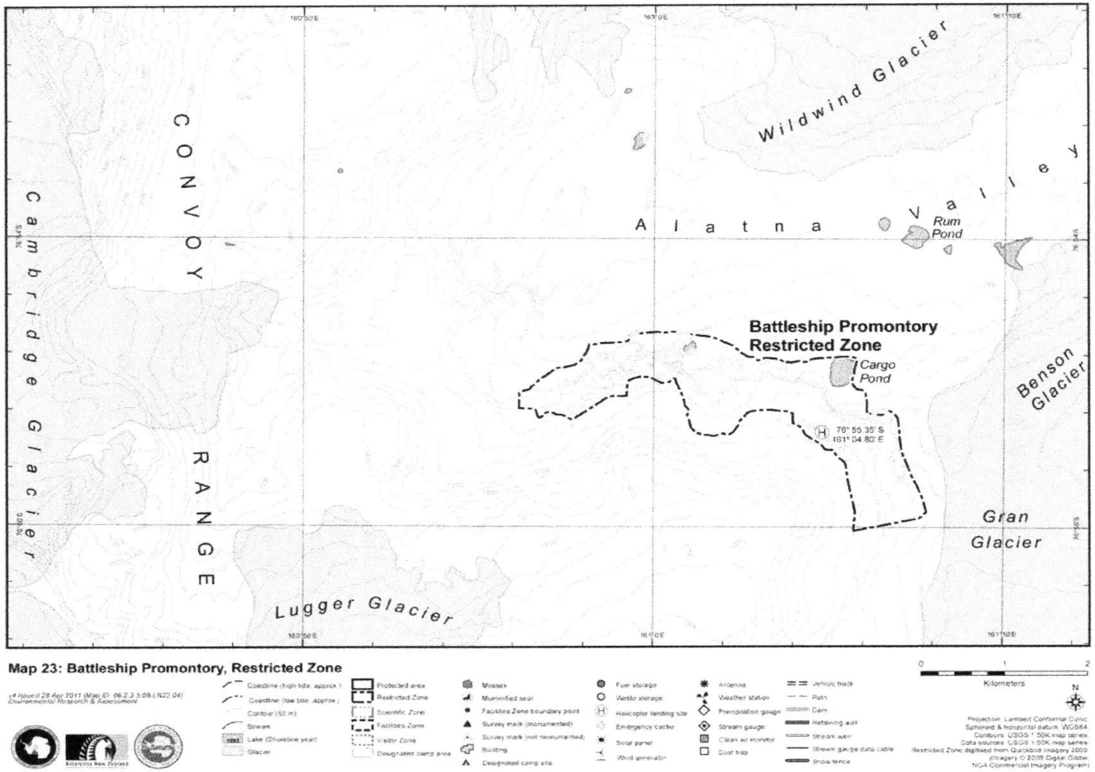

**Map 23: Battleship Promontory, Restricted Zone**

## *APPENDIX F:*

### *Guidelines for Visitor Zones*

The following site within the Area is designated a Visitor Zone:

- Taylor Valley

The Visitor Zone is located in the lower Taylor Valley near Canada Glacier. The location, boundaries, helicopter landing site, and features at the Visitor Zone are shown in Map 24.

The boundary of the Visitor Zone is defined as follows: proceeding in a clockwise direction from the northern limit of the zone on a low hill at 77° 37.523' S, 163° 03.189' E, the boundary extends 225 m southeast, past the designated helicopter landing site, to a point in moraine soils at 77° 37.609' S, 163° 03.585' E, thence extends 175 m southward ascending the summit of a small hill (elevation 60 m) at 77° 37.702' S, 163° 03.512' E. From this small hill, the boundary extends northwest 305 m towards and beyond a second small hill (summit elevation 56 m, marked nearby with a rock cairn and old survey marker), following a line ~30 m south of the main ridge joining the two hills, directly to a point on the western ridge of this second small hill at 77° 37.637' S, 163° 02.808' E. From this ridge, the boundary extends northeast 80 m directly to the western face of a prominent boulder located at 77° 37.603' S, 163° 02.933' E, which is ~70 m northwest from the cairn on the hill. The boundary thence extends northeast 130 m, descending parallel with the designated walking track (which follows a low moraine ridge) to a point near Bowles Creek at 77° 37.531' S, 163° 03.031' E. A mummified (dessicated seal) is located here, adjacent to a small area of mosses. The boundary thence extends eastward 65 m to return to the northern limit of the zone at 77° 37.523' S, 163° 03.189' E.

Special guidelines for activities within the Visitor Zone include that:

- Tour operators should ensure that all visitors to the Visitor Zone for which they are responsible have clean boots and equipment before visiting the site;
- Tour expedition helicopter landings should be made at the designated landing site at 77° 37.588' S, 163° 03.419' E (elevation 34 m);
- Tour operators should ensure that foot tracks within the Visitor Zone are clearly marked and that visitors stay on those routes. Markers used to mark tourist routes and sites of interest should be installed securely and removed at the end of each visit;
- Tents should only be erected at the designated tent site for health and safety reasons, and tour groups should not camp in the Visitor Zone except for reasons of safety;
- Tourist movement within the Visitor Zone should be conducted in small, guided groups;
- Stream and pond beds should be avoided; and
- Activities planned for and conducted within the Visitor Zone should be in accordance with ATCM Recommendation XVIII-1.

Further site-specific guidelines for the conduct of activities within the Visitor Zone are attached as the Antarctic Treaty Visitor Site Guide: Taylor Valley, Southern Victoria Land, Ross Sea (submitted as ATCM XXXIV WPXX).

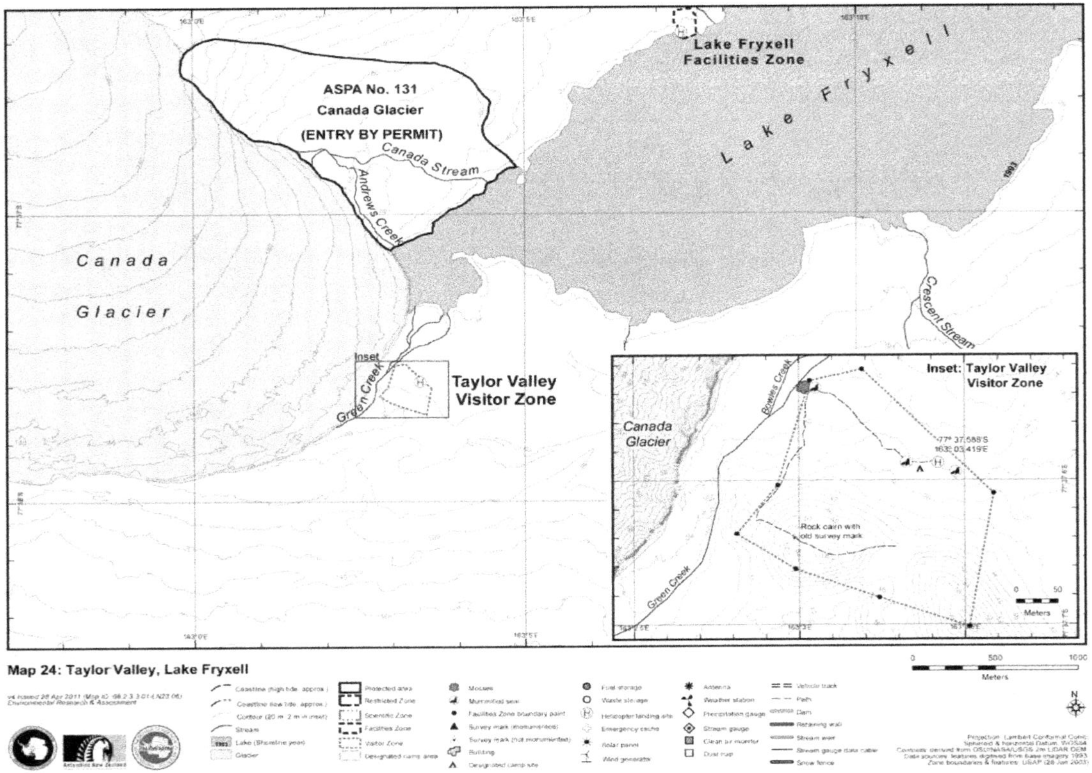

Map 24: Taylor Valley, Lake Fryxell

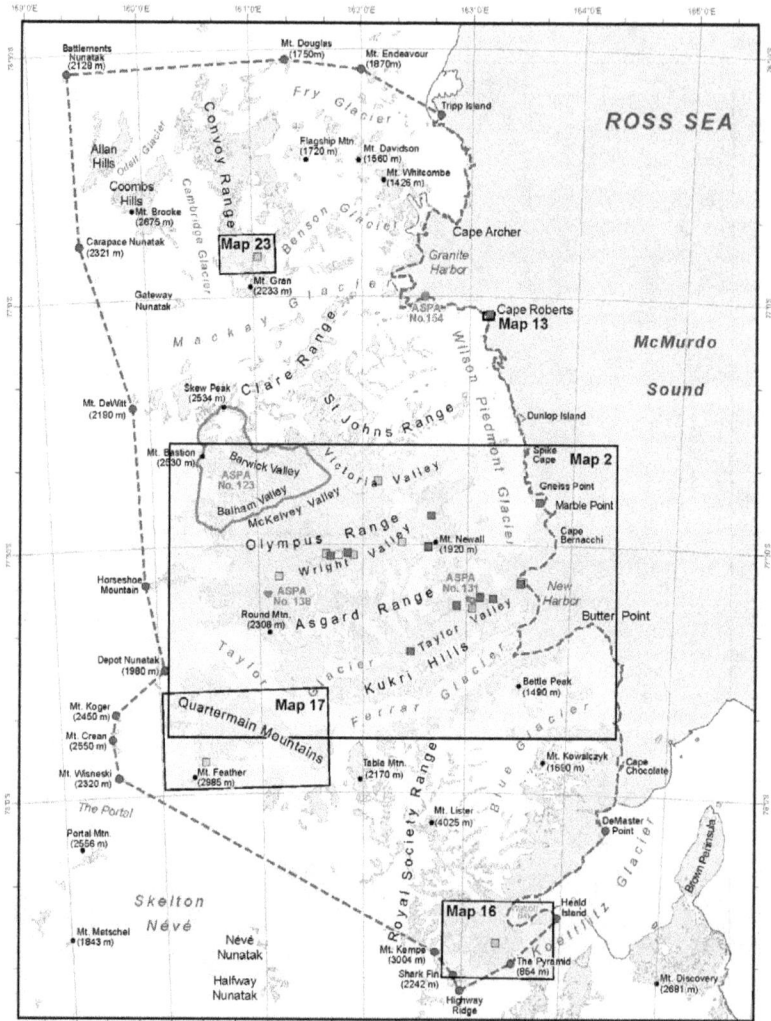

**Map 1: Overview**
**ASMA No. 2 McMurdo Dry Valleys: boundary & zones**

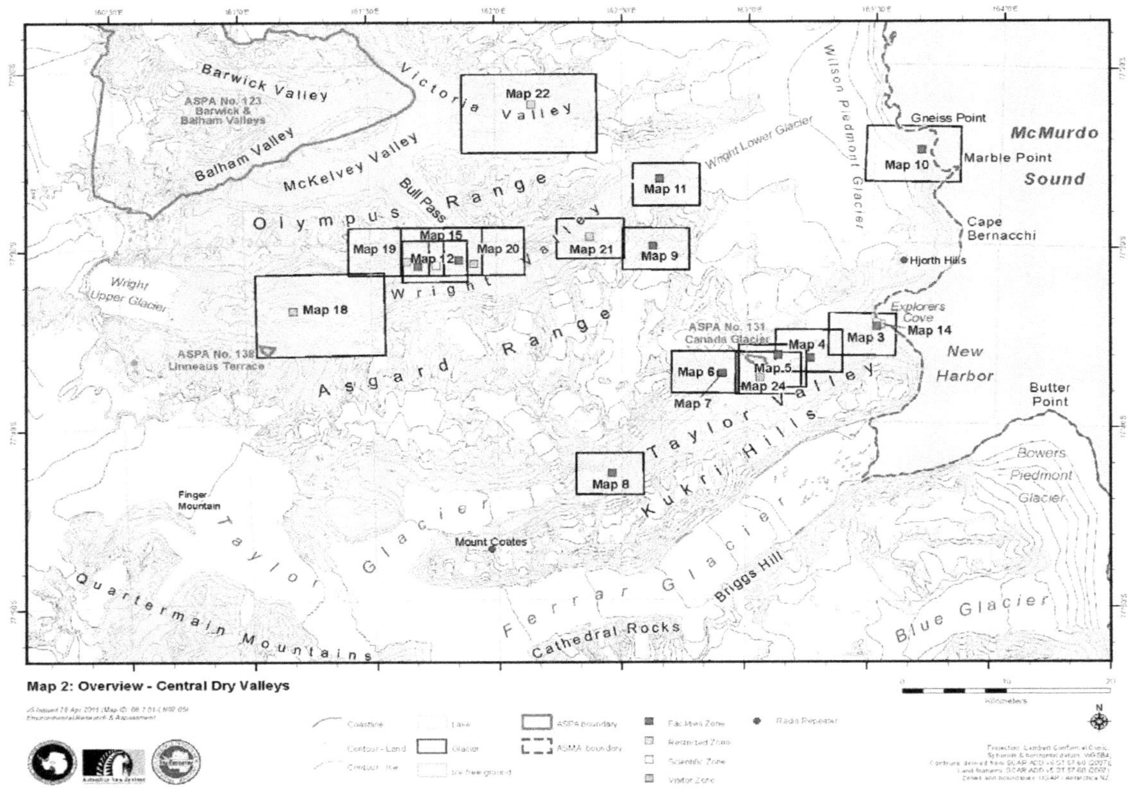

**Map 2: Overview - Central Dry Valleys**

# PART III

**Opening and Closing Addresses and Reports from ATCM XXIV**

# 1. Statements at the Session on Commemoration of the 50th Anniversary of the entry into force of the Antarctic Treaty

**Statement by Hector Timerman, Minister of Foreign Relations, International Trade and Worship of Argentina**

Foreign Ministers of the Republic of Chile and the Oriental Republic of Uruguay, Special Representatives and Delegates to the 34th Antarctic Treaty Consultative Meeting:

Argentina hosted the Antarctic Treaty Consultative Meeting in 1962 and 1981. Today, for the third time since its entry into force, on 23rd June 1961, we enjoy this great privilege once again.

Argentina is one of the 12 original signatory States to the Antarctic Treaty, which currently includes 48 State Parties. Using creativity and imagination, this instrument has made it possible to establish a legal framework enabling the development of scientific research and the protection of the vast Antarctic continent, against a background of peace and international cooperation.

This cooperation has so far always relied on a strong respect for the consensus principle, as a basis for the decision-making mechanism governing Consultative Meetings.

It is an honour for me to share this significant event with all of you, for the celebration of the 50th anniversary of the entry into force of the Antarctic Treaty. The permanence and efficacy of this international legal instrument demand that we give special recognition to all those involved in its drafting, and those who have worked throughout this last half century in order to consolidate its success.

In line with its principles and purposes, the Antarctic Treaty has made it possible to turn all the continent into a region of peace, science and cooperation, and into a representative example of how States can, united by a common goal, join their efforts and cooperate for the development of science and the protection of the environment in a continent whose preservation is essential to the lives of every inhabitant of this planet.

Allow me to reaffirm that the Argentine Republic is fully committed to the promotion of these principles and purposes.

By promoting the study and development of scientific knowledge in Antarctica, Argentina is committed to protecting the continent, confident that the best way to do so is through deep knowledge and increasing awareness of the unique conditions and special features of the region.

For the last 107 years, my country has enjoyed the privilege of operating the oldest permanent research station in Antarctica, the Orcadas Base. Established in 1904, it was for decades the only permanent station on Antarctic soil. Ever since, it has supplied meteorological data essential to much of the work performed at present in connection with climate change and global warming.

Likewise, the Argentine Antarctic Institute, established on 17th April 1951, was the first body in the world exclusively devoted to Antarctic research. Since then, it has conducted scientific research in Antarctica through its own highly specialised staff and in cooperation with the most renowned national and international scientific and academic institutions, upholding the paramount goals of gaining knowledge of Antarctica and protecting both the region and its resources, for the well being of all mankind.

The Argentine Republic has been consistent in its historical vision, as science has always played a key role in our activities in Antarctica, as well as in our efforts to preserve the environment and the resources in this continent.

In recent years the National Government has endorsed these policies through material actions, such as a significant increase in the number of Antarctic scientists and technicians, improvements and new facilities to enhance the Antarctic infrastructure, the implementation of alternative sources of energy to reduce the use of fossil fuels, and strict compliance with environmental protection measures.

The National Policy provides for the permanent upgrading of bases and for improvements in logistics, for better international cooperation in scientific research, technology and art projects. In this respect, projects with the active involvement of foreign researchers account for almost 60% of the work undertaken during the last Antarctic campaign, and current Argentine scientific stations have served as an excellent platform for the work we hope to improve in the future.

ATCM XXXIV Final Report

The redesigning and upgrading of the Almirante Irizar icebreaker in national shipyards will offer a modern platform, suitable for research in areas such as oceanography, biology and marine geology among other disciplines, and measures for the conservation of the Antarctic environment will be further streamlined.

The spirit of peace and international cooperation was what originally characterized the creation and entry into force of the Antarctic Treaty and the subsequent development of instruments that make up the whole system. This continues to be the basis of its current effectiveness. These first 50 years have clearly evidenced the irrefutable value of these instruments, achieved through consensus at a certain time in history, for the international community as well as for future generations.

Antarctica demands all our full respect. We must preserve its environment, its flora and fauna, gaining a deeper knowledge about it while creating awareness of its aesthetic values. The Parties have provided enough proof of the significance attached to these objectives during the first fifty years of the life of the Treaty. Today, the celebration of this anniversary in an atmosphere of peace and international cooperation is the best possible starting point to increase our efforts in the field of science and to protect the Antarctic environment, thus facing the challenges foreseen for the next decades and addressing them jointly as we have done so far.

Thank you very much.

## Statement by Alfredo Moreno Charme, Minister of Foreign Affairs of Chile

Ministers of Foreign Affairs of Argentina and Uruguay

Mr. Ariel Manzi, Chair of the meeting

Mr. Manfred Reinke, Executive Secretary of the Antarctic Treaty

Delegates and participants to this meeting

It is a great honour for me to have the opportunity to be present at the 34th Antarctic Treaty Consultative Meeting. Today, not only are we celebrating the annual meeting of the 48 States Parties gathered to discuss the Antarctic agenda, but we are also here to commemorate the 50 years during which the Antarctic Treaty has been in force. On June 23$^{rd}$, 1961, Argentina, Australia and Chile jointly submitted their ratifications which, in addition to those already presented by the United Kingdom, South Africa, Belgium, Japan, the United States, Norway, France, New Zealand and Russia, allowed this instrument to come into effect.

Prior to its signature in Washington, the Antarctic Treaty negotiation stage involved much more than 45 days of discussions. It was a complex task and there were clearly diverging political interests. Nevertheless, each of the twelve countries signatory to the Antarctic Treaty was able to compromise, and helped build a delicate political and legal balance. The signing of the Antarctic Treaty was an example of how, in spite of an adverse international context in the middle of the Cold War, challenges can be faced and overcome together.

As one of the 12 signatory countries, Chile played an important role in developing this agreement, as well as in the discussions and subsequent drafting. Ambassador Oscar Pinochet de la Barra, who is 91 today, and who was present for the subscription of this Treaty, stands out in this respect. He still shares his memories and experience of the principles and objectives that led to the agreements reached within this international instrument.

The Antarctic Treaty entailed a change of the existing paradigms. The climate of competition during the first half of the twentieth century gave way to an environment that favors collaboration between its members. Today, the Antarctic is a continent used exclusively for peaceful purposes. It is the only zone free of nuclear weapons in the world.

This Treaty has been, without doubt, a landmark agreement in many ways. The system has allowed the Contracting Parties to manage the territory collectively, without recourse to international arbitration yet without renouncing existing disputes, consensus being always the fundamental principle of all the decisions adopted. This concept is the key to the whole system, and even if it doesn't always permit us to go forward with sufficient speed, it lends a special legitimacy to all the recommendations, measures y decisions emanating from the System.

During these five decades, the Antarctic System has been developed on the basis of a commonality of national and international interests. This has allowed the merging of values such as scientific cooperation and peace with national interests. The stability of the System is demonstrated by the fact that not once during its application has any State taken a position which might endanger the Antarctic regime. However, this does not mean a permanent stability is guaranteed. During the 80's, the issue of mineral exploitation in the Antarctic generated a lot of discussion, as much within the System as without. This issue was resolved by prohibiting the exploration and exploitation of mineral resources in the Antarctic. The adoption of the Protocol on Environmental Protection to the Antarctic Treaty was a significant diplomatic success for Chile, in view of the important role it played as negotiator at the Eleventh Special Consultative Meeting in Viña del Mar and its leading role at the Madrid negotiations.

In a world of complex interdependence and scarce resources, the preservation of the Antarctic as a natural reserve, devoted to peace and science, with values and interests shared by all Parties, must strengthen the commitment of each Party to the System, and favor the common interest over the interests of each individual State.

Half a century after the signature of the Antarctic Treaty, it is clear that the development of the System which this legal instrument has made possible deserves the highest praise. The principles and objectives that inspired the diplomats who participated in the Antarctic Treaty negotiation process are still valid. They were instrumental in ensuring that the Antarctic continent is devoted to peace and science, without foregoing any sovereign rights.

Chile considers that the Antarctic Treaty and its System must be broadened and reinforced, as appears in our recently approved Antarctic Strategic Plan 2011-2014. In the face of global pollution and climate change, the Antarctic must be safeguarded, and preserved as our gift to future generations.

Scientific research has been and must continue to be the principal activity in the Antarctic. During the last decades, we have observed a significant increase in research projects, enabling even greater cooperation at international level and generating progress in areas such as biotechnology. Our country is following this trend. The projects undertaken by the Chilean Antarctic Institute have grown qualitatively and quantitatively, and involve joint work between a large number of countries. Currently, through its Antarctic capacities, Chile is able to offer logistic support to other Antarctic Treaty members, especially those who are developing projects in the Antarctic Peninsula zone.

Finally, may I use this opportunity to offer my sincere gratitude for the homage paid in this meeting to Ambassador Jorge Berguño, known to many of you, who recently passed away, and will be remembered with great affection. Mr. Jorge played a prominent role in the Antarctic Treaty System, not only as Head of the Delegation of Chile for many years, but also as a tireless contributor to the drafting of several Antarctic System instruments, especially the Protocol on Environmental Protection. His departure is a loss not only for Chile, but also for all those who have dedicated part of their lives to Antarctica.

Thank you very much.

## Statement by Luis Almagro Lemes, Minister of Foreign Affairs of Uruguay

Thank you President.

President of the thirty-fourth Antarctic Treaty Consultative Meeting,

Ambassador ARIEL MANZI.

Minister of Foreign Relations, International Trade and Cults of the

Argentine Republic, Mr. HECTOR TIMERMAN.

Minister of Foreign Relations of the Republic of Chile. Mr. LUIS MORENO

Executive Secretary of the Antarctic Treaty, Mr. MANFRED REINKE

Secretary of the Host Country, Minister JORGE ROBALLO,

Special Representatives, Delegates, Representatives of International Organizations.

Let me start by thanking and congratulating the Argentinean Government for hosting this meeting, which every year brings together this special group of countries committed to the protection of the continent of Antarctica and its use for peaceful ends, inspired this year with a special significance.

Let me also salute the Executive Secretariat of the Treaty, which, although it has been constituted in Buenos Aires for several years, is being officially inaugurated at this Meeting, after a prolonged negotiation process which ended last year on the occasion of the thirty-third Consultative Meeting, which my country had the honour of organizing.

Ministers, Delegates,

This thirty-fourth Antarctic Treaty Consultative Meeting is framed, as I have said, in particular circumstances on which I would like to comment and which constitute, in some sense, milestones in the history of Antarctica.

The first circumstance that I would like to mention is the commemoration, today, of the fiftieth anniversary of the entry into force of the Antarctic Treaty. The twelve Founder Members who gave birth to that generous effort of cooperation and understanding between men, in the world as it then existed of mistrust and confrontation, today number almost fifty, all committed to the preservation of the continent of Antarctica for carrying out scientific activities, free of any warlike activity. My country identifies fully with this focus, inscribed in the founding principles of the Charter of the United Nations, along with defence of international peace and security.

Today the world has changed to an extent that would have been hard to imagine five decades ago; we face new threats, and we are supported by new allies. In the face of the terrible effects of climate change, the depletion of the ozone layer, and global warming, modern developments are constantly opening new doors on the complex structure of scientific research. The scope of biotechnology, oceanography or atmospheric sciences, together with the extraordinary technological progress which has revolutionised the scientific world in recent years, encourage the hope that the activities carried on in Antarctica will provide a valuable contribution to the protection and preservation of the planet for future generations.

The second circumstance on which I would like to remark is the fact that we are also celebrating the twentieth anniversary of the opening for signature of the Madrid Protocol on Environmental Protection to the Antarctic Treaty. This Protocol has proved an effective instrument for consolidating the environmental objectives of the Antarctic Treaty, making it easier to establish limits to the possible negative repercussions of the activities carried on in the Antarctic environment and in the dependent and associated ecosystems.

My country is a firm promoter of environmental measures for the protection of Antarctica, and in this context it exhorts all those Treaty Members who have not yet ratified that Protocol to assume this commitment with determination, which is fundamental for the fulfilment of the objectives of the Treaty.

We have learnt much in recent decades about the harmful effects of human activity on the environment. In Antarctica, if we act with responsibility and commitment, we have an opportunity to mitigate those effects, and to avoid them in future, in the consciousness that our actions today will tomorrow affect this whole ecosystem which we are responsible for protecting.

Ministers, Delegates,

This Meeting is also held in the context of particular events which represent historical milestones for my country. Uruguay has been associated with the history of the Treaty as a Consultative Member for twenty-five years; that anniversary coincided last year with the organization of the thirty-third Consultative Meeting.

It is no small matter for the country which I represent to have trodden that long road. But this very circumstance obliges it today to review this history and project its future in the coming years.

Today, Uruguay faces the challenge of strengthening and expanding its participation in Antarctic activities, based on the two fundamental pillars of scientific research, and the protection and preservation of the Antarctic environment.

In this respect, my country is committed to a process of adapting its national institutions in order to continue to endow the executive organ of national policy in this area, the Uruguayan Antarctic Institute, with the human and material resources necessary to carry out more efficiently its proposed research activities.

In this context, Uruguay believes that the firm commitment of Members to deepen bilateral and multilateral cooperation in the different areas of Antarctic research, and the exchange of information for protection of the Antarctic environment, is fundamental; and will continue to promote cooperation agreements with other Members, in total compliance with the spirit and the letter of the Treaty.

There is one more ephemeral point which I must also mention, which marks the Antarctic vocation of Uruguay, while referring to the solidarity and courage of its men. This month is the ninety-fifth anniversary of the first incursion of a Uruguayan ship into Antarctic waters. On 9 June 1916, a small iron-hulled ship, under the command of Lieutenant Ruperto Elichiribehety, set sail to rescue the sailors of the British ship "Endurance", trapped on Elephant Island, who were finally rescued, after three frustrated attempts, by their captain, Ernest Shackleton. Although the expedition did not achieve its object, it was the decisive motive for a Uruguayan ship to sail, for the first time, to latitude 60 degrees south.

Ministers, Delegates,

The challenges facing the Antarctic Treaty in the next fifty years are not the same as those which gave rise to its existence. But what must be the same are the manner and spirit with which we confront them in order to solve them. Let us be guided always by the mandate of History, to conserve the Antarctic Continent free of all conflict; to preserve its use for peaceful ends, based on cooperation and free scientific research; and to protect and conserve its ecosystems.

Thank you very much.

## Statement by Ambassador Luiz Alberto Figueiredo Machado, Under Secretary of Environment, Energy, Science and Technology, Ministry of Foreign Relations of Brazil

Chancellor Héctor Timerman,

Ministers,

President of the XXXIV Antarctic Treaty Consultative Meeting,

Delegates,

It is a great pleasure for me to attend, in the name of the Minister of Foreign Relations, Ambassador Antonio Patriota, this ceremony to celebrate the 50th anniversary of the entry into force of the Antarctic Treaty, here in the charming city of Buenos Aires.

I congratulate the Argentinean Government, our neighbour, comrade, partner and ally in the construction of MERCOSUR, and the Secretariat of the Antarctic Treaty, for all their hard work to ensure the success of this meeting.

Ladies and Gentlemen,

Brazil signed the Antarctic Treaty in 1975. Its first expedition to Antarctica took place in 1982. The success of this operation led, in 1983, to the acceptance of Brazil as a Consultative Party to the Antarctic Treaty. Since then, Brazil has participated fully in the decision-making processes of the Treaty and in developing the legal regime for human activities in the region.

The decision to take part in scientific and exploration activities in Antarctica represented an important challenge for the country. With Operation Antarctica XXX, which will start next October, Brazil will complete 30 years of uninterrupted presence in Antarctica, a clear demonstration of the consolidation of the Brazilian Antarctic Programme. Our commemoration of the 50th anniversary of the Treaty, and 30 years of Brazilian presence in Antarctica, reinforces our responsibility and our commitment to the principles of the Antarctic Treaty System.

The logistical basis for carrying out research in Antarctica has been perfected. In recent years, Brazil has purchased the Antarctic vessel "Almirante Maximiano", fitted with modern scientific installations, and it continues to operate the oceanographic support vessel "Ary Rongel". It has refurbished and extended the Comandante Ferraz Antarctic Station, where it is installing a modern Environment Management system, based on the Madrid Protocol, to minimize the impacts of human activity.

The Antarctic region is an essential component of the world's climatic and environmental system. It exercises a profound influence on global climate, and consequently on ecosystems and life on earth. The western part of the Antarctic continent, where the Brazilian base is located, is the part of Antarctica which suffers the impacts of climate change most quickly. Atmospheric, oceanic and cryospheric processes which occur there have a direct effect on the climate in South America. Brazilian Antarctic research aims to understand those processes and their interaction with the phenomena which occur in Brazil, while at the same time focusing on study of the Antarctic environment, which is unique on the planet.

In recent years the Brazilian Government has increased the allocation of funds for research, allowing a significant increase in Brazilian scientific activities in Antarctica. This was evident in the IV International Polar Year, in which there was strong participation by Brazilian scientists.

Ladies and Gentlemen,

Today, as we celebrate the fiftieth anniversary of the entry into force of the Antarctic Treaty, it is worth remembering the scope of the discussions and the difficulty of the negotiations which led to the signing of the Treaty. The adoption of this regime was possible only with the demilitarization of the continent, and the skilful solution to territorial issues found in Article IV of the Treaty.

From an agreement motivated essentially by questions of strategy and security, it was possible to develop a network of international standards and agreements to make use of and conserve natural resources. It was further possible, through the Madrid Protocol, to develop a broad regime for environmental protection, which declares Antarctica to be "a natural reserve, devoted to peace and science".

Brazil supports the Declaration on Antarctic Cooperation which we have approved today, in all its dimensions. It is a declaration which celebrates the important victories won in these 50 years that the Antarctic Treaty has been in force.

To conclude, I would like to say that the greatest merit of the Treaty, which reflects very well its historic importance, is to have created a space for peace and cooperation directed towards scientific research, thus constituting a unique example of interaction between States.

Thank you very much.

## Statement by Michel Rocard, Special Representative for France

The signing of the Antarctic Treaty did not seem like an important event at the time and was of interest to few people. Yet over the years, the importance of what had just been created has become increasingly apparent.

As we celebrate, not without pride, the 50th Anniversary of the implementation of the Treaty, we must take a look at the world around us. During the 21st century, in other words for the last 11 years, all major international negotiations have failed, and this is also true of those which had begun during the 20th century, the Oslo peace talks, the Doha Development Round and the negotiations on climate change.

Amidst all this, the Antarctic Treaty stands firm. The 34th Antarctic Treaty Consultative Meeting (ATCM XXXIV) is now under way, bringing together 28 Consultative Parties to the Treaty. Within a peaceful and familiar framework, we will be discussing and voting on a number of resolutions. The world's only global commons is being managed peacefully, and whilst nothing else succeeds, as nations fail in their renewed efforts to regulate banking and finance, or in struggling to contain the greenhouse effect, this joint management of the Antarctic appears all the more exemplary.

This Treaty is indeed expanding and growing. The whole world is now faced with major environmental concerns. Biodiversity is under threat, pollution is choking the natural environment and destroying many of our living spaces.

In Antarctica, the Treaty has enabled countries to agree on important precautionary measures much more easily than in other regions. 1972 saw the conclusion of an agreement for the conservation of seals, followed in 1980 by an agreement for the conservation of marine flora and fauna. I am not sure these agreements could have been signed under the framework treaty of 1959.

But as a result, Antarctica has now become the object of peaceful exchanges. Nevertheless, minds change but slowly, and distrust recedes only with time. The demilitarisation of the Antarctic by the Treaty has changed the mindset of those countries involved, but it has been a slow process. Thirteen years went by between the signing of the Treaty and the first Protocol, which only deals with seals, and therefore not a great strategic commitment. It took another eight years to conclude the second Protocol, which only relates to marine flora and fauna. Still not a great strategic commitment. It took 21 years in all before more important issues could be broached.

The Wellington Agreement was intended to regulate the exploitation of mineral resources, iron, gas, oil and other resources. But how is it possible to reconcile environmental conservation and exploitation of those resources? A good document was produced and signed in 1988.

But the world had changed. Environmental political movements had multiplied and the expectations were much greater. Two prime ministers linked by their friendship, Robert Hawke from Australia and myself, announced they would not submit this convention to their respective parliaments for ratification and asked for much more ambitious negotiations to be set up. They were quickly followed by Italy and Belgium, then by Norway. The American Senate put pressure on the US President.

And lo and behold, a third Protocol to the Treaty was signed in Madrid in October 1991. It declared that Antarctica was « devoted to peace and science »« in the interest of mankind as a whole » and designated it as a natural reserve in which any activity relating to mineral resources shall be prohibited. Throughout its many pages, the Protocol sets out a code of environmental practices, and strengthens the management of the Treaty with a Committee for Environmental Protection, which meets at the same time as the Treaty's Council. You have just elected its President, my friend Yves Frenot.

This is a completely new venture. The whole world has joined together for the environmental management of part of its land surface. And it works. The tour operators grouped under the IAATO umbrella have become watchful guardians of the Protocol.

The beginnings of this growing global legal system, which now shines bright as it celebrates its 50th anniversary at a time when all attempts in the rest of the world are failing, is a major milestone. The system is indeed destined to grow and spread.

Here is my first example. A small incident with potentially huge effects. Two (French, unfortunately) sailors landed, celebrated and became rather drunk. They then smashed and damaged the hut known as *Wordie House*, designated as Antarctic Heritage. Attempts have been made since this incident to find ways to prosecute.

My second example is much more serious. In a few years time, countries and publicly owned operators will bring back to earth mineral samples from the Moon or Mars for analysis. Who will they belong to? Who will own them, and consequently who will be liable for any accidents, harmful damage or pollution which they may cause? The creation of space law is a matter of urgency. Lawyers are working on it. What has been their first task? A detailed examination of the Antarctic legal system.

Ladies and Gentlemen, this anniversary is not simply a commemoration. We are acknowledging the creation of a legal instrument which will be crucial for the human species in the years to come.

So there is one question left. How did this really happen? For those familiar with international relations, this amazing Antarctic system was clearly the result of two miracles.

First of those miracles, the Treaty itself. Let's go back to 1959, before the Cuban missile crisis. Everyone was convinced that the cold war would turn into a hot war. It was the days when civilian and military Headquarters, particularly in the United States and in Russia, would bombard their bosses with warnings that they should not trust anyone, should make high strategic demands and exert control and pressure on their counterparts.

And yet, Eisenhower and Khrushchev concluded the demilitarisation of Antarctica and a ban on all weapons in the region. It is amazing, and in my view, the history of the Treaty, in its usual form, is incomplete. What happened in the heads of those two great leaders? Which conversation led them to dispatch to the bin all the messages full of mistrust and antagonism which their generals and diplomats had sent, and sign a renouncement to military claims, a peace declaration and an agreement to sustain it.

The third Protocol is also a miracle. Our world is hungry for unlimited fishing, and desperate for gas and oil, and in the knowledge that these resources will become rare, an agreement was signed to restrict all those activities in Antarctica in order to protect them!

My friends, as delegates, we must not shroud our management of the implementation of the Treaty and of its Protocols with a discreet routine and an awkward silence. Antarctica is the place where the world has set itself a great example of collective responsibility which it cannot yet achieve anywhere else.

Let us say a loud and heartfelt Happy Birthday Antarctica!

## Statement by Ingo Winkelmann, Germany

Mr Chairman, Excellencies, distinguished delegates and colleagues,

The 50th anniversary of the entry into force of the Antarctic Treaty: we have every reason to celebrate at this year's 34th Consultative Meeting. We are grateful to our host, the Government of the Argentine Republic, for preparing this significant event, highlighted by today's celebration including a solemn Declaration agreed among States parties to the Treaty.

The Antarctic Treaty of 1959 paved the way for effective action through international cooperation. 50 years after its entry into force, the Treaty, supplemented by the 1991 Protocol on Environmental Protection, continues to provide a unique model for transnational good governance. The venue for our meeting, the Argentine capital Buenos Aires, has become home to the Treaty Secretariat.

The dramatic change in climate conditions underway at the North Pole has attracted greater attention to the Antarctic in Germany as well as throughout the world. Climate-related scientific research on the sixth continent is more important than ever. Changes in the polar climate have consequences for the climate around the world. Polar research makes a vital contribution to our understanding of past climate change, and its findings enable us to make better predictions regarding future climate change. By the same token: the effects of human intervention in the as yet largely untouched Antarctic environment are irreversible. Therefore, they must be reduced to a minimum.

This year, Germany looks back on 30 years of responsibility within the Antarctic Treaty system with a seat and a vote. Only two years ago, in 2009, Germany set up a new research station in the Antarctic. The new station, "Neumayer III", is a state-of-the-art station and has been built using environmentally-sound methods. The station is open to scientists and projects from all nations.

Germany, today and in the future, will remain unflagging in its commitment to the Treaty and to the protection of the Antarctic.

## Statement by Richard Rowe, Australia

Mr Chairman, Ministers, Distinguished Colleagues,

Successive Australian Governments have expressed a deep commitment to the Antarctic Treaty. We do so again today.

Australia takes great pride in its role in Antarctic affairs – on the ice in Antarctica and at the Antarctic Treaty Consultative Meetings. The Australian delegation is delighted to be in Buenos Aires, seat of the Treaty Secretariat, to join our Treaty partners in celebrating the 50th anniversary of the entry into force of the Antarctic Treaty.

As a people of the Southern Hemisphere, Australians are very conscious of their proximity to Antarctica. In winter, the cold air of Antarctica sweeps across our southern states and reminds us that across the ocean lies a great continent quite different from our normally hot, dry land. Our Antarctic connection comes in our climate, through the dynamics of the atmosphere and the Southern Ocean, the migrations of wildlife, and the geological continuity of Gondwana origins.

Our Antarctic connection also comes from the earliest days of discovery. The first Australian to winter in Antarctica was a scientist, a nineteenth century Tasmanian. 2011 sees Australia celebrate the centenary of Douglas Mawson's 1911-14 Australasian Antarctic Expedition – an iconic scientific expedition of the heroic era. Australia's stake in Antarctica was cemented by Mawson's return to Antarctica in 1929-31. Following formation in 1947 of Australia's permanent Antarctic program, in 1954 we established the oldest continuously operated station south of the Antarctic Circle, named in honour of Mawson. We now have three permanent stations in the Australian Antarctic Territory, multiple field camps, and the capacity for sustained research in the Southern Ocean.

As our capability has grown, so has our depth of knowledge. Increasingly our scientists are discovering critical information about Antarctica's past and present climate, and the influence that it has on Australia and the world. Such important research is undertaken in an environment that is not naturally kind to human visitors. Yet we continue to go to the Antarctic, as we have for over a century, because of the unique insights it provides into the natural world. This research will help us predict the climate of the future. For fifty years the Antarctic Treaty has allowed us the freedom to pursue such research wherever it needs to be done, and it has encouraged cooperation between the nations that engage in Antarctic science. Without the certainty that the Treaty provides, there is no doubt that work in Antarctica by Australians would be infinitely more difficult.

Our involvement in Antarctic matters is broader than science. Australia enthusiastically contributed to the negotiations that resulted in the 1959 Antarctic Treaty. As an original signatory, Australia is proud of the role it played in developing the Treaty, and the system which has evolved around it. At its core is the Treaty, devoid of complexity, elegant in its language, rich in its content. The principles of the Treaty have held up strongly and Australia celebrates the freedom of science and the commitment to peaceful use. The Antarctic Treaty shines a light on the quality of international relations where cooperation and consensus are the keys to success. We Australians consider it a privilege to work with our Treaty Party colleagues in this context.

This is an occasion to reflect on the significance of the Treaty over the last half-century and to celebrate what we have collectively achieved in that time – not only in terms of the increase in the number of Antarctic Treaty nations, but also with respect to the elaboration of the Treaty system. We now have a family of nations working cooperatively in a system that ensures peaceful use of the region. Australia is proud of its involvement in developing the instruments of the Treaty system, and the role that we have played in their implementation. We should recall that 2011 also represents the 20th anniversary of the adoption of the Protocol on Environmental Protection to the Antarctic Treaty. This was a landmark in the evolution of the Treaty system and one that now demands the greatest concentration of effort at our meetings. The Antarctic Treaty area's natural values, its place in the centre of global atmospheric and oceanographic processes, and its contribution to scientific understanding of the planet, give modern emphasis to the Treaty's obligation to work 'in the interests of all mankind'.

Fifty years ago, in 1961, Australia was pleased to host the first Antarctic Treaty Consultative Meeting in Canberra. At the opening of that meeting the Head of the Australian Delegation said:

*We are now embarking on a new voyage of exploration, a venture into uncharted territory of international cooperation. I am sure there will be the same camaraderie in this expedition as in the Antarctic itself. If crevasses of procedure or substance open up in our path, we shall be able to bridge them or, if we do slither deeply in, to crawl out without damage.*

I think I can confidently say that, after five decades, the crevasses of procedure have been few and any differences of substance have melted away in the warmth of good relations. Between us we have developed, from small beginnings, the most effective system for managing the Antarctic, and we have done this through consensus. We have established an admirably successful way of working with each other which will, I am sure, endure as we embark upon the next 50 years of close cooperation under the aegis of the Antarctic Treaty.

We particularly look forward to continuing our engagement with all Treaty Parties when we meet again, next year, at the 35th Antarctic Treaty Consultative Meeting which Australia will host in Hobart.

Thank you Mr Chairman.

## Statement of Belgium

Belgium, as original signatory of the Antarctic Treaty and Party to its Environment Protocol, would like to reaffirm its commitment to Antarctic cooperation and environmental protection.

Since 1961, Antarctic regulation has grown into the so-called Antarctic Treaty System, which includes, in particular, the Convention for the Conservation of Antarctic Marine Living Resources (CCAMLR) which came into force in 1982 and was followed in 1998 by the Environmental Protocol to the Antarctic Treaty.

Since then, the marine component of the Antarctic ecosystem has been subject to a growing number of scientific studies and interest from a number of industry sectors. Krill, an essential element of the Antarctic marine ecosystem, and marine biological resources generate increasing interest due to their economic and commercial potential. The Johannesburg summit agreed to establish by 2012 a representative global network of marine protected areas.

On one hand, the Antarctic regime is challenged by marine biological prospecting and predator communities are confronted with greater pressure from commercial krill catches. On the other hand, a process started in 2005 to establish marine protected areas in the Southern Ocean, with the first one created in 2010. Collaboration between the Committee for Environmental Protection of the Antarctic Treaty and CCAMLR was initiated in 2009 with a view to developing a representative network of marine protected areas.

Belgium strongly advocates the need to closely monitor key indicators of the environmental changes taking place in the Southern Ocean and to foster mechanisms to achieve the conservation of representative features of the world's largest ocean.

## Statement by Prof. Christo Pimpirev, Bulgaria

The Republic of Bulgaria confirms our ongoing commitments to the Antarctic Treaty System. The Treaty recognized Antarctica as a region reserved exclusively for peaceful purposes, freedom of scientific research, exchange of information and international cooperation. The Antarctic Treaty "provides an example to the world of how nations can successfully work together to preserve a major part of our planet for the benefit of all mankind"

Bulgaria started his polar activities in Antarctica in the austral summer 1987- 1988 when six Bulgarian scientists participated in joint projects with the British Antarctic Survey and the Russian Institute for Antarctic and Arctic Research. In the period 1993- 2011 we organized 19 successive Antarctic campaigns and a summer base named "St. Kliment Ohridski" was established on Livingston Island, South Shetland Islands.

Bulgaria adhered to the Antarctic Treaty in 1978, ratified the Madrid Protocol of environmental protection in 1998 and the same year become a Consultative member of the Treaty.

Most of the Antarctic issues are of global nature and Bulgarian polar explorers work closely with scientists from all over the world for the protection of the Antarctic environment and its associated ecosystems in relation of global climate change, particularly in the Antarctic Peninsula.

Over the past 50 years the Antarctic Treaty has developed into a system covering environmental protection. The Madrid Protocol that was adopted in 1991 is a key aspect of the continuance of international harmony in Antarctica and enshrines the sixth continent as a natural reserve dedicated to peace and science.The twentieth anniversary of the adoption of the Protocol is an opportunity to invite all the Parties to the Antarctic Treaty non-Parties to the Protocol to ratify as soon as possible.

This is a significant year for the Republic of Bulgaria, as it marks the 20th Bulgarian Antarctic expedition and also 80 years diplomatic relations between Argentina and Bulgaria. We would like to express our warm congratulations to Government of Argentina and the Secretariat of the Antarctic Treaty for the excellent organization of the Meeting and especially for the spectacular ceremony marked the 50th anniversary of the entry into force of the Antarctic Treaty.

## Statement by the Ambassador of China, His Excellency Yin Hengmin

Your Excellences,

Ladies and gentlemen,

This year marks the 50th anniversary of the entry into force of the Antarctic Treaty. I am very honored to be here, with friends old and new, to look back at the history and forward to the future. First, I would like to extend my warm congratulations to the ceremony and my heartfelt thanks to the thoughtful arrangements by the Government of Argentina and the Secretariat of the Antarctic Treaty.

Over the past 50 years, the Antarctic Treaty has developed into a system covering environmental protection, marine living resources and other relevant aspects. The scientific research in the Antarctic is booming. The utilization of Antarctic marine living resources is in good order. The Antarctic Treaty system has achieved tremendous success. We regard cooperation and consultation as the most important element for the success of the Antarctic Treaty system. It is with the spirit of cooperation and consultation that the Antarctic Treaty was concluded, laying aside disputes arising from territorial claims in a creative way, relieving the tension in the Antarctic, and establishing the important principles, i.e. the Antarctic can only be used for peaceful purposes; states enjoy the freedom of scientific research in the Antarctic; the consultative parties shall make decisions by consensus and so on. All these pave the way for further cooperation in the Antarctic. This spirit has been embodied in the development of the Antarctic Treaty system, the increase of the number of Treaty parties and the enhanced understanding between parties and non-parties. The Treaty has significantly contributed to the peace, stability and environmental protection of the Antarctic region, and set a successful example of international cooperation.

Currently, the Antarctic region is still facing serious challenges. Climate change and other global environmental problems pose increasingly severe impacts on the region. Antarctic tourism and environmental protection bring new tests for the wisdom of the Antarctic Treaty Consultative Parties. Most of Antarctic issues are of global nature. No single state could address them alone. All relevant states should put joint efforts to stress the fundamental role of scientific research and to improve the cooperation among scientists and to strengthen the interaction between scientists and policy makers. Cooperation should be enhanced within the frameworks of the Antarctic Treaty system, the United Nations Convention on the Law of the Sea and international maritime conventions, etc. Political wisdom should be exerted and necessary compromise should be made for common interests. China will continue, as always, to work together with scientists and policy makers from all over the world, and contribute to the peace, stability and sustainable development of the Antarctic region.

## Statement of Ecuador

During the XXXIV Consultative Meeting in Buenos Aires, in order to celebrate this important event, the fiftieth anniversary of the Antarctic Treaty, the Ecuadorean delegation extends its most sincere congratulations to all the countries which, through the regulations implemented by the Antarctic Treaty System, have made a commitment to scientific research and the conservation of this beautiful, frozen continent.

Ecuador, a country endowed with great biodiversity and lying at the mid-point of the planet, owns the Galapagos Islands, one of the natural wonders of the world, which we protect and care for with responsible national policies. This experience has enabled us to view Antarctica as a sensitive place, requiring the conservation and protection of its fragile ecosystems. Consistent with this posture, Ecuador has shown its interest in ensuring that the activities carried out in Antarctica always comply with Environmental Impact Studies, which guarantee not only the preservation and conservation of those ecosystems but also that the activities carried out on the white continent should cause the least possible impact.

As part of its commitment to Antarctica, Ecuador has concluded Environmental Impact Studies of the Pedro Vicente Maldonado Scientific station, which have been carried out based on the demanding standards laid down in our legislation. There is no doubt that when this Study is fully implemented, both the logistical and research activities carried out by Ecuador will comply with the objectives of responsibility, protection and conservation of the Antarctic environment.

During these fifty years since the Antarctic Treaty came into force, we have observed the efforts made by the Party States to care for and conserve this corner of the planet, efforts to which our country, as a lover of life and nature, subscribes with all its power, to preserve Antarctica as a place devoted to research, peace and preservation of the environment.

## Statement of the Russian Federation

Dear Mr. Minister,

Dear ladies and gentlemen,

Today in one of the most beautiful cities of the South America, the capital of Argentina, we celebrate the 50th anniversary of the Antarctic Treaty signed in Washington on December 1, 1959.

This Treaty was developed and adopted in the heat of the Cold War against the background of distrust and cautious attitude of the countries towards each other. Nevertheless a unique international instrument was created in those tense conditions that allowed to find a solution to one of the most difficult and the most important issues for the further development of mankind.

During the recent 50 years, the efforts of the Antarctic community have transformed the Treaty into a streamlined and expanded legal and organizational system aimed at implementation of various practical aspects of activity of the countries in the Southern polar region.

The viability of the Antarctic Treaty System is based on the integrity of its principles and at the same time on its capability of sensible adaptation to new challenges and menaces facing the international community: climate changes, increasing rate of natural disasters, globalization problems. This can be confirmed by a definitely important criterion of efficiency of the Treaty that new members continue joining the Treaty, with their total number more than 4 times greater than the number of initial members. Almost all countries taking the leading positions in political, economical, scientific and technical issues, representing all continents of the globe and over 65 % of the world population, are involved in the Antarctic issues joining their efforts in work, research and peaceful cooperation on the sixth continent.

The 2007-08 International Polar Year activities are a demonstrative example when the national Antarctic expeditions of the Consultative Parties joined their efforts, scientific, logistical and technical potential in reaching the common goals and tasks. The Russian Federation took an active part in those activities and continues close cooperation with many Antarctic Treaty member states supporting the basic principle of international cooperation established in the Antarctic Treaty.

Being one of the initiators of the Antarctic Treaty, our country adheres to maintaining and comprehensive strengthening of its regime, continuous implementation of its main objectives and principles, maintaining the peace and stability in the region and keeping Antarctica as a wildlife preservation for scientific research. This has been and remains to be a priority of the Russian policy in the Southern polar region.

Such approaches are determined in the Russian Federation Development Strategy for Antarctica till 2020 with a farther outlook adopted by the Russian Government at the end of 2010. This document determines the political line of our country with respect to the Antarctic Treaty and associated international legal acts. Adoption of the Strategy and its implementation will support a more persistent development of the Russian research efforts in Antarctica, create more favorable conditions for activities in this region, and ensure more rational use of the available material resources. And of course this document creates a strong foundation for development of a diversified and mutually beneficial cooperation of the Russian Federation with all stakeholders in Antarctica.

We are convinced that irrespective of the new problems facing the international community, the Antarctic Treaty will remain an excellent and demonstrative example of an opportunity to ensure objective solutions in harmonization of diversified national interests, objectives and goals and their implementation. For the recent 50 years we all have made sure that the principles and approaches embedded into various structures of the Antarctic Treaty and used in the spirit of cooperation will help to find new mutually beneficial solutions for the most problematic situations.

I congratulate all the Antarctic Treaty members on this wonderful anniversary!

## Statement of India

As the world celebrates 50th Anniversary of the Antarctic Treaty regime coming into force this day 50 years back, India as one of the consultative Party nations to the Antarctic Treaty, joins the world community in appreciating the visionary approach of the Treaty in visualizing the contribution of the icy continent and its associated ecosystem towards upholding the harmony among the nations and peaceful cooperation in the field of science for preservation, conservation and maintenance of the pristine environment and associated eco- system of the area. The Antarctic Treaty has withstood the test of the time and has become stronger with each passing year.

India reiterates its commitment to support the principles of Antarctic Treaty and the associated Protocols, such as the Protocol on the Environment protection to the Antarctic Treaty and its Annexes etc.

## Statement of the Ambassador of Italy, Guido Walter La Tella

Mr. Franco Frattini, Foreign Minister of Italy, who was unable to attend today due to previous commitments, has sent his regards.

Today, Italy takes part in the celebration of the 50th Anniversary of the entry into force of the Antarctic Treaty, proud to have worked in the interest of humanity in order to leave a worthy legacy to the generations to come.

This treaty, and the resulting legal system, represents a clear success in the peaceful use of Antarctica, especially in the fields of scientific research and environmental protection.

Through the years, the spirit of cooperation embodied in the Antarctic Treaty has helped acknowledge the priority of general interests over the national interests of each individual state.

Guided by these principles, Italy started to work in collaboration with other Treaty member states, initially scientifically and then politically to finally become a Consultative Party in 1987.

In the field of scientific cooperation, Italy has been noteworthy not only for the hospitality and logistical support it has offered foreign researchers at its "Mario Zucchelli" Station at Terranova Bay, but also for having established, in 1995, in association with France, the first base jointly managed by two states, the Concordia Dome C base. In this regard, the EPICA project, completed in 2003, also deserves special recognition.

In 1989, Italy also became a party to the Convention on the Conservation of Antarctic Marine Living Resources. Today, Italy reaffirms its commitment to continue guaranteeing the same level of protection to the Antarctic environment and to the resources in the Antarctic continent and waters, acknowledging the uniqueness of the Antarctic region as a whole.

In terms of political cooperation, Italy is committed to guaranteeing special protection to the Antarctic environment. To that end, in association with other states, it promoted the adoption of the Madrid Protocol, which designates Antarctica as a "natural reserve, devoted to peace and science".

This year we also celebrate the 20th Anniversary of the signing of the Protocol. Thanks to the fundamental principles on which it is based, the Protocol has now become an essential instrument. Therefore, Italy is convinced that as many member states as possible should be involved, and is striving towards this.

In terms of institutional development of the Antarctic Treaty system, Italy has taken an active part in the creation of the Antarctic Treaty Secretariat, having presided for two years over the working group in charge of drafting the Secretariat Charter. Throughout its seven years of work, the Secretariat, established here in Buenos Aires, has earned the recognition of the international community, and the praise of all Consultative Parties. It is highly valued for its key role in organising meetings, facilitating the exchange of information among the parties and, above all, providing the legal documents adopted at meetings. Thanks to the Secretariat, the Antarctic Treaty System has achieved the level of transparency demanded by the international community for decades, which has also earned the current international system greater credibility and effectiveness before third party States.

In this spirit of cooperation, and determined to safeguard the general interest above the specific needs of any individual state, Italy is determined to face any new political and legal challenges the Antarctic Treaty System may need to confront. Upcoming challenges include ensuring better discipline in tourism activities, and introducing an effective regulatory system for bioprospecting activities in the Antarctic, which we hope can be achieved as soon as possible.

The balance of these 50 years is very positive, and we are confident that the scientific and diplomatic achievements of the Antarctic Treaty System to date will be confirmed and further developed in the next decades.

Ambassador Guido Walter La Tella
Ambassador of Italy in Buenos Aires

## Statement by the Head of Delegation of Japan

### 1. Introduction

It is my great pleasure to be able to celebrate the 50th Anniversary of the entry into force of the Antarctic Treaty here in Buenos Aires, where the Secretariat of the Antarctic Treaty is located. I would like to extend my sincere appreciation for the untiring effort made by the Government of Argentina and the Secretariat. Let me also take this opportunity to express my heartfelt gratitude, on behalf of the people of Japan, for warm support and encouraging messages from all around the world, after the Great East Japan Earthquake hit my country in March.

### 2. Antarctic Observation and the use of Antarctica for peaceful purposes

Antarctica, as an unknown continent, has attracted many explorers including Japan's Lieutenant Nobu Shirase, for nearly two centuries. Antarctica also has been the centre of variety of observation activities, just like a natural laboratory without much human influence.

Japan started the observation of atmospheric total ozone in 1961. After continued regular observations, the stratospheric ozone depletion (or later called ozone hole) was discovered by the member of the 23rd JARE (Japanese Antarctic Research Expedition) in 1982. We still continue our observation of the ozone, and these observation results have made a great contribution to the international effort under the Montreal Protocol on Substances that Deplete the Ozone Layer.

At the Dome Fuji Station, scientists acquire data on the changes in temperature and greenhouse gases that have taken place over the past 720,000 years. These data will undoubtedly help to clarify the history of the global environment, and it is expected they will be utilized as we address issues like climate change.

Japan's achievements were made possible by the establishment of fundamental principles of the Antarctic Treaty, namely, "peaceful use" and "freedom of scientific investigation and international cooperation". Japan, as one of the countries signed the Treaty in 1959, has acted with responsibility as a consultative party. Japan is determined to continue to work to maintain the basic principles of the Treaty, and to actively engage with discussions on Antarctica.

### 3. Inspection

Japan, in order to fulfill its responsibility as a consultative party, conducted its first-ever inspection under the provisions of the Antarctic Treaty and the Protocol on Environmental Protection to the Treaty. The inspection took place in January 2010 for about two weeks and covered six stations. It took us almost two years to prepare for this inspection, with relevant ministries and experts repeatedly discussing its content and possible outcome.

Concluding inspections, we found that all inspected stations comply with the principle of the use of Antarctica for peaceful purposes, and endeavour to promote scientific investigation and international cooperation under physical and financial constraints, while trying to reduce extra burden on the Antarctic environment. The inspections also provided Japan with excellent opportunities to learn about operations of other stations, including those utilizing renewable energy with sophisticated technologies.

The system of inspection will increase its importance as human activities in Antarctica become more active in future. Japan hopes that this system will further enhance compliance to the Antarctic Treaty and the Environmental Protocol, as well as international cooperation in Antarctica.

### 4. Antarctic Tourism

In considering how to reduce extra burden of human activities on the Antarctic environment, we must think about how Antarctic tourism should be conducted. More than 30,000 people now visit Antarctica every year, frequently with large tourist vessels. Although Antarctic tourism itself can be a useful activity which provides opportunity of awareness raising and environmental learning, tourism activities must be conducted in a responsible manner not to interfere with the value of Antarctica as the place for scientific research or to adversely affect the Antarctic environment.

Japan has promoted environmental conservation in Antarctica by enacting the "Law Relating to Protection of the Environment in Antarctica", to ensure our full compliance with the provisions of the Protocol. Japan will continue to take part in the discussion on necessary actions on Antarctic tourism in good faith.

## 5. Conclusion

Antarctica is the place far from where we live. This uniqueness of Antarctica enables us to conduct pure observation of the impact of human activities on the environment, with little external influence. Antarctica is just like a mirror, reflecting how healthy our planet is.

All of us here have special responsibility to protect this special place. On this occasion of the 50th anniversary of the entry into force of the Treaty, Japan would like to renew its determination, to further promote research and observation and protect Antarctic environment, based on the principles of this historic Treaty.

Thank you very much.

## Statement of Peru

President:

The Peruvian Delegation to the XXXIV Antarctic Treaty Consultative Meeting expresses its enormous satisfaction in taking part in the acts to commemorate the entry into force of the Antarctic Treaty, exactly fifty years ago today.

President:

The Peruvian Delegation considers that this occasion offers us, as Consultative Party States, an opportunity to renew our commitment to the purposes and objectives of the Antarctic Treaty. This occasion also invites us to deploy our best efforts to ensure that this Consultative Meeting achieves its goals, and that it signifies positive progress in consolidating the system created by the Antarctic Treaty. Peru has a complete, irrevocable vocation for Antarctica. Part of the coast of Peru faces Antarctica directly. Peru is subject to the influence of the south polar system, and this interrelation is apparent in such crucial factors as, *inter alia*, climatic conditions, ocean currents, particularly the Humboldt Current, and the marine species on which the Peruvian fishing industry is based. These species are links in a biological chain which initiates in the southern oceans. These facts highlight the special meaning and importance of the Antarctic region, not only for the planet as a whole but particularly for southern hemisphere countries. The commemoration of the entry into force of the Antarctic Treaty fifty years ago today is, therefore, an opportunity which invites us to reflect on what we have achieved so far, and what we propose to use our presence in this important region of the planet to do in the future. The Antarctic Treaty has placed on the shoulders of the Consultative Party States the important and delicate task of directing the international administration of the Antarctic region. It is therefore our duty, as Consultative Party States of the Treaty, to honour this obligation.

Peru considers that a crucial aspect of how we view and appreciate the Antarctic region, is the permanent maintenance and preservation of Antarctica as a region of international peace and harmony, in which international cooperation will always be the preferred tool to guide the destiny of our common activities in the region. Cooperation, particularly for the preservation of the Antarctic environment, is, today more than ever, one of the prime objectives of our actions as members of the Antarctic system. The preservation of Antarctica will ensure a safer, and a more dependable and habitable planet for future generations, for all of humanity. Planet Earth is our common home, the only one which human civilization has. Preserving Antarctica is preserving the future of our planet and the presence of man in the universe.

President:

The Peruvian Delegation is proud to share, with all the Delegations taking part in this meeting in Buenos Aires, the privilege of witnessing, and bearing witness to, in this commemoration, a historic act which occurred fifty years ago: the entry into force of the Antarctic Treaty. The Antarctic Treaty has become the ideal international instrument, which today guarantees that the Antarctic region will always be used exclusively for peaceful purposes, and will not become the scene or object of international discord. On this propitious occasion, the Peruvian Delegation renews its commitment to the purposes and objectives of the Antarctic Treaty.

Thank you very much.

## Statement by Andrzej Misztal, Poland

Mr. Chairman,

Ladies and gentlemen,

Let me start by expressing my delight and personal satisfaction for representing the Minister of Foreign Affairs of the Republic of Poland at this very special and historic event. Since Mr. Minister Sikorski was unable to participate in this meeting, allow me to quote his personal letter directed to the host of this gathering H. E. Minister Hector Timerman:

Dear Minister,

I am pleased to write to you to thank you for your kind invitation of 9th February 2011 to take part in the commemoration of the 50th Anniversary of the entry into force of the Antarctic Treaty, signed in Washington on 1st December 1959, which will be held in the context of the XXXIV Consultative Meeting of the member countries of that Treaty. Unfortunately I will not be able to attend this significant event in person, due to engagements to which I am already committed.

The important place occupied by the Antarctic Treaty in modern international law is unquestionable, and even historic. Since its entry into force, it has evolved extensively with the development of a system of legal instruments, to become a unique regional regime: the Antarctic Treaty System, constantly developed and enriched.

A clear sign of the importance of the Antarctic Treaty for Poland is the fact that in 1977 we became the first non-signatory consultative country of the Treaty. The peaceful use of the Antarctic and the prohibition of any kind of weapons testing are particularly important for Poland, as well as the liberty to carry out scientific research in the territory. The Polish permanent base, the Henryk Arctowski scientific research station located on King George Island, has been operating in Western Antarctica for over 30 years.

I am certain that the commemorative events on 23rd June 2011 and the adoption of a declaration by those present will play an important role in the process of global dialogue on Antarctica, and will continue the impetus of International Polar Year (IPY).

Allow me to take this opportunity to inform you that during the visit of the Polish delegation, for the first time in the history of Polish-Argentine diplomatic relations, legal consultations will take place between our ministries.

I send you my very warmest wishes for this occasion.

Thank you for your attention.

## Statement by the Ambassador of the United Kingdom

Foreign Ministers, Ambassadors, Distinguished Colleagues and Heads of Delegations,

The United Kingdom would like to join those who have expressed thanks to the Government of Argentina for holding this anniversary event. It is fitting that we should continue to seek opportunities to celebrate all that the Antarctic Treaty has delivered over the past half century, and to raise the profile of the work undertaken through the Antarctic Treaty System to a wider audience.

The United Kingdom also, and without exception, confirms our ongoing commitment to the Antarctic Treaty System. We continue to hope that the framework provided by the Treaty will facilitate enhanced co-operation by all Governments in addressing the current and inevitable future challenges that face Antarctica.

The Antarctic Treaty is arguably one of the most successful international instruments of the last century and is a shining example of what international co-operation can inspire. This year also marks the 20th anniversary of the signing of the Protocol on Environmental Protection to the Antarctic Treaty. The continued protection these instruments collectively afford to one of the most unique and sensitive environments on earth is ever more important in the face of the rapid environmental changes already being experienced in many parts of the continent and the surrounding Southern Ocean. We must ensure that our collective efforts continue to secure and enhance this comprehensive and enduring protection.

The Antarctic Treaty provides an enduring framework for international scientific collaboration and, as the results of the International Polar Year 2007-08 continue to emerge, we can reflect on our enhanced understanding of Antarctica, yet also wonder in awe at how much we have yet to discover. As supported in the 2006 Edinburgh Declaration, we hope that the legacy of the International Polar Year will provide for even more scientific collaboration in the coming decades.

This is a particularly significant year for the United Kingdom, as it marks the centenary of when Captain Robert Falcon Scott and his Norwegian counter-part Roald Amundsen first set out on their expeditions to the South Pole. The early scientific pioneers on Captain Scott's expedition left a scientific legacy that continues to inspire British scientists to this day. That the Antarctic Treaty preserves the continent for peace and science is testimony to the legacy of those early scientists, who demonstrated the importance of Antarctica, not just as a unique laboratory in itself, but also its clear importance to the future climate and environmental changes of the rest of the world. From the early explorers to the discovery of the ozone hole and the proposed exploration of sub-glacial Lake Ellsworth, our scientists continue to see Antarctica as a global laboratory that has so much outstanding potential to help us unlock the secrets of our planet.

Climatic changes, particularly in the Antarctic Peninsula, however, potentially expose the Antarctic environment to new threats, whether from natural migration of flora and fauna from lower latitudes, or from increasing human accessibility. The Antarctic Treaty Parties must continue to work together to ensure that those who are fortunate enough to visit the region, in whatever capacity, do so in a safe and environmentally responsible way. We must redouble our efforts to ensure that the regulatory and management framework for all activities undertaken in Antarctica minimises any unnecessary additional human pressures to the already changing and fragile environment.

On behalf of the United Kingdom, may I once again thank the Government of Argentina for hosting this year's Antarctic Treaty Consultative Meeting. This renewed opportunity to reflect on the scientific and diplomatic endeavours of all those who have contributed to the Antarctic Treaty System over the past 50 years, reminds us once again of how much has been achieved, as well as the global importance of continuing this vital work.

## Statement by the Ambassador of South Africa, Mr Tony Leon

Ministers, Chairman, Delegates and Distinguished Guests:

On behalf of the South African Government and the South African Delegation here at these important proceedings, allow me to add my thanks to the Argentinean Government for initiating and arranging this important event to commemorate the 50th Anniversary of the operationalization of the Antarctic Treaty of 1959. As one of the twelve founding country –Parties to the milestone agreement, it is of particular relevance to South Africa.

The Antarctic Treaty is, in its own way, remarkable. If you think of the many things which the world and the 12 founding Treaty Countries had got wrong back in 1959 (my own country, South Africa included), this Treaty – with its efficiency, flexibility, longevity and visionary farsightedness – represents one of the big things which the international community, or some of its member states, got right back then: sparing the Antarctic from a global arms race and insulating it from disputed territorial claims, were two of its initial achievements. But with the addition of the 1991 Madrid Protocol on Environmental Protection, the Treaty was signaling the centrality in the world climate system of the pristine Antarctic ecosystem. Its determination to exercise effective stewardship over the seventh continent would prove to be seminal in the battle to be fought against the yet-to-be-named enemy of "climate change".

The Antarctic Treaty is an unique instrument for international cooperation with science as its common objective. But the Treaty has also allowed the world's seventh, and only uninhabited, continent to be preserved from the predations of the other six. Furthermore, through the provisions of the Treaty, it has become the common workplace for people from across the globe, of different races and cultures and national origins, to unite and work together, harmoniously, to meet and mitigate the effects of climate change.

As an original signatory, South Africa - with a proud track record of continuous involvement and responsible custodianship in the Antarctic, looks forward to continued international co-operation with Treaty Parties and to share scientific knowledge and data for this generation, and for the future preservation of mankind.

South Africa remains the only African Treaty Party on the Antarctic. Yet, we know that global changes in weather and climate will, ironically and disproportionately, perhaps effect Africa more than any other continent. It is therefore appropriate that in the 50th anniversary year of the commencement of this Treaty, my country will be host in November and December of this year, to the UNFCCC COP 17 (United Nations Conference on Climate Change) in Durban. It is the sincere wish of South Africa's Minister of International Relations and Co-operation, that the world will unite, later at this meeting to meet the challenges of global change, with as much wisdom and courage as the Treaty Parties displayed 52 years ago in protecting the Antarctic.

May we also express our appreciation to the Argentinean Government for hosting the XXXIV ATCM and for the excellence of the arrangements. Our delegation looks forward to productive deliberations and positive outcomes over the next two weeks.

## Statement by the Ambassador of Sweden, H.E. Charlotte Wrangberg

Mr Chairman, Dear Delegates,

It is an honour for me to represent my Minister for Foreign Affairs, Mr. Carl Bildt, at this important meeting of the ATCM XXXIV to commemorate the 50th anniversary of the entry into force of the Antarctic Treaty.

The Antarctic Treaty and the other elements of the Antarctic Treaty system together form a unique legal and institutional framework for the management of human activities on the Antarctic continent and in the Southern Ocean.

Sweden is proud to be one of the 28 Consultative Parties to the Antarctic Treaty. Collectively and individually, the Consultative Parties have a responsibility to ensure that the Antarctic Treaty system remains robust. We need to continuously strengthen it and adapt it to meet new challenges. Biological prospecting for example.

We must also ensure that all the elements of the Antarctic Treaty system are effectively and fully implemented through adequate national regulation!

The Environmental Protocol provides for everlasting protection of the Antarctic environment. The Convention on the Conservation of Antarctic Marine Living Resources is an integral part of the Antarctic Treaty system. The work of the CEP and the CCAMLR institutions needs to be better coordinated to ensure effective protection of the Antarctic marine environment and its associated and dependant ecosystems.

Swedish scientists perform advanced scientific research and monitoring in close cooperation with scientists from other countries. The "International Polar Year 2007-2008" provided a major boost to international scientific cooperation on polar issues. Its legacy is now inspiring further advances in science and innovative formats for Antarctic cooperation. In particular, the IPY highlighted the need for concerted efforts to sustain long-term observation and monitoring throughout the whole Antarctic Treaty area.

Data from scientific research and monitoring shall be freely available and easily accessible. The ATCM electronic information system is a useful tool that could be further expanded to facilitate dissemination of data and other relevant information.

Global climate change creates new challenges to Antarctica and to human activities there. All Antarctic living organisms are potentially impacted by the effects of climate change. The marine ecosystems seem to be particularly at risk. Too little is still known about the effects of ocean acidification and of the warming of the waters in the Southern Ocean.

It is essential to minimize the cumulative footprint of all human activities in Antarctica - scientific research, tourism and fishing.

Safety and security aspects of Antarctic operations should also be reviewed in light of climate change.

All our management decisions need to be guided by the precautionary approach. This is particularly urgent and critical for fishing and fishing-related activities.

Thank you for your attention.

## Statement by the Ambassador of Ukraine, Oleksandr Taranenko

Dear Mr.Chairman,

Distinguished Heads of Delegations,

Ladies and Gentlemen,

On behalf of Ukraine I would like to express my gratitude to the Government of Argentina for its warm welcome, and for having perfectly organised the XXXIV[th] Antarctic Treaty Consultative Meeting, which coincides with the 50th anniversary of the entry into force by the Antarctic Treaty and takes place 30 years after the previous consultative meeting in Argentina.

This symbolic coincidence takes place now that Argentina has entered its modern era, as has Ukraine, which this year celebrates the 20th anniversary of its independence. The independence my country gained 15 years ago, on February 6, 1996, meant it could unfurl its flag in Antarctica, become actively involved in the efforts of the international community aimed at securing use of Antarctica exclusively for peaceful purposes, and make its own contribution to scientific knowledge through international cooperation in scientific investigation in Antarctica. Ukraine's active participation in the Antarctic Treaty System was underlined by the fact that in 2008, four years after it had achieved the status of Consultative Party, Ukraine hosted the XXXI[th] Antarctic Treaty Consultative Meeting in its capital.

Let me also mention another fact important to Ukraine. The first Ukrainian ever to set foot in Antarctica was a member of Robert Scott's expedition to the South Pole in 1911-1912. The whole Antarctic Community will shortly be celebrating the 100th anniversary of this remarkable event in the context of Antarctic exploration. For a long time, Ukraine had been taking an active part in large-scale comprehensive researches as part of the Soviet Antarctic expeditions. Using domestic towing snowmobiles, repeated transcontinental towed sled expeditions into the depth of Antarctica, including the South Pole and the Pole of Inaccessibility, were successfully conducted in 1957-1967.

In 1992, Ukraine joined the Antarctic Treaty, and in 1995, the first Ukrainian Antarctic expedition began its work at Great Britain's Faraday Research Station. Following successful negotiations between the Governments of Great Britain and Ukraine, the Faraday Research Station was transferred to Ukraine and renamed in honour of the academician Volodymyr Vernadsky, the first president of the Academy of sciences of Ukraine, developer of the concepts of the Earth's bio- and noosphere.

The Vernadsky Research Station is a unique geophysical observatory which benefits from continuous meteorological data from the Antarctic Peninsula. It was indeed at this research base that the ozone hole was discovered in the 1980s, and that the ensuing investigations started. The base is surrounded by a network of sampling points providing data about environmental changes. The scientific legacy of the base therefore means it will have a key role to play in future research.

At the moment, no scientific issue of global significance can be solved without taking into account large-scale phenomena or processes on a scale equivalent to Antarctica. The risks associated with observed climate changes, as well as a rapid increase in unpredictable catastrophes, are the kind of problems which could be solved through well-rounded research projects. Multi-disciplinary research on this scale in the South Polar region requires permanent collaboration between National Antarctic Programs and relevant authorities.

In November 2010, the Government of Ukraine adopted its State Antarctic Research Program for the period of 2011-2020. The main objectives of this program are to continue supporting fundamental and applied research in Antarctica, to conduct the scientific evaluation of the biological and mineral potential of the region, to maintain efficiently the Vernadsky Research Station, which serves as a base for the 16th Ukrainian Antarctic Expedition, and to meet our international commitments in accordance with the Antarctic Treaty. These are the priorities which Ukraine has set for itself in Antarctica for the next decade.

One of the subjects this Consultative Meeting has been examining is the implementation of Annex VI to the Protocol on Environmental Protection to the Antarctic Treaty. In line with this, I would like to remark that

Ukraine has the firm intention to ratify this document when it passes national legislation on activities in the Antarctic, which is currently going through the legislative process.

In addition, on the occasion of the 20th anniversary of the adoption of the Protocol on Environmental Protection to the Antarctic Treaty (known as the Madrid Protocol), allow me to stress that Ukraine supports the joint proposal presented by the Governments of Australia, France and Spain, which encourages accession to the Protocol of the Parties that have not yet done so. In our opinion, this would contribute to a more efficient multilateral diplomacy, which has always fostered the development of international cooperation in scientific research and environmental protection as a means of strengthening peace.

Last but not least, the Ukrainian delegation supports the Declaration on Antarctic Cooperation inasmuch as it meets obligations stemming from the Antarctic Treaty which have emerged since it came into force.

In conclusion, I would like to thank again the host country and the Secretariat of this Consultative meeting, and express my best wishes for a fruitful and mutually beneficial cooperation.

Thank you for your attention!

# 2. Closing remarks by the Chairman of the XXXIV ATCM

## Closing remarks by Ambassador Ariel Mansi, Chairman of the XXXIV ATCM

Distinguished Delegates: we have reached the closing of the XXXIV Antarctic Treaty Consultative Meeting which I had the honor of chairing. At this Meeting we have made progress in the adoption of provisions aimed at achieving a better management and protection of Antarctica. Among the more outstanding developments, I would like to highlight the Buenos Aires Declaration on Antarctic Cooperation on the Occasion of the 50th Anniversary of the entry into force of the Antarctic Treaty, adopted on Thursday June 23rd. I cannot go without mentioning that for the initial drafts which served as the basis for the negotiations of the text of the Declaration, we received the valuable contributions of Ambassador Juan Carlos Beltramino, who was present here at our opening session and who was also delegate at the Washington Conference at which the Antarctic Treaty was signed in 1959. We have had to regret however, the absence due to personal reasons, of our very esteemed colleague, and renowned Antarctic expert, Dr. Roberto Puceiro Ripoll, from Uruguay, the Chair of the Punta del Este Consultative Meeting last year.

As expected, the work of the Committee for Environmental Protection has proven especially fruitful, and I would like to congratulate Dr. Yves Frenot for his very efficient work as Chair and for the results achieved. An important part of this Meeting's Recommendations has been the result of the Committee's work. Among other important topics, the CEP considered the Comprehensive Environmental Evaluations for the exploration at the Ellsworth Subglacial Lake as well as the one undertaken for the construction of the new Korean Station Jang Bogo. Ten management plans for Antarctic Specially Protected Areas were revised and a new historic monument was adopted. New site visitor guidelines were adopted for certain sites and others were revised. In addition the CEP also continues to make progress to minimize the introduction of non native species into Antarctica.

I also extend my congratulations and gratitude to Dr. José Retamales, Chair of the Operations Working Group, to Ambassador Don McKay, Chair of the Tourism and Non Governmental activities Working Group, as well as to Ambassador Richard Rowe for chairing the Legal and Institutional Working Group.

On the matter of inspections, those undertaken by Japan and Australia have evidenced the efforts made by Parties to fully comply with Treaty and Protocol requirements. We have also begun consideration of the evaluation of tsunami risks, a problem which highlighted serious concerns for stations located on the coastal areas in Antarctica, and regarding which I have been tasked with requesting the International Hydrographic Organization to present information on bathymetric charting for tsunami forecasting at the next ATCM.

In the area of tourism and non governmental activities, three main topics were considered: a substantive exchange of opinions on strategic Antarctic tourism issues took place; also, issues pertaining tourism supervision mechanisms; and aspects related to the operation of leisure vessels and yachts in Antarctica. We also considered the ways to prevent unauthorized entries into Antarctica, bearing in mind problems associated with identification of visitors who enter without the adequate permits as well as aspects of judicial proceedings when illegal conducts are detected. Furthermore, it was decided to undertake a revision of the existing legal provisions which regulate tourism in order to analyze in 2012 if additional measures are required. It was further highlighted that in order to optimize future management, it is necessary to achieve better cooperation through more active sharing of information and technologies.

We have completed the revision on the status of ATCM Recommendations on sites and monuments and protected areas and on environmental issues other than area protection and management, adopting a Decision which points out which Measures are no longer current and requesting the Secretariat to undertake pending work regarding Recommendations on operational matters. We have also adopted the revision of the ATCM and CEP Rules of Procedure, as well as procedures for the presentation, translation and distribution of documents and have incorporated to such Rules, provisions regarding the handling of information requests on ATCM activities presented by international organizations. With the aim of reinforcing the Madrid Protocol, there has also been a call to Parties to the Antarctic Treaty which are not party to the Protocol to become party to the Protocol and that Australia, Spain and France coordinate with other Consultative Parties to take the appropriate steps to that effect.

The Meeting adopted the Secretariat proposals for the 2011/2012 budget as well as budgetary provisions for the 2012/2013 period. We began considerations on how to make our work more efficient, leading to an exchange of views regarding multiyear strategic planning and reduction in duration of future meetings without losing any of the essential elements required to insure good performance. In this respect a work schedule for the eight day Meeting in Hobart was adopted.

I wish to thank the Chair of SCAR for his contribution to our work, as well as for his excellent Conference for Delegates on Wednesday of last week, and also thank COMNAP and CCAMLR for their important contributions as well.

On everyone's behalf I would like to thank Dr. Manfred Reinke and his team at the Antarctic Treaty Secretariat for their proven efficiency in their work, as well to the rapporteurs, interpreters and translators. My gratitude be made extensive to all the members of the Host State Secretariat without whose tireless hard work over several months, it would not have been possible for our Meeting to run appropriately.

Finally, my recognition to all delegations for their constructive spirit, which allowed us to achieve satisfactory results and for the Meeting developments to be conducted under a true sentiment of cooperation.

Next year it is Australia's turn to host the XXXV ATCM, and to its organizers we wish the very best. Almost following the footsteps of Amundsen's Norwegian expedition, travelling from Buenos Aires to Australia, to approach the maximum latitudes thus reaching the South Pole in December of 1911, the Consultative Meetings function on the basis of cooperation which appears in every aspect in Antarctica as well as at our meetings.

With no further matters to consider, and hoping to meet you again in Hobart in June 2012, I understand we may now conclude and close this XXXIV Antarctic Treaty Consultative Meeting.

It is so decided.

I wish you all a safe return to your respective countries.

# 3. Reports by Depositaries and Observers

**Report of the Depositary Government of the Antarctic Treaty and its Protocol in accordance with Recommendation XIII-2**

**Information Paper submitted by the United States**

This report covers events with respect to the Antarctic Treaty and the Protocol on Environmental Protection.

In the past year, there have been no accessions to the Antarctic Treaty or to the Protocol on Environmental Protection. There are forty-eight (48) Parties to the Treaty and thirty-four (34) Parties to the Protocol.

The following countries have provided notification that they have designated the persons so noted as Arbitrators in accordance with Article 2(1) of the Schedule to the Protocol on Environmental Protection:

| | | |
|---|---|---|
| Bulgaria | Mrs. Guenka Beleva | 30 July 2004 |
| Chile | Amb. María Teresa Infante | June 2005 |
| | Amb. Jorge Berguño | June 2005 |
| | Dr. Francisco Orrego | June 2005 |
| Finland | Amb. Holger Bertil Rotkirch | 14 June 2006 |
| India | Prof. Upendra Baxi | 6 October 2004 |
| | Mr. Ajai Saxena | 6 October 2004 |
| | Dr. N. Khare | 6 October 2004 |
| Japan | Judge Shunji Yanai | 18 July 2008 |
| Rep. of Korea | Prof. Park Ki Gab | 21 October 2008 |
| United States | Prof. Daniel Bodansky | 1 May 2008 |
| | Mr. David Colson | 1 May 2008 |

Lists of Parties to the Treaty, to the Protocol, and of Recommendations/Measures and their approvals are attached.

**Date of most recent action: January 29, 2010**

**The Antarctic Treaty**

Done:              Washington; December 1, 1959

Entry into force:  June 23, 1961
                   In accordance with Article XIII, the Treaty was subject to ratification by the signatory
                   States and is open for accession by any State which is a Member of the United Nations,
                   or by any other State which may be invited to accede to the Treaty with the consent of
                   all the Contracting Parties whose representatives are entitled to participate in the
                   meetings provided for under Article IX of the Treaty; instruments of ratification and
                   instruments of accession shall be deposited with the Government of the United States of
                   America. Upon the deposit of instruments of ratification by all the signatory States, the
                   Treaty entered into force for those States and for States which had deposited instruments
                   of accession to the Treaty. Thereafter, the Treaty enters into force for any acceding
                   State upon deposit of its instrument of accession.

*Legend:* (no mark) = ratification; a = accession; d = succession; w = withdrawal or equivalent action

| Participant | Signature | Consent to be bound | | Other Action | Notes |
|---|---|---|---|---|---|
| Argentina | December 1, 1959 | June 23, 1961 | | | |
| Australia | December 1, 1959 | June 23, 1961 | | | |
| Austria | | August 25, 1987 | a | | |
| Belarus | | December 27, 2006 | a | | |
| Belgium | December 1, 1959 | July 26, 1960 | | | |
| Brazil | | May 16, 1975 | a | | |
| Bulgaria | | September 11, 1978 | a | | |
| Canada | | May 4, 1988 | a | | |
| Chile | December 1, 1959 | June 23, 1961 | | | |
| China | | June 8, 1983 | a | | |
| Colombia | | January 31, 1989 | a | | |
| Cuba | | August 16, 1984 | a | | |
| Czech Republic | | January 1, 1993 | d | | i |
| Denmark | | May 20, 1965 | a | | |
| Ecuador | | September 15, 1987 | a | | |
| Estonia | | May 17, 2001 | a | | |
| Finland | | May 15, 1984 | a | | |
| France | December 1, 1959 | September 16, 1960 | | | |
| Germany | | February 5, 1979 | a | | ii |
| Greece | | January 8, 1987 | a | | |
| Guatemala | | July 31, 1991 | a | | |
| Hungary | | January 27, 1984 | a | | |
| India | | August 19, 1983 | a | | |
| Italy | | March 18, 1981 | a | | |
| Japan | December 1, 1959 | August 4, 1960 | | | |
| Korea (DPRK) | | January 21, 1987 | a | | |
| Korea (ROK) | | November 28, 1986 | a | | |
| Monaco | | May 31, 2008 | a | | |
| Netherlands | | March 30, 1967 | a | | iii |
| New Zealand | December 1, 1959 | November 1, 1960 | | | |

| | | | | | |
|---|---|---|---|---|---|
| Norway | December 1, 1959 | August 24, 1960 | | | |
| Papua New Guinea | | March 16, 1981 | d | | iv |
| Peru | | April 10, 1981 | a | | |
| Poland | | June 8, 1961 | a | | |
| Portugal | | January 29, 2010 | a | | |
| Romania | | September 15, 1971 | a | | v |
| Russian Federation | December 1, 1959 | November 2, 1960 | | | vi |
| Slovak Republic | | January 1, 1993 | d | | vii |
| South Africa | December 1, 1959 | June 21, 1960 | | | |
| Spain | | March 31, 1982 | a | | |
| Sweden | | April 24, 1984 | a | | |
| Switzerland | | November 15, 1990 | a | | |
| Turkey | | January 24, 1996 | a | | |
| Ukraine | | October 28, 1992 | a | | |
| United Kingdom | December 1, 1959 | May 31, 1960 | | | |
| United States | December 1, 1959 | August 18, 1960 | | | |
| Uruguay | | January 11, 1980 | a | | viii |
| Venezuela | | March 24, 1999 | a | | |

---

[i] Effective date of succession by the Czech Republic. Czechoslovakia deposited an instrument of accession to the Treaty on June 14, 1962. On December 31, 1992, at midnight, Czechoslovakia ceased to exist and was succeeded by two separate and independent states, the Czech Republic and the Slovak Republic.

[ii] The Embassy of the Federal Republic of Germany in Washington transmitted to the Department of State a diplomatic note, dated October 2, 1990, which reads as follows:

"The Embassy of the Federal Republic of Germany presents its compliments to the Department of State and has the honor to inform the Government of the United States of America as the depositary Government of the Antarctic Treaty that, t[h]rough the accession of the German Democratic Republic to the Federal Republic of Germany with effect from October 3, 1990, the two German states will unite to form one sovereign state which, as a contracting party to the Antarctic Treaty, will remain bound by the provisions of the Treaty and subject to those recommendations adopted at the 15 consultative meetings which the Federal Republic of Germany has approved. From the date of German unity, the Federal Republic of Germany will act under the designation of "Germany" within the framework of the [A]ntarctic system.
"The Embassy would be grateful if the Government of the United States of America could inform all contracting parties to the Antarctic Treaty of the contents of this note.
"The Embassy of the Federal Republic of Germany avails itself of this opportunity to renew to the Department of State the assurances of its highest consideration."

Prior to unification, the German Democratic Republic deposited an instrument of accession to the Treaty, accompanied by a declaration, on November 19, 1974, and the Federal Republic of Germany deposited an instrument of accession to the Treaty, accompanied by a statement, on February 5, 1979.

[iii] The instrument of accession to the Treaty by the Netherlands states that the accession is for the Kingdom in Europe, Suriname and the Netherlands Antilles; as of January 1, 1986, Aruba as a separate entity.

[iv] Date of deposit of notification of succession by Papua New Guinea; effective September 16, 1975, the date of its independence.

[v] The instrument of accession to the Treaty by Romania was accompanied by a note of the Ambassador of the Socialist Republic of Romania to the United States of America, dated September 15, 1971, which reads as follows:
"Dear Mr. Secretary:
"Submitting the instrument of adhesion of the Socialist Republic of Romania to the Antarctic Treaty, signed at Washington on December 1, 1959, I have the honor to inform you of the following:

'The Council of State of the Socialist Republic of Romania states that the provisions of the first paragraph of the article XIII of the Antarctic Treaty are not in accordance with the principle according to which the multilateral treaties whose object and purposes are concerning the international community, as a whole, should be opened for universal participation.'

"I am kindly requesting you, Mr. Secretary, to forward to all parties concerned the text of the Romanian instrument of adhesion to the Antarctic Treaty, as well as the text of this letter containing the above mentioned statement of the Romanian Government.

"I avail myself of this opportunity to renew to you, Mr. Secretary, the assurances of my highest consideration."

Copies of the Ambassador's letter and the Romanian instrument of accession to the Treaty were transmitted to the Antarctic Treaty parties by the Secretary of State's circular note dated October 1, 1971.

[vi] The Treaty was signed and ratified by the former Union of Soviet Socialist Republics.  By a note dated January 13, 1992, the Russian Federation informed the United States Government that it "continues to perform the rights and fulfil the obligations following from the international agreements signed by the Union of Soviet Socialist Republics."

[vii] Effective date of succession by the Slovak Republic.  Czechoslovakia deposited an instrument of accession to the Treaty on June 14, 1962.  On December 31, 1992, at midnight, Czechoslovakia ceased to exist and was succeeded by two separate and independent states, the Czech Republic and the Slovak Republic.

[viii] The instrument of accession to the Treaty by Uruguay was accompanied by a declaration, a Department of State English translation of which reads as follows:

"The Government of the Oriental Republic of Uruguay considers that, through its accession to the Antarctic Treaty signed at Washington (United States of America) on December 1, 1959, it helps to affirm the principles of using Antarctica exclusively for peaceful purposes, of prohibiting any nuclear explosion or radioactive waste disposal in this area, of freedom of scientific research in Antarctica in the service of mankind, and of international cooperation to achieve these objectives, which are established in said Treaty.

"Within the context of these principles Uruguay proposes, through a procedure based on the principle of legal equality, the establishment of a general and definitive statute on Antarctica in which, respecting the rights of States as recognized in international law, the interests of all States involved and of the international community as a whole would be considered equitably.

"The decision of the Uruguayan Government to accede to the Antarctic Treaty is based not only on the interest which, like all members of the international community, Uruguay has in Antarctica, but also on a special, direct, and substantial interest which arises from its geographic location, from the fact that its Atlantic coastline faces the continent of Antarctica, from the resultant influence upon its climate, ecology, and marine biology, from the historic bonds which date back to the first expeditions which ventured to explore that continent and its waters, and also from the obligations assumed in conformity with the Inter-American Treaty of Reciprocal Assistance which includes a portion of Antarctic territory in the zone described in Article 4, by virtue of which Uruguay shares the responsibility of defending the region.

"In communicating its decision to accede to the Antarctic Treaty, the Government of the Oriental Republic of Uruguay declares that it reserves its rights in Antarctica in accordance with international law."

# PROTOCOL ON ENVIRONMENTAL PROTECTION TO THE ANTARCTIC TREATY

Signed at Madrid on October 4, 1991*

| State | Date of Signature | Date deposit of Ratification, Acceptance (A) or Approval (AA) | Date deposit of Accession | Date of entry into force | Date Acceptance ANNEX V** | Date of entry into force of Annex V |
|---|---|---|---|---|---|---|
| **CONSULTATIVE PARTIES** | | | | | | |
| Argentina | Oct. 4, 1991 | Oct. 28, 1993 [3] | | Jan. 14, 1998 | Sept. 8, 2000 (A) | May 24, 2002 |
| Australia | Oct. 4, 1991 | Apr. 6, 1994 | | Jan. 14, 1998 | Aug. 4, 1995 (B) | May 24, 2002 |
|  |  |  |  |  | Apr. 6, 1994 (A) |  |
| Belgium | Oct. 4, 1991 | Apr. 26, 1996 | | Jan. 14, 1998 | June 7, 1995 (B) | May 24, 2002 |
|  |  |  |  |  | Apr. 26, 1996 (A) |  |
| Brazil | Oct. 4, 1991 | Aug. 15, 1995 | | Jan. 14, 1998 | Oct. 23, 2000 (B) | May 24, 2002 |
|  |  |  |  |  | May 20, 1998 (B) |  |
| Bulgaria | | | April 21, 1998 | May 21, 1998 | May 5, 1999 (AB) | May 24, 2002 |
| Chile | Oct. 4, 1991 | Jan. 11, 1995 | | Jan. 14, 1998 | Mar 25, 1998 (B) | May 24, 2002 |
| China | Oct. 4, 1991 | Aug. 2, 1994 | | Jan. 14, 1998 | Jan. 26, 1995 (AB) | May 24, 2002 |
| Ecuador | Oct. 4, 1991 | Jan. 4, 1993 | | Jan. 14, 1998 | May 11, 2001 (A) | May 24, 2002 |
|  |  |  |  |  | Nov. 15, 2001 (B) |  |
| Finland | Oct. 4, 1991 | Nov. 1, 1996 (A) | | Jan. 14, 1998 | Nov. 1, 1996 (A) | May 24, 2002 |
|  |  |  |  |  | Apr. 2, 1997 (B) |  |
| France | Oct. 4, 1991 | Feb. 5, 1993 (AA) | | Jan. 14, 1998 | Apr. 26, 1995 (B) | May 24, 2002 |
|  |  |  |  |  | Nov. 18, 1998 (A) |  |
| Germany | Oct. 4, 1991 | Nov. 25, 1994 | | Jan. 14, 1998 | Nov. 25, 1994 (A) | May 24, 2002 |
|  |  |  |  |  | Sept. 1, 1998 (B) |  |
| India | July 2, 1992 | Apr. 26, 1996 | | Jan. 14, 1998 | May 24, 2002 (B) | May 24, 2002 |
| Italy | Oct. 4, 1991 | Mar. 31, 1995 | | Jan. 14, 1998 | May 31, 1995 (A) | May 24, 2002 |
|  |  |  |  |  | Feb. 11, 1998 (B) |  |
| Japan | Sept. 29, 1992 | Dec. 15, 1997 (A) | | Jan. 14, 1998 | Dec. 15, 1997 (AB) | May 24, 2002 |
| Korea, Rep. of | July 2, 1992 | Jan. 2, 1996 | | Jan. 14, 1998 | June 5, 1996 (B) | May 24, 2002 |
| Netherlands | Oct. 4, 1991 | Apr. 14, 1994 (A) [6] | | Jan. 14, 1998 | Mar 18, 1998 (B) | May 24, 2002 |
| New Zealand | Oct. 4, 1991 | Dec. 22, 1994 | | Jan. 14, 1998 | Oct. 21, 1992 (B) | May 24, 2002 |
| Norway | Oct. 4, 1991 | June 16, 1993 | | Jan. 14, 1998 | Oct. 13, 1993 (B) | May 24, 2002 |
| Peru | Oct. 4, 1991 | Mar. 8, 1993 | | Jan. 14, 1998 | Mar 8, 1993 (A) | May 24, 2002 |
|  |  |  |  |  | Mar 17, 1999 (B) |  |
| Poland | Oct. 4, 1991 | Nov. 1, 1995 | | Jan. 14, 1998 | Sept. 20, 1995 (B) | May 24, 2002 |
| Russian Federation | Oct. 4, 1991 | Aug. 6, 1997 | | Jan. 14, 1998 | June 19, 2001 (B) | May 24, 2002 |
| South Africa | Oct. 4, 1991 | Aug. 3, 1995 | | Jan. 14, 1998 | June 14, 1995 (B) | May 24, 2002 |
| Spain | Oct. 4, 1991 | July 1, 1992 | | Jan. 14, 1998 | Dec. 8, 1993 (A) | May 24, 2002 |
|  |  |  |  |  | Feb. 18, 2000 (B) |  |
| Sweden | Oct. 4, 1991 | Mar. 30, 1994 | | Jan. 14, 1998 | Mar 30, 1994 (A) | May 24, 2002 |
|  |  |  |  |  | Apr. 7, 1994 (B) |  |

# ATCM XXXIV Final Report

| | | | | | |
|---|---|---|---|---|---|
| Ukraine | | | May 25, 2001 | June 24, 2001 | May 25, 2001 (A) | May 24, 2002 |
| United Kingdom | Oct. 4, 1991 | Apr. 25, 1995 [5] | | Jan. 14, 1998 | May 21, 1996 (B) | May 24, 2002 |
| United States | Oct. 4, 1991 | Apr. 17, 1997 | | Jan. 14, 1998 | Apr. 17, 1997 (A) / May 6, 1998 (B) | May 24, 2002 |
| Uruguay | Oct. 4, 1991 | Jan. 11, 1995 | | Jan. 14, 1998 | May 15, 1995 (B) | May 24, 2002 |

** The following denotes date relating either
to acceptance of Annex V or approval of Recommendation XVI-10
(A) Acceptance of Annex V    (B) Approval of Recommendation XVI-10

-2-

| State | Date of Signature | Ratification Acceptance or Approval | Date deposit of Accession | Date of entry into force | Date Acceptance ANNEX V** | Date of entry into force of Annex V |
|---|---|---|---|---|---|---|
| **NON-CONSULTATIVE PARTIES** | | | | | | |
| Austria | Oct. 4, 1991 | | July 16, 2008 | Aug. 15, 2008 | | |
| Belarus | | | | | | |
| Canada | Oct. 4, 1991 | Nov. 13, 2003 | | Dec. 13, 2003 | | |
| Colombia | Oct. 4, 1991 | | | | | |
| Cuba | | | | | | |
| Czech Rep. [1,2] | Jan. 1, 1993 | Aug. 25, 2004 [4] | | Sept. 24, 2004 | | |
| Denmark | July 2, 1992 | | | | | |
| Estonia | | | | | | |
| Greece | Oct. 4, 1991 | May 23, 1995 | | Jan. 14, 1998 | | |
| Guatemala | | | | | | |
| Hungary | Oct. 4, 1991 | | | | | |
| Korea, DPR of | Oct. 4, 1991 | | | | | |
| Monaco | | | July 1, 2009 | July 31, 2009 | | |
| Papua New Guinea | | | | | | |
| Romania | Oct. 4, 1991 | Feb. 3, 2003 | | Mar. 5, 2003 | Feb. 3, 2003 | Mar. 5, 2003 |
| Slovak Rep. [1,2] | Jan. 1, 1993 | | | | | |
| Switzerland | Oct. 4, 1991 | | | | | |
| Turkey | | | | | | |
| Venezuela | | | | | | |

• Signed at Madrid on October 4, 1991; thereafter at Washington until October 3, 1992.
The Protocol will enter into force initially on the thirtieth day following the date of deposit of instruments of ratification, acceptance, approval or accession by all States which were Antarctic Treaty Consultative Parties at the date on which this Protocol was adopted. (Article 23)

**Adopted at Bonn on October 17, 1991 at XVIth Antarctic Consultative Meeting.

1. Signed for Czech & Slovak Federal Republic on Oct. 2, 1992 - Czechoslovakia accepts the jurisdiction of the International Court of Justice and Arbitral Tribunal for the settlement of disputes according to Article 19, paragraph 1. On December 31, 1992, at midnight, Czechoslovakia ceased to exist and was succeeded by two separate and independent states, the Czech Republic and the Slovak Republic.

2. Effective date of succession in respect of signature by Czechoslovakia which is subject to ratification by the Czech Republic and the Slovak Republic.

3. Accompanied by declaration, with informal translation provided by the Embassy of Argentina, which reads as follows: "The Argentine Republic declares that in as much as the Protocol to the Antarctic Treaty on the Protection of the Environment is a Complementary Agreement of the Antarctic Treaty and that its Article 4 fully respects what has been stated in Article IV, Subsection 1, Paragraph A) of said Treaty, none of its stipulations should be interpreted or be applied as affecting its rights, based on legal titles, acts of possession, contiguity and geological continuity in the region South of parallel 60, in which it has proclaimed and maintained its sovereignty."

4. Accompanied by declaration, with informal translation provided by the Embassy of the Czech Republic, which reads as follows: "The Czech Republic accepts the jurisdiction of the International Court of Justice and of the Arbitral Tribunal under Article 19, paragraph 1, of the Protocol on Environmental Protection to the Antarctic Treaty, done at Madrid on October 4, 1991."

5. Ratification on behalf of the United Kingdom of Great Britain and Northern Ireland, the Bailiwick of Guernsey, the Isle of Man, Anguilla, Bermuda, the British Antarctic Territory, Cayman Islands, Falkland Islands, Montserrat, St. Helena and Dependencies, South Georgia and the South Sandwich Islands, Turks and Caicos Islands and British Virgin Islands.

6. Acceptance is for the Kingdom in Europe. At the time of its acceptance, the Kingdom of the Netherlands stated that it chooses both means for the settlement of disputes mentioned in Article 19, paragraph 1 of the Protocol, i.e. the International Court of Justice and the Arbitral Tribunal. A declaration by the Kingdom of the Netherlands accepting the Protocol for the Netherlands Antilles was deposited on October 27, 2004 with a statement confirming that it chooses both means for the settlement of disputes mentioned in Article 19, paragraph 1 of the Protocol.

Department of State,
Washington, May 9, 2011.

Approval, as notified to the Government of the United States of America, of measures relating to the furtherance of the principles and objectives of the Antarctic Treaty

| | 16 Recommendations adopted at First Meeting (Canberra 1961) Approved | 10 Recommendations adopted at Second Meeting (Buenos Aires 1962) Approved | 11 Recommendations adopted at Third Meeting (Brussels 1964) Approved | 28 Recommendations adopted at Fourth Meeting (Santiago 1966) Approved | 9 Recommendations adopted at Fifth Meeting (Paris 1968) Approved | 15 Recommendations adopted at Sixth Meeting (Tokyo 1970) Approved |
|---|---|---|---|---|---|---|
| Argentina | ALL | ALL | ALL | ALL | ALL | ALL |
| Australia | ALL | ALL | ALL | ALL | ALL | ALL |
| Belgium | ALL | ALL | ALL | ALL | ALL | ALL |
| Brazil (1983)+ | ALL | ALL | ALL | ALL | ALL | ALL (except 10) |
| Bulgaria (1998)+ | | | | | | |
| Chile | ALL | ALL | ALL | ALL | ALL | ALL |
| China (1985)+ | ALL | ALL | ALL | ALL | ALL | ALL (except 10) |
| Ecuador (1990)+ | | | | | | |
| Finland (1989)+ | | | | | | |
| France | ALL | ALL | ALL | ALL | ALL | ALL |
| Germany (1981)+ | ALL | ALL | ALL (except 8) | ALL (except 16-19) | ALL (except 6) | ALL (except 9) |
| India (1983)+ | ALL | ALL | ALL (except 8***) | ALL (except 18) | ALL | ALL (except 9 & 10) |
| Italy (1987)+ | ALL | ALL | ALL | ALL | ALL | ALL |
| Japan | ALL | ALL | ALL | ALL | ALL | ALL |
| Korea, Rep. (1989)+ | ALL | ALL | ALL | ALL | ALL | ALL |
| Netherlands (1990)+ | ALL (except 11 & 15) | ALL (except 3, 5, 8 & 10) | ALL (except 3, 4, 6 & 9) | ALL(except 20, 25, 26 & 28) | ALL (except 1, 8 & 9) | ALL (except 15) |
| New Zealand | ALL | ALL | ALL | ALL | ALL | ALL |
| Norway | ALL | ALL | ALL | ALL | ALL | ALL |
| Peru (1989)+ | ALL | ALL | ALL | ALL | ALL | ALL |
| Poland (1977)+ | ALL | ALL | ALL | ALL | ALL | ALL |
| Russia | ALL | ALL | ALL | ALL | ALL | ALL |
| South Africa | ALL | ALL | ALL | ALL | ALL | ALL |
| Spain (1988)+ | ALL | ALL | ALL | ALL | ALL | ALL |
| Sweden (1988)+ | | | | | | |
| U.K. | ALL | ALL | ALL | ALL | ALL | ALL |
| Uruguay (1985)+ | ALL | ALL | ALL | ALL | ALL | ALL |
| U.S.A. | ALL | ALL | ALL | ALL | ALL | ALL |

* IV-6, IV-10, IV-12, and V-5 terminated by VIII-2
*** Accepted as interim guideline
+ Year attained Consultative Status. Acceptance by that State required to bring into force Recommendations or Measures of meetings from that year forward.

Approval, as notified to the Government of the United States of America, of measures
relating to the furtherance of the principles and objectives of the Antarctic Treaty

| | 9 Recommendations adopted at Seventh Meeting (Wellington 1972) Approved | 14 Recommendations adopted at Eighth Meeting (Oslo 1975) Approved | 6 Recommendations adopted at Ninth Meeting (London 1977) Approved | 9 Recommendations adopted at Tenth Meeting (Washington 1979) Approved | 3 Recommendations adopted at Eleventh Meeting (Buenos Aires 1981) Approved | 8 Recommendations adopted at Twelfth Meeting (Canberra 1983) Approved |
|---|---|---|---|---|---|---|
| Argentina | ALL | ALL | ALL | ALL | ALL | ALL |
| Australia | ALL | ALL | ALL | ALL | ALL | ALL |
| Belgium | ALL | ALL | ALL | ALL | ALL | ALL |
| Brazil (1983)+ | ALL (except 5) | ALL | ALL | ALL | ALL | ALL |
| Bulgaria (1998)+ | | | | | | |
| Chile | ALL | ALL | ALL | ALL | ALL | ALL |
| China (1985)+ | ALL (except 5) | ALL | ALL | ALL | ALL | ALL |
| Ecuador (1990)+ | | | | | | |
| Finland (1989)+ | | | | | | |
| France | ALL | ALL | ALL | ALL | ALL | ALL |
| Germany (1981)+ | ALL (except 5) | ALL (except 2 & 5) | ALL | ALL (except 1 & 9) | ALL | ALL |
| India (1983)+ | ALL | ALL | ALL | ALL (except 1 & 9) | ALL | ALL |
| Italy (1987)+ | ALL (except 5) | ALL | ALL | ALL | ALL | ALL |
| Japan | ALL | ALL | ALL | ALL | ALL | ALL |
| Korea, Rep. (1989)+ | ALL | ALL | ALL | ALL | ALL | ALL |
| Netherlands (1990)+ | ALL | ALL | ALL (except 3) | ALL (except 9) | ALL (except 2) | ALL |
| New Zealand | ALL | ALL | ALL | ALL | ALL | ALL |
| Norway | ALL | ALL | ALL | ALL | ALL | ALL |
| Peru (1989)+ | ALL | ALL | ALL | ALL | ALL | ALL |
| Poland (1977)+ | ALL | ALL | ALL | ALL | ALL | ALL |
| Russia | ALL | ALL | ALL | ALL | ALL | ALL |
| South Africa | ALL | ALL | ALL | ALL | ALL | ALL |
| Spain (1988)+ | ALL | ALL | ALL | ALL (except 1 & 9) | ALL (except 1) | ALL |
| Sweden (1988)+ | ALL | ALL | ALL | ALL | ALL | ALL |
| U.K. | ALL | ALL | ALL | ALL | ALL | ALL |
| Uruguay (1985)+ | ALL | ALL | ALL | ALL | ALL | ALL |
| U.S.A. | ALL | ALL | ALL | ALL | ALL | ALL |

\* IV-6, IV-10, IV-12, and V-5 terminated by VIII-2

\*\*\* Accepted as interim guideline

+ Year attained Consultative Status. Acceptance by that State required to bring into force Recommendations or Measures of meetings from that year forward.

# 3. Reports by Depositaries and Observers

Approval, as notified to the Government of the United States of America, of measures relating to the furtherance of the principles and objectives of the Antarctic Treaty

| | 16 Recommendations adopted at Thirteenth Meeting (Brussels 1985) | 10 Recommendations adopted at Fourteenth Meeting (Rio de Janeiro 1987) | 22 Recommendations adopted at Fifteenth Meeting (Paris 1989) | 13 Recommendations adopted at Sixteenth Meeting (Bonn 1991) | 4 Recommendations adopted at Seventeenth Meeting (Venice 1992) | 1 Recommendation adopted at Eighteenth Meeting (Kyoto 1994) |
| --- | --- | --- | --- | --- | --- | --- |
| | **Approved** | **Approved** | **Approved** | **Approved** | **Approved** | **Approved** |
| Argentina | ALL | ALL | ALL | ALL | ALL | ALL |
| Australia | ALL | ALL | ALL | ALL | ALL | ALL |
| Belgium | ALL | ALL | ALL | ALL | ALL | ALL |
| Brazil (1983)+ | ALL | ALL | ALL | ALL | ALL | ALL |
| Bulgaria (1998)+ | | | | XVI-10 | | |
| Chile | ALL | ALL | ALL | ALL | ALL | ALL |
| China (1985)+ | ALL | ALL | ALL | ALL | ALL | ALL |
| Ecuador (1990)+ | | | | XVI-10 | | |
| Finland (1989)+ | | | ALL | ALL | | |
| France | ALL | ALL | ALL | ALL | ALL | ALL |
| Germany (1981)+ | ALL | ALL | ALL (except 3,8,10,11&22) | ALL | ALL | ALL |
| India (1983)+ | ALL | ALL | ALL | ALL | ALL | ALL |
| Italy (1987)+ | | ALL | ALL | ALL | ALL | ALL |
| Japan | ALL | ALL | ALL (except 1-11, 16, 18, 19) | XVI-10 | ALL | ALL |
| Korea, Rep. (1989)+ | ALL | ALL | ALL (except 22) | ALL (except 12) | ALL (except 1) | ALL |
| Netherlands (1990)+ | ALL | ALL (except 9) | ALL | ALL | ALL | ALL |
| New Zealand | ALL | ALL | ALL | ALL | ALL | ALL |
| Norway | ALL | ALL | ALL | ALL | ALL | ALL |
| Peru (1989)+ | ALL | ALL | ALL (except 22) | ALL (except 13) | ALL | ALL |
| Poland (1977)+ | ALL | ALL | ALL | ALL | ALL | ALL |
| Russia | ALL | ALL | ALL | ALL | ALL | ALL |
| South Africa | ALL | ALL | ALL | ALL | ALL | ALL |
| Spain (1988)+ | | | ALL | ALL | ALL | ALL |
| Sweden (1988)+ | | | ALL | ALL | ALL | ALL |
| U.K. | ALL (except 2) | ALL (except 2) | ALL (except 3, 4, 8, 10, 11) | ALL (except 4, 6, 8, & 9) | ALL | ALL |
| Uruguay (1985)+ | ALL | ALL | ALL | ALL | ALL | ALL |
| U.S.A. | ALL | ALL | ALL (except 1-4, 10, 11) | ALL | ALL | ALL |

* IV-6, IV-10, IV-12, and V-5 terminated by VIII-2

*** Accepted as interim guideline

+ Year attained Consultative Status.  Acceptance by that State required to bring into force Recommendations or Measures of meetings from that year forward.

Approval, as notified to the Government of the United States of America, of measures relating to the furtherance of the principles and objectives of the Antarctic Treaty

| | 5 Measures adopted at Nineteenth Meeting (Seoul 1995) Approved | 2 Measures adopted at Twentieth Meeting (Utrecht 1996) Approved | 5 Measures adopted at Twenty-First Meeting (Christchurch 1997) Approved | 2 Measures adopted at Twenty-Second Meeting (Tromso 1998) Approved | 1 Measure adopted at Twenty-Third Meeting (Lima 1999) Approved |
|---|---|---|---|---|---|
| Argentina | ALL | ALL | ALL | ALL | ALL |
| Australia | ALL | ALL | ALL | ALL | ALL |
| Belgium | ALL | ALL | ALL | ALL | ALL |
| Brazil (1983)+ | ALL | ALL | ALL | ALL | ALL |
| Bulgaria (1998)+ | | | | | |
| Chile | ALL | ALL | ALL | ALL | ALL |
| China (1985)+ | ALL | ALL | ALL | ALL | ALL |
| Ecuador (1990)+ | | | | | |
| Finland (1989)+ | ALL | ALL | ALL | ALL | ALL |
| France | ALL | ALL | ALL | ALL | ALL |
| Germany (1981)+ | ALL | ALL | ALL | ALL | ALL |
| India (1983)+ | ALL | ALL | ALL | ALL | ALL |
| Italy (1987)+ | ALL | ALL | ALL | ALL | ALL |
| Japan | | | | | |
| Korea, Rep. (1989)+ | ALL | ALL | ALL | ALL | ALL |
| Netherlands (1990)+ | ALL | ALL | ALL | ALL | ALL |
| New Zealand | ALL | ALL | ALL | ALL | ALL |
| Norway | ALL | ALL | ALL | ALL | ALL |
| Peru (1989)+ | ALL | ALL | ALL | ALL | ALL |
| Poland (1977)+ | ALL | ALL | ALL | ALL | ALL |
| Russia | ALL | ALL | ALL | ALL | ALL |
| South Africa | ALL | ALL | ALL | ALL | ALL |
| Spain (1988)+ | ALL | ALL | ALL | ALL | ALL |
| Sweden (1988)+ | ALL | ALL | ALL | ALL | ALL |
| U.K. | ALL | ALL | ALL | ALL | ALL |
| Uruguay (1985)+ | ALL (except 2, 3, 4 and 5) | ALL (except 2) | ALL (except 3, 4 and 5) | ALL (except 2) | ALL |
| U.S.A. | ALL | ALL | ALL | ALL | ALL |

"+Year attained Consultative Status. Acceptance by that state required to bring into force Recommendations or Measures of meetings from that Year forward."

Approval, as notified to the Government of the United States of America, of measures relating to the furtherance of the principles and objectives of the Antarctic Treaty

| | 2 Measures adopted at Twelfth Special Meeting (The Hague 2000) Approved | 3 Measures adopted at Twenty-Fourth Meeting (St. Petersburg 2001) Approved | 1 Measure adopted at Twenty-Fifth Meeting (Warsaw 2002) Approved | 3 Measures adopted at Twenty-Sixth Meeting (Madrid 2003) Approved | 4 Measures adopted at Twenty-Seventh Meeting (Cape Town 2004) Approved |
|---|---|---|---|---|---|
| Argentina | ALL | ALL | * | XXVI-1, XXVI-2 *, XXVI-3 ** | XXVII-1 *, XXVII-2 *, XXVII-3 ** |
| Australia | ALL | ALL | ALL | XXVI-1, XXVI-2 *, XXVI-3 ** | XXVII-1 *, XXVII-2 *, XXVII-3 ** |
| Belgium | ALL | ALL | ALL | ALL | ALL |
| Brazil (1983)+ | | | ALL | ALL | XXVII-1, XXVII-2, XXVII-3 |
| Bulgaria (1998)+ | ALL | ALL | * | XXVI-1, XXVI-2 *, XXVI-3 ** | XXVII-1, XXVII-2, XXVII-3 ** |
| Chile | ALL | ALL | ALL | ALL | ALL |
| China (1985)+ | | | ALL | ALL | XXVII-1 *, XXVII-2 *, XXVII-3 ** |
| Ecuador (1990)+ | | | * | XXVI-1, XXVI-2 *, XXVI-3 ** | XXVII-1 *, XXVII-2 *, XXVII-3 ** |
| Finland (1989)+ | ALL | ALL | * | XXVI-1, XXVI-2 *, XXVI-3 ** | XXVII-1 *, XXVII-2 *, XXVII-3 **, XXVII-4 |
| France | ALL (except SATCM XII-2) | ALL | * | XXVI-1, XXVI-2 *, XXVI-3 ** | XXVII-1 *, XXVII-2 *, XXVII-3, XXVII-4 |
| Germany (1981)+ | ALL | ALL | ALL | ALL | XXVII-1 *, XXVII-2 *, XXVII-3 ** |
| India (1983)+ | ALL | ALL | ALL | ALL | XXVII-1 *, XXVII-2 *, XXVII-3 ** |
| Italy (1987)+ | | | * | XXVI-1, XXVI-2 *, XXVI-3 ** | XXVII-1 *, XXVII-2 *, XXVII-3 ** |
| Japan | | | * | ALL | XXVII-1 *, XXVII-2 *, XXVII-3 **, XXVII-4 |
| Korea, Rep. (1989)+ | ALL | ALL | * | XXVI-1, XXVI-2 *, XXVI-3 ** | XXVII-1 *, XXVII-2 *, XXVII-3 ** |
| Netherlands (1990)+ | ALL | ALL | ALL | ALL | ALL |
| New Zealand | ALL | ALL | ALL | ALL | XXVII-1 *, XXVII-2 *, XXVII-3 **, XXVII-4 |
| Norway | | ALL | * | XXVI-1, XXVI-2 *, XXVI-3 ** | XXVII-1 *, XXVII-2 *, XXVII-3 ** |
| Peru (1989)+ | ALL | ALL | ALL | XXVI-1, XXVI-2 *, XXVI-3 ** | XXVII-1 *, XXVII-2 *, XXVII-3 ** |
| Poland (1977)+ | | ALL | ALL | ALL | ALL |
| Russia | ALL | ALL | ALL | XXVI-1, XXVI-2, XXVI-3 ** | XXVII-1 *, XXVII-2 *, XXVII-3 ** |
| South Africa | ALL | ALL | ALL | ALL | ALL |
| Spain (1988)+ | | | * | XXVI-1, XXVI-2 *, XXVI-3 ** | XXVII-1 *, XXVII-2 *, XXVII-3 ** |
| Sweden (1988)+ | ALL | ALL | | ALL | XXVII-1 *, XXVII-2 *, XXVII-3 ** |
| Ukraine (2004)+ | | | | | XXVII-1 *, XXVII-2 *, XXVII-3 ** |
| U.K. | ALL (except SATCM XII-2) | ALL (except XXIV-3); ALL (except XXIV-1 and XXIV-2) | ALL | ALL | XXVII-1 *, XXVII-2 *, XXVII-3 **, XXVII-4 |
| Uruguay (1985)+ | ALL | ALL | * | XXVI-1, XXVI-2 *, XXVI-3 | XXVII-1 *, XXVII-2 *, XXVII-3 ** |
| U.S.A. | ALL | ALL | * | XXVI-1, XXVI-2 *, XXVI-3 ** | XXVII-1 *, XXVII-2 *, XXVII-3 ** |

"+Year attained Consultative Status. Acceptance by that state required to bring into force Recommendations or Measures of meetings from that Year forward."

* Management Plans annexed to this Measure were deemed to have been approved in accordance with Article 6(1) of Annex V to the Protocol on Environmental Protection to the Antarctic Treaty and the Measure not specifying a different approval method.

** Revised and updated List of Historic Sites and Monuments annexed to this Measure was deemed to have been approved in accordance with Article 8(2) of Annex V to the Protocol on Environmental

Protection to the Antarctic Treaty and the Measure not specifying a different approval method.

Approval, as notified to the Government of the United States of America, of measures relating to the furtherance of the principles and objectives of the Antarctic Treaty

| | 5 Measures adopted at Twenty-Eighth Meeting (Stockholm 2005) Approved | 4 Measures adopted at Twenty-Ninth Meeting (Edinburgh 2006) Approved | 3 Measures adopted at Thirtieth Meeting (New Delhi 2007) Approved | 14 Measures adopted at Thirty-first Meeting (Kyiv 2008) Approved | 16 Measures adopted at Thirty-second Meeting (Baltimore 2009) Approved |
|---|---|---|---|---|---|
| Argentina | XXVIII-2 *, XXVIII-3 *, XXVIII-4 *, XXVIII-5 **, | XXIX-1 *, XXIX-2 *, XXIX-3 **, XXIX-4 *** | XXX-1 *, XXX-2 *, XXX-3 ** | XXXI-1 *, XXXI-2 *, … XXXI-14 * | XXXII-1 *, XXXII-2 *, … XXXII-14 ** |
| Australia | XXVIII-2 *, XXVIII-3 *, XXVIII-4 *, XXVIII-5 **, | XXIX-1 *, XXIX-2 *, XXIX-3 **, | XXX-1 *, XXX-2 *, XXX-3 ** | XXXI-1 *, XXXI-2 *, … XXXI-14 * | XXXII-1 *, XXXII-2 *, … XXXII-14 ** |
| Belgium | ALL except Measure 1 | XXIX-4 ***, ALL | ALL | XXXI-1 *, XXXI-2 *, … XXXI-14 * | XXXII-1 *, XXXII-2 *, … XXXII-14 ** |
| Brazil (1983)+ | ALL except Measure 1 | XXIX-1 *, XXIX-2 *, XXIX-3 **, XXIX-4 *** | XXX-1 *, XXX-2 *, XXX-3 ** | XXXI-1 *, XXXI-2 *, … XXXI-14 * | XXXII-1 *, XXXII-2 *, … XXXII-14 ** |
| Bulgaria (1998)+ | XXVIII-2 *, XXVIII-3 *, XXVIII-4 *, XXVIII-5 **, | XXIX-1 *, XXIX-2 *, XXIX-3 **, XXIX-4 *** | XXX-1 *, XXX-2 *, XXX-3 ** | XXXI-1 *, XXXI-2 *, … XXXI-14 * | XXXII-1 *, XXXII-2 *, … XXXII-14 ** |
| Chile | ALL except Measure 1 | XXIX-1 *, XXIX-2 *, XXIX-3 **, XXIX-4 *** | XXX-1 *, XXX-2 *, XXX-3 ** | XXXI-1 *, XXXI-2 *, … XXXI-14 * | XXXII-1 *, XXXII-2 *, … XXXII-14 ** |
| China (1985)+ | XXVIII-2 *, XXVIII-3 *, XXVIII-4 *, XXVIII-5 **, | XXIX-1 *, XXIX-2 *, XXIX-3 **, XXIX-4 *** | XXX-1 *, XXX-2 *, XXX-3 ** | XXXI-1 *, XXXI-2 *, … XXXI-14 * | XXXII-1 *, XXXII-2 *, … XXXII-14 ** |
| Ecuador (1990)+ | XXVIII-2 *, XXVIII-3 *, XXVIII-4 *, XXVIII-5 **, | XXIX-1 *, XXIX-2 *, XXIX-3 **, XXIX-4 *** | XXX-1 *, XXX-2 *, XXX-3 ** | XXXI-1 *, XXXI-2 *, … XXXI-14 * | XXXII-1 *, XXXII-2 *, … XXXII-14 ** |
| Finland (1989)+ | XXVIII-1, XXVIII-2 *, XXVIII-3 *, XXVIII-4 *, XXVIII-5 ** | XXIX-1 *, XXIX-2 *, XXIX-3 **, XXIX-4 *** | XXX-1 *, XXX-2 *, XXX-3 ** | XXXI-1 *, XXXI-2 *, … XXXI-14 * | XXXII-1 *, XXXII-2 *, … XXXII-14 **, XXXII-16 |
| France | XXVIII-2 *, XXVIII-3 *, XXVIII-4 *, XXVIII-5 **, | XXIX-1 *, XXIX-2 *, XXIX-3 **, XXIX-4 *** | XXX-1 *, XXX-2 *, XXX-3 ** | XXXI-1 *, XXXI-2 *, … XXXI-14 * | XXXII-1 *, XXXII-2 *, … XXXII-14 **, XXXII-15 |
| Germany (1981)+ | XXVIII-2 *, XXVIII-3 *, XXVIII-4 *, XXVIII-5 **, | XXIX-1 *, XXIX-2 *, XXIX-3 **, XXIX-4 *** | XXX-1 *, XXX-2 *, XXX-3 ** | XXXI-1 *, XXXI-2 *, … XXXI-14 * | XXXII-1 *, XXXII-2 *, … XXXII-14 ** |
| India (1983)+ | XXVIII-2 *, XXVIII-3 *, XXVIII-4 *, XXVIII-5 **, | XXIX-1 *, XXIX-2 *, XXIX-3 **, XXIX-4 *** | XXX-1 *, XXX-2 *, XXX-3 ** | XXXI-1 *, XXXI-2 *, … XXXI-14 * | XXXII-1 *, XXXII-2 *, … XXXII-14 ** |
| Italy (1987)+ | XXVIII-2 *, XXVIII-3 *, XXVIII-4 *, XXVIII-5 **, | XXIX-1 *, XXIX-2 *, XXIX-3 **, XXIX-4 *** | XXX-1 *, XXX-2 *, XXX-3 ** | XXXI-1 *, XXXI-2 *, … XXXI-14 * | XXXII-1 *, XXXII-2 *, … XXXII-14 **, XXXII-16 |
| Japan | XXVIII-2 *, XXVIII-3 *, XXVIII-4 *, XXVIII-5 **, | XXIX-1 *, XXIX-2 *, XXIX-3 **, XXIX-4 *** | XXX-1 *, XXX-2 *, XXX-3 ** | XXXI-1 *, XXXI-2 *, … XXXI-14 * | XXXII-1 *, XXXII-2 *, … XXXII-14 **, XXXII-15 |
| Korea, Rep. (1989)+ | ALL except Measure 1 | ALL | ALL | XXXI-1 *, XXXI-2 *, … XXXI-14 *, ALL | XXXII-1 *, XXXII-2 *, … XXXII-14 ** |
| Netherlands (1990)+ | XXVIII-2 *, XXVIII-3 *, XXVIII-4 *, XXVIII-5 **, | XXIX-1 *, XXIX-2 *, XXIX-3 **, XXIX-4 *** | XXX-1 *, XXX-2 *, XXX-3 ** | XXXI-1 *, XXXI-2 *, … XXXI-14 * | XXXII-1, XXXII-2 *, … XXXII-14 |
| New Zealand | XXVIII-2 *, XXVIII-4 *, XXVIII-5 **, | XXIX-1 *, XXIX-2 *, XXIX-3 **, XXIX-4 *** | XXX-1 *, XXX-2 *, XXX-3 ** | XXXI-1 *, XXXI-2 *, … XXXI-14 * | XXXII-1 *, XXXII-2 *, … XXXII-14 ** |

| | XXVIII | XXIX | XXX | XXXI | XXXII |
|---|---|---|---|---|---|
| Norway | XXVIII-2 *, XXVIII-3 *, XXVIII-4 *, XXVIII-5 **, XXVIII-1, XXVIII-2 *, XXVIII-3 *, XXVIII-4 ** | XXIX-1 *, XXIX-2 *, XXIX-3 **, XXIX-4 *** | XXX-1 *, XXX-2 *, XXX-3 ** | XXXI-1 *, XXXI-2 *, .... XXXI-14 * | XXXII-1 *, XXXII-2 *, .... XXXII-14 ** |
| Peru (1989)+ | XXVIII-3 *, XXVIII-4 *, XXVIII-5 ** | XXIX-1 *, XXIX-2 *, XXIX-3 **, XXIX-4 *** | XXX-1 *, XXX-2 *, XXX-3 ** | XXXI-1 *, XXXI-2 *, .... XXXI-14 ** | XXXII-1 *, XXXII-2 *, .... XXXII-14 ** |
| Poland (1977)+ | ALL | ALL | ALL | XXXI-1 *, XXXI-2 *, .... XXXI-14 ** | XXXII-1 *, XXXII-2 *, .... XXXII-14 ** |
| Russia | XXVIII-2 *, XXVIII-3 *, XXVIII-4 *, XXVIII-5 **, XXVIII-2 *, XXVIII-3 *, | XXIX-1 *, XXIX-2 *, XXIX-3 **, XXIX-4 *** | XXX-1 *, XXX-2 *, XXX-3 ** | XXXI-1 *, XXXI-2 *, .... XXXI-14 * | XXXII-1 *, XXXII-2 *, .... XXXII-14 ** |
| South Africa | XXVIII-4 *, XXVIII-5 **, XXVIII-1, XXVIII-2 *, | ALL | XXX-1 *, XXX-2 *, XXX-3 ** | XXXI-1 *, XXXI-2 *, .... XXXI-14 * | XXXII-1 *, XXXII-2 *, .... XXXII-14 ** |
| Spain (1988)+ | XXVIII-3 *, XXVIII-4 *, XXVIII-5 **, XXVIII-1, XXVIII-2 *, XXVIII-3 *, XXVIII-4 *, XXVIII-5 ** | XXIX-1 *, XXIX-2 *, XXIX-3 **, XXIX-4 *** | XXX-1 *, XXX-2 *, XXX-3 ** | XXXI-1 *, XXXI-2 *, .... XXXI-14 * | XXXII-1 *, XXXII-2 *, .... XXXII-14 ** |
| Sweden (1988)+ | XXVIII-2 *, XXVIII-3 *, XXVIII-4 *, XXVIII-5 ** | XXIX-1 *, XXIX-2 *, XXIX-3 **, XXIX-4 *** | XXX-1 *, XXX-2 *, XXX-3 ** | XXXI-1 *, XXXI-2 *, .... XXXI-14 * | XXXII-1 *, XXXII-2 *, .... XXXII-14 ** |
| Ukraine (2004)+ | XXVIII-2 *, XXVIII-3 *, | XXIX-1 *, XXIX-2 *, XXIX-3 **, XXIX-4 *** | XXX-1 *, XXX-2 *, XXX-3 ** | XXXI-1 *, XXXI-2 *, .... XXXI-14 * | XXXII-1 *, XXXII-2 *, .... XXXII-14 ** |
| U.K. | XXVIII-2 *, XXVIII-3 *, | XXIX-1 *, XXIX-2 *, XXIX-3 **, XXIX-4 *** | XXX-1 *, XXX-2 *, XXX-3 ** | XXXI-1 *, XXXI-2 *, .... XXXI-14 * | XXXII-1 *, XXXII-2 *, .... XXXII-14 ** |
| Uruguay (1985)+ | XXVIII-4 *, XXVIII-3 *, XXVIII-2 *, XXVIII-3 *, | XXIX-1 *, XXIX-2 *, XXIX-3 **, XXIX-4 *** | XXX-1 *, XXX-2 *, XXX-3 ** | XXXI-1 *, XXXI-2 *, .... XXXI-14 * | XXXII-1 *, XXXII-2 *, .... XXXII-14 ** |
| U.S.A. | XXVIII-4 *, XXVIII-5 ** | XXIX-1 *, XXIX-2 *, XXIX-3 **, XXIX-4 *** | XXX-1 *, XXX-2 *, XXX-3 ** | XXXI-1 *, XXXI-2 *, .... XXXI-14 * | XXXII-1 *, XXXII-2 *, .... XXXII-14 ** |

"+Year attained Consultative Status. Acceptance by that state required to bring into force Recommendations or Measures of meetings from that Year forward."

* Management Plans annexed to this Measure deemed to have been approved in accordance with Article 6(1) of Annex V to the Protocol on Environmental Protection to the Antarctic Treaty and the Measure not specifying a different approval method.

** Revised and updated List of Historic Sites and Monuments annexed to this Measure deemed to have been approved in accordance with Article 8(2) of Annex V to the Protocol on Environmental Protection to the Antarctic Treaty and the Measure not specifying a different approval method.

*** Modification of Appendix A to Annex II to the Protocol on Environmental Protection to the Antarctic Treaty deemed to have been approved in accordance with Article 9(1) of Annex II to the Protocol on Environmental Protection to the Antarctic Treaty and the Measure not specifying a different approval method.

Approval, as notified to the Government of the United States of America, of measures relating to the furtherance of the principles and objectives of the Antarctic Treaty

**15 Measures
adopted at Thirty-third Meeting
(Punta del Este 2010)**

**Approved**

| | |
|---|---|
| Argentina | XXXIII-1 - XXXIII-14* and XXXIII-15** |
| Australia | XXXIII-1 - XXXIII-14* and XXXIII-15** |
| Belgium | XXXIII-1 - XXXIII-14* and XXXIII-15** |
| Brazil (1983)+ | XXXIII-1 - XXXIII-14* and XXXIII-15** |
| Bulgaria (1998)+ | XXXIII-1 - XXXIII-14* and XXXIII-15** |
| Chile | XXXIII-1 - XXXIII-14* and XXXIII-15** |
| China (1985)+ | XXXIII-1 - XXXIII-14* and XXXIII-15** |
| Ecuador (1990)+ | XXXIII-1 - XXXIII-14* and XXXIII-15** |
| Finland (1989)+ | XXXIII-1 - XXXIII-14* and XXXIII-15** |
| France | XXXIII-1 - XXXIII-14* and XXXIII-15** |
| Germany (1981)+ | XXXIII-1 - XXXIII-14* and XXXIII-15** |
| India (1983)+ | XXXIII-1 - XXXIII-14* and XXXIII-15** |
| Italy (1987)+ | XXXIII-1 - XXXIII-14* and XXXIII-15** |
| Japan | XXXIII-1 - XXXIII-14* and XXXIII-15** |
| Korea, Rep. (1989)+ | ALL |
| Netherlands (1990)+ | XXXIII-1 - XXXIII-14* and XXXIII-15** |
| New Zealand | XXXIII-1 - XXXIII-14* and XXXIII-15** |
| Norway | XXXIII-1 - XXXIII-14* and XXXIII-15** |
| Peru (1989)+ | XXXIII-1 - XXXIII-14* and XXXIII-15** |
| Poland (1977)+ | XXXIII-1 - XXXIII-14* and XXXIII-15** |
| Russia | XXXIII-1 - XXXIII-14* and XXXIII-15** |
| South Africa | XXXIII-1 - XXXIII-14* and XXXIII-15** |
| Spain (1988)+ | XXXIII-1 - XXXIII-14* and XXXIII-15** |
| Sweden (1988)+ | XXXIII-1 - XXXIII-14* and XXXIII-15** |
| Ukraine (2004)+ | XXXIII-1 - XXXIII-14* and XXXIII-15** |
| U.K. | XXXIII-1 - XXXIII-14* and XXXIII-15** |
| Uruguay (1985)+ | XXXIII-1 - XXXIII-14* and XXXIII-15** |
| U.S.A. | XXXIII-1 - XXXIII-14* and XXXIII-15** |

"+Year attained Consultative Status.  Acceptance by that state required to bring into force Recommendations or Measures of meetings from that Year forward."

* Management Plans annexed to these Measures deemed to have been approved in accordance with Article 6(1) of Annex V to the Protocol on Environmental Protection to the Antarctic Treaty and the Measure not specifying a different approval method.

** Addition to List of Historic Sites and Monuments deemed to have been approved in accordance with Article 8(2) of Annex V to the Protocol on Environmental Protection to the Antarctic Treaty and the Measure not specifying a different approval method.

Office of the Assistant Legal Adviser for Treaty Affairs
Department of State
Washington, May 9, 2011.

**Report Submitted to Antarctic Treaty Consultative Meeting XXXIV by the Depositary Government for the Convention for the Conservation of Antarctic Seals in Accordance with Recommendation XIII-2, Paragraph 2(D)**

**Submitted by the United Kingdom**

This report covers events regarding the Convention for the Conservation of Antarctic Seals (CCAS) for the reporting year 1 March 2009 to 28 February 2010.

The summary at Annex A lists all capturing and killing of Antarctic seals by Contracting Parties to CCAS during the reporting period. A report of events in the 2010 – 2011 year will be submitted to ATCM XXXV, once the June 2011 deadline for exchange of information has passed.

The United Kingdom would like to remind Contracting Parties to CCAS that the reporting period for the Exchange of Information is from 1 March to the end of February each year. The reporting period was changed to the above dates during the September 1988 Meeting to Review the Operation of the Convention. This is documented in Paragraph 19(a) of the Report of that Meeting.

The Exchange of Information, referred to in Paragraph 6(a) in the Annex to the Convention, should be submitted to other Contracting Parties and to SCAR by **30 June** each year, including nil returns. The UK would like to thank all Contracting Parties to CCAS for providing this information in time to enable the UK to submit a complete report to ATCM XXXIV. The UK would, however, continue to encourage all Contracting Parties to CCAS to submit returns by the 30 June deadline to ensure that all relevant information has been provided.

Since ATCM XXXIII, there have been no accessions to CCAS. A list of countries which were original signatories to the Convention, and countries which have subsequently acceded is attached to this report (Annex B).

*March 2011*

## CONVENTION FOR THE CONSERVATION OF ANTARCTIC SEALS (CCAS)

Synopsis of reporting in accordance with Article 5 and the Annex of the Convention: Capturing and killing of seals during the period 1 March 2009 to 28 February 2010.

| Contracting Party | Antarctic Seals Captured | Antarctic Seals Killed |
|---|---|---|
| Argentina | 34[a] | Nil |
| Australia | Nil | Nil |
| Belgium | Nil | Nil |
| Brazil | 103[b] | Nil |
| Canada | Nil | Nil |
| Chile | Nil | Nil |
| France | 150[c] | Nil |
| Germany | Nil | Nil |
| Italy | Nil | Nil |
| Japan | Nil | Nil |
| Norway | Nil | Nil |
| Poland | Nil | Nil |
| Russia | Nil | Nil |
| South Africa | Nil | Nil |
| United Kingdom | Nil | Nil |
| United States of America | 1210[d] | 1[e] |

[a] 34 Elephant Seals
[b] 103 Southern Elephant Seals
[c] 150 Weddell Seals
[d] 630 Antarctic Fur Seals, 460 Weddell Seals, 50 Southern Elephant Seals, 30 Leopard Seals, 35 Crabeater Seals, 5 Ross Seals
[e] 1 Weddell Seal

All reported capturing was for scientific research.

## CONVENTION FOR THE CONSERVATION OF ANTARCTIC SEALS (CCAS)

London, 1 June – 31 December 1972

(The Convention entered into force on 11 March 1978)

| *State* | Date of Signature | Date of deposit (Ratification or Acceptance) |
|---|---|---|
| Argentina[1] | 9 June 1972 | 7 March 1978 |
| Australia | 5 October 1972 | 1 July 1987 |
| Belgium | 9 June 1972 | 9 February 1978 |
| Chile[1] | 28 December 1972 | 7 February 1980 |
| France[2] | 19 December 1972 | 19 February 1975 |
| Japan | 28 December 1972 | 28 August 1980 |
| Norway | 9 June 1972 | 10 December 1973 |
| Russia[1,2,4] | 9 June 1972 | 8 February 1978 |
| South Africa | 9 June 1972 | 15 August 1972 |
| United Kingdom[2] | 9 June 1972 | 10 September 1974[3] |
| United States of America[2] | 28 June 1972 | 19 January 1977 |

**ACCESSIONS**

| *State* | Date of deposit of Instrument of Accession |
|---|---|
| Brazil | 11 February 1991 |
| Canada | 4 October 1990 |
| Germany, Federal Republic of | 30 September 1987 |
| Italy | 2 April 1992 |
| Poland | 15 August 1980 |

[1] Declaration or Reservation
[2] Objection
[3] The instrument of ratification included the Channel Islands and the Isle of Man
[4] Former USSR

**Report of the Depositary Government for the Convention on the Conservation of Antarctic Marine Living Resources (CCAMLR)**

### Summary

A report is provided by Australia as depositary of the Convention on the Conservation of Antarctic Marine Living Resources 1980 on the status of the Convention.

### Depositary report

Australia, as depositary of the Convention on the Conservation of Antarctic Marine Living Resources 1980 (the Convention) is pleased to report to the Thirty-fourth Antarctic Treaty Consultative Meeting on the status of the Convention.

Australia advises the Antarctic Treaty Parties that, since the Thirty-third Antarctic Treaty Consultative Meeting, no States have acceded to the Convention.

A copy of the status list for the Convention is available via the internet on the Australian Treaties Database at the following address: http://www.austlii.edu.au/au/other/dfat/treaty_list/depository/CCAMLR.html

The status list is also available upon request to the Treaties Secretariat of the Australian Government Department of Foreign Affairs and Trade. Requests can be conveyed through Australian diplomatic missions.

## Report of the Depositary Government for the Agreement on the Conservation of Albatrosses and Petrels (ACAP)

### Summary

A report is provided by Australia as depositary of the Agreement on the Conservation of Albatrosses and Petrels 2001 on the status of the Agreement.

### Depositary report

Australia, as depositary of the Agreement on the Conservation of Albatrosses and Petrels 2001 (the Agreement) is pleased to report to the Thirty-fourth Antarctic Treaty Consultative Meeting on the status of the Agreement.

Australia advises the Antarctic Treaty Parties that, since the Thirty-third Antarctic Treaty Consultative Meeting, no States have acceded to the Agreement.

A copy of the status list for the Agreement is available via the internet on the Australian Treaties Database at the following address:

http://www.austlii.edu.au/au/other/dfat/treaty_list/depository/consalbnpet.html

The status list is also available upon request to the Treaties Secretariat of the Australian Government Department of Foreign Affairs and Trade. Requests can be conveyed through Australian diplomatic missions.

# Report by the CCAMLR Observer to the Thirty-Fourth Antarctic Treaty Consultative Meeting

## Introduction

1.     The Twenty-ninth Annual Meeting of the Commission for the Conservation of Antarctic Marine Living Resources was held in Hobart, Tasmania, Australia, from 25 October to 5 November 2010. It was chaired by Ambassador D. MacKay (New Zealand).

2.     All 25 Members of the Commission were represented.

## Standing Committee on Administration and Finance

3.     The Commission received SCAF's advice with respect to the Executive Secretary's proposal to undertake a review of the 2002 Strategic Plan and report the results of that review to CCAMLR-XXX.

4.     In addition, the Commission endorsed SCAF's recommendations that an open-ended informal group consider, inter alia, a comprehensive review of the CCAMLR Financial Regulations and, where appropriate, developing draft amendments to the Financial Regulations including drafting of investment principles.

## Scientific Committee

### Harvested species

*Krill resources*

5.     In 2009/10, six Members fished for krill in Subareas 48.1, 48.2 and 48.3 and most of the catch was taken in Subarea 48.1. The reported catch to 24 October 2010 was 211 180 tonnes[1].

6.     The krill fishery in Subarea 48.1 was closed when the catch reached 99% of the trigger level for the subarea (155 000 tonnes). The catch in Subarea 48.1 was the highest ever recorded in that subarea, and this was the first time that a subarea had been closed because catches had reached one of the apportioned trigger levels introduced in 2009 (Conservation Measure (CM) 51-07).

7.     Notifications for krill fishing in 2010/11 were received from seven Members covering 15 vessels with a notified total predicted catch of 410 000 tonnes; there was no notification for exploratory krill fisheries.

8.     The Commission endorsed the Scientific Committee's advice on the calculation of $B_0$ estimates for krill. The revised $B_0$ estimate for Subareas 48.1, 48.2, 48.3 and 48.4 was 60.3 million tonnes with a sampling CV of 12.8%, and this represented the best estimate of krill biomass derived from the CCAMLR-2000 Survey.

9.     The Commission endorsed the Scientific Committee's revised precautionary catch limit for krill of 5.61 million tonnes for Subareas 48.1 to 48.4 and agreed that this value would be appropriate for a revision of CM 51-01. The Commission noted that the current trigger level is not linked to the assessment of $B_0$ and would remain at 620 000 tonnes for Subareas 48.1 to 48.4.

10.    The Commission also noted the need to investigate the potential impact of climate change on recruitment variability, and agreed that a full review of the influence of recruitment variability on the calculation of sustainable yield be undertaken.

*Toothfish resources*

---

[1]    The reported total catch of krill in the Convention Area in 2009/10 was 211 974 tonnes (China 1 946 tonnes; Japan 29 919 tonnes; Republic of Korea 45 648 tonnes; Norway 119 401 tonnes; Poland 6 995 tonnes; and Russia 8 065 tonnes) (*CCAMLR Statistical Bulletin*, Volume 23, 2011).

11.     In 2009/10, 11 Members fished for toothfish in Subareas 48.3, 48.4, 48.6, 58.6, 58.7, 88.1 and 88.2 and Divisions 58.4.1, 58.4.2, 58.4.3b, 58.5.1 and 58.5.2; Japan also conducted research fishing in Divisions 58.4.4a and 58.4.4b. The reported total catch to 24 September 2010 was 11 860 tonnes[2].

*Icefish resources*

12.     In 2009/10, three Members fished for icefish in Subarea 48.3 and Division 58.5.2 and the catch reported to 24 September 2010 was 378 tonnes[3].

**Climate change**

13.     The Commission noted the findings of the SCAR Antarctic Climate Change and Environment (ACCE) report and the recommendations of the Scientific Committee on potential responses of CCAMLR to the protection of sites and species that might be particularly vulnerable to climate change.

14.     The Chair of the Scientific Committee noted that, while there was no substantive advice on the issue of climate change at this meeting, it remains an important part of the agenda of the Committee.

**Scientific Committee activities**

15.     The Commission noted the important discussions undertaken in the Scientific Committee on its work over the next 2 to 3 years and endorsed the three priority areas of (i) feedback management of the krill fishery, (ii) assessment of toothfish fisheries (especially in exploratory fisheries), and (iii) MPAs and the allocation of tasks to its working groups.

16.     The Commission endorsed the terms of the CCAMLR Scientific Scholarship. While the scheme should be funded from the General Science Capacity Special Fund, the long-term nature of the scheme was dependent on additional funding from the Commission and Members.

## *Bottom Fishing*

17.     The Commission noted the discussions and advice regarding bottom fishing and VMEs which had been provided by the Scientific Committee which included:

(i)     the development of a glossary of terms and conceptual diagram;

(ii)     consideration of two alternative approaches to defining the term 'Vulnerable Marine Ecosystem';

(iii)     estimation of the cumulative impact of bottom longline fishing on benthic communities and VME taxa;

(iv)     review of preliminary impact assessments provided by Members' who had notified their intention to participate in exploratory fisheries in 2010/11;

(v)     consideration of VMEs notified in accordance with CM 22-06 and potential encounters with VMEs notified in accordance with CM 22-07;

(vi)     development by WG-FSA of a Report on Bottom Fisheries and Vulnerable Marine Ecosystems.

18.     The Commission endorsed the following aspects of the Scientific Committee's work:

(i)     a glossary of terms and conceptual diagram relevant to the consideration and management of VMEs in the Convention Area;

---

[2]     The reported total catch of toothfish in the Convention Area in 2009/10 was 14 518 tonnes (*CCAMLR Statistical Bulletin*, Volume 23, 2011).

[3]     The reported total catch of icefish in the Convention Area in 2009/10 was 364 tonnes (*CCAMLR Statistical Bulletin*, Volume 23, 2011).

(ii)    development of advice on precautionary management actions that can be taken to mitigate immediate risks to VMEs without the definition of a VME;

(iii)   revision of CM 22-06, Annex A, in order to facilitate the work on the estimation of the spatial footprint and potential impact of notified fishing activities in forthcoming fishing seasons;

(iv)   inclusion into the VME Register of two new sites which were identified during a fishery-independent trawl survey in Subarea 48.2.

19.    The Commission noted the Scientific Committee's work plan on VMEs and related matters, most of which was scheduled for 2012 and 2013 and agreed to review CM 22-07 in 2012.

## Incidental Mortality of Seabirds and Marine Mammals during Fishing Operations

20.    The Commission noted that even though the Working Group on Incidental Mortality Associated with Fishing (WG-IMAF) had not met this year, it was important to continue to review IMAF-related information.

## Marine Protected Areas

21.    The Commission endorsed the terms of reference and potential workshop outputs from an MPA Workshop to be hosted in France in August 2011. It is proposed the workshop will review progress, share experience on different approaches to the selection of candidate sites for protection, review draft proposals for MPAs in the CAMLR Convention Area and determine a work program for the identification of MPAs in as many of the priority regions as possible.

22.    The Commission endorsed the revised management plan for ASPA No. 149, Cape Shirreff and San Telmo Islands.

23.    The Commission endorsed the recommendation that the process for designation of an MPA include the development of a research and monitoring program to be conducted within a specified timetable (e.g. 3 to 5 years), and that the development of a designation process and a monitoring plan may proceed in a step-wise fashion or both processes may occur simultaneously.

## IUU Fishing in the Convention Area

24.    Seven vessels had been reported to have engaged in IUU fishing in the Convention Area during 2009/10 and all were believed to be using gillnets.

## New and Exploratory Fisheries

25.    The Commission noted that WG-FSA and the Scientific Committee had reviewed progress in assessing the exploratory fisheries for *Dissostichus* spp. Many of these fisheries were considered to be 'data-poor exploratory fisheries' in, for example, Subareas 48.6 and 58.4, because data are currently insufficient to undertake a stock assessment and in some instances this is despite many years of a structured research and tagging program.

## Conservation Measures

26.    Conservation measures and resolutions adopted at CCAMLR-XXIX have been published in the *Schedule of Conservation Measures in Force 2010/11* (www.ccamlr.org/pu/e/e_pubs/cm/drt.htm).

## Cooperation with other Elements of the Antarctic Treaty System

### Cooperation with Antarctic Treaty Consultative Parties

27.     The Commission noted the discussion in the ATCM with respect to the development of the IMO's Guidelines for Ships Operating in Polar Waters and encouraged Members to fully engage in this process, as well as in the work of the Hydrographic Commission on Antarctica (HCA) of the International Hydrographic Organization (IHO), noting that many areas within the CAMLR Convention Area have not been surveyed to modern standards.

28.     There were no resolutions or decisions arising from ATCM XXXIII and CEP XIII requiring decisions to be made at CCAMLR-XXIX, although the Commission noted the adopted Resolution 5 (2010) 'Coordination Among Antarctic Treaty Parties on Antarctic Proposals under Consideration in the IMO' and Decision 1 'Compilation of Key Documents of the Antarctic Treaty System'.

### Cooperation with SCAR

29.     The Commission endorsed the terms of reference of a Joint CCAMLR–SCAR Action Group to improve the strategic alliance between the two organisations, noting that this would address objectives of the Commission as well as the Scientific Committee.

## Implementation of Convention Objectives

### Performance Review

30.     The Commission determined that the Performance Review should remain a matter for priority attention at future Commission meetings.  The status of the Commission's considerations of the recommendations arising from the Review is available at  www.ccamlr.org/pu/E/revpanrep.htm.

## Election of Chair

31.     The Commission elected Norway as Chair of the Commission from the end of the 2010 meeting until the conclusion of the 2012 meeting.

### Date and location of the next meeting

32.     The Commission agreed that its Thirtieth Meeting will be held from 24 October to 4 November 2011, in Hobart, Australia.

### 30th Anniversary of the CAMLR Convention

33.     7 April 2012 will mark the 30th anniversary for the entry into force of the Convention for the Conservation of Antarctic Marine Living Resources.

**CCAMLR-XXIX References for Topics and Decisions**

**The CCAMLR-XXIX Report is downloadable from:**
www.ccamlr.org/pu/e/e_pubs/cr/drt.htm

| Topics and Decisions | CCAMLR-XXIX Paragraphs |
|---|---|
| 1. Finance and Administration | 3.1-3.33 |
| 1. General Fishery Matters | |
|     1.1    Fisheries Catches in 2009/10 | 4.5-4.58 |
|     1.2    Fishery Regulation Measures | 12.1–12.78 |
|     1.3    Bottom Fishing + VMEs | 5.1–5.7, 12.12–12.13 |
|     1.4    Mitigation Measures | 6.1, 6.3–6.7 |
|     1.5    Scheme International Scientific Observation | 4.75, 10.1–10.6 |
|     1.6    Climate Change | 4.31, 4.59–4.61, 13.8 |
|     1.7    New and Exploratory Fisheries | 11.1–11.27 |
| 2. IUU fishing in Convention Area | |
|     2.1    Current Levels | 9.1–9.9 |
|     2.2    IUU Vessel Lists | 9.16–9.35 |
| 3. General Compliance | |
|     3.1    Compliance with Conservation Measures | 8.2–8.8 |
|     3.2    Market-Related Measures | 8.1–8.22 |
|     3.3    Compliance Evaluation        Procedure | 8.9–8.10 |
| 4. Ecosystem Approach to Fisheries Management | |
|     4.1    Krill Ecosystem-Based Management | 4.7–4.32 |
|     4.2    Incidental Mortality Seabird/Mammals | 6.3–6.7 |
|     4.3    Marine Debris | 6.2 |
| 5. Marine Protected Areas | |
|     5.1    Protected Areas | 7.1–7.20 |
| 6. Cooperation Antarctic Treaty System | |
|     6.1    ATCM | 13.1–13.6 |
|     6.2    SCAR | 13.7–13.8 |
| 7. Cooperation Other International Organisations | |
|     7.1    ACAP | 14.1 |
|     7.2    Others | 14.2–14.5 |
| 8. CCAMLR Performance Review | |
|     7.1    General | 15.1–15.9 |

**Summary of the Annual Report for 2010 of the Scientific Committee on Antarctic Research (SCAR)**

## 1. Background

The Scientific Committee on Antarctic Science (SCAR) is a non-governmental, Interdisciplinary Scientific Body of the International Council of Science (ICSU), and Observer to the Antarctic Treaty and the United Nations Framework Convention on Climate Change.

SCAR's mission is to be the leading, independent, non-governmental facilitator, coordinator, and advocate of excellence in Antarctic and Southern Ocean science and research. Secondly, SCAR's mission is to provide independent, sound, scientifically-based advice to the Antarctic Treaty System and other policy makers including the use of science to identify emerging trends and bring these issues to the attention of policy makers.

## 2. Introduction

SCAR's scientific research adds value to national efforts by enabling national researchers to collaborate on large-scale scientific programmes to accomplish objectives not easily obtainable by any single country. SCAR's members currently include scientific academies of 36 nations and 9 ICSU scientific unions.

SCAR provides independent scientific advice in support of the wise management of the Antarctic environment, in partnership with the Antarctic Treaty Parties and other bodies such as the CEP, CCAMLR, COMNAP, and ACAP.

SCAR's success depends on the quality and timeliness of its scientific outputs, which in most cases are assessed through external peer-review. Descriptions of SCAR's research programmes and scientific outputs are available at www.scar.org and are summarised in this paper.

SCAR produces an electronic quarterly Newsletter highlighting relevant science and other SCAR related issues (http://www.scar.org/news/newsletters/issues2011/SCARnewsletter26_Mar2011.pdf). Please email info@scar.org if you would like to be added to the mailing list.

## 3. SCAR Past and Future Highlights

### (i) SCAR Highlights for 2010:

1. SCAR published its new Strategic Plan 2011-2016 (http://www.scar.org/strategicplan2011/) "Antarctic Science and Policy Advice in a Changing World". SCAR's new Strategic Plan 2011-2016 aims to foster a sense of dedication and commitment in SCAR members and the community it serves to ensure realisation of the organisation's vision, mission and goals. The Strategic Plan guides collective decision-making about priorities and resource allocation.

2. In August 2010 SCAR held its Business meetings, Open Science Conference and Delegates' Meeting in Buenos Aires, Argentina. The Open Science Conference attendance was over 800 and it was particularly gratifying to see a large number of students and early career researchers attending.

3. Several new SCAR research groups were officially approved at the Delegates' Meeting in Buenos Aires, including the Scientific Research Programme Astronomy and Astrophysics from Antarctica (AAA), Action Groups on Southern Ocean Acidification, Multibeam Data Acquisition, and Antarctic Clouds and Aerosols. New Expert groups on Advancing TecHnological and ENvironmental stewardship for subglacial exploration in Antarctica (ATHENA) and Operational Meteorology in the Antarctic (OPMet) were also established. For further details see the full SCAR report or www.scar.org.

4. Planning for next generation of SCAR Scientific Research Programmes moved ahead in earnest with four new planning groups approved (State of the Antarctic Ecosystem (AntEco), Antarctic Ecosystems: Adaptations, Thresholds and Resilience (AntETR), Past and Future Change of the Antarctic Environment (PACE) and Solid Earth Responses and Influences on Cryospheric Evolution (SERCE) – For further details see the full SCAR report or www.scar.org.

5. Monaco became the latest country to join the SCAR family, having successfully applied to become an Associate Member of SCAR in 2010.

6. Professor Helen Fricker was awarded the 2010 Martha T Muse Prize for Science and Policy in Antarctica. Professor Fricker is widely recognized for her discovery of active subglacial lakes. She has shown that these lakes form dynamic hydrologic systems where one lake can drain into another in a short period of time. She is also known for her innovative research into Antarctic ice shelf mass budget processes such as iceberg calving and basal melting and freezing.

7. A Southern Ocean Observing System (SOOS) International Project Office was established in Australia, supported by the new Institute for Marine and Antarctic Studies at the University of Tasmania in Hobart (www.imas.utas.edu.au). This is a crucial step in implementing the SOOS.

8. SCAR, with the Association of Polar Early Career Scientists (APECS), and the International Arctic Science Committee (IASC) were awarded funding from the International Council for Science (ICSU) for a project "Education and Outreach Lessons from the International Polar Year".

9. The Ice Sheet Mass Balance and Sea Level: A Science Plan (ISMASS, http://www.scar.org/publications/reports/Report_38.pdf) was finalised. ISMASS is also now co-sponsored by the International Arctic Science Committee (IASC).

10. The Census of Antarctic Marine Life (CAML, www.caml.aq), which has identified more that 1000 new species, officially ended in 2010. The final legacy of CAML is still being explored, with a follow-up workshop in 2011 in Aberdeen, Scotland.

11. SCAR appointed a new SCAR Executive Officer, Dr Renuka Badhe. Renuka is from India, and holds dual Indian (OCI) and British citizenship. She is a marine biologist (PhD from the British Antarctic Survey) but with some policy background (Mphil from Cambridge University in Environmental Policy) and work experience with IUCN.

12. Several important publications of note were completed in 2010, including the International Polar Year Summary Report (http://www.arcticportal.org/ipy-joint-committee); a new book on the 'History of the International Polar Years' (http://www.springer.com/earth+sciences+and+geography/oceanography/book/978-3-642-12401-3) and a book on Science Diplomacy: Antarctica, Science and the Governance of International Spaces (http://www.scholarlypress.si.edu/index.cfm) that was written as an outcome of the Antarctic Treaty Summit (www.atsummit50.aq). Printed copies of the Antarctic Climate Change and the Environment report are available on-line. For further details please email info@scar.org.

## SCAR: Future Highlights

SCAR is involved in several major meetings over the next year (http://www.scar.org/events/),including:

- A Workshop on Antarctic Conservation for the 21st Century (31st May to 2nd June 2011), Nelspruit, South Africa – S. Chown will present a "non-paper" to the CEP, updating Parties on the preliminary outcomes of this workshop.

- ISAES XI - 11th International Symposium on Antarctic Earth Sciences 10 - 15 July 2011, Edinburgh, Scotland, UK (http://www.isaes2011.org.uk/)

- SCAR Executive Committee Meeting, 18 - 19 July 2011, Edinburgh, UK

- Symposium on Research Urgencies in the Polar Regions, 23 - 24 September 2011, Siena, Italy (http://www.mna.it/english/News/ICSU_symposium/)

The next SCAR science conference entitled "Antarctic Science and Policy Advice in a Changing World" will be in Portland, USA (July 16-19, 2012). This will follow the International Polar Year (IPY) Conference - "From Knowledge to Action" in Montreal, Canada (http://www.mna.it/english/News/ICSU_symposium/) (http://www.ipy2012montreal.ca/001_welcome_e.shtml).

Several other workshops are in the planning stages, for example on Ice Sheet Mass Balance and the relation to sea level and on Observing Systems in the Antarctic and Southern Ocean region.

For further details on SCAR activities see the full report, www.scar.org or email info@scar.org.

## The Annual Report for 2010 of the Council of Managers of National Antarctic Programs (COMNAP)

COMNAP is the organisation of National Antarctic Programs which brings together, in particular, the Managers of those Programs, that is, the national officials responsible for planning, conducting and managing support to science in Antarctica on behalf of their respective governments, all Consultative Parties to the Antarctic Treaty.

COMNAP has grown into an international association whose Members are the National Antarctic Programs from 28 Antarctic Treaty Parties from Africa (1), the Americas (7), Asia (4), Australasia (2) and Europe (14).

COMNAP's Constitution asserts its purpose: to develop and promote best practice in managing the support of scientific research in the Antarctic. As an organisation, COMNAP acts to add value to National Antarctic Program's efforts by serving as a forum to develop practices that improve effectiveness of activities in an environmentally responsible manner, by facilitating and promoting international partnerships, and by providing opportunities and systems for information exchange.

COMNAP also strives to provide the Antarctic Treaty System with objective, practical, technical and non-political advice drawn from the National Antarctic Programs' extensive pool of expertise and their first-hand knowledge of the Antarctic.

Increasingly complex science questions are being poised which can only be answered by multi-disciplinary and often multi-national science teams. This complexity, along with more demanding environmental measures and, in some cases, reduced funding, contribute to added pressure on National Antarctic Programs and to an even greater need for international collaboration. COMNAP works in support of greater collaboration between National Antarctic Programs and recognises the need for robust partnerships with organisations with similar goals. COMNAP has also progressively assumed responsibility for the production of a number of practical tools related to safety and information exchange.

For more information on COMNAP, generally, please refer to ATCM XXXII IP078 *COMNAP's 20 years: a New Constitution and a New Way of Working to Continue Supporting Science and the Antarctic Treaty System.*

### Highlights and Achievements for 2010

**COMNAP/SCAR Action Group**

This Action Group (AG) was formed at the joint Executive Committee meeting in August 2009, Punta Arenas. The AG met formally in March 2010 and developed a list of areas to collaborate together. These areas include education, outreach and communications, sustainability, non-native species, and the King George Island Project, to name only a few.

**Inaugural COMNAP Research Fellowship**

Noting that education and capacity-building was an area of mutual interest to both SCAR and COMNAP, and in recognition of the depth and breadth of talent within National Antarctic Programs, COMNAP has established, in conjunction with SCAR, the first COMNAP Research Fellowship. The COMNAP Research Fellowship was jointly launched with the Annual SCAR Science Fellowships, is being promoted jointly and applications will be reviewed by a joint selection panel. This inaugural fellowship was made possible by a grant from Antarctica New Zealand to COMNAP. The deadline for applications was 15 May 2011. It is hoped COMNAP can offer a Research Fellowship on an annual basis.

**COMNAP Symposium**

The "Responding to Change through New Approaches" Symposium took place on 11 August, in Buenos Aires. Over 120 people attended, with 12 presentations and 15 posters that were selected by a Symposium Review Committee. Symposium Proceedings were published and distributed to all COMNAP Members in November 2010 (ISBN 978-0-473-17888-8). Additional copies have been brought to this ATCM for distribution to those who wish a copy.

**Non-native Species Workshop and the Non-Native Species Checklists for Supply Chain Managers**

The COMNAP/SCAR Non-native Species Workshop was convened by Dr. Yves Frenot on the margins of the COMNAP Annual General Meeting (AGM) 2010 (8 August 2010, Buenos Aires, Argentina) in order to continue to raise awareness of the risks of non-native species introductions by human vectors. The preliminary results of the IPY "Aliens in Antarctica" project were discussed. COMNAP took very seriously the discussions held during the workshop and noted, especially, the need to develop simple and inexpensive awareness tools which could be used by National Antarctic Program supply chain managers (see COMNAP ATCM XXXIV Working Paper *Raising awareness of non-native species introductions: Workshop results and checklists for supple chain managers*). The checklists were made available to all National Antarctic Programs in November, are available in many formats for ease of use, in both English and Spanish, and copies of the checklists can be found at www.comnap.aq/nnsenvironment. Paper copies are also available at this meeting should anyone wish a copy. At the COMNAP AGM, August 2010 in Buenos Aires, it was noted by the Environmental Expert Group leader that cooperation with the CEP on the issue of the introduction of non-native species into the Antarctic was, the most significant, current environmental issue and also said that engaging in the CEP's work program on non-native species was considered a high priority task. COMNAP through its Environmental Expert Group continues to focus attention on education regarding non-native species and on sharing best practice as regards prevention of non-native species introduction in the Antarctic region.

**Energy Management Workshop**

Considering the discussion that took place at ATCM XXXIII and the discussions and recommendations of the ATME, it was agreed that a COMNAP Energy Management Workshop would be held on 8 August 2010, in Buenos Aires. The workshop, convened by Energy and Technology Expert Group Leader, David Blake with oversight from COMNAP EXCOM Vice Chair, Kazuyuki Shiraishi included presentations and also allowed time for discussion in order to share best practice related to energy management in Antarctica (see COMNAP ATCM XXXIV IP008 *COMNAP Energy Management Workshop*).

**IPY Outreach Workshop**

COMNAP Outreach Expert Group members met in Tromso and Oslo in June 2010 on the margins of the IPY Science Conference. The group held workshop meetings, provided 'masterclass' sessions for the Association of Early Polar Career Scientists (APECS) colleagues, and worked together in the IPY Press Centre to promote the science and operations from members' organisations. These combined activities afforded the Expert Group sufficient time together to share best professional practice and discuss past examples of successful joint communication and outreach projects and examine in-depth how this network would continue to work successfully post-IPY.

**Medical Expert Group – Workshop and Restructure**

The Medical Expert Group met on the margins of the AGM on 8 August in Buenos Aires to discuss pandemic management in Antarctica. The Expert Group on Human Biology and Medicine, Life Sciences Standing Scientific Group of SCAR and the Medical Expert Group of COMNAP proposed to combine the two groups in order to be more effective and reduce duplication of efforts. The proposal was first discussed by the joint Executive Committees, and in November 2010, the COMNAP EXCOM agreed to the proposal. The combined group will be known as the Joint Advisory Group on Antarctic Human Science and Medicine. It will remain responsive to the needs of both SCAR and COMNAP, but will have a reporting line via COMNAP alone.

## COMNAP Products and Tools

### COMNAP Ship Position Reporting System (SPRS)

The SPRS (www.comnap.aq/sprs) is an optional, voluntary system for exchange of information about National Antarctic Program ship operations. Its primary purpose is to facilitate collaboration between National Antarctic Programs, however, it can also make a very useful contribution to safety with all SPRS information made available to the Rescue Coordination Centres (RCCs) which cover the Antarctic region, as an additional source of information complementing all other national and international systems in place.

### The Antarctic Flight Information Manual (AFIM)

AFIM is a handbook of aeronautical information published by COMNAP as a tool towards safe air operations in Antarctica as recommended by the ATCM Recommendation XV-20 *Air safety in Antarctica*. An in-depth review of the AFIM is in progress. The AFIM continues to be updated via information from National Antarctic Programs and revisions are prepared and distributed on an annual basis to all National Antarctic Programs and to other subscribers.

### Antarctic Telecommunications Operators Manual (ATOM)

ATOM is an evolution of the handbook of telecommunications practices to which ATCM Recommendation X-3 *Improvement of Telecommunications in Antarctica and the Collection and Distribution of Antarctic Meteorological Data* refers. COMNAP members and Search and Rescue authorities have access to the latest version (March 2011) at www.comnap.aq/membersonly/atom (login required).

### Accident, Incident and Near-Miss Reporting (AINMR)

Information on problems encountered in Antarctica has always been exchanged. The very first ATCM recommended in Recommendation I-VII Exchange *of Information on Logistics Problems* that this should be so (effective 30 April 1962). COMNAP Annual General Meetings offer an opportunity for Members to exchange such information and also a new, comprehensive AINMR System is under development as one of COMNAP's projects. The AINMR's primary objective is: To capture outline information about events that had, or could have had, serious consequences; and/or reveal lessons to be learned; and/or are novel, very unusual events. So that National Antarctic Programs can learn from each other to reduce the risk of serious consequences occurring in the course of their activities.

––––––––––

For more information, please visit COMNAP's web site at www.comnap.aq or email us at info@comnap.aq.

## Appendix 1. COMNAP officers, projects and expert groups

### Executive Committee (EXCOM)

The COMNAP Chair and Vice-Chairs are elected officers of COMNAP. The elected officers plus the Executive Secretary, compose the COMNAP Executive Committee as follows:

| Position | Officer | Term expires |
|---|---|---|
| Chair | José Retamales (INACH) jretamales@inach.cl | Aug-2011 |
| Vice-Chair | Kazuyuki Shiraishi (NPRI) kshiraishi@nipr.ac.jp | Aug-2011 |
| | Maaike Vancauwenberghe (BELSPO) maaike.vancauwenberghe@belspo.be | AGM 2012 |
| | Yuansheng Li (PRIC) lysh@pric.gov.cn | AGM 2013 |
| | Mariano Memolli (DNA) drmemolli@gmail.com | AGM 2013 |
| Executive Secretary | Michelle Rogan-Finnemore michelle.finnemore@comnap.aq | 30 Sept 2015 |

Table 1 – COMNAP Executive Committee.

### Projects

| Project | Project Manager | EXCOM officer (oversight) |
|---|---|---|
| Antarctic glossary | Valerie Lukin | Mariano Memolli |
| AFIM – Consideration of the results of the review | Brian Stone & Giuseppe De Rossi | Maaike Vancauwenberghe |
| AINMR Reporting System & implementation | Robert Culshaw | Kazuyuki Shiraishi |
| King George Island project (APASI) | Michelle Rogan-Finnemore | Jose Retamales |
| Energy standard terminology development | David Blake | Kazuyuki Shiraishi |
| Review of equipment available at Antarctic stations for oil spill response | To be determined | Mariano Memolli |

Table 2 – COMNAP Projects currently in progress.

### Expert Groups

| Expert Group (topic) | Expert Group leader | EXCOM officer (oversight) |
|---|---|---|
| Science | Heinz Miller | Jose Retamales |
| Outreach | Linda Capper | Michelle Rogan-Finnemore |
| Air | Giuseppe De Rossi | Maaike Vancauwenberghe |
| Environment | Sandra Potter | Maaike Vancauwenberghe |
| Training | Veronica Vlasich | Mariano Memolli |
| Medical | Iain Grant | Mariano Memolli |
| Shipping | Juan Jose Danobeitia | Jose Retamales |
| Safety | Robert Culshaw | Kazuyuki Shiraishi |
| Energy & Technology | David Blake | Yuansheng Li |
| Data Management | Michelle Rogan-Finnemore | Jose Retamales |
| External Relationships | Michelle Rogan-Finnemore | EXCOM All |
| Strategic Framework | Michelle Rogan-Finnemore | Jose Retamales |

Table 3 – COMNAP Expert Groups.

## *Appendix 2. Meetings*

**Previous 12 months**

**9 - 12 August, 2010, COMNAP Annual General Meeting (COMNAP XXII) & IX Symposium, Buenos Aires, Argentina** hosted by the COMNAP member for Argentina, Direccion Nacional del Antartico (DNA).

**17 – 19 November, 2010, COMNAP Executive Committee (EXCOM) Meeting, Shanghai, China** hosted by COMNAP Vice Chair, Yuansheng Li of the Polar Research Institute of China (PRIC).

**Upcoming 12 months**

**1 – 3 August, 2011, COMNAP Annual General Meeting (COMNAP XXIII), Stockholm, Sweden,** hosted by the Swedish Polar Research Secretariat. In conjunction with COMNAP XXIV, two workshops will be held on the margins of the AGM. These are "The Management Implications of a Changing Antarctica" and "Inland Traversing".

**2012 COMNAP Annual General Meeting (COMNAP XXIV), Portland, Oregon, USA** (dates to be confirmed) in conjunction with the SCAR Open Science Conference and associated meetings.

# 4. Reports by Experts

## Report of the Antarctic and Southern Ocean Coalition (ASOC)

### 1. Introduction

ASOC is pleased to be in the Argentine Republic for the annual Antarctic Treaty Consultative Meeting. This report briefly describes ASOC's work over the past year, and outlines some key issues for this ATCM.
ASOC Worldwide

ASOC maintains its Secretariat office in Washington DC, USA. Our website (http://www.asoc.org) provides details about the organisation and its activities.

ASOC has 27 full member groups in eleven countries. ASOC campaigns are coordinated by teams of experts located in Argentina, Australia, Brazil, Chile, France, Japan, Netherlands, New Zealand, Norway, South Africa, South Korea, Spain, Russia, Ukraine, UK and USA.

### 2. ASOC Intersessional Activities Since XXXIII ATCM

Since XXXIII ATCM ASOC participated in intersessional discussions in the ATCM and CEP fora, contributing actively to the discussions on tourism; non-native species; revision of CEEs; subsidiary group on management plans; the development of the IMO mandatory Polar Code; Historic Sites and Monuments; and preparations for the upcoming ASMA workshop.

ASOC representatives attended:

- CCAMLR's 29th Meeting in October-November 2010, introducing papers on Antarctic krill management, Marine Protected Areas, the Ross Sea, fishing vessels, IUU fishing, and impacts of climate change.
- International Maritime Organization (IMO) meetings, including the 61st Marine Environment Protection Committee session, and the 54th and 55th sessions of the Ship Design and Equipment sub-committee regarding development of a mandatory Polar Code for ships operating in polar waters.
- Antarctic Krill in a Changing Ocean – Scientific workshop on effects of environmental change on Antarctic krill and implications for ecosystem-based management, April 2011 in Texel, The Netherlands.
- SCAR workshop on Antarctic Conservation in the 21st Century, held in June 2011 in Kruger National Park, South Africa.

### 3. Information Papers for XXXIV ATCM

ASOC has introduced twelve Information Papers, which address a range of topics that ASOC regard as particularly important for environmental management and conservation. The Information Papers contain recommendations for the ATCM and CEP that will help to achieve a more effective protection of Antarctica.

**An Antarctic Climate Change Communication Plan (IP 83)** – The ATME on Implications of Climate Change for Antarctic Management and Governance recommended that the ATCM consider developing an Antarctic climate change communication plan to bring the findings of the SCAR's Antarctic Climate Change and Environment report to the attention of other decision makers, the general public and the media [Recommendation 2]. In this paper, ASOC provides a draft communication plan to help implement this recommendation.

**Ocean Acidification and the Southern Ocean (IP 88)** – This paper provides an overview of the growing problem of ocean acidification, which poses severe potential threats to marine environments. The unique characteristics of the Southern Ocean suggest that ocean acidification will have its greatest initial impacts in the waters surrounding Antarctica if greenhouse gas emissions continue at present rates. More research is needed to fill current knowledge gaps on Southern Ocean acidification and its impacts.

**The Ross Sea: A Valuable Reference Area to Assess the Effects of Climate Change (IP 92)** – This paper discusses how International Panel on Climate Change models predict that the Ross Sea will be the last portion of the Southern Ocean with sea ice year round. The Ross Sea constitutes an important reference area to gauge the ecosystem effects of climate change and distinguish those effects from the effects of human activities elsewhere. This, in conjunction with a range of other scientific and biological reasons underpins why the Ross Sea should be included as a key component of a network of Southern Ocean marine protected areas.

**The Southern Ocean MPA Agenda – Matching words and spirit with action (IP 90)** – CCAMLR Members and ATCPs need to increase their resources directed towards a representative system of marine protected areas by 2012. ASOC urges ATCPs to make effective use of the upcoming MPA workshop this August in Brest, France. This will ensure that the words and the spirit of the agreements and conventions that make up the ATS and of recent discussions on MPAs are matched with action. ASOC looks forward to all participants coming to the workshop with well-justified MPA proposals.

**Antarctic Tourism – What Next? Key Issues to Address with Binding Rules (IP 84)** – This paper addresses issues that require particular attention from regulatory entities. Current trends suggest that tourism will continue to expand and diversify, adopting new modalities and penetrating further into the Antarctic mainland and along its coasts. It is important that ATCPs take proactive steps to constrain tourism within ecologically sustainable limits.. Making better use of existing regulatory mechanisms would be a good first step.

**Land-Based Tourism in Antarctica (IP 87)** – This paper examines the interface between commercial land-based tourism and the use of national program infrastructures, as well as recent developments in land-based tourism. The improvement of land-based facilities such as runways and camps, and the broad array of land activities now available to tourists, indicate that land-based tourism is growing. If no actions are taken soon, land-based tourism may well become consolidated as a major activity.

**An Antarctic Vessel Traffic Monitoring and Information System (IP 82)** – This paper provides information on the value of vessel traffic monitoring and information systems for improving safety and environmental protection. It uses as an example the development of a European VTMIS as a direct response to disasters in European waters. It summarises the existing tools and initiatives for tracking and monitoring of vessels, which could provide increased safety and environmental protection in Antarctica. ASOC calls on the ATCM to adopt a Resolution or Decision on development of an Antarctic Vessel Traffic Monitoring and Information System.

**Developing a Mandatory Polar Code – Progress and Gaps (IP 85)** – This paper provides information on the development of a Mandatory Polar Code and identifies issues needing further consideration, including a requirement for only polar class vessels to operate in waters where ice presents a hazard; and an Environmental Protection Chapter. ASOC calls on the ATCM to adopt a Resolution on taking collaborative actions to ensure that the Mandatory Polar Code provides appropriate safety and environmental protection standards for all vessel operations in Antarctica.

**Vessel Protection and Routeing – Options Available to Reduce Risk and Provide Enhanced Environmental Protection (IP 91)** –Ships' routeing and environmental protection measures developed to reduce risk and prevent marine pollution have not been used extensively in Antarctica. This paper provides information on the range of IMO measures available. A review of opportunities for reducing the risks of collision and groundings and protecting the most vulnerable areas through the use of IMO measures should be considered. ASOC calls on the ATCM to adopt a Resolution on a review of measures to address these issues.

**The Antarctic Environmental Protocol, 1991-2011 (IP 89)** – This paper reflects on Antarctic environmental protection since the signature of the Protocol on Environmental Protection. There have been some significant accomplishments, some issues remain outstanding, and some events seem incompatible with the original commitments. While overall the Antarctic region is protected, it is also under growing environmental pressures. The challenge for ATCPs is to respond effectively to emerging pressures, and not let national interests prevail over international obligations and the global benefits of protecting the Antarctic.

**Review of the Implementation of the Madrid Protocol: Annual reports by Parties (Article 17) (IP 113)** – This paper, addresses the annual reporting duty set out in Article 17 of the Protocol.. The level of compliance by Parties since the entry into force of the Protocol, while showing an increasing trend, is still relatively low. Information papers submitted to the CEP and the Electronic Information Exchange System (EIES) are the most effective ways available to Parties for complying with annual information exchange requirements.

**Evolution of Footprint: Spatial and Temporal Dimensions of Human Activities (IP 86)** – This paper discusses why the concept of footprint is essential in quantifying the impacts of human activities on Antarctica. This concept has been largely discussed since the first meeting of the CEP and needs to be applied more rigorously to address the complex aspects of a growing human presence in Antarctica. ASOC has also prepared a poster that illustrates the human footprint in Antarctica.

## 4. Other Important Issues for XXXIV ATCM

- Bringing **Annex VI on Liability Arising from Environmental Emergencies** into force as rapidly as possible should be a high priority for all ATCPs. ASOC urges all Parties to redouble their efforts over the next year to solve the remaining implementation problems, so that Annex VI can be ratified and come into force in 2012.

- **Biological prospecting** is not yet adequately regulated. ASOC supports a framework for managing it, including much more transparent sharing of data and information by Parties. Following Resolution 9 (2009), ASOC urges all Parties to re-start the discussions of bioprospecting.

## 5. Concluding Remarks

Antarctica is facing many pressures from global climate change and a wide range of activities.. ASOC looks forward to the ATCPs taking concrete actions in Buenos Aires that will help protect Antarctica over the longer term.

# Report of the International Association of Antarctica Tour Operators 2010-11

## Under Article III (2) of the Antarctic Treaty

## *Introduction*

The International Association of Antarctica Tour Operators (IAATO) is pleased to report on its activities to ATCM XXXIV, under Article III (2) of the Antarctic Treaty.

In its 20th anniversary year, IAATO continues to focus activities in support of its mission statement to ensure:

- Effective day-to-day management of member activities in Antarctica;
- Educational outreach, including scientific collaboration; and
- Development and promotion of Antarctic tourism industry best practices.

A detailed description of IAATO, its mission statement, primary activities and recent developments can be found in the *2010-11 Fact Sheet*, and on the IAATO website: www.iaato.org.

### *IAATO Membership and Activities during 2010-11*

IAATO is comprised of 108 Members, Associates and Affiliates. Member offices are located worldwide, representing 57% of the Antarctic Treaty Consultative Party countries, and carrying nationals from nearly all Treaty Parties annually to Antarctica.

During the 2010-11 Antarctic tourism season, the overall number of visitors decreased 8.3% to 33,824 from the previous season (36,875 visitors in 2009-10). These numbers reflect only those traveling with IAATO member companies. Details on tourism statistics can be found in ATCM XXXIV IP106 *IAATO Overview of Antarctic Tourism: 2010-11 Season and Preliminary Estimates for 2011-12*. The Membership Directory and additional statistics on IAATO member activities can be found at ***www.iaato.org***.

### *IAATO Annual Meeting and Participation at Other Meetings during 2010-11*

IAATO Secretariat staff and member representatives participated in internal and external meetings, liaising with National Antarctic Programs, governmental, scientific, environmental and industry organizations.

- The IAATO 22nd Annual Meeting (May 9-12, 2011, Hobart, Tasmania, Australia) hosted over 80 participants. Treaty Party representatives from Australia and Chile attended, along with representatives from CCAMLR, COMNAP, IHO/HCA and other Antarctic stakeholders. Notable outcomes of the meeting included:

    - Agreement to move forward with the IAATO Enhanced Observer Scheme. For details, see ATCM XXXIV IP107 *Towards an IAATO Enhanced Observer Scheme*.

    - A sustained commitment to education efforts aimed at non-IAATO Antarctica-bound yachts. For details, see ATCM XXXIV IP014 *IAATO Yacht Outreach Campaign*.

    - A report on success achieved with the IAATO Field Staff Online Assessment. More than 70 expedition leaders (ELs) and assistant expedition leaders (AELs) working with IAATO member-companies have now taken the test, which is designed to supplement the training and knowledge of field staff on the contents of the *IAATO Field Operations Manual* (FOM). Nearly all IAATO vessel operators have supported and participated in the test, and one Member-company requires it as a condition of employment for ELs and AELs. For 2011-12, the assessment will be expanded beyond its current focus on vessel-based operations in the Peninsula to include the Ross Sea/East Antarctica region. A version for land tourism operators is being developed. The assessment can now be taken online by all field staff.

- An update by the IAATO Climate Change Working Group. For details, see ATCM XXXIV IP0103 *IAATO Climate Change Working Group: Report of Progress.*

IAATO members, representatives from the Australian Antarctic Division (AAD) and other Antarctic stakeholders participated in an informal round table discussion at AAD offices in Kingston, Tasmania May 12, 2011 on issues pertaining to Antarctic tourism. A summary report on the discussion is forthcoming and will be available to Treaty Parties.

- One IAATO representative attended COMNAP XXII in Buenos Aires, Argentina, including the Non-Native Species Workshop. Efforts by IAATO members to eliminate the introduction of non-native species were commended at the workshop, and additional preventative recommendations were made and passed on to IAATO operators. IAATO gave a presentation on its risk-assessment approach at IMO Polar Code deliberations, and expressed interest in participating in the development of an accident, incident and near-miss database to facilitate lessons-learned and improved safety. IAATO supports further cooperation and collaboration between its members and National Antarctic Programs.

- Four IAATO representatives attended the 10th International Hydrographic Organization / Hydrographic Commission on Antarctica (IHO/HCA) Meeting in Cambridge, UK. Options for IAATO vessels, as "ships of opportunity," to contribute useful hydrographic information were discussed, including the rendering of mud maps and annotated charts; the use of simple data loggers; surveys and calibration of IAATO vessel sensors by hydrographic offices (HO); and the carrying of HO survey teams. An IAATO representative also agreed to provide comments on the current survey prioritization plan to HCA. IAATO will continue to recommend IAATO vessels as ships of opportunity for hydrographic data collection.

- IAATO sent a representative to the International Maritime Organization (IMO) Design and Equipment (D&E) Subcommittee's 54th and 55th meetings in London, as an advisor for Cruise Lines International Association (CLIA). Aware of the importance of the development of a mandatory Polar Code, IAATO participated in the working groups at both meetings, and will engage in the intersessional correspondence group currently underway. IAATO continues to work with an independent maritime safety consultant to develop an in-depth risk assessment study.

- An IAATO representative attended the Conservation of Antarctica Workshop in South Africa, May 2011, hosted by the Scientific Committee on Antarctic Research (SCAR). The workshop examined current and future challenges to the conservation of Antarctica, and ways in which these challenges can be addressed.

- IAATO was invited to participate in the Antarctic Tourism Conference, November 6, 2010 in Punta Arenas, Chile. Highlights of the conference were presentations by President Sébastian Piñera of Chile and President Rafael Correa of Ecuador. IAATO was pleased to provide a presentation on its role and mission in Antarctica.

- The IAATO 23rd Annual Meeting is scheduled for May 1-3, 2012 in Providence, Rhode Island, USA. Interested Treaty Parties that would like to attend or participate should contact IAATO at iaato@iaato.org.

### Environmental Monitoring

IAATO continues to provide ATCM and CEP with detailed information on member activities in Antarctica. For details see ATCM XXXIV IP106 *IAATO Overview of Antarctic Tourism: 2010-11 Season and Preliminary Estimates for 2011-12 Antarctic Season* and ATCM XXXIV IP105 *Report on IAATO Operator use of Antarctic Peninsula Landing Sites and ATCM Visitor Site Guidelines, 2009-10 & 2010-11 Seasons.* IAATO continues to welcome opportunities for collaborative work with scientific institutions to address specific issues on environmental monitoring, such as the work with Oceanites, Antarctic Site Inventory and University of Maryland and University of Stellenbosch reported in ATCM XXXIII IP112 *Report of the International Association of Antarctica Tour Operators* and ATCM XXXIII IP2 *Spatial Patterns of Tour Ship Traffic in the Antarctic Peninsula Region.*

**Tourism Incidents 2010-11; Update on Tourism Incidents 2008-09 and 2009-10**

Incidents during the 2010-11 season included:

- Arctic Trucks, a subcontractor to IAATO Member TAC, did not follow NGO guidelines for ASMA No. 5 Amundsen-Scott South Pole Station, South Pole. IAATO discussed the incident with NSF in February 2011, and the general issue of ensuring subcontractors are aware of their obligations has been raised within IAATO.

- Possible harmful disturbance of an elephant seal at Hannah Point. For details, see ATCM XXXIV IP104 *Proposed Amendment to Antarctic Treaty Site Guidelines for Hannah Point*.

- The *MV Clelia II* sustained a broken bridge window and electrical/communications malfunction when it was struck by a large wave in heavy seas in the Drake Passage December 7, 2010. The vessel returned safely to Ushuaia with no reported injuries to passengers and a minor injury sustained by one crew member.

- The *MV Polar Star* struck an un-surveyed rock while anchoring just north of Detaille Island on January 31, 2011. Following an underwater inspection at Arctowski Station, the flag state (Barbados) recommended that passengers be transferred to other vessels for the return to Ushuaia. This was accomplished on February 3, with all passengers returning to Ushuaia aboard other IAATO vessels, the *MV Marina Svetaeva*, *MV Expedition* and *MV Ushuaia*, on February 6. There were no reported injuries to passengers or crew, and the *MV Polar Star* also returned safely to Ushuaia.

Updates on previous season incidents:

- IAATO Marine Committee reviewed a draft report from Panama on the *MV Ushuaia* grounding in 2008 and the subsequent mitigation actions that were enacted by the operator, noting that the actions taken by the operator provided a good example of useful lessons learned.

- IAATO has requested and awaits a final flag-state report from the Bahamas regarding the grounding of the *MV Ocean Nova*, which occurred February 17, 2009.

- IAATO was informed by Malta that no flag-state report is warranted relative to the damaged propeller and shaft incurred when the *MV Clelia II* hit a rock at Petermann Island, December 6, 2009.

### Scientific and Conservation Support

During the 2010-11 season, IAATO members cost-effectively transported more than 100 scientific, support and heritage conservation staff, as well as equipment and supplies used by these personnel, to and from stations, field sites and gateway ports.

In addition, IAATO members and their passengers contributed $316,500 to scientific and conservation organizations active in Antarctica and the sub-Antarctic, such as Save the Albatross, South Georgia Heritage Trust, UK Antarctic Heritage Trust, Last Ocean, Mawson Huts Foundation, NZ Antarctic Heritage Trust, Oceanites and the World Wildlife Fund.

### With Thanks – Cooperation with National Programs, Antarctic Treaty Parties and all Antarctic Stakeholders

IAATO appreciates the opportunity to work cooperatively with Antarctic Treaty Parties, COMNAP, SCAR, CCAMLR, IHO/HCA, ASOC and others toward the long-term protection of Antarctica.

**Report by the International Hydrographic Organization (IHO) on "Cooperation in hydrographic surveying and charting of Antarctic waters"**

### *Introduction*

The International Hydrographic Organization (IHO) is the competent international organization, as referred to in the United Nations Convention on the Law of the Sea, which coordinates on a worldwide basis the setting of standards for the production of hydrographic data and the provision of hydrographic services to support safety of navigation and the protection and sustainable use of the marine environment. The IHO's mission is to create a global environment in which States provide adequate and timely hydrographic data, products and services for their widest possible use.

In order to concentrate its effort, the IHO has several Regional Hydrographic Commissions and has established a Hydrographic Commission on Antarctica (HCA) dedicated to promoting technical co-operation in the domains of hydrographic surveying, marine cartography, and nautical information within the Antarctic region. This Report provides a brief summary of the key coordination activities since the last ATCM.

The IHO is working closely with different organizations concerned with and interested in Antarctica, aiming at strengthening cooperation to improve safety of life at sea, safety of navigation, protection of the marine environment and contribute to marine scientific research in Antarctica.

### *1.- Key Coordination Activities (in chronological order)*

#### 1.1. IHO/HCA participation in Annual 21$^{st}$ IAATO Meeting

At the 21$^{st}$ Annual Meeting of IAATO that took place in Turin, Italy, 21-24 June 2010, the HCA and the HCA Hydrographic Survey Prioritization Working Group Chairmen made a set of presentations under the title "Importance of Hydrographic Activities in Antarctica".

The objective of these presentations was to raise awareness at the operational level of the importance of hydrographic activity in the Antarctica; to achieve a better understanding of IAATO on the existing risks associated to the present status of charting in the region and what IHO/HCA is doing to fill the gaps and, finally, to jointly explore on what and how IAATO can contribute to IHO/HCA efforts to improve the situation.

The first presentation covered IHO and IHO/HCA involvement in Antarctica; the role, priorities and achievements of HCA; SOLAS V Regulation 9 and the Antarctic and IHO/IAATO relationship. A second presentation included a description of the Maritime Shipping Routes (MSRs) and approach to charting priorities; work done and future work plans. Some case studies were offered as well as how hydrographic knowledge reduces the risk. Finally some proposals were considered as they could be put in practice by IAATO to contribute to improve availability of reliable nautical charts of Antarctic waters. Particularly the Guidelines for the Collection and Rendering of Hydrographic Data obtained by "Ships of Opportunity" in Antarctic waters was explained.

Participants appreciated the opportunity to discuss in detail matters concerning safety to navigation and their potential involvement in contributing to improve the hydrographic knowledge of Antarctic waters. Particular interest was expressed with regard to technologies to be incorporated on cruise ships as data collected was felt to be a concrete potential contribution from IAATO to the IHO/HCA, if such data is collected following standards. IAATO confirmed that it stands ready to continue cooperating with and participating in IHO/HCA meetings. In conclusion, the participation of the IHO/HCA representatives in the IAATO Annual Meeting has opened up new opportunities for mutual cooperation and collaboration aiming at improving safety to navigation and protection of the marine environment in Antarctic waters.

## 1.2. The 10th Meeting of the IHO Hydrographic Commission on Antarctica

The 10th Meeting of the Hydrographic Commission on Antarctica (HCA) took place in Cambridge, United Kingdom, 20-22 September 2010, organized by the UKHO and with the support of the British Antarctic Survey (BAS).

Dr. Nick OWENS, Director of the BAS welcomed all participants and highlighted the importance of the work of the HCA. The Chairman, Capt GORZIGLIA (IHB Director), thanked him for his kind words and also welcomed the 16 out of 23 IHO Member States (see **Annex A**) present (Argentina, Australia, Brazil, Chile, Ecuador, France, Germany, India, Korea (Rep. of), New Zealand, Norway, Peru, South Africa, Spain, United Kingdom and USA), as well as 5 international organizations and projects (COMNAP, IAATO, IALA, GEBCO, IBCSO). A representative of the UK Foreign and Commonwealth Office also attended and participated actively in the event.

The Commission elected Commodore Rod NAIRN (Australia) as Vice Chairman of the HCA; reviewed the status of the actions agreed at the last meeting; discussed the progress achieved and realized that almost all actions had been completed. The reports provided by IAATO, IALA, GEBCO and IBCSO as well as those provided by IHO Member States were commented. The reports on the progress made regarding the INT chart scheme; ENC scheme and production; the C-55 status with regard to the Antarctica; and an Antarctic GIS under development at the IHB, were also considered and discussed. Several actions were identified to progress further the actions. The Commission regretted that there were no representatives and no reports from IMO, IOC and AT Secretariat.

The Commission noted with satisfaction the constant support and contribution made by IAATO. At this meeting the IAATO delegation was formed by four representatives in a clear demonstration of interest in the HCA work. The Commission discussed at great length the outcome of the seminar delivered by HCA at the last IAATO Annual Meeting in June 2010, as well as the technical visits paid to IAATO ships before heading to Antarctica, briefing Captains on the procedure to collect and render hydrographic data collected as Ships of Opportunity. With regard to this last topic, IAATO offered to collect and make available all old available bathymetric data collected by IAATO ships; it was agreed to continue the practice of ships' visits and a group was established to study complementary future actions to implement the existing procedure.

A special discussion took place on availability of ENC covering Antarctic waters. It was agreed to include in the IHO report to the next ATCM the status on ENC production and a call to enhance ENC availability as a mechanism to improve safety to navigation and protection of the marine environment in the region. It was also agreed to prepare a paper to be submitted to IMO to report on the real ENC coverage of Antarctic waters by 2012 due to poor bathymetric data availability, datum mis-adjustment and other relevant factors. The IHB, as the coordinator of the INT Chart of Antarctica, was requested to develop and propose a large-scale ENC scheme for consideration by the HCA.

The Hydrographic Survey Prioritization Working Group continues to analyze the needs and its work will be improved with input from a new assessment of Maritime Shipping Routes and survey requirements that will be made by all HCA Members. Input is also awaited from IAATO who agreed to review the HCA survey plans.

Following a kind invitation from the Australian Hydrographic Service, the Commission decided to have the 11th HCA meeting in Hobart, Tasmania, Australia on 5 – 7 October 2011.

## 1.3 IHO/HCA participation in the Arctic-Antarctic Seafloor Mapping Meeting

This meeting - aimed at bringing together key players conducting bathymetric mapping in Arctic and Antarctic waters - was organized by Prof. Martin Jakobsson (IBCAO) from the Stockholm University, Sweden and Dr. Hans-Werner Schenke (IBCSO) from the Alfred Wegener Institute for Polar and Marine Research, Germany, under the name "Arctic-Antarctic Seafloor Mapping Meeting 2011", took place in Stockholm, Sweden, 3-5 May, hosted by the Department of Geological Sciences, Stockholm University.

The International Bathymetric Chart of the Arctic Ocean (IBCAO) and the International Bathymetric Chart of the Southern Ocean (IBCSO) are two projects whose objective is to compile the most up-to-date bathymetric portrayals of these two regions. The meeting was identified as a coordination mechanism to improve IBCAO and IBCSO and to discuss the uses and technical requirements of regional bathymetric compilations.

The opening keynote speech was made by the IOC Executive Secretary on "Why do we need to learn more about the Arctic and Southern Ocean? and the IHO/HCA Chairman reported on the "Status of Hydrographic Surveying and Nautical Charting in Antarctica". Around 50 people from 15 different countries were in attendance and over 11 oral presentations were given on Arctic Seafloor Mapping and 7 on Antarctic Seafloor Mapping. Also five presentations covered new data compilation methods and the situation regarding IBCAO and IBCSO, followed by separate breakout sessions on Arctic and Antarctic. In addition, a poster session was held.

Both IBC projects got organized and identified Members of their respective Editorial Boards. The coordination between these two IBCs, the Arctic Regional Hydrographic Commission and the Hydrographic Commission on Antarctica, respectively, was considered vital for the improvement of the Sea Floor Mapping of these regions. Technical details and deliverables were also identified and its execution coordinated. The GEBCO parent organizations, the IOC and particularly the IHO, were recognized for the efforts made to provide support to the development of the projects. GEBCO Nippon Foundation Project was identified as a potential support for the development of an Antarctic project, aimed at the continuation of the bathymetric compilation work so far conducted by IBCSO. In order to follow up and gain momentum, it was decided to have the next joint coordination meeting in May 2012, venue to be decided.

### 1.4 IHO/HCA participation in Annual 22nd IAATO Meeting.

At the 22nd Annual Meeting of IAATO that took place in Hobart, Australia, 10 May 2011, the IHO/HCA was given the opportunity to provide participants a follow-up on the actions and outcomes since the last HCA meeting in Cambridge that involves IAATO. The HCA Vice Chair represented the IHO/HCA at this event.

**Action 10/1:** Invites IAATO to make past bathymetric data available, with a view to improving the decision making process with regard to hydrographic survey priority assignment. Data can be provided to the IHB or directly to the HSPWG Chair

Outcome - the contribution from IAATO has started and data has been received at the IHB, allowing the IHB to contact producer nations and make them aware of the existence of such information for the benefit of the INT Charts series. This is something ongoing. In fact data has been passed to the UKHO. This is a positive sign that should be recognized and promoted to encourage further data submissions.

**Action 10/2 :** Develop further complementary future actions to implement ship visits and guidelines on the IAATO ship visit process. IHB to disseminate such procedures to relevant parties.

Outcome  - the development of the procedure is in progress.

**Action 10/3 :** Coordinate the visit of hydrographic surveyors from Argentina, Australia, Brazil, Chile, New Zealand and UK through HMS Scott to IAATO ships, when calling in ports on her way to Antarctica, or in Antarctica, to advise on the collection and rendering of hydrographic data, and report experience to HCA11.

Outcome - invite IAATO to consider contacting directly the relevant HCA Member States at all practicable port calls made before and after heading to Antarctica to ensure fluent exchange of information so that the collection of hydrographic data be done in accordance with established protocols and to facilitate the timely delivery of the data and information collected. IAATO ships jointly with relevant HOs are implementing this action.

The presentation given also referred to the concern raised by IAATO that some of the international charts did not contain the most comprehensive information. To overcome this, the following actions have been undertaken:

a) Specific actions have been placed on Member States to provide their additional survey data to the INT CHART producing nation.

b) A Catalogue of National Charts in the Antarctic has been compiled and was published in February 2011 on the HCA web site.

As regards to ENC availability, it was indicated that National Hydrographic Offices have been frantically working to complete ENC coverage of their coast waters and EEZs – to meet IHO deadlines ahead of IMO implementation of Compulsory carriage of ECDIS. Now that the initial ENC coverage deadline has passed and most coastal states have completed ENC coverage of their own EEZs, a rapid improvement in the coverage of ENC in the Antarctic can be expected. Nevertheless, it has to be considered that an ENC is only as good as the data that it is based on – if the existing paper chart is inadequate (unsurveyed areas etc), then a derived ENC will be similarly inadequate.

The IHO/HCA representative seeks continuing cooperation with IAATO in particular to:

(i) Encourage nations with Antarctic programs to collect as much hydrographic information as possible and share that information with the International Chart producing nation (and/or the IHB).

(ii) Keep pressure on National Governments / Hydrographic Offices to increase the priority of Antarctic Chart production.

(iii) Encourage all ships navigating in the Antarctic to routinely collect hydrographic information and provide it to the IHO/Charting Authority

(iv) Seek methods and systems to automate the data collection and simplify the rendering of the information whilst maintaining the necessary metadata to make it assessable and useful.

## 2.- Status of Hydrographic Surveys and Nautical Chart Production

### 2.1 Hydrographic Surveys

Out of the 13 National Reports submitted to the last HCA meeting, only 6 indicated that some systematic hydrographic surveys had taken place during the 2009/2010 season. Of these, two correspond to surveys conducted by scientific vessels engaged in projects of a wider scope, where bathymetry has been collected and we understand has been rendered to the national hydrographic offices for its use in the improvement of nautical charts. There is no assessment yet with respect to the 2010/2011 season.

It is expected that, with the commission of new survey ships and modern equipment installed on hydrographic survey ships, in the near future there will be improved capacity to conduct surveys in Antarctica.

The contribution made by IAATO ships and other Ships of Opportunity is appreciated and data collected is providing useful information to charting authorities.

The HCA Hydrographic Survey Prioritizing Working Group, with cooperation from COMNAP and IAATO, continues to progress its mandate and the preparation of graphics reflecting the status of hydrographic surveys assets, in the short list priority areas and related INT Charts.

### 2.2 Nautical Chart Production

Until the early 1990's, nautical chart coverage in Antarctica was limited to that produced by a number of IHO Member States' Hydrographic Offices for their areas of interest. Coverage was inconsistent, with much duplication.

In order to harmonize chart coverage, optimize production costs and better serve the mariner, the IHO adopted an international (INT) chart scheme for Antarctic waters, based on the following criteria:

- Adequate cover for international shipping.
- Conformance to IHO chart specifications.
- Number of charts kept to a minimum.
- Specific coverage for access to permanent scientific bases and those areas most frequently visited by cruise vessels.
- Responsibility for chart production shared by IHO Member States on a voluntary basis.
- Adoption of WGS-84 as the common geodetic datum.

The overall result is a consistent INT chart scheme of some 108 charts with approximately half of them covering the Antarctic Peninsula. The scheme includes a continuous coastal series at small scales (1:10,000,000 and 1: 2,000,000), charts at medium scales (1:150,000 to 1:500,000) in the approaches to scientific bases, and charts at large scales (1:10,000 to 1:50,000) around those bases and in critical passages.

The production of these INT charts is shared by the following 17 IHO Member States: Argentina, Australia, Brazil, Chile, France, Germany, India, Italy, Japan, New Zealand, Norway, Peru, Russian Federation, South Africa, Spain, United Kingdom and USA. As of March 2011, some 65 INT charts have been published; see **Annex B**.

 The driving force behind progressing INT chart production is the availability of good quality hydrographic survey data for the areas concerned. In many areas not yet covered, there is either no data or it is old data of unsatisfactory quality. Any significant progress towards completion of production for the whole scheme will therefore depend upon the capability of conducting hydrographic surveys to modern standards.

The remoteness and hostile environment of the area result in high costs for surveys. This fact and the priority given by IHO Member States to surveying their own national waters are both limiting factors to the progression of INT chart production for Antarctica.

Substantial efforts are being made to prepare Electronic Navigational Charts (ENC) of Antarctica.

It has been so far defined that volunteering Hydrographic Offices that have assumed the responsibility to produce the paper INT Charts covered in the INT Chart Scheme, will also be in charge of the production of the corresponding ENCs covering that area.

The IHO/HCA has already agreed on a small and medium scale scheme for ENCs covering Antarctic waters and it is working on the preparation of a large scale scheme, based on existing paper charts and other requirements.

Several Hydrographic Offices have started the production of ENC covering Antarctic waters. So far 48 ENCs cells are available (see **Annex C**) and the production program for the near future looks promising. Nevertheless those areas for which there are no reliable data and information to produce the INT Charts in paper format will likely face the same problem in its ENC version, so we should not expect the actual gaps to be covered by ENCs in the short or medium term, as the progress will only be possible after new hydrographic surveys are conducted.

## 3.- Conclusions

**13.** The IHO/HCA continues to be concerned about the extremely slow progress achieved in terms of bathymetric data gathering in the period 2009/2010, due to few hydrographic surveys being conducted.

14. Several Hydrographic Offices are progressing in the production of ENC covering Antarctic waters, following the ENC scheme agreed by the IHO/HCA. Nevertheless it has to be kept in mind that an ENC is only as good as the data that it is based on.

15. The IHO/HCA acknowledges and appreciates the cooperation and contribution received from several international organizations, particularly from IAATO and research institutions, who have made ancient collections of bathymetric informative data available, as well as new standardized hydrographic surveying data. This collective effort goes in direct support of the production of INT Charts and ENC covering Antarctic waters.

## 4.- Recommendations

It is recommended that the XXXIV ATCM:

1. Takes note of the IHO Report.

2. Considers encouraging the Hydrographic Offices of the countries belonging to the AT System to accelerate the production of ENC based on existing information, and to conduct hydrographic surveys of the missing parts of the priority areas identified by the IHO/HCA so that INT charts may be produced and made available at the soonest possible.

Monaco, May 2011.

**Annex A**

**HCA MEMBERSHIP**

**(May 2011)**

**MEMBERS:**

Argentina

Australia

Brazil

Chile

China

Ecuador

France

Germany

Greece

India

Italy

Japan

Korea, Republic of

New Zealand

Norway

Peru

Russian Federation

South Africa

Spain

United Kingdom

Uruguay

USA

Venezuela

**OBSERVER ORGANIZATIONS:**

Antarctic Treaty Secretariat (ATS)

Council of Managers of National Antarctic Programmes (COMNAP)

Standing Committee on Antarctic Logistics and Operations (SCALOP)

International Association of Antarctic Tour Operators (IAATO)

Scientific Committee on Antarctic Research (SCAR)

International Maritime Organization (IMO)

Intergovernmental Oceanographic Commission (IOC)

General Bathymetric Chart of the Oceans (GEBCO)

International Bathymetric Chart of the Southern Ocean (IBCSO)

IHO Data Center for Digital Bathymetry (DCDB)

Australian Antarctic Division

Antarctica New Zealand

**Annex B**

**INT Chart Present Production Status (May 2011)**

## STATUS OF INTERNATIONAL CHART PRODUCTION IN ANTARCTICA
### (1 of 2)

............... Not published

_____ Published

_____ In preparation

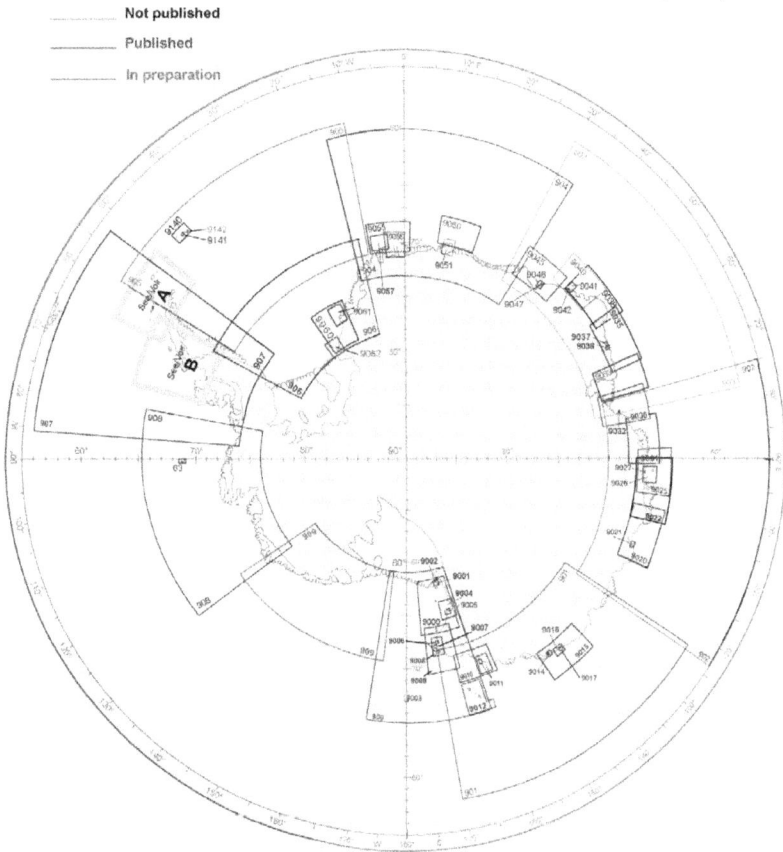

## STATUS OF INTERNATIONAL CHART PRODUCTION IN ANTARCTICA
### (2 of 2)

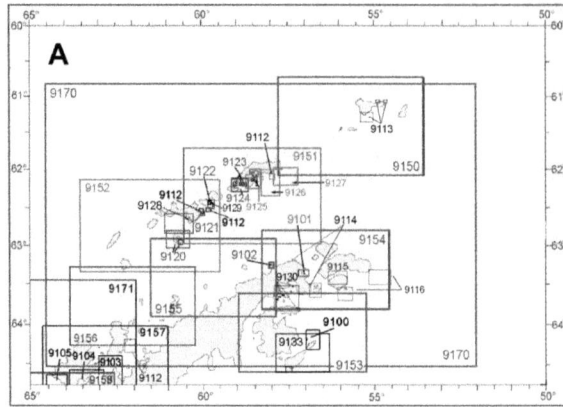

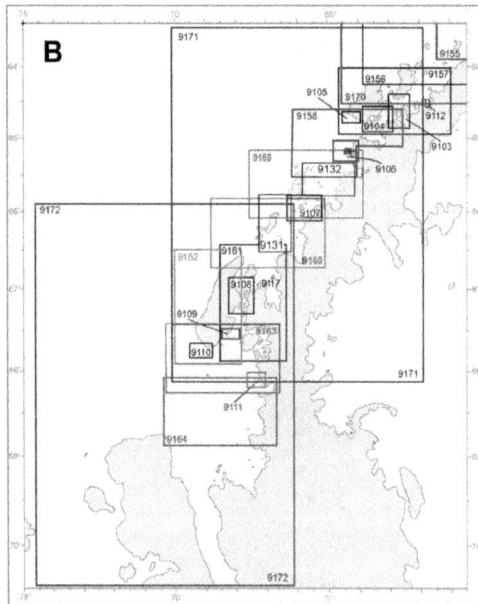

Not published
Published
In preparation

**Annex C**

**ENC Production (May 2011)**

**STATUS OF ENC PRODUCTION IN ANTARCTICA (1 of 3)**
**SMALL-SCALE «OVERVIEW» ENCs**
(based on the 1: 10M and 1: 2M INT Chart Series)

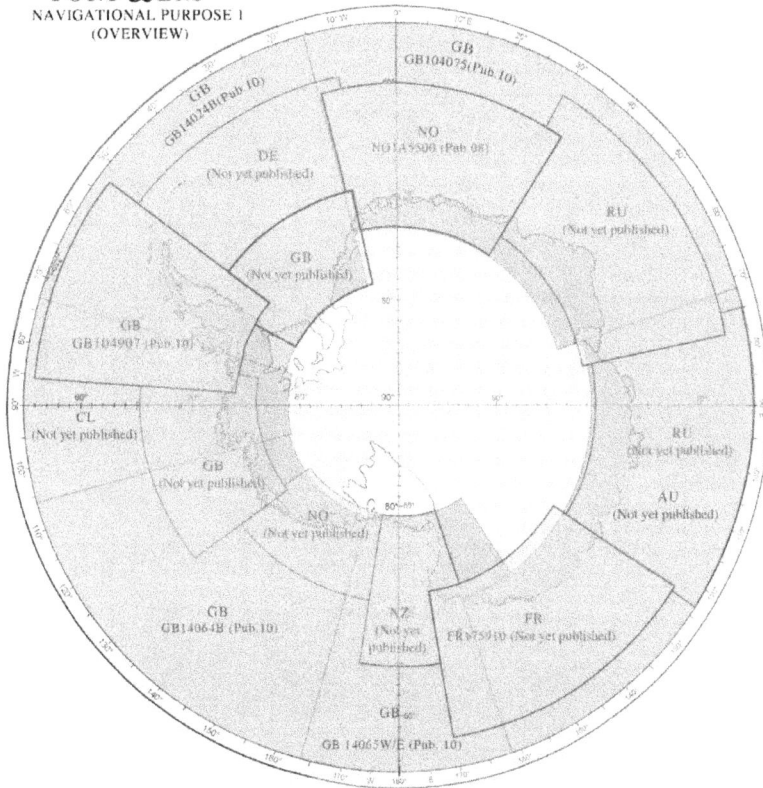

10M & 2M
NAVIGATIONAL PURPOSE 1
(OVERVIEW)

# STATUS OF ENC PRODUCTION IN ANTARCTICA (2 of 3)
## MEDIUM-SCALE « GENERAL» and «COASTAL» ENCs

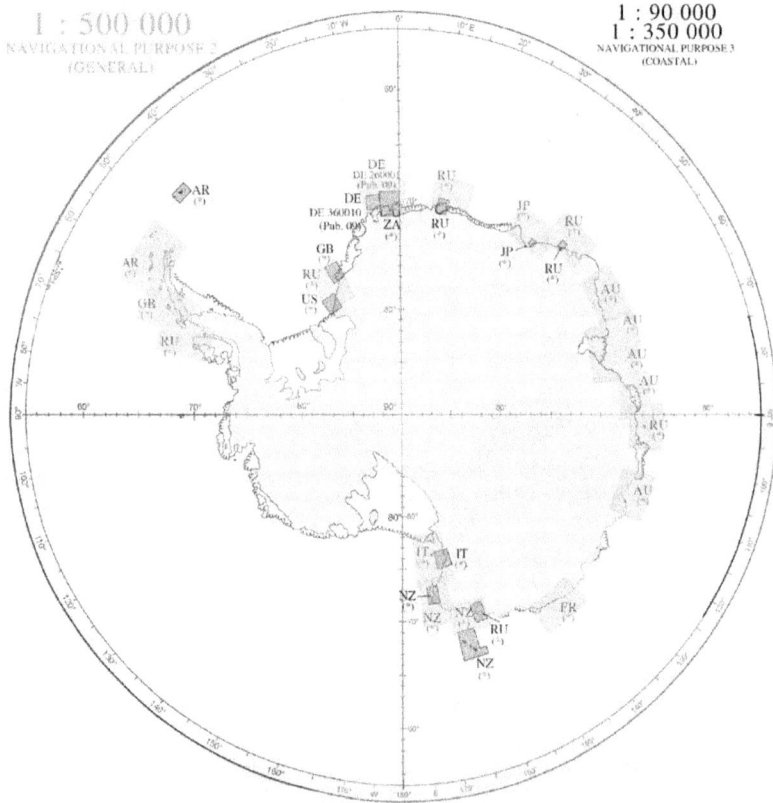

(°) Not yet published

## STATUS OF ENC PRODUCTION IN ANTARCTICA (3 of 3)
### MEDIUM-SCALE «COASTAL» ENCs
(based on the medium-scale INT Chart Series)

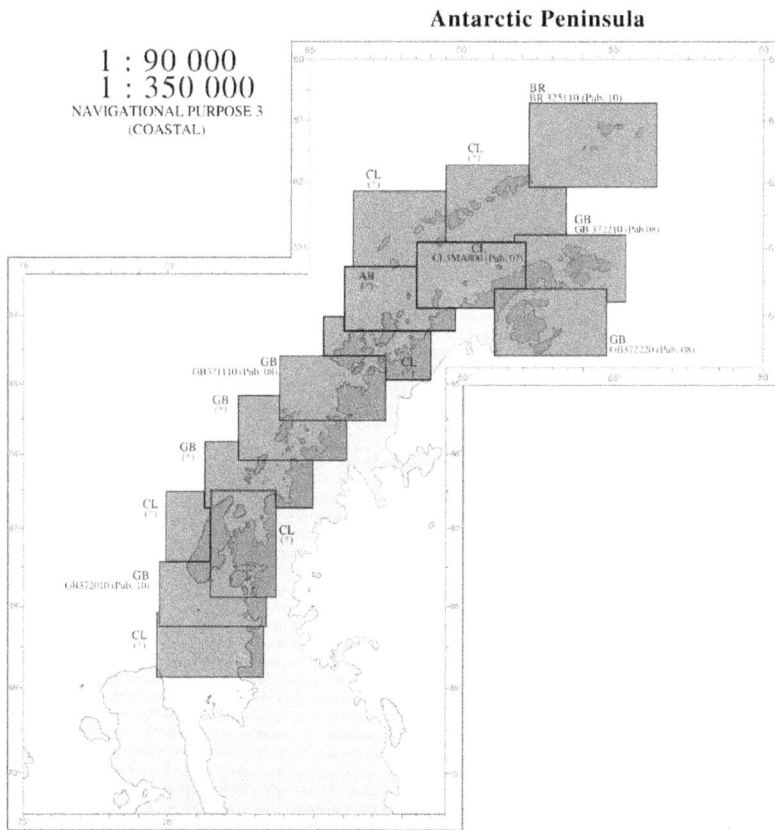

**Antarctic Peninsula**

1 : 90 000
1 : 350 000
NAVIGATIONAL PURPOSE 3
(COASTAL)

(*) Not yet published

Note: Additionally, 12 large-scale ENCs have been published by Brazil (2 ENCs), Chile (3 ENCs), France (2 ENCs), Italy (1 ENC) and United Kingdom (4 ENCs), including 9 ENCs in the Antarctic Peninsula.

# PART IV

**Additional Documents
from XXXIV ATCM**

# 1. Additional Documents

## Abstract of SCAR Lecture

### Detecting the Imprint of Humans on Antarctic: A Case Study

### By Mahlon Kennicutt II

The SCAR Lecture for 2011 "Detecting the Imprint of Humans on Antarctic: A Case Study" was given by the SCAR President, Mahlon "Chuck" Kennicutt II. The US National Science Foundation has funded a long-term monitoring program that examines the impacts of science and logistics at McMurdo Station, Antarctica's largest scientific base. The lecture was based on two IPs (IP 1 and IP 2).

The first of these (IP1) discusses how analyses of soil samples have shown that the most common contaminants are hydrocarbons from fuel, occurring at levels so low that acute or chronic biological responses are not expected. Similarly, contaminant metals generally occur at or near background levels and are not expected to elicit acute or chronic biological effects. Due to remediation efforts, there was not a strong correlation between known spill locations and soil contaminant levels. However, hydrocarbon levels were highest in areas where fuel is either stored or transferred to vehicles and in vehicular traffic and parking areas.

Marine sediments were contaminated by past (pre-1980) disposal practices. Polychlorinated biphenyls (PCBs), petroleum hydrocarbons, and metals were detectable in the sediments close to the Station at concentrations expected to elicit biological responses. PCB concentrations are highest near the sewage outfall.

Hydrocarbons in both terrestrial and marine samples were biodegraded, indicating that the area around McMurdo Station has an indigenous population of hydrocarbon-degrading bacteria. PCBs, however, were unaltered indicating that *in situ* microbes have limited capacities to degrade synthetic chemicals.

From a management perspective, these data are useful for

- Identifying monitoring indicators and protocols that work well in the Antarctic environment;
- Assessing program design elements; and
- Informing monitoring efforts elsewhere in Antarctica.

The second Information paper (IP2) show how using aerial photographs taken between 1956 and 2005, researchers identified areas where the ground surface has been visibly altered by anthropogenic activities (e.g., roads, buildings, disappearance of the original periglacial microrelief pattern of polygons). Geographic Information Systems (GIS) analyses of historic and current aerial photographs have shown that most of the disturbance of physical surfaces on land (i.e. the creation of the station's physical footprint) occurred during the early years of the station's history and the footprint has not expanded much since the 1970s.

From a management perspective, these data are useful for

- Placing observed environmental impacts in their historical perspective;
- Providing an understanding of the current state of the environment around McMurdo Station;
- Assessing station design elements; and
- Informing monitoring efforts elsewhere in Antarctica.

The presentation is available in pdf format from: http://www.scar.org/communications/ATCM 2011 SCAR Lecture/Kennicutt ATCM.pdf

# 2. List of Documents

## 2. List of Documents

| Working Papers | | | | | | | | |
|---|---|---|---|---|---|---|---|---|
| Number | Ag. Items | Title | Submitted By | E | F | R | S | Attachments |
| WP001 | ATCM 11 CEP 10 | Inspection undertaken by Japan in accordance with Article VII of the Antarctic Treaty and Article XIV of the Protocol on Environmental Protection | Japan | X | X | X | X | |
| WP002 rev.1 | ATCM 9 | Early Warning System for Antarctica of the arrival of waves generated by earthquakes | Argentina | X | X | X | X | |
| WP003 | CEP 7a | Review of the management plan for ASPA No. 120, Pointe-Géologie Archipelago, Terre Adélie | France | X | X | X | X | ASPA 120. Revised Management Plan |
| WP004 | CEP 7a | Management Plan for ASPA No. 166, Port-Martin, Terre Adélie. Proposal to extend the existing Management Plan | France | X | X | X | X | |
| WP005 | CEP 7b | Proposed addition of No.1 Building Commemorating China's Antarctic Expedition at Great Wall Station to the List of Historic Sites and Monument | China | X | X | X | X | |
| WP006 | CEP 7a | Revised Management Plan for Antarctic Specially Protected Area No. 149 Cape Shirreff and San Telmo Island, Livingston Island, South Shetland Islands | United States Chile | X | X | X | X | ASPA 149 Map 1 ASPA 149 Map 2 ASPA 149 Map 3 ASPA 149 Revised Management Plan |
| WP007 | CEP 6a | Report of the intersessional open-ended contact group to consider the draft CEE for the "Construction and Operation of the Jang Bogo Station, Terra Nova Bay, Antarctica" | Australia | X | X | X | X | |
| WP008 | ATCM 20 CEP 14 | Proposed schedule for the 35th Antarctic Treaty Consultative Meeting, Hobart, 2012 | Australia | X | X | X | X | |
| WP009 | CEP 7a | Revised Management Plan for Antarctic Specially Protected Area No. 122 Arrival Heights, Hut Point Peninsula, Ross Island | United States | X | X | X | X | ASPA 122 Map 1 ASPA 122 Map 2 ASPA 122 Revised Management Plan |
| WP010 | CEP 7a | Developing a plan for Special protection at Taylor Glacier and Blood Falls, Taylor Valley, McMurdo Dry Valleys Victoria Land | United States | X | X | X | X | Appendix A – Protected Area Boundary Options |
| WP011 | ATCM 10 | Follow-up to the unauthorized presence of French yachts within the Treaty area and damage caused to the hut known as Wordie House - Observations on the consequences of the affair | France | X | X | X | X | |
| WP012 | CEP 8a | Raising awareness of non-native species introductions: Workshop results and checklists for | COMNAP SCAR | X | X | X | X | COMNAP/SCAR Checklists for Supply Chain Managers COMNAP/SCAR NNS Workshop Report |

| Working Papers | | | | | | | | |
|---|---|---|---|---|---|---|---|---|
| Number | Ag. Items | Title | Submitted By | E | F | R | S | Attachments |
| | | supply chain managers | | | | | | |
| WP013 | CEP 7a | Subsidiary Group on Management Plans – Report on Terms of Reference #4 and #5: Improving Management Plans and the Process for their Intersessional Review | Australia | X | X | X | X | Resolution 2 (2011) - Annex |
| WP014 | CEP 6a | Report of the Intersessional Open-ended Contact Group to Consider the Draft CEE for the "Proposed Exploration of Subglacial Lake Ellsworth, Antarctica" | Norway | X | X | X | X | |
| WP015 rev.1 | CEP 9 | Remote Sensing Techniques for Improved Monitoring of Environment and Climate Change in Antarctica | United Kingdom | X | X | X | X | |
| WP016 | CEP 6a | Draft Comprehensive Environmental Evaluation (CEE) for the Proposed Exploration of Subglacial Lake Ellsworth, Antarctica | United Kingdom | X | X | X | X | Non-technical summary |
| WP017 | CEP 7c | Revision of Site Guidelines for Whalers Bay, Deception Island, South Shetland Islands | United Kingdom Argentina Chile Norway Spain United States | X | X | X | X | Revised Site guidelines for Whalers Bay |
| WP018 | CEP 7a | Proposed monitoring activities within Antarctic Specially Protected Area (ASPA) No. 107 Emperor Island, Dion Islands, Marguerite Bay, Antarctic Peninsula | United Kingdom | X | X | X | X | |
| WP019 | ATCM 10 | The Assessment of Land-Based Activities in Antarctica | United Kingdom | X | X | X | X | |
| WP020 | ATCM 10 | Data Collection and Reporting on Yachting Activity in Antarctica in 2010/11 | United Kingdom | X | X | X | X | |
| WP021 | ATCM 10 | Antarctic Tourism: Towards a strategic and pro-active approach via an inventory of outstanding questions | Netherlands United Kingdom | X | X | X | X | |
| WP022 | ATCM 5 | An additional procedure for intersessional consultations among ATCPs | Netherlands Germany | X | X | X | X | |
| WP023 | CEP 7a | Revision of the Management Plan for Antarctic Specially Protected Area (ASPA) No. 140 Parts of Deception Island, South Shetland Islands | United Kingdom | X | X | X | X | ASPA 140 - Revised Management Plan |
| WP024 | ATCM 5 | Progress Report of the Intersessional Contact Group on Review of ATCM Recommendations | Argentina | X | X | X | X | |
| WP025 | ATCM 5 CEP 4 | Timely Submission of Papers in Advance of ATCMs | Germany United States | X | X | X | X | |

| Working Papers | | | | | | | |
|---|---|---|---|---|---|---|---|
| Number | Ag. Items | Title | Submitted By | E | F | R | S | Attachments |
| WP026 | ATCM 10 | ATCM Review of Tourism Rules and Regulations | United States France Germany Netherlands New Zealand | X | X | X | X | |
| WP027 | CEP 7b | Report of the Informal Discussions on Historic Sites and Monuments | Argentina | X | X | X | X | |
| WP028 | CEP 12 | Environmental issues related to the practicality of repair or remediation of environmental damage | Australia | X | X | X | X | |
| WP029 | CEP 7a | Revised management plan for Antarctic Specially Protected Area No. 167, Hawker Island, Princess Elizabeth Land | Australia | X | X | X | X | ASPA 167 Map A ASPA 167 Map B ASPA 167 Revised Management Plan |
| WP030 | CEP 7c | Site Guidelines for the Taylor Valley Visitor Zone, Southern Victoria Land | New Zealand United States | X | X | X | X | Site Guidelines for Taylor Valley Site Guidelines Taylor Valley Image 1 Site Guidelines Taylor Valley Map 1 Site Guidelines Taylor Valley Map 2 Site Guidelines Taylor Valley Overview |
| WP031 | CEP 7a | Revision of Management Plan for Antarctic Specially Protected Area No. 116: New College Valley, Caughley Beach, Cape Bird, Ross Island | New Zealand | X | X | X | X | ASPA 116 Map A ASPA 116 Map B ASPA 116 Revised Management Plan |
| WP032 | CEP 7f | Enhancing the Antarctic Protected Areas Database to help assess and further develop the protected areas system | Australia | X | X | X | X | |
| WP033 | CEP 7a | Revision of Management Plan for Antarctic Specially Protected Area No. 131: Canada Glacier, Lake Fryxell, Taylor Valley, Victoria Land | New Zealand | X | X | X | X | ASPA 131 Map A ASPA 131 Map B ASPA 131 Revised Management Plan |
| WP034 | CEP 8a | Report of the Intersessional Contact Group on Non-Native Species 2010-2011 | New Zealand | X | X | X | X | Resolution 6 (2011) - Annex |
| WP035 | CEP 7d | Understanding concepts of Footprint and Wilderness related to protection of the Antarctic environment | New Zealand | X | X | X | X | |
| WP036 | ATCM 5 CEP 4 | A proposed new approach to the handling of Information Papers | Australia France New Zealand | X | X | X | X | |
| WP037 | ATCM 10 | Yacht guidelines to complement safety standards of ship traffic around Antarctica | Germany Australia Norway United Kingdom United States | X | X | X | X | |
| WP038 | CEP 8c | Antarctic Discussion Forum of Competent Authorities (DFCA) – Impacts of underwater sound to Antarctic waters – | Germany | X | X | X | X | |
| WP039 | CEP 7a | Revised Management Plan for Antarctic Specially Managed Area No. 2 | New Zealand United States | X | X | X | X | ASMA 2 Appendix A ASMA 2 Appendix B ASMA 2 Appendix C |

| | | | Working Papers | | | | | |
|---|---|---|---|---|---|---|---|---|
| Number | Ag. Items | Title | Submitted By | E | F | R | S | Attachments |
| | | McMurdo Dry Valleys, Southern Victoria Land | | | | | | ASMA 2 Appendix D<br>ASMA 2 Appendix E<br>ASMA 2 Appendix F<br>ASMA 2 Map 1<br>ASMA 2 Map 2<br>ASMA 2 Revised Management Plan |
| WP040 | ATCM 5 | Strengthening Support for the Madrid Protocol | France<br>Australia<br>Spain | X | X | X | X | Call to restart the ratification process of the Madrid Protocol |
| WP041 | CEP 7f | Fourth Progress Report on the Discussion of the International Working Group about Possibilities for Environmental Management of Fildes Peninsula and Ardley Island | Chile<br>Germany | X | X | X | X | |
| WP042 | CEP 6a | The Draft Comprehensive Environmental Evaluation for the construction and operation of the Jang Bogo Antarctic Research Station, Terra Nova Bay, Antarctica | Korea (ROK) | X | X | X | X | Annex A. Non-technical summary |
| WP043 | CEP 5 | Developing a Simple Methodology for Classifying Antarctic Specially Protected Areas According to their Vulnerability to Climate Change | United Kingdom<br>Norway | X | X | X | X | |
| WP044 | ATCM 13<br>CEP 5 | Progress report on ATME on Climate Change | United Kingdom<br>Norway | X | X | X | X | |
| WP045 | CEP 7c | Report of the open-ended intersessional contact group on revision of environmental elements of Recommendation XVIII-1 | Australia | X | X | X | X | Resolution X (2011) Guidelines for visitors to the Antarctic |
| WP046 | ATCM 10 | Limitation of tourism and non-governmental activities to sites under Guidelines for Site Visits only | France | X | X | X | X | |
| WP047 | CEP 7a | Subsidiary Group on Management Plans – Report on Terms of Reference #1 to #3: Review of Draft Management Plans | Australia | X | X | X | X | ASPA 126 Revised Management Plan |
| WP048 | ATCM 10 | Report of the Intersessional Contact Group on Supervision of Antarctic Tourism | Argentina | X | X | X | X | DRAFT MODULE OF QUESTIONS FOR VISITORS' IN-FIELD ACTIVITIES |
| WP049 | ATCM 10<br>CEP 7c | Guidelines for the north-east beach of the Ardley Peninsula (Ardley Island), King George Island / Isla 25 de Mayo, South Shetland Islands | Chile<br>Argentina | X | X | X | X | Visitor site guidelines Ardley Island<br>Visitor site guidelines Ardley Island |
| WP050 | CEP 7a | Revised Management Plan for Antarctic Specially Protected Area (ASPA) No. 165 Edmonson Point, Ross Sea | Italy | X | X | X | X | ASPA 165 Map 1<br>ASPA 165 Map 2<br>ASPA 165 Map 3<br>ASPA 165 Map 4<br>ASPA 165 Revised Management Plan |
| WP051 | ATCM 11<br>CEP 10 | Australian Antarctic Treaty and Environmental Protocol inspections: | Australia | X | X | X | X | |

| | | | Working Papers | | | | | |
|---|---|---|---|---|---|---|---|---|
| Number | Ag. Items | Title | Submitted By | E | F | R | S | Attachments |
| | | January 2010 and January 2011 | | | | | | |
| WP052 rev.1 | CEP 7c | Visitor site guide for Mawson's Huts and Cape Denison, East Antarctica | Australia | X | X | X | X | |
| WP053 | CEP 8a | Measures to reduce the risk of non-native species introductions to the Antarctic region associated with fresh foods | SCAR | X | X | X | X | |
| WP054 | CEP 6b | Technology for investigating water strata of subglacial Lake Vostok | Russian Federation | X | X | X | X | |
| WP055 | ATCM 5 | On strategy for the development of the Russian Federation activities in the Antarctic for the period until 2020 and longer-term perspective | Russian Federation | X | X | X | X | |
| WP056 | ATCM 9 | Ensuring safety of shipping in Antarctic waters adopted in the Russian Federation | Russian Federation | X | X | X | X | |
| WP057 | CEP 7f | On the need of constant monitoring of the values of Antarctic Specially Protected Areas and Antarctic Specially Managed Areas | Russian Federation | X | X | X | X | |
| WP058 | CEP 7a | Revised Management Plan for Antarctic Specially Protected Area No. 127 "HASWELL ISLAND" (Haswell Island and Adjacent Emperor Penguin Rookery on Fast Ice) Revised Management Plan | Russian Federation | X | X | X | X | ASPA 127 Revised Management Plan |
| WP059 | CEP 7b | Proposal of Modification for the Historic Monument No. 82. Installation of Commemorative Plaques at the Monument to the Antarctic Treaty | Chile | X | X | X | X | |
| WP060 | ATCM 18 | Proposal for shortening the Antarctic Treaty Consultative Meetings | Norway | X | X | X | X | |
| WP061 rev.1 | CEP 7f | Report of the CEP Workshop on Marine and Terrestrial Antarctic Specially Managed Areas. Montevideo, Uruguay, 16-17 June 2011 | Australia Uruguay | X | X | X | X | |

| Information Papers | | | | | | | | |
|---|---|---|---|---|---|---|---|---|
| Number | Ag. Items | Title | Submitted By | E | F | R | S | Attachments |
| IP001 | CEP 7d | Temporal and spatial patterns of anthropogenic disturbance at McMurdo Station, Antarctica | United States | X | | | | Kennicutt et al. 2010 Temporal and spatial patterns of anthropogenic disturbance at McMurdo Station, Antarctica |
| IP002 | CEP 7d | The historical development of McMurdo Station, Antarctica, An environmental perspective. | United States | X | | | | Klein et al. 2008 The historical development of McMurdo station, Antarctica, an environmental perspective. |
| IP003 | ATCM 4 | Report Submitted to Antarctic Treaty Consultative Meeting XXXIV by the Depositary Government for the Convention for the Conservation of Antarctic Seals in Accordance with Recommendation XIII-2, Paragraph 2(D) | United Kingdom | X | X | X | X | |
| IP004 | ATCM 11 CEP 10 | Japanese Inspection Report 2010 | Japan | X | | | | |
| IP005 | ATCM 12 | 60th Anniversary of the Argentine Antarctic Institute | Argentina | X | | X | | |
| IP006 | ATCM 9 | Report on the Evacuation of an Altitude Sickness-suffered Expeditioner at the Kunlun Station in Dome A | China | X | | | | |
| IP007 | ATCM 12 | Brief Introduction of the Fourth Chinese National Arctic Expedition | China | X | | | | |
| IP008 | ATCM 13 CEP 5 | COMNAP Energy Management Workshop | COMNAP | X | | | | |
| IP009 | ATCM 10 CEP 7c | Antarctic Site Inventory: 1994-2011 | United States | X | | | | |
| IP010 | ATCM 4 CEP 11 | The Annual Report for 2010 of the Council of Managers of National Antarctic Programs (COMNAP) | COMNAP | X | X | X | X | |
| IP011 | ATCM 13 | Permafrost and climate change in the maritime Antarctic. 5 Years of permafrost research at the St Kliment Ohridski Station in Livingston Island | Bulgaria Portugal | X | | | | |
| IP012 | CEP 7c | Guidelines of environmental behavior of the expedition participants and visitors to the Bulgarian Base in Antarctica | Bulgaria | X | | | | |
| IP013 | CEP 6a | The Draft Comprehensive Environmental Evaluation (CEE) for the Proposed Exploration of Subglacial Lake Ellsworth, Antarctica | United Kingdom | X | | | | Draft CEE for the Proposed Exploration of Subglacial Lake Ellsworth |
| IP014 | ATCM 10 | IAATO Yacht Outreach Campaign | IAATO | X | | | | Yacht Outreach Pamphlet Yacht Outreach Poster |
| IP015 | ATCM 10 | Training Course for Yachts intending to visit Antarctica | United Kingdom | X | | | | |
| IP016 | ATCM 17 | Report on the recent bioprospecting activities carried out by Argentina during the period 2010-2011 | Argentina | X | | X | | |

| | | Information Papers | | | | | | |
|---|---|---|---|---|---|---|---|---|
| Number | Ag. Items | Title | Submitted By | E | F | R | S | Attachments |
| IP017 | ATCM 12 | Bioremediation of Antarctic soils contaminated with hydrocarbons. Rational design of bioremediation strategies | Argentina | X | | | X | |
| IP018 | ATCM 10 ATCM 9 | The Berserk Incident, Ross Sea, February 2011 | New Zealand Norway United States | X | X | X | X | |
| IP019 | ATCM 14 CEP 6a | The Draft Comprehensive Environmental Evaluation for the construction and operation of the Jang Bogo Antarctic Research Station, Terra Nova Bay, Antarctica | Korea (ROK) | X | | | | Full Draft CEE of Korean Jang Bogo Station in Antarctica |
| IP020 | ATCM 10 | Report on Antarctic tourist flows and cruise ships operating in Ushuaia during the 2010/2011 austral summer season | Argentina | X | | | X | |
| IP021 rev.1 | ATCM 10 | Non-commercial pleasure and/or sport vessels which travelled to Antarctica through Ushuaia during the 2010/2011 season | Argentina | X | | | X | |
| IP022 | ATCM 4 | Report of the Depositary Government of the Antarctic Treaty and its Protocol in accordance with Recommendation XIII-2 | United States | X | X | X | X | Antarctic Treaty Status table List of Recommendations/Measures and their approvals Protocol Status table |
| IP023 | ATCM 10 CEP 7c | Antarctic Peninsula Compendium, 3rd Edition | United States United Kingdom | X | | | | Appendix A - Antarctic Peninsula Compendium Maps and Tables |
| IP024 | CEP 7f | Progress Report on the Research Project "Current Environmental Situation and Management Proposals for the Fildes Region (Antarctic)" | Germany | X | | | | |
| IP025 | ATCM 10 | Notice on environmental impacts by small tourist groups within the overall frame of Antarctic tourism | Germany | X | | | | |
| IP026 | CEP 8a | Progress Report on the Research Project "The role of human activities in the introduction of non-native species into Antarctica and in the distribution of organisms within the Antarctic" | Germany | X | | | | |
| IP027 | CEP 8c | Progress Report on the Research Project 'Whale Monitoring Antarctica' | Germany | X | | | | |
| IP028 | ATCM 10 | Technical safety standards and international law affecting yachts with destination Antarctica | Germany | X | | | | |
| IP029 | CEP 8c | Potential of Technical Measures to Reduce the Acoustical Effects of Airguns | Germany | X | | | | Evaluation of the Potential of Technical Measures to Reduce the Acoustical Effects of Airguns |
| IP030 rev.1 | ATCM 10 | Areas of tourist interest in the Antártica Peninsula (Antarctic Peninsula) and Orcadas del Sur Islands (South Orkney Islands) | Argentina | X | | | X | |

| | | Information Papers | | | | | | |
|---|---|---|---|---|---|---|---|---|
| Number | Ag. Items | Title | Submitted By | E | F | R | S | Attachments |
| | | region. 2010/2011 austral summer season | | | | | | |
| IP031 | CEP 11 | Report by the SC-CAMLR Observer to the Fourteenth Meeting of the Committee for Environmental Protection | CCAMLR | X | X | X | X | |
| IP032 | CEP 8a | Report on IPY Oslo Science Conference Session on Non-Native Species | France | X | | | | |
| IP033 | CEP 8c | SCAR's code of conduct for the exploration and research of subglacial aquatic environments | SCAR | X | | | | |
| IP034 | ATCM 8 | Implementation of Annex II and VI of the Protocol on Environmental Protection to the Antarctic Treaty and Measure 4(2004) | Finland | X | | | | |
| IP035 | CEP 9 | Environmental Monitoring and Ecological Activities in Antarctica, 2010-2012 | Romania | X | | | | |
| IP036 | ATCM 12 | ERICON AB Icebreaker FP7 Project. A new era in the polar research | Romania | X | | | | |
| IP037 | ATCM 12 | Law- Racovita Base. An example of cooperation in Antarctica | Romania | X | | | | |
| IP038 | ATCM 19 | Statement of the Romanian delegation at the celebration of the 50th anniversary of the entry into force of the Antarctic Treaty | Romania | X | | | | |
| IP039 | ATCM 11 CEP 10 | Australian Antarctic Treaty and Environmental Protocol inspections January 2010 | Australia | X | | | | |
| IP040 | ATCM 11 CEP 10 | Australian Antarctic Treaty and Environmental Protocol inspections January 2011 | Australia | X | | | | |
| IP041 | ATCM 12 | Japan's Antarctic research highlights in 2010–2011 including those related to climate change | Japan | X | | | | |
| IP042 | ATCM 12 | Legacy of IPY 2007–2008 for Japan | Japan | X | | | | |
| IP043 | CEP 7d | Discovery of human activity remains, pre-1958 in the north coast of the King George Island / 25 de Mayo. | Uruguay | X | | | X | Caracterización de la zona y descripción de los hallazgos |
| IP044 | ATCM 9 | Exploration, search and rescue training activities in support of the scientific, technical and logistical operational tasks | Uruguay | X | | | X | |
| IP045 | ATCM 15 | Publication of the book "The Elephant Island. The Adventure of the Uruguayan Pioneers in Antarctica" | Uruguay | X | | | X | |
| IP046 | ATCM 15 | Publication of the book "Antarctic Verses" in occasion of the 25th anniversary of "Uruguay | Uruguay | X | | | X | |

| | | Information Papers | | | | | | |
|---|---|---|---|---|---|---|---|---|
| Number | Ag. Items | Title | Submitted By | E | F | R | S | Attachments |
| | | Consultative Member of the Antarctic Treaty" | | | | | | |
| IP047 | ATCM 15 | Commemorative postage stamp issue: "25th anniversary of Uruguay consultative member of the Antarctic Treaty" | Uruguay | X | | | X | |
| IP048 | CEP 12 | Thala Valley Waste Removal | Australia | X | | | | |
| IP049 | ATCM 14 CEP 12 | Renewable Energy and Energy Efficiency Initiatives at Australia's Antarctic Stations | Australia | X | | | | |
| IP050 | CEP 8a | Colonisation status of known non-native species in the Antarctic terrestrial environment (updated 2011) | United Kingdom Uruguay | X | | | | |
| IP051 | ATCM 12 CEP 9 | The Southern Ocean Observing System (SOOS): An update | SCAR Australia | X | | | | |
| IP052 | ATCM 13 CEP 5 | Antarctic Climate Change and the Environment – 2011 Update | SCAR | X | | | | |
| IP053 | CEP 8c | SCAR's Code of Conduct for the Use of Animals for Scientific Purposes in Antarctica | SCAR | X | | | | |
| IP054 | ATCM 18 ATCM 4 CEP 11 CEP 3 | Summary of SCAR's Strategic Plan 2011-2016 | SCAR | X | | | | |
| IP055 | ATCM 12 | Summary Report on IPY 2007–2008 by the ICSU-WMO Joint Committee | SCAR | X | | | | IPY Summary Contents Table IPY Summary Cover |
| IP056 | ATCM 13 CEP 5 CEP 7e | Marine spatial protection and management under the Antarctic Treaty System: new opportunities for implementation and coordination | IUCN | X | | | | |
| IP057 | CEP 11 | Report of the CEP Observer to SC-CAMLR's Working Group on Ecosystem Monitoring and Management (WG-EMM) | CCAMLR | X | X | X | X | |
| IP058 | ATCM 12 | IPY Legacy Workshop | Norway | X | | | | IPY Legacy Report |
| IP059 | ATCM 9 | The grounding of the Polar Star | Norway | X | | | | |
| IP060 | ATCM 9 | Working group on the development of a mandatory code for ships operating in polar waters, IMO | Norway | X | | | | IMO Report DE 55/WP.4 |
| IP061 | ATCM 12 CEP 12 | The SCAR Antarctic Climate Evolution (ACE) Programme | SCAR | X | | | | |
| IP062 | ATCM 17 | A case of Biological Prospecting | Netherlands | X | | | | |
| IP063 | ATCM 14 | Renovación del Parque de Tanques de combustible de la Base Científica Antártica Artigas (BCAA) | Uruguay | | | | X | Fotografías del Parque de Tanques |
| IP064 | CEP 6b | Final Comprehensive Environmental Evaluation (CEE) of New Indian Research Station at | India | X | | | | |

| | | | Information Papers | | | | | |
|---|---|---|---|---|---|---|---|---|
| Number | Ag. Items | Title | Submitted By | E | F | R | S | Attachments |
| | | Larsemann Hills, Antarctica and Update on Construction Activity | | | | | | |
| IP065 | CEP 5 | Frontiers in Understanding Climate Change and Polar Ecosystems Workshop Report | United States | X | | | | Frontiers in Understanding Climate Change |
| IP066 | ATCM 4 | Report of the Depositary Government for the Agreement on the Conservation of Albatrosses and Petrels (ACAP) | Australia | X | X | X | X | |
| IP067 | ATCM 4 | Report of the Depositary Government for the Convention on the Conservation of Antarctic Marine Living Resources (CCAMLR) | Australia | X | X | X | X | |
| IP068 | CEP 8a | Alien Species Database | Australia SCAR | X | | | | |
| IP069 | CEP 7f | Summary of key features of Antarctic Specially Managed Areas | Australia | X | | | | |
| IP070 | ATCM 12 | The Dutch Science Facility at the UK's Rothera Research Station | Netherlands United Kingdom | X | | | | |
| IP071 | CEP 4 | Annual Report pursuant to Article 17 of the Protocol on Environmental Protection to the Antarctic Treaty. 2009-2010 | Italy | X | | | | |
| IP072 | CEP 6b | Methodology for clean access to the subglacial environment associated with the Whillans Ice Stream | United States | X | | | | |
| IP073 | CEP 7a | Amundsen-Scott South Pole Station, South Pole Antarctica Specially Managed Area (ASMA No. 5) 2011 Management Report | United States | X | | | | ASMA 5 South Pole - Revised Map 3 ASMA 5 South Pole - Revised Map 4 Guideline for NGO Visitors to South Pole Station 2011 2012 Revised Appendix A Additional Guidelines for Non-Governmental Organizations at the South Pole |
| IP074 | ATCM 13 | Assessment of wind energy potential at the Norwegian research station Troll | Norway | X | | | | |
| IP075 | ATCM 10 | The legal aspects of the Berserk Expedition | Norway | X | | | | |
| IP076 | CEP 6a | The Initial Responses to the Comments on the Draft CEE for Construction and Operation of the Jang Bogo Antarctic Research Station, Terra Nova Bay, Antarctica | Korea (ROK) | X | | | | |
| IP077 | ATCM 12 | Scientific & Science-related Collaborations with Other Parties During 2010-2011 | Korea (ROK) | X | | | | |
| IP078 | ATCM 14 | The First Antarctic Expedition of Araon (2010/2011) | Korea (ROK) | X | | | | |
| IP079 | CEP 7a | Report of the Larsemann Hills Antarctic Specially Managed Area (ASMA) | Australia China India | X | | | | |

| | | Information Papers | | | | | | |
|---|---|---|---|---|---|---|---|---|
| Number | Ag. Items | Title | Submitted By | E | F | R | S | Attachments |
| | | Management Group | Romania Russian Federation | | | | | |
| IP080 | ATCM 4 | Report by the CCAMLR Observer to the Thirty-Fourth Antarctic Treaty Consultative Meeting | CCAMLR | X | X | X | X | |
| IP081 | ATCM 4 | Summary of the Annual Report for 2010 of The Scientific Committee on Antarctic Research (SCAR) | SCAR | X | X | X | X | |
| IP082 | ATCM 14 | An Antarctic Vessel Traffic Monitoring and Information System | ASOC | X | | | | |
| IP083 | ATCM 13 CEP 5 | An Antarctic Climate Change Communication Plan | ASOC | X | | | | |
| IP084 | ATCM 10 CEP 6b | Antarctic Tourism – What Next? Key Issues to Address with Binding Rules | ASOC | X | | | | |
| IP085 | ATCM 9 | Developing a Mandatory Polar Code – Progress and Gaps | ASOC | X | | | | |
| IP086 | CEP 7d | Evolution of Footprint: Spatial and Temporal Dimensions of Human Activities | ASOC | X | | | | |
| IP087 | ATCM 10 CEP 6b | Land-Based Tourism in Antarctica | ASOC | X | | | | |
| IP088 | ATCM 13 CEP 5 | Ocean Acidification and the Southern Ocean | ASOC | X | | | | |
| IP089 rev.1 | ATCM 18 ATCM 5 CEP 3 | The Antarctic Environmental Protocol, 1991-2011 | ASOC | X | | | | |
| IP090 | CEP 7e | The Southern Ocean MPA Agenda – Matching words and spirit with action | ASOC | X | | | | |
| IP091 | ATCM 9 | Vessel Protection and Routeing – Options Available to Reduce Risk and Provide Enhanced Environmental Protection | ASOC | X | | | | |
| IP092 | ATCM 13 CEP 7e | The Ross Sea: A Valuable Reference Area to Assess the Effects of Climate Change | ASOC | X | | | | |
| IP093 | CEP 4 CEP 7a | Annual Report Pursuant to Article 17 of the Protocol on Environmental Protection to the Antarctic Treaty | Ukraine | X | | | | |
| IP094 | ATCM 10 CEP 8c | Use of dogs in the context of a commemorative centennial expedition | Norway | X | | | | |
| IP095 | ATCM 5 CEP 12 | Paying for Ecosystem Services of Antarctica? | Netherlands | X | | | | |
| IP096 | ATCM 12 | Scientific workshop on Antarctic krill in the Netherlands | Netherlands | X | | | | |
| IP097 | ATCM 12 | Current status of the Russian drilling project at Vostok station | Russian Federation | X | | X | | |
| IP098 | ATCM 13 | New approach to study of climate change based on global albedo monitoring | Russian Federation | X | | X | | |

| | | | | | | | | |
|---|---|---|---|---|---|---|---|---|
| | | **Information Papers** | | | | | | |
| **Number** | **Ag. Items** | **Title** | **Submitted By** | **E** | **F** | **R** | **S** | **Attachments** |
| IP099 | ATCM 17 | Microbiological monitoring of coastal Antarctic stations and bases as a factor of study of anthropogenic impact on the Antarctic environment and the human organism | Russian Federation | X | | X | | |
| IP100 | ATCM 12 | Preliminary results of Russian scientific studies in the Antarctic in 2010 | Russian Federation | X | | X | | |
| IP101 rev.1 | ATCM 12 | Russian proposals on the International Polar Decade Initiative | Russian Federation | X | | X | | Nuuk Declaration |
| IP102 | CEP 7f | Present zoological study at Mirny station area and at ASPA No 127 "Haswell Island" | Russian Federation | X | | X | | |
| IP103 | ATCM 13 CEP 5 | IAATO Climate Change Working Group: Report of Progress | IAATO | X | | | | |
| IP104 | CEP 7c | Proposed Amendment to Antarctic Treaty Site Guidelines for Hannah Point | IAATO | X | | | | |
| IP105 | ATCM 10 CEP 7c | Report on IAATO Operator use of Antarctic Peninsula Landing Sites and ATCM Visitor Site Guidelines, 2009-10 & 2010-11 Seasons | IAATO | X | | | | |
| IP106 rev.1 | ATCM 10 | IAATO Overview of Antarctic Tourism: 2010-11 Season and Preliminary Estimates for 2011-12 Season | IAATO | X | | | | |
| IP107 | ATCM 10 | Towards an IAATO Enhanced Observer Scheme | IAATO | X | | | | Appendix 1 IAATO Member Internal Review Scheme Appendix 2 IAATO Member External Review Mechanism Appendix 3 IAATO Observer Report Form ship based w landings 2011 Appendix 4 IAATO Observer Report Form Cruise Only 2011 Appendix 5 IAATO Observer Report Form Land 2011 |
| IP108 | ATCM 4 | Report of the International Association of Antarctica Tour Operators 2010-11 | IAATO | X | X | X | X | |
| IP109 | CEP 7f | Cooperation Management Activities at ASPAs in 25 de Mayo (King George) Island, South Shetland Islands | Korea (ROK) Argentina | X | | | X | |
| IP110 | CEP 7c | Ukraine policy regarding visits by tourists to Vernadsky station | Ukraine | X | | X | | Site Guidelines for Vernadsky Station |
| IP111 | ATCM 13 | Installation of new meteorological equipment at Vernadsky Station | Ukraine | X | | X | | |
| IP112 | ATCM 12 | Ukrainian research in Antarctica, 2002-2011 | Ukraine | X | | X | | |
| IP113 | ATCM 16 CEP 4 | Review of the Implementation of the Madrid Protocol: Annual report by Parties (Article 17) | UNEP ASOC | X | | | | |
| IP114 | ATCM 4 | Report by the International | IHO | X | X | X | X | Annexes A, B and C |

| Information Papers | | | | | | | | |
|---|---|---|---|---|---|---|---|---|
| Number | Ag. Items | Title | Submitted By | E | F | R | S | Attachments |
| | | Hydrographic Organization (IHO) on "Cooperation in hydrographic surveying and charting of antarctic waters" | | | | | | |
| IP115 | CEP 7a | Fauna Survey of the ASPA 171 Narębski Point, ASPA 150 Ardley Island and ASPA 132 Potter Peninsula in 2010-11 | Korea (ROK) | X | | | | |
| IP116 | ATCM 19 | Statement by the Head of Japanese Delegation on the occasion of the 50th Anniversary of the entry into force of the Antarctic Treaty | Japan | X | | | | |
| IP117 | CEP 7b | Inauguración de la instalación de Placas Conmemorativas en el Monumento al Tratado Antártico | Chile | | | | X | |
| IP118 | ATCM 12 | Contribuciones chilenas al conocimiento científico de la Antártica: Expedición 2010/11 | Chile | | | | X | |
| IP119 | ATCM 12 | Programa Chileno de Ciencia Antártica PROCIEN: Un Programa Abierto Al Mundo | Chile | | | | X | |
| IP120 rev.1 | ATCM 9 | Navegación Aérea Segura, hacia la Base Antártica Presidente Eduardo Frei, en la isla Rey Jorge | Chile | | | | X | |
| IP121 | ATCM 14 | Medical evacuation reported by the Combined Antarctic Naval Patrol | Argentina Chile | X | X | | X | |
| IP122 | ATCM 10 | Perceptions of Antarctica from the modern travellers' perspective | Argentina | X | | | X | |
| IP123 | CEP 6b | Estudio de Impacto Ambiental Ex-post de la Estación Científica Ecuatoriana "Pedro Vicente Maldonado". Isla Greenwich-Shetland del Sur-Antártida, 2010-2011. | Ecuador | | | | X | |
| IP124 | ATCM 15 | I Concurso Intercolegial sobre Temas Antárticos (CITA, 2010) | Ecuador | | | | X | |
| IP125 | ATCM 12 | Cooperación en Investigación Científica entre Ecuador y Venezuela | Ecuador Venezuela | | | | X | |
| IP126 | ATCM 10 CEP 7c | Manejo turístico para la isla Barrientos | Ecuador | | | | X | |
| IP127 | CEP 12 | The Construction of an Orthodox Chapel at Vernadsky Station | Ukraine | X | | X | | |
| IP128 | ATCM 15 | The excitement "Antarctica" distance in itself invisible | Bulgaria | X | | | | |
| IP129 | ATCM 4 | Report of the Antarctic and Southern Ocean Coalition (ASOC) | ASOC | X | X | X | X | |
| IP130 | CEP 7b | Update on enhancement activities for HSM 38 "Snow Hill" | Argentina | X | | | X | |
| IP131 | CEP 7a | Deception Island Specially | Argentina | X | | | | |

| Information Papers | | | | | | | | |
|---|---|---|---|---|---|---|---|---|
| Number | Ag. Items | Title | Submitted By | E | F | R | S | Attachments |
| | | Managed Area (ASMA) Management Group Report | Chile Norway Spain United Kingdom United States | | | | | |
| IP132 | ATCM 12 | Report on the Research Activities: Czech Research Station J. G. Mendel, James Ross Island, and Antarctic Peninsula, Season 2010/11 | Czech Republic | X | | | | |
| IP133 | ATCM 12 CEP 7d | Report on all-terrain vehicles impact on deglaciated area of James Ross Island, Antarctica | Czech Republic | X | | | | |
| IP134 | ATCM 9 | Situación SAR en los últimos 5 años en el área de la Antártica de responsabilidad de Chile | Chile | | | | X | |
| IP135 | ATCM 9 | Patrulla de rescate terrestre Argentina-Chilena PARACACH (Bases Antárticas "Esperanza" y "O'Higgins") | Argentina Chile | | | | X | |
| IP136 | CEP 7f | Report of the CEP Workshop on Marine and Terrestrial Antarctic Specially Managed Areas Montevideo, Uruguay, 16-17 June 2011 | Australia Uruguay | X | | | | |
| IP137 | ATCM 19 | Declaración del Perú en conmemoración del 50 Aniversario de la entrada en vigencia del Tratado Antártico | Peru | | | | X | |

| Secretariat Papers | | | | | | | | |
|---|---|---|---|---|---|---|---|---|
| Number | Ag. Items | Title | Submitted By | E | F | R | S | Attachments |
| SP001 rev.1 | ATCM 1 CEP 1 | ATCM XXXIV and CEP XIV Agenda and Schedule | ATS | X | X | X | X | |
| SP002 rev.2 | ATCM 6 | Secretariat Report 2010/11 | ATS | X | X | X | X | Audited Financial Report 2009/10 Contributions Received by the Antarctic Treaty Secretariat 2010/11 Decision 3 (2011) Annex 1 Decision 3 (2011) Annex 2 Letter Jan Huber concerning the Staff Termination Fund |
| SP003 | ATCM 6 | Secretariat Programme 2011/12 | ATS | X | X | X | X | Contribution scale 2012/13 Five years forward budget profile 2011 to 2016 Prov. Report 2010/11, Budget 2011/12, Forecast Budget 2012/13 Salaries Scale |
| SP004 rev.1 | ATCM 6 | Contributions Received by the Antarctic Treaty Secretariat 2008-2012 | ATS | X | X | X | X | |
| SP005 rev.1 | CEP 6b | Annual list of Initial Environmental Evaluations (IEE) and Comprehensive Environmental Evaluations (CEE) prepared between April 1st 2010 and March 31st 2011 | ATS | X | X | X | X | |
| SP006 | CEP 7e | Summary of the work of the CEP on Marine Protected Areas | ATS | X | X | X | X | |
| SP007 | CEP 7a | Status of Antarctic Specially Protected Area and Antarctic Specially Managed Area Management Plans | ATS | X | X | X | X | |

# 3. List of Participants

# 3. List of Participants

| Participants: Consultative Parties | | | | |
|---|---|---|---|---|
| Party | Title | Contact | Position | Email |
| Argentina | Mrs | Balsalobre, Silvina | Advisor | |
| Argentina | Secretary | Barreto, Juan | Delegate | bat@mrecic.gov.ar |
| Argentina | Mr | Bunge, Carlos | Advisor | carlosbunge73@yahoo.com.ar |
| Argentina | Mr | Casela, Hugo | Advisor | |
| Argentina | Dr | Coria, Néstor | Advisor | |
| Argentina | Mr | Correa, Manuel | Advisor | |
| Argentina | Mrs | Daverio, María Elena | Advisor | medaverio@arnet.com.ar |
| Argentina | Dr | del Valle, Rodolfo | Advisor | |
| Argentina | Mrs | del Valle, Verónica | Advisor | |
| Argentina | Mr | Di Vincenzo, Andrés | Advisor | |
| Argentina | Mr | Figueroa, Victor Hugo | Advisor | |
| Argentina | Counsellor | Gowland, Máximo | Alternate | gme@mrecic.gov.ar |
| Argentina | Mr | Graziano, Pablo | Delegate | zgp@mrecic.gov.ar |
| Argentina | Mrs | Gucioni, Paola | Delegate | |
| Argentina | Mrs | Hourcade, Odile | Advisor | |
| Argentina | Mr | Irusta, Adolfo Guillermo | Advisor | |
| Argentina | Min | López Crozet, Fausto | Head of Delegation | flc@mrecic.gov.ar |
| Argentina | Mr | Lusky, Jorge | Advisor | |
| Argentina | Dr | MacCormack, Walter | Delegate | |
| Argentina | Mr | Maldonado, Gabriel | Advisor | gfmaldo@live.com.ar |
| Argentina | Ambassador | Mansi, Ariel | ATCM Chairman | rpc@mrecic.gov.ar |
| Argentina | Dr | Marenssi, Sergio | Delegate | smarenssi@dna.gov.ar |
| Argentina | Dr | Marschoff, Enrique | Delegate | marschoff@dna.gov.ar |
| Argentina | Dr | Memolli, Mariano A. | CEP Representative | mmemolli@dna.gov.ar |
| Argentina | Ms | Molina Carranza, Maria Isabel | Advisor | mmcarr@minagri.gob.ar |
| Argentina | Mrs | Motta, Luciana | Advisor | |
| Argentina | Mrs | Nuviala, Victoria | Advisor | |
| Argentina | Mrs | Ortúzar, Patricia | Advisor | portuzar@dna.gov.ar |
| Argentina | Mr | Palet, Guillermo | Advisor | clamos41@yahoo.com.ar |
| Argentina | Dr | Perlini, Gabriel | Advisor | |
| Argentina | Dr | Quartino, Liliana | Advisor | |
| Argentina | Mr | Sala, Hérnan | Advisor | |
| Argentina | Mr | Sánchez, Rodolfo | Delegate | rsanchez@dna.gov.ar |
| Argentina | Mr | Santillana, Sergio | Advisor | |
| Argentina | Ms | Vereda, Marisol | Advisor | |
| Argentina | Ms | Vlasich, Verónica | Delegate | veronicavlasich@hotmail.com |
| Australia | Ms | Davidson, Lisa | Delegate | |
| Australia | Mr | Davis, Robert (Bob) | Delegate | Bob.Davis@dfat.gov.au |
| Australia | Mr | Gunn, John | Delegate | john.gunn@aad.gov.au |
| Australia | Mr | Jackson, Andrew | Delegate | andrew.jackson@aad.gov.au |
| Australia | Mr | McIvor, Ewan | CEP Representative | ewan.mcivor@aad.gov.au |
| Australia | Mr | Mundy, Jason | Delegate | Jason.Mundy@dfat.gov.au |
| Australia | Mr | Nicoll, Rob | Advisor | RNicoll@wwf.org.au |
| Australia | Ms | Ralston, Kim | Delegate | Kim.Ralston@dfat.gov.au |
| Australia | Mr | Richardson, John | Alternate | John.Richardson@dfat.gov.au |
| Australia | Dr | Riddle, Martin | Delegate | martin.riddle@aad.gov.au |
| Australia | Mr | Rowe, Richard | Head of Delegation | Richard.Rowe@dfat.gov.au |
| Australia | Dr | Tracey, Phillip | Delegate | phil.tracey@aad.gov.au |
| Australia | Ms | Trousselot, Chrissie | Advisor | chrissie.trousselot@development.tas.gov.au |
| Belgium | Mr | de Lichtervelde, Alexandre | CEP Representative | alexandre.delichtervelde@health.fgov.be |
| Belgium | Ms | Vancauwenberghe, Maaike | Delegate | maaike.vancauwenberghe@belspo.be |
| Belgium | Mr | Vanden Bilcke, Christian | Head of Delegation | christian.vandenbilcke@diplobel.fed.be |
| Belgium | Ms | Wilmotte, Annick | Advisor | awilmotte@ulg.ac.be |
| Brazil | Rear Admiral | de Carvalho Ferreira, Marcos José | Alternate | proantar@secirm.mar.mil.br |
| Brazil | Commander | do Amaral Silva, Marco Antonio | Delegate | amaral.silva@secirm.mar.mil.br |
| Brazil | Ms | Leal Madruga, Jaqueline | Delegate | jaqueline.madruga@mma.gov.br |
| Brazil | Commander | Leite, Márcio | Delegate | marcio.leite@secirm.mar.mil.br |
| Brazil | Mr | Moesch, Ricardo | Advisor | ricardo.moesch@turismo.gov |
| Brazil | Mr | Polejack, Andrei | Delegate | andrei.polejack@mct.gov.br |
| Brazil | Mr | Rosa da Silveira, Carlos | Delegate | carlos.rosa@itamaraty.gov.br |

| Participants: Consultative Parties | | | | |
|---|---|---|---|---|
| Party | Title | Contact | Position | Email |
| Brazil | Mrs | Soares Leite, Patricia | Delegate | pleite@brasil.org.ar |
| Brazil | Minister | Vaz Pitaluga, Fábio | Head of Delegation | dmae@itamaraty.gov.br |
| Bulgaria | Mr | Ivchev, Encho | Delegate | embular@uolsinectis.com.ar |
| Bulgaria | Prof. | Pimpirev, Christo | Head of Delegation | polar@gea.uni-sofia.bg |
| Chile | Mr | Cariceo Yutronic, Yanko Jesús | Advisor | ycariceo.12@mma.gob.cl |
| Chile | Ms | Carvallo, María Luisa | Delegate | mlcarvallo@minrel.gov.cl |
| Chile | Colonel | Castillo, Rafael | Delegate | castillo.antartica@gmail.com |
| Chile | Second Secretary | Concha, Andrea | Advisor | aconcha@minrel.gov.cl |
| Chile | Captain | Lubascher, Pablo | Advisor | |
| Chile | Colonel | Madrid, Santiago | Delegate | smadrid@fach.cl |
| Chile | Third Secretary | Marin, Juan Cristobal | Delegate | jmarin@minrel.gov.cl |
| Chile | Mr | Olguin, Carlos | Advisor | colguin@minrel.gov.cl |
| Chile | Dr | Retamales, José | Alternate | jretamales@inach.cl |
| Chile | Mr | Riquelme, Hernan | Delegate | hriquelme@emdn.cl |
| Chile | Counsellor | Sanhueza, Camilo | Head of Delegation | csanhueza@minrel.gov.cl |
| Chile | Ms | Sardiña, Jimena | Delegate | jsardina@inach.cl |
| Chile | Captain | Sepúlveda, Víctor | Delegate | vsepulveda@armada.cl |
| Chile | Ms | Tellez Rubina, Andrea | Advisor | cruiz@sernatur.cl |
| Chile | Ms | Vallejos, Verónica | CEP Representative | vvallejos@inach.cl |
| Chile | Captain | Velásquez, Ricardo | Delegate | mcabrerad@directemar.cl |
| Chile | Ms | Verdugo, Manola | Delegate | mverdugo@minrel.gov.cl |
| China | Miss | Fang, Lijun | Advisor | |
| China | Mr | Liu, Shaoqing | Advisor | |
| China | Mr | Wang, Chen | Delegate | wang_chen@mfa.gov.cn |
| China | Mr | Wei, Long | CEP Representative | chinare@263.net.cn |
| China | Mr | WU, Jun | Delegate | |
| China | Mr | Zhang, Xia | Advisor | |
| China | Ms | Zhao, Wenting | Advisor | zhao_wenting@mfa.gov.cn |
| China | Mr | Zhou, Jian | Head of Delegation | zhou_jian@mfa.gov.cn |
| Ecuador | Dr | BORBOR, MERCY | Head of Delegation | mborbor@ambiente.gob.ec |
| Ecuador | Msc. | CAJIAO, DANIELA | Delegate | danicajiao@gmail.com |
| Ecuador | Dr | MIELES, JOSE LUIS | Head of Delegation | jmieles@midena.gob.ec |
| Ecuador | Mr | Olmedo Morán, José | Delegate | inae@gye.satnet.net |
| Ecuador | Dr | Proaño, Pilar | Delegate | |
| Ecuador | Ambassador | SUAREZ, ALEJANDRO | Delegate | cartografia@mmrree.gob.ec |
| Finland | Mr | Kalakoski, Mika | Delegate | mika.kalakoski@fiMrfi |
| Finland | Ms | Mähönen, Outi | CEP Representative | outi.mahonen@ely-keskus.fi |
| Finland | Ambassador | Meres-Wuori, Ora | Head of Delegation | ora.meres-wuori@formin.fi |
| Finland | Ms | Pohjanpalo, Maria | Alternate | maria.pohjanpalo@formin.fi |
| France | Ambassador | Asvazadourian, Jean-Pierre | Advisor | jean-pierre.asvazadourian@diplomatie.gouv.fr |
| France | Mrs | Belna, Stéphanie | CEP Representative | stephanie.belna@developpement-durable.gouv.fr |
| France | Dr | Choquet, Anne | Delegate | anne.choquet@univ-brest.fr |
| France | Ms | Dalmas, Dominique | CEP Representative | dominique.dalmas@interieur.gouv.fr |
| France | Dr | Frenot, Yves | CEP Representative | yves.frenot@ipev.fr |
| France | Mr | Lebouvier, Marc | CEP Representative | marc.lebouvier@univ-rennes1.fr |
| France | Mr | Maxime, Reynaud | Delegate | maxime.reynaud@diplomatie.gouv.fr |
| France | Mr | Mayet, Laurent | Advisor | lmayet@lecerclepolaire.com |
| France | Mr | Pottier, Stanislas | Advisor | stanislas.pottier@dgtresor.gouv.fr |
| France | Mr | Reuillard, Emmanuel | Delegate | emmanuel.reuillard@taaf.fr |
| France | Ambassador | Rocard, Michel | Head of Delegation | stanislas.pottier@dgtresor.gouv.fr |
| France | Mr | Segura, Serge | Head of Delegation | serge.segura@diplomatie.gouv.fr |
| Germany | Dr | Gaedicke, Christoph | Advisor | |
| Germany | Dr | Herata, Heike | Advisor | heike.herata@uba.de |
| Germany | Dr | Läufer, Andreas | Advisor | andreas.laeufer@bgr.de |
| Germany | Mr | Lehmann, Harry | Advisor | |
| Germany | Mr | Liebschner, Alexander | Advisor | alexander.liebschner@bfn-vilm.de |
| Germany | Mr | Lindemann, Christian | Advisor | christian.lindemann@bmu.bund.de |
| Germany | Prof. Dr | Miller, Heinrich | Advisor | heinrich.miller@awi.de |
| Germany | Dr | Ney, Martin | Head of Delegation | |
| Germany | Dr | Nixdorf, Uwe | Advisor | Uwe.Nixdorf@awi.de |
| Germany | Dr | Vöneky, Silja | Advisor | svoeneky@mpil.de |
| Germany | Dr | Winkelmann, Ingo | Alternate | 504-RL@diplo.de |
| India | Dr | Chaturvedi, Sanjai | Delegate | |
| India | Dr | Rangreji, Luther | Delegate | rangreji@yahoo.com |

**Participants: Consultative Parties**

| Party | Title | Contact | Position | Email |
|---|---|---|---|---|
| India | Dr | Ravindra, Rasik | Head of Delegation | rasik@ncaor.org |
| India | Dr | Tiwari, Anoop | Delegate | anooptiwari@ncaor.org |
| Italy | Amb. | Fornara, Arduino | Head of Delegation | arduino.fornara@esteri.it |
| Italy | Dr | Mecozzi, Roberta | Staff | roberta.mecozzi@enea.it |
| Italy | Mr | Paparo, Gabriele | Delegate | scient.buenosaires@esteri.it |
| Italy | Dr | Tamburelli, Gianfranco | Staff | gtamburelli@pelagus.it |
| Italy | Ms | Tomaselli, Maria Stefania | Staff | tomaselli.stefania@minambiente.it |
| Italy | Dr | Torcini, Sandro | Staff | sandro.torcini@casaccia.enea.it |
| Italy | Ms | Vigni, Patrizia | Alternate | vigni@unisi.it |
| Japan | Ms | Fujimoto, Masami | Delegate | masami.fujimoto@mofa.go.jp |
| Japan | Mr | Hasegawa, Shuichi | Delegate | SHUICHI_HASEGAWA@env.go.jp |
| Japan | HE | Ishida, Hitohiro | Head of Delegation | masami.fujimoto@mofa.go.jp |
| Japan | Mr | Kawashima, Tetsuya | Delegate | tetsuya_kawashima@nm.maff.go.jp |
| Japan | Ms | Konagaya, Yuki | Delegate | yuki.konagaya@mofa.go.jp |
| Japan | Dr | Suginaka, Atsushi | Head of Delegation | atsushi.suginaka@mofa.go.jp |
| Japan | Mr | Uno, Kenya | Delegate | kenya.uno@mofa.go.jp |
| Japan | Prof | Watanabe, Kentaro | Delegate | |
| Japan | Prof | Yamanouchi, Takashi | Delegate | |
| Korea (ROK) | Ms | Cho, Ji I | Delegate | jicho07@mofat.go.kr |
| Korea (ROK) | Dr | Choi, Jaeyong | Delegate | jaychoi@cnu.ac.kr |
| Korea (ROK) | Mr | Hwang, Jun Gu | Advisor | hwangjg@kimst.re.kr |
| Korea (ROK) | Mr | Kang, Myong-il | Alternate | mikang94@mofat.go.kr |
| Korea (ROK) | Dr | Kim, Ji Hee | Delegate | jhalgae@kopri.re.kr |
| Korea (ROK) | Dr | Kim, Yeadong | CEP Representative | ydkim@kopri.re.kr |
| Korea (ROK) | Dr | Lee, Yoo Kyung | Delegate | yklee@kopri.re.kr |
| Korea (ROK) | Mr | Lee, Key Cheol | Head of Delegation | kclee85@mofat.go.kr |
| Korea (ROK) | Mr | Lee, Young-joon | Advisor | yjlee@kei.re.kr |
| Korea (ROK) | Mr | Lim, Hyun Taek | Delegate | pado21@korea.kr |
| Korea (ROK) | Dr | Seo, Hyun kyo | Delegate | shkshk@kopri.re.kr |
| Korea (ROK) | Mr | Yang, Jae-gook | Delegate | jgyang91@mofat.go.kr |
| Netherlands | Prof. Dr | Bastmeijer, Kees | Advisor | c.j.bastmeijer@uvt.nl |
| Netherlands | Ms | Elstgeest, Marlynda | Advisor | |
| Netherlands | Mr | Hernaus, Reginald | CEP Representative | Reggie.hernaus@minvrom.nl |
| Netherlands | Mr | Lefeber, René J.M. | Alternate | rene.lefeber@minbuza.nl |
| Netherlands | Dr | Martijn, Peijs | Advisor | w.f.peijs@minlnv.nl |
| Netherlands | Dr | van der Kroef, Dick A. | Advisor | d.vanderkroef@nwo.nl |
| Netherlands | Mr | van Zeijst, Vincent | Head of Delegation | vincent-van.zeijst@minbuza.nl |
| Netherlands | Mrs | Willems, Gerrie | Advisor | gerrie.willems@minbuza.nl |
| New Zealand | Mr | Gaston, David | Advisor | david.gaston@mfat.govt.nz |
| New Zealand | Dr | Keys, Harry | Advisor | hkeys@doc.govt.nz |
| New Zealand | Ms | Leslie, Nicola | Advisor | nicola.leslie@mfat.govt.nz |
| New Zealand | Mr | MacKay, Don | Advisor | don_maria_mackay@msn.com |
| New Zealand | Mr | Martin, Peter | Advisor | peter.martin@mfat.govt.nz |
| New Zealand | Ms | Newman, Jana | Advisor | j.newman@antarcticanz.govt.nz |
| New Zealand | Mr | Sanson, Lou | Advisor | l.sanson@antarcticanz.govt.nz |
| New Zealand | Mrs | Schwalger, Carolyn | Head of Delegation | carolyn.schwalger@mfat.govt.nz |
| New Zealand | Dr | Sharp, Ben | Advisor | Ben.Sharp@fish.govt.nz |
| Norway | Ms | Askholt, Kjerstin | Alternate | kjerstin.askholt@jd.dep.no |
| Norway | Mr | Halvorsen, Svein Tore | Delegate | sth@md.dep.no |
| Norway | H.E. | Haugstveit, Nils | Delegate | nils.haugstveit@mfa.no |
| Norway | Ms | Holten, Inger | Delegate | iho@mfa.no |
| Norway | Ms | Ingebrigtsen, Hanne Margrethe | Delegate | hanne.margrethe.ingebrigtsen@jd.dep.no |
| Norway | Mr | Klepsvik, Karsten | Head of Delegation | karsten.klepsvik@mfa.no |
| Norway | Ms | Njaastad, Birgit | CEP Representative | njaastad@npolar.no |
| Norway | Mr | Pettersen, Terje Hernes | Delegate | terje-hernes.pettersn@nhd.dep.no |
| Norway | Mr | Rognhaug, Magnus H. | Delegate | mar@md.dep.no |
| Norway | Mr | Rosenberg, Stein Paul | Alternate | |
| Norway | First Secretary | Tapia, Eugenia | Delegate | |
| Norway | Dr | Winther, Jan-Gunnar | Delegate | |
| Peru | Mr | Farje Orna, Alberto Alejandro | Advisor | |
| Peru | Amb. | Isasi-Cayo, Fortunato | Delegate | fisasi@rree.gob.pe |
| Peru | Mr | Sandiga Cabrera, Luis | Head of Delegation | lsandiga@rree.gob.pe |
| Poland | Mr | Misztal, Andrzej | Head of Delegation | |
| Poland | Ambassador | Wolski, Jakub T. | Head of Delegation | jakub.wolski@msz.gov.pl |

| Participants: Consultative Parties | | | | |
|---|---|---|---|---|
| Party | Title | Contact | Position | Email |
| Russian Federation | Mrs | Bystramovich, Anna | Delegate | antarc@mcc.mecom.ru |
| Russian Federation | Mr | Gevorgyan, Kirill | Head of Delegation | dp@mid.ru |
| Russian Federation | Mr | Lukin, Valery | Delegate | lukin@aari.nw.ru |
| Russian Federation | Mr | Makoedov, Anatoly | Delegate | |
| Russian Federation | Mr | Masolov, Valery | Delegate | |
| Russian Federation | Mr | Pomelov, Victor | Delegate | pom@aari.nw.ru |
| Russian Federation | Mr | Timokhin, Konstantin | Delegate | dp@mid.ru |
| Russian Federation | Mr | Titushkin, Vassily | Alternate | tvj2000@mail.ru |
| Russian Federation | Ms | Varigina, Tatiana | Staff | dp@mid.ru |
| South Africa | Ms | Jacobs, Carol | CEP Representative | cjacobs@deat.gov.za |
| South Africa | Dr | Mphepya, Jonas | Delegate | jmphepya@environment.gov.za |
| South Africa | Dr | Siko, Gilbert | Advisor | Gilbert.Siko@dst.gov.za |
| South Africa | Mr | Smit, Danie | CEP Representative | dsmit@deat.gov.za |
| South Africa | Mr | Stemmet, Andre | Delegate | StemmetA@dirco.gov.za |
| South Africa | Mr | Valentine, Henry | Head of Delegation | hvalentine@environment.gov.za |
| Spain | Ambassador | Martinez-Cattaneo, Juan Antonio | Head of Delegation | juan.mcattaneo@maec.es |
| Spain | Mrs | Ramos, Sonia | Delegate | cpe@micinn.es |
| Sweden | Research Coordinator | Jonsell, Ulf | Delegate | ulf.jonsell@polar.se |
| Sweden | Dr | Melander, Olle | Alternate | olle.melander@polar.se |
| Sweden | Ambassador | Ödmark, Helena | Head of Delegation | helena.odmark@foreign.ministry.se |
| Sweden | Environment Officer | Selberg, Cecilia | CEP Representative | cecilia.selberg@polar.se |
| Ukraine | Counsellor | Boietskyi, Taras | Alternate | embucra@embucra.com.ar |
| Ukraine | Mr | Fedchuk, Andrii | Delegate | andriyf@gmail.com |
| Ukraine | Ambassador | Taranenko, Oleksandr | Head of Delegation | embucra@embucra.com.ar |
| United Kingdom | Mr | Bowman, Rob | CEP Representative | rob.bowman@fco.gov.uk |
| United Kingdom | Ms | Clarke, Rachel | Delegate | racl@bas.ac.uk |
| United Kingdom | Mr | Culshaw, Robert | Delegate | rocl@bas.ac.uk |
| United Kingdom | Ms | Dickson, Susan | Delegate | susan.dickson@fco.gov.uk |
| United Kingdom | Mr | Downie, Rod | Delegate | rhd@bas.ac.uk |
| United Kingdom | Ms | Durham, Anna | Delegate | anna.durham@fco.gov.uk |
| United Kingdom | Dr | Hughes, Kevin | Delegate | kehu@bas.ac.uk |
| United Kingdom | HMA | Morgan, Shan | Delegate | |
| United Kingdom | Ms | Rumble, Jane | Head of Delegation | Jane.Rumble@fco.gov.uk |
| United Kingdom | Dr | Shears, John | Delegate | jrs@bas.ac.uk |
| United Kingdom | Mr | Siegert, Martin | Delegate | M.J.Siegert@ed.ac.uk |
| United Kingdom | Ms | Whitehouse, Natasha | Delegate | |
| United States | Mr | Bloom, Evan T. | Head of Delegation | bloomet@state.gov |
| United States | Ms | Cohun, Kelly | Delegate | cohunka@state.gov |
| United States | Ms | Dahood-Fritz, Adrian | Delegate | adahood@nsf.gov |
| United States | Mr | Edwards, David | Delegate | |
| United States | Mr | Foster, Harold D. | Alternate | fosterhd@state.gov |
| United States | Mr | Gilanshah, Bijan | Delegate | bgilansh@nsf.gov |
| United States | Ms | Hessert, Aimee | Delegate | |
| United States | Dr | Karentz, Deneb | Advisor | karentzd@usfca.edu |
| United States | Ms | LaFratta, Susanne | Delegate | slafratt@nsf.gov |
| United States | Mr | McDonald, Samuel | Delegate | |
| United States | Mr | Naveen, Ron | Advisor | |
| United States | Dr | Penhale, Polly A. | CEP Representative | ppenhale@nsf.gov |
| United States | Ms | Perrault, Michele | Advisor | |
| United States | Mr | Rudolph, Lawrence | Delegate | lrudolph@nsf.gov |
| United States | Mr | Spangler, Bryson | Delegate | Bryson.T.Spangler@uscg.mil |
| United States | Ms | Toschik, Pamela | Delegate | |
| United States | Mr | Watters, George | Delegate | George.Watters@noaa.gov |
| United States | Ms | Wheatley, Victoria | Advisor | |
| Uruguay | Mr | Abdala, Juan | CEP Representative | jabdala@iau.gub.uy |
| Uruguay | CA | Burgos, Manuel | Head of Delegation | presidente@iau.gub.uy |
| Uruguay | Mrs | Caula, Nicole | CEP Representative | ambiente@iau.gub.uy |
| Uruguay | Mr | Escayola, Carlos | Delegate | secretaria@atcm2010.gub.uy |
| Uruguay | Mr | Fontes, Waldemar | Delegate | dirsecretaria@iau.gub.uy |
| Uruguay | Dr | Grillo, Bartolome | Advisor | cakrill@redfacil.com.uy |
| Uruguay | Mr | Lluberas, Albert | Advisor | alexllub@iau.gub.uy |
| Uruguay | Mr | Pollack, Raúl | Delegate | urubaires@embajadadeluruguay.com.ar |
| Uruguay | Mr | Schunk, Ricardo | Advisor | rschunk@iau.gub.uy |

**Participants: Consultative Parties**

| Party | Title | Contact | Position | Email |
|---|---|---|---|---|
| Uruguay | Mr | Somma, Gustavo | Alternate | |
| Uruguay | Mr | Vignali, Daniel | Advisor | secretaria@atcm2010.gub.uy |

**Participants: Non-Consultative Parties**

| Party | Title | Contact | Position | Email |
|---|---|---|---|---|
| Colombia | Ms | Lozano Pinilla, Mery | Advisor | mery.lozano@cancilleria.gov.co |
| Colombia | Mr | Restrepo Hurtado, Alvaro | Advisor | |
| Czech Republic | Mr | Bartak, Milos | Advisor | mbartak@sci.muni.cz |
| Czech Republic | Mr | Venera, Zdenek | CEP Representative | zdenek.venera@geology.cz |
| Greece | Mr | Konstantinou, Konstantinos | Head of Delegation | grembsecr.bay@mfa.gr |
| Romania | Mr | Iftimescu, Daniel | Head of Delegation | dvifti@yahoo.com |
| Romania | Mr | Iftimescu, Adrian | Delegate | dvifti@yahoo.com |
| Switzerland | Mrs | Gerber, Evelyne | Head of Delegation | evelyne.gerber@eda.admin.ch |
| Venezuela | Dr | Alfonso, Juan A. | Advisor | jalfonso@ivic.gob.ve |
| Venezuela | Captain | Leon Fajardo, Reinaldo | Delegate | operacionesdhn@gmail.com |
| Venezuela | Admiral | Ortega Hernandez, Jesus | Head of Delegation | dihn@dhn.mil.ve |
| Venezuela | Captain | Pereira, Adolfo | Delegate | adolfojosepereira@hotmail.com |
| Venezuela | Mr | Quintero, Alberto | Advisor | ajquinte@ivic.gob.ve |
| Venezuela | Captain | Rodriguez, Hector | Delegate | hrodriguezp63@yahoo.com |

**Participants: Observers**

| Party | Title | Contact | Position | Email |
|---|---|---|---|---|
| CCAMLR | Dr | Agnew, David | CEP Representative | d.agnew@mrag.co.uk |
| CCAMLR | Dr | Reid, Keith | Advisor | keith@ccamlr.org |
| CCAMLR | Mr | Wright, Andrew | Head of Delegation | andrew_wright@ccamlr.org |
| COMNAP | Ms | Rogan-Finnemore, Michelle | Head of Delegation | michelle.finnemore@comnap.aq |
| SCAR | Dr | Badhe, Renuka | Delegate | rb302@cam.ac.uk |
| SCAR | Prof. | Kennicutt, Mahlon (Chuck) | Delegate | m-kennicutt@tamu.edu |
| SCAR | Dr | Sparrow, Mike | Head of Delegation | mds68@cam.ac.uk |

**Participants: Experts**

| Party | Title | Contact | Position | Email |
|---|---|---|---|---|
| ASOC | Mr | Barnes, James | Head of Delegation | jimbo0628@mac.com |
| ASOC | Ms | Barrett, Jill | Advisor | j.barrett@BIICL.ORG |
| ASOC | Ms | Christian, Claire | Advisor | Claire.Christian@asoc.org |
| ASOC | Ms | Cirelli, Verónica | Advisor | oceanosaustrales@vidasilvestre.org.ar |
| ASOC | Ms | Di Pangracio, Ana | Advisor | adipangracio@farn.org.ar |
| ASOC | Mr | Leiva, Sam | Advisor | |
| ASOC | Ms | Park, Jie-Hyun | Advisor | sophile@gmail.com |
| ASOC | Ms | Prior, Judith Sian | Advisor | Karen.Sack@wdc.greenpeace.org |
| ASOC | Mr | Roura, Ricardo | CEP Representative | ricardo.roura@worldonline.nl |
| ASOC | Mr | Weller, John | Advisor | jweller@indra.com |
| ASOC | Mr | Werner Kinkelin, Rodolfo | Advisor | rodolfo.antarctica@gmail.com |
| IAATO | Dr | Crosbie, Kim | CEP Representative | kimcrosbie@iaato.org |
| IAATO | Ms | Hohn-Bowen, Ute | Delegate | ute@antarpply.com |
| IAATO | Ms | Machado-D'Oliveira, Suzana | Delegate | Oisuzana@yahoo.com |
| IAATO | Mr | Rootes, David | Delegate | david.rootes@antarctic-logistics.com |
| IAATO | Ms | Schillat, Monika | Delegate | Monika@antarpply.com |
| IAATO | Mr | Wellmeier, Steve | Head of Delegation | swellmeier@iaato.org |
| IHO | Capt. | Gorziglia, Hugo | Head of Delegation | hgorziglia@ihb.mc |

**Participants: Secretariats**

| Party | Title | Contact | Position | Email |
|---|---|---|---|---|
| ATS | Mr | Acero, José Maria | Alternate | tito.acero@ats.aq |
| ATS | Mr | Agraz, José Luis | Staff | pepe.agraz@ats.aq |
| ATS | Ms | Balok, Anna | Staff | annabalok@live.com |

| Participants: Secretariats | | | | |
|---|---|---|---|---|
| Party | Title | Contact | Position | Email |
| ATS | Mr | Davies, Paul | Staff | littlewest2@googlemail.com |
| ATS | Mr | Fennell, Alan | Staff | alan.fennell@ats.aq |
| ATS | Ms | Fontan, Gloria | Staff | gloria.fontan@ats.org.ar |
| ATS | Ms | Guretskaya, Anastasia | Staff | a.guretskaya@googlemail.com |
| ATS | Dr | Reinke, Manfred | Head of Delegation | manfred.reinke@ats.aq |
| ATS | Dr | Reinke, Friederike | Staff | friederike.reinke@uni-bremen.de |
| ATS | Mr | Wainschenker, Pablo | Staff | pablo.wainschenker@ats.aq |
| ATS | Mr | Walton, David W H | Staff | dwhw@bas.ac.uk |
| ATS | Mr | Wydler, Diego | Staff | diego.wydler@ats.aq |
| HCS | Mr | Acosta, Adolf | Advisor | gringo19145@hotmail.com |
| HCS | Ms | Aguirre, Aldana Rocío | Staff | |
| HCS | Ms | Alsina, Andrea Isabel | Staff | andreaalsin@yahoo.com.ar |
| HCS | Ms | Alvarez, Miguel | Advisor | paisaje34@hotmail.com |
| HCS | Ms | Ameri, Carolina | HCS Staff | info@atcm2011.gov.ar |
| HCS | Mr | Arzani, Leandro | HCS Staff | info@atcm2011.gov.ar |
| HCS | Mr | Ayala, Nicolas Pablo | Staff | ayalanp@gmail.com |
| HCS | Mr | Barrandeguy, Martin Horacio | Staff | |
| HCS | Mrs | Bazterrica Benson, Victoria | Staff | vicky.bazte@hotmail.com |
| HCS | Mr | Bizzozero, Andres | HCS Staff | info@atcm2011.gov.ar |
| HCS | Counsellor | Bovone, Silvana M. | HCS Staff | sbo@mrecic.gov.ar |
| HCS | Mr | Briloni, Fernando Ruben | HCS Staff | info@atcm2011.gov.ar |
| HCS | Mr | Cabrera, Hugo Sebastián | Staff | |
| HCS | Mr | Canio, Alejandro | HCS Staff | info@atcm2011.gov.ar |
| HCS | Ms. | Casanovas, Paula | HCS Staff | paulacasanovas@gmail.com |
| HCS | Ms. | Castelanelli, Adriana | HCS Staff | info@atcm2011.gov.ar |
| HCS | Ms. | Caviglia, Lucila | HCS Staff | lucaviglia@hotmail.com |
| HCS | Secretary | Conde Garrido, Rodrigo | HCS Staff | xgr@mrecic.gov.ar |
| HCS | Mr | Crilchuk, Guido | HCS Staff | info@atcm2011.gov.ar |
| HCS | Ms | Deimundo Roura, Lucila | HCS Staff | info@atcm2011.gov.ar |
| HCS | Ms | Erceg, Diane | Advisor | |
| HCS | Mr | Flesia, Carlos Felix | HCS Staff | |
| HCS | Mr | Gomez, Gonzalo | HCS Staff | ggomez@cancilleria.gov.ar |
| HCS | Mr | Gonzalez Vaillant, Joaquín | HCS Staff | joacogv@hotmail.com |
| HCS | Mrs | Graziani, Maria | HCS Staff | maria@mariagraziani.com |
| HCS | Mr | Hirsch, Federico Gabriel | HCS Staff | info@atcm2011.gov.ar |
| HCS | Ms | Idiens, Melissa | HCS Staff | melissa.idiens@canterbury.ac.nz |
| HCS | Mr | Jimenez, Nicanor | HCS Staff | info@atcm2011.gov.ar |
| HCS | Mr | JULIA, Gustavo | HCS Staff | gusjulia@gmail.com |
| HCS | Mr | Kestelboim, Juan Cesar | Advisor | juankestel@gmail.com |
| HCS | Mr | Lopez Crozet, Martiniano | HCS Staff | sirmartiniano@gmail.com |
| HCS | Ms | Mallmann, Heidi | Staff | heidi.mallmann@gmail.com |
| HCS | Mr | Massa, Gustavo | Staff | gustavo.massa@gmail.com |
| HCS | Mr | Massuh, Carlos | Staff | muh@mrecic.gov.ar |
| HCS | Mr | Meli, Facundo | HCS Staff | facundo.meli@gmail.com |
| HCS | Mr | Molinari, Angel Ernesto | HCS Staff | iae@mrecic.gov.ar |
| HCS | Mr | Munafo, Oscar | HCS Staff | info@atcm2011.gov.ar |
| HCS | Ms | Oberti, Tamara | HCS Staff | info@atcm2011.gov.ar |
| HCS | Mr | Ortea Sabitay, Maximiliano | HCS Staff | info@atcm2011.gov.ar |
| HCS | Mr | Otegui, Jose | HCS Staff | info@atcm2011.gov.ar |
| HCS | Mr | Palermo, Blas Alberto | HCS Staff | info@atcm2011.gov.ar |
| HCS | Mr | Quiroga, Ariel Fernando | HCS Staff | |
| HCS | Mr | Rabinstein, Mariano | Advisor | mrabinstein@hotmail.com |
| HCS | Min. | Roballo, Jorge | HC Executive Secretary | jjr@atcm2011.gov.ar |
| HCS | Mr | Sakamoto, Leonardo Martin | HCS Staff | martinsakamoto@hotmail.com |
| HCS | Ms. | Salkin, Paula Daniela | HCS Staff | info@atcm2011.gov.ar |
| HCS | Ms. | Sanchez Acosta, Sofia | HCS Staff | info@atcm2011.gov.ar |

**Participants: Secretariats**

| Party | Title | Contact | Position | Email |
|---|---|---|---|---|
| HCS | Miss | Sulikowski, Chavelli | HCS Staff | csulik@gmail.com |
| HCS | Miss | Tuttle, Robin | HCS Staff | robltut@yahoo.com |
| HCS | Ms | Urdaniz, Belen | Staff | belenurdaniz@gmail.com |
| HCS | Mr | Vega, Rodrigo | Advisor | rodrigo_vega@live.com.ar |
| HCS | Ms | Vicente Lago, Emilia | Staff | evl@mrecic.gov.ar |
| Translation & Interpretation | Ms | Alal, Cecilia | Staff | conference@oncallinterpreters.com |
| Translation & Interpretation | Mr | Aroustian, Aramais | Staff | conference@oncallinterpreters.com |
| Translation & Interpretation | Mr | Avella, Alex | Staff | conference@oncallinterpreters.com |
| Translation & Interpretation | Ms | Bouladon, Sabine | Staff | conference@oncallinterpreters.com |
| Translation & Interpretation | Ms | Christopher, Vera | Staff | conference@oncallinterpreters.com |
| Translation & Interpretation | Ms | Coussaert, Joelle | Staff | conference@oncallinterpreters.com |
| Translation & Interpretation | Ms | de Bassi, Teresa | Staff | conference@oncallinterpreters.com |
| Translation & Interpretation | Ms | de Choch Asseo, Ana | Staff | conference@oncallinterpreters.com |
| Translation & Interpretation | Mr | Doubine, Vadim | Staff | conference@oncallinterpreters.com |
| Translation & Interpretation | Dr | Hale, Sandra | Staff | conference@oncallinterpreters.com |
| Translation & Interpretation | Mr | Iatsenko, Viktor | Staff | conference@oncallinterpreters.com |
| Translation & Interpretation | Mr | Ivacheff, Alexey | Staff | conference@oncallinterpreters.com |
| Translation & Interpretation | Ms | Lacey, Roslyn | Staff | conference@oncallinterpreters.com |
| Translation & Interpretation | Ms | Lieve, Marisol | Staff | conference@oncallinterpreters.com |
| Translation & Interpretation | Ms | Lira, Isabel | Staff | conference@oncallinterpreters.com |
| Translation & Interpretation | Mrs | McGrath, Peps | Staff | peps.mcgrath@oncallinterpreters.com |
| Translation & Interpretation | Mr | Orlando, Marc | Staff | conference@oncallinterpreters.com |
| Translation & Interpretation | Ms | Poblete, Verónica | Staff | conference@oncallinterpreters.com |
| Translation & Interpretation | Ms | Rosenstein, Cecilia | Staff | conference@oncallinterpreters.com |
| Translation & Interpretation | Ms | Stern, Ludmila | Staff | conference@oncallinterpreters.com |
| Translation & Interpretation | Mr | Tanguy, Philippe | Staff | conference@oncallinterpreters.com |
| Translation & Interpretation | Ms | Ulman, Irene | Staff | conference@oncallinterpreters.com |
| Translation & Interpretation | Ms | Weschler, Doralia | Staff | conference@oncallinterpreters.com |
| Translation & Interpretation | Dr | Wilson, Hilary | Staff | conference@oncallinterpreters.com |

**Participants: Invited Guests**

| Party | Title | Contact | Position | Email |
|---|---|---|---|---|
| Malaysia | Mr | Othman, Mohd Hafiz | Advisor | hafizwp@kln.gov.my |
| Malaysia | His Excellency | Yaacob, Dato´Zulkifli | Head of Delegation | aizzaty@kln.gov.my |

www.ingramcontent.com/pod-product-compliance
Lightning Source LLC
Chambersburg PA
CBHW081456200326
41518CB00015B/2279